Lead Agency

Dresdner Schriften zu Recht und Politik der Vereinten Nationen

Dresden Papers on Law and Policy of the United Nations

Herausgegeben von/edited by
Sabine von Schorlemer

Zentrum für Internationale Studien/
School of International Studies,
Technische Universität Dresden/
University of Dresden

Band 17

PL ACADEMIC RESEARCH

Martin Gerner

Lead Agency

UNESCO's Global Leadership and Co-ordination Role for the United Nations Decade of Education for Sustainable Development (2005–2014)

PL ACADEMIC RESEARCH

Bibliographic Information published by the Deutsche Nationalbibliothek
The Deutsche Nationalbibliothek lists this publication in the Deutsche Nationalbibliografie; detailed bibliographic data is available in the internet at http://dnb.d-nb.de.

Zugl.: Dresden, Techn. Univ., Diss., 2012

Library of Congress Cataloging-in-Publication Data

Gerner, Martin, author.
Lead agency : UNESCO's global leadership and co-ordination role for the United Nations Decade of Education for Sustainable Development (2005-2014) / Martin Gerner.
pages cm. — (Dresden Papers on Law and Policy of the United Nations ; Band 17)
"PL Academic Research."
Doctoral Technische Universität Dresden, Juristische Fakultät 2012.
Includes bibliographical references and index.
ISBN 978-3-631-64423-2
1. UNESCO. 2. United Nations Decade of Education for Sustainable Development, 2005-2014. 3. Law and economic development. 4. Sustainable development—Law and legislation. 5. International agencies—Law and legislation I. Title.
K3710.G47 2013
001.06'01—dc23

2013014293

88

ISSN 1862-443X
ISBN 978-3-631-64423-2

www.peterlang.de

Foreword

The UNESCO, a specialized agency of the United Nations with its headquarters in Paris, also has a mandate to identify and articulate pivotal emerging issues in the fields of education, science, culture and communication, making this organisation what is frequently considered the *intellectual hub* of the United Nations.

The present volume, *Lead agency – UNESCO's global leadership and co-ordination role for the United Nations Decade of Education for Sustainable Development (2005–2014)*, focuses on the leadership and co-ordination role of the UNESCO in the field of education for sustainable development, an issue that was first mentioned by the Brundtland Report *Our Common Future* in 1987. This concept is now firmly established on an international scale and undeniably plays a significant role, particularly in professional circles but also beyond.

The approach opted for in this book has been taken with careful deliberation for its theoretical value and practical relevance. The primacy of a single organization within the United Nations system and its potential claim for leadership in view of the United Nations Decade of Education for Sustainable Development (2005–2014) implicitly calls for efficiency by avoiding at the same time the duplication of efforts within the existing structural framework of the United Nations. Wherever leadership and co-ordination are efficiently accomplished, problems of both overlapping responsibilities and diverging spheres of influence diminish. As is well-known the latter reflects one of the main failures of the United Nations and has been harshly criticized over the past years.

Beyond any doubt it is the profound analysis and assessment of this very complex UNESCO mandate that represents the most important strength of the present publication. Such an in-depth and comprehensive interdisciplinary collection of articles has not been available to date. Analysis at the interface of education, politics and law truly adds cutting-edge value to ongoing discourses.

In a word, this present publication provides an encouraging strategic focus on a leadership of an unflinchingly independent United Nations decisively positioning itself in an ever-changing world; likewise, most notably through the novel concept of *lead agency,* this volume actively contributes to the theory and practice of international organizations.

Gerd Michelsen

Abstract

Abstract

The *United Nations Educational, Scientific and Cultural Organization* (UNESCO) is mandated *lead agency* for the *United Nations Decade of Education for Sustainable Development* which takes place from 2005 until 2014. This global mandate comprises both leadership and co-ordination. An in-depth look is taken at how UNESCO meets normative expectations and accomplishes its challenging mission. In doing so, the objectives crucially envisaged are twofold: Providing comprehensive understanding of the United Nations decade in accordance with the organisation's functional mandate, and discussing the implementing commitment on the basis of sound regime criteria. To this end, theory-based techniques are combined with document and data analysis in order to obtain well-balanced views on institutional effectiveness, efficiency, compliance, leadership, topicality, context and power. As a result, UNESCO's performance as *lead agency* ranges between accomplished, attainable and challenging, most notably diverging in regional perspective. Moreover, this study of its kind aims to describe, explain and qualify general mechanisms that constitute and affect leadership assignments of international organisations.

Key words: lead agency; sustainable development; UNESCO; decade; mandate; leadership; education; regime theory; new institutionalism

Resumen

La *Organización de las Naciones Unidas para la Educación, la Ciencia y la Cultura* (UNESCO) tiene como mandato como *lead agency* para el *Decenio de las Naciones Unidas de la Educación para el Desarrollo Sostenible* que tiene efecto desde 2005 hasta 2014. Este mandato global afecta tanto al liderazgo así como a la coordinación. Merece la pena echar un vistazo profundo a la cuestión de en qué medida UNESCO alcanza las expectativas normativas y cumple su exigente misión. En este sentido, los fines más importantes a discutir se bifurcan: Tener un panorama general del decenio de las Naciones Unidas de acuerdo con el papel fundamental funcional de la organización, y discutir el compromiso de su realización en cuanto a los criterios de régimen con valor informativo. Por lo tanto, los métodos basados en teoría se combinan con el análisis de documentos y datos con el fin de obtener argumentos equilibrados con respecto a la eficacia, la eficiencia, el cumplimiento, el liderazgo, la actualidad, el contexto y el poder institucional. En resumen, la capacidad de la UNESCO en terminos de *lead agency* oscila entre lograda, alcanzable y complicada, sobre todo con divergencias a nivel regional. Además, este tipo de estudio se fija como meta describir, aclarar y calificar mecanismos generales, los cuales constituyen y afectan el encargo de liderazgo para organizaciones internacionales.

Palabras clave: lead agency; desarrollo sostenible; UNESCO; decenio; mandato; liderazgo; educación; teoría de régimen; neoinstitucionalismo

Abrégé

L'*Organisation des Nations unies pour l'Education, la Science et la Culture* (UNESCO) est l'instance mandatée comme *lead agency* de la *Décennie des Nations Unies pour l'éducation en vue du développement durable* qui a lieu de 2005 à 2014. Ce mandat global comporte à la fois la direction et la co-ordination de l'opération. Nous accorderons une attention particulière à la manière dont l'UNESCO assume les attentes normatives et réalise son ambitieuse mission. L'objectif à atteindre est double: faire comprendre en détail la décennie des Nations Unies en accord avec le mandat fonctionnel de l'organisation, et délibérer sur sa mise en œuvre sur la base des critères de régime. Pour ce faire, les techniques issues de la théorie sont combinées à l'analyse de documents et de données, afin d'obtenir une perspective balancée sur l'efficacité, l'efficience, la politique de respect des règles, la direction, l'actualité, le contexte et le pouvoir de l'institution. Il en résulte que la performance de l'UNESCO comme *lead agency* se situe entre accomplie, atteignable et compliquée, divergeant particulièrement d'une région à l'autre. En outre, une telle étude vise à décrire, expliquer et qualifier les mécanismes qui constituent et influencent les missions directives des organisations internationales.

Mots-clés: lead agency; développement durable; UNESCO; décennie; mandat; direction; éducation; théorie de régime; théorie néo-institutionnelle

Acknowledgments

This publication, accepted as doctoral thesis by the *Faculty of Law* of the *Technische Universität Dresden* (Germany), has arisen out of research that has been conducted intensively for some years. In this time, I have had the privilege to work with many people whose contributions to research in various forms and towards the drafting of this thesis deserve special mention. It is therefore my pleasure to convey my gratitude to all of them in this humble acknowledgment.

I wish first of all to record my gratitude to my doctoral supervisor, the State Minister for Science and the Arts of the Free State of Saxony (Germany), Prof. Sabine von Schorlemer[1] for her supervision, advice and guidance from the earliest stages of my research to the point of publication. Prof. von Schorlemer has, first and foremost, provided encouragement and support in numerous ways, and wholly unflinchingly. Her truly scientific intuition has contributed significantly to the generation of new ideas and of appealing approaches in science – this has been a source of significant inspiration, enriching my perspective on research as well as providing me with memorable experiences throughout the work on the thesis. I have appreciated her pragmatic and strategic method of thinking which has been of particular assistance in times of doubts and uncertainty. Lastly, I wish to thank her for her tacit confidence in me, my skills and my expertise! I am more indebted to Prof. von Schorlemer than she can ever know.

In a similar vein, I gratefully acknowledge the vital and motivational commitment of Prof. Gerd Michelsen[2] and his team. I wish to thank him for his technical advice and professional guidance, and, in particular, for his support during the process of writing-up. Furthermore, as an expert in this field of research, Prof. Michelsen has unselfishly supported me in establishing valuable research contacts. He has been the backbone of this project. I have greatly appreciated his unpretentious and direct involvement, as well as his constructive comments. I have found his originality and cordial understatement to be personally and intellectually enriching, and from this I shall continue to draw benefit. I wish to extend my appreciation and gratitude to his entire team for providing me with opportunities to present and discuss the project which have been extremely beneficial to its completion.

This project has been made possible through the generous financial support of the *German Federal Ministry of Education and Research* (BMBF) and the *Friedrich Naumann Foundation for Freedom* (*Friedrich-Naumann-Stiftung für*

1 Prof. Dr. jur. habil. Dr. rer. pol. habil. Sabine von Schorlemer. *UNESCO Chair in International Relations, Technische Universität Dresden* (Germany).

2 Prof. Dr. rer. pol. Dr. phil. habil. Gerd Michelsen. *Chair of the Institute for Environmental and Sustainability Communication / UNESCO Chair in Higher Education for Sustainable Development, Leuphana Universität Lüneburg* (Germany).

die Freiheit, FNF). I appreciate enormously both the intellectual and financial investment that has made possible a great number of experiences and programmatic discussions, plenty of professional and social networking, and the freedom to commit to the project. Particular thanks to the Dresden scholarship group and Prof. Hans Vorländer for patiently lending an ear to me and certain matters of concern! Above all, my personal thanks go to the foundation's scholarship department and the *International Academy for Leadership* (IAF), in particular to Marie-Luise Wohlleben, Michael Gold, Renate Brassat, Dr. Petra Weckel, Ingrid Hirthe, Mohammad Shahpari and Birgit Lamm. Thank you all for your down-to-earth approach and your confidence combined with a pleasant individual touch!

The completion of this project would not have been possible without the advice, assistance and support of various persons and institutions. First of all, I am extremely grateful to all interviewees for sharing their expert knowledge with me. For their openness, analytic expertise and kind support I thank the following: Astrid Hollander (Germany and Chile); Carol Salgado (Chile); Beatriz Macedo (Uruguay, Chile and France); Gilberto Gallopin (Argentina and Chile); Karl Böhmer (Chile); Tito Gallardo (Chile); Joseluis Samaniego (Chile); Rodrigo Arrué Rodriguez (Chile); Octavio Gajardo Gabelo (Chile); Vicente Ossa (Chile) and Fernando Berrios (Peru). ¡Muchas gracias! Special thanks are also due to distinguished experts who have made considerable effort towards the provision of valuable insider information through informal briefings, chats or spontaneous telephone calls. Merci beaucoup, Marianna Bolshakova (*United Nations Economic Commission for Europe* (UNECE)), Shivali Lawale (UNESCO), Gabriele Göttelmann-Duret (*International Institute for Educational Planning* (IIEP-UNESCO)), Olivier Laboulle and Bernard Combes (UNESCO).

In addition, several institutions and affiliated members have given substantial assistance to the project. Their congeniality and the excellence of their respective facilities have contributed greatly to this project. I therefore thank the following: at the UNESCO in Bonn, Germany: Bianca Bilgram and Katja Römer (*German Commission for UNESCO* (DUK)), Cathrine Caspari and Dr. Alexander Leicht (*Education for Sustainable Development in Germany* (*Bildung für Nachhaltige Entwicklung*, BNE)); at the UNESCO in Paris, France: Aline Bory-Adams, Shivali Lawale, Bernard Combes and Olivier Laboulle (*Division for the Co-ordination of UN Priorities in Education*), Beatriz Macedo, (*Education Sector*), Carole Mongrenier and Petra van den Born (library); at the UNESCO in Buenos Aires, Argentina: Margarita Poggi, Mariana Clucellas, Néstor López and Emilio Tenti Fanfani (*Instituto Internacional de Planeamiento de la Educación* (IIPE-UNESCO)); at the United Nations Geneva, Switzerland: Marianna Bolshakova (*United Nations Economic Commission for Europe* (UN-ECE)); at the *Organización de Estados Iberoamericanos para la Educación, la Ciencia y la Cultura* (OEI) in Buenos Aires, Argentina: Prof. María Fernanda

Gilardoni; at the UNESCO Lima, Perú: Inés Castro; at the UNESCO in Montevideo, Uruguay: María Ana Paz Echeverriarza; at the UNESCO in Santiago, Chile: Astrid Hollander, Carol Salgado, Nora Mora and Usune Zuazo; at the *Ministerio de Educación de Chile* (MINEDUC) in Santiago: Patricia Lobos, Ana María Foxley and Roberto Hiran Gonzalez Munizaga; at the *Programa de las Naciones Unidas para el Desarrollo* (PNUD) in Santiago, Chile: María Luisa Sierra, Enrique Ganuza and Flavio Fuertes; and at the United Nations in Santiago, Chile: Verónica Aldunate and Loreto Ariztía (*Comisión Económica para América Latina* (CEPAL)).

Numerous people have helped in various ways to determine how certain scientific concepts might feasibly be discussed in this thesis. I have considered this academic debate a crucial process of developing and harmonising them. For her vital methodological advice I am deeply indebted to Prof. Monika Medick-Krakau (Dresden). I wish to thank for having painstakingly managed my individual concerns, Megan Runow, Friederike May, Maritta Brückner, Dr. Nina Christiane Lück, Dr. Rainer Schröder and Dr. Alexander Brand (Dresden)! Dr. Maik Adomßent, Dr. Marco Rieckmann and Uschi Jänicke (Lüneburg) have earned my gratitude for taking numerous telephone calls and allowing me participate in their summer school. I have also benefited from the advice and guidance of Prof. Daniella Tilbury and Ingrid Mulà Pons de Vall from the *International Research Institute in Sustainability* (IRIS) (Gloucestershire). They have always been generous with their time in providing me with useful information and in answering my questions. I thank them for their swift and gracious communications.

My appreciation goes to those who have substantially contributed to this success, either as scientific advisors, facilitators or associated mentors: Prof. Erdmute Alber, Prof. Dieter Neubert, Prof. Peter Oberender and Dr. Peter Kistler (Bayreuth), Prof. Heinz Neuser (Bielefeld), Prof. Wilhelm Loewenstein (Bochum), Prof. Wolfram Hilz and Dr. Peter Wolff (Bonn), Prof. Beate Neuss, Prof. Jürgen Straub, Dr. Willy Spanjers, Prof. Manfred Moldaschl and Prof. Fritz Helmedag (Chemnitz), Prof. Wolfgang Burr (Erfurt), Prof. Sergio Costa and Prof. Stephan Panther (Flensburg), Prof. Hans-Jürgen Puhle (Frankfurt on the Main), Prof. Hans-Rimbert Hemmer (Gießen), Dr. Susan Steiner, Dr. Dirk Kohnert, Prof. Detlef Nolte and Prof. Robert Kappel (Hamburg), Prof. Stephan Klasen, Ph.D. (Göttingen), Prof. Ingo Pies and Prof. Reinhard Rode (Halle), Prof. Javier Revilla Diez (Hanover), Prof. Uwe Cantner and Dr. Andreas Meder (Jena), Prof. Ulf Engel, Prof. Hartmut Elsenhans and Prof. Rolf H. Hasse (Leipzig), Prof. Ingo Moerth (Linz), Prof. Ulrich Wengenroth, Prof. Edgar Grande and Dr. Thomas Wieland (Munich), Prof. Harald Fuhr (Potsdam), Prof. Manfred M. Fischer, Dr. Klaus Schuch (Vienna), and Prof. Katja Michaelowa (Zurich). I have been extraordinarily fortunate in having Prof. Claus Scholl as a professor, mentor and partner in lively conversation. To him I am grateful in every conceivable way.

A number of friends have kept me in touch with normality, and I thank them for their understanding, support and discussion! Ilja and Sebastian, with your help I have finally managed to manoeuvre through some *shallow waters*. Particularly Albert Einstein's unmistakably unique pieces of wisdom are due your lovely sharp tongue, Ilja! Inken and Steffi have willingly provided advice and personal perspectives, shaping up my ideas and research.

I am grateful to my dear friends in Lüneburg, Martina, Fabian, Andreas and Wolfgang, for their cordial hospitality during my stopovers. I look forward in particular to keeping our stimulating scientific and political discussions alive! I thank also all my international friends for helping and cordially hosting me during my research stays: Elisabeth and Florent, Beatriz and Thomas, Christelle and Isabel, Ángela and Eduardo, Patricia, and Dieter.

I wish to acknowledge my colleagues at the *Faculty of Law* of the *Technische Universität Dresden* both collectively and individually. I am much indebted to them for their valuable advice and comments. It has been a pleasure with Heidi, Sylvia, Birgit, Nina and Jana, and I thank them for the invigorating, helpful and memorable company, either occasionally during lunch, while patiently listening to the organ or buying baby clothes.

Many thanks go in particular to Ursula Schmidt-Liermann and Dr. Rüdiger Graichen for their hospitality when working with them during my stays in Latin America. I apologise for my impatience and persistence, but, by means of consolation, they have had the privilege of having been acquainted firsthand with my permanently changing plans! For friendship whenever and wherever I thank them.

I wish to thank Dr. Carsten Linnemann (MdB) and Prof. Cornelia Manger-Nestler for their intuitive engagement from the very beginning of this project. I wish them good luck in their respective fields of science and politics.

Many thanks go to Mabyn Troup (Oxford) and Patrick Howard (London) for their patience and straightforwardness in proofreading! They have had the tricky task of transforming a German's mediocre academic English into the smooth and readable parlance of Anglo-Saxon science. I thank Katy for offering her assistance also. In this vein, I am grateful also to the two *language pioneers* Francis-Joseph Minogue and Dr. Rolf Freier. It must have been an insufferable task to dedicate their precious time to an initial evaluation of my poor English!

I would also like to acknowledge the entire team of *Swiss Academic Software*. Your programme *Citavi* has turned reference management into an entirely pleasant activity. Frieder, thank for your snappy technical assistance in backing up and transferring data! Peter, I very much appreciate your twenty-four-hour hotline for inspiring technical support! Especial thanks go to the team of *Peter*

Lang Publishing Group for their professional guidance of the entire publication process.

I am very grateful to Irene Spindler (Buenos Aires) and Anke Kessler (Santiago de Chile) of the *Goethe-Institut* for their kind help in finding accommodation. Many thanks go to Holger Baum, Ingo Konrads, Friederike Kraft, Nancy El-Deiry of *MediaCompany – Agentur für Kommunikation* for the opportunity to attend and subsequently to enjoy the 2009 *UNESCO World Conference in Bonn on Education for Sustainable Development*. Isabella Pfaff, in view of *www.tagesblick.de* I have enjoyed some beautiful journalistic *distraction* during the work. Thank you for your kind support and curiosity!

Where would I be without my family? Words cannot express my appreciation, and their contribution is entirely beyond description. My parents deserve special mention for their unconditional support, sympathy and confidence. Their dedication and love have relieved the most grievous of burdens. My brother Michael has, though younger than me, beat me to graduation and become as a consequence an outstanding motivational coach! I deeply owe a dept of gratitude to him for unselfishly letting his intelligence and ambitions collide with mine. I am very much indebted to my grandparents. They watched the process of writing with particular interest as well as their thoughtful support, and I am sure that my grandpa would have loved to see this project finished. Thank you very much!

Finally, I would like to thank those who have been important to the successful realisation of this project, and can only I apologise for not being able to mention everybody by name.

I dedicate this book to my grandpa, in loving gratitude.

Table of contents

List of figures

List of tables

I Introduction

For years everyone has been talking about sustainability and now, through the United Nations Decade of Education for Sustainable Development, this principle has been given institutional recognition over a ten-year period from 2005 until 2014. This chapter will introduce the reader to the primary concern of the subsequent analyses.

1 Preface

"I never think of the future. It comes soon enough." This well-known and untroubled quotation made by Albert Einstein represents his very pragmatic and unperturbed attitude as scientist. For obvious reasons, there is not a single glimpse of positivist or normative thinking, let alone vision-building!

The *United Nations Decade of Education for Sustainable Development* (2005–2014) is about convincing people that the opposite is true: caring for the future matters. Therefore, any and every aspect of *Education for Sustainable Development* incorporates an element of dynamism and orientation towards the future.[3] This is the case for *education*, *sustainability* and *development*.

3 See *Figure 1* in chapter I 1 *Preface* on page 2, and *Figure 2* in chapter I 1 *Preface* on page 3.

Figure 1: *Official symbol of globally addressing sustainability literacy*[4]

All three aspects are vital and have profound contemporary relevance, and for this reason the *United Nations Decade of Education for Sustainable Development* coincides and connects with manifold global trends in multiple spheres of interest. The decade's main focus is education, first and foremost: education establishes the strategic and procedural requirements of sustainable development. UNESCO has, with good cause, been mandated to take on responsibility for leading the *United Nations Decade of Education for Sustainable Development.*

4 Only two simple graphic elements are used to convey the key message. The *opened book* obviously refers to education as means of prospect investment to achieve awareness and capacities in view of sustainability. The *globe* certainly stresses its geographically overarching ambit as global concern.
See UNESCO (ed.) (2007k): The UN Decade of Education for Sustainable Development (DESD 2005–2014). The First Two Years. Paris: UNESCO publishing, p. 5.

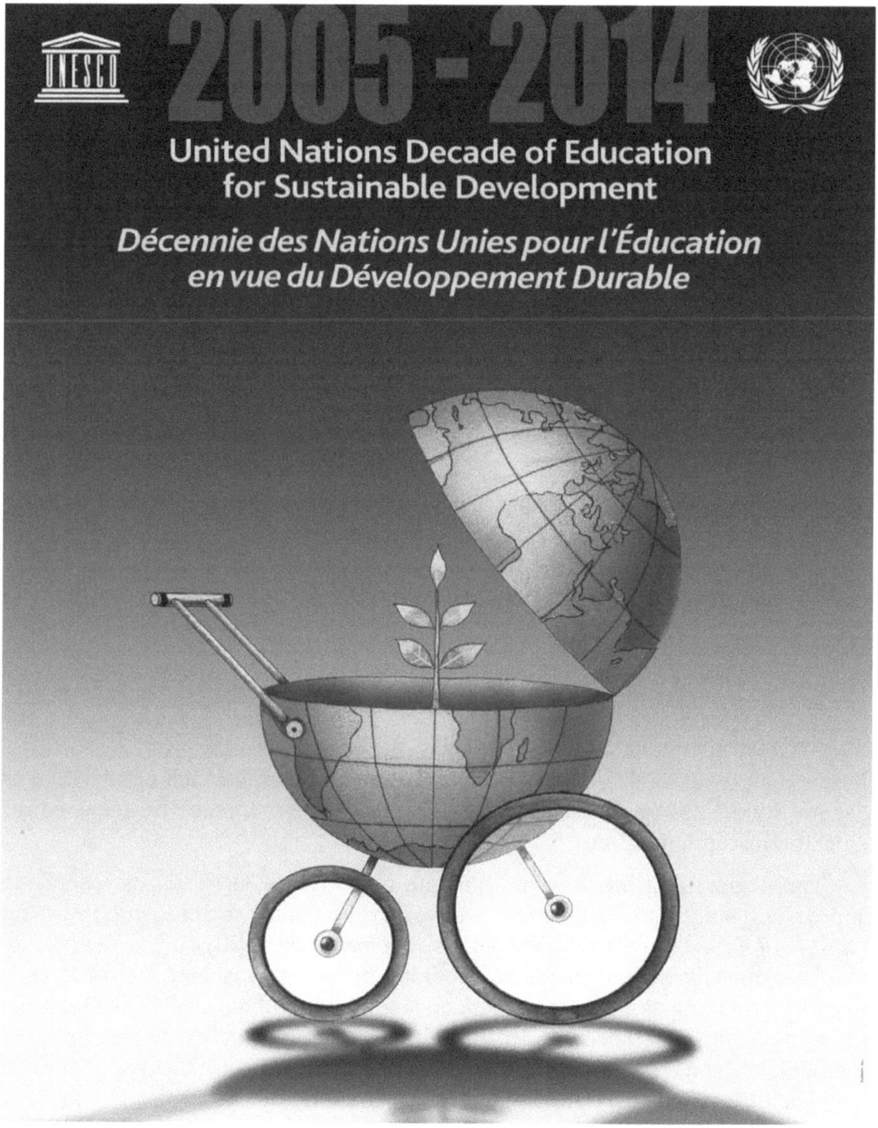

Figure 2: DESD: Joint challenges – common responsibilities[5]

5 This visual campaign shows sustainability to be an international concern in its fledgling stages which must be cared for during the process of maturation. Sustainable development is therefore already a present and lively concern.
See UNESCO (ed.) (2007k) (cf. *footnote 4* op. cit.), p. 7.

2 Objectives

The primary concern of further considerations is a substantial elucidation of UNESCO's specific role in the course of the *United Nations Decade of Education for Sustainable Development* (2005–2014). To this end, a discussion will take place from a normative perspective on *how* the organisation manages its leadership and co-ordination assignment as the designated *lead agency*. For the purpose of this study, attention is paid primarily to the two principal objectives of:

1. Providing a comprehensive and general overview of the *United Nations Decade of Education for Sustainable Development*; as well as
2. Illustrating the focal points of regional implementation of the *United Nations Decade of Education for Sustainable Development*.

3 Structure

The research design is constructed with the intention of meeting both key objectives. It encompasses four main lines of enquiry:

a) Introducing and concluding the research assignment;
b) Adopting the set of terms, theory and methodology;
c) Developing the normative outline; and
d) Discussing relevant aspects of its application.

In this regard, research is organised into different domains which either serve as general guidelines (general research question) or refer to specific focal points (specific research question).

The overarching intention is illustrate how UNESCO fulfils its leadership and co-ordination mandate as *lead agency* in the course of the *United Nations Decade of Education for Sustainable Development* (2005–2014).

Two objectives are critical: to elaborate, in the first instance, on the decade itself by providing comprehensive understanding in relation to UNESCO's functional mandate; and, secondly, to introduce and discuss in depth examples of regional implementation in order to underline the decade's practical relevance.

Scientific value may therefore be conferred in two respects: On the one hand, by providing a theorisation of the term *lead agency*[6] and, on the other hand, by embedding the conception of *lead agency* into the complex functional background of an organisational mandate.

---

6 See chapter VI 2.1 *Lead agency* on page 125.

In the matter of division into chapters, each research question relates to one particular aspect that fits into the global research context.[7]

Table 1: Chapter-related research questions

Chapter	Related research question
Introduction	What is the primary concern to be discussed in depth?
Definitions	Which key terms require direct clarification prior to further considerations?
Theory	Which theoretical setting best serves to support the research objective?
Methodology	Which methodological approach provides a suitable connection between theory and research objectives?
Framework for action	To what extent does UNESCO provide regulatory frames of reference that may facilitate the *United Nations Decade of Education for Sustainable Development*?
Mandate for leadership	Which features and competences constitute and define the UNESCO mandate for the *United Nations Decade of Education for Sustainable Development* leadership?
Background information	In what way is the *United Nations Decade of Education for Sustainable Development* grounded and affiliated to evolutions in practice?
Obligation of compliance	Which means of force and effect does UNESCO employ in order to facilitate effective implementation of the *United Nations Decade of Education for Sustainable Development*?
Implementation practices	How does UNESCO co-ordinate and monitor the implementation of the *United Nations Decade of Education for Sustainable Development*?
Conclusion	What are the principal results of research to be reviewed and critically acclaimed?

4 Notion

In devising intentions and expectations at the very beginning, it is important to emphasise that this thesis does not deal with education, sustainability or development as single issues; nor does it deal with education for sustainable development as a whole. Admittedly, this may sit incongruously with the context of the *United Nations Decade of Education for Sustainable Development*. In fact, the concept dealt with is far more technical and less concerned with the subject matter of the *United Nations Decade of Education for Sustainable Development* proper. What matters is addressing UNESCO's institutional performance and not the fully-fledged discourses taking place in terms of education, sustainability

7 See *Table 1* in chapter I 3 *Structure* on page 5.

or development. Still, detailed cross-references to those are only to be expected in cases where these themes impact on the organisational mandate.

Furthermore, this treatise ought to be considered *interdisciplinary*, since it involves different strands supporting arguments from several scientific disciplines. Basically, the author claims the thesis to be dedicated to the field of international relations by virtue of both subject matter and scope.[8] Analysis predominantly moves into the realms of public international law[9] and political science[10] touching on diverse socio-economic aspects[11], in addition.[12]

5 State of the art

Before launching analytically *in medias res*, a brief outline follows explaining where and how this thesis begins. Given this intention, two critical aspects must carefully be distinguished:

a) On the one hand, the quantity of discourse on each component of the *United Nations Decade of Education for Sustainable Development* is immense. Increasing importance is attributed to education, sustainability and development. Documented publications in these fields are multi-faceted, substantial, often interdisciplinary and large in number, and due to the constraints imposed by the research strategy these are neither to be dealt with *in extenso* nor a summary of their content provided; and
b) On the other hand, the discourse on leadership mandates is far more focussed and manageable, precisely because, as yet, little research has been carried out on lead agencies. Though relatively new, the political concept of *lead agency* has been astonishingly under-represented in scientific discourse thus far. On the international scale, these mandatory assignments receive relatively little coverage. Few reported cases labeled *lead agency* are referenced, particularly

8 See *Table 28* in chapter IX 1.2.1 *Programmes* on page 260, and chapter IX 1.7 *Cross-cutting* on pages 271 et seqq, for instance.

9 See particularly chapter V *Framework for action* on pages 97 et seqq, and chapter VIII *Obligation of compliance* on pages 197 et seqq.

10 See particularly chapter III *Theory* on pages 37 et seqq, chapter V *Framework* on pages 97 et seqq, chapter VI *Mandate for leadership* on pages 121 et seqq, chapter VII *Background information* on pages 149 et seqq, chapter IX *Implementation practices* on pages 255 et seqq, and chapter X *Conclusion* on pages 481 et seqq.

11 See particularly chapter II *Definitions* on pages 11 et seqq, chapter IV *Methodology* on pages 71 et seqq, chapter VII *Background* on pages 149 et seqq, chapter VIII *Obligation* on pages 197 et seqq, and chapter IX *Implementation* on pages 255 et seqq.

12 See *footnote 2418* in chapter X 3 *Implications* on page 514.

in the realm of organisational leadership in particular domains,[13] and an approach based on the systematic and comprehensive assessment of long-term leadership principles practically does not exist yet.

These two contrastive considerations apply to the bibliographical background accordingly. The *United Nation Decade of Education for Sustainable Development* is a process in motion, and the context is thus highly dynamic and reaches far beyond the time frame of the intended decade. Of course, this major characteristic must be taken into especial consideration as far as a review of existing literature is concerned. At first glance, official, *primary-source* documents seem to outweigh *secondary-source* literature by far in terms of quantity (as a result of

13 In the realm of, for example: education (UNESCO – *United Nations Educational, Scientific and Cultural Organization* and UNICEF – *United Nations International Children's Emergency Fund*), humanitarian assistance (UNHCR – *United Nations High Commissioner for Refugees*), environment (UNEP – *United Nations Environment Programme* and FAO – *Food and Agriculture Organisation*), development (UNDP – *United Nations Development Programme*), and health care (WHO – *World Health Organisation*).
Cf. King, Kenneth (1993): Multilateral agencies in the construction of the global agenda on education. In: Comparative Education, Volume 43, Issue 3, pp. 377–391; Imber, Mark F. (1993): The United Nations' role in sustainable development. In: Environmental Politics, Volume 2, Issue 4, pp. 121–136; Jönsson, Christer (1996): From 'Lead Agency' to 'Integrated Programming': The Global Response to AIDS in the Third World. Green Globe Yearbook 1996. Fridtjof Nansen Institute. In: Green Globe Yearbook (GGY), pp. 65–72, pp. 65–66, 69–70; UNHCR Cunliffe, S. Alex (1996): The UNHCR as Lead Agency in the Former Yugoslavia. In: The Journal of Humanitarian Assistance; Pugh, Michael; Cunliffe, S. Alex (1997): The Lead Agency Concept in Humanitarian Assistance: The Case of the UNHCR. In: Security Dialogue, Volume 28, Issue 1, pp. 17–30, pp. 17–18; WHO Lee, Kelley (1998): Shaping the future of global health cooperation: where can we go from here? World Health. In: The Lancet, Volume 351, March 21, pp. 899–902, p. 901; Oestreich, Joel E. (1998): UNICEF and the Implementation of the Convention on the Rights of the Child. In: Global Governance, Volume 4, Issue 183, pp. 183–198; Pigozzi, Mary Joy (ed.) (1999): Education in Emergencies and for Reconstruction: A developmental approach. UNICEF/PD/ED/99–1. New York: UNICEF Programme Division Education (Working Paper Series), pp. 10–11; Hofer, Thomas; McGuire, Douglas (2003): Beyond the International Year of Mountains: A Preliminary Assessment by the FAO, the United Nations Lead Agency for IYM2002. In: Mountain Research and Development, Volume 23, Issue 1, pp. 80–83, pp. 80, 82; Bauer, Steffen; Biermann, Frank (eds.) (2004): Partners or Competitors? Policy Integration for Sustainable Development between United Nations Agencies. The Case of the United Nations Environment Programme and the United Nations Development Programme. 2004 Berlin Conference on the Human Dimensions of Global Environmental Change: Greening of Policies-Interlinkages and Policy Integration. Berlin, pp. 10, 14; Jones, Phillip Worner; Coleman, David (2005): The United Nations and education. Multilateralism, development and globalisation. London / New York: Routledge Falmer, pp. 1, 44, 222.

the ongoing process of implementation). *Primary-source* documents[14] can be classified according to the document type and purpose of publication. By and large, these are:

- Declarations and resolutions as first-hand documents which prescribe, in an official capacity, primarily institutional positions, both governmental and non-governmental;
- Progress reports as a means of describing proceedings and states of development which are provided mainly from an internal point of view; and
- Conference reports as indices of the merger of different aspects and perspectives, opening up discourses for the scientific and journalistic public, and contributing to the formation of opinions and public perception;
- Guidelines as background documents for implementation and co-ordination which are considered powerful instruments of guidance, advice and monitoring; and
- Online resources serving as up-to-date sources of information and tool kits for practical application in quotidian contexts.

Secondary-source documents[15] deal in greater depth with different aspects and single issues related to the *United Nation Decade of Education for Sustainable Development*. Discussion of such literature offers additional information and allows the researcher to embed previous developments in, and establish a connection with current tendencies. *Secondary-source* documents are intended to provide an essential research basis through the definition and interpretation of the unchallenged foil concepts of education, sustainability and development.

6 Technical remarks

Because of a strong dislike for abbreviations and for the sake of enhanced readability, only two *authorised* and italicised abbreviations are used in order to keep explanations short and simple:

- *DESD* stands for *The United Nations Decade of Education for Sustainable Development* as the official and institutionalised process; whereas
- *ESD* refers to *Education for Sustainable Development* as the unaffiliated and more theoretical entity.

In all other cases, full titles are preferred and are frequently accompanied by lists of abbreviations or acronyms.

14 See chapter IV 3.1 *Primary-source materials* on page 85.
15 See chapter IV 3.2 *Secondary-source materials* on page 86.

Unless otherwise stated or acknowledged, all contents herein with the inclusion of images are the author's own and original intellectual property.

Technical terms and related concepts are explained in the appended glossary. The searching and navigation of keywords is supported through an additional subject index.

II Definitions

How does UNESCO fulfil its distinct mandate of leadership and co-ordination as lead agency in the United Nations Decade of Education for Sustainable Development (2005–2014)? Taking this question of global research to constitute a further programme of inquiry, different key terms must be defined within this context to ensure understanding. Thus, this chapter will provide a classification of the key terms which require direct clarification prior to further considerations. Terminology is subject to two paradigms: firstly, the identification and immediate definition of fundamental content-based concepts – education, sustainability, development, DESD –; and secondly, the provision of structural or strategy-related terms to be analysed in the course of work.

1 Education

"Education is a fundamental human right. Education is essential for development. (...) (E)ducation makes a difference – it can help people to work together to find new solutions to their problems and can lead to new opportunities. [...]"[16]

Education is a multi-faceted and highly politicised term. Derived from Latin *educare*[17] and *educere*,[18] it refers to the process of learning, training and teach-

16 See UNESCO (ed.) (2005g): UN Decade of Education for Sustainable Development: Links between the Global Initiatives in Education. Education for Sustainable Development in Action. Technical Paper N°1. Paris: UNESCO workshops, p. 6.

17 I.e. to rear or to foster.

18 I.e. to draw out or to develop.

ing in order to develop applicable skills and knowledge.[19] *Education* is comprised of these concepts, which distinguish between three constitutive elements:[20]

a) Development through learning;
b) Transformation through training and instruction; and
c) Transmission through teaching.

Education is only possible when basic provisions of the fundamental and globally recognised *right to education*[21] are adequately made, by, *inter alia*, eliminating discrimination and facilitating access to educational systems.[22]

---

19 Cf. Leicht, Alexander; Plum, Jacqueline; Fuchs, Max (2007): Kulturelle Bildung für nachhaltige Entwicklung. Sankt Augustin / Berlin: Konrad-Adenauer-Stiftung (IM PLENUM), pp. 15, 22.

20 Cf. United Nations Economic Commission for Europe (UNECE); United Nations Economic and Social Council (ECOSOC) (eds.) (2004d): Draft UNECE Strategy for Education for Sustainable Development. Addendum. Explanatory Notes. Second regional meeting on education for sustainable development (Rome, 15–16 July 2004). CEP/AC.13/2004/8/Add.2. New York: United Nations, p. 1; United Nations Economic Commission for Europe (UNECE) (ed.) (2006): UNECE Strategy for Education for Sustainable Development. Guidance for reporting. Expert Group on Indicators for ESD. Geneva: United Nations, p. 6.

21 See Article 26 United Nations (ed.) (1948): Universal Declaration of Human Rights. A/RES/217(III)[A]. Geneva / New York: United Nations Publications (Resolutions adopted by the General Assembly during its 3rd session, 1), p. 76.
Cf. UNESCO Education Sector (ed.) (2005): Contributing to a More Sustainable Future: Quality Education, Life Skills and Education for Sustainable Development. ED/PEQ/IQL/2005/PI/H/2. Paris: UNESCO publishing, p. 2; UNESCO (ed.) (2006b): Definitions of legal terms concerning normative and standard setting instruments. Paris: UNESCO publishing, p. 1;Foreign Office of the Federal Republic of Germany / German Commission for UNESCO (ed.) (2007): The Role of UNESCO. Contribution to the Debate by Germany. Berlin / Bonn: Gebrüder Kopp, p. 6; Fernandez, Alfred (2007): Fostering Access to Education and Knowledge. Ensuring Equal Opportunities in Education. In: Yusuf, Abdulqawi A. (ed.): Normative action in education, science and culture. Essays in commemoration of the sixtieth anniversary of UNESCO. French edition. Paris / Leiden / Boston: UNESCO publishing; Martinus Nijhoff Publishers (UNESCO reference works series, 1), pp. 331–339, p. 334.

22 Cf. United Nations (ed.) (1989 / 1990): Convention on the Rights of the Child. A/RES/44/25. New York: United Nations, pp. 7–12; UNESCO Education Sector (ed.) (2005) (cf. *footnote 21* op. cit.), p. 5; Tooley, James; Dixon, Pauline (eds.) (2005): Private Education is Good for the Poor: A Study of Private Schools Serving the Poor in Low-Income Countries. White Paper. Washington, D. C.: Cato Institute (Policy Studies), pp. 44, 45; Benedek, Wolfgang (2007): Fostering Access to Education and Knowledge. The Normative Implications of Education for All (EFA): The Right to Education. In: Yusuf, Abdulqawi A. (ed.): Normative action in education, science and culture. Essays in commemoration of the sixtieth anniversary of UNESCO. French edition. Paris / Leiden / Boston: UNESCO publishing; Martinus Nijhoff Publishers

1.1 Learning

Learning is the far-reaching process[23] of acquiring certain knowledge, values and skills with the intention of effecting continuous change in individual and societal behaviour.[24] *Learning* is about absorbing information and incorporating reflections obtained from this process into individual or collective decision-making. Again, the way information is obtained and processed is dependent upon available knowledge, experience, philosophies of living, and culturally-bound norms and values. *Learning* takes place in various modes, settings and multiple *learning spaces*,[25] with the following considerations:

- The distinction between individual and collective responsibility for differentiating between a *learning person* with individual skills, auto-development and an individual position in society, a *learning organisation* making internal efforts to improve the quality of its own structure and performance, and a *learning society* with cumulative effects, both individually and collectively.[26]
- The inclusion of *lifelong learning*[27] or continuing *"(e)ducation, beginning with basic literacy and extending throughout life (...)"*.[28] This *passport to*

(UNESCO reference works series, 1), pp. 311–329; Fernandez, Alfred (2007) (cf. *footnote 21* op. cit.), p. 334; Centre for Environment and Sustainability (GMV); Chalmers University of Technology; University of Gothenburg (eds.) (2009): The Gothenburg Recommendations on Education for Sustainable Development. Adopted November 12, 2008. Edited by Pernilla Ottosson; Bo E. Samuelsson. Göteborg: Eskils Tryckeri, p. 50.

23 Cf. UNESCO (ed.) (2005c): Draft International Implementation Scheme for the United Nations Decade of Education for Sustainable Development. 171 EX/7. Paris: UNESCO publishing, p. 20.

24 Cf. Deutsche UNESCO-Kommission e. V. (DUK) (ed.) (2007): Education for Sustainable Development Worldwide. Conference Report. International Workshop on the UN Decade of Education for Sustainable Development. 28–29 November 2006, Bonn. Edited by Alexander Leicht; Charlotte Schmitz; Lina Franken. Bonn: Deutsche UNESCO-Kommission / German Commission for UNESCO, p. 9.

25 See UNESCO (ed.) (2005c) (cf. *footnote 23* op. cit.), pp. 22 et seqq; UNESCO (ed.) (2006f): Framework for the UN DESD International Implementation Scheme. ED/DESD/2006/PI/1. Paris: UNESCO workshops, p. 21.

26 Cf. Leicht, Alexander; Plum, Jacqueline; Fuchs, Max (2007) (cf. *footnote 19* op. cit.), p. 9; United Nations Economic Commission for Europe (UNECE) (ed.) (2006) (cf. *footnote 20* op. cit.), p. 7.

27 See United Nations Economic Commission for Europe (UNECE); United Nations Economic and Social Council (ECOSOC) (eds.) (2004f): Draft UNECE Strategy for Education for Sustainable Development. Explanatory Notes. Second regional meeting on education for sustainable development Rome, 15–16 July 2004. CEP/AC.13/2004/8/Add.2. Geneva: United Nations, p. 2; UNESCO Education Sector (ed.) (2008): Quality Education, Equity and Sustainable Development. A holistic vision through UNESCO's four World Education Conferences 2008–2009. Paris:

lifelong learning[29] will be considered by addressing various levels of education from early childhood to adult life.[30]

- Encompassing different *categories*[31] of *learning*. *Formal learning* is primarily related to education and training institutions that award recognised diplomas and qualifications. *Non-formal learning* takes place outside, or in parallel with *mainstream systems of education and training*[32] without formal certification provided by *non-state* or *third-party* stakeholders.[33] *Informal learning* can be described as everyday learning that is neither necessarily intentional nor consciously recognised.[34]

"Education, like society, is full of contradictions and paradoxes. It is called upon to reconcile divergent aims and trends, to embody both continuity and renewal, to encourage conformity and innovation at the same time. Furthermore, like much human endeavour, the practice of education is always a blend be-

---

UNESCO publishing, p. 4; Centre for Environment and Sustainability (GMV); Chalmers University of Technology; University of Gothenburg (eds.) (2009) (cf. *footnote 22* op. cit.), p. 7.

28 See Matsuura, Koïchiro (01/03/2005): Address by Mr Koïchiro Matsuura Director-General of the United Nations Educational, Scientific and Cultural Organization (UNESCO) on the occasion of the International launch of the United Nations Decade on Education for Sustainable Development (2005–2014). DG/2005/036. Manuscript. Officially released and issued on 01/03/2005, United Nations Headquarters, New York, p. 2.

29 See UNESCO (ed.) (1996): Learning: The treasure within. Report to UNESCO of the International Commission on Education for the Twenty-first Century. Edited by Jacques Delors. Paris: UNESCO publishing; Editions Odile Jacob, p. 22.

30 E.g., pre-primary education, primary education, lower-secondary education, upper-secondary education, post-secondary education, tertiary education.
Cf. United Nations Economic Commission for Europe (UNECE) (ed.) (2006) (cf. *footnote 20* op. cit.), p. 11.
See *Figure 3* in chapter II 1.1 *Learning* on page 16.

31 See United Nations Economic Commission for Europe (UNECE); United Nations Economic and Social Council (ECOSOC) (eds.) (2004d) (cf. *footnote 20* op. cit.), p. 2; Centre for Environment and Sustainability (GMV); Chalmers University of Technology; University of Gothenburg (eds.) (2009) (cf. *footnote 22* op. cit.), p. 49.

32 See United Nations Economic Commission for Europe (UNECE) (ed.) (2006) (cf. *footnote 20* op. cit.), p. 7.

33 E.g., private sector, civil society, organisations and specialised groups (trade unions, associations, communities).
Cf. Tooley, James; Dixon, Pauline (eds.) (2005) (cf. *footnote 22* op. cit.).

34 Cf. UNESCO (ed.) (2004c): United Nations Decade of Education for Sustainable Development (2005–2014). Draft International Implementation Scheme. Paris: UNESCO publishing, pp. 22–23; United Nations Economic Commission for Europe (UNECE) (ed.) (2006) (cf. *footnote 20* op. cit.), p. 7.

tween a long-range vision and the urgency of day-to-day practice. Neither can be sacrificed, neither can be entirely satisfied, at any time."[35]

It is unquestionable that *learning models* are based upon certain beliefs and values pertaining to the ideal form of educations. Because of such divergence in visions of education, UNESCO introduced its own four-pillar interpretation or *memorandum of understanding* of *learning* priorities that addresses all spheres of learning, including cognitive, emotional and behavioural aspects.[36]

Table 2: The four pillars of education[37]

Pillar	Notion
Learning to live together	Capability of developing understanding and recognition of others, their history, traditions and spiritual values, and creating awareness of growing interdependence, common risks and challenges of the future
Learning to know	Capability of combining broad general education with the possibility of in-depth work on selected subjects
Learning to do	Capability of enabling people to deal with a variety of situations
Learning to be	Capability of fostering stronger personal responsibility for the attainment of common goals due to greater independence and judgement

35 See UNESCO (ed.) (1996) (cf. *footnote 29* op. cit.), pp. 21–23.

36 See *Table 2* in chapter II 1.1 *Learning* on page 15.

37 This *four-pillar model* of education is the outcome of the *International Commission on Education for the Twenty-first Century* prepared by the correspondent *UNESCO Task Force* under the presidency of *Jacques Delors* published in 1996.
Cf. UNESCO (ed.) (1996) (cf. *footnote 29* op. cit.), pp. 21–23; UNESCO (ed.) (July 2003): United Nations Decade of Education for Sustainable Development (January 2005 – December 2014). Framework for a Draft International Implementation Scheme. Paris: UNESCO publishing, pp. 3–4; UNESCO (ed.) (2005f): Report by the Director-General on the United Nations Decade of Education for Sustainable Development. International Implementation Scheme and UNESCO's Contribution to the Implementation of the Decade. 172 EX/11. Paris: UNESCO publishing, p. 24; Schuchardt, Erika; Mbeki, Thabo (eds.) (2005): Brückenbau: 15 Jahre Begegnungsschulen im Südlichen Afrika. Erfolgsmodell deutscher Auswärtiger Kulturpolitik. Berlin: IBA, p. 241; Bory-Adams, Aline (2010): Looking beyond the Decade: UNESCO's contribution. In: Witthaus, Michele; McCandless, Karen; Lambert, Rebecca (eds.): Tomorrow today. Leicester, United Kingdom: Tudor Rose; UNESCO publishing, pp. 175–178, pp. 176–177.

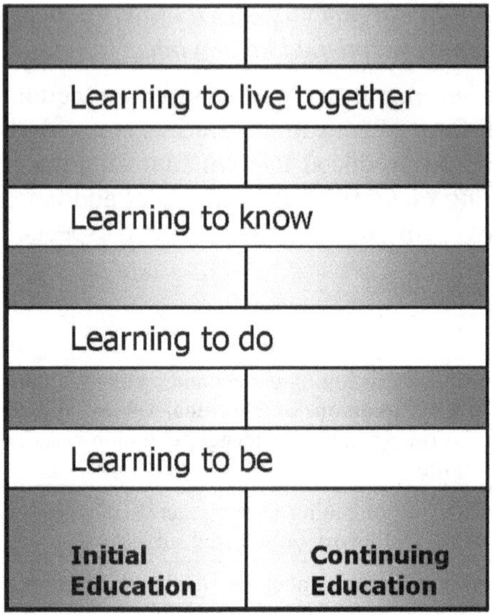

Figure 3: Linking education stages with pillars of learning[38]

1.2 Training

Training reveals another critical aspect of education that is related more pertinently to *capacity-building*[39] and for this reason includes practical application. *Continuing education or training* covers specific *"activities aimed at updating, refreshing or extending knowledge and skills gained during basic education (or) training".*[40]

38 Education is considered holistic and continuous. Differentiating between initial and continuing education is arbitrary, even though meaningful in order to meet certain stage-specific requirements by applying the *four-pillar model.*

39 Capacity-building is consequently defined as a *"process whereby individuals, institutions, organisations and countries acquire, adapt, strengthen, deploy and maintain their capacities or abilities".*
See UNESCO (ed.) (2007j): Report by the Director-General on the follow-up to decisions and resolutions adopted by the Executive Board and the General Conference at their previous sessions. Progress in the development of cross-sectoral capacity-building programmes. 176 EX/5 Add.2. Paris: UNESCO publishing, p. 18.

40 See United Nations Economic Commission for Europe (UNECE) (ed.) (2006) (cf. *footnote 20* op. cit.), p. 7; UNESCO (ed.) (2007j) (cf. *footnote 39* op. cit.), pp. 18 et seqq.

Capacity-building aims at building knowledge, life skills, perspectives, attitudes and values. This may be achieved through effective exchange of information, multiplication[41] of reliable experience and expertise, and purposeful training of human resources in both public and private sectors. All of them primarily contribute to the development of strategic and management capacities in terms of policy development and implementation, the promotion, distribution and use of technology as well as the development and transfer of skills.[42]

1.3 Teaching

Teaching is closely related to the personal and technical competences that are crucial for a *quality education*,[43] proclaiming or envisioning:[44]

- Education as a human right;
- Education as a four-pillar concept, namely learning to know, learning to do, learning to live together and with others, and learning to be;
- Education as a learner-centric affiliation viewing learners as individuals, family and community members, and global citizens capable of creating individual competency in all four roles;
- Education as a sustainable ideal;
- Education as a context-based effort taking into consideration social, economic, environmental and cultural inclinations;

41 E.g., through train-the-trainer programmes.
Cf. Mayor, Federico (17/10/1992): Address by Mr Federico Mayor at the opening of the World Congress for Education and Communication on Environment and Development (ECO-ED). Education for Sustainable Development: Taking up the Challenge of Rio. DG/92/43. Manuscript. Officially released and issued on 17/10/1992, Toronto, Ontario, p. 4.

42 E.g., attaining cultural education through means of capacity-building.
Cf. UNESCO (ed.) (2005a): Convention on the Protection and Promotion of the Diversity of Cultural Expressions. General Conference 33rd session. CLT-2005/CONVENTION DIVERSITE-CULT REV. Paris: UNESCO publishing, p. 9; Leicht, Alexander; Plum, Jacqueline; Fuchs, Max (2007) (cf. *footnote 19* op. cit.), pp. 18, 31, 42; Maclean, Rupert; Fien, John; Park, Man-Gon (eds.) (2009): Work, Learning and Sustainable Development. Opportunities and Challenges. Dordrecht: Springer Netherlands (Springer-11648 [Dig. Serial], 8), p. xxii.

43 See UNESCO (ed.) (2005f) (cf. *footnote 37* op. cit.), p. 24.
See *Figure 4* in chapter II 1.3 *Teaching* on page 18.

44 Cf. UNESCO (ed.) (2005j): United Nations Decade of Education for Sustainable Development (2005–2014). International Implementation Scheme. ED/DESD/2005/PI/01. Paris: UNESCO workshops, p. 27; UNESCO (2006): UNESCO's role, vision and challenges for the UN Decade of Education for Sustainable Development (2005–2014). In: Connect, Volume 31, 1–2, pp. 1–28, pp. 1–2; UNESCO Education Sector (ed.) (2008) (cf. *footnote 27* op. cit.), pp. 4–10.

- Education as a flexible approach that adapts to particular conditions by shaping curricula or programmes according to locally relevant and culturally appropriate needs;
- Education as a continual redefinition informed by indigenous and traditional knowledge of the past, relevant to the present, and which prepares individuals for the future;
- Education as a capacity-building concept of knowledge, life skills, perspectives, attitudes and values;
- Education as tool of societal transformation; and
- Education as measurable.

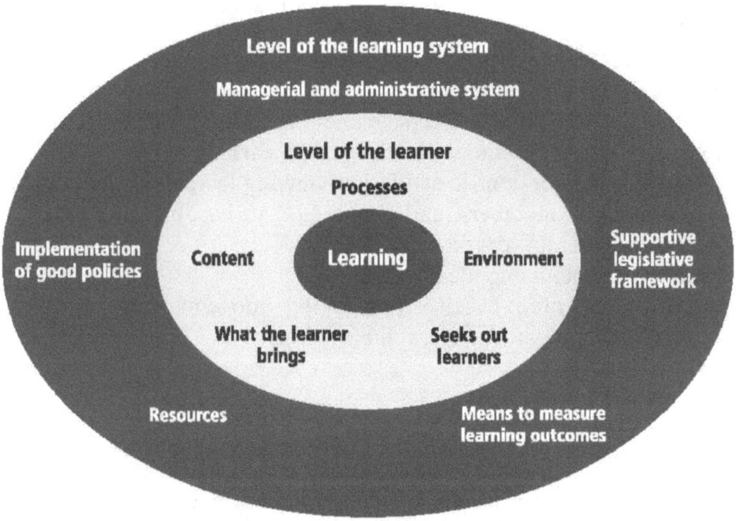

Figure 4: From educating to learning: a framework for quality education[45]

2 Sustainability

Sustainability comprises an immense and difficult scope[46] as *"(d)efinitions of sustainability and sustainable development are (supposedly) commonplace,*

45 See UNESCO Education Sector (ed.) (2005) (cf. *footnote 21* op. cit.), p. 3. This chart depicts how UNESCO relates the concept of *quality education* to both the individual learner and the supporting systems of education. This learner-centric perspective enables defining and setting teaching and training objectives accordingly.

46 Cf. Taylor, Jerry (August 2002): Sustainable Development. A Dubious Solution in Search of a Problem. The Cato Institute. In: Policy Analysis, Issue 449, p. 2; UNESCO

(but) often elusive as to their intent and meaning, and vague enough to allow almost anyone to participate under the sustainability banner".[47]

Since *sustainability* has been *en vogue* for only a few decades, its origins in a much earlier stage of history are frequently neglected. Formerly, *sustainability* was an environmental, economic and social necessity in yield forestry during the 18th century: vast areas of woods cut down for timber and heating had to be re-forested in anticipation of the need to ensure continuing harvests and marketable incomes. Introduced by the German tax accountant and mining administrator Hans Carl von Carlowitz, the formula is quite simple: prospective harvests are only possible if resources have been planted and grown cyclically. In other words, sustainable yield forestry requires adaptive and future-oriented thinking.

A broad attempt at defining *sustainability "(...) refers to the capacity of people to adapt and cope with their environments as individuals and as a part of social organisations".*[48] Certainly the most prominent, readily acknowledged and cited definition of *sustainability* is that given by the so called *Brundtland Report*[49] in 1987.[50] In fact, this definition paved the way for an increasing global awareness of *sustainability*. For the very first time *sustainability* was defined as *"(...) development that meets the needs of the present without compromising the ability of future generations to meet their own needs. It contains within it two key concepts:*

(ed.) (2007b): Drivers and Barriers for Implementing Learning for Sustainable Development in Pre-School through Upper Secondary and Teacher Education. Education for Sustainable Development in Action. Göteborg Workshop 27–29 March 2006. Technical Paper N° 4. Edited by Inger Björneloo; Eva Nyberg. Paris: UNESCO publishing, p. 15.

47 See Fien, John; Goldney, David; Murphy, Tom (2009): Rethinking Development: As if the Planet and its People Really Mattered. In: Maclean, Rupert; Fien, John; Park, Man-Gon (eds.): Work, Learning and Sustainable Development. Opportunities and Challenges. Dordrecht: Springer Netherlands (Springer-11648 [Dig. Serial], 8), pp. 19–33, p. 21.

48 See Thomas, Elwyn (2009): Sustainable Development: The Challenges and Prospects for a Sustainability Curriculum. In: Maclean, Rupert; Fien, John; Park, Man-Gon (eds.): Work, Learning and Sustainable Development. Opportunities and Challenges. Dordrecht: Springer Netherlands (Springer-11648 [Dig. Serial], 8), pp. 77–92, p. 77.

49 Cf. United Nations (ed.) (1987b): Report of the World Commission on Environment and Development. General Assembly Resolution. A/RES/42/187. New York: United Nations; United Nations (ed.) (1987c): Report of the World Commission on Environment and Development. Brundtland Report (Annex "Our Common Future"). A/43/427. New York: United Nations.

50 Cf. Morris, Julian (ed.) (2002): Sustainable Development. Promoting progress or perpetuating poverty? London: Profile Books Ltd, p. 1; Magraw Barstow, Daniel; Hawke, Lisa D. (2007): Sustainable Development. In: Bodansky, Daniel; Brunée, Jutta; Hey, Ellen (eds.): The Oxford handbook of international environmental law. Oxford: Oxford University Press (Oxford handbooks), pp. 613–638, pp. 618–622.

- *(T)he concept of 'needs', in particular the essential needs of the world's poor, to which overriding priority should be given; and*
- *(T)he idea of limitations imposed by the state of technology and social organisation on the environment's ability to meet present and future needs".*[51]

This definition emphasises two critical aspects: firstly, there are certain human needs that must be satisfied through constant development through the exploitation of any resource; secondly, given limited resources, such development must guarantee future generations at least the same opportunities to fulfil their particular needs.[52]

It must subsequently be asked how to tackle *sustainability* as a concept. More precisely, what methods of reasoning must be considered? With this in mind, three interdependent approaches or dimensions are proposed:[53]

- *Analytical dimension*: *sustainability* features a qualification of different states and processes within a continuum of feasible states and processes;
- *Normative dimension*: *sustainability* constitutes an imperative to achieve compatibility between divergent claims and commitments, such as social, cultural, economic and environmental goals at all levels; and
- *Strategical dimension*: *sustainability* requires that, firstly, different goals, secondly, appropriate ways and means of implementation, thirdly, processes of critical re-evaluation and assessment of assigned institutions and institutional arrangements, and fourthly, the management of potential actors and respective conflicts of interest among them be identified.

Sustainability is characterised by a gradual transformation and qualitative improvement from term to conception.[54] In defining *sustainability* in 1987 for the very first time, the term became established for the first time in international

---

51 See United Nations; Brundtland, Gro Harlem (1991): Our common future. (In 1987 published and transmitted to UN General Assembly as annex to document A/42/42). Volume 13. imprint. Oxford: Oxford University Press (Oxford paperbacks), p. 54. Cf. Singer, S. Fred (22/04/2011): The Sustainable Development Hoax. In: American Thinker, April 2011, p. 1.

52 Cf. Deutscher Bundestag (ed.) (1998): Konzept Nachhaltigkeit. Vom Leitbild zur Umsetzung = The concept of sustainability. Abschlußbericht der Enquete-Kommission "Schutz des Menschen und der Umwelt – Ziele und Rahmenbedingungen einer nachhaltig zukunftsverträglichen Entwicklung" des 13. Deutschen Bundestages. Bonn / Berlin: Deutscher Bundestag Referat Öffentlichkeitsarbeit (Drucksache 13/11200, 98,4), pp. 30 et seqq; UNESCO (ed.) (2005c) (cf. *footnote 23* op. cit.), pp. 8–9, 13; UNESCO (2007): Welcome to Education for Sustainable Development. UNESCO.

53 Cf. Becker, Egon; Jahn, Thomas; Stieß, Immanuel, et al. (eds.) (1997): Sustainability: A Cross-Disciplinary Concept for Social Transformations. Paris / Frankfurt am Main: UNESCO publishing (Management of Social Transformation (MOST) Policy Papers, 6), pp. 21–22.

54 See *Figure 5* in chapter II 2 *Sustainability* on page 21.

law. *Sustainability* later developed into an acknowledged principle of guidance for further discourse as a *law-like* or rule-based manifesto. *DESD* finally elevated *sustainability* to a more conceptually comprehensive position in identifying it as process of constituting and forming concise ideas and plans of implementation.

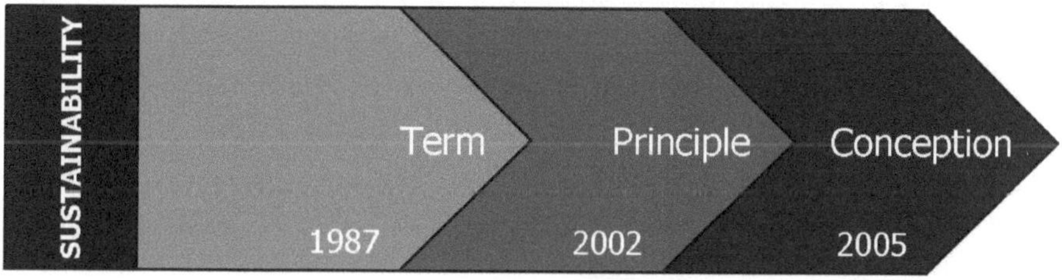

Figure 5: Sustainability – from term to conception[55]

"However, sustainability remains a nebulous concept that is variously defined, debated and deconstructed."[56] As a consequence it is useful to distinguish between different notions of *sustainability*.

2.1 Environmental or ecological sustainability

It is presumed that *environmental or ecological sustainability* ranges among the most common and comprehensible understanding of sustainability, since it takes into account the fundamental notion of *green* pioneering work.[57] Both in scien-

---

55 *Sustainability* has undergone an evolutionary process of transforming from coining the term in 1987 (*Brundtland Report*), establishing an agreed-upon principle of institutional guidance in 2002 (*Johannesburg Declaration*), and providing conception-like frameworks of implementation starting from 2005 (*DESD*).
Cf. UNESCO (ed.) (2005c) (cf. *footnote 23* op. cit.), pp. 8, 13; Selby, David (2009): The Firm and Shaky Ground of Education for Sustainable Development. In: Chalkley, Brian; Haigh, Martin J.; Higgitt, David (eds.): Education for sustainable development. Papers in honour of the United Nations Decade of Education for Sustainable Development (2005–2014). London / New York: Routledge, pp. 199–213, pp. 200 et seqq.

56 See Higgitt, David (2009b): Finding Space for Education for Sustainable Development in the Enterprise Economcy. In: Chalkley, Brian; Haigh, Martin J.; Higgitt, David (eds.): Education for sustainable development. Papers in honour of the United Nations Decade of Education for Sustainable Development (2005–2014). London / New York: Routledge, pp. 99–110, p. 99.
Cf. Selby, David (2009) (cf. *footnote 55* op. cit.), pp. 203 et seqq.

57 Cf. Carson, Rachel (1962 / 2002): Silent spring. Volume 40th anniversary edition / 1st Mariner Books edition. Boston: Houghton Mifflin; United Nations Economic Commission for Europe (UNECE); United Nations Economic and Social Council

tific and public discourse this *resource sustainability*[58] relates to *"an awareness of the resources and fragility of the physical environment and the affects on it of human activity and decisions, with a commitment to factoring environmental concerns into social and economic policy development"*.[59] Notable conceptions of *environmental* or *ecological sustainability* include:[60]

- Sustainable development and natural *carrying capacity*;
- Eco-space, ecological footprint, natural capitalism and natural resource accounting;
- Eco-efficiency and life-cycle analysis;
- Triple-bottom-line reporting and environmental management systems; and
- Biodiversity, inter-species equity as well as intra- and inter-generational equity.

2.2 Social sustainability

Social sustainability aims at providing *"an understanding of social institutions and their role in change and development, as well as the democratic and participatory systems which give opportunity for the expression of opinion, the selection of governments, the forging of consensus and the resolution of differences"*.[61] Reliance and reliability in time are core elements of revolving and future-oriented societies. This is usually referred to as *inter-generational equity*[62] or *–responsibility*,[63] claiming that social wellbeing will not decline substantially over the course of time.[64] Major efforts and achievements in terms of *social sustainability* are envisioned in the fields of:[65]

(ECOSOC) (eds.) (2004f) (cf. *footnote 27* op. cit.), p. 7; Bodansky, Daniel; Brunée, Jutta; Hey, Ellen (eds.) (2007): The Oxford handbook of international environmental law. Oxford: Oxford University Press (Oxford handbooks).

58 See Taylor, Jerry (August 2002) (cf. *footnote 46* op. cit.), p. 6.

59 See UNESCO (ed.) (2005c) (cf. *footnote 23* op. cit.), pp. 8, 17.

60 Cf. Gallopin, Gilberto (ed.) (March 2003): A systems approach to sustainability and sustainable development. LC/L.1864-P/I. Santiago de Chile: Naciones Unidas (medio ambiente y desarrollo, 64), pp. 13–16; Maclean, Rupert; Fien, John; Park, Man-Gon (eds.) (2009) (cf. *footnote 42* op. cit.), pp. xxvi–xxx.

61 See UNESCO (ed.) (2005c) (cf. *footnote 23* op. cit.), pp. 8, 17.

62 Cf. Shelton, Dinah (2007e): Equity. In: Bodansky, Daniel; Brunée, Jutta; Hey, Ellen (eds.): The Oxford handbook of international environmental law. Oxford: Oxford University Press (Oxford handbooks), pp. 639–662, pp. 642–643.

63 Cf. Selby, David (2009) (cf. *footnote 55* op. cit.), pp. 203 et seqq.

64 Cf. Becker, Egon; Jahn, Thomas; Stieß, Immanuel, et al. (eds.) (1997) (cf. *footnote 53* op. cit.); Taylor, Jerry (August 2002) (cf. *footnote 46* op. cit.), p. 4.

65 Cf. Maclean, Rupert; Fien, John; Park, Man-Gon (eds.) (2009) (cf. *footnote 42* op. cit.), pp. xxx–xxxiv.

- Respect for (cultural) diversity;
- Gender equality, participation and citizenship;
- Teamwork and workplace relations; and
- Safety.

2.3 Economic sustainability

Economic sustainability emphasises the basics of resource-dependent growth[66] in order to attain *"sensitivity to the limits and potential of economic growth and their impact on society and on the environment, with a commitment to assess personal and societal levels of consumption out of concern for the environment and for social justice"*.[67] At the same time it serves as a critique of conventional performance-oriented conditions of economic growth.[68] Considering that *"economic growth is not necessarily synonymous with material economic growth"*,[69] *economic sustainability* deals with alternative questions of *non-material* economic growth,[70] such as the gradual replacement of natural resources through adequate means of technological change. Important issues of economic sustainability are, amongst others:[71]

- Economic literacy;
- Sustainable production;
- Sustainable consumption; and
- Small enterprise management.

66 Cf. Choucri, Nazli (1995): Global accord. Environmental challenges and international responses. Volume 1. paperback edition. Cambridge, Massachusetts: MIT Press (Global Environmental Accord: Strategies for Sustainability and Institutional Innovation), pp. 67 et seqq; Taylor, Jerry (August 2002) (cf. *footnote 46* op. cit.), p. 1.

67 See UNESCO (ed.) (2005c) (cf. *footnote 23* op. cit.), pp. 8, 17.

68 Cf. North, Douglass Cecil (1997): Economic Performance Through Time. Nobel Prize Lecture. December 9, 1993. In: Persson, Torsten (ed.): Nobel Lectures. Economic sciences. 1991–1995. Singapore: World Scientific Publishing Company (Nobel lectures), pp. 112–126, pp. 6, 10.
E.g., indefinite patterns of consumption, availability of scarce (human and natural) resources, etc.
Cf. Taylor, Jerry (August 2002) (cf. *footnote 46* op. cit.), p. 2.

69 See Gallopin, Gilberto (ed.) (March 2003) (cf. *footnote 60* op. cit.), p. 36.

70 Cf. Gallopin, Gilberto (ed.) (March 2003) (cf. *footnote 60* op. cit.), pp. 5, 25.

71 Cf. Maclean, Rupert; Fien, John; Park, Man-Gon (eds.) (2009) (cf. *footnote 42* op. cit.), pp. xxiv–xxvi.

2.4 Cultural sustainability

"Sustainable development and the flourishing of culture are interdependent."[72] Recently, it has not been commonplace to state that *"(c)ultural diversity and intercultural education contribute to the social and cultural aspects of sustainability"*.[73] Meanwhile, *cultural sustainability* is increasingly gaining importance.[74] This is mainly due to the findings that *"(t)he values, diversity, knowledge, languages and worldviews associated with culture strongly influence the way issues of (sustainability) are dealt with in specific (...) contexts. In this sense, culture is just not a collection of particular manifestations (...), but a (promising) way of being, relating, behaving, believing and acting through which people live out in their lives and that is in a constant process of change"*.[75] In other words, *"being aware that cultural diversity creates a rich and varied world, which increases the range of choices and nurtures human capacities and values, and therefore is a mainspring for sustainable development for communities, peoples and nations (...)"*.[76]

The shifting paradigm of cultural diversity[77] as a *key action theme*[78] adopted by UNESCO is attested by practices of international law-making, laid down in

72 See UNESCO (ed.) (1998): Action Plan on Cultural Policies for Development. adopted in by the Intergovernmental Conference on Cultural Policies for Development. 2 April 1998, Stockholm, Sweden. Paris / Stockholm: UNESCO Networking & Information Section, p. 2.

73 See Lasonen, Johanna (2009): Intercultural Education: Promoting Sustainability in Education and Training. In: Maclean, Rupert; Fien, John; Park, Man-Gon (eds.): Work, Learning and Sustainable Development. Opportunities and Challenges. Dordrecht: Springer Netherlands (Springer-11648 [Dig. Serial], 8), pp. 187–202, p. 187.

74 Cf. Pérez Cuéllar, Javier de (ed.) (1995 / 1996): Our creative diversity. Report of the World Commission on Culture and Development. CLT-96/WS-6. Volume 2. edition, revised. Paris: UNESCO publishing; UNESCO (ed.) (2005c) (cf. *footnote 23* op. cit.), p. 15; UNESCO (ed.) (2008b): Convention on the Protection and Promotion of the Diversity of Cultural Expressions. Culture in Sustainable Development: Insights for the future implementation of art. 13. CE/08/Throsby/Art.13. Edited by David Throsby. Sydney: UNESCO publishing, p. 2.

75 See UNESCO (ed.) (2005c) (cf. *footnote 23* op. cit.), pp. 8, 17.

76 See digit 3 UNESCO (ed.) (2005a) (cf. *footnote 42* op. cit.), p. 2.

77 Cf. UNESCO (ed.) (2001): UNESCO Universal Declaration on Cultural Diversity. General Conference 31st session. Volume No. 1, 2002. Paris: Copyright Bulletin (Vol. XXXVI), p. 5; Deutsche UNESCO-Kommission e. V. (DUK) (2007): Kultur – Deutsche UNESCO-Kommission. Supported by: Offenhäußer, Dieter; Schlünkes, Kurt and Möller, Lutz; Inglis, Christine (2008): Planning for cultural diversity. Paris: UNESCO publishing (Fundamentals of Educational Planning, 87), p. 37; Alkoby, Asher (2008): Theories of Compliance with International Law and the Challenge of Cultural Difference. In: Journal of International Law and International Relations, Volume 4, Issue 1, pp. 151–198, pp. 153 et seqq.

different documents related to *cultural sustainability* and development, and, in particular:[79]

- *The UNESCO Universal Declaration on Cultural Diversity* (2001);[80] and
- *The Convention on the Protection and Promotion of the Diversity of Cultural Expressions* (2005).[81]

In summary, culture is highly recognised as valuable source, resource and constitutive element of change,[82] particularly in the matter of sustainability.[83] Thus,

---

78 See UNESCO (2007): Key Action Themes. Cultural Diversity. Published by: UNESCO Education Sector.

79 Cf. UNESCO (2007n): Conventions, Recommendations, Declarations and Charters adopted by UNESCO (1948–2006). Paris / Leiden: UNESCO publishing; Martinus Nijhoff Publishers (UNESCO reference works series, 2).

80 Cf. UNESCO (ed.) (2001) (cf. *footnote 77* op. cit.).
"Article 3 – Cultural diversity as a factor in development: Cultural diversity widens the range of options open to everyone; it is one of the roots of development, understood not simply in terms of economic growth, but also as a means to achieve a more satisfactory intellectual, emotional, moral and spiritual existence."
See UNESCO (ed.) (2001) (cf. *footnote 77* op. cit.), p. 6; UNESCO (ed.) (2002b): Cultural Diversity: A Conceptual Platform. Sustainable Diversity: The indivisibility of culture and development. Edited by Katérina Stenou. Paris: UNESCO publishing (Cultural Diversity Series, No. 1).

81 Cf. UNESCO (ed.) (2005a) (cf. *footnote 42* op. cit.).
"Article 2 (Paragraph 6) – Principle of sustainable development: Cultural diversity is a rich asset for individuals and societies. The protection, promotion and maintenance of cultural diversity are an essential requirement for sustainable development for the benefit of present and future generations.
Article 13 – Integration of culture in sustainable development: Parties shall endeavour to integrate culture in their development policies at all levels for the creation of conditions conducive to sustainable development and, within this framework, foster aspects relating to the protection and promotion of the diversity of cultural expressions."
See UNESCO (ed.) (2008b) (cf. *footnote 74* op. cit.), p. 2.

82 I.e. UNESCO definition of *culture*.
Cf. Fuchs, Max (2002): Dialog zwischen den Kulturen. Kulturtheoretische und -politische Anmerkungen. Online-Magazin der Deutschen UNESCO-Kommission. In: unesco heute online, Volume März 2002, Issue 3.

83 I.e. technically and structurally linking culture and sustainable development.
Cf. Scott, William A. H.; Gough, Stephen R. (2003): Sustainable development and learning. Framing the issues. Volume 1. edition. London / New York: Routledge Falmer, pp. 10–11; Kono, Toshiyuki (2007): Safeguarding the World's Cultural and Natural Heritage. UNESCO and Intangible Cultural Heritage from the Viewpoint of Sustainable Development. In: Yusuf, Abdulqawi A. (ed.): Normative action in education, science and culture. Essays in commemoration of the sixtieth anniversary of UNESCO. French edition. Paris / Leiden / Boston: UNESCO publishing; Martinus Nijhoff Publishers (UNESCO reference works series, 1), pp. 249–280; UNESCO (ed.) (2008a): Approved Programme and Budget 2008–2009. 34 C/5 Approved. Paris:

"(i)n the development of (...) sustainability (...), it is clear that cultural context has to be taken into account if it is to be a success".[84]

3 Development

Development describes a multi-faceted process of measurable and directional progress. *"(D)evelopment is a qualitative process of realisation of potentialities which may or may not involve economic growth (a quantitative increase in wealth)."*[85] As discussed, *development* is not restricted or equivalent to economic growth alone.[86] On the contrary: it affects many different spheres of life.[87] More recently, for instance, mounting emphasis and awareness-raising may be observed in consideration of the nexus between (cultural) education and *development.*[88] Therefore, *"UNESCO should reaffirm the centrality of education for development. As United Nations lead agency, UNESCO should advocate a more coherent co-ordination (...)".*[89] Similar observations are equally applicable to

---

UNESCO workshops, p. 196; Gambini, Barbara (2009): Cultural Assumptions against Sustainability: An International Survey. In: Chalkley, Brian; Haigh, Martin J.; Higgitt, David (eds.): Education for sustainable development. Papers in honour of the United Nations Decade of Education for Sustainable Development (2005–2014). London / New York: Routledge, pp. 111–127, p. 125.

84 See Thomas, Elwyn (2009) (cf. *footnote 48* op. cit.), p. 85.

85 See Gallopin, Gilberto (ed.) (March 2003) (cf. *footnote 60* op. cit.), p. 36.

86 Cf. Soubbotina, Tatyana P. (2004): Beyond economic growth. An introduction to sustainable development. HD75.S684 2000. Volume 2. edition. Supported by: Sheram, Katherine A. Washington, D. C.: World Bank (WBI learning resources series), p. 1.

87 Cf. Soubbotina, Tatyana P. (2004) (cf. *footnote 86* op. cit.), pp. 7–8.

88 I.e. culture meets development: Culture enables and facilitates economic development. E.g., implementing the *United Nations World Decade for Cultural Development* (1988–1997).
Cf. UNESCO Culture Sector (ed.) (1997): From weaving to websites ... UNESCO celebrates culture. Culture and Development. Rethinking development: the World Decade for Cultural Development, 1988–1997. Edited by Malachy Quinn. Paris: Paragraphic L'UNION, pp. 29–30; Bernecker, Roland; Leicht, Alexander (eds.) (1998): Kultur und Entwicklung. Zur Umsetzung des Stockholmer Aktionsplans. Bonn: Deutsche UNESCO-Kommission; UNESCO (ed.) (1998) (cf. *footnote 72* op. cit.), p. 1; Kuhn, Katina (März 2006): Zur kulturellen Dimension nachhaltiger Entwicklung – Eine metatheoretische und diskursanalytische Bestandsaufnahme. INFU-Diskussionsbeiträge 28/06. Supervised by: Michelsen, Gerd; Adomßent, Maik; Barth, Matthias and Godemann, Jasmin. Lüneburg. Universität Lüneburg / University of Lüneburg, Institut für Umweltkommunikation (INFU), pp. 22–29; Kono, Toshiyuki (2007) (cf. *footnote 83* op. cit.), pp. 253 et seqq.

89 See Bokova, Irina (2009): UNESCO in a Globalised World: New Humanism for the 21st Century. Mission statement by the Director-General of UNESCO. 15 November 2009. UNESCO.

the social and human dimension of *development*. The unalienable *human right* to *development* was approved by United Nations resolution *A/RES/41/128* as *Declaration on the Right to Development* in 1986.[90]

3.1 Sustainable development

"Sustainable Development (SD) has been a huge success in the talking shops of the world. In think-tanks, universities, P(ublic) R(elations) agencies and the UN, it has been a triumph."[91]

Sustainable development relates to a particular aspect of development that is directed towards sustainability.[92] One can indisputably question this nexus by referring to sustainable development as an *oxymoron*.[93] Conversely, it is *"(...) the social, economic, (perhaps cultural) and environmental capacity to maintain an intentional path of continuing development"*.[94] In contrast to interpretations of development mainly built on external or *steady-state*[95] assumptions, *"(s)ustainable development (gives) a more dynamic notion, emphasizing the need for individuals and organisations to actively learn and develop"*.[96]

Only to a markedly lesser extent may *sustainable development* be regarded as a neutral term of development. Since it depends on values,[97] commonly shared perspectives and targeted aims, *sustainable development* constitutes a

90 Cf. United Nations (ed.) (1987a): Declaration on the Right to Development. Resolution adopted by the General Assembly. A/RES/41/128. New York: United Nations (Resolutions and decisions adopted by the General Assembly during its 41st session, 53), pp. 164 et seqq.

91 See North, Richard D. (2005): Sustainable Development: A concept with a Future? Volume First Edition. Berlin: Comdok GmbH (OccasionalPaper, 11), p. 3.
Cf. Singer, S. Fred (22/04/2011) (cf. *footnote 51* op. cit.), p. 1.

92 Cf. Soubbotina, Tatyana P. (2004) (cf. *footnote 86* op. cit.), pp. 9–10; Kuhn, Katina (März 2006) (cf. *footnote 88* op. cit.), pp. 21–22.

93 See Selby, David (2009) (cf. *footnote 55* op. cit.), p. 203.

94 See Matsuura, Koïchiro (01/03/2005) (cf. *footnote 28* op. cit.), p. 2.

95 See World Bank (ed.) (2003): Sustainable development in a dynamic world. Transforming institutions, growth, and quality of life. 24705. New York: Oxford University Press (World development report, 25), p. 14.

96 See Thomas, Elwyn (2009) (cf. *footnote 48* op. cit.), p. 77.

97 I.e. minimum underlying values and consensus are the respect for the dignity and human rights of all people, the respect for the human rights of future generations and a commitment to inter-generational responsibility, the respect and care for the greater community of life in all its diversities, and the respect for cultural diversity and commitment for a culture of tolerance.
Cf. Selby, David (2009) (cf. *footnote 55* op. cit.), pp. 200 et seqq.

normative concept or even a *paradigm*.[98] Therefore, *"the belief that sustainable development, which implies meeting the needs of the present without compromising the ability of future generations to meet their own needs, should become a central (and integrated) guiding principle (of human development) [...]"*.[99]

Sustainable development must identify in actual terms *added value* exempt from ideology in order to avoid provoking radical criticism: *"(t)o put it bluntly: because people insist that sustainable development legitimises either economic development or green romanticism – or that it can reconcile them – its whole value is thrown away. Its real value is that it frames debate"*.[100]

3.2 Characteristics

Controversy still exists as to how *sustainable development* may be conceptualised in theory[101] and practice,[102] and first and foremost as to how it may be appropriately implemented: *"In practice, sustainable development is a nebulous concept, a chimera that can be adapted, contradicted and contested, and caricatured as a 'large, diverse and rapidly expanding field of enquiry populated by heterogeneous discourses, multiple approaches and a variety of recommendations as to the ways forward'"*.[103]

98 See Bartholomäi, Reinhard (1997): Sustainable Development und Völkerrecht. Nachhaltige Entwicklung und intergenerative Gerechtigkeit in der Staatenpraxis. Baden-Baden: Nomos Verlagsgesellschaft (Gießener Abhandlungen zum Umweltrecht, 2), p. 82.

99 See United Nations (ed.) (1987b) (cf. *footnote 49* op. cit.), p. 1; Deutsche UNESCO-Kommission e. V. (DUK) (ed.) (2003b): Tätigkeitsbericht 2002. Vertrauen schaffen, Nachhaltigkeit gestalten. Bonn: Deutsche UNESCO-Kommission (Online-Magazin der Deutschen UNESCO-Kommission, 7), p. 22.

100 See North, Richard D. (2005) (cf. *footnote 91* op. cit.), p. 3.

101 E.g., *"(o)ther advocates of sustainable development describe regimes in which the natural resource base would be allowed to deteriorate as long as biological resources are maintained at a minimum critical level and the wealth generated by the exploitation of natural resources is preserved for future generations, who would otherwise be 'robbed' of their rightful inheritance"*.
See Taylor, Jerry (August 2002) (cf. *footnote 46* op. cit.), p. 2.

102 Cf. Bartholomäi, Reinhard (1997) (cf. *footnote 98* op. cit.), pp. 72–81; Morris, Julian (ed.) (2002) (cf. *footnote 50* op. cit.), pp. 1–10; Deutsche UNESCO-Kommission e. V. (DUK) (ed.) (2007) (cf. *footnote 24* op. cit.), pp. 15–16.

103 See Higgitt, David (2009a): Approaching the UN Decade of Education for Sustainable Development: Prospects and Challenges. In: Chalkley, Brian; Haigh, Martin J.; Higgitt, David (eds.): Education for sustainable development. Papers in honour of the United Nations Decade of Education for Sustainable Development (2005–2014). London / New York: Routledge, pp. 1–12, p. 3; Wiliams, Colin C.; Millingtin, Andrew C. (2004): The diverse and contested meanings of sustainable development. In: Geographical Journal, Volume 170, Issue 2, pp. 99–104, p. 99.

Sustainable development cannot be regarded as the heir of an outdated and uniform ideation of *orderliness* in the ecosystem.[104] There is neither a concrete quality nor any tendency towards stability inherent in perspectives on this concept. In fact, *sustainable development* ought to be considered as the realistic conception of disorder characterised by the short-lived, unfathomable, unquantifiable or indefinable. As already mentioned, there is a need for interdisciplinary or cross-cutting perspectives.[105] In summary, *"(s)ustainable development is a dynamic and evolving concept with many dimensions and interpretations and reflects locally relevant and culturally appropriate visions for a (sustainably-developing) world (...)"*.[106]

104 Cf. Selby, David (2009) (cf. *footnote 55* op. cit.), p. 210.

105 Cf. Selby, David (2009) (cf. *footnote 55* op. cit.), pp. 210 et seqq.

106 See UNESCO (ed.) (July 2003) (cf. *footnote 37* op. cit.).
See *Figure 6* in chapter II 3.2 *Characteristics* on page 30.

Figure 6: Key characteristics of sustainable development[107]

4 Education for Sustainable Development

4.1 Concept

"Education for sustainable development (ESD) is a dynamic concept that encompasses a new vision of education seeking to empower people of all ages to assume responsibility for creating and enjoying a sustainable future."[108]

ESD binds together three conceptual components: sustainability, development and education. Added value is to be created through combining *"(...) all aspects of public awareness, education and training to create or enhance an un-*

107 This catalogue of multiple characteristics reveals the UNESCO-driven view of sustainable development that is most relevant to *DESD*.
Cf. UNESCO (ed.) (July 2003) (cf. *footnote 37* op. cit.), p. 12; UNESCO (ed.) (2004c) (cf. *footnote 34* op. cit.), p. 16; UNESCO (ed.) (July 2003) (cf. *footnote 37* op. cit.), p. 10; UNESCO (ed.) (2005c) (cf. *footnote 23* op. cit.), p. 18; UNESCO (ed.) (2005j) (cf. *footnote 44* op. cit.), pp. 30–31; UNESCO (2007) (cf. *footnote 52* op. cit.).

108 See Lasonen, Johanna (2009) (cf. *footnote 73* op. cit.), p. 187.

derstanding of the linkages among the issues of sustainable development and to develop the knowledge, skills, perspectives and values which will empower people of all ages to assume responsibility for creating and enjoying a sustainable future".[109]

Importantly, *"(e)ducation for sustainable development should not (exclusively*[110]*) be equated with environmental education".*[111] Instead, *ESD* is concerned more with addressing a *range* of issues and thereby generating spillover effects.[112] Despite the fact that *"(t)here is no (solely) valid definition of ESD"*,[113] there is at least a *"uniformly agreed definition of the scope of ESD".*[114] It encompasses both the *multi-dimensional* approach of sustainability and development, and the *four-pillar* UNESCO conception of education: *"(q)uality education is a prerequisite for education for sustainable development at all levels and in all modalities of education".*[115]

---

109 See UNESCO (ed.) (2003b): United Nations Decade of Education for Sustainable Development (2005–2014). Framework for the International Implementation Scheme. 32 C/INF.9. Paris: UNESCO publishing, pp. 2–3.

110 Of course, there are effective contributions of environmental education to sustainable development, particularly the process orientation and participatory practices. Notwithstanding, *DESD* is larger in scope.
Cf. Haigh, Martin J. (2009): Promoting Environmental Education for Sustainable Development: The Value of Links between Higher Education and Non-Governmental Organizations (NGOs). In: Chalkley, Brian; Haigh, Martin J.; Higgitt, David (eds.): Education for sustainable development. Papers in honour of the United Nations Decade of Education for Sustainable Development (2005–2014). London / New York: Routledge, pp. 175–197.

111 See UNESCO (ed.) (2005c) (cf. *footnote 23* op. cit.), p. 18.
See *Figure 7* in chapter II 4.1 *Concept* on page 32.

112 Cf. United Nations Economic Commission for Europe (UNECE) (ed.) (2006) (cf. *footnote 20* op. cit.), p. 6; Deutsche UNESCO-Kommission e. V. (DUK) (ed.) (2007) (cf. *footnote 24* op. cit.), p. 26.

113 See UNESCO; The Earth Charter Initiative (ECI) (eds.) (Marzo 2007): Encuentro Latinoamericano: Construyendo una Educación para el Desarrollo Sostenible. Estrategia Regional: Construyendo una Educación para el Desarrollo Sostenible en América Latina y el Caribe. Paris / San José: Producciones ALPI, p. 13; Selby, David (2009) (cf. *footnote 55* op. cit.), p. 209.

114 See Higgitt, David (2009b) (cf. *footnote 56* op. cit.), p. 99.

115 See UNESCO (ed.) (2003b) (cf. *footnote 109* op. cit.), p. 2.

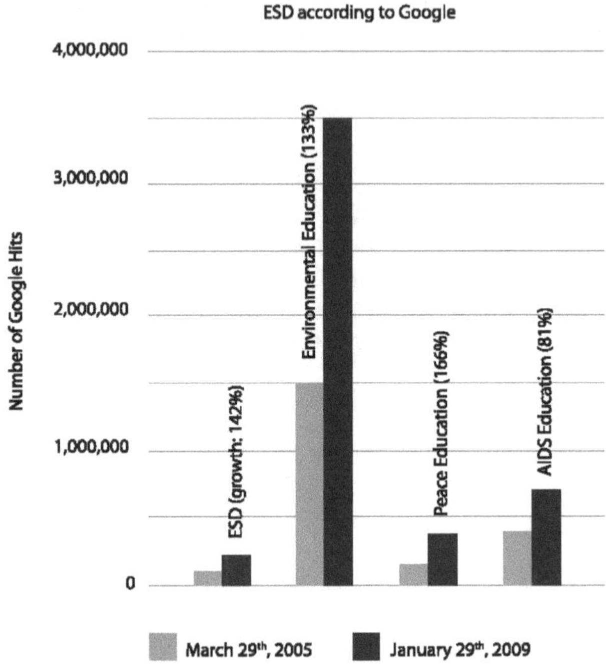

Figure 7: ESD – marginal or growing concern?[116]

For obvious reasons, changes in behaviours require two prerequisites: positive attitude *and* capacity to modify lifestyles. Given a benevolent acquiescence towards future-oriented societies, the question arises of how to achieve sustainable behaviour in reality. This is where capacity-building through education becomes increasingly important. *"Emphasizing that education is an indispensable element for achieving sustainable development"*,[117] the success of the latter de-

116 Measuring the development of public perception of *ESD* by hits, environmental education remains by far the predominant pillar of *ESD*. Even compared to other educational issues, such like HIV / AIDS or peace, *ESD* must be considered a marginal concern in public perception only.
Cf. UNESCO Section for DESD Coordination (ed.) (2009): Learning for a sustainable world. Review of Contexts and Structures for Education for Sustainable Development. 2009 DESD Global Report. Edited by Daniella Tilbury; Saïd Belkachla; Abelardo Brenes; Elaine Unterhalter; Pierre Varcher; Roel van Raiij; Alex Michalos; Govinda Rangachar; Shivali Lawale; Overson Shumba. Paris: UNESCO workshops, p. 10.

117 See United Nations (ed.) (2002 / 2003): United Nations Decade of Education for Sustainable Development. Resolution adopted by the General Assembly. A/RES/57/254. New York: United Nations, p. 1.

pends accordingly on education-based societies alone.[118] Education constitutes a *conditio sine qua non*[119] of learning sustainability.[120] *"Thus, education is the primary agent of transformation towards sustainable development, increasing people's capacities to transform their visions for society into reality."*[121]

(Sustainability + Development) ∗ Education

=

Education for **S**ustainable **D**evelopment

Figure 8: Calculating ESD[122]

4.2 United Nations Decade of Education for Sustainable Development

"The Decade of Education for Sustainable Development (DESD) is a far-reaching and complex undertaking. Its conceptual basis, socio-economic implications, and environmental and cultural connections make it an enterprise, which potentially touches on every aspect of life. [...] (It) presents three key areas of sustainable development – society, environment and economy with culture as an underlying dimension. [...] The basic vision of the DESD is a world where everyone has the opportunity to benefit from education and learn the values, be-

---

118 Cf. UNESCO (ed.) (2005c) (cf. *footnote 23* op. cit.), p. 17; Deutsche UNESCO-Kommission e. V. (DUK) (ed.) (2007) (cf. *footnote 24* op. cit.), p. 5.
See *Figure 8* in chapter II 4.1 *Concept* on page 33.

119 See UNESCO (ed.) (2004c) (cf. *footnote 34* op. cit.), p. 12.

120 Cf. Deutsche UNESCO-Kommission e. V. (DUK) (ed.) (2003a): Nachhaltigkeit lernen: Hamburger Erklärung der Deutschen UNESCO-Kommission zur Dekade der Vereinten Nationen "Bildung für nachhaltige Entwicklung" (2005–2014). Bonn: Deutsche UNESCO-Kommission; Scott, William A. H.; Gough, Stephen R. (2003) (cf. *footnote 83* op. cit.), pp. xiv, 31 et seqq; UNESCO (ed.) (2007c): Education for Sustainable Development: Linking Learning and Happiness. APE/ESD/07/OP/065–500. Edited by Joel E. Bacha; Sombath Somphone; Lawrence Surendra. Bangkok: UNESCO Asia and Pacific Regional Bureau for Education, p. 14.

121 See UNESCO (ed.) (July 2003) (cf. *footnote 37* op. cit.), p. 4; UNESCO (ed.) (2005j) (cf. *footnote 44* op. cit.), pp. 30–31.

122 This hypothetical equation compiles the most critical components of *ESD* consisting of sustainability and development multplied by appropriate means of education.

haviour and lifestyles required for a sustainable future and for positive societal transformation."[123]

DESD stands for the *United Nations Decade of Education for Sustainable Development* which constitutes the institutionalised process of dealing with *Education for Sustainable Development* (ESD) worldwide from 2005 until 2014. As the prepositions within the title indicate, *DESD* is a momentum-building process *for* sustainable development and not just *about* sustainable development.[124] This fact turns the issue from a passive *object* into an active, comprehensive and participatory *subject* function. *DESD* must be adopted and driven by the common people and less by theorists or bureaucrats.

Organised under the umbrella of United Nations and led by UNESCO *"(i)t is a framework of partnership and collaboration, bringing together a great diversity of interests and concerns. It is an instrument of mobilisation and advocacy. And it is a vehicle of accountability through which governments, international organisations, civil society, the private sector and local communities around the world can demonstrate their practical commitment to learning to live sustainably".*[125]

5 Conclusion

To cope adequately with defining different terms, a meaningful distinction was made at the outset: *content-based* versus *structure or strategy-related* terms.[126] In a concise and illustrative way this chapter aimed to define exclusively *content-based* terms. Why is it necessary to define *content-based* characteristics, given in a more technical type of work? In the first place, such definitions are necessary because they are fundamental to further contextual understanding. In the second place, because *grosso modo* these are fixed in terms of independence of analytical interpretation and reasoning. All relevant *structure or strategy-related* terms are therefore defined *in situ*.

123 Cf. UNESCO (ed.) (2004c) (cf. *footnote 34* op. cit.), p. 5.
See chapter VII 1 *Vision* on page 149.

124 Cf. UNESCO (05/07/2003): Position Paper. Education for Sustainable Development. Eighth Draft. Manuscript. Officially released and issued on 05/07/2003, Paris, p. 5; Centre for Environment Education (CEE); UNESCO (2007): Comprendre l'Éducation pour le développement durable. ED/EO/KMS/031. Directed by: Nambiar, Prithi. Supported by: Mewada, Ashok (Compilation). Format: CD (Image). Paris: UNESCO Multimedia Archives; Selby, David (2009) (cf. *footnote 55* op. cit.), p. 207.

125 See Matsuura, Koïchiro (01/03/2005) (cf. *footnote 28* op. cit.), p. 3.

126 See *Table 3* in chapter II 5 *Conclusion* on page 35.

Table 3: Content-based versus structure or strategy-related terminology

Content-based	*Structure or strategy-related*
Education	Leadership
Sustainability	Co-ordination
Development	Lead agency
Education for Sustainable Development	Mandate

What principal findings may be drawn from these *content-based* definitions for strategic incorporation into the proceedings of this thesis? In other words, what implications do these definitions have upon further and subsequent considerations?

- Coping with diversity: definitions and concepts derived are all relative. They are therefore subject to divergent perspectives that must be taken into account.
- Coping with interdependence: sustainability, development and education are interdependent learning concepts. Context-based interpretations are therefore required.[127]
- Coping with institutionalism: *ESD* takes place in an institutional setting. All relevant agents and their background must be appreciated appropriately.[128]
- Coping with aspects of normativity: specific qualities and requirements of *structure or strategy-related* characteristics, such as leadership, co-ordination, *lead agency* or mandate are *intrinsic*, or context-bound. They must therefore be interpreted within the system's normative scope.[129]

127 See chapter II *Definitions* on pages 11 et seqq.

128 See chapter III *Theory* on pages 37 et seqq.

129 In this case all multi-faceted and dynamic terms are subject to the normative framework of strategy proposed by the UNESCO entitlement to education, first and foremost.
Cf. Yusuf, Abdulqawi A. (ed.) (2007): Normative action in education, science and culture. Essays in commemoration of the sixtieth anniversary of UNESCO. Volume French edition. Paris / Leiden / Boston: UNESCO publishing; Martinus Nijhoff Publishers (UNESCO reference works series, 1); Yusuf, Abdulqawi A. (2007b): Elaborating and Implementing UNESCO's Standard-setting Instruments. UNESCO Practices and Procedures for the Elaboration of Standard-setting Instruments. In: Yusuf, Abdulqawi A. (ed.): Normative action in education, science and culture. Essays in commemoration of the sixtieth anniversary of UNESCO. French edition. Paris / Leiden / Boston: UNESCO publishing; Martinus Nijhoff Publishers (UNESCO reference works series, 1), pp. 31–49; Yusuf, Abdulqawi A. (2007a): Beyond Treaty Law: The Influence of the Legal Instruments Adopted by UNESCO on General International Law. Introduction. In: Yusuf, Abdulqawi A. (ed.): Normative action in education, science and culture. Essays in commemoration of the sixtieth anniversary of UNESCO. French edi-

To conclude: "*(e)ducation for sustainable development is a dynamic concept that utilises all aspects of public awareness, education and training to create or enhance an understanding of the linkages among the issues of sustainable development and to develop the knowledge, skills, perspectives and values which will empower people of all ages to assume responsibility for creating and enjoying a sustainable future*".[130] The only way to address leadership issues adequately is to take into account the structural requirements of all contributing components. This is to say that given three multi-faceted conceptions of education, sustainability and development, *ESD* can only be dealt with holistically. In turn, this leads to considerable consequences in terms of institutional *ESD* structures which are to be introduced and applied accordingly through theory and methodology.

---

tion. Paris / Leiden / Boston: UNESCO publishing; Martinus Nijhoff Publishers (UNESCO reference works series, 1), pp. 369–370.
See chapter V *Framework* on pages 97 et seqq, and chapter VIII *Obligation* on pages 197 et seqq.

130 See UNESCO (ed.) (2003b) (cf. *footnote 109* op. cit.), pp. 2–3.

III Theory

In an analysis of UNESCO's role as lead agency for DESD the question of both the theoretical and methodological foundations inevitably arises. Defining the appropriate theoretical background depends on the nature of DESD alone. To this end, this chapter will clarify which theoretical setting best serves to support the research objective. The approach presented here argues for DESD to be regarded as an international regime embedded in the theoretical setting of new institutionalism.

1 Nature

In international relations three main concepts may be discussed to describe actors' relations according to their specific strategies of dealing with problems.[131] Networks, regimes and institutions symbolise not only different degrees of normative and executive power, but also point at diverging philosophies, such as *positivist*[132] and *constructivist*[133] positions of institutionalism. In the positivist

---

131 Cf. Hasenclever, Andreas; Mayer, Peter (2007): Einleitung. Macht und Ohnmacht internationaler Institutionen. In: Hasenclever, Andreas; Rittberger, Volker (eds.): Macht und Ohnmacht internationaler Institutionen. Festschrift für Volker Rittberger. Frankfurt am Main: Campus Verlag, pp. 9–37, p. 13.

132 From a positivist perspective, institutional legitimacy is obtained through legally binding acts, such as norms, rules or treaties.

133 From a constructivist or rational-choice point of view, norms and compliance arise interactively as result of social constitution and interdependent behavioural expectations (*presuppositions*).

view, two major strands of institutionalism in political science may be distinguished:[134]

a) Dealing with domestic affairs (domestic political institutions); or
b) Dealing with international relations (*regime theory*).[135]

Since *DESD* is set up globally,[136] the concepts of international relations therefore apply.

1.1 Networks

Networks are *"relatively permanent, not formally arranged, non-hierarchical modes of communicative relations fostered by interdependence and commonly shared expectations or orientations of behaviour"*.[137] The normative structure is rather loose and usually established by the stakeholders themselves. Problems are dealt with in an *ad-hoc* manner either according to fields of policy or in an interdisciplinary way.[138]

Networks are closely tied to global governance, because *"(f)or many, global governance refers to the network of interstate agencies and the rules which order their relations and increasingly shape their (...) institutions. For others, global governance is a more pervasive system of diffuse, often private, authority*

Cf. Gehring, Thomas (2002): Die Europäische Union als komplexe internationale Organisation. Wie durch Kommunikation und Entscheidung soziale Ordnung entsteht. Volume 1. Auflage. Baden-Baden: Nomos Verlagsgesellschaft, pp. 61–68.

134 Cf. DiMaggio, Paul Joseph; Powell, Walter Woody (1991 / 2004 / 2008): Introduction. In: Powell, Walter Woody; DiMaggio, Paul Joseph (eds.): The new institutionalism in organizational analysis. Reprint. Chicago / London: University of Chicago Press, pp. 1–38, p. 5.

135 I.e. to *„pertain to particular sets of issues in international politics"*.
See Keohane, Robert O. (1989a): Neoliberal Institutionalism: A Perspective on World Politics. In: Keohane, Robert O. (ed.): International institutions and state power. Essays in international relations theory. Boulder: Westview Press, pp. 1–20, p. 4.

136 Cf. United Nations (ed.) (2002 / 2003) (cf. *footnote 117* op. cit.).

137 Translation from German into English: *„Bei Netzwerken handelt es sich (...) um relativ dauerhafte, nicht formal organisierte, nicht hierarchische, durch wechselseitige Abhängigkeiten und gemeinsame Verhaltenserwartungen bzw. Verhaltensorientierungen stabilisierte Kommunikationsbeziehungen"*.
See Hasenclever, Andreas; Mayer, Peter (2007) (cf. *footnote 131* op. cit.), p. 15.
Cf. Gehring, Thomas (2002) (cf. *footnote 133* op. cit.), p. 61.

138 E.g., G-8-Summit, G-20-Summit, Club of Rome, etc.
Cf. Hasenclever, Andreas; Mayer, Peter (2007) (cf. *footnote 131* op. cit.), p. 15.

stemming from globalization, which organizes and disciplines the affairs of communities and nations in the industrial and developing worlds".[139]

1.2 Regimes

Regimes may be defined as conglomerations of *"social institutions consisting of agreed upon principles, norms, rules, procedures and programs that govern the interactions of actors in specific areas".*[140] In other words, *"regimes are institutions in a particular political arena without stakeholder status. They are concerned only with directing the behaviour of international actors along ordained paths in relying on the normative methods available to them".*[141] This regime-based concept of *patterned behaviours*[142] has been derived from the game- and rational-choice theories of institutional economics. It may be regarded as high-level institutionalisation[143] culminating in *"some central authority system".*[144]

---

139 Cf. Sinclair, Timothy J. (ed.) (2004): Global Governance. London / New York: Routledge Chapman & Hall (Critical Concepts in Political Science, Volume I).

140 See Young, Oran R. (ed.) (1999a): The effectiveness of international environmental regimes. Causal connections and behavioral mechanisms. Cambridge, Massachusetts: MIT Press, p. 1; Jansen, Dorothea (27/06/2000): Der neue Institutionalismus. Antrittsvorlesung. Volume Lehrstuhl für Soziologie der Organisation. Speyer: Deutsche Hochschule für Verwaltungswissenschaften Speyer, p. 11.
Cf. Fischer-Lescano, Andreas; Teubner, Gunther (2006): Regime-Kollisionen. Zur Fragmentierung des globalen Rechts. Volume Originalausgabe. Frankfurt am Main: Suhrkamp (Suhrkamp Taschenbuch Wissenschaft, 1803), p. 18.

141 Translation from German into English: *„Regime sind politikfeldspezifische Institutionen ohne Akteursqualität. Sie beschränken sich darauf, das Verhalten internationaler Akteure allein mit Hilfe ihres normativen Apparats in geordnete Bahnen zu lenken".*
See Hasenclever, Andreas; Mayer, Peter (2007) (cf. *footnote 131* op. cit.), p. 14.
Cf. Ruggie, John Gerard (2004 / 2006): International regimes, transactions, and change. Embedded liberalism in the postwar economic order. In: Sinclair, Timothy J. (ed.): Global Governance: Critical Concepts in Political Science. London / New York / London: Taylor & Francis, Inc.; Routledge (Critical Concepts in Political Science, Volume II), Volume International Organization 36 (2) (1982): 379–415, pp. 387–425, p. 388; Alvarez, José Enrique (2006): International organizations as law-makers. Oxford: Oxford University Press, pp. 338–339.

142 See Peters, Brainard Guy (2005): Institutional theory in political science. The 'new institutionalism'. Volume 2. edition. London: Continuum, p. 130.

143 *"(F)ormal organisational structures arise in highly institutionalised contexts."*
See Meyer, John W.; Rowan, Brian (1991 / 2004 / 2008a): Institutionalized Organizations: Formal Structure as Myth and Ceremony. In: Powell, Walter Woody; DiMaggio, Paul Joseph (eds.): The new institutionalism in organizational analysis. Reprint. Chicago / London: University of Chicago Press, pp. 41–62, p. 41.

Assuming the presence of rational actors,[145] regimes simply appear whenever the costs of communication, transaction, monitoring and enforcement are low compared to the benefits derived from joining.[146] Regimes are based either on treaties,[147] conventional agreements or other *"explicitly codified rules and sanctions without embodiment in a formal organizational apparatus"*.[148]

Conventions are framework structures of international law *"which reflect the common stakeholder understanding of their social environment"*[149] with

---

144 See Jepperson, Ronald L. (1991 / 2004 / 2008): Institutions, Institutional Effects, and Institutionalism. In: Powell, Walter Woody; DiMaggio, Paul Joseph (eds.): The new institutionalism in organizational analysis. Reprint. Chicago / London: University of Chicago Press, pp. 143–163, p. 150.

145 In this context, this refers to a *calculus* rather than *cultural approach.*
Cf. Dietz, Hella (1998): Der soziologische Neo-Institutionalismus von James G. March und Johan P. Olsen. Auf dem Weg zur eigenständigen Methodologie oder Katalysator und Korrektiv für gegenwärtige politikwissenschaftliche Theorien? Semesterarbeit WS 1997 / 1998. Supervised by: Wiesenthal, Helmut. Berlin. Humboldt-Universität Berlin, Fachbereich Sozialwissenschaften, p. 4.

146 *"When it is costly to transact, then institutions matter. And it is costly to transact."*
See North, Douglass Cecil (1997) (cf. *footnote 68* op. cit.).
Cf. North, Douglass Cecil (1990 / 2007): Institutions, institutional change and economic performance. Volume 24. print. Cambridge: Cambridge University Press (Political Economy of Institutions and Decisions), p. 12; Dietz, Hella (1998) (cf. *footnote 145* op. cit.), p. 5.
This pragmatic argument is supported by many authors: stakeholder-specific preferences do not necessarily occur as result of target-oriented decisions of institutions, but instead in most cases not until decision-making processes are already under way. In this context, rules evolve due to particular role expectations and the logic of situation appropriateness.
Cf. DiMaggio, Paul Joseph; Powell, Walter Woody (1991 / 2004 / 2008) (cf. *footnote 134* op. cit.), p. 10; Cowhey, Peter F. (2004 / 2006): The international telecommunications regime. The political roots of regimes for high technology. In: Sinclair, Timothy J. (ed.): Global Governance: Critical Concepts in Political Science. London / New York / London: Taylor & Francis, Inc.; Routledge (Critical Concepts in Political Science, Volume II), Volume International Organization 44 (2) (1990): 169–199, pp. 426–456, p. 427; Alvarez, José Enrique (2006) (cf. *footnote 141* op. cit.), pp. 346–347; Kailitz, Steffen (2007): Schlüsselwerke der Politikwissenschaft. James G. March / Johan P. Olsen, Rediscovering Institutions. The Organizational Basis of Politics, New York / London 1989. pp. 278–281. Wiesbaden: VS Verlag für Sozialwissenschaften; GWV Fachverlage GmbH Wiesbaden (SpringerLink), pp. 278–279.

147 E.g., The international telecommunications regime; The International Regime for the Protection of the Stratospheric Ozone Layer; The Fisheries Regime of the Exclusive Economic Zone, etc.

148 See Jepperson, Ronald L. (1991 / 2004 / 2008) (cf. *footnote 144* op. cit.), p. 150.

149 Translation from German into English: *„Eine Konvention spiegelt (...) ein gemeinsames Verständnis der beteiligten Akteure von ihrer sozialen Umwelt wider".*
See Gehring, Thomas (2002) (cf. *footnote 133* op. cit.), pp. 62–63.

varying extents of legally-binding provisions. *"Conventions consist of cognitive expectations accompanied by the preparedness to learn cooperatively. They become useless if they no longer have the potential to carry out this prognostic function."*[150] From a positivist perspective, conventions pave the way for potential organisations, regimes and networks.[151] Conventions are external points of reference which foster co-ordinating behaviour and normative expectations.[152] In this context a conventional agreement serves three major purposes:[153]

1. Reflecting balanced expectations as internal, but target-oriented patterns of stakeholders as involved in the given framework conditions of the situation;
2. Depicting co-ordinating behaviour without any specific *normative* content; and
3. Serving as a baseline of evaluation of stakeholder behaviour.

Regimes are characterised by both a specific intellectual or political perspective on a problem and the presumed capacity of governance[154] to solve a given problem. *"One principal advantage of conceptualizing international politics in regime and institutional terms is that it helps to move the debate in that subdiscipline away from power politics to thinking about consonance, at least within specific policy areas."*[155] This requires functioning institutional settings, the distribution of capabilities and entrepreneurial leadership.[156]

By consequence the following principles may be derived directly from the definition of regime:[157]

150 Translation from German into English: *„Konventionen (bilden) also lediglich von Lernbereitschaft begleitete kognitive Erwartungen, die unbrauchbar werden, wenn sie diese Prognosefunktion nicht mehr zu erfüllen vermögen".*
See Gehring, Thomas (2002) (cf. *footnote 133* op. cit.), pp. 62–63.

151 Cf. Hasenclever, Andreas; Mayer, Peter (2007) (cf. *footnote 131* op. cit.), p. 14.

152 Cf. Novak Talavera, Fabián; García Corrochano Moyano, Luis (2002): Derecho Internacional Público. Sujetos de derecho internacional. Volume 1. edición. Lima: Pontificia Universidad Católica del Perú Fondo Editorial (Derecho internacional público / Fabián Novak Talavera Luis García-Corrochano Moyano, Tomo II, Volumen II), p. 26.

153 Cf. Gehring, Thomas (2002) (cf. *footnote 133* op. cit.), pp. 61–62.

154 Cf. Sinclair, Timothy J. (ed.) (2004) (cf. *footnote 139* op. cit.).

155 See Peters, Brainard Guy (2005) (cf. *footnote 142* op. cit.), p. 139.

156 See Young, Oran R. (ed.) (1999a) (cf. *footnote 140* op. cit.), pp. 1 et seqq.

157 Cf. Young, Oran R.; Levy, Marc A. (1999): The Effectiveness of International Environmental Regimes. In: Young, Oran R. (ed.): The effectiveness of international environmental regimes. Causal connections and behavioral mechanisms. Cambridge, Massachusetts: MIT Press, pp. 1–32, pp. 1–18; Ruggie, John Gerard (2004 / 2006) (cf. *footnote 141* op. cit.).

- Regimes operate as concerted and pragmatic entities in well-defined international fields of action and with specific issues, relevant within the confines of an *overarching society*.[158]
- Regimes exert normative authority up to an agreed extent.
- Regimes acquire their right to exist from effectiveness of their problem-solving capacity and from their administrative efficiency.
- Regimes are in need of integrated and specialised institutions.

As a result of the various expectations and regime requirements, specific functions are attributed to them. Commonly-shared axioms on regime functions encompass, amongst others:

a) Regimes as utility modifiers.[159]

It is presumed that institutions are self-interested utility maximizers which balance the costs and benefits of each individual stakeholder. Institutional behaviour is guided by certain arrangements in line with well-defined utility functions and driven by an instinct of self-preservation. At this point regimes may serve as unitary and rational utility maximizers by proposing alternative behavioural pathways in order to enhance norm-driven behaviour, to promote social learning and to enhance the operation of social roles;

b) Regimes as enhancers of co-operation.[160]

It is presumed that problems of joint action are solved through interaction. Regimes are entities concerned with negotiating in favour of collective outcomes or *joint gains*;[161]

c) Regimes as *bestowers* of authority.[162]

It is presumed that social norms guide the behaviour of individuals and collective entities through their unanimous legitimacy or authoritativeness. This

---

158 See Breitmeier, Helmut; Young, Oran R.; Zürn, Michael (2006): Analyzing international environmental regimes. From case study to database. Cambridge, Massachusetts: MIT Press (Global Environmental Accord: Strategies for Sustainability and Institutional Innovation), p. 1.

159 Cf. Young, Oran R.; Levy, Marc A. (1999) (cf. *footnote 157* op. cit.), pp. 21–22.

160 Cf. Keohane, Robert O. (ed.) (1989): International institutions and state power. Essays in international relations theory. Boulder: Westview Press, p. 2; Young, Oran R.; Levy, Marc A. (1999) (cf. *footnote 157* op. cit.), p. 23.

161 See Young, Oran R.; Levy, Marc A. (1999) (cf. *footnote 157* op. cit.), p. 23.
E.g., approaching the *pareto-optimal equilibrium* frontier by reducing *transaction costs*.

162 Cf. Young, Oran R.; Levy, Marc A. (1999) (cf. *footnote 157* op. cit.), pp. 23–24; Cowhey, Peter F. (2004 / 2006) (cf. *footnote 146* op. cit.), p. 427.
See chapter VIII 1.6 *Summary* on pages 237 et seqq.

agreed habit of obedience to regimes implies compliance coerced by means of norms and setting standards;

d) Regimes as learning facilitators.[163]

It is presumed that institutions are places of social learning, inspiration and innovation. Regimes may therefore be regarded as dynamic and *epistemic* learning communities;[164]

e) Regimes as role definers.[165]

It is presumed that institutions operate constitutively, shaping identities and influencing behaviour through processes of bargaining. Regimes may be considered capable of defining and allocating roles to participating stakeholders; and

f) Regimes as agents of internal re-alignments.[166]

It is presumed that regimes have the potential to innovatively create new constituencies, re-direct behaviour or shift existing balances.

1.3 Institutions

"Institutions are comprehensive patterns or systems of regulation in which stakeholders such as individuals, organizations or nation states are embedded."[167] More concisely, institutions are durable *"social entities which produce stability of expectation in interdependent relations. They consist primarily of a set of principles, norms and rules"*.[168]

---

163 Cf. Young, Oran R.; Levy, Marc A. (1999) (cf. *footnote 157* op. cit.), pp. 24–25.

164 E.g., by improving roles of individual leaders and groups of experts.

165 Cf. Young, Oran R.; Levy, Marc A. (1999) (cf. *footnote 157* op. cit.), pp. 25–26; Young, Oran R. (1999b): Governance in world affairs. Ithaca, New York: Cornell University Press.

166 Cf. Young, Oran R.; Levy, Marc A. (1999) (cf. *footnote 157* op. cit.), pp. 26–27; Cowhey, Peter F. (2004 / 2006) (cf. *footnote 146* op. cit.), p. 427.

167 Translation from German into English: *„Institutionen sind (...) umfangreiche Muster oder Regelungssysteme, in die Akteure wie Individuen, Organisationen und Nationalstaaten eingebettet sind".*
See Hasse, Raimund; Krücken, Georg (2005): Neo-Institutionalismus. Volume 2. vollständig überarbeitete Auflage. Bielefeld: Transcript-Verlag, p. 8.

168 Translation from German into English: *„Institutionen sind soziale Einrichtungen, die in interdependenten Beziehungen Erwartungsstabilität produzieren. Sie bestehen in erster Linie aus einem Set von Prinzipien, Normen und Regeln".*
See Hasenclever, Andreas; Mayer, Peter (2007) (cf. *footnote 131* op. cit.), p. 13.
Cf. Scott, William Richard (Dick) (2008): Institutions and organizations. Ideas and interests. Volume 3rd edition. Los Angeles: SAGE Publications, p. 48; Dietz, Hella (1998) (cf. *footnote 145* op. cit.), p. 13; Jansen, Dorothea (27/06/2000) (cf. *footnote*

"Institutions are a means for eluding (a) fundamental problem of collective action. Institutions provide a set of agreed upon rules that map preferences into decisions."[169] Functionally, institutions have a considerable impact on society since:

- They provide meaningful frameworks of social norms which are permanent, binding and relevant for decision making;[170]
- They provide organisational support with regard to the interpretation and formation of opinion, co-ordination of interaction and assignment of tasks;[171] and
- They provide effective patterns for stakeholder relationships.[172]

The classification of different types of institutions both in terms of technical scope[173] and according to three criteria or pillars *"identified to as making up or supporting institutions"*[174] is broadly supported by institutional theory.[175]

---

140 op. cit.), pp. 1–2; Walgenbach, Peter; Meyer, Renate E. (2008): Neoinstitutionalistische Organisationstheorie. Stuttgart: Kohlhammer, p. 56.

169 See Peters, Brainard Guy (2005) (cf. *footnote 142* op. cit.), p. 49.
Cf. Alvarez, José Enrique (2006) (cf. *footnote 141* op. cit.), p. 358.

170 Cf. Jachtenfuchs, Markus; Knodt, Michèle (eds.) (2002): Regieren in internationalen Institutionen. Festschrift für Beate Kohler-Koch. Opladen: Leske & Budrich; Senge, Konstanze; Hellmann, Kai-Uwe; Scott, William Richard (Dick) (eds.) (2006): Einführung in den Neo-Institutionalismus. Volume 1. Auflage. Wiesbaden: VS Verlag für Sozialwissenschaften, p. 35; Walgenbach, Peter; Meyer, Renate E. (2008) (cf. *footnote 168* op. cit.), p. 56.

171 Cf. Walgenbach, Peter; Meyer, Renate E. (2008) (cf. *footnote 168* op. cit.), p. 55.

172 Considering interactive and interdependent stakeholder co-relations, *trade-off* situations are most likely to occur: *„Institutions institute and shape the structure and the action of social actors. In turn, protagonists generate, maintain or change institutions and are ultimately responsible for their dissolution".*
Translation from German into English: *„Institutionen fundieren und formen die Gestalt sowie das Handeln sozialer Akteure – Akteure wiederum erzeugen, erhalten sowie verändern Institutionen und lassen sie letztlich erodieren".*
See Koch, Sascha; Schemmann, Michael (2009b): Neo-Institutionalismus und Erziehungswissenschaft – Eine einleitende Verhältnisbestimmung. In: Koch, Sascha; Schemmann, Michael; Göhlich, Michael (eds.): Neo-Institutionalismus in der Erziehungswissenschaft. Grundlegende Texte und empirische Studien. Organisation und Pädagogik 6. 1. Auflage. Wiesbaden: VS Verlag für Sozialwissenschaften, pp. 7–18, p. 7.

173 E.g., differentiating primarily between political, economic, social, cultural, etc. institutions.
Cf. Sjöblom, Gunnar (1993): Some Critical Remarks on March and Olsen's Rediscovering Institutions. In: Journal of Theoretical Politics, Volume 5, Issue 3, pp. 397–407, pp. 5, 8; Jansen, Dorothea (27/06/2000) (cf. *footnote 140* op. cit.).

174 Cf. Scott, William Richard (Dick) (2008) (cf. *footnote 168* op. cit.), pp. 50 et seqq; Dietz, Hella (1998) (cf. *footnote 145* op. cit.), pp. 13–14; Hasse, Raimund; Krücken,

Table 4: Types of institutions[176]

Type of institution	Means of conformity	Systematically supported through
Regulative	Coercion	Statutes, rules, treaties, titles, etc.
Normative	Obligation	Morally binding, commonly shared norms and values
Cognitive-cultural	Conviction	General attitudes, ideologies and meaning

1. Regulative: Institutions work both to empower or to constrain and regularise social behaviour.[177] This takes place either explicitly or implicitly through various kinds of regulatory procedures and legal or quasi-legal requirements (laws and regulations) such as rule-setting, monitoring, sanctions or more informal mechanisms. In this respect, law is considered to be more suitable for concise and collective interpretation. Thus, due to its effects of *incentivisation*, greater reliance on cognitive and normative elements should be preferred to coercive elements;[178]
2. Normative: Institutions are normative systems that recognise values and norms[179] as moral obligations and integrate joint attitudes into social life through the introduction of a prescriptive, evaluative and obligatory dimension and through defining certain goals, assets or objectives;[180] and

---

Georg (2005) (cf. *footnote 167* op. cit.), p. 64; Senge, Konstanze (2006): Zum Begriff der Institution im Neo-Institutionalismus. In: Senge, Konstanze; Hellmann, Kai-Uwe; Scott, William Richard (Dick) (eds.): Einführung in den Neo-Institutionalismus. 1. Auflage. Wiesbaden: VS Verlag für Sozialwissenschaften, pp. 35–47, pp. 38–41.

175 See *Table 4* in chapter III 1.3 *Institutions* on page 45, and *Figure 9* in chapter III 1.3 *Institutions* on page 47.

176 Following Senge, Konstanze (2006) (cf. *footnote 174* op. cit.), pp. 38–41; Scott, William Richard (Dick) (2008) (cf. *footnote 168* op. cit.), pp. 50 et seqq.

177 This includes both explicit norms and, alternatively, more implicit types of regulation, such as customs, routines or social conventions.
Cf. Hasse, Raimund; Krücken, Georg (2005) (cf. *footnote 167* op. cit.), p. 14; Jepperson, Ronald L. (1991 / 2004 / 2008) (cf. *footnote 144* op. cit.), p. 145.

178 Cf. Alvarez, José Enrique (2006) (cf. *footnote 141* op. cit.), p. 364; Scott, William Richard (Dick) (2008) (cf. *footnote 168* op. cit.), p. 54; Jansen, Dorothea (27/06/2000) (cf. *footnote 140* op. cit.), p. 3.

179 In this context values can be defined as *"conceptions of the preferred or the desirable, together with the construction of standards to which existing structures or behaviours can be compared or assessed"*. Norms *"specify how things should be done; they define legitimate means to pursue valued ends"*.
See Scott, William Richard (Dick) (2008) (cf. *footnote 168* op. cit.), pp. 54–55.

180 Cf. Scott, William Richard (Dick) (2008) (cf. *footnote 168* op. cit.), p. 54.
Choosing a *utilitarian* approach, normative binding must be embedded into a benefit-incentive system that rewards compliance on the one hand and punishes non-compliance on the other. In economic theory, an illustration frequently employed is the

3. Cultural-cognitive: Institutions are self-regulatory and interactive bodies both by virtue of their internal processes of interpretation and external cultural frameworks. The *"cultural-cognitive dimension of institutions (is) the major distinguishing feature of neo-institutionalism with sociology".*[181]

Intended to reflect different levels of institutional legitimacy, these three dimensions or pillars depict an *approach of smooth transition* ranging from *"the conscious to the unconscious, from the legally enforced to the taken for granted".*[182] It is commonly accepted in international relations that matters of legitimacy define the success[183] of an institution or an international organisation in particular.[184] *"Legitimacy is a generalized perception or assumption that the actions of an entity are desirable, proper, or appropriate within some socially constructed system of norms, values, beliefs, and definitions."*[185]

---

opportunity-costs concept which considers profits in case of compliance (winning the game, making profit, establishing comparative advantage, making progress), versus costs in case of non-compliance (sanctions, payments of avoidance, damage of public image).

181 See Scott, William Richard (Dick) (2001): Institutions and organizations. Volume 2nd edition. Thousand Oaks, California: SAGE Publications, p. 57.
Cf. Sjöblom, Gunnar (1993) (cf. *footnote 173* op. cit.), p. 5; Grendstad, Gunnar; Selle, Per (1995): Cultural Theory and the New Institutionalism. In: Journal of Theoretical Politics, Volume 7, Issue 1, pp. 5–27, pp. 6–10; Jansen, Dorothea (27/06/2000) (cf. *footnote 140* op. cit.), pp. 2, 3; Dietz, Hella (1998) (cf. *footnote 145* op. cit.), p. 4.

182 Cf. Scott, William Richard (Dick) (2008) (cf. *footnote 168* op. cit.), p. 50.

183 Success defined in (economic) terms of *effectiveness* (goal achievement) and *efficiency* (least-cost criterion), for instance.

184 Cf. Jansen, Dorothea (27/06/2000) (cf. *footnote 140* op. cit.), pp. 2, 13 et seqq; Walgenbach, Peter; Meyer, Renate E. (2008) (cf. *footnote 168* op. cit.), p. 63.

185 See Suchman, Mark C. (1995): Managing legitimacy: strategic and institutional approaches. In: Academy of Management Review, Volume 20, Issue 3, pp. 571–610, p. 574.

	Regulative	*Normative*	*Cultural-Cognitive*
Basis of compliance	Expedience	Social obligation	Taken-for-grantedness
			Shared understanding
Basis of order	Regulative rules	Binding expectations	Constitutive schema
Mechanisms	Coercive	Normative	Mimetic
Logic	Instrumentality	Appropriateness	Orthodoxy
Indicators	Rules	Certification	Common beliefs
	Laws	Accreditation	Shared logics of action
	Sanctions		Isomorphism
Affect	Fear guilt / Innocence	Shame / Honor	Certainty / Confusion
Basis of legitimacy	Legally sanctioned	Morally governed	Comprehensible
			Recognizable
			Culturally supported

Figure 9: Three pillars of institutions[186]

Staying with the positivist principle of *form follows function*, the subsequent question must be how these institutional pillars translate into manageable frameworks for effective analysis.[187] The concept mentioned proposes an analytic framework based on different variables:[188]

a) *Symbolic systems* prescribe behavioural guidance by means of rules, values and norms, classifications, representations, frames, schemata, prototypes and scripts;[189]
b) *Relational systems* are patterned or pre-structured interactions connected to networks of social positions (*open-role systems*);[190]
c) *Routines* can be defined as types of repetitive performance programmes;[191] and

186 See Scott, William Richard (Dick) (2008) (cf. *footnote 168* op. cit.), p. 51.
187 Cf. Scott, William Richard (Dick) (2008) (cf. *footnote 168* op. cit.), pp. 62 et seqq.
188 Cf. Scott, William Richard (Dick) (2008) (cf. *footnote 168* op. cit.), pp. 79 et seqq. See *Figure 10* in chapter III 1.3 *Institutions* on page 48.
189 Cf. Scott, William Richard (Dick) (2008) (cf. *footnote 168* op. cit.), pp. 81–82; Dietz, Hella (1998) (cf. *footnote 145* op. cit.), p. 14.
190 Cf. Scott, William Richard (Dick) (2008) (cf. *footnote 168* op. cit.), pp. 81–82; Koch, Sascha; Schemmann, Michael (2009a): Entstehungskontexte und Grundlegungen neo-institutionalistischer Organisationsanalyse. In: Koch, Sascha; Schemmann, Michael; Göhlich, Michael (eds.): Neo-Institutionalismus in der Erziehungswissenschaft. Grundlegende Texte und empirische Studien. Organisation und Pädagogik 6. 1. Auflage. Wiesbaden: VS Verlag für Sozialwissenschaften, pp. 20–27, p. 21; Jepperson, Ronald L. (1991 / 2004 / 2008) (cf. *footnote 144* op. cit.), p. 145.
191 Cf. Scott, William Richard (Dick) (2008) (cf. *footnote 168* op. cit.), p. 82.

d) *Artefacts* stand for *"material cultural element(s) consciously produced or transformed by human activity under the influence of the physical and cultural environment".*[192]

	Pillars		
	Regulative	*Normative*	*Cultural-Cognitive*
Symbolic systems	Rules	Values	Categories
	Laws	Expectations	Typifications
			Schema
Relational systems	Governance systems	Regimes	Structural isomorphism
	Power systems	Authority systems	Identities
Routines	Protocols	Jobs	Scripts
	Standard operating procedures	Roles	
		Obedience to duty	
Artifacts	Objects complying with mandated specifications	Objects meeting conventions and standards	Objects possessing symbolic value

Figure 10: Institutional pillars and respective carriers[193]

This systematic approach clearly underpins the long-term rather than the immediate conception of institutional settings.[194] *"Institutions are to some extent shaped by enduring cultural, professional, legal and historical processes. (They) are physically and temporarily bound together by forces which reach far beyond particular actors and the constellations of their interests."*[195] Institutions are characterised by permanence of existence, objectivity and external independence, meaning and regulation.[196]

"Formal organizations are generally understood to be systems of coordinated and controlled activities that arise when work is embedded in complex networks of technical relations and boundary-spanning exchanges."[197]

Institutions and organisations are not interchangeable terms.[198] The distinction between institutions in general terms and (international) organisations as

192 Cf. Scott, William Richard (Dick) (2008) (cf. *footnote 168* op. cit.), pp. 83–84.

193 See Scott, William Richard (Dick) (2008) (cf. *footnote 168* op. cit.), p. 79.

194 Cf. Jansen, Dorothea (27/06/2000) (cf. *footnote 140* op. cit.), p. 3.

195 Translation from German into English: *„Institutionen (sind) von zum Teil sehr lang anhaltenden kulturellen, professionellen, rechtlichen und historischen Charakteristika geprägt; räumlich und zeitlich von Kräften gebunden, die weit über spezifische Akteurs- und Interessenskonstellationen hinausreichen".*
See Hasse, Raimund; Krücken, Georg (2005) (cf. *footnote 167* op. cit.), p. 9.
Cf. Jansen, Dorothea (27/06/2000) (cf. *footnote 140* op. cit.), p. 7.

196 Cf. Koch, Sascha; Schemmann, Michael (2009a) (cf. *footnote 190* op. cit.), p. 22.

197 See Meyer, John W.; Rowan, Brian (1991 / 2004 / 2008a) (cf. *footnote 143* op. cit.), p. 41.

particular institutions lies in the mere existence of established and agreed upon governing and decision-making structures:[199]

"An international organisation is rather like a company in that it has legal personality separate from its members. This makes the organisation a subject of international law, with rights and duties under it."[200] These represent *"collections of interrelated rules and routines that define appropriate actions in terms of relations between roles and situations. The process involves determining what the situation is, what role is being fulfilled, and what obligation of that role in that situation is".*[201] *International organisations* are therefore those institutions with existing, effective and autonomous competences[202] in decision-making with respect to particular *trans-disciplinary* fields of action.[203] *"Depending on their mandate fulfillment (and range of mandatory assignment) they can carry out independently up to a certain extent."*[204]

---

198 Cf. Fridtjof Nansens Institutt / The Fridtjof Nansens Institute (ed.) (2005): The Commission on Sustainable Development. A Study of Institutional Design, Distribution of Capabilities and Entrepreneurial Leadership. Edited by Stine Madland Kaasa. Lysaker: Fridtjof Nansen Institute (FNI report, 5), p. 12.

199 For example: secretary, executive board, general conference, general assembly, etc. Cf. Hasenclever, Andreas; Mayer, Peter (2007) (cf. *footnote 131* op. cit.), p. 14; Woyke, Wichard (ed.) (2008): Handwörterbuch internationale Politik. Volume 11. überarbeitete und aktualisierte Auflage. Opladen: Budrich (UTB für Wissenschaft, 702), pp. xiii–xiv.

200 See Aust, Anthony (2006): Handbook of international law. Volume Reprint. Cambridge: Cambridge University Press, p. 198.

201 See March, James G.; Olsen, Johan P. (1989): Rediscovering Institutions. The organizational basic of politics. Volume 1.edition, 3. print. New York: Free Press, p. 160.

202 Autonomy (power of veto, dispute settlement, transferring competences, genuine bureaucratic mechanisms) and effectiveness (impact) are recognised as driving characteristics of international institutions. Both terms are causally interrelated: There is no such output orientation (effectiveness) without sources of autonomy in decision-making or action and vice versa.
Cf. Hasenclever, Andreas; Mayer, Peter (2007) (cf. *footnote 131* op. cit.), pp. 26 et seqq, 29 et seqq.

203 Cf. Frowein, Jochen Abraham (1989): The Internal and External Effects of Resolutions by International Organizations. In: Zeitschrift für ausländisches öffentliches Recht und Völkerrecht (ZaöRV) / Heidelberg Journal of International Law (HJIL), Volume 49, pp. 778–790, p. 780; Novak Talavera, Fabián; García Corrochano Moyano, Luis (2002) (cf. *footnote 152* op. cit.), p. 30; Krott, Maximilian (2002): Evaluation of Transdisciplinary Research. In: UNESCO (ed.): Knowledge for sustainable development. An insight into the Encyclopedia of life support systems. 3 Volumes. Oxford / Paris / London: UNESCO publishing; Encyclopedia of Life Support Systems (EOLSS) Publishers (Environment and Development series), Volume 3, pp. 965–973, p. 966; Fischer-Lescano, Andreas; Teubner, Gunther (2006) (cf. *footnote 140* op. cit.), p. 18.

204 Translation from German into English: *„Internationale Organisationen sind Institutionen mit Entscheidungsbefugnissen. Sie (...) können bei der Erfüllung ihres Auftrags*

Formal organisational structures arise from sets of rationalised institutional patterns. Incorporating these commonly shared settings into an established framework ultimately justifies the existence of a self-contained organisation:[205] *"An autonomous international organization has some degree of independence in making its own decisions without dictation from outside actors (...) 'valued for itself, not as a tool but as an institutional fulfillment of group integrity and aspiration'".*[206] Correspondingly, designated to provide stability and order[207] organisations feature three constitutive elements:[208]

1. Resources and stability: autonomous action requires appropriate both material and non-material resources.[209]
2. Information: decision-making requires essential technical information and expertise in a specific field of action. This knowledge platform constitutes a comparative advantage *sui generis*, creating a unique-selling proposition.
3. Acceptability and credibility: Carrying out a particular mission requires support and legitimacy either created implicitly by social standing and reputation or by explicitly attributed and enforceable rights and obligations.

In sum, organisations possess all the mentioned characteristics of institutions: They may be regulative, normative and cultural-cognitive. Conversely, organisations are more specific in terms of mandatory binding: *"Autonomy for international organizations means the development of political organizations and procedures that are not simply expressions of the interests of particular states or*

(und in Abhängigkeit ihres Mandates) in begrenztem Umfang selbstständig tätig werden".
See Hasenclever, Andreas; Mayer, Peter (2007) (cf. *footnote 131* op. cit.), p. 14.

205 Cf. Fischer-Lescano, Andreas; Teubner, Gunther (2006) (cf. *footnote 140* op. cit.), p. 33; Meyer, John W.; Rowan, Brian (2009b): Institutionalisierte Organisationen. Formale Struktur als Mythos und Zeremonie. In: Koch, Sascha; Schemmann, Michael; Göhlich, Michael (eds.): Neo-Institutionalismus in der Erziehungswissenschaft. Grundlegende Texte und empirische Studien. Organisation und Pädagogik 6. 1. Auflage. Wiesbaden: VS Verlag für Sozialwissenschaften, pp. 28–56.

206 See Keohane, Robert O. (2004 / 2006b): Institutionalization in the United Nations General Assembly. In: Sinclair, Timothy J. (ed.): Global Governance: Critical Concepts in Political Science. London / New York / London: Taylor & Francis, Inc.; Routledge (Critical Concepts in Political Science, Volume II), Volume International Organization 23 (4) (1969): 859–896, pp. 225–262, p. 227.

207 Cf. Scott, William Richard (Dick) (2008) (cf. *footnote 168* op. cit.), p. 48.

208 Cf. Alvarez, José Enrique (2006) (cf. *footnote 141* op. cit.), p. 338; Scott, William Richard (Dick) (2008) (cf. *footnote 168* op. cit.), p. 59.

209 Cf. Meyer, John W.; Rowan, Brian (2009b) (cf. *footnote 205* op. cit.).
Material resources are, for instance: financial endowments (budget, funding), real estate, physical resources (materials), facilities (communication, information technology), etc. *Non-material* resources are meant to be, for example: specialists and experts, employees, skills and knowledge, etc.

other international actors",[210] but oriented towards *genuine* organisation-related targets and performance.

1.4 Synthesis

Although clear and indisputable distinctions between network, regime and institution are not easily made, there are key categories that permit some tendentious elements to be reasoned out:[211]

Table 5: Summary scheme distinguishing between network, regime and institution

Category	Network	Regime	Institution
Organisational degree	Low	Medium	High
Normative basis	Presupposition	Treaty or convention	Treaty or mandate
Scope	Rather international	International	National or international
Autonomy	Limited	Limited	High
Formality	Non-formal	Semi-formal	Formal
Objective	Communication	Co-ordination, co-operation and commitment	Decision-making and compliance
Content	Codes of conduct	Principles, norms, rules, procedures or programmes	Principles, norms and rules
Temporal orientation	Permanent	Intermediate	Long-term
Problem-solving	Ad-hoc	Target-oriented	Process-oriented
Philosophy	Constructivist	Constructivist / Positivist	Positivist

Following these characteristics, regimes obtain an *intermediary* position between networks and institutions. In other words, regimes share certain elements of both networks and institutions. They certainly do matter in producing a significant impact on collective decisions.[212]

210 See Keohane, Robert O. (2004 / 2006b) (cf. *footnote 206* op. cit.), p. 227.

211 See *Table 5* in chapter III 1.4 *Synthesis* on page 51.

212 Cf. Underdal, Arild (2002a): Conclusions. Patterns of Regime Effectiveness. In: Miles, Edward L. (ed.): Environmental regime effectiveness. Confronting theory with evidence. Cambridge, Massachusetts: MIT Press (Global Environmental Accord: Strategies for Sustainability and Institutional Innovation), pp. 433–466, p. 456.

Given the definitions and relevant features detailed above, the question arises of whether *DESD* may possibly be characterised as *regime* according to the following constituent arguments:

- Existence of social institutions

DESD is primarily based upon agencies, state and non-state bodies, enterprises and organisations carrying out social functions in the field of education, sustainability and development. UNESCO is declared the *lead agency* which serves as the normative and regulatory organisation with autonomy according to scope both for *DESD*[213] and beyond;[214]

- Presence of agreed-upon principles, norms, rules, procedures or programmes

DESD represents more than merely a number of aggregated institutions. The various stakeholders are tied together by unanimously adopted self-binding resolutions, procedural agreements and programmes;[215]

- Governance of stakeholders' actions

DESD is an action plan in itself. Guidance for stakeholders is mainly provided by UNESCO through plans of action or implementation;[216]

- Absence of stakeholder status

DESD follows a multi-stakeholder approach. Despite being led by UNESCO as an institution with proper stakeholder status, *DESD* does not automatically confer the status of an independent stakeholder;

- Dedication to a specific area

DESD covers, in accordance with its own definition and mandate, the specific area of education aiming at sustainable strategies of development;[217]

- Necessity of directing behaviour

---

213 Cf. chapter V 3 *Standard-setting* on page 109.

214 Cf. Novak Talavera, Fabián; García Corrochano Moyano, Luis (2002) (cf. *footnote 152* op. cit.), pp. 118–119; Foreign Office of the Federal Republic of Germany / German Commission for UNESCO (ed.) (2007) (cf. *footnote 21* op. cit.).

215 Cf. United Nations (ed.) (2002 / 2003) (cf. *footnote 117* op. cit.).

216 Cf. United Nations (ed.) (2002 / 2003) (cf. *footnote 117* op. cit.); UNESCO (ed.) (2005i): UNESCO's Contribution to the Implementation of the United Nations Decade of Education for Sustainable Development (2005–2014). Report by the Director-General on the United Nations Decade of Education for Sustainable Development: International Implementation Scheme and UNESCO's Contribution to the implementation of the decade. 172 EX/INF.4. Paris: UNESCO publishing; UNESCO (ed.) (2005j) (cf. *footnote 44* op. cit.); UNESCO (ed.) (2007m): United Nations Decade of Education for Sustainable Development (2005–2014). Summary of the UNESCO Action Plan For DESD. Final Draft. Paris: UNESCO publishing.

217 Cf. UNESCO (2007) (cf. *footnote 52* op. cit.).

DESD aims to integrate principles, values, and practices of sustainable development into all aspects of education and learning. Effectively implementing principles of *DESD* requires active guidance in order to re-direct stakeholder behaviour;

- Application of normative instruments

DESD relies essentially on normative *soft-law* instruments, such as United Nations General Assembly resolutions, declarations or recommendations;[218]

- Consistency by treaty or convention

DESD is not treaty-based. Moreover, *DESD* refers to a conventional agreement characterised by target-oriented stakeholder expectations, expressed needs for co-ordinating behaviour and proper means of measuring stakeholder commitment through reporting, monitoring and evaluation;[219]

- Capacity of problem-solving

DESD claims to gradually change stakeholder behaviour towards more sustainable approaches. The measures taken up by UNESCO and its participating stakeholders might be suitable for success;[220] and

- Availability of appropriate institutional setting, capabilities and leadership

DESD is embedded in a comprehensive framework of activities. These are on the one hand related to sustainable development with its different dimensions, yet on the other hand they refer to various ongoing educational processes. Due to its interdisciplinary expertise as a specialised United Nations agency in the field of education[221] and because of its long experience in organisational management, UNESCO was appointed as the executive authority charged with leading *DESD*.

---

218 Cf. UNESCO (ed.) (2006b) (cf. *footnote 21* op. cit.).

219 Cf. Tilbury, Daniella (2007): Evaluating the UN Decade of Education for Sustainable Development (DESD). Monitoring and Evaluation during the UN Decade of Education for Sustainable Development. In: Journal of Education for Sustainable Development, Volume Vol. 1, Issue 2, pp. 239–254; UNESCO (ed.) (2008h): UN DESD Global Monitoring and Evaluation Framework (GMEF). Operational Plan. Edited by Daniella Tilbury. Paris: UNESCO publishing.

220 Cf. Underdal, Arild (2002c): One question, two answers. In: Miles, Edward L. (ed.): Environmental regime effectiveness. Confronting theory with evidence. Cambridge, Massachusetts: MIT Press (Global Environmental Accord: Strategies for Sustainability and Institutional Innovation), pp. 3–46, p. 3.

221 Cf. Novak Talavera, Fabián; García Corrochano Moyano, Luis (2002) (cf. *footnote 152* op. cit.), pp. 118–119.
Cf. chapter V 3 *Standard-setting* on page 109.

1.5 Conclusion

As a preliminary result, sound justifications exist for considering *DESD* as particular regime under the appropriate theoretical umbrella.[222] Of course, this conclusion is not considered an end in itself. Clarifying the status of *DESD* at an early stage by definition enables the further application of both appropriate theoretical and methodological frameworks. For instance, looking at regimes in a more economic sense, questions of *regime effectiveness*[223] and efficiency will be addressed in greater detail.

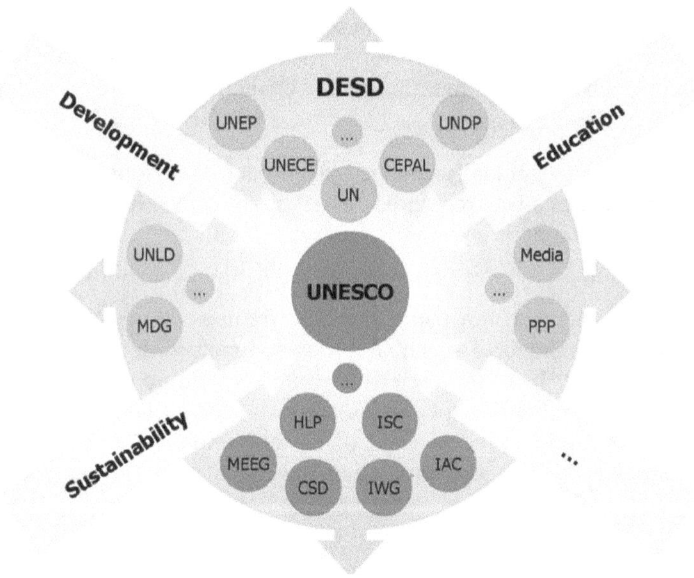

Figure 11: DESD considered as international regime[224]

222 See *Figure 11* in chapter III 1.5 *Conclusion* on page 54.
223 See Underdal, Arild (2002c) (cf. *footnote 220* op. cit.), p. 4.
224 The figure illustrates how *DESD* can be interpreted in a multi-level perspective embedded in structures of network, regime and institutions:
1. *DESD* is linked to a number of existing networks operating in the fields of education, development and sustainability, among other things.
2. *DESD* takes place in a regime environment consisting of certain degrees of stakeholder commitment in a particular principle-based field of action.
3. *DESD* is managed by institutions or institution-like entities that are linked together either by mandatory assignment (UNESCO) or by an established means of active decision-making.

2 New institutionalism

The subject of institutions has reached a decisive crossroads following the proclamation of post-war sociology that separate mainstreams existed in Europe and in North America.[225] European approaches have considered a more comprehensive study of institutions to serve as foundations for political sciences.

In contrast, North American scientists have stressed individualistic assumptions made by approaches based on behaviour and rational-choice approaches: individuals act autonomously based either on socio-psychological characteristics or on a rational calculation of their personal utility.[226]

Thus, in institutional and organisational analysis respectively two paradigms dominate and compete in scientific discourses: *classic institutionalism* versus *new institutionalism*.[227] Both differ in their integration into theory of either fixed or adaptable assumptions with regard to context.

Therefore, the so-called *new institutionalism* can be defined in sharp contrast to the conventional *classic institutionalism*.[228] The latter is primarily related to *status quo* analysis which interrogates above all contextual and stakeholder dynamics.[229] Likewise, the former considers context to be an essential element of *new institutionalism* as a programme of research.[230]

"Historical (Old) institutionalism is based on the assumption that a historically constructed set of institutional constraints and feedbacks structure the behaviour of political actors and interest groups during the policy-making process."[231]

On the contrary, *"(t)he new institutionalism in organization theory and sociology comprises a rejection of rational-actor models, an interest in institutions as independent variables, a turn toward cognitive and cultural explanations, and an interest in properties of supra-individual units of analysis that cannot be*

225 Cf. Dietz, Hella (1998) (cf. *footnote 145* op. cit.), p. 1.

226 Cf. Peters, Brainard Guy (2005) (cf. *footnote 142* op. cit.), pp. 1–6; Dietz, Hella (1998) (cf. *footnote 145* op. cit.), p. 5.

227 See *Table 6* in chapter III 2.1 *Comparison* on page 58.

228 Alternatively be referred to as *old or historical institutionalism*, too.
See Béland, Daniel (2005): Ideas, Interests, and Institutions: Historical Institutionalism Revisited. In: Lecours, André (ed.): New Institutionalism. Theory and Analysis. Toronto / Buffalo / Toronto: University of Toronto Press (Studies in Comparative Political Economy and Public Policy, 23), pp. 29–50.

229 Cf. Hasse, Raimund; Krücken, Georg (2005) (cf. *footnote 167* op. cit.), p. 102.

230 Cf. Hasse, Raimund; Krücken, Georg (2005) (cf. *footnote 167* op. cit.), p. 102.

231 See Béland, Daniel (2005) (cf. *footnote 228* op. cit.), p. 29.

reduced to aggregations or direct consequences of individuals' attributes or motives".[232]

Constituent elements of *new institutionalism* in organisational analysis are:[233]

1. Need for institutional holism and legitimacy;[234]
2. Need for autonomy, effectiveness and efficiency;[235]
3. Existence of appropriate organisational fields;[236]
4. Integration of contexts and socio-cultural settings;[237]
5. Acquisition of insights and theorisations based on empirical studies (research);[238]
6. Presence of cross-cutting institutional characteristics;[239] and
7. Capacity to actively adopt perceptions and interpretations of institutional factors (*taken-for-granted axioms*).[240]

---

232 See Powell, Walter Woody; DiMaggio, Paul Joseph (eds.) (1991 / 2004 / 2008): The new institutionalism in organizational analysis. Volume Reprint. Chicago / London: University of Chicago Press, p. 8.
See *Figure 12* in chapter III 2 *New institutionalism* on page 57.

233 Cf. Hasse, Raimund; Krücken, Georg (2005) (cf. *footnote 167* op. cit.), pp. 22 et seqq.

234 This refers to social, spatial and temporal ambits.
Cf. Hasse, Raimund; Krücken, Georg (2005) (cf. *footnote 167* op. cit.), p. 22; Walgenbach, Peter; Meyer, Renate E. (2008) (cf. *footnote 168* op. cit.), p. 65.

235 Cf. Hasse, Raimund; Krücken, Georg (2005) (cf. *footnote 167* op. cit.), p. 22.

236 Cf. Hasse, Raimund; Krücken, Georg (2005) (cf. *footnote 167* op. cit.), p. 25.

237 Cf. Hasse, Raimund; Krücken, Georg (2005) (cf. *footnote 167* op. cit.), p. 28.

238 E.g., in politics, society, economics, etc.
Cf. Hasse, Raimund; Krücken, Georg (2005) (cf. *footnote 167* op. cit.), pp. 33 et seqq.

239 Cf. Hasse, Raimund; Krücken, Georg (2005) (cf. *footnote 167* op. cit.), p. 102.

240 Cf. Hasse, Raimund; Krücken, Georg (2005) (cf. *footnote 167* op. cit.), p. 102.

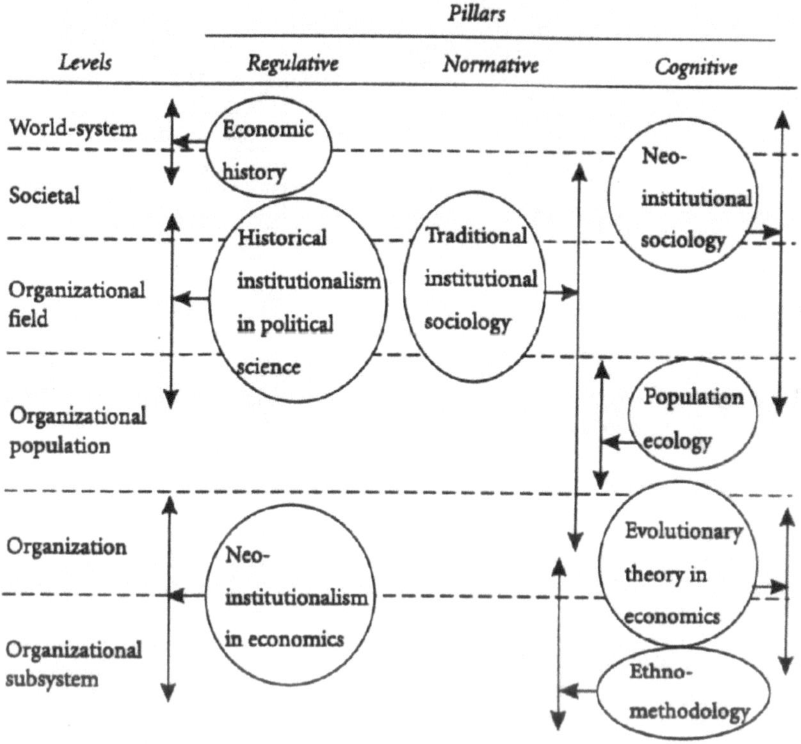

Figure 12: Schools of old and new institutionalism: institutional pillars and levels[241]

2.1 Comparison

In brief, the *classic (old)* and the *new institutionalism* may be sketched according to the following distinctions:[242]

241 Unlike *classic institutionalism,* new institutional theories rather tend to involve both regulative and even more cognitive dimensions.
See Scott, William Richard (Dick) (2001) (cf. *footnote 181* op. cit.), p. 87.

242 See *Table 6* in chapter III 2.1 *Comparison* on page 58.

Table 6: Differences between new institutionalism and classic (old) institutionalism[243]

Element	*Classic institutionalism*	*New institutionalism*
Approach	History matters[244]	Contexts matter[245]
Philosophy	Material structures[246]	Immaterial structures[247]
Autonomy	Path dependency[248]	Path independency
Institutional change	Exogenous[249]	Endogenous[250]

243 This table roughly summarises the stylised and typified differences between those two major schools of institutionalism.
Cf. Lecours, André (ed.) (2005): New Institutionalism. Theory and Analysis. Toronto / Buffalo / Toronto: University of Toronto Press (Studies in Comparative Political Economy and Public Policy, 23); Lecours, André (2005): New Institutionalism: Issues and Questions. In: Lecours, André (ed.): New Institutionalism. Theory and Analysis. Toronto / Buffalo / Toronto: University of Toronto Press (Studies in Comparative Political Economy and Public Policy, 23), pp. 3–25; Harty, Siobhán (2005): Theorizing Institutional Change. In: Lecours, André (ed.): New Institutionalism. Theory and Analysis. Toronto / Buffalo / Toronto: University of Toronto Press (Studies in Comparative Political Economy and Public Policy, 23), pp. 51–79, p. 56; Dietz, Hella (1998) (cf. *footnote 145* op. cit.), p. 4; Peters, Brainard Guy (2005) (cf. *footnote 142* op. cit.), pp. 6–24; Peters, Brainard Guy (2005) (cf. *footnote 142* op. cit.), pp. 25 et seqq; Rutherford, Malcolm (1994 / 2008): Institutions in Economics. The Old and the New Institutionalism. Volume Reprint. Cambridge: Cambridge University Press (Historical Perspectives in Modern Economics); March, James G.; Olsen, Johan P. (2004): The new institutionalism. Organizational factors in political life. In: Sinclair, Timothy J. (ed.): Global Governance. London / New York: Routledge Chapman & Hall (Critical Concepts in Political Science, Volume I), Volume The American Political Science Review, Vol. 78, No. 3. (1984), pp. 734–749, pp. 271–299, pp. 2–11.

244 That is, cultivating *historicism* by exclusively embedding historical, socio-economic and cultural developments as analytic foundation. The premise of *"legacy of the past"* explains the dominance of decisions made early in the existence of a programme or organisation.
Cf. Peters, Brainard Guy (2005) (cf. *footnote 142* op. cit.), pp. 6 et seqq, 63, 76; Harty, Siobhán (2005) (cf. *footnote 243* op. cit.), p. 56.

245 Namely, context-based, interdependent and interactive institutions.
Cf. Koch, Sascha; Schemmann, Michael (2009b) (cf. *footnote 172* op. cit.), p. 10.

246 Institutions and corresponding functions primarily defined by, for example, government or state.

247 Adding beliefs, values as well as cognitive and behavioural *scripts* to the general analytic scope.

248 Cf. Harty, Siobhán (2005) (cf. *footnote 243* op. cit.), p. 56.

249 Politics are interpreted as subordinate to and derivate of exogenous forces (*external effects*): differences in social status, geography, climate, ethnicity, language, culture, economic conditions, demography, technology, ideology, religion, etc.
Cf. March, James G.; Olsen, Johan P. (2004) (cf. *footnote 243* op. cit.), p. 3.

Element	*Classic institutionalism*	*New institutionalism*
Reductionism	Deductive[251]	Inductive[252]
Approval	Legalism[253]	Decision-making[254]
Legacy	Structuralism[255]	Inputism[256]
Openness	Holism[257]	Theory[258]
Conception	Normative analysis[259]	Cognitive basis[260]

250 Due to lack of legitimacy, calculation of opportunity costs, for example. Political structures and processes are perceived as a function of endogenous variables (integrative and holistic approach).
Cf. March, James G.; Olsen, Johan P. (2004) (cf. *footnote 243* op. cit.), p. 7.

251 Explaining political phenomena as aggregated macro (social) consequences of micro (individual) behaviour (deductive and extrinsic approach).
Cf. March, James G.; Olsen, Johan P. (2004) (cf. *footnote 243* op. cit.), p. 4.

252 Outcomes are determined by the interactions of individuals acting consistently in terms of the axioms of individual behaviour (inductive and intrinsic approach); for example the theory of markets, ecological theory of environmental competition, etc.
Cf. March, James G.; Olsen, Johan P. (2004) (cf. *footnote 243* op. cit.), p. 4.

253 I.e. law regarded as constituent framework to govern and affect citizen's behaviour.
Cf. Peters, Brainard Guy (2005) (cf. *footnote 142* op. cit.), pp. 6 et seqq.

254 This might involve refraining from a-priori assumptions regarding socio-economic, political and legal settings by stressing proper and rational decision-making competencies.
Cf. Peters, Brainard Guy (2005) (cf. *footnote 142* op. cit.), p. 4.

255 Namely, being represented through established and functioning institutional features within a particular political system – presidential, parliamentary, etc.
Cf. Peters, Brainard Guy (2005) (cf. *footnote 142* op. cit.), pp. 6 et seqq.

256 Representing an *anti-normative* basis replacing legalism by *inputism* related with commitment and participation.
Cf. Peters, Brainard Guy (2005) (cf. *footnote 142* op. cit.), p. 14.

257 Relating to formal structures of theory and methodology by directing analysis away from comparative aspects.
Cf. Peters, Brainard Guy (2005) (cf. *footnote 142* op. cit.), pp. 6 et seqq.

258 Demanding the functional theory and methodology of institutional individualism (*open system*).
Cf. Peters, Brainard Guy (2005) (cf. *footnote 142* op. cit.), pp. 6 et seqq; Rutherford, Malcolm (1994 / 2008) (cf. *footnote 243* op. cit.), p. 37; Koch, Sascha; Schemmann, Michael (2009b) (cf. *footnote 172* op. cit.).

259 Recalling a positivist normative basis of rule following of changing behaviour (*homo sociologicus*) in favour of *good government* or *good governance*, respectively.
Cf. Peters, Brainard Guy (2005) (cf. *footnote 142* op. cit.), p. 10; Rutherford, Malcolm (1994 / 2008) (cf. *footnote 243* op. cit.), p. 51; Gerner, Martin (2008): Global Governance und Internationales Ressourcenmanagment – aktuelle Aspekte, Entwicklung und Herausforderungen. Seminar paper. Supervised by: Schorlemer, Sabine von. Dresden.

Element	*Classic institutionalism*	*New institutionalism*
Leadership	*Broker*[261]	*Facilitator*[262]
Constitution	Collectivist	Evolutionary[263]

2.2 Approaches

New institutionalism is not at all constituted by homogenous ways of thinking and theorising, but provides instead a thoroughly multi-faceted vision and understanding.

Thus, different methods result from diverging approaches or competing paradigms: *calculus* versus *cultural approach.*[264] *New institutionalism* primarily addresses three basic questions:

- First, how do stakeholders behave?
- Second, how do institutions influence decision-making in politics and society?
- Third, how do institutions persist in time?[265]

Underlying the analytic pattern of *calculus* versus *cultural approach* brief answers to these questions follow:[266]

Technische Universität Dresden, Juristische Fakultät / Lehrstuhl für Völkerrecht, Recht der EU und Internationale Beziehungen, pp. 4–5, 7, 15, 25.

260 Being more attached to some conventional rational-choice conception (*homo oeconomicus*), but simultaneously recognising its enlarged scope towards behavioural and cognitive matters.
Cf. Rutherford, Malcolm (1994 / 2008) (cf. *footnote 243* op. cit.), p. 51.

261 Providing information, identifying coalitions, and ensuring common implicit understanding.

262 Encouraging stakeholder interaction, education, stimulation, interpretation, stimulating commitments, and providing legitimacy.
Cf. March, James G.; Olsen, Johan P. (2004) (cf. *footnote 243* op. cit.), p. 7.

263 Cf. Rutherford, Malcolm (1994 / 2008) (cf. *footnote 243* op. cit.), p. 103.

264 See Dietz, Hella (1998) (cf. *footnote 145* op. cit.), p. 4.

265 Cf. Dietz, Hella (1998) (cf. *footnote 145* op. cit.), p. 4.

266 See *Table 7* in chapter III 2.2 *Approaches* on page 61.

Table 7: Major approaches in new institutionalism[267]

Issues	Approach	
	Calculus	*Cultural*
How do stakeholders behave?	Human behaviour and action is directed by strategic cost-benefit thinking and the calculation of the rational utility depending on individual preferences.	Human behaviour and action is influenced by collective socio-cultural patterns and particular conditions of view of life (*Weltanschauung*).
How do institutions influence decision-making in politics and society?	Institutions are based on strategic interaction of their various stakeholders by providing stability of planning through shared expectations (presuppositions), information and compliance.	Institutions are regarded as the context-based framework for individual decision and preference, making containing symbols and routines to support processes of interpretation and self-reflection.
How do institutions persist in time?	Economically speaking, relevant stakeholders keep firmly attached to institutions if conformity and rule compliance are more highly remunerated than deviant behaviour.[268]	Sociologically speaking, stakeholders voluntarily and subconsciously assist institutional conventions and norms that are embedded and widely accepted in society.[269]

2.3 Modes

By consequence, these two major mainstream perceptions further distinct types of *new institutionalism* appropriate for the explanation of ranging developments by certain modes in new institutional theories.[270]

267 Cf. Dietz, Hella (1998) (cf. *footnote 145* op. cit.), pp. 4–5; Walgenbach, Peter; Meyer, Renate E. (2008) (cf. *footnote 168* op. cit.), p. 55.

268 In economics this explanation is subsumed under the rational-choice solution concept, called the *Nash-equilibrium*: given two or more players involved in decision making and further assuming that each player knows the preferred *equilibrium* strategies of the other players, each player chooses exactly the strategy a) by which no player can benefit more by b) changing its proper strategy without changing any of the other players. Only in this case do the established set of strategy choices and the corresponding pay-offs constitute a durable equilibrium.
Cf. also Dietz, Hella (1998) (cf. *footnote 145* op. cit.), p. 5.

269 It is argued that, in accordance with the *cultural approach*, institutions are less likely or able to be reformed as stakeholders alone make the decision.
Cf. Dietz, Hella (1998) (cf. *footnote 145* op. cit.), p. 5.

270 Cf. Dietz, Hella (1998) (cf. *footnote 145* op. cit.), pp. 5 et seqq; Peters, Brainard Guy (2005) (cf. *footnote 142* op. cit.), pp. 25 et seqq.

Table 8: Modes of new institutionalism

Mode	*Characteristics*	*Proponents*
Normative institutionalism[271]	• Logic of functional and contextual appropriateness • Logic of real consequentiality (routines, patterns and rules)	James G. March Johan P. Olsen
Rational choice institutionalism[272]	• Utility-maximising decisions of individuals • Actor-centred approach • Internalisation of given external effects[273] • Rational-choice based institutions[274]	Fritz W. Scharpf Hans Keman Barry R. Weingast Jack Knight
Empirical institutionalism[275]	• Classifying institutions by various empirical data • Determining the real occurring performance impact	Kent R. Weaver Bert A. Rockman
Historical institutionalism[276]	• Distinguishing between *calculus* and *cultural approach* • Recognising given asymmetric power relations among stakeholders • Path dependency of institutional evolution • Causal connectivity of institutions encouraging ideas and innovation	Peter A. Hall Rosemary C. R. Taylor Stephen D. Krasner

See *Table 8* in chapter III 2.3 *Modes* on page 62.

271 Normative institutionalism is considered to represent *"the roots of the 'new institutionalism'"*.
See Peters, Brainard Guy (2005) (cf. *footnote 142* op. cit.), p. 25.
Cf. March, James G.; Olsen, Johan P. (1989) (cf. *footnote 201* op. cit.), p. 160.

272 Cf. Peters, Brainard Guy (2005) (cf. *footnote 142* op. cit.), p. 43; Dietz, Hella (1998) (cf. *footnote 145* op. cit.), p. 6.

273 Individual preferences and definitions of personal interest are considered endogenous to the institution.

274 This may be characterised by common set of assumptions, common set of problems, idea of innovative *tabula rasa* (determined by nature of incentives and constraints).
Cf. Peters, Brainard Guy (2005) (cf. *footnote 142* op. cit.), pp. 46–47.

275 Cf. Peters, Brainard Guy (2005) (cf. *footnote 142* op. cit.), pp. 87, 96.

276 Cf. Dietz, Hella (1998) (cf. *footnote 145* op. cit.), pp. 5–6.

Mode	*Characteristics*	*Proponents*
Sociological institutionalism[277]	• Understanding and explaining the cognitive and normative accounts of institutions within sociology • Elucidating conceptual deficits in providing resources[278] • State-society relationships	Herbert A. Simon
International institutionalism[279]	• Considering the entire international system as institution of regimes • Institutions serving as normative intermediary of particular interests	Stephen D. Krasner Volker Rittberger Petr Kratchovil Robert O. Keohane Oran R. Young John G. Ruggie

2.4 Nexus

There is neither a uniform interpretation nor a simple application of *new institutionalism.*[280] All derived concepts have certain features in common; for instance, outcome orientation, rule-based institutions and, last but not least, the immanent problem of appropriate impact assessment. There are also major differences: for example, the diverging definitions of institutions based either on values, incentives or on constraints and on contrastive preferences and structures.[281] Theories of *new institutionalism* are to some extent compatible, aiming at reconciling dichotomised methodological approaches.[282]

Why deal with *new institutionalism* in the context of networks, regimes and institutions? There is obviously an undeniable link between those concepts and *new institutionalism* in treating regimes as social institutions.[283] New institutionalism considers institutions to be links between organisations and civil soci-

277 This is also known as *societal institutionalism* or *organisational theory.*
Cf. Peters, Brainard Guy (2005) (cf. *footnote 142* op. cit.), pp. 97, 110; Dietz, Hella (1998) (cf. *footnote 145* op. cit.), pp. 6–7.

278 These may include major restraints on time, information, perception, communication, etc.

279 Cf. Peters, Brainard Guy (2005) (cf. *footnote 142* op. cit.), pp. 126–140.

280 Cf. Peters, Brainard Guy (2005) (cf. *footnote 142* op. cit.), p. 141.

281 There is some controversy over whether to relate new institutionalism with normative or rational-choice concepts.
Cf. Peters, Brainard Guy (2005) (cf. *footnote 142* op. cit.), pp. 25 et seqq; Rutherford, Malcolm (1994 / 2008) (cf. *footnote 243* op. cit.).

282 See Rutherford, Malcolm (1994 / 2008) (cf. *footnote 243* op. cit.).

283 Cf. Breitmeier, Helmut; Young, Oran R.; Zürn, Michael (2006) (cf. *footnote 158* op. cit.), pp. 1–21.

ety.[284] Confined to international institutionalism, regimes apply to *regime theory* as institutional theory in any of their a) interest-based, b) power-based, and c) knowledge-based manifestations.[285] Likewise, several features of *new institutionalism* are applicable to regime theory. For example, *new institutionalism* promulgates certain sets of values accepted as appropriate for regime stakeholders.[286] Furthermore, grass root work is successfully carried out in terms of differentiating regimes encountered in different areas of policy and with varying *thresholds* of compliance.[287]

2.5 Regime theory

Regime theory deals with international regimes and the question under which conditions of international co-operation occur.[288] Recalling the consolidated definition of regimes as *"sets of implicit or explicit principles norms, rules and decision-making procedures around which actors' expectations converge in a given area of international relations"*,[289] this involves examining institutions which, above all, promote co-operation. On an international scale in particular, regime theory stresses the necessity of governance aspects: *"International regimes are social institutions created to respond to the demand for governance relating to specific issues arising in a social setting that is anarchical in the sense that it lacks a centralized public authority or a government in the ordinary meaning of the term"*.[290]

Regime theory was launched in the 1970s as a reaction to the emerging formalism of mainstream work on international organisations. Revealing the growing demand for governance and organisational arrangements, the regime-

284 Cf. Senge, Konstanze; Hellmann, Kai-Uwe; Scott, William Richard (Dick) (eds.) (2006) (cf. *footnote 170* op. cit.), p. 19.

285 Since the beginning of the 1980s theorists have, under the influence of new institutionalism increasingly subsumed the issues of the United Nations and the International Monetary Fund under regime theory.
Cf. Peters, Brainard Guy (2005) (cf. *footnote 142* op. cit.), pp. 126 et seqq.

286 Given diverging stakeholder-centered approaches for institutional co-operation, *calculus* versus *cultural*, it is meaningful to consider the fact that the fragility of regimes in terms of formation and institutional change depends mainly on the stakeholders themselves and nothing for which the institution can be blamed in the first instance.
Cf. Peters, Brainard Guy (2005) (cf. *footnote 142* op. cit.), pp. 126 et seqq.

287 Cf. Peters, Brainard Guy (2005) (cf. *footnote 142* op. cit.), p. 138.

288 Cf. DiMaggio, Paul Joseph; Powell, Walter Woody (1991 / 2004 / 2008) (cf. *footnote 134* op. cit.), p. 6.

289 See Krasner, Stephen D. (ed.) (2004): International regimes. Volume 11. print. Ithaca, New York: Cornell University Press, p. 2.

290 See Breitmeier, Helmut; Young, Oran R.; Zürn, Michael (2006) (cf. *footnote 158* op. cit.), p. 3.

theoretical approach was at first applied in international political economy and international environmental politics. *Regime theory* pleads for holistic concepts by integrating positivist and constructivist positions on the one hand and dealing equally with state and non-state actors on the other. For that matter, *regime theory* aims at:[291]

a) Understanding processes through which issues or problems find their way onto the international agenda through public policy; and
b) Creating appropriate institutional arrangements for legislative and institutional bargaining by agreement in the form of conventions, treaties or declaration setting.

2.6 Topics

Expertise in dealing with international regimes with regard to *new institutionalism* can be illustrated via a number of prominent issues, among others:[292]

Table 9: New institutionalism – practice and achievements

Domain	*Functional range*
International political economy[293]	• Strategic choice and management • Reduction of transaction costs • Market-value analysis • Constrained-efficiency approach • Organisational-ecology approach • Business-systems approach • Negotiated-order approach

291 Cf. Breitmeier, Helmut; Young, Oran R.; Zürn, Michael (2006) (cf. *footnote 158* op. cit.), p. 6.
292 See *Table 9* in chapter III 2.6 *Topics* on page 65.
293 Cf. Breitmeier, Helmut; Young, Oran R.; Zürn, Michael (2006) (cf. *footnote 158* op. cit.), pp. 1–21; Walgenbach, Peter; Meyer, Renate E. (2008) (cf. *footnote 168* op. cit.), pp. 147 et seqq.

Domain	*Functional range*
International environmental politics[294]	• Baltic sea regime • Regime to manage trade in hazardous chemicals and pesticides • European air pollution regime • Acid rain in Europe and North America • End of dumping in the North Sea • Sea dumping of low-level radioactive waste • Barents sea fisheries • Management of tuna fisheries in the Pacific • Ozone regime (*Vienna Convention* and *Montreal Protocol* on ozone layer depletion) • Land-based pollution control in the North Sea • Convention on long-range trans-boundary air pollution • Management of high seas salmon in the North Pacific • Mediterranean action plan • Oil pollution from ships at sea • International trade in endangered species • International whaling commission • Convention for the conservation of Antarctic marine living resources • International vessel-source oil pollution
Culture[295]	• Cultural institutions • Ethno-methodology • Phenomenology

294 Cf. Breitmeier, Helmut; Young, Oran R.; Zürn, Michael (2006) (cf. *footnote 158* op. cit.), pp. 1–21; Biermann, Frank; Bauer, Steffen (2004): Assessing the effectiveness of intergovernmental organisations in international environmental politics. In: Global Environmental Change, Volume 14, Issue 2, pp. 189–193; Miles, Edward L. (ed.) (2002): Environmental regime effectiveness. Confronting theory with evidence. Cambridge, Massachusetts: MIT Press (Global Environmental Accord: Strategies for Sustainability and Institutional Innovation); Skjærseth, Jon Birger; Stokke, Olav Schram; Wettestad, Jørgen (2006): Soft Law, Hard Law, and Effective Implementation of International Environmental Norms. In: Global Environmental Politics, Volume 6, Issue 3, pp. 104–120; Skodvin, Tora; Andresen, Steinar (2006): Leadership Revisited. Negotiating International Environmental Regimes. In: Global Environmental Politics, Volume 6, Issue 3, pp. 13–28; Victor, David G.; Raustiala, Kal; Skolnikoff, Eugene (1998): The implementation and effectiveness of international environmental commitments. Theory and practice. Cambridge, Massachusetts: MIT Press; Young, Oran R. (ed.) (1999a) (cf. *footnote 140* op. cit.); Young, Oran R. (2002): Evaluating the success of international environmental regimes: Where are we now? In: Global Environmental Change, Volume 12, Issue 1, pp. 73–77; Young, Oran R.; Levy, Marc A. (1999) (cf. *footnote 157* op. cit.), pp. 5–6.

Domain	*Functional range*
Education[296]	• Lifelong-learning initiatives worldwide • Quality management in professional training • Social milieus of educators • Private education
Sustainability[297]	• Sustainable development leadership[298]

2.7 Conceptions of order

New institutionalism pays particular attention to *institutional conceptions of order*[299] in order to structure systematically both relevant protagonists and their respective issues. In full alignment with regime theory, order may be produced either *"by political contracts and reflected in constitutions, laws, and other stable rules, or by a community of moral obligation (...)"*.[300]

Furthermore, institutional order is either established through concluding declarations of intent based on good faith (*bona fide*) or is to be imposed by competition and coercion. *Order* by reason is based on the *cultural approach* of *"ideas of rationality and intentional action; it finds institutional expression in the hierarchical organization of means and ends"*; and thus finally results *"in formally planned institutions"*. *Order* by competition and coercion, more related to the *calculus approach*, are *"recognized in ideas of conflict of interest, power,*

295 This refers to the classification of cultures as institutions to be subsumed under *regime theory*.
Cf. Grendstad, Gunnar; Selle, Per (1995) (cf. *footnote 181* op. cit.), pp. 3, 6–11, 12.

296 Cf. Koch, Sascha; Schemmann, Michael; Göhlich, Michael (eds.) (2009): Neo-Institutionalismus in der Erziehungswissenschaft. Grundlegende Texte und empirische Studien. Organisation und Pädagogik 6. Volume 1. Auflage. Wiesbaden: VS Verlag für Sozialwissenschaften; Koch, Sascha; Schemmann, Michael (2009b) (cf. *footnote 172* op. cit.); Meyer, Heinz-Dieter (ed.) (2006): The new institutionalism in education. Albany, New York: State University of New York Press.

297 Cf. Fridtjof Nansens Institutt / The Fridtjof Nansens Institute (ed.) (2005) (cf. *footnote 198* op. cit.); Kaasa, Stine Madland (2007): The UN Commission on Sustainable Development: Which Mechanisms Explains Its Accomplishments? In: Global Environmental Politics, Volume 7, Issue 3, pp. 107–130; Kiss, Alexandre (2003): Commentary and Conclusions. In: Shelton, Dinah (ed.): Commitment and Compliance. The Role of Non-Binding Norms in the International Legal System. Published new in paperback. Oxford / New York: Oxford University Press, pp. 223–242.

298 For example, *United Nations Commission for Sustainable Development* (CSD), *Agenda 21*.

299 Cf. March, James G.; Olsen, Johan P. (2004) (cf. *footnote 243* op. cit.), pp. 11–12; Dietz, Hella (1998) (cf. *footnote 145* op. cit.), pp. 11–13.

300 See March, James G.; Olsen, Johan P. (2004) (cf. *footnote 243* op. cit.), p. 11.

bargaining, survival, and war; they find institutional expression in elections and policymaking".[301]

There is broad support for the classification of *institutional conceptions of order* according to the following six category criteria of:[302]

a) Historical order:

Historical order shows appreciation for the value of historical processes and learning. In institutional theory historical order specifies how historical processes are affected by specific characteristics of (political) institutions. This includes adaptive standard-operating procedures, professions and learning institutions as well as expertise in storing and recalling institutional history;

b) Temporal order:

Temporal order considers the correlation and co-occurrence of some given problem to be solved and its current manifestation. This aspect of topicality is closely related to queuing theory by embedding current discussions into consequential structures. Therefore, institutional means are linked to their appropriate ends. By consequence, topics arise in cycles due to specific effects and procedures;

c) Endogenous order:

Endogenous order stresses the fact that processes of internal, institutional decision-making are directly affected by the distribution of preferences, resource management or the control of power. Thus, the context in which institutional action takes place is of great importance;

d) Normative order:

Normative order highlights the commonplace observation, proven by empirical evidence, that social behaviour is constrained and dictated by cultural patterns and social norms. Normative structures are transformed by culturally bound relations between norms and time paths, and which receive particular expression in conventions;

e) Demographic order:

Demographic order refers to institutions that are subject to change due to interactively driven cohort structures, such as the pursuit of careers and professional standards; and

f) Symbolic order:

Symbolic order draws attention to symbolic functions of institutional action: myths may serve as the ordering force of symbols, rituals, ceremonies, stories and drama in political life. Institutional action is both purposeful and symbolic.

---

301 See March, James G.; Olsen, Johan P. (2004) (cf. *footnote 243* op. cit.), p. 11.
302 Cf. March, James G.; Olsen, Johan P. (2004) (cf. *footnote 243* op. cit.), pp. 11–12.

2.8 Conclusion

Given that *DESD* is considered a regime, how can *new institutionalism* (settings), *regime theory* (conditions) and *institutional conceptions of order* (principles) affect further considerations?

1. Dynamics and potentials

Institutional settings must be interpreted through aspects of interdependence, facilitation, consequentiality of action, and governance.

2. Scope and approach

Institutional conditions must be read and understood in terms of cross-cutting, interdisciplinary or multi-dimensional criteria.[303]

3. Assessment and critique

Institutional principles must be used to properly assess and measure performance.[304]

3 Closing remarks

Embedding *DESD* into a theoretical framework cannot of course be an end in itself but must instead enable further considerations of its role. Recalling that the general research question is on UNESCO's role as global *lead agency* for *DESD*, theory should contribute to the problem of how to address this particular issue of international co-operation. One promising approach is to argue for *DESD* as a regime within the context of new institutionalism.

This chapter highlighted different *DESD*-related mechanisms of co-operation on an international scale. *DESD* is attached, first and foremost, to institutional patterns that are rule-based and stakeholder-oriented. Having intensely studied functions, characteristics and related types of institutions, it becomes clear that *DESD* cannot be regarded as a stand-alone institution *eo ipso*. In fact, *DESD* reveals interdependent, networking institutions. In this respect,

303 This is done in reference to a holistic theoretical approach by integrating appropriate context-based means of explanation, *inter alia* rational-choice, cognitive, socio-cultural, normative or behavioural instruments. Methodology accordingly applies to as: a) endogenous, highly contextualised and input oriented, b) inductive, evolutionary and experimental, and c) interpretative and self-reflective.

304 Questions are addressed in relation to legitimacy, acceptance, autonomy and impact (effectiveness and efficiency), *inter alia* related to: a) theory and empirical research within b) corresponding interest-, power- and knowledge-based organisational fields and due to c) a matrix of determining elements of order (historical, temporal, endogenous, normative, demographic and symbolic).

DESD can be considered a network specialised in *ESD* without proper stakeholder status. This in turn is the decisive characteristic in support of a definition of *DESD* as a regime: according to its principles and functions, *DESD* takes place in the particular field of *ESD*, provides normative action and exercises not a self-contained stakeholder function but an overarching function. Secondly, unlike *old* institutionalist theory, *new* institutionalism enables the flexible application of certain regime criteria to *DESD*. Assuming that institutions related to *DESD* are interactively linked and exposed to changing circumstances, stakeholders and decision-makers are consistently and dynamically bidden to exercise responsibility.

According to new institutionalism and regime theory, UNESCO's challenge is to provide order in terms of institutional settings, conditions and principles in relation to *DESD* as a regime. Keeping in mind that leadership implies the application of order, appropriate patterns of meaningful criteria must be established in order to achieve commitment as a result of compliance.

IV Methodology

Given the theoretical background in which DESD is considered as a regime, appropriate criteria are the conditio sine qua non for the proper elucidation of both assignment and performance. Which methodological approach, in accordance with regime theory and new institutionalism, provides a suitable connection between theory and research objectives? This chapter will discuss sets of criteria which will be devised primarily through triangulation, or analysis grounded in three independent sources of theory-oriented, document-based and data-based research.

1 Introduction

Form follows function, and that which applies to modern architecture relates to methodological instruments also. They must be derived from the theoretical orientation alone. Structures need to support reasoning by facilitating appropriately conducted argumentation. Choosing a methodological approach must depend on theoretical intent alone.

Taking into account the notional background of *DESD qua* regime, analytical methods must reflect, reliably, the nature of theoretical concepts such as *new institutionalism* (settings), *regime theory* (conditions) and *institutional conceptions of order* (principles). Methodological instruments must therefore be appropriate and manageable for an examination of UNESCO's role within *DESD* with particular reference to:

1. Dynamics and potentials;
2. Scope and approach; and
3. Assessment and critique.

With a theoretical basis, analysis typically follows deductive guidelines: reference to general considerations in relation to *DESD* leads first to particular case studies[305] that enrich and validate findings from different and interdisciplinary perspectives.[306] In doing so, a reconciliation is effected between two contrastive research models: the *normative paradigm* and the *interpretative paradigm*.[307]

Table 10: Normative versus interpretative paradigms in research[308]

Paradigm	*Normative*	*Interpretative*
Orientation	Quantitative	Qualitative
Approach	Classifying given symbolic material through scientifically-skilled observation and expertise	Interpreting symbol- and communication-driven processes of interaction by means of scientific discourse
Prerequisites	Existing rules of explicit categorisation and schematic procedures	Existing research layout and collected data material
Objectives	Collection of data	Assessment of data
	Support or disproving of hypotheses	Establishment of theories
Criteria	Objectivity	Openness[309]
	Systematic	Communicative
	Quantifiability	Naturalness
	Content-based	Explication and interpretation

305 Cf. Tilbury, Daniella (2007) (cf. *footnote 219* op. cit.), p. 2.

306 I.e. conception of *methodological triangulation*.
Cf. Becker, Egon; Jahn, Thomas; Stieß, Immanuel, et al. (eds.) (1997) (cf. *footnote 53* op. cit.); Flick, Uwe; Kardorff, Ernst von; Steinke, Ines (eds.) (2005): Qualitative Forschung. Ein Handbuch. Reinbek bei Hamburg: Rowohlt-Taschenbuch-Verlag (Rororo Rowohlts Enzyklopädie, 55628), p. 318; Bohnsack, Ralf; Marotzki, Winfried; Meuser, Michael (eds.) (2006): Hauptbegriffe qualitativer Sozialforschung. Volume 2. Auflage. Opladen: Budrich (UTB Erziehungswissenschaft Sozialwissenschaft, 8226); Flick, Uwe (2006): Qualitative Sozialforschung. Eine Einführung. Volume 4. Auflage, vollständig überarbeitet und erweiterte Neuausgabe. Reinbek bei Hamburg: Rowohlt-Taschenbuch-Verlag (Rororo Rowohlts Enzyklopädie, 55654), pp. 330–332.

307 See *Table 10* in chapter IV 1 *Introduction* on page 72.

308 Cf. Lamnek, Siegfried (2005): Qualitative Sozialforschung. Lehrbuch. Volume 4. vollständig überarbeitete Auflage. Weinheim: Beltz-Verlag (Beltz-PVU), pp. 479–480, 493–505, 505–546.

309 I.e. refraining from over-reliance on prior knowledge and *axioms*.

The methodological approach applied at this point consists of a selection of three independent but closely intertwined components:

1. Theory-oriented analysis;
2. Document-based analysis; and
3. Data-based analysis.

2 Theory-oriented analysis

Theory-oriented analysis aims to identify key factors of institutional performance.[310] Data is derived directly from the theoretical background of *new institutionalism* and *regime theory* by deducing definitive criteria of regime success, relating, for instance, to regime performance and -effectiveness.

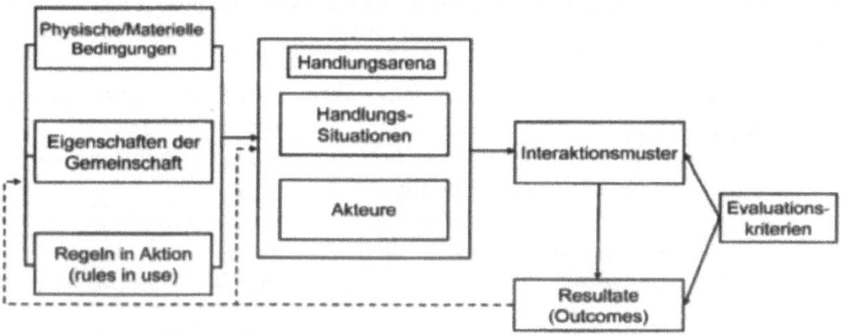

Physical and material conditions	Context of action		
Stakeholder characteristics	Situations of action	Patterns of interaction	Criteria of assessment
Rules in use	Stakeholders	Outcomes	

Figure 13: Framework for institutional analysis[311]

In the case of UNESCO and *DESD*, two different theory-based sources must be taken into consideration:

310 See *Figure 13* in chapter IV 2 *Theory-oriented analysis* on page 73.

311 According to the model elaborated by Elinor Ostrom (1999), the influence of decisions is subject to structural and normative factors of institutions. Criteria of success and imperatives of action have to be fully consistent with a) initial institutional *conditions*, b) institutional *characteristics*, and c) *rules* in use within specific contexts.
Cf. Schneider, Volker; Janning, Frank (2006): Politikfeldanalyse. Akteure, Diskurse und Netzwerke in der öffentlichen Politik. Wiesbaden: VS Verlag für Sozialwissenschaften; GWV Fachverlage GmbH Wiesbaden (Springer-11776 [Dig. Serial]), p. 91.

- Internal or *in-house* criteria that refer expressly to internationally recognised functions of UNESCO; and
- External criteria which define regime catalogue criteria to *DESD*.

2.1 Functions

UNESCO's functions are frequently prescribed in various official documents, primarily those that record medium-term strategies.[312] Five principal tasks are widely recognised: *"Throughout its activities and projects, UNESCO will perform and assume a range of functions corresponding to its role as the international lead agency for education, the sciences, culture and communication:*

- *a laboratory of ideas: UNESCO will play a key role in anticipating and defining, in the light of the ethical principles that it champions, the most important emerging problems in its spheres of competence, and in identifying appropriate strategies and policies to deal with them;*
- *a standard-setter: UNESCO will serve as a central forum for articulating the ethical, normative and intellectual issues of our time, fostering multidisciplinary exchange and mutual understanding, working – where possible and desirable – towards universal agreements on these issues, benchmarking targets and mobilizing international opinion;*
- *a clearing house: UNESCO has a role in gathering, transferring, disseminating and sharing available information, knowledge and best practices in its fields of competence, identifying innovative solutions and testing them through pilot projects;*
- *a capacity-builder in Member States: UNESCO will organise international cooperation for servicing its stakeholders, especially its Member States, in building human and institutional capacities in all its fields of competence;*
- *a catalyst for international cooperation: UNESCO as a technical multidisciplinary agency will assume a catalytic role for development cooperation in its fields of competence. To that end it will seek to ensure that the objectives, principles and priorities it promotes are followed suit by other multi- and bilateral programmes and that projects are implemented, in particular at regional and national levels, through innovation, effective interventions and wise practices".*[313]

---

312 Cf. UNESCO (ed.) (2002f): Medium-Term Strategy for 2002–2007. 31 C/4 Approved. Paris: UNESCO workshops, p. 13; Foreign Office of the Federal Republic of Germany / German Commission for UNESCO (ed.) (2007) (cf. *footnote 21* op. cit.), p. 14; UNESCO (ed.) (2008e): Medium-Term Strategy for 2008–2013. 34 C/4 (CLD-8.8). Paris: UNESCO workshops, p. 8.

313 See UNESCO (ed.) (2002f) (cf. *footnote 312* op. cit.), p. 13.

Taking into account UNESCO's various strategic programme objectives,[314] almost one third of which correspond to *DESD* issues in an interdisciplinary manner,[315] some focal functions receive particular emphasis. They include *"[...] evidence-based policy advice, normative and standard-setting activities, research and foresight, policy advice, benchmarking, monitoring and evaluation as well as country-level operational engagement in particular institutional and human capacity-building [...]"*.[316] Expressed in a more concisely and in a more condensed manner, UNESCO *modalities of action*[317] are:

a) The formulation of global policies and policy advice;
b) The setting of standards; and
c) The monitoring of normative actions.

These given functions also play an important role in the methodological sphere. They are not only the strategic driving factors in UNESCO governance,[318] but also the fundamental analytic layer of cross-cutting *in-house* criteria.

2.2 Criteria

In addition to the underlying UNESCO *in-house* criteria, certain performance criteria, which originate in the prior theoretical consideration of interpreting *DESD* as an international regime[319], have to be taken into account. In this regard, *regime theory* provides a distinctly manifold toolkit of instruments. Most of them are either attached to or, by analogy, derived from environmental regimes, particularly in the case of analytic criteria of effectiveness.[320] Incorporat-

314 Cf. UNESCO (ed.) (2008e) (cf. *footnote 312* op. cit.), pp. 16 et seqq.

315 *DESD*-related strategic UNESCO programme objectives are reflected in: *"2 – Developing policies, capacities and tools for quality education for all and lifelong learning as well as promoting education for sustainable development; 9 – Strengthening the contribution of culture to sustainable development; 11 – Sustainably protecting and enhancing cultural heritage"*.
See UNESCO (ed.) (2008e) (cf. *footnote 312* op. cit.), pp. 18, 25, 28.

316 See UNESCO (ed.) (2008e) (cf. *footnote 312* op. cit.), p. 8.

317 See Foreign Office of the Federal Republic of Germany / German Commission for UNESCO (ed.) (2007) (cf. *footnote 21* op. cit.), p. 14.

318 Cf. Gehring, Thomas (2002) (cf. *footnote 133* op. cit.), p. 74.

319 Cf. *Figure 11* in chapter III 1.5 *Conclusion* on page 54.

320 Cf. Young, Oran R. (ed.) (1999a) (cf. *footnote 140* op. cit.); Young, Oran R. (2002) (cf. *footnote 294* op. cit.); Stokke, Olav Schram (2007): Qualitative Comparative Analysis, Shaming, and International Regime Effectiveness. In: Journal of Business Research, Volume 60, Issue 5, pp. 501–511; Andresen, Steinar (2007): The Effectiveness of UN Environmental Institutions. In: International Environmental Agreements: Politics, Law and Economics, Volume 7, Issue 4, pp. 317–336; Young, Oran R.; King, Leslie A; Schroeder, Heike (eds.) (2008): Institutions and environmental change. Prin-

ing these into the methodological framework will lead to a *catalogue* or *scheme of criteria*[321] that is most likely to profitably approach UNESCO's performance during *DESD*.

2.2.1 Effectiveness

Effectiveness is an elusive concept which encompasses normative, scientific and historical judgments.[322] Effectiveness is defined as *"(...) a measure of the extent to which an activity achieves its objectives".*[323] *Behavioural effectiveness*[324] involves solving problems[325] by channeling social conduct through *behavioural mechanisms*.[326]

Discussion frequently reveals little knowledge of the effectiveness of regimes and international organisations, and this is due to the limited value assigned to conceptual models.[327] However, *"(t)he assessment of (such) institutions is ultimately an evaluation of how real institutions interact with other real institutions and human behaviour to produce real consequences".*[328] The level at which these results are achieved constitutes the definitive, major differences between the assessment of regime effectiveness and that of organisational effectiveness.[329] This *functional effectiveness*[330] is determined by both structural and contextual variables.[331] In particular, effective *performance*[332] depends on the following characteristics:[333]

---

cipal findings, applications, and research frontiers. Cambridge, Massachusetts: MIT Press.

321 Cf. Lamnek, Siegfried (2005) (cf. *footnote 308* op. cit.), p. 502.
See *Table 11* in chapter III 1.5 *Conclusion* on page 79.

322 Cf. Young, Oran R.; Levy, Marc A. (1999) (cf. *footnote 157* op. cit.), p. 3.

323 See Dicke, Klaus; Hüfner, Klaus (1987): Die Leistungsfähigkeit des VN-Systems. Politische Kritik und wissenschaftliche Analyse. Bonn: Deutsche Gesellschaft für die Vereinten Nationen; UNO-Verlag (UN-Texte, 37), p. 32.

324 See Underdal, Arild (2002a) (cf. *footnote 212* op. cit.), p. 436.

325 Cf. Young, Oran R.; Levy, Marc A. (1999) (cf. *footnote 157* op. cit.), p. 1.

326 Personal incentives and benefits encourage stakeholders' contributions to solve problems that motivate actors to invest more time and energy (the *participatory approach*). Determinants within the behavioural complex consist of a constellation of actors, interests and interactions centered on a specific issue or issue area. They may be bound internally (system based or management dependent) or externally (*external effects*).
Cf. Young, Oran R. (2002) (cf. *footnote 294* op. cit.), p. 76; Underdal, Arild (2002c) (cf. *footnote 220* op. cit.), p. 18.

327 Cf. Biermann, Frank; Bauer, Steffen (2004) (cf. *footnote 294* op. cit.), pp. 190–191.

328 See March, James G.; Olsen, Johan P. (1989) (cf. *footnote 201* op. cit.), p. 129.

329 Cf. Biermann, Frank; Bauer, Steffen (2004) (cf. *footnote 294* op. cit.), p. 191.

330 See Underdal, Arild (2002a) (cf. *footnote 212* op. cit.), p. 436.

331 *Structural variables* are: formal competencies, degree of regime *embeddedness*, organisational structure, problem of scope, availability of resources, stakeholder involve-

- Context supporting the necessity and commitment to co-operate;[334]
- Legislative practice and codification that ensures precision and quality of interpretation;
- Legitimacy;
- Inclusion;
- Democratic representation; and
- Distribution of power.

There are different conceptual models of how to approach effectiveness from a methodological perspective.[335] In consideration of the contribution made by *DESD* and UNESCO the following three models are considered to be relevant.

The *classic* approach of organisational theory is to calibrate assessment in accordance with three dimensions:[336]

a) *Output* refers to the actual activity or product of an organisation represented by the quantity and quality in generating principles, norms, rules, procedures and decisions;
b) *Outcome* refers to changing the behaviour of societal actors by adapting policies in accordance with particular normative requirements;[337] and

---

ment, decision-making procedures, internal mechanisms of conflict resolution, mechanisms for external representation, recruitment of human resources, etc.
Contextual variables are: external factors, such as belief systems, state of economy, technological breakthroughs, etc; and internal factors, such as positive attitude, personal characteristics, professional ethos, etc.
Cf. Biermann, Frank; Bauer, Steffen (2004) (cf. *footnote 294* op. cit.), pp. 192–193; Alvarez, José Enrique (2006) (cf. *footnote 141* op. cit.), pp. 363–364.

332 Cf. Fridtjof Nansens Institutt / The Fridtjof Nansens Institute (ed.) (2005) (cf. *footnote 198* op. cit.), p. 6.

333 Cf. Hasenclever, Andreas; Mayer, Peter (2007) (cf. *footnote 131* op. cit.), pp. 31–32.

334 Cf. Young, Oran R. (2002) (cf. *footnote 294* op. cit.), p. 75.

335 Cf. Young, Oran R.; Levy, Marc A. (1999) (cf. *footnote 157* op. cit.), pp. 10–16; Young, Oran R. (2004b): The Consequences of International Regimes. In: Underdal, Arild; Young, Oran R. (eds.): Regime consequences. Methodological challenges and research strategies. Dordrecht: Kluwer Academic Publishers, pp. 3–24, p. 11.
See *Table 12* in chapter IV 2.3 *Overview* on page 84.

336 Cf. Young, Oran R. (2002) (cf. *footnote 294* op. cit.), p. 74; Börzel, Tanja; Risse, Thomas (2002): Die Wirkung internationaler Institutionen. Von der Normanerkennung zur Normeinhaltung. In: Jachtenfuchs, Markus; Knodt, Michèle (eds.): Regieren in internationalen Institutionen. Festschrift für Beate Kohler-Koch. Opladen: Leske & Budrich, pp. 141–182, p. 144; Underdal, Arild (2002c) (cf. *footnote 220* op. cit.), pp. 5–6; Biermann, Frank; Bauer, Steffen (2004) (cf. *footnote 294* op. cit.), p. 190; Fridtjof Nansens Institutt / The Fridtjof Nansens Institute (ed.) (2005) (cf. *footnote 198* op. cit.), p. 6; Breitmeier, Helmut; Young, Oran R.; Zürn, Michael (2006) (cf. *footnote 158* op. cit.); Hasenclever, Andreas; Mayer, Peter (2007) (cf. *footnote 131* op. cit.), p. 29; Andresen, Steinar (2007) (cf. *footnote 320* op. cit.), p. 3; Kaasa, Stine Madland (2007) (cf. *footnote 297* op. cit.), pp. 108–109.

c) *Impact* refers to *broader consequences*[338] in terms of changes effected in policy targets by fulfilling the objectives.[339]

Another model relates to the character of the problem in reference to the problem-solving capacity of a regime or an organisation.[340] This *steady-state* approach examines the interplay between the distribution of capabilities and the relevant institutional settings.[341]

Effectiveness may thirdly be assessed according to both causal and chronological sequentiality: on the one hand major achievements are attributed to causal connections between institutions and collective outcomes.[342] On the other hand, real contributions and successful developments are evaluated in an *ex ante* and *ex post* perspective according to a *counterfactual*[343] or *what-might-have-happened* scenario.[344]

---

337 E.g., governments, institutions, non-governmental lobbyist groups and organisations, scientists, media or individual actors.

338 See Underdal, Arild; Young, Oran R. (eds.) (2004): Regime consequences. Methodological challenges and research strategies. Dordrecht: Kluwer Academic Publishers, pp. 1–2.

339 E.g., quantifiable long-term benefits and improvements.

340 Cf. Young, Oran R. (2004b) (cf. *footnote 335* op. cit.), p. 7; Fridtjof Nansens Institutt / The Fridtjof Nansens Institute (ed.) (2005) (cf. *footnote 198* op. cit.), pp. 9–13; Kaasa, Stine Madland (2007) (cf. *footnote 297* op. cit.), pp. 109–112.

341 E.g., secretariat structure, aspects of entrepreneurial leadership, access and participation of stakeholders or the contribution of state sectors.

342 I.e. direct (due to *short* causal chains) and indirect (due to *longer* causal chains) effects.

343 Counterfactual can be described as *"a strategy that involves systematically reconstructing how the course of event would have developed in the absence of a regime or an institution"*.
See Fridtjof Nansens Institutt / The Fridtjof Nansens Institute (ed.) (2005) (cf. *footnote 198* op. cit.), p. 16.

344 Measuring effectiveness includes the analysis of beneficial and inhibitive effects (good or bad effects). These can only be emphasised by an appropriate benchmark. Alternatively, some hypothetical means of assessment can be considered:
Laboratory or quasi-experiments directed towards the exploration of comparisons (differences and commonalities); or
Thought experiments working with methods of *counterfactuals* in order to provide thinking in alternatives. *"A counterfactual analysis can be described as a thought experiment where the expected decisions and efforts in the absence of the institution are identified, and then compared with the actual events."*
See Fridtjof Nansens Institutt / The Fridtjof Nansens Institute (ed.) (2005) (cf. *footnote 198* op. cit.), p. 16.
Cf. Young, Oran R. (1999a): Regime Effectiveness: Taking Stock. In: Young, Oran R. (ed.): The effectiveness of international environmental regimes. Causal connections and behavioral mechanisms. Cambridge, Massachusetts: MIT Press, pp. 249–279, pp. 265–268; Young, Oran R.; Levy, Marc A. (1999) (cf. *footnote 157* op. cit.), pp. 17–18.

Table 11: Survey of different modes of assessing effectiveness

Approach	*Detail*	*Critical remarks*
Results	Classification of regime or organisational results.	Difficult to distinguish.
Problem-solving[345]	Elimination or alleviation of the problem related to problem-solving capacity.	Difficult to find a substantive bottom line and to be aware of own limitations (self-reflection).
Causal-temporal	Linking institutions and outcomes causally and chronologically *ex ante* and *ex post*.	Difficult to substantiate nexus due to non-laboratory conditions, lack of alternatives and too many determining factors.
Legal[346]	Meeting contractual obligations.	Difficult to ensure compliance with rules, initiated policies and programmes.
Economic[347]	Incorporating minimal cost criteria into fulfillment of contractual obligations.	Difficult to tackle efficiency in practice due to calculations based on theoretical models and lack of empirical observation of alternative regimes (*opportunity costs*).
Normative[348]	Achieving normative values (fairness, justice, stewardship, commitment, etc.).	Difficult to set up measurable values.
Political[349]	Treating international problems as functions of specific constellations of actors, interests or institutions.	Difficult to isolate own contribution to effective regime change due to minimum required behavioural change.

Prerequisites for the assessment of effectiveness are:[350]

---

345 Cf. Young, Oran R.; Levy, Marc A. (1999) (cf. *footnote 157* op. cit.), p. 4.

346 Cf. Young, Oran R.; Levy, Marc A. (1999) (cf. *footnote 157* op. cit.), p. 4.

347 Cf. Young, Oran R.; Levy, Marc A. (1999) (cf. *footnote 157* op. cit.), pp. 4–5.

348 Cf. Young, Oran R.; Levy, Marc A. (1999) (cf. *footnote 157* op. cit.), p. 5.

349 Prominent examples of effective environmental regimes are the oil pollution regime, the fishery regime and the regime against air pollution.
Cf. Young, Oran R.; Levy, Marc A. (1999) (cf. *footnote 157* op. cit.), pp. 5–6.

350 Cf. Underdal, Arild (1992): The Concept of Regime 'Effectiveness'. In: Cooperation and Conflict, Volume 27, Issue 3, pp. 227–240, pp. 228–238; Underdal, Arild (2004d): Methodological challenges in the Study of Regime Effectiveness. In: Underdal, Arild; Young, Oran R. (eds.): Regime consequences. Methodological challenges and research strategies. Dordrecht: Kluwer Academic Publishers, pp. 27–48, p. 31; Fridtjof Nansens Institutt / The Fridtjof Nansens Institute (ed.) (2005) (cf. *footnote 198* op. cit.), p. 6.

1. Full awareness of the object of evaluation (*What?*): does one assess the effectiveness of the regime itself or just its problem-solving efforts?
2. Clarity of points of reference for evaluation (*By which means?*): Are there any particular standards or units of measurement?[351] Is an assessment of relative or collective improvement best?[352]
3. Preparedness for measurement (*How?*): Does one refer to comparative case studies or to a catalogue of criteria?

2.2.2 Efficiency

Efficiency may be said to constitute the economic counterpart or an *add-on* principle to effectiveness.[353] Economically speaking, efficiency refers to the criterion of least or minimal cost that requires the minimal use of allocated resources. Theories of new institutionalism explicitly call on efficiency of regimes and organisations while performing tasks.[354] Applying efficiency to institutions implies the *optimal* – not necessarily the least – allocation of means and resources in order to accomplish given objectives within a certain range. The criterion of efficiency then serves as a legal normative.[355]

2.2.3 Compliance

Compliance is probably one of the most difficult terms employed in the assessment regime performance. By definition, compliance encompasses the behavioural practice of obeying either particular rules or requests made by people in authority or institutions as appropriate. Two different wordings suit the description conformity to behaviour, either to act in accordance with or in fulfilment of something.

Compliance may encompass both an explicit and an implicit tacit dimension as vividly illustrated thus: *"(Institutions) are perfectly analogous to the rules of*

351 For instance, does one focus on *hard result-oriented* indicators or maybe on *soft process-oriented* indicators, too, such as: agenda-setting, participation, comprehensiveness and institution-building?
Cf. Andresen, Steinar (2007) (cf. *footnote 320* op. cit.), p. 4.

352 E.g., using individual baseline indicators for marginal changes or referring to collective concepts of maximising the sum of net benefits, such as the so called *pareto frontier*.

353 Cf. Underdal, Arild (2004d) (cf. *footnote 350* op. cit.), p. 27.

354 Cf. Hasse, Raimund; Krücken, Georg (2005) (cf. *footnote 167* op. cit.), p. 24.

355 Cf. Dicke, Klaus (1994): Effizienz und Effektivität internationaler Organisationen. Darstellung und kritische Analyse eines Topos im Reformprozeß der Vereinten Nationen. Berlin / Kiel: Duncker & Humblot (VIIR 116), p. 355; Foreign Office of the Federal Republic of Germany / German Commission for UNESCO (ed.) (2007) (cf. *footnote 21* op. cit.), p. 16.

the game in a competitive team sport. That is, they consist of formal written rules as well as typically unwritten codes of conduct that underlie and supplement formal rules. (...) (T)he rules and informal codes are sometimes violated and punishment is enacted. Therefore, an essential part of the functioning of institutions is the costliness of ascertaining violations and the severity of punishment (opportunity costs)".[356]

In order to assess compliance the following key questions must be addressed and taken into consideration:

1. Compliance involves varying types or domains: signing an agreement or its ratification does not necessarily ensure compliance and commitment to its implementation;
2. Compliance must be considered a matter of degree. In other words, partial compliance is perfectly possible in practice. Compliance is a gradual or dynamic concept that cannot be limited to binary terms of either yes or no;
3. Compliance does not necessarily demand causality. This means that compliance by default and without any causal commitment is quite reasonable; and
4. Compliance must be clearly distinguished from regime effectiveness. *"Effectiveness is the question whether the goals of the norm are achieved, and may be independent of compliance."*[357] To provide an example, there are recorded cases of little behavioural change at the highest level of compliance.[358] The nexus between compliance and effectiveness may be explicated only with difficulty. Employment of the degree of compliance as an exclusive indicator of effectiveness inevitably leads to the problem of validity.[359]

In this respect, compliance can be considered in connection with distinctive mechanisms of behavioural regulation or modes of regime activity:[360]

a) Coercing compliance;
b) Enmeshing states through launching particular programmatic activities;
c) Shaping expectations and common understanding; and

356 See North, Douglass Cecil (1990 / 2007) (cf. *footnote 146* op. cit.), p. 4.

357 See Shelton, Dinah (ed.) (2000): Commitment and Compliance. The Role of Non-Binding Norms in the International Legal System. Oxford: Oxford University Press, p. 5; Shelton, Dinah (2003c): Law, Non-Law and the Problem of 'Soft Law'. In: Shelton, Dinah (ed.): Commitment and Compliance. The Role of Non-Binding Norms in the International Legal System. Published new in paperback. Oxford / New York: Oxford University Press, pp. 1–18, p. 5.

358 Cf. Underdal, Arild (1998): Explaining Compliance and Defection. Three Models. In: European Journal of International Relations, Volume 4, Issue 1, pp. 5–30, p. 6.

359 Cf. Fridtjof Nansens Institutt / The Fridtjof Nansens Institute (ed.) (2005) (cf. *footnote 198* op. cit.), p. 6.

360 Cf. Young, Oran R. (1999a) (cf. *footnote 344* op. cit.), pp. 265–268; Shelton, Dinah (ed.) (2000) (cf. *footnote 357* op. cit.), p. 1.

d) Promoting gradated processes.

Additionally, effective regulation that leads ultimately to compliance depends on a mutual belief in co-operation. It is coercive tactics employed by any higher power that will facilitate compliance, but good management and institutionalised mechanisms of incentive. To conclude, compliance is dependent on *goodwill* and a thoroughly positive attitude towards behavioural changes in action or policy.[361]

2.2.4 Leadership

One major difference between international institutions and regimes that emerge spontaneously from those specially constituted in a purposeful and planned sense concerns the impact of directing behavioural change. Specialised institutions, agencies and regimes are established to exercise meaningful influence on changing behavioural patterns in order to reach substantial results through negotiation.[362] This does not just require stakeholder commitment. For various reasons, theories of rational co-operation are limited in their explanation of how stakeholders exert momentum for successful regime performance.[363]

Constructivist approaches of co-operation therefore propose coercive selection in well-defined situations of negotiation. Regimes may provide this platform of decision-making through offering opportunities to realise the benefits of co-operation and through governance.[364] To work effectively those processes need facilitation through *broker*-like[365] and sometimes informal leadership in the provision of information, identification of coalitions for decisions, communication and management of competencies.[366] Leadership in this very sense aims at establishing commonly shared expectations and implicit understanding through-

---

361 Cf. Breitmeier, Helmut; Young, Oran R.; Zürn, Michael (2006) (cf. *footnote 158* op. cit.), pp. 63–65.

362 Cf. Gehring, Thomas (2002) (cf. *footnote 133* op. cit.), p. 69.

363 Problems of regime co-operation arise where rational-choice assumptions fail. This particularly applies to individual and collective decision making in the case of the strategic *prisoners' dilemma* or *free-rider phenomena*, for instance. Prominent examples on an international scale may be found in the fields of environmental protection or free-trade negotiations.
Cf. Keohane, Robert O. (ed.) (1989) (cf. *footnote 160* op. cit.), p. 2.

364 Relations between stakeholders and institutions are expressed by a cybernetic model referring to stakeholder-institution-stakeholder-institution reciprocally.
Cf. Gehring, Thomas (2002) (cf. *footnote 133* op. cit.), pp. 71, 74.

365 See March, James G.; Olsen, Johan P. (2004) (cf. *footnote 243* op. cit.), p. 739.

366 Cf. Gehring, Thomas (2002) (cf. *footnote 133* op. cit.), p. 78; Underdal, Arild (2002a) (cf. *footnote 212* op. cit.), p. 451.

out evolving negotiations in accordance with situation-specific models of what is preferable.[367]

2.2.5 Topicality

Another prominent criterion relates to the question of whether a regime is considered to be timely enough to get its message across. Should regimes wish to perform favourably they must adopt the driving topics of society in order to justify the needs of their foundation. Topical issues significantly contribute to a positive image of the regime and the way it is visualised in the public perception.[368]

2.2.6 Context

Regimes do not arise out of nowhere. Context constitutes the overall framework or *window of opportunity* in which effective regime activities take place.[369] The conditions of context influence to a considerable extent the positioning of topical issues on the agendas of international regimes.[370] Once strategically placed, context plays a pivotal role in the establishment of binding forums of negotiations by recognising the situation dependent order of individual stakeholder preferences.[371]

2.2.7 Power

The concept of power can be applied, with justification, to international institutions and regimes when the consideration that power is not an end in itself is borne in mind.[372] In order to achieve full recognition and justification power must be related to productive creativity and also to encouragement of leadership functions. International institutions and regimes are organised to exert power in three different ways:[373]

---

367 Cf. Gehring, Thomas (2002) (cf. *footnote 133* op. cit.), pp. 79 et seqq.

368 Cf. Walgenbach, Peter; Meyer, Renate E. (2008) (cf. *footnote 168* op. cit.), p. 151.

369 Cf. Lamnek, Siegfried (2005) (cf. *footnote 308* op. cit.), p. 535.

370 Cf. Shelton, Dinah (ed.) (2000) (cf. *footnote 357* op. cit.), pp. 14–17; March, James G.; Olsen, Johan P. (2004) (cf. *footnote 243* op. cit.), p. 744.

371 Cf. Gehring, Thomas (2002) (cf. *footnote 133* op. cit.), p. 70.

372 Cf. Peters, Brainard Guy (2005) (cf. *footnote 142* op. cit.), p. 126; Hasenclever, Andreas; Rittberger, Volker (eds.) (2007): Macht und Ohnmacht internationaler Institutionen. Festschrift für Volker Rittberger. Frankfurt am Main: Campus Verlag.

373 Cf. Betz, Joachim (2007): Macht und Ohnmacht der internationalen Finanzinstitutionen – IWF und Weltbank. In: Hasenclever, Andreas; Rittberger, Volker (eds.): Macht und Ohnmacht internationaler Institutionen. Festschrift für Volker Rittberger. Frankfurt am Main: Campus Verlag, pp. 314–342, p. 315.

- *Deciding power* by asserting and implementing decisions subject to material and normative resources;
- *Institutional power* constituted in terms of agenda-setting activities, stakeholder assistance or participation; and
- *Productive power* directed towards defining problems and deficits, proposing viable solutions and taking action effectively.

2.3 Overview

Table 12: DESD catalogue of criteria

Functions	*Criterion*	*Aspects*
Standard-setting – Policy advice – Monitoring	Effectiveness	• Implementation and monitoring • Co-ordination
	Efficiency	• Proportionality • Flexibility • Validity
	Compliance	• Responsibility • Commitment • Accountability
	Leadership	• Promotion • Integration • Consultancy • Governance
	Topicality	• Continuity • Frequency • Image • Visibility • Communication
	Context	• Resources • Structure • Expertise
	Power	• Deciding • Institutional • Productive

3 Document-based analysis

Document-based analysis clearly marks the core activity of research due to the fact that major findings are deduced primarily from comparative and interpretative textual analysis.[374] *Content analysis* is applied in a rather free-style technique to systematically explore, extract, condense and re-arrange information in accordance with the relevant research question.[375]

The documentary basis applied may ideally be divided into two different types:

- Primary-source materials; and
- Secondary-source materials.

3.1 Primary-source materials

Primary-source materials are written or non-written *first-hand accounts*; original materials directly related to the issue of investigation either through co-occurrence or by participation. They are the most trustworthy and objective source of contemporary evidence. In particular, primary sources recognise varying contexts and changing conditions.

Primary sources are primarily official documents. Arranged according to document type and intended purpose of publishing, they include:

- Documents prescribing official positions and legal status provisions, such as treaties, conventions, constitutions, statutes, resolutions, declarations, recommendations, protocols, speeches or any other regulatory sources of binding legal authority;
- Documents describing progress and development from an internal perspective, such as progress reports, schemes of implementation and reporting;
- Documents providing communication, merging different aspects and perspectives and opening up discourse for public opinion making, such as conference reports, reviews and scientific or journalistic publications;
- Documents displaying in-house decisions such as manuscripts, working papers, strategies, publicity or image campaigns;
- Documents focusing on external assessment by other governmental and non-governmental institutions such as recommendations, scientific assistance, research reports, support or critique;

---

374 Cf. Lamnek, Siegfried (2005) (cf. *footnote 308* op. cit.), p. 502.

375 Cf. Atteslander, Peter; Cromm, Jürgen (eds.) (2003): Methoden der empirischen Sozialforschung. Volume 10. neu bearbeitete und erweiterte Auflage. Berlin: de Gruyter (De-Gruyter-Studienbuch), pp. 215–239; Lamnek, Siegfried (2005) (cf. *footnote 308* op. cit.), pp. 478 et seqq.

- Documents providing up-to-date information such as online sources, databases and toolkits; and
- Expert interviews, such as personal correspondence, official records of interviews and results of informal briefings.

3.2 Secondary-source materials

Based upon primary sources, secondary-source materials are documents containing generalisations, abstracts of analysis, synthesis, interpretation or evaluation of original information. In contrast to primary sources, secondary ones lack the immediacy or authenticity of the original; they are indirect, possibly biased and subjective replica of the primary record. Thus, it is vital to be aware of the fact that secondary documents always contain interpreted, commented or criticised, analysed, adapted or information otherwise processed. Advantageously, by assessing, re-arranging, re-packaging, compressing and re-distributing information, these sources make information more accessible and *digestible* – essentially, a well-defined *added value*, however debatable.

In this case, secondary-source materials are used to establish the analytical framework of theory and methodology. Furthermore, secondary sources are intended to provide essential background information by means of defining and interpreting, illustrated as follows:

- Documents commenting on key concepts and issues, such as reference books or textbooks, technical dictionaries, encyclopedias, journal articles, conference proceedings and book reviews;
- Documents dealing with questions of theory and methodology in search of an appropriate research approach, such as handbook entries, position papers; term papers or dissertations; and
- Documents containing additional information that embeds current affairs in, and connects them with, previous and future developments such as declarations of intent or mid- and long-term reports on scheduled follow-up activities, future issues, budgetary planning as well as adjustments and changes in staff and the availability of resources.

4 Data-based analysis

As mentioned, *methodological triangulation* refers to the attempt to improve research validity by combining various techniques.[376] The blend of multiple methods is considered a guiding principle that ensures full use is made of differ-

---

376 Cf. Bohnsack, Ralf; Marotzki, Winfried; Meuser, Michael (eds.) (2006) (cf. *footnote 306* op. cit.), pp. 161–162.

ent sources of information and approaches in order to present sound and methodologically-grounded results.[377]

Starting with theory-based analysis, by sketching the analytical framework of performance criteria, facts are generated and structured in a further progression through document-based analysis of primary and secondary sources. The third step of triangulation suggests validation of these facts by means of data-based analysis.[378]

Empirical data analysis is applied in the collection and processing of relevant information. The aim is to gather data that relies upon an *evidence-based* and *bottom-up* approach.[379] With regard to the collection of empirical data, research is either qualitatively or quantitatively oriented. There are major conceptual differences in the planning of qualitative and quantitative research.[380]

Table 13: Characteristics of qualitative and quantitative research – a synthesis[381]

	Qualitative	*Quantitative*
Nature	Comprehensive	Explicative
	Interactive-explorative	Analytic
	Inductive	Deductive
	Subjective	Objective
	Interpretative	Causal
	Idiographic	Nomothetic
Approach	Data-based (grounded)	Theory-based
	Stakeholder-driven	Factor-specific
Scope	Commonalities	Differences
	Pluralist	Limited

377 Cf. Mayring, Philipp (2002): Einführung in die qualitative Sozialforschung. Eine Anleitung zu qualitativem Denken. Volume 5. überarbeitete und neu ausgestattete Auflage. Weinheim: Beltz-Verlag (Beltz Studium), pp. 147–148; Cropley, Arthur J. (2005): Qualitative Forschungsmethoden. Eine praxisnahe Einführung. Volume 2. überarbeitete Auflage. Eschborn bei Frankfurt am Main: Klotz, pp. 112–113; Lamnek, Siegfried (2005) (cf. *footnote 308* op. cit.), pp. 274–291; Bohnsack, Ralf; Marotzki, Winfried; Meuser, Michael (eds.) (2006) (cf. *footnote 306* op. cit.), pp. 161–162.

378 Cf. Flick, Uwe; Kardorff, Ernst von; Steinke, Ines (eds.) (2005) (cf. *footnote 306* op. cit.), pp. 309–318; Flick, Uwe (2006) (cf. *footnote 306* op. cit.), pp. 330–332.

379 Cf. UNESCO (ed.) (2003b) (cf. *footnote 109* op. cit.), p. 5.

380 See *Table 13* in chapter IV 4 *Data-based analysis* on page 87.

381 Cf. Atteslander, Peter; Cromm, Jürgen (eds.) (2003) (cf. *footnote 375* op. cit.), p. 238; Lamnek, Siegfried (2005) (cf. *footnote 308* op. cit.), pp. 242–272; Flick, Uwe (2006) (cf. *footnote 306* op. cit.), pp. 16–20, 67–75; Walgenbach, Peter; Meyer, Renate E. (2008) (cf. *footnote 168* op. cit.), pp. 171, 178.

	Qualitative	*Quantitative*
	Historic	A-historic
Design	Circular-reflective[382]	Linear[383]
	Dynamic	Static
	Flexible	Fixed
Methods	Holistic	Particularistic
	Open	Closed
	Identification	Distance
Results	Relevant	Representative
Assessment	Low-level	High-level
	Micro-founded	Reductive

Dealing with qualitative and quantitative data is not an end in itself but explicitly required as an integral outcome of theory-based performance criteria:[384] *"Qualitative and quantitative evaluation methods will be necessary (...) – aspects such as the adoption of values and changes in behaviour cannot be adequately captured by numbers alone. As far as quantitative approaches are concerned, a wide range of data (particularly ethnographic) can be collected".*[385]

4.1 Qualitative approach

Qualitative means of research are vital in order to properly address different aspects of an issue: not all research questions can be purposefully tackled with simply any theoretical or documentary method. In the case of implicit structures

382 Although target-oriented and unidirectional, the process of *qualitative* modeling involves various *loops* of interdependence and reciprocity.

383 In a nutshell, the linear model of designing *quantitative* research consists in: 1) Establishing theory; 2) Formulating hypotheses; 3) Creating sound criteria for assessment (operationalisation); 4) Defining the sampling; 5) Collecting data; 6) Analyzing data; and 7) Validating data.

384 Cf. Young, Oran R. (ed.) (1999a) (cf. *footnote 140* op. cit.), pp. 281–287; Breitmeier, Helmut; Young, Oran R.; Zürn, Michael (2006) (cf. *footnote 158* op. cit.), pp. 1–20.

385 See UNESCO (ed.) (2005c) (cf. *footnote 23* op. cit.), p. 46.
Cf. UNESCO (ed.) (2005c) (cf. *footnote 23* op. cit.), pp. 45–47; Tilbury, Daniella (2007) (cf. *footnote 219* op. cit.), pp. 241 et seqq; United Nations Economic Commission for Europe (UNECE); United Nations Economic and Social Council (ECOSOC) (eds.) (2007b): Indicators for Education for Sustainable Development. Progress report on the work of the Expert Group. Second meeting, Geneva, 4–5 December 2006. ECE/CEP/AC.13/2006/5. New York: United Nations, pp. 2–3.

of knowledge, comprehensive information can be gathered only through a more flexible approach. Qualitative research enables this by providing a vaster methodological scope. Some will be applied and explained in more detail.[386]

What functions in particular does qualitative empiric research play? The following elements serve to justify its application by elaborating the necessary requirements:

- Stakeholder behaviour and appropriate strategies must be examined both in isolation and in responsive interaction with varying contexts and situational specifics;[387]
- The creation and evaluation of *narrative accounts qua tendency-finding analysis*[388] enables an illustration of the institutional role as a determinant of collective outcomes in an international society and a description of individual regime members' performances simultaneously;[389]
- Empirical case studies are widely recognised tools of organisational research, and, accordingly, include qualitative indicators of performance analysis;[390]
- *"Evaluation methods and indicators for the implementation of ESD, in particular qualitative ones, should be developed".*[391]

---

386 Cf. Strauss, Anselm Leonard (1998): Grundlagen qualitativer Sozialforschung. Datenanalyse und Theoriebildung in der empirischen soziologischen Forschung. Volume 2. Auflage. München: Fink (UTB für Wissenschaft, 1776, Soziologie), pp. 25–29; Underdal, Arild (2002b): Methods of analysis. In: Miles, Edward L. (ed.): Environmental regime effectiveness. Confronting theory with evidence. Cambridge, Massachusetts: MIT Press (Global Environmental Accord: Strategies for Sustainability and Institutional Innovation), pp. 47–62, pp. 48–49.

387 Cf. Walgenbach, Peter; Meyer, Renate E. (2008) (cf. *footnote 168* op. cit.), pp. 171 et seqq.

388 See Young, Oran R. (ed.) (1999a) (cf. *footnote 140* op. cit.), p. 285.

389 I.e. processes and results are not self-explanatory, but need to permanently reconstruct the forces at work that shape stakeholder behaviour, particularly at critical moments in regime development. Causal pathways have to be clearly indicated by openly addressing problems and actions taken or by using the method of *counterfactuals* in order to describe what would have happened in the absence of this international regime.
Cf. Young, Oran R. (ed.) (1999a) (cf. *footnote 140* op. cit.), pp. 285–287; Underdal, Arild (2002b) (cf. *footnote 386* op. cit.), p. 50.

390 Adequate methods of organisational empirical research, for instance, consist of observation, interview, questionnaire, simulation and first-hand archival information.
Cf. Powell, Walter Woody; DiMaggio, Paul Joseph (eds.) (1991 / 2004 / 2008) (cf. *footnote 232* op. cit.); Strati, Antonio (2000): Theory and method in organization studies. Paradigms and choices. London: SAGE Publications, p. 134; Stokke, Olav Schram (2007) (cf. *footnote 320* op. cit.), pp. 5 et seqq.

391 See United Nations Economic Commission for Europe (UNECE); United Nations Economic and Social Council (ECOSOC) (eds.) (2004g): Framework for the Implementation of the UNECE Strategy for Education for Sustainable Development. Eleventh session (Geneva, 13–15 October 2004). CEP/2004/17 / CEP/AC.13/2004/10. New

Case studies are used to explore a particular issue and draw conclusions about it.[392] Case-study research that addresses institutional contexts is most effectively carried out by referring to different methods simultaneously. This usually involves the joint use of stakeholder observation, in-depth interviews and additional archival information.[393] Case-oriented research requires the right choice of cases to be made with care, and the access to and availability of information or resources, amongst other things, to be taken into account.[394]

An *interview* is knowingly and purposefully arranged, and a *formal* appointment made between participants in order to exchange meaningful information through patterned structures of discourse. The type of interview depends on how communication asymmetries between interviewer and interviewee are addressed in the posing and answering of questions.[395]

Conducting interviews may be a productive tool of case studies for eliciting valuable, directly relevant information. Applied as source of data generation, comparison and validation, modes of interviewing inherently privilege a *via regia*[396] both in quantitative and qualitative empiric research.[397]

Expert interviews are conducted in a *semi-structured* way:[398] On the one hand a questionnaire prepared in advance orientates the proceedings and additionally guarantees easy handling for comparing results. On the other hand, sufficient flexibility is retained to adapt and extend conversations if necessary.[399]

York: United Nations, p. 2; United Nations Economic Commission for Europe (UNECE); United Nations Economic and Social Council (ECOSOC) (eds.) (2004b): Draft UNECE Strategy for Education for Sustainable Development. High-level meeting of Environment and Education Ministries (Vilnius, 17–18 March 2005). CEP/AC.13/2005/3. New York: United Nations, p. 14; United Nations Economic Commission for Europe (UNECE); United Nations Economic and Social Council (ECOSOC) (eds.) (2005f): UNECE Strategy for Education for Sustainable Development. High-level meeting of Environment and Education Ministries (Vilnius, 17–18 March 2005). CEP/AC.13/2005/3/Rev.1. New York: United Nations, p. 14.

392 Cf. United Nations Economic Commission for Europe (UNECE); United Nations Economic and Social Council (ECOSOC) (eds.) (2004d) (cf. *footnote 20* op. cit.), p. 6.

393 Cf. Strati, Antonio (2000) (cf. *footnote 390* op. cit.), pp. 133–134, 164 et seqq.

394 Cf. Stokke, Olav Schram (2007) (cf. *footnote 320* op. cit.), p. 6.

395 Cf. Atteslander, Peter; Cromm, Jürgen (eds.) (2003) (cf. *footnote 375* op. cit.), pp. 120–121; Lamnek, Siegfried (2005) (cf. *footnote 308* op. cit.), pp. 329–330.

396 See Lamnek, Siegfried (2005) (cf. *footnote 308* op. cit.), p. 329.

397 Cf. Lamnek, Siegfried (2005) (cf. *footnote 308* op. cit.), pp. 330–332; Bohnsack, Ralf; Marotzki, Winfried; Meuser, Michael (eds.) (2006) (cf. *footnote 306* op. cit.), pp. 94–98.

398 Cf. Atteslander, Peter; Cromm, Jürgen (eds.) (2003) (cf. *footnote 375* op. cit.), pp. 156–159; Flick, Uwe (2006) (cf. *footnote 306* op. cit.), pp. 127 et seqq.
See *Table 14* in chapter IV 4.1 *Qualitative approach* on page 91.

399 E.g., significantly tending more towards narrative elements rather than towards questions and answers.

Experts have well-defined expertise. They are not necessarily always agency officials but also free-lance specialists without any particular institutional affiliation.[400]

Table 14: Opportunities and challenges of semi-structured interviews[401]

Opportunities	*Challenges*
Providing guidance through questionnaire	Dealing with additionally raised or follow-up questions during an interviewing situation?
Balancing competencies and asymmetries between interviewer and interviewee	Promoting flexibility in order to avoid bureaucratic attitudes?
Achieving comparability of data and reducing mistakes	Ensuring coherence of questions and answers between interviewer and interviewee?
Generating structured, consolidated and easily accessible data	Remaining active participants during interviews in order to avoid conversational passivity.
Achieving subject-centred orientation and high level of data reliability	Avoiding technical deficiencies.

The successful collection of interview data is predominantly a matter of respecting certain guiding principles. These consist of:[402]

- Manifest intention and interest;
- Openness and relevance of questions and answers;
- Neutrality and authenticity;
- Sensitivity towards situation and context;
- Flexibility towards specific interview arrangements;
- Accuracy and reliability of communication;
- Clarity and non-ambiguity as essential elements for maximising data validity;
- Interview calibrated towards and grounded in process to prioritise generation rather than validation of theory; and
- Responsiveness between subject and object of analysis.

Cf. Flick, Uwe (2006) (cf. *footnote 306* op. cit.), pp. 117–145; Bohnsack, Ralf (2007): Rekonstruktive Sozialforschung. Einführung in qualitative Methoden. Volume 6. durchgesehene und aktualisierte Auflage. Opladen: Verlag Barbara Budrich (UTB Erziehungswissenschaft Sozialwissenschaft, 8242), pp. 91–104.

400 Cf. Strati, Antonio (2000) (cf. *footnote 390* op. cit.), pp. 146–148.

401 Cf. Atteslander, Peter; Cromm, Jürgen (eds.) (2003) (cf. *footnote 375* op. cit.), pp. 156–159; Lamnek, Siegfried (2005) (cf. *footnote 308* op. cit.), pp. 335–336, 341; Flick, Uwe (2006) (cf. *footnote 306* op. cit.), pp. 117–145.

402 Cf. Mayring, Philipp (2002) (cf. *footnote 377* op. cit.), pp. 68 et seqq; Atteslander, Peter; Cromm, Jürgen (eds.) (2003) (cf. *footnote 375* op. cit.), pp. 120–195; Lamnek, Siegfried (2005) (cf. *footnote 308* op. cit.), pp. 329–401.

The assessment of interview material is limited in this case to the analysis of content. Processes such as literal transcription, single-case analysis and general considerations are either abbreviated or omitted entirely. The intention is to provide a consolidated *synopsis* of answers based on the questionnaire referring both to common tendencies as well as to distinctive facts. Data analysis is therefore much more focussed on the accumulation of *hard facts*. A strategy of five steps is proposed in order to analyse *semi-structured* interview data properly:[403]

a) Defining analytical categories based on questionnaire and interview materials;
b) Developing a code of guidelines according to the analytical categories;
c) Coding and structuring interview data;
d) Quantifying phenomena by comparing and indicating their frequency of occurrence; and
e) Interpreting selected cases more specifically as appropriate.[404]

The comprehensive comparison of interview data aims to prove theory to be conceptually dense, typologically differentiated and context-independent in its basic assumptions. This may be reached through:[405]

1. Clearly constituting and categorising case subjects intended for comparison;
2. Strategically selecting cases according to contents (*principle of relevance*) and points of comparison (*theoretical sampling*); and
3. Profoundly carrying out subject-centred analysis before the point of theoretical saturation.[406]

Briefings are *narrative accounts* less formally arranged than interviews. Due to their *informal* character,[407] the information gained must be handled with particu-

---

403 Cf. Schmidt, Christiane (2005): Analyse von Leitfadeninterviews. Kapitel 5.10. In: Flick, Uwe; Kardorff, Ernst von; Steinke, Ines (eds.): Qualitative Forschung. Ein Handbuch. Reinbek bei Hamburg: Rowohlt-Taschenbuch-Verlag (Rororo Rowohlts Enzyklopädie, 55628), pp. 447–456, pp. 448–456.

404 E.g., proving strategies, examining or validating new hypotheses, differentiating concepts of terminology, revisiting theoretic frameworks, etc.
Cf. Schmidt, Christiane (2005) (cf. *footnote 403* op. cit.), pp. 448–455.

405 Cf. Deppermann, Arnulf (2001): Gespräche analysieren. Eine Einführung. Volume 2. durchgesehene Auflage. Opladen: Leske & Budrich (Qualitative Sozialforschung, 3), pp. 84–93, 94–104.

406 In particular, this includes *co-occurrence* in terms of synchronised communicative styles and practices of argumentation as well as parallel structures of content.

407 Cf. Atteslander, Peter; Cromm, Jürgen (eds.) (2003) (cf. *footnote 375* op. cit.), p. 156; Gerner, Martin (30/07/2009): DESD: Monitoring and evaluating. Informal briefing. Interviewee: Lawale, Shivali. Format: Personal notes. Paris; Gerner, Martin (10/08/2009): DESD in progress. Informal briefing. Interviewee: Laboulle, Olivier. Format: Personal notes. Paris; Gerner, Martin (11/08/2009): International Institute for

lar care, because not every insight is explicitly intended to be made public and might even differ from institutional positions.[408] Therefore, together with all experiences obtained through working in institutions of relevance, data is used to serve as background information. Whether or not directly applicable, briefings offer important perspectives for the scrutiny of individual regimes at work.[409]

4.2 Quantitative approach

Quantitative research is applied to measure people's behaviour as evidenced by particular ways of thinking and acting. It is usually carried out through comprehensive surveys, including large samples. Unlike qualitative approaches, quantitative research is principally characterised by:[410]

- Fields of research clearly indicated by focusing on those *hard cases* which affect the content of collective outcomes;
- A manifest outcome in direction and expectation;
- The quest for precise measurement and analysis of target concepts;
- Use of structured surveys and focused questionnaires by incorporating closed questions with a choice set responses;
- Efficiency in testing and systematic assessment of rival hypotheses;
- *Variation-finding techniques*, such as experiments involving variation on the independent variable under similar situations and conditions with differing outcomes *ex ante* and *ex post* as appropriate; and
- The threat of spurious correlation and the risk of failing to detect essential causal links.

In the present context quantitative research achieves its principal relevance in two forms:

1. Certain mechanisms of reporting are introduced in order to document progress. These reporting formats consist of sets of mostly quantitative indicators related to baseline data. They must be taken into consideration when evaluating;[411] and

Educational Planning (IIEP) and DESD. Informal briefing. Interviewee: Göttelmann-Duret, Gabriele. Format: Personal notes. Paris; Gerner, Martin (14/09/2009): DESD and UNECE. Informal briefing. Interviewee: Bolshakova, Marianna. Format: Personal notes. Geneva.

408 I.e. personal statements, work in progress, critical remarks, diplomatically sound expressions.

409 Cf. Strati, Antonio (2000) (cf. *footnote 390* op. cit.), p. 150.

410 Cf. Young, Oran R. (ed.) (1999a) (cf. *footnote 140* op. cit.), pp. 281–284.

411 Cf. United Nations Economic Commission for Europe (UNECE); United Nations Economic and Social Council (ECOSOC) (eds.) (2005c): Indicators for Education for Sus-

2. Database entries which enable optional research on compliance, rules of decision-making or specifically programmatic regime activities.

Progress and development is displayed, officially, by the commitment displayed in individual reporting. Stakeholders are obliged to report to authorities in order to prove compliant behaviour, or at least a *spirit of goodwill*.[412] This procedure is internationally accepted and widely favoured. Substantial efforts made in the format of reporting on a regional[413] or international scale must be appreciated and interpreted.

A regime database may serve as a methodologically useful tool in the readjustment of analysis among case study and global assignments. This implies an imperative to *"move regime analysis from its current emphasis on the use of discrete case studies to the use of a relational database encompassing comparable data on a large number of cases and (...) facilitate quantitative as well as qualitative analyses of hypotheses dealing with international regimes"*.[414]

5 Research assignment

In asking how UNESCO fulfills its leadership and co-ordination mandate as *lead agency* in the course of the *United Nations Decade of Education for Sustainable Development (2005–2014)* (DESD), the two following objectives are crucial: on the one hand, to elaborate on *DESD* itself by providing comprehensive understanding of its nature in relation to UNESCO; and, on the other hand, to discuss examples of regional implementation practices in order to demonstrate the actual relevance of *DESD*. Each objective is linked to specific research questions.

---

tainable Development. Progress Report on the work of the Expert Group. First meeting, Geneva, 13–14 December 2005. CEP/AC.13/2005/9. New York: United Nations, p. 2.

412 Cf. Hüfner, Klaus; Reuther, Wolfgang (eds.) (2005): UNESCO-Handbuch. Volume Neuausgabe, 2. Auflage. Bonn: UNO-Verlag, p. 29.

413 E.g., UNECE initiative on *DESD* indicators and reporting formats.
Cf. United Nations Economic Commission for Europe (UNECE) (26/10/2006): Format for Reporting on Implementation of the UNECE Strategy for Education for Sustainable Development. Within the framework of the United Nations Decade of Education for Sustainable Development (2005–2014). ECE/CEP/AC.13/2006/5/Add.1. UNECE Steering Committee on Education for Sustainable Development. Geneva.

414 See Young, Oran R.; Zürn, Michael (2006): The International Regimes Database: Designing and Using a Sophisticated Tool for Institutional Analysis. In: Global Environmental Politics, Volume 6, Issue 3, pp. 121–143.
Cf. Breitmeier, Helmut; Young, Oran R.; Zürn, Michael (2006) (cf. *footnote 158* op. cit.), p. 21.

Theory- and document-based analyses contribute mainly to the first aspect by unfolding and structuring *DESD* in an interdisciplinary manner. By contrast, data-based analysis focuses more on the second aspect of implementation.[415]

Table 15: Methodological research assignments

Approach	*Assignment*
Theory-based analysis	*DESD* co-ordination and facilitation
Document-based analysis	
Data-based analysis	*DESD* implementation

6 Conclusion

Methodology must meet the specific requirements of the underlying *regime theory*, underpinning in particular:

a) Dynamics and potentials;
b) Scope and approach; and
c) Assessment and critique.

This will be achieved by reconciling and combining deductive and inductive means of research.[416] First and foremost, methodological triangulation is applied in order to make the most use of data available, and specifically through:[417]

- Theory-based analysis as a source of meaningful criteria, both UNESCO's *in-house* criteria or those which relate to *regime theory*;
- Document-based analysis with reference to primary and secondary materials; and
- Data-based analysis as an empirical means of qualitative and quantitative validation.

415 See *Table 15* in chapter IV 5 *Research assignment* on page 95.
416 Cf. Underdal, Arild (2002b) (cf. *footnote 386* op. cit.), p. 47.
417 See *Figure 14* in chapter IV 6 *Conclusion* on page 96.

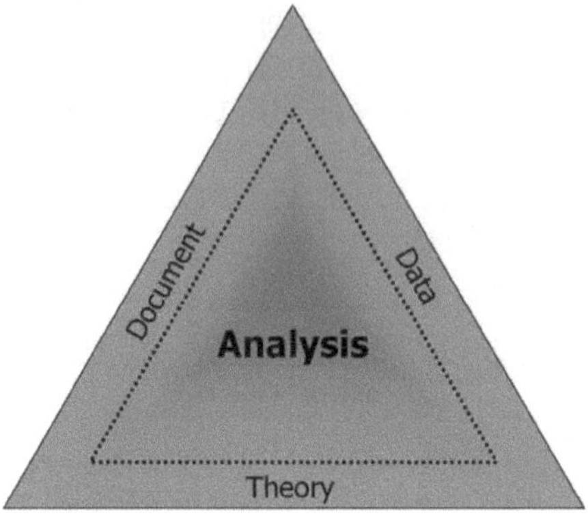

Figure 14: Methodological triangulation[418]

A number of promising facts are connected with this methodological approach. Particularly advantageous are:

- Existing strategic instruments of analysis that serve as a sound *storyboard* and constitute a purposeful connection between theory and methodology;
- The avoidance of a *selection-bias* by referring to many sets of methods including strong and *grounded* criteria; and
- A substantial and systematic contribution towards the concept of *lead agency*.

There are also some problematic aspects. That which must be considered further is primarily related to:

- Finding an adequate balance between theoretical considerations and data-bound techniques;
- Anchoring regime criteria effectively and comprehensively; and
- Refraining from counterproductive *trade-offs* between descriptiveness and analysis.

This methodology is proven appropriate both to address *DESD* and to support the relevant research questions. It connects with theory by applying *regime theory* to *DESD* as appropriate; it explicitly pursues the holistic and interdisciplinary intent of *ESD* through research represented by a multi-method approach, and it enables answers to the research questions to be pre-structured and well-defined.

418 In this case triangulation refers to three different sources of methodology for analyis, to be specific theory-based, document-based and data-based.

V Framework for action

To what extent does UNESCO provide regulatory frames of reference that may facilitate DESD? This thesis is concerned with UNESCO as a whole institutional framework, and not specifically with DESD. Questions of the organisation's global mandate in role and function must first be addressed. This chapter will outline three basic methods conceived of by UNESCO for carrying out its global assignment in the formulation of global policies and the provision of policy advice, standard-setting, and monitoring.

1 Global assignment

Both the foundational background and the present global assignment of UNESCO are informed by three fundamental and universally understood principles of the United Nations:[419]

a) No application of force and arms;
b) Peaceful settlement of disputes; and
c) An obligation to promote social and economic progress by peaceful means.

---

419 Cf. Faundez, Julio (2007): Promoting Dignity, Equality and Mutual Respect among Human Beings. Introduction. In: Yusuf, Abdulqawi A. (ed.): Normative action in education, science and culture. Essays in commemoration of the sixtieth anniversary of UNESCO. French edition. Paris / Leiden / Boston: UNESCO publishing; Martinus Nijhoff Publishers (UNESCO reference works series, 1), pp. 177–195, p. 177.

Given this spirit UNESCO contributes as *specialised United Nations lead agency*[420] *"with the function of advising the United Nations on the educational, scientific and cultural aspects of matters of concern to the latter"*.[421] UNESCO has been deemed particularly successful within the process of globalisation in consideration of its concern for democratic participation, sustainable development and cultural diversity.[422]

However, UNESCO faces a number of global challenges which considerably influence its assignment: On the one hand there is no international consensus concerning global governance. On the other hand, nation-states are increasingly incapable of compliance with the social and economic rights which, ultimately, effect changes in the contexts of political regimes.[423] In this respect, UNESCO earns its reputation and comparative advantage by emphasising its mandatory policy-fields, namely education, science and culture.[424] Additionally, UNESCO ensures adequate *equilibrium* in handling the potential dominance of financial and commercial organisations.

---

420 See Article 57–59 of the *Charter of the United Nations* and Article X of the *Constitution of the United Nations Educational, Scientific and Cultural Organization*.
Articles 57 to 63, particularly Article 61, of the *Charter of the United Nations* state the principle of functional decentralisation of *specialised agencies* affiliated with United Nations.
Cf. United Nations (ed.) (1945): Charter of the United Nations. San Francisco / New York: UN Treaty Collection (Certified True Copies), p. 12; UNESCO (ed.) (1945): Constitution of the United Nations Educational, Scientific and Cultural Organization. Adopted in London on 16 November 1945. Volume 2004 edition. Paris: UNESCO workshops (Basic texts), pp. 18, 173; Schrijver, Nico (2007): Beyond Treaty Law: The Influence of the Legal Instruments Adopted by UNESCO on General International Law. UNESCO's Role in the Development and Application of International Law: An Assessment. In: Yusuf, Abdulqawi A. (ed.): Normative action in education, science and culture. Essays in commemoration of the sixtieth anniversary of UNESCO. French edition. Paris / Leiden / Boston: UNESCO publishing; Martinus Nijhoff Publishers (UNESCO reference works series, 1), pp. 385–405, pp. 390–394.

421 See UNESCO (ed.) (1945) (cf. *footnote 420* op. cit.), p. 173.

422 Cf. Foreign Office of the Federal Republic of Germany / German Commission for UNESCO (ed.) (2007) (cf. *footnote 21* op. cit.), p. 10; Faundez, Julio (2007) (cf. *footnote 419* op. cit.), p. 178.

423 Cf. Faundez, Julio (2007) (cf. *footnote 419* op. cit.), p. 178.

424 Cf. UNESCO (ed.) (2003b) (cf. *footnote 109* op. cit.), p. 2; Finnemore, Martha (2004 / 2006): International organizations as teachers of norms. The United Nations educational, scientific, and cultural organization and science policy. In: Sinclair, Timothy J. (ed.): Global Governance: Critical Concepts in Political Science. London / New York / London: Taylor & Francis, Inc.; Routledge (Critical Concepts in Political Science, Volume II), Volume International Organization 47 (4) (1993): 565–597, pp. 302–335, pp. 585–586; Faundez, Julio (2007) (cf. *footnote 419* op. cit.), p. 179; Maclean, Rupert; Fien, John; Park, Man-Gon (eds.) (2009) (cf. *footnote 42* op. cit.), p. xxii.

These aspects of UNESCO's mandate impact upon the *DESD* framework. The objectives of *DESD* mesh particularly well with the global objective of working in favour of social and economic progress *"so that we can learn to make a better world"*.[425] UNESCO's contribution to and within the United Nations system can be analysed and evaluated in two different ways, with reference to either specific functions in particular spheres of operation or in stressing its global strategic role.

1.1 Functions

"UNESCO's comparative advantage within the United Nations system is its ability to respond to complex contemporary problems in a comprehensive and relevant manner through inter-sectoral and interdisciplinary action."[426] The organisation's functional orientation is defined thus:[427]

- Laboratory of ideas: anticipating and defining important and emerging problems in its spheres of specialisation and identifying appropriate strategies and policies of negotiating them;
- Standard-setter: forging universal agreements on emerging ethical issues by fostering multi-disciplinary exchange and mutual understanding;
- Clearinghouse: gathering, transferring, disseminating and sharing available information, knowledge and best practices in its fields of specialisation in order to identify innovative solutions to be tested through pilot projects (research, networks of exchanging results and training);
- Capacity-builder: focusing on human and institutional capacities in all fields of specialisation by means of *technical co-operation* or *technical (advisory) assistance*; and
- Catalyst for international co-operation: promoting international co-operation for the concentration of labour as a technical multi-disciplinary agency among its member and associate member states in all relevant fields.

---

425 See Matsuura, Koïchiro (01/03/2005) (cf. *footnote 28* op. cit.), p. 4.

426 See UNESCO (ed.) (2008e) (cf. *footnote 312* op. cit.), p. 6.

427 Cf. Matsuura, Koïchiro (01/03/2005) (cf. *footnote 28* op. cit.), p. 3; UNESCO (ed.) (2007f): Highlights on DESD Progress to Date. January 2007. Paris: UNESCO publishing, p. 2; Matsuura, Koïchiro (2007): Foreword. In: Yusuf, Abdulqawi A. (ed.): Normative action in education, science and culture. Essays in commemoration of the sixtieth anniversary of UNESCO. French edition. Paris / Leiden / Boston: UNESCO publishing; Martinus Nijhoff Publishers (UNESCO reference works series, 1), pp. 11–14.
See *Figure 15* in chapter V 1.1 *Functions* on page 100.

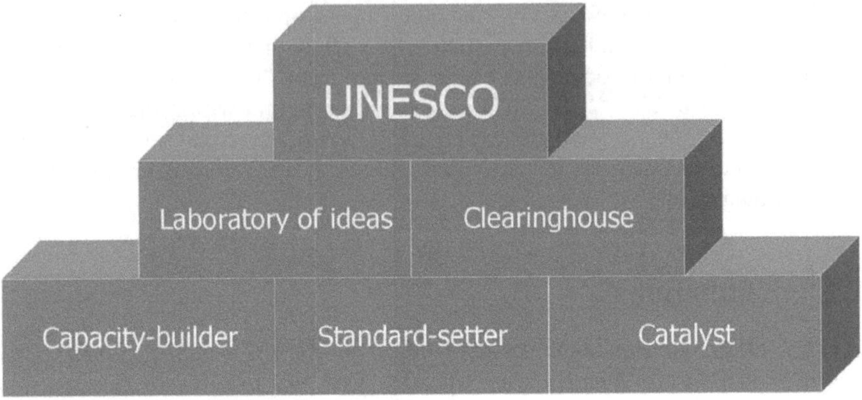

Figure 15: UNESCO's functional assignment[428]

Given the *DESD* leadership mandate, UNESCO may comfortably make use of all five organisational functions. Due to the nature of *ESD*, the functions of capacity-building and acting as a catalyst are certainly the most obviously suitable. Nonetheless, carrying out clearinghouse tasks is crucial in order to publicise and create awareness of *ESD* and its practices. The same undoubtedly applies to the development of new concepts and visions of *ESD* from the perspectives of content and methodology. Standard-setting is one of the most prominent UNESCO spheres of activity.[429] It is surely desirable to the setting of standards in the field of *ESD*; however, due to the structural quality of *ESD*, the available means of implementation are rather limited.

1.2 Role

According to the UNESCO constitutional act,[430] the organisation is mandated to adopt means of international law-making intended to produce direct external effects.[431] This relates to the adoption of conventions, first and foremost, but also to the formulation of recommendations or declarations.[432] The provision in

428 UNESCO's functions are equally important in the organisation's general scope, but do apply differently in the specific case of *DESD*.

429 Cf. Yusuf, Abdulqawi A. (ed.) (2007) (cf. *footnote 129* op. cit.).

430 I.e. *Constitution of the United Nations Educational, Scientific and Cultural Organization*.
Cf. UNESCO (ed.) (1945) (cf. *footnote 420* op. cit.); Schrijver, Nico (2007) (cf. *footnote 420* op. cit.), pp. 385–390; Matsuura, Koïchiro (2007) (cf. *footnote 427* op. cit.), pp. 11–14.

431 Cf. Matsuura, Koïchiro (2007) (cf. *footnote 427* op. cit.), p. 12.

432 Cf. UNESCO (ed.) (1945) (cf. *footnote 420* op. cit.), pp. 113, 117.

support of UNESCO *normative action* makes a substantial impact on international law as proved by the divergent natures of conventions, recommendations, and declarations in various spheres of activity.[433] UNESCO's *normative action* ranges in functional and legal scope,[434] carrying:

a) No function: the adoption of recommendations or declarations without specifically binding character;
b) Declarative or declaratory function: announcement of future (customary) law;
c) Interpretative function: enhancing understanding of legally-binding instruments;
d) Catalyst function: presentation of new fields or evolving domainsw of international law; or
e) Programmatic function: setting agendas, defining problems and setting standards referred to as *programmatic law*.

UNESCO applies normative tools in the progressive fulfillment of its global functions.[435] UNESCO's global role is threefold and includes strategic aspects of generating, applying and monitoring international law.[436] This specific role of *normative action* consists of:[437]

- The formulation of global policies and policy advice,
- Standard-setting, and
- Monitoring.

2 Formulation of global policies and policy advice

Building visions of global policies and providing policy advice are two closely interrelated activities with which UNESCO is concerned. Both form part of *policy cycles* which explain the circular process from the emergence of needs to

433 E.g., field of human rights, education, anti-discrimination, cultural rights, property rights, cultural heritage and bio-ethics.
Cf. Schrijver, Nico (2007) (cf. *footnote 420* op. cit.), pp. 394–400; Boyle, Bill; Christie, Tom (1996): Issues in setting standards. Establishing comparabilities. London: Routledge Falmer.

434 I.e. differing in compliance with norms, for instance, according to context of norm-creation, content of the norm, institutional setting or targets of the norm.
Cf. Shelton, Dinah (ed.) (2000) (cf. *footnote 357* op. cit.), pp. 14–17; Schrijver, Nico (2007) (cf. *footnote 420* op. cit.), pp. 403–405.

435 Cf. Matsuura, Koïchiro (2007) (cf. *footnote 427* op. cit.), p. 12.

436 Cf. Schrijver, Nico (2007) (cf. *footnote 420* op. cit.), p. 385.

437 Cf. Foreign Office of the Federal Republic of Germany / German Commission for UNESCO (ed.) (2007) (cf. *footnote 21* op. cit.), pp. 12, 14.

innovative solutions.[438] Thus, policy cycles are future-oriented, but based primarily upon present requirements. The same applies to UNESCO when formulating global policies and offering policy advice: Firstly, it is vitally important to recognise the implications of emerging trends and the need for action. Subsequently, policies must be developed and issued that are forward-thinking and timely.[439] This is extremely pertinent to the discourse on sustainability.

It is very interesting to analyse how UNESCO actually entered into the field of sustainable development which certainly did not previously belong to the organisation's focal issues in the commercial world. Ultimately, it successfully entered the agenda because of an emphasis on the link between education and sustainable development.[440] Today, UNESCO advocates sustainability and sustainable development by turning it, step by step, into an understood global principle of cross-cutting policies.

2.1 Instruments

Two general tools, *strategy* and *framework*, are presented as examples of *policy cycles* in order to illustrate UNESCO's global formulation and presentation of policy.[441]

2.1.1 Strategy

UNESCO policies are developed as part of a clearly defined and coherent strategy that constitutes a plan of action with a particular objective. Each strategy therefore suggests different focal issues, targets and periods of time.[442] Strategic policy planning and advocacy should principally be based on certain steps or

438 Cf. Underdal, Arild (2002a) (cf. *footnote 212* op. cit.), p. 436.

439 Cf. Foreign Office of the Federal Republic of Germany / German Commission for UNESCO (ed.) (2007) (cf. *footnote 21* op. cit.), pp. 12 et seqq; Young, Oran R.; King, Leslie A; Schroeder, Heike (eds.) (2008) (cf. *footnote 320* op. cit.).

440 Cf. UNESCO (1997b): The Declaration of Thessaloniki. International Conference on Environment and Society: Education and Public Awareness for Sustainability. 8–12 December 1997. Published by: UNESCO; UNESCO (ed.) (2002c): Education for Sustainability. From Rio to Johannesburg: Lessons learnt from a decade of commitment. Paris: UNESCO publishing; UNESCO (ed.) (2002d): Enhancing Global Sustainability. Preparatory Committee for the World Summit on Sustainable Development (WSSD) 3rd Session New York, 25 March 2002. Position Paper and Proposals by UNESCO. Paris / New York: UNESCO publishing.

441 See *Figure 16* in chapter V 2.2 *Summary* on page 104.

442 E.g., biennial strategies, mid-term strategies, etc.
Cf. UNESCO (ed.) (2002f) (cf. *footnote 312* op. cit.); UNESCO (ed.) (2008e) (cf. *footnote 312* op. cit.).

phases, commonly referred to as *policy cycles*. Speaking in terms of strategic planning, different arrangements and compilations are possible.[443] Most of them share at least some of the subsequent characteristics proposed for the present case of UNESCO and *DESD*:

a) Identifying focal issue(s);
b) Formulating specific policies;
c) Analising policies;
d) Determining goals and objectives;
e) Developing respective instruments of implementation; and
f) Adopting the strategy and its instruments.

2.1.2 Framework

In the case of practical guidance, policy development must be oriented towards applicability and *manoeuvrability*.[444] Frameworks are institutionalised patterns that support the implementation of strategy. They must be flexible enough to respond to changing conditions.[445] UNESCO supports different frameworks that range from the binding to the declaratory as well as from those that pertain to communication, implementation, and assessment.

2.2 Summary

DESD ideally represents this twofold model of strategic planning and consecutive application: UNESCO serves both elements at once by proposing one consolidated and consistent approach.[446]

443 Cf. Schröder, Peter (2011): Politische Strategien. Potsdam: Friedrich-Naumann-Stiftung für die Freiheit, pp. 51 et seqq.

444 Cf. Chinkin, Christine (2003): Normative Development in the International Legal System. In: Shelton, Dinah (ed.): Commitment and Compliance. The Role of Non-Binding Norms in the International Legal System. Published new in paperback. Oxford / New York: Oxford University Press, pp. 21–42, pp. 37 et seqq.

445 Cf. Burgstaller, Markus (2005): Theories of compliance with international law. Leiden: Martinus Nijhoff Publishers; Brill Academic Publishers (Developments in International Law, 52); Higgitt, David (2009b) (cf. *footnote 56* op. cit.).

446 Cf. UNESCO (ed.) (2005j) (cf. *footnote 44* op. cit.), pp. 6 et seqq, 16 et seqq.

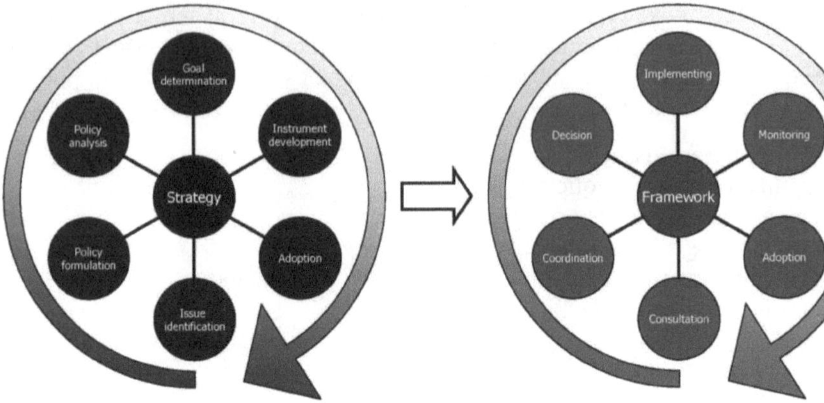

Figure 16: Policy cycles in strategic planning and framework[447]

3 Standard-setting

"Standard-setting represents one of the main constitutional functions of UNESCO and an important tool for realising the goals for which the Organisation was created."[448]

UNESCO embodies an integrative and value-based working style. As *"[...] a standard-setter: UNESCO will serve as a central forum for articulating the ethical, normative and intellectual issues of our time, fostering multidisciplinary exchange and mutual understanding, working – where possible and desirable – towards universal agreements on these issues, benchmarking targets and mobilizing international opinion [...]".*[449] This is achieved primarily through the generation and implementation of appropriate, normative methods of operation.[450]

Classic standard-setting achieved notable prominence shortly after the Industrial Revolution of the 19th century. Economic growth and rising cross-border activities required reliable standards in organisation and course of action in order to reconcile competing interests. To begin with, standards were introduced

447 Both planning strategies and designing frameworks may be regarded as circular processes with embedded feedback mechanisms. As to *DESD*, UNESCO copes with each component of policy cycles simultaneously.
Cf. Schröder, Peter (2011) (cf. *footnote 443* op. cit.), p. 52.

448 See Yusuf, Abdulqawi A. (ed.) (2007) (cf. *footnote 129* op. cit.).

449 See UNESCO (ed.) (2002f) (cf. *footnote 312* op. cit.), p. 13.

450 Remark: The following terms may be used interchangeably unless otherwise noted: *normative actions = standard-setting = normative instruments.*
Cf. Schrijver, Nico (2007) (cf. *footnote 420* op. cit.), p. 405.

with applicability to economic sectors only.[451] In raising efficiency considerably, voluntary and privately-owned co-operation towards standardisation became more and more popular at the beginning of the 20th century across different economic sectors. It was much later that standard-setting came to be organised publicly through state authorities or through treaties at international scale. Nowadays, in times of globalisation, standard-setting procedures qua *international phenomena*[452] are at a turning point, given the diminishing power of effective state regulation systems. *Global governance* structures are faced with a plurality of stakeholders and networks.[453]

Although the implementation of classic standard-setting procedures came into effect more than a century ago, the term nonetheless remains legally ambiguous.[454] Standard-setting is *"the proper following of a prescribed, rational system of rules (norms) or procedures resulting in the assignment of a number to differentiate between two or more states or degrees of performance".*[455] *"Norms includes all rules of conduct, while standards refer to the measures of compliance or technical objectives."*[456] Standards result from *"(...) instrumental alignment confined to a specific purpose and with specific scope (...)"*[457] composed of features such as:[458]

a) Being applicable as an *instrument*[459] of harmonisation for
b) Setting *de-facto* provisions of regulation[460] through

---

451 Standardisation of time zones and weights and measures let to the foundation of different international organisations and agencies, for instance the *International Telecommunication Union* (ITU) in 1865 or the *Universal Postal Union* (UPU) in 1874.

452 See Röhl, Hans Christian (2007): Internationale Standardsetzung. In: Möllers, Christoph; Vosskuhle, Andreas; Walter, Christian (eds.): Internationales Verwaltungsrecht. Tübingen: Mohr Siebeck (Jus internationale et Europaeum, 16), pp. 319–343, p. 319.

453 Cf. Gerner, Martin (2008) (cf. *footnote 259* op. cit.), pp. 7, 23.

454 Cf. Röhl, Hans Christian (2007) (cf. *footnote 452* op. cit.).

455 See Cizek, Gregory J.; Bunch, Michael B. (2006): Standard setting. A guide to establishing and evaluating performance standards on tests. Thousand Oaks, California: SAGE Publications, p. 15.

456 See Shelton, Dinah (ed.) (2000) (cf. *footnote 357* op. cit.), p. 5; Shelton, Dinah (2003c) (cf. *footnote 357* op. cit.), p. 5.

457 Translation from German into English: *„Bei Standards handelt es sich um eine instrumentelle Normierung, die mit einem bestimmten Zweck auf einen Gegenstandsbereich begrenzt wird".*
See Lepsius, Oliver (2007): Standardsetzung und Legitimation. In: Möllers, Christoph; Vosskuhle, Andreas; Walter, Christian (eds.): Internationales Verwaltungsrecht. Tübingen: Mohr Siebeck (Jus internationale et Europaeum, 16), pp. 345–373, p. 347.

458 Cf. Röhl, Hans Christian (2007) (cf. *footnote 452* op. cit.), p. 319; Lepsius, Oliver (2007) (cf. *footnote 457* op. cit.), p. 347.

459 *"Instruments are the variety of texts in which (norms or standards) are contained."*
See Shelton, Dinah (ed.) (2000) (cf. *footnote 357* op. cit.), p. 5; Shelton, Dinah (2003c) (cf. *footnote 357* op. cit.), p. 5.

c) Pursuing determined purposes by
d) Limiting the scope and field of action.

Standard-setting, on the other hand, *„(...) is periodically the result of focused, organised and procedurally structured processes of defining norms"*.[461]

It can often be difficult to determine whether standards belong to public, private, national or international law.[462] Four types of *legal standards* may therefore be distinguished:[463]

1. Rules that are not at all coercive, such as technical standards;
2. Rules that must be complied with, such as technical prescriptions;
3. Rules that are international norms, either *a priori* binding provisions as opposed to *a posteriori* binding dynamic provisions that must be incorporated primarily into domestic jurisdiction; and
4. Rules that result from private-sector commitment in private international law in co-operation with public institutions[464] and which serve as a *template* for prospective public legislation.

In the field of international law in particular the question of the legal status of standards remains controversial: do they constitute rights and obligations or do they constitute social norms based on shared values and moral binding? Largely uncontroversial is the contention that standards do not exist autonomously, constituting neither proper *de-jure* status among multiple stakeholders nor affecting any mechanisms of compliance.[465]

---

460 *Regulatory* power may vary depending on *minimum* versus *enhanced* standards: Declaring minimum or enhanced practice requirements.
Cf. NSW Ageing and Disability Department (ed.) (1998): Standards In Action Manual. Edited by Margarete Verick; Deborah Fullwood. Sydney: Ageing and Disability Department, p. 9.

461 Translation from German into English: *„Standardsetzung ist regelmäßig das Ergebnis eines gezielten, organisierten und verfahrensmäßig strukturierten Normsetzungsprozesses"*.
See Lepsius, Oliver (2007) (cf. *footnote 457* op. cit.), p. 347.

462 In a consolidated way standard-setting is defined as *blended approach* of involving both state authorities and civil society.
Cf. Lepsius, Oliver (2007) (cf. *footnote 457* op. cit.), p. 350.

463 Cf. Röhl, Hans Christian (2007) (cf. *footnote 452* op. cit.), p. 329.

464 I.e. *Public-Private-Partnerships* (PPP).

465 E.g., private-sector agreements (*International Organization for Standardization* (ISO)), recommended rules of conduct (*Codex Alimentarius* of the *World Health Organisation* (WHO) and *Food and Agriculture Organisation* of the United Nations (FAO)), technical annex provisions of international law supplementary to treaties or (*International Civil Aviation Organization* (ICAO) or *International Maritime Organization* (IMO)) and institutional accords of co-operation.

Moreover, standard-setting activities are considered informal, unless they are incorporated into existing legal frameworks. Only in this case do they acquire a legally binding, normative nature consisting of rights and obligations which are subject to legal sanction. Standards cannot thus be regarded *per se* as instruments of autonomous *law-making.*[466] Irrespective of sufficient regulation content standards also require formal legitimisation in accordance with democratic procedures.[467] There are two conceivable scenarios in law:[468]

a) Reference (*legal standards*): the incorporation of standards into the binding secondary or tertiary frameworks of national or international law; and
b) Commitment (*recommended practices*):[469] Generating effective brands of conducive, extra-legal compliance.[470]

"Standards are, therefore, only one of number of normative methods needful of legitimation by the measure of democratic principles when being related as legal references incorporated into legal frameworks which may ultimately be imposed by coercive means. As long the implementation of standards is pursued by means of personal commitment alone, there is no issue of legitimation from the perspective of constitutional law."[471]

To receive recognition and support, standard-setting should adhere to certain procedural stipulations, among them requirements pertaining to constitutional considerations, transparency, context, participation, expertise, technical ration-

---

Cf. Lepsius, Oliver (2007) (cf. *footnote 457* op. cit.), p. 349; Röhl, Hans Christian (2007) (cf. *footnote 452* op. cit.), pp. 321–322; Bernstein, Stephen; Hannah, Erin (2008): Non-state global standard setting and the WTO: Legitimacy and the need for regulatory space. In: Journal of International Economic Law, Volume 11, Issue 3, pp. 575–608.

466 Cf. UNESCO (ed.) (2006b) (cf. *footnote 21* op. cit.), p. 1.

467 Cf. Shelton, Dinah (ed.) (2000) (cf. *footnote 357* op. cit.), pp. 14–17; Lepsius, Oliver (2007) (cf. *footnote 457* op. cit.), pp. 358–360.

468 Cf. Röhl, Hans Christian (2007) (cf. *footnote 452* op. cit.), p. 319; Lepsius, Oliver (2007) (cf. *footnote 457* op. cit.), pp. 363–369.

469 See Röhl, Hans Christian (2007) (cf. *footnote 452* op. cit.), pp. 321–322.

470 E.g., by impeding or anticipating law enforcement through the incorporation of *de-facto* standards, by creating supporting institutional settings (neutrality, plurality of interests, stakeholder participation and representation, etc.), by intensifying economic and social (*peer-group*) pressure.

471 Translation from German into English: *„Standards sind nur dann ein am Maßstab des Demokratieprinzips legitimationsbedürftiger Normtyp, wenn ihnen rechtliche Fremdbindung zukommt, wenn sie also Bestandteil der Rechtsordnung werden und mit Zwang durchgesetzt werden können. Solange Standards mit den Mitteln der Selbstbindung befolgt werden, besteht aus verfassungsrechtlicher Sicht kein Legitimationsproblem".*
See Lepsius, Oliver (2007) (cf. *footnote 457* op. cit.), p. 367.

ale, political legitimacy and implementation.[472] *"Considered as a means of normalisation, standards can only exist in a nebulous form of non-binding legality. Should one wish to elevate standards to the status of law (with the prerequisites of validity and legitimation), there would be no requirement for the regulatory form of a standard. Appeal to national, international or supranational law and to their forms of jurisdiction would remain possible."*[473] International standard-setting is structured in a twofold way according to the:[474]

1. Need for authorisation explicitly given; and
2. Need for democratic legitimisation in organisation and implementation.

Does UNESCO constitute a recognised standard-setting organisation? UNESCO has great expertise in standard-setting[475] and thereby in *"creating new evidence for acceptance of new modes of law-making"*.[476] As already illustrated, UNESCO has a *de-jure* obligation under its own constitutional law to adopt normative procedures.[477] UNESCO offers viable and applicable *de-facto* solutions to a growing number of problems of co-ordination.[478] UNESCO's standard-setting activities are thus evidenced through many cases and focal issues.[479]

---

472 Cf. Lepsius, Oliver (2007) (cf. *footnote 457* op. cit.), pp. 369–374; Röhl, Hans Christian (2007) (cf. *footnote 452* op. cit.), pp. 339 et seqq.
See *Figure 17* in chapter V 3 *Standard-setting* on page 110.

473 Translation from German into English: *„Als Normtyp können Standards nur in einer diffusen Form rechtlicher Unverbindlichkeit existieren. Wer Standards zu Recht erheben wollte (mit seinen entsprechenden Voraussetzungen der Geltung und Legitimation), bräuchte die Regelungsform des Standards nicht. Man könnte auf nationales, internationales oder supranationales Recht und seine jeweilige Geltungsformen zurückgreifen"*.
Cf. Lepsius, Oliver (2007) (cf. *footnote 457* op. cit.), p. 371.

474 Cf. Röhl, Hans Christian (2007) (cf. *footnote 452* op. cit.), pp. 339–342; UNESCO (2007): General introduction to the standard-setting instruments of UNESCO. Published by: UNESCO, p. 1.

475 UNESCO's international standard-setting and legislation is well documented by 28 adopted conventions and a total number of 44 recommendations and declarations respectively.
Cf. Hüfner, Klaus; Reuther, Wolfgang (eds.) (2005) (cf. *footnote 412* op. cit.), p. 29; Yusuf, Abdulqawi A. (ed.) (2007) (cf. *footnote 129* op. cit.).

476 See Shelton, Dinah (ed.) (2000) (cf. *footnote 357* op. cit.), p. 5.

477 Cf. UNESCO (ed.) (1945) (cf. *footnote 420* op. cit.); UNESCO (2007) (cf. *footnote 474* op. cit.), p. 1.

478 Cf. Eisemann, Pierre Michel (2007): Elaborating and Implementing UNESCO's Standard-setting Instruments. Introduction. In: Yusuf, Abdulqawi A. (ed.): Normative action in education, science and culture. Essays in commemoration of the sixtieth anniversary of UNESCO. French edition. Paris / Leiden / Boston: UNESCO publishing; Martinus Nijhoff Publishers (UNESCO reference works series, 1), pp. 25–30, pp. 27–28.

479 Cf. Yusuf, Abdulqawi A. (ed.) (2007) (cf. *footnote 129* op. cit.).

The most prominent and typical example of standard-setting is the domain of education as one of UNESCO's comparative and relative advantage.[480]

480 Cf. United Nations (ed.) (2002b): Resolution adopted by the General Assembly [on the report of the Third Committee (A/56/572)]. United Nations Literacy Decade: Education for All. A/RES/56/116. New York: United Nations; UNESCO (ed.) (2003b) (cf. *footnote 109* op. cit.); Hüfner, Klaus; Reuther, Wolfgang (eds.) (2005) (cf. *footnote 412* op. cit.), pp. 44 et seqq; UNESCO (ed.) (2005g) (cf. *footnote 16* op. cit.); UNESCO Education Sector (ed.) (2005) (cf. *footnote 21* op. cit.); Foreign Office of the Federal Republic of Germany / German Commission for UNESCO (ed.) (2007) (cf. *footnote 21* op. cit.), pp. 16 et seqq; Benedek, Wolfgang (2007) (cf. *footnote 22* op. cit.); Benedek, Wolfgang (2007) (cf. *footnote 22* op. cit.); UNESCO; Oficina Regional de Educación de la UNESCO para América Latina y el Caribe (OREALC) (eds.) (2007b): Quality Education for All: A Human Rights Issue. Educational policies within the framework of the II Intergovernmental Meeting of the Regional Project in Education for Latin America and the Caribbean (EFA/PRELAC). Background document. March 29–30, 2007; Buenos Aires, Argentina. Santiago de Chile: UNESCO Santiago; Fernandez, Alfred (2007) (cf. *footnote 21* op. cit.); Wade, Ros; Parker, Jenneth (eds.) (2008): EFA-ESD Dialogue: Educating for a sustainable world. ED.2008/WS/49. Paris: UNESCO publishing (Education for sustainable development policy dialogue, 1); UNESCO Education Sector (ed.) (2008) (cf. *footnote 27* op. cit.); UNESCO; UNESCO Associated Schools (eds.) (2008b): First Collection of Good Practices for Quality Education. ED-2008/WS/41. Edited by Amina Hamshari. Paris: UNESCO Press; Lind, Agneta (2009): Literacy for all. Making a difference. Paris: UNESCO publishing (Fundamentals of Educational Planning, 89); Oficina Regional de Educación de la UNESCO para América Latina y el Caribe (OREALC) (ed.) (2010): Activity Review 2009. OREALC/2010/PI/H/1. Santiago de Chile: UNESCO Santiago.

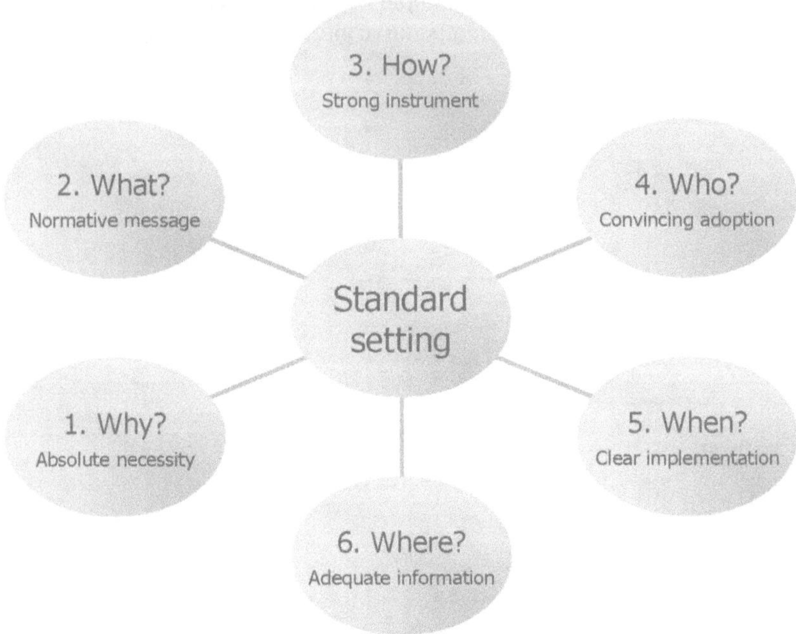

Figure 17: Creating normative instruments – standard-setting[481]

3.1 Instruments

Paragraph 4 of Article IV of the *UNESCO constitution*[482] emphasises different normative instruments, not neglecting the fact that one must *"draw(...) also (...) attention to the difference in the legal nature (...)".*[483] The distinction between *soft-law* versus *hard-law* instruments as an expression of the varying extents of legal binding is one commonly established in theoretical discourse.[484] In order to overcome fruitless discussions on terminological dichotomy and to meet the real

481 Means of standard-setting should be indicated and necessary, consist of normative content, relate to powerful instruments, encourage stakeholder adoption, express realistic indications of time, and provide respective information.
Cf. Eisemann, Pierre Michel (2007) (cf. *footnote 478* op. cit.), pp. 26–30.

482 Cf. UNESCO (ed.) (1945) (cf. *footnote 420* op. cit.), pp. 11, 117.

483 See UNESCO (ed.) (1945) (cf. *footnote 420* op. cit.), p. 117.

484 Cf. Matsuura, Koïchiro (2007) (cf. *footnote 427* op. cit.), pp. 11 et seqq; Yusuf, Abdulqawi A. (2007b) (cf. *footnote 129* op. cit.), p. 36.

concerns of complexity,[485] UNESCO's range of normative instruments best fits into the framework of *gradual normativity.*[486]

The driving factor of evidence-based *opinio iuris*[487] is a positive obligation and a voluntary commitment to act, a re-orientation of the international law of co-existence towards an international law of co-operation.[488] Due to available and applied instruments of normative action, UNESCO demonstrates remarkable expertise in standard-setting. This in turn leads to the organisation's representation as internationally renowned skills factory and competence centre.[489]

The most common normative instruments applied by UNESCO are explained in more detail below:[490]

- Convention;
- Recommendation, charters and frameworks or plans of actions;
- Declaration; and
- Other.

3.1.1 Convention

"A convention is a binding formal agreement drafted and adopted by international bodies such as UNESCO or the United Nations."[491] Conventions must be ratified[492] by state or other stakeholder parties in order to take effect and to then

485 E.g., diversity of instruments, dynamic of international norms on the international law system, appropriate modeling of civil-society interaction, difficulties in analyzing phases and processes international customary law.
Cf. Dupuy, Pierre-Marie (2007): Beyond Treaty Law: The Influence of the Legal Instruments Adopted by UNESCO on General International Law. The Impact of Legal Instruments Adopted by UNESCO on General International Law. In: Yusuf, Abdulqawi A. (ed.): Normative action in education, science and culture. Essays in commemoration of the sixtieth anniversary of UNESCO. French edition. Paris / Leiden / Boston: UNESCO publishing; Martinus Nijhoff Publishers (UNESCO reference works series, 1), pp. 371–384, p. 371.

486 See Yusuf, Abdulqawi A. (2007a) (cf. *footnote 129* op. cit.), p. 369.

487 See Chinkin, Christine (2003) (cf. *footnote 444* op. cit.), p. 30; Dupuy, Pierre-Marie (2007) (cf. *footnote 485* op. cit.), p. 383.

488 Cf. Abi-Saab, Georges (2007): Conclusions. General Conclusions. In: Yusuf, Abdulqawi A. (ed.): Normative action in education, science and culture. Essays in commemoration of the sixtieth anniversary of UNESCO. French edition. Paris / Leiden / Boston: UNESCO publishing; Martinus Nijhoff Publishers (UNESCO reference works series, 1), pp. 417–423, pp. 418–421.

489 Cf. Yusuf, Abdulqawi A. (ed.) (2007) (cf. *footnote 129* op. cit.); UNESCO (2007n) (cf. *footnote 79* op. cit.).

490 Cf. UNESCO (ed.) (2006b) (cf. *footnote 21* op. cit.), p. 1.

491 See UNESCO (ed.) (2006b) (cf. *footnote 21* op. cit.), pp. 1–2.

492 I.e. process of ratification: signature, compliance with domestic legislative requirements (hearing or vote), depositary notification.

become functioning and directly applicable law.[493] Once signed, only those parties adopting and ratifying the convention are legally bound by the text.[494] Reservations about certain articles in a convention are accepted, unless such reservations contradict the main objective and purpose of the convention.

Since conventions are legally binding among their signatory (member state) stakeholders, they become justiciable. This means they produce force and effect between the beneficiaries or *rights-holder* and state or *primary duty-bearer* using any available legal means to secure compliance.[495] For this very reason most conventions consist of mutually agreed mechanisms of monitoring on a regular basis that involve reporting structures and evaluation panels.[496] These are frequently formed by independent international committees of experts tasked to issue confidential or publicly accessible proceedings and reports containing non-legally binding conclusions and recommendations.[497]

3.1.2 Recommendation

Recommendations, charters, frameworks or plans of actions[498] are unlike conventions in that they are not legally-binding by nature but rather their character is declamatory by nature.[499] No instrument mentioned is subject to ratification or to legally-enforced compliance.[500] However, in most cases, well-intentioned commitments are made in signing the document, or through other expressions of intent. The comparative advantage of recommendations, charters, frameworks or plans of action lies in the flexible mechanisms of their implementation, in particular accordance with domestic needs, general agreements and codes of conduct.[501]

---

493 E.g., UNESCO (ed.) (2005a) (cf. *footnote 42* op. cit.).

494 Cf. Matsuura, Koïchiro (2007) (cf. *footnote 427* op. cit.), p. 12.

495 E.g., up to the binding force of dispute settlement bodies or courts' decisions. Cf. UNESCO (ed.) (2006b) (cf. *footnote 21* op. cit.), p. 1.

496 Cf. Boisson de Chazournes, Laurence (2007): Elaborating and Implementing UNESCO's Standard-setting Instruments. Monitoring, Supervision and Coordination of the Standard-setting Instruments of UNESCO. In: Yusuf, Abdulqawi A. (ed.): Normative action in education, science and culture. Essays in commemoration of the sixtieth anniversary of UNESCO. French edition. Paris / Leiden / Boston: UNESCO publishing; Martinus Nijhoff Publishers (UNESCO reference works series, 1), pp. 51–73, p. 53.

497 Cf. UNESCO (ed.) (2006b) (cf. *footnote 21* op. cit.), p. 2; UNESCO (2007n) (cf. *footnote 79* op. cit.); Schrijver, Nico (2007) (cf. *footnote 420* op. cit.), pp. 394 et seqq.

498 Cf. Chinkin, Christine (2003) (cf. *footnote 444* op. cit.).

499 Cf. UNESCO (ed.) (2006b) (cf. *footnote 21* op. cit.), p. 2; Schrijver, Nico (2007) (cf. *footnote 420* op. cit.), p. 403.

500 Cf. Yusuf, Abdulqawi A. (2007b) (cf. *footnote 129* op. cit.), p. 36.

501 Cf. Matsuura, Koïchiro (2007) (cf. *footnote 427* op. cit.), p. 12; UNESCO (2007n) (cf. *footnote 79* op. cit.).

Particular importance can be attributed to recommendations in terms of:

- Monitoring and guidance: *Internally* contributing to report system and individual communication, and *externally* integrating multiple international stakeholders to ensure compliance;[502] and
- Co-ordination: *Ex ante* furthering of normative instruments for standard-setting (*lex feranda*); and *ex post* strengthening of institutional co-operation through normalisation and standardisation, and creation of coherence by normative instruments within the current system of international (*lex lata*).[503]

3.1.3 Declaration

"In addition to conventions and recommendations, the declarations adopted by the General Conference promulgate principles and norms intended to inspire the action of Member States in specific fields of activity."[504]

Although declarations are not an explicitly mentioned instrument of normative action in the UNESCO constitution, this particular method is becoming increasingly important.[505] The reason for this is that stakeholders *"(...) adhering to these declarations and recommendations thereby subscribe to moral commitments and strive towards international consensus"*.[506] Due to the very fact of *intentional power*[507] stakeholders may abide by declarations *"even though there are no legal penalties for non-compliance"*.[508] In addition, declarations may also lead to legally-binding accords upon their passage into recognised international customary law.[509]

Any resolution adopted either by the United Nations General Assembly or by the UNESCO General Conference[510] may be considered an example of *declaratory effect*.[511]

---

502 E.g., by *ad-hoc* joint experts commissions or supervision by other institutions. Cf. Boisson de Chazournes, Laurence (2007) (cf. *footnote 496* op. cit.), pp. 59–68.

503 Cf. Boisson de Chazournes, Laurence (2007) (cf. *footnote 496* op. cit.), pp. 68–71.

504 See Yusuf, Abdulqawi A. (ed.) (2007) (cf. *footnote 129* op. cit.).

505 Cf. Matsuura, Koïchiro (2007) (cf. *footnote 427* op. cit.), p. 12; UNESCO (2007n) (cf. *footnote 79* op. cit.); Schrijver, Nico (2007) (cf. *footnote 420* op. cit.), pp. 394 et seqq; Vitzthum, Wolfgang Graf; Bothe, Michael (eds.) (2007): Völkerrecht. Volume 4. neu bearbeitete Auflage. Supported by: Dolzer, Rudolf; Hailbronner, Kay and Klein, Eckard et al. Berlin: de Gruyter (Recht), p. 12.

506 See UNESCO (ed.) (2006b) (cf. *footnote 21* op. cit.), p. 2.

507 See Chinkin, Christine (2003) (cf. *footnote 444* op. cit.), pp. 37 et seqq.

508 See UNESCO (ed.) (2006b) (cf. *footnote 21* op. cit.), p. 2. Cf. Boisson de Chazournes, Laurence (2007) (cf. *footnote 496* op. cit.), pp. 52, 56–59.

509 E.g., *Universal Declaration of Human Rights* (UDHR) (1948). Cf. UNESCO (ed.) (2006b) (cf. *footnote 21* op. cit.), p. 2.

510 Cf. Bothe, Michael (1980): Legal and Non-Legal Norms – a meaningful distinction in international relations? In: Netherlands Yearbook of International Law Review, Vol-

3.1.4 Other

Further normative, albeit legally non-binding instruments are guidelines, commentaries, studies or other documents of reference.[512] Such documents are intended to contribute to a better understanding of the significance and application of standard-setting instruments.[513] They may be explanatory, interpretative, trend-setting or offer guidance.[514]

3.2 Illustration

Due to changing patterns of manifesting commitment there is an ongoing debate about prioritising the crafting of new normative instruments of action, including their adoption, implementation and monitoring.[515] This particularly refers to such instruments as legally non-binding or *soft law*. It appears that UNESCO's standard-setting activities correspond to this tendency.[516]

---

ume 11 / XI, pp. 65–95, p. 75; Skubiszewski, Krzysztof; Bernhardt, Rudolf (eds.) (1981): Die Bedeutung der Resolutionen der Generalversammlung der Vereinten Nationen. Volume 1. Auflage. Baden-Baden: Nomos Verlagsgesellschaft (Fünftes Deutsch-Polnisches Juristen-Kolloquium); Conforti, Benedetto (1995): Diritto internazionale. Volume 4. edizione, ristampa (con aggiornamenti). Napoli / Padova: Edizione Scientifica (Diritto internazionale, 16); Brownlie, Ian (2002): Principles of public international law. Volume 5. edition, reprinted. Oxford: Clarendon Press; Kälin, Walter; Baldegger, Mirjam (eds.) (2006): Völkerrecht. Eine Einführung. Volume 2. Auflage. Bern: Stämpfli, p. 218; Krajewski, Markus (2006): Wirtschaftsvölkerrecht. Heidelberg: C. F. Müller Verlag, pp. 25–26; Hörtreiter, Isabel (2007): Die Vereinten Nationen und Wirtschaftsunternehmen – zwischen Kooperation und Kontrolle. Steuerungsformen zur Stärkung menschenrechtlicher Unternehmensverantwortung unter dem Dach der Vereinten Nationen. Frankfurt am Main: Peter Lang GmbH, p. 278.

511 See Hobe, Stephan; Kimminich, Otto (2004): Einführung in das Völkerrecht. Volume 8. vollständig neu bearbeitete und erweiterte Auflage. Tübingen / Basel: A. Francke Verlag, p. 196.

512 I.e. concepts, prerequisites, guidance, implementing schemes, means of monitoring and coaching, regional and national agenda setting, or progress reports.

513 Cf. UNESCO (ed.) (2006b) (cf. *footnote 21* op. cit.), p. 2.

514 E.g., provisions within legal instruments, methodological tools, guidelines of interpretation and implementation or comprehensive frameworks for enhanced understanding. Cf. UNESCO (ed.) (2006b) (cf. *footnote 21* op. cit.), p. 2.

515 Cf. Matsuura, Koïchiro (2007) (cf. *footnote 427* op. cit.), pp. 13–14; Vitzthum, Wolfgang Graf; Bothe, Michael (eds.) (2007) (cf. *footnote 505* op. cit.), p. 12.

516 Particularly the cultural sector of UNESCO, considering cultural property and heritage, cultural expression, diversity and life, cultural co-operation, or cultural diffusion, appropriately reveals far more non-binding instruments than binding ones. Cf. UNESCO (2007n) (cf. *footnote 79* op. cit.); UNESCO (ed.) (2005a) (cf. *footnote 42* op. cit.).

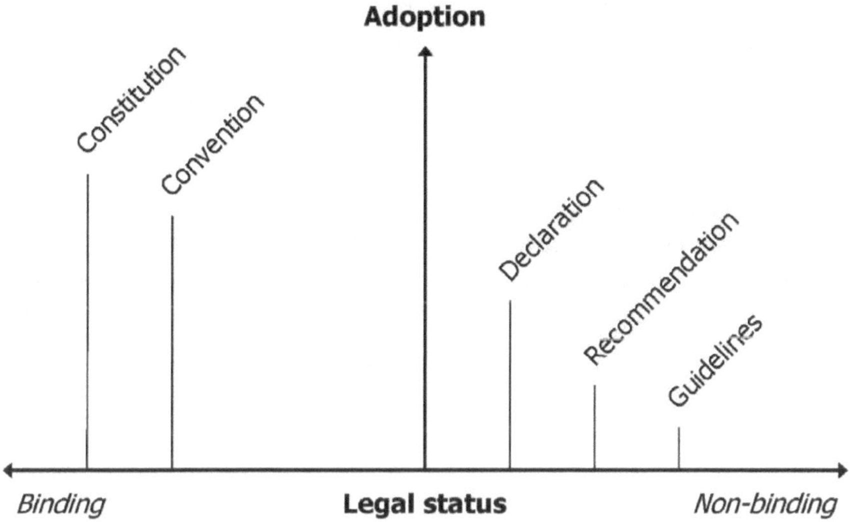

Figure 18: Gradual normativity in UNESCO standard-setting[517]

Standard-setting in *ESD* is, in general, worthwhile, but, legally speaking, realised only with difficulty. As will be explained later, the provision of *de-jure* standards on *ESD* is nigh on impossible. This is subject to the basic strategic and programmatic structure of *DESD* which is intended to be primarily declarative and non-binding. Thus, no UNESCO binding instruments discussed above, and namely the constitution and convention, apply to *ESD*. However, even declarations can be instrumental in creating *de-facto* standards through forms of momentum-building and self-commitment. In this respect, UNESCO offers respective options of extra-legal co-ordination through recommended practices, for instance.

4 Monitoring

In discussing normative instruments no means of monitoring may be omitted, for the simple reason that they constitute an essential part of the whole operational UNESCO framework mandates to assess the effectiveness of applied

See *Figure 18* in chapter V 3.2 *Illustration* on page 115.

517 Strictly speaking and given the quality of adoption, *DESD* corresponds to UNESCO's standard-setting instruments that are non-binding according to their legal status.

means of normative action.[518] This is realised through specifically-designed *steering systems*[519] used to evaluate and ensure compliance.[520] Given the variety of UNESCO's normative means and bodies, monitoring must meet these *polycentric*[521] requirements.[522] UNESCO distinguishes three types of monitoring functions:[523]

1. Initiative function towards norm respect;
2. Control function for effective implementation; and
3. Informative function directed to norm-compliant communication.

UNESCO's monitoring expertise is particularly relevant in development-related issues.[524] Monitoring progress in development ultimately depends upon effective reporting using sound indicators.

---

518 Cf. Foreign Office of the Federal Republic of Germany / German Commission for UNESCO (ed.) (2007) (cf. *footnote 21* op. cit.), p. 14.

519 See Young, Oran R. (2002) (cf. *footnote 294* op. cit.), p. 76.

520 Cf. Shelton, Dinah (ed.) (2000) (cf. *footnote 357* op. cit.), p. 5; Shelton, Dinah (2003c) (cf. *footnote 357* op. cit.), pp. 3–5; Weiss, Edith Brown (2003): Conclusions: Understanding Compliance with Soft Law. In: Shelton, Dinah (ed.): Commitment and Compliance. The Role of Non-Binding Norms in the International Legal System. Published new in paperback. Oxford / New York: Oxford University Press, pp. 535–553, p. 538; Abi-Saab, Georges (2007) (cf. *footnote 488* op. cit.), p. 420.

521 See Boisson de Chazournes, Laurence (2007) (cf. *footnote 496* op. cit.), p. 52.

522 Cf. Eisemann, Pierre Michel (2007) (cf. *footnote 478* op. cit.), pp. 26–28.

523 Cf. Boisson de Chazournes, Laurence (2007) (cf. *footnote 496* op. cit.), pp. 72–73.

524 Cf. UNESCO (ed.) (1987b): World Decade for Cultural Development Report by the Director-General. General Conference Twenty-fourth Session, Paris 1987. 24 C/23. Paris: UNESCO publishing; Pérez Cuéllar, Javier de (ed.) (1995 / 1996) (cf. *footnote 74* op. cit.); United Nations Conference on Trade and Development (UNCTAD); UNESCO; United Nations Children's Fund (UNICEF) (eds.) (2001): Education for All and Sustainable Development in LDCs. Issue Paper. Third United Nations Conference on the Least Developed Countries (LDC III) Brussels, 14–20 May 2001. Interactive Thematic Session on Education for All 16 May 2001. Brussels: UNESCO publishing; UNESCO (ed.) (2002c) (cf. *footnote 440* op. cit.); UNESCO (ed.) (2001) (cf. *footnote 77* op. cit.); UNESCO (ed.) (2002b) (cf. *footnote 80* op. cit.); World Bank (ed.) (2003) (cf. *footnote 95* op. cit.); Blaze Corcoran, Peter; Maathai, Wangari (2005): The Earth Charter in action. Amsterdam: KIT Publishers BV; UNESCO (ed.) (2005a) (cf. *footnote 42* op. cit.); Foreign Office of the Federal Republic of Germany / German Commission for UNESCO (ed.) (2007) (cf. *footnote 21* op. cit.); Foreign Office of the Federal Republic of Germany / German Commission for UNESCO (ed.) (2007) (cf. *footnote 21* op. cit.), pp. 16 et seqq; Gambini, Barbara (2009) (cf. *footnote 83* op. cit.).

4.1 Instruments

When monitoring documents' development, instruments of monitoring must consist of at least two elements in sequence: *reporting* and *evaluation*. There is no feasible evaluation without meaningful reporting.

4.1.1 Reporting

Reporting is institutionalised *follow-up*[525] to the implementation and application of normative instruments.[526] It constitutes the necessary, facilitating precondition for effective evaluation to take place. At the same time, reporting may serve as the first indication of stakeholder compliance. Classic reporting mechanisms might be, for instance, bulletins, résumés, questionnaires, statements, policy and working papers, panel and board results, but also includes (expert) interviews and (informal) briefings.

4.1.2 Evaluation

Evaluation or assessment[527] is based upon reporting mechanisms[528] and refers to a systematic and specialised approach of opinion-making using *sound* criteria.[529] These consist both of technical indicators, but also those of good and best practices of action.

---

525 See Jabloner, Clemens; Okresek, Wolf (1983): Theoretische und praktische Anmerkungen zu Phänomenen des "soft law". In: Österreichische Zeitschrift für öffentliches Recht und Völkerrecht, Volume 34, Issue 2, pp. 217–241, p. 222.

526 Cf. Kälin, Walter; Baldegger, Mirjam (eds.) (2006) (cf. *footnote 510* op. cit.), pp. 223–225.

527 I.e. evaluation encompasses assessment; assessment for its part encompasses testing:
Evaluation is usually conceptualised as broader in scope and concerned with the overall programme, the wider process of interpreting data (feedback, interview, discussion, etc.) in order to make profound judgments about a particular programme or a range of programmes.
Assessment is more related to performance analysis in a *given* circumstance or set of processes through which judgments are created about the level of skills and knowledge, attitude, effort and personal progress involving stakeholders and their specific criteria.
Testing again is considered an instrument or systematic procedure for measuring just one sample of behaviour.
Cf. Boyle, Bill; Christie, Tom (1996) (cf. *footnote 433* op. cit.), p. 33.

528 Cf. Jabloner, Clemens; Okresek, Wolf (1983) (cf. *footnote 525* op. cit.), p. 222.

529 Cf. Boisson de Chazournes, Laurence (2007) (cf. *footnote 496* op. cit.), p. 53.
See *Table 16* in chapter V 4.1.2 *Evaluation* on page 118.

Table 16: Examples of evaluation guidelines[530]

Dimension of evaluation	Criteria of evaluation
Procedural	Explicitness
	Practicability
	Implementation
	Feedback
	Documentation
Internal	Methodological consistency
	Intra-participant consistency
	Inter-participant consistency
	Decision-making consistency
External	Comparison to other standard-setting methods
	Comparison to other sources of information

UNESCO's practice of monitoring proves two combined categories of evaluation:[531]

a) *Summative evaluation* refers to information gathered right at the end of the process to be scrutinised in order to prove and to make decisions; and
b) *Formative evaluation* is carried out during the process mainly in order to improve and to serve as guidance, so that corrections can be made flexibly.

If applicable, results of evaluation find their way directly into the formulation of global policies or policy advice.

4.2 Summary

DESD and UNESCO monitoring go together by virtue of their similar methods of initiating, controlling and informing.[532] In line with instruments of strategy and framework, mechanisms of reporting and assessment – both *summative* and *formative* – complement *ESD* implementation.[533]

530 Cf. Cizek, Gregory J.; Bunch, Michael B. (2006) (cf. *footnote 455* op. cit.), p. 60.
531 Cf. Boyle, Bill; Christie, Tom (1996) (cf. *footnote 433* op. cit.), pp. 33–34.
532 Cf. UNESCO (ed.) (2008h) (cf. *footnote 219* op. cit.).
533 Cf. Wals, Arjen E. J. (July 2009): A Mid-DESD Review. Key Findings and Ways Forward. In: Journal of Education for Sustainable Development, Volume 3, Issue 2, pp. 195–204, pp. 3, 13, 27–30.

5 Conclusion

To conclude, UNESCO represents a high-level institutional framework conditioned by well-defined and sufficiently tested means of normative action. The organisation is permanently confronted with the challenge of building momentum and commitment among its stakeholders within specific fields of action. Particular emphasis must be placed on three interdependent pillars of global function. They are all of the same value or status, though slightly differing in interaction: standard-setting requires effective monitoring in order to facilitate policy advice. At the same time, monitoring does have immediate impact on standard-setting procedures and vice versa.[534]

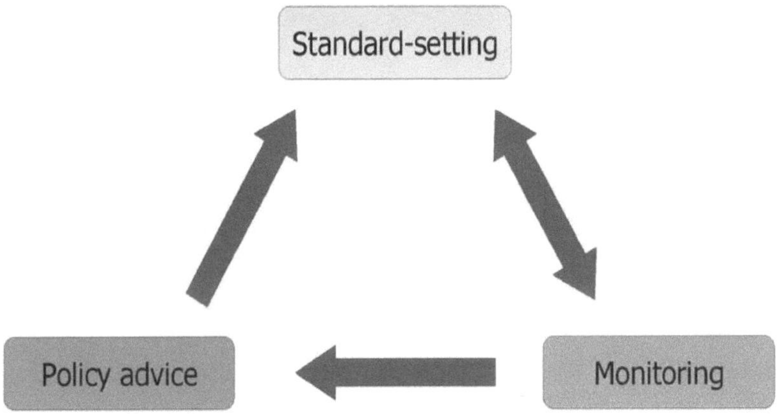

Figure 19: Correlation between UNESCO's global functions[535]

For important reasons, UNESCO provides framework conditions that facilitate *DESD*:

1. The organisation's global assignment can be considered to be in full alignment with the vision and mission ascribed to *ESD*;
2. The organisation's operational profile coincides with the actual needs of *ESD*-related processes and leadership, requiring particular expertise in capacity-building and catalyst aspects; and
3. The organisation's normative role is well reflected and represented regarding *ESD* both as:

534 See *Figure 19* in chapter V 5 *Conclusion* on page 119.

535 All three global functions of UNESCO are closely interrelated. However, standard-setting particularly relies upon policy advice and sound means of monitoring.

- *Integrated mandate* characterised by the holistic approach of programmatic planning (*ESD*); and
- *Composite mandate* consisting of single-issue aspects of educational standard-setting (*E*), policy advice in sustainability issues (*S*), and reporting in the range of development (*D*).

VI Mandate for leadership

Which features and competences constitute and define the UNESCO mandate for DESD leadership? This chapter will present essential information that relates to the DESD mandate. However, the primary focus is on structure and organisation, and focuses to a lesser extent on practical implementation of this mandate.

1 Competences

The notion of a *mandate* consists of three critical elements:

- *Authority* given to do something;
- *Power* assigned for a specific period of time; and
- *Order* given to perform a particular task in an official capacity.

There are a number of other United Nations agencies, multilateral bodies and independent institutions entitled to deal with different issues of sustainability.[536] Most of them share certain characteristics, such as *co-ordination functions*,[537] but are not necessarily assigned to, or legitimised by, a particular mandate of implementation.

Given that there are multiple potentially relevant institutions, UNESCO must prove its *unique* aptitude to fulfil the *DESD* mandate better than these other institutions. In this respect, one crucial United Nations principle is the di-

536 E.g., *Committee on Sustainable Development* (CSD), *United Nations Development Programme* (UNDP), *United Nations Environment Programme* (UNEP), *United Nations Conference on Trade and Development* (UNCTAD), etc.
Cf. King, Kenneth (2007): Multilateral agencies in the construction of the global agenda on education. In: Comparative Education, Volume 43, Issue 3, pp. 377–391.

537 See Andresen, Steinar (2007) (cf. *footnote 320* op. cit.), p. 2.

vision of tasks according to manifest core competences.[538] Another is the creation of *comparative advantage*[539] through the use of synergies within given fields of competence. One must thus ask which particular competences specifically qualify UNESCO to lead *DESD*.

UNESCO is firstly considered *the* driving agency with the acknowledged normative competence and commitment in the field of worldwide education.[540] In expanding the acronyms *UNESCO* and *DESD* it becomes obvious that *education* is one of UNESCO's principal fields of activity, stated as the *key* to any form of social, economic and sustainable development.[541]

Secondly, according to the global mission statement, UNESCO's mandate as *lead agency* for *DESD* can be considered to be in full accordance with the organisation's functional orientation involving all its competences.[542] This means that effective leadership of *DESD* relates to all three UNESCO functions, such as monitoring, policy advice and standard-setting.[543] Aside from the topical relevance and renowned expertise in education, science and culture,[544] the aspect of functional impact must be raised. The designation of United Nations *lead agency* by mandate must, of course, create a meaningful difference with respect to conduct and outcomes in international law. In terms of rights and obligations,

538 Cf. Foreign Office of the Federal Republic of Germany / German Commission for UNESCO (ed.) (2007) (cf. *footnote 21* op. cit.), pp. 16 et seqq.

539 See UNESCO (ed.) (2005h): UNESCO and Sustainable Development. Edited by Monique Perrot-Lanaud; Sabrina Sidhu; Stéphanie Tang; Marine Samson. Paris: UNESCO publishing, p. 6.

540 Cf. UNESCO (ed.) (1990 / 2000): World Declaration on Education for All. Adopted by the World Conference on Education for All. Meeting Basic Learning Needs, Jomtien, Thailand, 5–9 March 1990. ED-2000/WS/27. Edited by Ulrika Peppler Barry. Paris: UNESCO publishing, pp. 75 et seqq; Benedek, Wolfgang (2007) (cf. *footnote 22* op. cit.); Fernandez, Alfred (2007) (cf. *footnote 21* op. cit.), p. 334; Foreign Office of the Federal Republic of Germany / German Commission for UNESCO (ed.) (2007) (cf. *footnote 21* op. cit.), p. 4.
Cf. chapter V 1 *Global assignment* on pages 97 et seqq.

541 Cf. Mayor, Federico (17/10/1992) (cf. *footnote 41* op. cit.), p. 2; UNESCO (ed.) (2000): The Dakar Framework for Action: Education for All: Meeting our Collective Commitments. Adopted by the World Education Forum Dakar, Senegal, 26–28 April 2000. ED-2000/WS/27. Edited by Ulrika Peppler Barry. Paris: UNESCO publishing, p. 8; UNESCO (2007) (cf. *footnote 52* op. cit.).
Cf. chapter II 1 *Education* on pages 11 et seqq, and chapter II 4 *Education for Sustainable Development* on pages 30 et seqq.

542 Cf. Matsuura, Koïchiro (01/03/2005) (cf. *footnote 28* op. cit.), p. 3; UNESCO (ed.) (2007f) (cf. *footnote 427* op. cit.), p. 2; Foreign Office of the Federal Republic of Germany / German Commission for UNESCO (ed.) (2007) (cf. *footnote 21* op. cit.), pp. 12 et seqq; Gerner, Martin (10/08/2009) (cf. *footnote 407* op. cit.).

543 Cf. Foreign Office of the Federal Republic of Germany / German Commission for UNESCO (ed.) (2007) (cf. *footnote 21* op. cit.), pp. 10, 14.

544 Cf. Faundez, Julio (2007) (cf. *footnote 419* op. cit.), pp. 178–179.

are member states more prepared and willing to comply with *DESD* as a direct result of UNESCO's leadership qualities?

2 Leadership

Leadership is the proactive ability to perceive the need for action and the capacity to influence behaviour through:

a) Convincing others – without imposition or coercion – to share individual visions, aims, values and codes of conduct;
b) Encouraging transparent processes of decision-making; and
c) Serving, by oneself, as an example of best practice.[545]

Two types or styles of *leadership* are often distinguished: *Charismatic leadership* mainly refers to *vision* as the initiator of creativity, directional innovation and change. *Bureaucratic leadership* is more related to the handling of change through systems of management and power-based administration.[546] In reality, both types of leadership are required to effect notable change.[547]

545 Cf. Skodvin, Tora; Andresen, Steinar (2006) (cf. *footnote 294* op. cit.), pp. 14–15.

546 Cf. Cox, Robert W. (2004 / 2006): The Executive Head. An Essay on Leadership in International Organization. In: Sinclair, Timothy J. (ed.): Global Governance: Critical Concepts in Political Science. London / New York / London: Taylor & Francis, Inc.; Routledge (Critical Concepts in Political Science, Volume II), Volume International Organization 23 (2) (1969): 205–230, pp. 199–224, p. 203; Skodvin, Tora; Andresen, Steinar (2006) (cf. *footnote 294* op. cit.), p. 15.

547 Cf. Cox, Robert W. (2004 / 2006) (cf. *footnote 546* op. cit.), p. 207.
See *Figure 20* in chapter VI 2 *Leadership* on page 124.

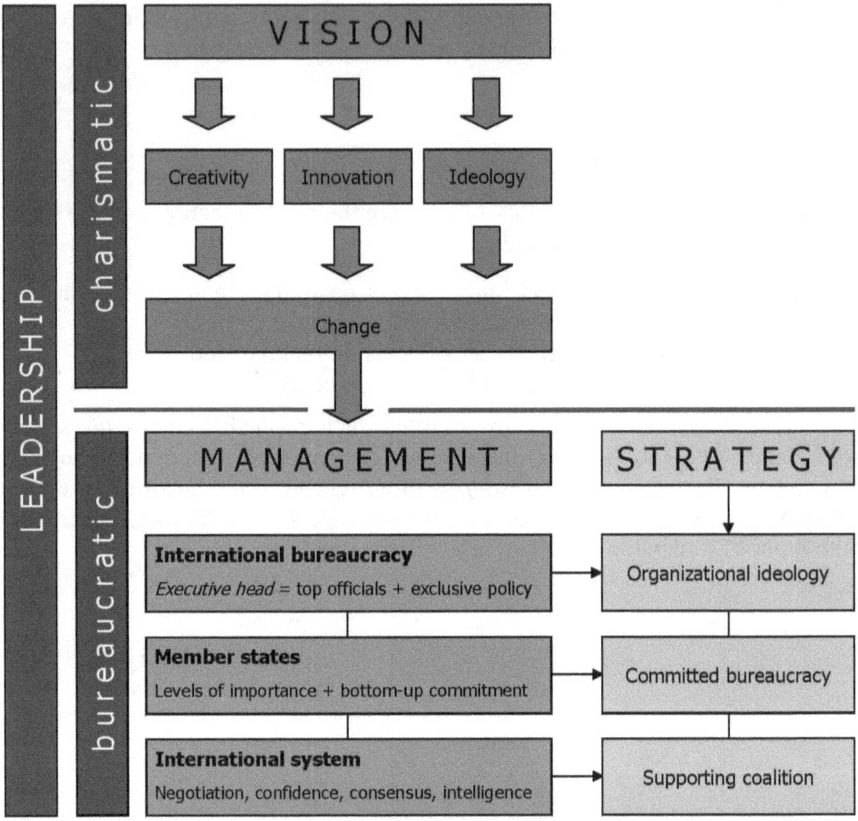

Figure 20: Dual character of leadership[548]

The understanding of *leadership* has changed significantly in recent decades. While *new institutionalism* has gradually taken the place of old institutionalism, the image and role of a leader have been shifting from those of a *broker* to those of a *facilitator*.[549] This coincides with the very need to introduce *entrepreneurial leadership*[550] into organisational theory and practice.[551] In this respect

548 The so called *Haas strategy* offers valid guidelines for executive leadership in organisational management. These are encapsulated formulaically in stating that management success is due to organisational ideology *plus* committed bureaucracy *plus* supporting coalitions.
Cf. Cox, Robert W. (2004 / 2006) (cf. *footnote 546* op. cit.), pp. 207 et seqq, 221, 229.

549 Cf. March, James G.; Olsen, Johan P. (2004) (cf. *footnote 243* op. cit.), p. 276.

550 See Skodvin, Tora; Andresen, Steinar (2006) (cf. *footnote 294* op. cit.), p. 15.

strong leadership[552] requires a broadly negotiated and unanimously approved *leadership agreement.*[553]

2.1 Lead agency

Assigning mandates for leadership applies fully to the United Nations *lead agency* concept. They result from the evolution of specific responsibilities, and this has been the case since the 1960s in particular. *"One common denominator of most efforts to achieve co-ordination among the variety of national and international agencies concerned with global issues is the search for formal mechanisms which introduce an element of hierarchy. The 'lead agency' concept within the (United Nations) family represents a manifestation of this belief in hierarchical solutions."*[554] In subsequent decades the vocabulary of leadership responsibility has been in a state of constant change. New wordings show different conceptions ranging from *under the auspices*[555] and *leader*[556] to *lead agency.* It is only since the end of the 1980s that stakeholder responsibilities have been officially institutionalised by the appointment of specialised agencies for effective and successful leadership.[557]

The term *lead agency* is conspicuously new, and there is still no official or legal definition of *lead agency* in any relevant document or publication.[558] Consequently, an alternative and thoroughly viable way of conceptualising *lead agency* is according to key characteristics. Which characteristics might therefore constitute UNESCO as a *lead agency*? One major benchmark and point of reference from which suitable characteristics may be derived is the *World Decade for Cultural Development.*[559] Between 1988 and 1997 the entire leadership of

551 Cf. Krott, Maximilian (2002) (cf. *footnote 203* op. cit.), p. 966; Fridtjof Nansens Institutt / The Fridtjof Nansens Institute (ed.) (2005) (cf. *footnote 198* op. cit.), pp. 12 et seqq.

552 See UNESCO (ed.) (2007f) (cf. *footnote 427* op. cit.), p. 2.

553 Cf. Foreign Office of the Federal Republic of Germany / German Commission for UNESCO (ed.) (2007) (cf. *footnote 21* op. cit.), p. 16.

554 See Jönsson, Christer (1996) (cf. *footnote 13* op. cit.), p. 70.

555 E.g., dating from 1988 to 1997.
See UNESCO (ed.) (1987b) (cf. *footnote 524* op. cit.), p. 2.

556 See UNESCO (ed.) (1987b) (cf. *footnote 524* op. cit.), p. 3.

557 Cf. UNESCO (ed.) (2002d) (cf. *footnote 440* op. cit.), pp. 15–16; United Nations (2009): International Decades Designated by the General Assembly. Periods, topics and respective resolutions. R02086. Published by: United Nations. United Nations Dag Hammarskjöld Library.

558 Cf. Pugh, Michael; Cunliffe, S. Alex (1997) (cf. *footnote 13* op. cit.), p. 22.

559 Cf. UNESCO (ed.) (1987a): Report by the Director-General on the proposed setting-up of an Intergovernmental Committee to be responsible for following and evaluating the

UNESCO was accounted for, for the very first time.[560] Since there is in all probability no single UNESCO-related documentary basis for establishing *DESD* leadership, the following general mechanisms of *lead agencies* serve as a *blueprint* for UNESCO's leadership role in the course of *DESD*.[561] A *lead agency* is considered:

- To achieve legitimacy by mandatory assignment[562] and relevant technical background;[563]
- To be officially launched and scheduled;[564]
- To attract and encourage multiple stakeholders;[565]
- To address interdisciplinary and meaningful topics;[566]

---

implementation of the World Decade for Cultural Development. Executive Board. 126 EX/24. Paris: UNESCO publishing, p. 2.

560 Cf. UNESCO (ed.) (1987a) (cf. *footnote 559* op. cit.), p. 2; UNESCO (ed.) (1987b) (cf. *footnote 524* op. cit.), pp. 1–2; United Nations; UNESCO (eds.) (1994): Rethinking development. World Decade for Cultural Development 1988–1997. Edited by Birgitta Leander. Paris: UNESCO publishing (Culture Plus), p. 6.

561 Cf. UNESCO (ed.) (2007f) (cf. *footnote 427* op. cit.), p. 2; UNESCO (ed.) (2007k) (cf. *footnote 4* op. cit.).

562 I.e. based upon United Nations resolutions, e.g., A/RES/41/187 (1986), A/RES/44/238 (1989); A/RES/45/189 (1990); A/RES/46/157 (1991).
Cf. UNESCO (ed.) (1997a): Resolutions and Recommendations adopted by various bodies and organizations of the United Nations System concerning the World Decade for Cultural Development. Intergovernmental Committee of the World Decade for Cultural Development; Fifth regular session (Paris, 21–25 April 1997). CLT/DEC/1997/05. Paris: UNESCO publishing, pp. 3–4, 5–6, 7–8, 9–10.

563 Cf. UNESCO (ed.) (1987b) (cf. *footnote 524* op. cit.), p. 2; UNESCO (ed.) (1990b): World Decade for Cultural Development 1988–1997. Plan of Action. CC-89/WS-20. Paris: UNESCO workshops.

564 Cf. Mayor, Federico (21/01/1988): Address by Mr Federico Mayor Director-General of the United Nations Educational, Scientific and Cultural Organization (UNESCO) on the occasion of the launching of the World Decade for Cultural Development. Manuscript. Officially released and issued on 21/01/1988, Paris; UNESCO (ed.) (1990c): World Decade for Cultural Development 1988–1997. Strategy for the Implementation of the Plan of Action. CC-89/WS-19. Paris: UNESCO workshops, p. 32.

565 I.e. integrating and co-ordinating 70 non-governmental organisations, 14 intergovernmental organisations and 166 member states.
Cf. UNESCO Culture Sector (ed.) (1997) (cf. *footnote 88* op. cit.), p. 7; UNESCO (ed.) (1987a) (cf. *footnote 559* op. cit.), p. 3; UNESCO (ed.) (1987b) (cf. *footnote 524* op. cit.), p. 3; United Nations; UNESCO (eds.) (1994) (cf. *footnote 560* op. cit.), p. 6.

566 I.e. addressing cross-cutting topics linking culture and development with issues such as: migration, minorities, poverty, environment, sustainable development, empowerment and participation, etc.
Cf. UNESCO Culture Sector (ed.) (1997) (cf. *footnote 88* op. cit.), p. 8; Goncalves G., María Paola (ed.) (1998): A Cultural Decade. Reflections on the World Decade for Cultural Development 1988–1997. CLT-98AVSI8. Paris: UNESCO publishing (Stud-

- To work on a project basis;[567]
- To provide institutional settings, strategic structures and decision-making bodies;[568]
- To provide appropriate co-ordination, implementation, evaluation and follow-up structures;[569] and
- To make public good and best practices.[570]

Given these elements, one provisional definition for *lead agency* may read as follows: a *lead agency* constitutes any formally appointed, mandated, designated or otherwise legitimated institutional body that is officially launched and scheduled for a particular mission.[571] A *lead agency* provides certain institutional settings in order to inspire and manage simultaneously a range of divergent stakeholders and issues under the auspices of different projects. A *lead agency* develops structural provisions and specific guidelines essential in order to guarantee effective leadership performance in the fields of co-ordination, implementation, communication and assessment.

---

ies and Reports of the Unit of Cultural Research and Management, 5); Pérez Cuéllar, Javier de (ed.) (1995 / 1996) (cf. *footnote 74* op. cit.), pp. 77 et seqq, 129 et seqq, 135–137, 175 et seqq, 205 et seqq, 268–269; UNESCO Culture Sector (ed.) (1997) (cf. *footnote 88* op. cit.), p. 6.

567 I.e. including 1,179 officially recognised decade activities.
Cf. UNESCO Culture Sector (ed.) (1997) (cf. *footnote 88* op. cit.), p. 7.

568 E.g., Intergovernmental Committee, secretariat, statutes, rules of procedure, etc.
Cf. UNESCO (ed.) (1987a) (cf. *footnote 559* op. cit.), pp. 2 et seqq; UNESCO (ed.) (1987b) (cf. *footnote 524* op. cit.), pp. 3 et seqq; UNESCO (ed.) (1990a): World Decade for Cultural Development 1988–1997. Statutes and Rule of Procedures. CC-89/WS-21. Paris: UNESCO workshops; UNESCO (ed.) (1990c) (cf. *footnote 564* op. cit.), pp. 33–41; UNESCO (ed.) (1997a) (cf. *footnote 562* op. cit.).

569 I.e. plan of action, reporting progress mechanisms, etc.
Cf. UNESCO (ed.) (1987a) (cf. *footnote 559* op. cit.), p. 2; UNESCO (ed.) (1987b) (cf. *footnote 524* op. cit.), pp. 3 et seqq; UNESCO (ed.) (1987b) (cf. *footnote 524* op. cit.), pp. 4 et seqq; UNESCO (ed.) (1990c) (cf. *footnote 564* op. cit.); UNESCO (ed.) (1990b) (cf. *footnote 563* op. cit.); UNESCO (ed.) (1991): Report by the Director-General on the Process in the implementation of the aims and programmes of the World Decade for Cultural Development. General Conference Twenty-sixth Session, Paris 1991. 26 C/94. Paris: UNESCO publishing; UNESCO (ed.) (1997a) (cf. *footnote 562* op. cit.), p. 15; Pérez Cuéllar, Javier de (ed.) (1995 / 1996) (cf. *footnote 74* op. cit.); Goncalves G., María Paola (ed.) (1998) (cf. *footnote 566* op. cit.); Pugh, Michael; Cunliffe, S. Alex (1997) (cf. *footnote 13* op. cit.), p. 18.

570 Cf. UNESCO (ed.) (1990c) (cf. *footnote 564* op. cit.), pp. 42–45; United Nations; UNESCO (eds.) (1994) (cf. *footnote 560* op. cit.).

571 See *Figure 21* in chapter VI 2.1 *Lead agency* on page 128.

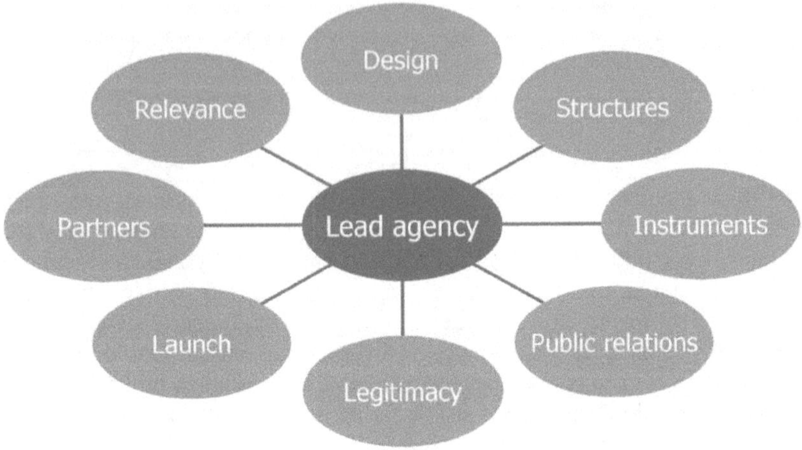

Figure 21: Lead agency[572]

How does the term *lead agency* apply to UNESCO's specific leadership role for *DESD*? In order to support this case-specific interpretation, this catalogue of proposed characteristics is appropriate.[573]

As to *legitimacy*, designated as *lead agency* for *DESD* by resolution *A/RES/57/254*[574] adopted by the United Nations General Assembly in December 2002, UNESCO is officially mandated to carry out an ambitious *dual role* both as:

- *"(I)nternational coordinator and facilitator for the Decade"*; and
- *"(S)ubstantive implementer of Education for Sustainable Development (ESD)".*[575]

UNESCO has consequently achieved *intra-vires* legitimacy to lead *DESD* by the assignation of a mandate and the suitability of its technical background.[576]

As to *launch*, *DESD* came into force as of 1st March 2005 and lasts until 2014.[577] It can therefore be stated that *DESD* has been officially launched and scheduled by UNESCO in accordance with its mandate.

---

572 Being aware of the fact that this list of items cannot be exhaustive, these characteristics are proposed to contain and define what a lead agency may be like.

573 At this point, *scanning* for terminological evidence knowingly omits in-depth discussion of the role proper, for instance in terms of its extent and its responsibilities, obligations and functions.

574 Cf. United Nations (ed.) (2002 / 2003) (cf. *footnote 117* op. cit.).

575 See Matsuura, Koïchiro (01/03/2005) (cf. *footnote 28* op. cit.), p. 2.
Cf. *Figure 63* in chapter IX 2.3 *Summary* on page 289.

576 Cf. Bory-Adams, Aline (2010) (cf. *footnote 37* op. cit.), pp. 175–176.

As to *partners*, by its very nature *"UNESCO is a multi-stakeholder forum which seeks to bring the best out of a variety of global, regional, national and local networks. (The) primary purpose, therefore, is (...) the promotion of linkages and dialogue through which (different) entities can contribute to peace, development and other goals pursued by the Organisation"*.[578] From the outset, this networking principle has particular relevance to DESD.[579] UNESCO therefore attempts in a partnership approach to attract and encourage multiple stakeholders to participate in DESD.

As to *relevance*, UNESCO concentrates on both relevant and timely issues related to *DESD*[580] focusing on links and synergies through the *"sharing of innovative (...) programmes, practices and policies"*.[581] UNESCO successfully addresses interdisciplinary and significant *DESD* topics.

As to *design*, the development, recognition and appraisal of strategic projects or project clusters in support of *DESD* through UNESCO are both intentional and thus highly appreciated.[582] UNESCO explicitly promotes project-based work on *DESD*.

As to *structures*, UNESCO provides a productive infrastructure dedicated to the needs of *DESD*. These mechanisms involve leadership, structures of governance, administrative support, human, material and financial resources, operating procedures, accountability, vision-building, engagement and retention.[583] As a

---

577 Cf. Matsuura, Koïchiro (01/03/2005) (cf. *footnote 28* op. cit.), pp. 1, 3.

578 See UNESCO (ed.) (2006j): UNESCO-Private Sector Partnerships: Making a Difference. ERC/CFS/MLT/2006/PI/1. Paris: UNESCO publishing, pp. 1, 24.

579 Cf. UNESCO (ed.) (2003b) (cf. *footnote 109* op. cit.), p. 4; UNESCO (ed.) (2004c) (cf. *footnote 34* op. cit.); UNESCO (ed.) (2005j) (cf. *footnote 44* op. cit.), pp. 9–15; UNESCO (ed.) (2006j) (cf. *footnote 578* op. cit.), p. 24; UNESCO (ed.) (2006i): Promotion for a Global Partnership for the UN Decade of Education for Sustainable Development (2005–2014). The International Implementation Scheme for the Decade in brief. ED-2006/WS/60. Paris: UNESCO workshops; UNESCO (ed.) (2008h) (cf. *footnote 219* op. cit.), p. 6; UNESCO (2007) (cf. *footnote 52* op. cit.); UNESCO (2009): UN Decade of Education for Sustainable Development. DESD in Close-up. Published by: UNESCO Education Sector.

580 Cf. UNESCO (ed.) (2005j) (cf. *footnote 44* op. cit.), p. 7; UNESCO (ed.) (2008h) (cf. *footnote 219* op. cit.); UNESCO (ed.) (2008g): The contribution of early childhood education to a sustainable society. The Role of Early Childhood Education for a Sustainable Society Göteborg, Sweden, 2–4 May 2007. ED-2008/WS/14 – CLD 3427.7. Edited by Ingrid Pramling Samuelsson; Yoshie Kaga. Paris: UNESCO publishing; Haigh, Martin J. (2009) (cf. *footnote 110* op. cit.).

581 See UNESCO (ed.) (2003b) (cf. *footnote 109* op. cit.), p. 2.
Cf. UNESCO (ed.) (2005g) (cf. *footnote 16* op. cit.); UNESCO (ed.) (2005j) (cf. *footnote 44* op. cit.), pp. 8–9, 18, 31.

582 Cf. UNESCO (ed.) (2005j) (cf. *footnote 44* op. cit.), pp. 8: 14.

583 Cf. UNESCO (ed.) (2005j) (cf. *footnote 44* op. cit.), pp. 23–24; UNESCO (ed.) (2005i) (cf. *footnote 216* op. cit.), p. 3; UNESCO (ed.) (2007k) (cf. *footnote 4* op. cit.), p. 10.

result, UNESCO affords *DESD* specific institutional settings, strategic and decision-making structures.

As to *instruments*, given its institutional settings, UNESCO facilitates *DESD* performance, such as the evaluation, tracking and reporting of mechanisms, in order to guarantee standards of implementation and monitoring results.[584] As a result, UNESCO provides the structures of co-ordination, implementation and evaluation suitable to *DESD*.

As to *public relations*, sharing and learning from good practices requires information. UNESCO fosters processes of capacity-building and instruction materials in the pursuit of transparency in the publication and communication of *DESD*.[585] UNESCO actively makes known and appraises, in a public forum, good and best practices relating to *DESD*.

In summary, in the course of leading *DESD*, UNESCO has proactively and in an interdisciplinary manner set its institutional sights on the success of *DESD*. The priority it gives to the strength of its role as leader and co-ordinator at an international level is clearly displayed by a substantial agenda of co-ordination. Its role as *lead agency* consists of:[586]

- Performing to the full its strategic role in relation to *ESD*;
- Acting as a catalyst for new partnerships with the private sector, youth and media groups;
- Serving as a forum for bringing together important stakeholders, such as leading representatives of key multinationals, faith-based institutions, youth associations, indigenous people, etc.;
- Promoting a research agenda and serving as a platform for relevant research on *ESD*;

---

584 Cf. UNESCO (ed.) (2005j) (cf. *footnote 44* op. cit.), pp. 9–16, 16–24; UNESCO (ed.) (2008h) (cf. *footnote 219* op. cit.).

585 Cf. UNESCO (ed.) (2005j) (cf. *footnote 44* op. cit.), pp. 16, 19; UNESCO (ed.) (2007d): Framework for a DESD Communication Strategy in support of the UN Decade of Education for Sustainable Development. ED-2007/WS/20. Paris: UNESCO workshops; UNESCO; The Earth Charter Initiative (ECI) (eds.) (2007d): Good Practices in Education for Sustainable Development Using the Earth Charter. Education for Sustainable Development in Action. Good Practices No. 3. Paris / San José: Earth Charter Center; UNESCO publishing; UNESCO (ed.) (2007e): Good Practices in Education for Sustainable Development: Teacher Education Institutions. Education for Sustainable Development in Action. Good Practices N°1. Edited by Rosalyn McKeown. Paris: UNESCO workshops; UNESCO; UNESCO Associated Schools (eds.) (2008b) (cf. *footnote 480* op. cit.); UNESCO; UNESCO Associated Schools (eds.) (2009b): Second Collection of Good Practices. Education for Sustainable Development. ED-2009/WS/11. Edited by Amina Hamshari. Paris: UNESCO Press.

586 Cf. Matsuura, Koïchiro (01/03/2005) (cf. *footnote 28* op. cit.), p. 3; UNESCO (ed.) (2005j) (cf. *footnote 44* op. cit.), pp. 15–16; UNESCO (ed.) (2007f) (cf. *footnote 427* op. cit.), p. 2.

- Convening *ad-hoc* working groups on particular topics;
- Linking member states and aiding in the implementation of *ESD* curricula, policies, research, etc., in those member states which require assistance;
- Encouraging monitoring and evaluation; and
- Sharing good *ESD* practices and expertise.

2.2 Expertise

Expertise is an acquired set of expert knowledge, skills and competences obtained in a specific domain. In the case of UNESCO and *DESD*, which *expertise* qualifies UNESCO to act as the *lead agency* for United Nations decades in general and *DESD* in particular? In order to answer this question properly, all United Nations decades with UNESCO as *lead agency* have to be taken into consideration. Only if the organisation is explicitly mentioned in, assigned or differently appointed to such leadership functions, regardless of the extent to which it is performed, is such analysis undertaken.

Apart from *ESD*, UNESCO supports and leads a range of *single-issue* initiatives. As *memorandum of understanding* they are all embedded in the organisation's mission. Remarkably, this *expertise* is primarily related to education as several examples clearly illustrate:

- Human rights education;[587]
- Early-childhood education;[588]
- Literacy and education for development;[589]
- Right and access to education;[590]
- Education and cultural development;[591] or
- Cultural education and diversity.[592]

---

587 *United Nations Decade for Human Rights Education* (1995–2004): UNESCO assigned as body of co-ordination and liaison with other organisations involved in the promotion of a culture of peace.
Cf. Mahler, Claudia; Mihr, Anja; Toivanen, Reetta (2009): The United Nations Decade for Human Rights Education and the inclusion of national minorities. Volume 1. Auflage. Frankfurt am Main: Peter Lang Publishing Incorporation.

588 Cf. UNESCO (ed.) (2008g) (cf. *footnote 580* op. cit.).

589 Cf. UNESCO (ed.) (2005g) (cf. *footnote 16* op. cit.); Lind, Agneta (2009) (cf. *footnote 480* op. cit.).

590 Cf. Benedek, Wolfgang (2007) (cf. *footnote 22* op. cit.); Fernandez, Alfred (2007) (cf. *footnote 21* op. cit.).

591 Cf. United Nations; UNESCO (eds.) (1994) (cf. *footnote 560* op. cit.); Pérez Cuéllar, Javier de (ed.) (1995 / 1996) (cf. *footnote 74* op. cit.), pp. 14 et seqq; Goncalves G., María Paola (ed.) (1998) (cf. *footnote 566* op. cit.), p. 26; Inglis, Christine (2008) (cf. *footnote 77* op. cit.), pp. 39 et seqq.

As a result, for several reasons UNESCO's conception of education nurtures and favours *DESD*. In first place, the organisation's programmatic notion of education can be regarded as very well elaborated and worldwide fully recognised.[593] In second place, the organisation's education concept has already been installed, tested and approved, most notably within the realms of institutional leadership responsibility.[594] In third place, even though UNESCO's definition of education applies universally, the concept remains thoroughly adaptable to various changing contexts and conditions.[595]

UNESCO *expertise* applies in various ways. Medium-term programmes and project activities led by respective sectors, bureaus or designated task forces are the most common applications of *expertise*. Another demanding instrument which provides the unique opportunity to share a more holistic notion of *expertise* is institutional leadership. Working intensely on a few focal issues over a longer period of time requires a specific effort in order to succeed, along with high-performance structures, promising topics and persistency. Since the 1980s, these elements of *expertise* have been attested by UNESCO's leadership of a number of United Nations decades in full or shared responsibility.[596]

Table 17: UNESCO expertise in acting as designated lead agency[597]

Period	Topic	Resolution
2005–2014	United Nations Decade of Education for Sustainable Development	*A/RES/57/254*
2003–2012	United Nations Literacy Decade: Education for All	*A/RES/56/116*
2001–2010	International Decade for a Culture of Peace and Non-violence for the Children of the World	*A/RES/53/25* *A/RES/60/3*
1995–2004	United Nations Decade for Human Rights Education	*A/RES/49/184*
1993–2003	Third Decade to Combat Racism and Racial Discrimination	*A/RES/48/91*
1991–2000	United Nations Decade against Drug Abuse	*A/RES/S-17/2*

592 Cf. UNESCO (ed.) (2001) (cf. *footnote 77* op. cit.); Inglis, Christine (2008) (cf. *footnote 77* op. cit.), pp. 39 et seqq.

593 Cf. chapter II 1 *Education* on page 11, and chapter VI 1 *Competences* on page 121.

594 Cf. *Table 23* in chapter VII 14 *United Nations decades* on page 193, and *footnote 587* on page 131.

595 I.e. in terms of focal issues, regions, target groups etc.
Cf. *Table 23* in chapter VII 14 *United Nations decades* on page 193, *Figure 105* in chapter IX 6.5.5 *Issues* on page 472, *Figure 57* in chapter IX 1.1 *Regional strategies* on page 258, and VII 12 *Stakeholders* on page 167.

596 See *Table 17* in chapter VI 2.2 *Expertise* on page 132.

597 Cf. United Nations (2009) (cf. *footnote 557* op. cit.); UNESCO (2009): International Decades proclaimed by the United Nations General Assembly. Published by: UNESCO Education Sector.

1988–1997	United Nations World Decade for Cultural Development	*A/RES/41/187*

Full participation	*Lead agency*
Partial participation	*Shared, contributing or complementary responsibility*

When referring to *DESD* and UNESCO's present mandate as *lead agency*, neither general nor specific cross-references are made either publicly or within documents to previous decades and *lead agency* mandates.[598] The conclusion may thus be drawn that recollection of *lead agency* experiences is either not relevant or intended, and not even implicitly shared as part of the organisation's institutional memory. The impression is given that each and every mandate starts from the very beginning, although, as indicated earlier, this is not the case. Key characteristics have meanwhile been established through practical application which may be interpreted as *lead agency* standards or as professional UNESCO *expertise*.

2.3 Resources

"Implementing the DESD will require leadership, planning and resources – both human and financial. So far, much of the financing of the DESD is coming through reallocating resources from existing initiatives and few new resources have been allocated."[599]

Extensive instruction in accounting and control is certainly not appropriate here, and indeed the objective is to provide an overall idea and understanding of how UNESCO's *lead agency* mandate is provided for and supported in terms of human and financial resources. Economically speaking, UNESCO pursues a strategy of maximising *utility* according to the *maximisation principle,* whose principal aim is *"to maximise quality and impact with available human and financial resources"*.[600]

598 For instance, it was only in 2002 that UNESCO was referred to *ex post* as *lead agency* in for the very first time. Before that, the term *responsible* was used without specific definition of meaning and content.
Cf. Dyroff, Hans-Dieter (ed.) (1994): Weltdekade für kulturelle Entwicklung (1988–1997). Deutsche Beiträge. Bonn: Deutsche UNESCO-Kommission; Goncalves G., María Paola (ed.) (1998) (cf. *footnote 566* op. cit.), p. 29; Bernecker, Roland; Leicht, Alexander (eds.) (1998) (cf. *footnote 88* op. cit.); Bell, Imogen (ed.) (2002): Eastern Europe, Russia and Central Asia. Volume Third edition. London: Publications Office of the European Union / Europa Publications Ltd. (Regional Surveys of the World), p. 610.

599 See UNESCO (ed.) (2005j) (cf. *footnote 44* op. cit.), p. 24.

600 See UNESCO (ed.) (2003b) (cf. *footnote 109* op. cit.), p. 3.

2.3.1 Staffing

It must firstly be stated that there is very little publicly available information on UNESCO personnel and staff concerned with *DESD*. Given an ambitious UNECSO agenda and in consideration of the cross-cutting and decentralised organisation of *DESD*, it is improbable that it constitutes a full-time occupation for the majority of its stakeholders. *DESD* must necessarily be understood as flexible division of labour without either exclusive or shared areas of *DESD* responsibility.

However, UNESCO's overall leadership of *DESD* constitutes an exception to the above observation. UNESCO headquarters does house staff particularly involved in *DESD* co-ordination through the *DESD Secretariat* or *Section for DESD Co-ordination* (ED/UNP/DESD) and who are located in the *Education for Sustainable Development Section of the Division for the Co-ordination of United Nations Priorities in Education.*[601]

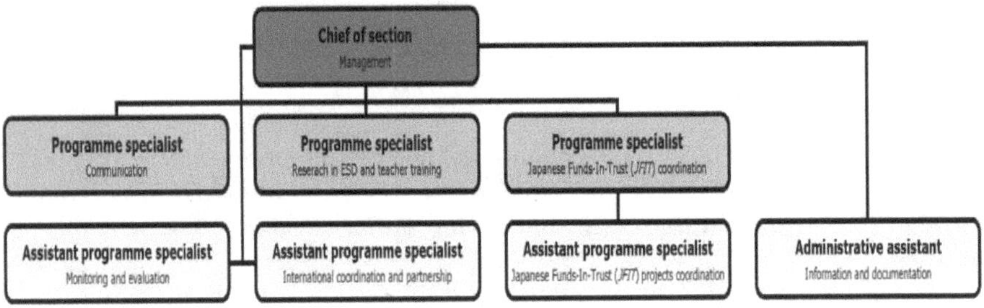

Figure 22: UNESCO headquarters staff in DESD co-ordination – ED/UNP/DESD[602]

2.3.2 Financing

Financial aspects are important, but not easily dealt with and this is particularly true of UNESCO's mandate for *DESD* leadership. This is due on the one hand to the structure of *DESD* and on the other hand dependent upon the availability of relevant data. *DESD* is financially supported both by member states and by UNESCO itself.[603]

601 See *Figure 22* in chapter VI 2.3.1 *Staffing* on page 134.
602 Clearly set and de-centralised management structures including third-party-funded posts.
603 See *Figure 23* in chapter VI 2.3.2 *Financing* on page 135.

<table>
<tr><th>Source / Institution</th><th>Regular</th><th>Extra-budgetary</th></tr>
<tr><td>Member states</td><td>✓</td><td rowspan="2">✓</td></tr>
<tr><td>UNESCO</td><td>✓</td></tr>
</table>

Figure 23: DESD financing[604]

Member-state financing relates to the de-centralised approach of extra-UNESCO resources *"urg(ing) governments and other potential funding sources to assess the existing resources and needs related to ESD in their jurisdictions and to re-allocate existing resources and find ways to create new resources"*.[605]

As is also true of UNESCO's global budget, the budget for *DESD* has two components: approved *regular* and *extra-budgetary* resources. Both forms are important. The regular budget provided through member state contributions enables budgetary planning according to the criteria of cost and efficiency of activities. Extra-budgetary resources are unpredictable as far as voluntary contributions of member states or other donors are concerned.

In this context, only the regular budget matters. For two reasons, no extra-budgetary resources are included: first, as mentioned above these contributions are very often arbitrarily and unpredictably made or strategically placed and differ considerably in their extent;[606] secondly, emphasising the *lead agency* aspect, UNESCO must necessarily rely upon proper financial resources (core-funding) in order to act independently in the execution of its strategic functions and assigned mandates. Considering extra-budgetary contributions as a credible index of commitment in UNESCO practice, the following observations give an approximate outline of UNESCO's approved regular budget in relation to *DESD*.

Technically speaking, the budget is administered in line with programme planning through biennial plans, the so called *C-documents*, which contain information on budgetary spending relating to different sectors and UNESCO's various fields of action. *DESD* constitutes one *main line*, or field of action. Unlike other programme activities, *DESD* action cannot be reduced to one expense item only. In accordance with its interdisciplinary nature *DESD* is varia-

604 Apart from UNESCO's mandatory *DESD* funding both regular member states' contributions and extra-budgetary funding activities are highly appreciated.

605 See UNESCO (ed.) (2005j) (cf. *footnote 44* op. cit.), p. 24.

606 *Extra-budgetary* contributions are a highly politicised domain which is subject to self-interest and the influence of political agenda.
Cf. Gerner, Martin (10/08/2009) (cf. *footnote 407* op. cit.); Gerner, Martin (14/09/2009) (cf. *footnote 407* op. cit.).

bly distributed among different sectors and it is thus included in UNESCO biennial planning. It is therefore difficult to provide an exact budget for the implementation of *DESD*.

There are numerous occasions for difficulty to arise. The following three scenarios are possible:

a) *DESD* is not yet accounted for or even mentioned;
b) *DESD* is mentioned, but neither scheduled nor planned for in the budget; or
c) *DESD* is mentioned, scheduled and planned for, but subsumed into other programmes.

Only the last case merits further discussion, because it is the only manifest *DESD* reference in the absence of different bases and benchmarks of assessment. It is thus impossible to provide any detailed budgetary information. However, two principal forms of *DESD* financing can instead be distinguished:

1. *Sectoral financing* is the classic method of allocating portions of the UNESCO budget to clearly marked expenditure within a particular programme sector. It follows the *investment*-like principle of linking programmes through main lines of action with their expected results. *DESD* is a strategically established part of UNESCO's Education Sector.[607] As a result, financial resources are allocated primarily to the *DESD Secretariat* or *Section for DESD Co-ordination* (ED/UNP/DESD) located in the *Education for Sustainable Development Section of the Division for the Co-ordination of United Nations Priorities in Education*.

607 See *Figure 24* in chapter VI 2.3.2 *Financing* on page 137.

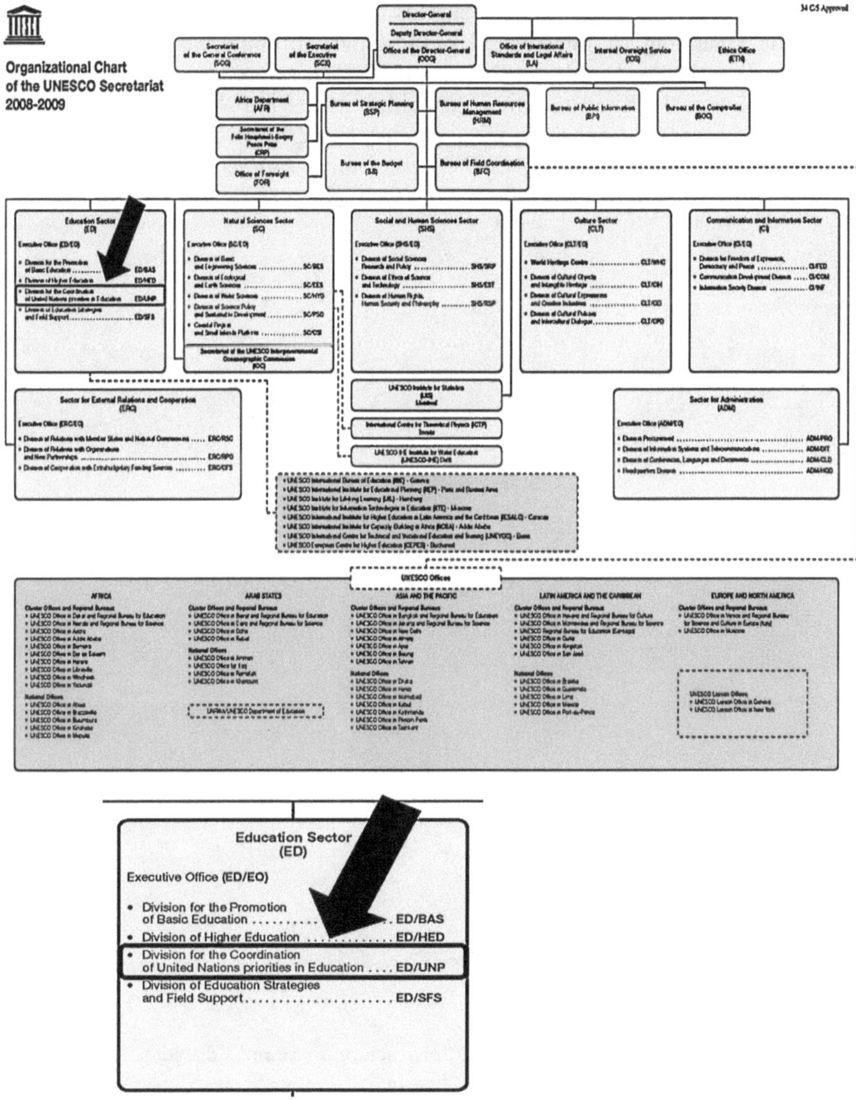

Figure 24: Intricate budgetary pathway of DESD expenditure[608]

608 The regular budget allocated to *DESD* is primarily assigned by the the organisation's education sector. *DESD* ranges among and thus internally competes with other inter- and intra-sectoral priorities sharing respective resources, of course.
See UNESCO (ed.) (2008a) (cf. *footnote 83* op. cit.), p. 304.

2. *Inter-sectoral financing* is the relatively novel UNESCO approach of cross-cutting financing of interrelated programmes through the means of inter-sectoral platforms. Firstly, in the case of *DESD*, reference is made to the appropriate cross-cutting initiative by making use of introductory phrases, such as *in the context of* or *within the framework of DESD*. Secondly, the sector-specific contributions to the *ESD Inter-sectoral Platform*[609] are specified as *"indicative allocations from the following major programmes"*.[610]

609 Cf. Dhillon, Sam (2008): UNESCO Intersectoral Platform: Education for sustainable development. Published by: UNESCO.
See *Figure 25* in chapter VI 2.3.2 *Financing* on page 139.

610 See, for instance, *Approved Programme and Budget 2008–2009: 34 C/5 Approved* UNESCO (ed.) (2008a) (cf. *footnote 83* op. cit.), p. 191.
Major programmes represent the five *UNESCO Sectors*: Education (I), Natural Sciences (II), Social and Human Sciences (III), Culture (IV) and Communication and Information (V).
See chapter IX 1.7 *Cross-cutting* on page 271, and chapter IX 2.2.3 *Developing public awareness of sustainability* on pages 282 et seqq.

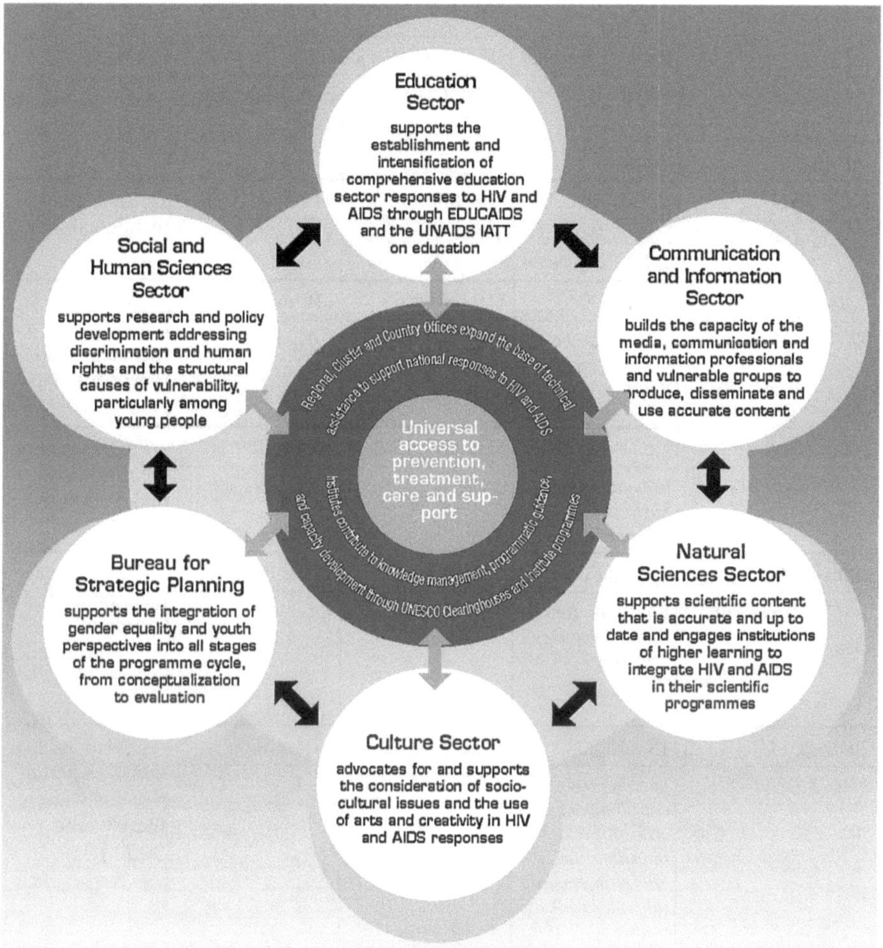

Figure 25: UNESCO inter-sectoral co-operation and financing[611]

Bearing in mind the deficiencies concerning the classification and accrual of expenses, the sole objective of the following table is to provide an idea of how much money is spent by UNESCO on *DESD* compared to the organisation's overall regular budget.[612]

---

611 This chart illustrates the functioning of UNESCO's *inter-sectoral platform*, both in terms of functional co-operation and finance, taking the example of comprehensive HIV-AIDS prevention programmes of treatment, care and support. See UNESCO (ed.) (2008a) (cf. *footnote 83* op. cit.), p. 188.

612 See *Table 18* in chapter VI 2.3.2 *Financing* on page 140.

Table 18: UNESCO's DESD spending as ratio of DESD expenditures to global budget[613]

	Regular biennial budget (in US-Dollar)			Comment
Biennium	Spent	UNESCO global	Education Sector total	
Document	*Scope*	%	%	
2002–2003	3,137,300	544 million	94 million	*DESD* not yet mentioned
31 C/5 Approved[614]	*Education for a sustainable future*	0.58	3.3	
2004–2005	5,480,600	610 million	110 million	*DESD* mentioned, but neither scheduled (yet) nor budgeted
32 C/5 Approved[615]	*Improving the quality of education*	0.89	5.0	
2006–2007	1,621,900	610 million	108 million	*DESD* explicitly mentioned and budgeted as a separate item
33 C/5 Approved[616]	*Education for Sustainable Development*	0.27	1.5	
2008–2009	1,160,000	631 million	108 million	*DESD* explicitly mentioned, but subsumed in a cumulative and inter-sectoral approach
34 C/5 Approved[617]	*Education for Sustainable Development*	0.18	1.1	
2010–2011	13,170,200	653 million	119 million	*DESD* mentioned as part of a sector-wide framework
35 C/5 Draft[618]	*Leading the education agenda: co-ordinating international efforts in education and tracking trends*	2.0	11.1	

613 The table illustrates by trend how much of UNESCO's global and the organisation's education sector budget is approximately spent on *DESD*.

614 Cf. UNESCO (ed.) (2002a): Approved Programme and Budget 2002–2003. 31 C/5 Approved. Paris: UNESCO workshops, pp. XXIII, 11, 31–32, 237.

615 Cf. UNESCO (ed.) (2004a): Approved Programme and Budget 2004–2005. 32 C/5 Approved. Paris: UNESCO workshops, pp. 19, 35, 38, 48–49, 307.

616 Cf. UNESCO (ed.) (2006a): Approved Programme and Budget 2006–2007. 33 C/5 Approved. Paris: UNESCO workshops, pp. xix, 17, 22, 36, 44–45, 282.

617 Cf. UNESCO (ed.) (2008a) (cf. *footnote 83* op. cit.), pp. xv, 19, 190–191, 269.

618 Cf. UNESCO (ed.) (2009a): Draft Programme and Budget 2010–2011. Revised version. 35 C/5 Draft. Paris: UNESCO workshops (Volumes 1and 2), pp. 3, 9, 26–27, 15 (Annex I), 18 (Vol. 2), 159 et seqq (Vol. 2).

As previously noted, it is important and necessary to recall that these figures cannot form part of a deductive leap from budgetary spending to the quality of UNESCO's execution of its mandate as *lead agency*. If any two biennial terms reflect UNESCO's budgetary commitment towards *DESD* in a more or less representative way, it is because *DESD* is dealt with in a more focussed and concise way given its separate budgetary disclosure. The following approximation is therefore possible:[619]

Table 19: DESD spending in comparison to UNESCO's Education Sector budget[620]

	Regular biennial budget (in US-Dollar)			Comment
Biennium	Spent	UNESCO global	Education Sector total	
Document	*Scope*	%	%	
2006–2007	1,621,900	610 million	108 million	*DESD* explicitly mentioned and separately budgeted
33 C/5 Approved[621]	*Education for Sustainable Development*	0.27	1.5	
2008–2009	1,160,000	631 million	108 million	*DESD* explicitly mentioned, but subsumed in a cumulative and intersectoral approach
34 C/5 Approved[622]	*Education for Sustainable Development*	0.18	1.1	

Given the information available, UNESCO's financial support of *DESD* appears limited. Although given high priority by the global leadership mandate, it must be conceded that few budgetary resources are procured for *DESD* compared to the UNESCO Education Sector spending in total. In other words, this implies that there have to be other priorities within this domain that must be fulfilled or managed as matters of prime importance. In terms of budgetary matters, *DESD* is insufficiently prioritised.

With regard to financial resources that are exclusively available for the *DESD Secretariat* or *Section for DESD Co-ordination* (ED/UNP/DESD), the

619 See *Table 19* in chapter VI 2.3.2 *Financing* on page 141.

620 Two biennial terms of budget regularly allocated to *DESD* serve as a shining example of which proportion of the global and sectoral UNESCO assignment are available for programmatic spending.

621 Cf. UNESCO (ed.) (2006a) (cf. *footnote 616* op. cit.), pp. xix, 17, 22, 36, 44–45, 282.

622 Cf. UNESCO (ed.) (2008a) (cf. *footnote 83* op. cit.), pp. xv, 19, 190–191, 269.

assignment of funds gains more substance. Still, it remains wholly impossible to rate these figures qualitatively.[623]

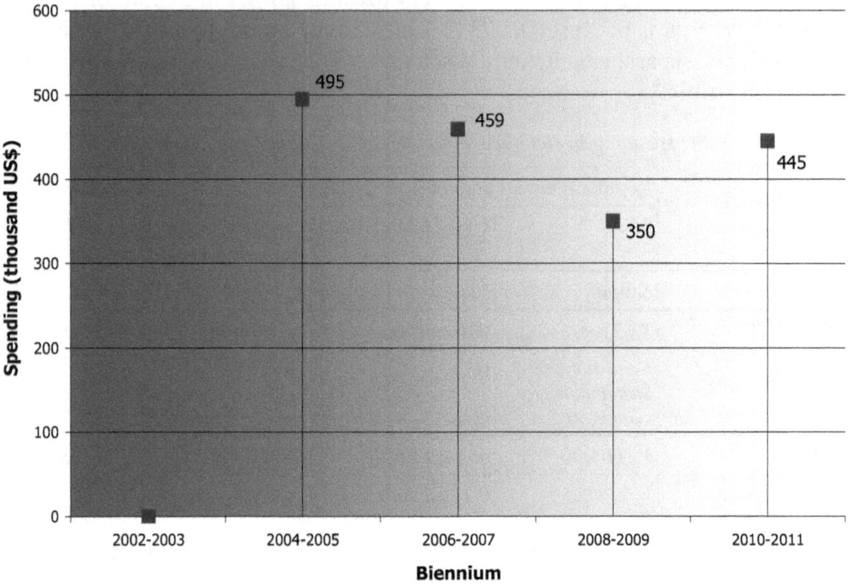

Figure 26: DESD spending at UNESCO headquarters[624]

It is extremely difficult to make any reliable statement according to the financial strength of *DESD* and for various reasons. Firstly, there is no publicly available information on *DESD* financing. Secondly, there is no appropriate benchmark with which to compare spending on *DESD*. Thirdly, there is neither consistency in scope nor distinctness in classification with regard to *ESD*. It is therefore almost impossible to deduce, at first glance, the financial significance of *DESD* for UNESCO from budgetary planning.

623 See *Figure 26* in chapter VI 2.3.2 *Financing* on page 142.

624 This table visualises the resources applicable for managing *DESD*. Roughly one third of the overall UNESCO *DESD* budget is spent for co-ordination at the UNESCO headquarters.
Cf. Combes, Bernard P. Y. (12/05/2010): Ressources DESD. Paris. E-Mail to: Gerner, Martin compared to *Table 19* in chapter VI 2.3.2 *Financing* on page 141.

3 Scope

The functional scope of UNESCO's leadership mandate for *DESD* is twofold. It can *grosso modo* be divided into:

a) Co-ordinating and facilitating *DESD*; and
b) Implementing *DESD*.

This distinction leads to two envisaged requirements, but at the same time these areas are closely interrelated.[625] In other words, they are complementary: no implementation without co-ordination; and no facilitation without implementation.

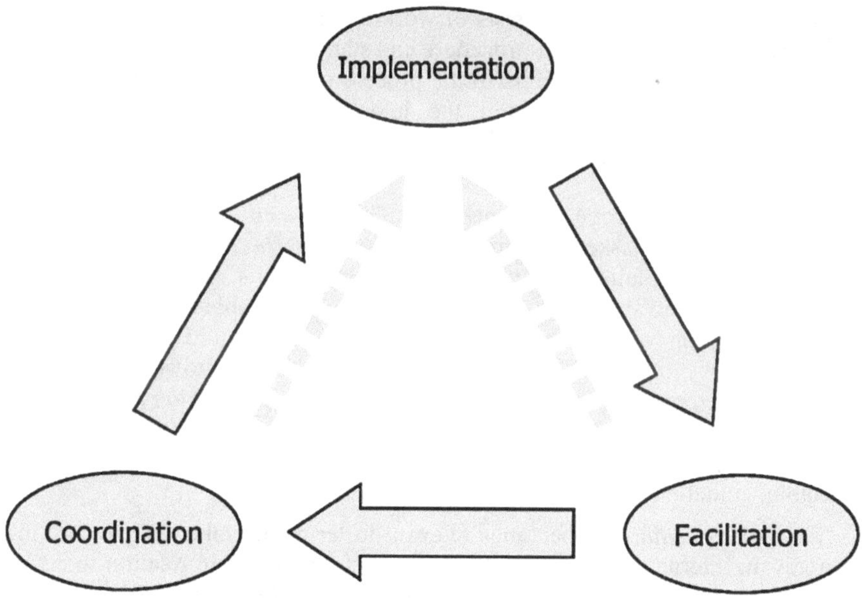

Figure 27: Functional relationship between co-ordination, facilitation and implementation[626]

625 See *Figure 27* in chapter VI 3 *Scope* on page 143.

626 Co-ordination, implementation and facilitation are strategically linked with each other. Means of implementation were certainly ineffective without proper facilitating and co-ordinating mechanisms.

3.1 Co-ordination and facilitation

Co-ordination describes the process of organising both the different parts of an activity or work programme, and the people involved in it so that it functions without complications. *Facilitation* is the practice of enabling processes and making them work effectively. Both terms refer to the management aspect of leadership.

UNESCO takes the assigned responsibility of guiding the global *DESD* process *"to reorient education in support of sustainable development in national policies and education systems"*.[627] This mandate involves two forms of *co-ordination*:[628]

- *Ex-ante co-ordination*[629] consists of working on (normative) instruments for setting agreed-upon rules of procedure and standards; and
- *Ex-post co-ordination*[630] refers to the process of establishing coherence with (normative) instruments within the international law system (*lex lata*) through normalisation and standardisation by means of institutional co-operation.

In order to fulfill the scope of an international *ex-ante co-ordinator* and *facilitator*, UNESCO was asked to provide a draft *International Implementation Scheme* (IIS)[631] explaining how to turn multiple actors into stakeholders of *DESD* by raising awareness of the importance of sustainable development. Following an extensive process of consultation and a multi-party approach, UNESCO *"has painstakingly engaged all major players"*[632] to actively contribute to the development of this draft *International Implementation Scheme* (IIS), by paying attention to their specific needs and implementation requirements. Finally, the adopted *International Implementation Scheme* (IIS) can be seen as a timetable, guideline and framework throughout *DESD*.

Ex-post co-ordination becomes relevant in terms of embedding *DESD* into the relevant international legal and extra-legal frameworks in relation to education and sustainable development. To some extent the *International Implementation Scheme* (IIS) contributes to this both by linking major stakeholders and by correlating existing or ongoing initiatives with *DESD*.[633]

---

627 See Matsuura, Koïchiro (01/03/2005) (cf. *footnote 28* op. cit.), p. 2.
628 Cf. Boisson de Chazournes, Laurence (2007) (cf. *footnote 496* op. cit.), pp. 68–71.
629 See Boisson de Chazournes, Laurence (2007) (cf. *footnote 496* op. cit.), p. 68.
630 See Boisson de Chazournes, Laurence (2007) (cf. *footnote 496* op. cit.), p. 70.
631 Cf. UNESCO (ed.) (2005j) (cf. *footnote 44* op. cit.), p. 5.
632 See Matsuura, Koïchiro (01/03/2005) (cf. *footnote 28* op. cit.), p. 2.
633 Cf. UNESCO (ed.) (2005j) (cf. *footnote 44* op. cit.), p. 25.

3.2 Implementation

Implementation refers to the action of starting and carrying out something that has been officially decided, purposefully planned and scheduled. In contrast to co-ordination and facilitation, any process of *implementation* cannot be externally driven or controlled. Instead, it must be self-contained, autonomous and subject to individual accountability. *Implementation* applies both to the visionary and managerial aspects of leadership.

Fully in line with the *International Implementation Scheme* (IIS), UNESCO provides its own independent *"broad-based inter-sectoral action plan"*[634] which contains the guidelines of the specific organisation's efforts and initiatives.[635] These are recorded as part of the *UNESCO Action plan*[636] and the related *DESD Communication Strategy*.[637] In the course of *DESD*, UNESCO focuses on promoting education as *"a basis for a more sustainable human society and will encourage the integration of sustainable development issues and practices, including local knowledge and culture, into education systems at all levels"*.[638]

Unlike an emphasis on executive management or on the logistical aspects of co-ordination and facilitation, *implementation* has more to do with principles or acting upon maxims. *DESD* is not about a neutral attitude, but about directing behaviour. Thus, *DESD implementation* requires *drive* in terms of a programmatic method of *implementation*. In order to meet these expectations UNESCO proposes certain criteria of *DESD* implementation. However, the list of criteria should not be seen as *self-imposed*, for the following reason. Given both the organisation's philosophical background and actions already undertaken, these catalogue criteria must be considered as a matter of course, or as a mandatory consequence. UNESCO aims to meet the needs of *DESD implementation* in a unique and multi-faceted way.[639]

634 See Matsuura, Koïchiro (01/03/2005) (cf. *footnote 28* op. cit.), p. 2.
635 Cf. UNESCO (ed.) (2005i) (cf. *footnote 216* op. cit.), p. 1.
636 Cf. UNESCO (ed.) (2007m) (cf. *footnote 216* op. cit.).
637 Cf. UNESCO (ed.) (2007d) (cf. *footnote 585* op. cit.).
638 See Matsuura, Koïchiro (01/03/2005) (cf. *footnote 28* op. cit.), p. 2.
639 See *Figure 28* in chapter VI 3.2 *Implementation* on page 146.

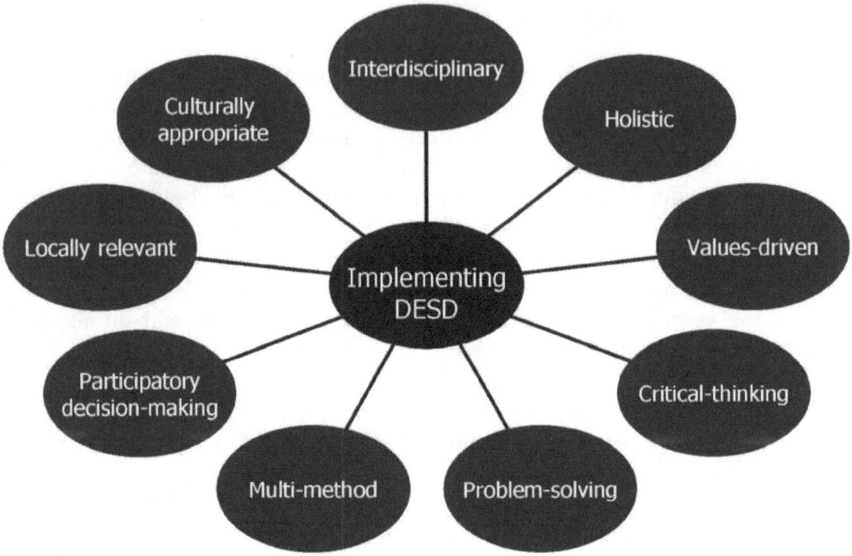

Figure 28: Catalogue of DESD implementation criteria[640]

Taking into account these characteristics, UNESCO envisages a flexible *implementation* framework which favours diversity. This position originates in the organisation's conviction that *"(t)here is no universal model of education for sustainable development. While there will be overall agreement on the concept, there will be nuanced differences according to local contexts, priorities and approaches. Each country has to define its own priorities and actions. The goals, emphases and processes must, therefore, be locally defined to meet the local environmental, social and economic conditions in culturally appropriate ways. Education for sustainable development is equally relevant and critical for both developed and developing countries".*[641] What sounds suitable in theory might turn out to be rather problematic in practice, given that *DESD* ought to be im-

640 The self-imposed catalogue of *DESD* implementation criteria can be considered both extensive and ambitious. However, at the same time it represents the range of core principles and philosophies of UNESCO.
See Becker, Egon; Jahn, Thomas; Stieß, Immanuel, et al. (eds.) (1997) (cf. *footnote 53* op. cit.); UNESCO (ed.) (2004c) (cf. *footnote 34* op. cit.), p. 16; UNESCO (2007) (cf. *footnote 52* op. cit.); UNESCO (2009) (cf. *footnote 579* op. cit.).

641 See UNESCO (2004): Education. Concepts. Published by: UNESCO Education Sector; Higgitt, David (2009b) (cf. *footnote 56* op. cit.), p. 100.

plemented *"in equal measure"*[642] because it is *"(...) equally relevant and important (...)"*[643] to all.

Effective *implementation* depends upon feedback. *Autonomous* mechanisms of monitoring must therefore be developed and established. They can be divided into several stages of reporting followed by evaluation, best realised externally.[644] UNESCO explicitly *"encourage(s) monitoring and evaluation"*[645] by introducing appropriate structures of global *in-house* monitoring of *DESD*.[646]

4 Conclusion

This chapter has dealt with UNESCO's mandate as *lead agency* for *DESD*. Based on considerations regarding the definition and notion of *mandate* in terms of *authority*, *power*, and *order*, UNESCO's competences were rated promising and compatible with – if not best-suited to – the requirements of leadership for *DESD*. Two leadership models were introduced: *charismatic leadership* related to vision-building versus *bureaucratic leadership* related to qualities of management.

Because of the lack of any legal definition of *lead agency* and given UNESCO's expertise, different features were discussed proving the suitability of the organisation's character for the leadership of *DESD*. Followed by a brief *tour d'horizon* of the mandate's resource provision in terms of staffing and finance, its functional scope was assessed. It consists of two closely related aspects: *co-ordination* and *facilitation* on the one hand, and criteria-based *implementation* on the other.

In a nutshell, three points may be emphasised:

1. UNESCO is thoroughly capable of rising to the challenge of leading *DESD*, taking into conscious account the paucity of available resources;
2. UNESCO's mandate as *lead agency* covers both charismatic *and* bureaucratic leadership: *DESD* requires both visionary and managerial qualities[647]; and

642 Cf. UNESCO (ed.) (2004c) (cf. *footnote 34* op. cit.), p. 24.
643 See UNESCO (ed.) (2005j) (cf. *footnote 44* op. cit.), p. 30.
644 Cf. Gerner, Martin (30/07/2009) (cf. *footnote 407* op. cit.).
645 See UNESCO (ed.) (2007f) (cf. *footnote 427* op. cit.), p. 2.
646 Cf. Weiss, Edith Brown (2003) (cf. *footnote 520* op. cit.), p. 538; UNESCO (ed.) (2008h) (cf. *footnote 219* op. cit.); UNESCO Section for DESD Coordination (ed.) (2009) (cf. *footnote 116* op. cit.).
See chapter IX 5.4 *Evaluation* on page 378.
647 Cf. *Figure 20* in chapter VI 2 *Leadership* on page 124.

3. UNESCO may potentially profit from *DESD* by broadening its organisational leadership profile from culture and development towards education and sustainable development.

VII Background information

In what way is DESD grounded and affiliated to evolutions in practice? In this respect context is very important. There is no development without good reason and the same general principle of evolution can also be said to apply to DESD. For this purpose, this chapter will outline the required context by following three principal elements: firstly, an explanation of DESD in terms of strategic reasons based on vision, mission and obstacles followed by programmatic aspects outlined through perspectives, objectives, focal issues and general principles of conduct; secondly, background information on the characteristics, intended schedule and main motivations of DESD as well as brief descriptions of stakeholders; thirdly and finally, contextualisation of DESD in a framework of past developments, current affairs and future obstacles in order to make its circumstances clear.

1 Vision

Building visions is a future-oriented and stylised capacity of positive and creative thinking directed towards a desirable steady state.[648] *"The basic vision of the DESD is a world where everyone has the opportunity to benefit from education and learn the values, behaviour and lifestyles required for a sustainable future and for positive societal transformation."*[649]

Visions are highly imaginative – sometimes even utopian – and for this reason not attached to any *a priori* consideration of feasibility. Hence, *"(e)ducation*

648 Cf. UNESCO (ed.) (2007k) (cf. *footnote 4* op. cit.), p. 7.
649 Cf. UNESCO (ed.) (2004c) (cf. *footnote 34* op. cit.), p. 5.

for sustainable development is a vision of education that seeks to balance human and economic well-being with cultural traditions and respect for the Earth's natural resources. It emphasises aspects of learning that enhance the transition towards sustainability including future education; citizenship education; education for a culture of peace; gender equality and respect for human rights; health education; population education; education for protecting and managing natural resources; and education for sustainable consumption. Pursuing sustainable development through education requires educators and learners to reflect critically on their own communities".[650]

Visions are value-driven, goal-oriented and designed in a normative way. As far as *DESD* concerns *"(t)he overall goal (...) is to integrate the values inherent in sustainable development into all aspects of learning in order to encourage changes in behaviour that allow for a more sustainable, economically viable and just society for all, a world where everyone has the opportunity to benefit from education and learn the values, behaviour and lifestyles required for a sustainable future and for positive societal transformation".*[651]

In summary, *DESD* is an ongoing ambition that envisages *sustainability literacy*[652] in society. Developing any kind of *sustainability literate society* calls for:[653]

- An understanding of the urgent need for change towards a sustainable way of doing things, both individually and collectively;
- Sufficient knowledge and skills to decide and act adequately towards sustainable development; and
- The capacity to recognise and appreciate the decisions of others, their commitment and their actions in favour of sustainable development.

---

650 See UNESCO (ed.) (2005g) (cf. *footnote 16* op. cit.), p. 11.

651 See UNESCO (ed.) (2005i) (cf. *footnote 216* op. cit.), p. 2.

652 See Forum for the Future; Higher Education Partnership for Sustainability (HEPS) (eds.) (2004): Learning and skills for sustainable development. Developing a sustainability literate society. Guidance for Higher Education Institutions. Edited by Fiona Brookes; Elizabeth White. London: Severnprint; Selby, David (2009) (cf. *footnote 55* op. cit.), p. 208.

653 Cf. Forum for the Future; Higher Education Partnership for Sustainability (HEPS) (eds.) (2004) (cf. *footnote 652* op. cit.), p. 9; Bhola, Harbans S. (2008): Adult Literacy for Sustainable Development: Creating a Knowledge-based Discourse for Action. In: Bhola, Harbans S.; Valdivielso Gómez, Sofía (eds.): Signposts to literacy for sustainable development. Complementary studies. Hamburg: UNESCO Institute for Lifelong Learning, pp. 1–76; Richmond, Mark (2010): Envisioning, coordinating and implementing the UN Decade of Education for Sustainable Development. In: Witthaus, Michele; McCandless, Karen; Lambert, Rebecca (eds.): Tomorrow today. Leicester, United Kingdom: Tudor Rose; UNESCO publishing, pp. 19–22, p. 19.
See *Figure 29* in chapter VII 1 *Vision* on page 151.

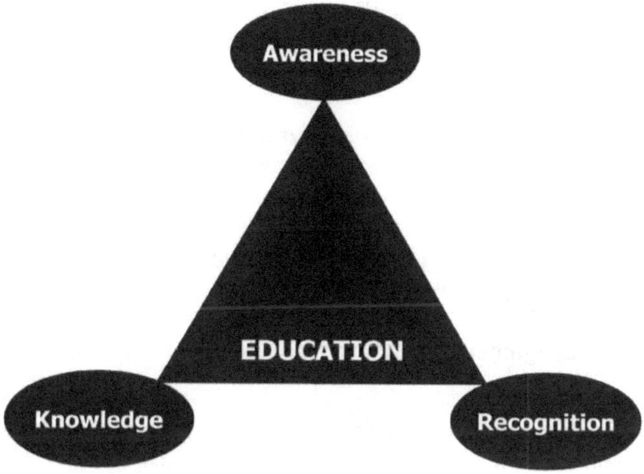

Figure 29: DESD and sustainability literacy[654]

2 Mission

DESD must be seen as much more than merely a period-specific event – scheduled from 2005 until 2014 – and a specific scope of action. Instead, major protagonists tend to evoke a long-term and priority-based perspective, usually referred to as a mission.[655] Missions are derived from visions. In other words, the mission of *DESD* can be described as the translation of vision vis-à-vis *DESD* into programmatic practice. The main goals to be pursued can be synthesised from selected mission statements.

When launching *DESD* in 2005, United Nations Secretary-General Kofi Annan officially stated that *"(o)ur biggest challenge in this new century is to take an idea that sounds abstract – sustainable development – and turn it into a reality for all the world's people".*[656]

Koïchiro Matsuura, Director-General of the *United Nations Educational, Scientific and Cultural Organization* (UNESCO), explains the task with which *DESD* is confronted: *"At the heart of the Decade of Education for Sustainable*

654 Education towards *sustainability literacy* may be taken into consideration by the triad of recognition, knowledge and awareness-raising.

655 E.g., López Ospina, Gustavo (2003): Planetary Sustainability in the Age of the Information and Knowledge Society. For a Sustainable World and Future. Working toward 2015. ED-2004/WS/15. Paris / Quito: UNESCO publishing, pp. 19 et seqq.

656 Cf. Matsuura, Koïchiro (01/03/2005) (cf. *footnote 28* op. cit.), pp. 4–5.

Development is a simple idea with complex implications, namely, after being taught over past centuries to live unsustainably, we now have to learn to live sustainably. And the greatest part of this challenge, I believe, is to learn the lessons of interdependence".[657]

More concisely: *"(e)ducation for a sustainable future is a formidable challenge. How can we better understand the complexity of the world around us? What relationships are there between the problems of our world and what does this mean for resolving them? What kind of world do we wish for the future, within the constraints imposed by the systems supporting the life on our Earth? How can we reconcile the requirements of the economy, society and the environment?"*[658]

Key *DESD* assignments simultaneously mentioned in all mission statements consist of:

- *Challenge* of changing social behaviour;
- *Simple* concept vis-à-vis *complex* global implications;
- *Understanding* and *learning*; and
- *Interdependence* and broad interdisciplinary approach.

3 Challenges

Carrying out the *DESD* mission creates four substantial challenges to be overcome. *"Nevertheless, conceptual fuzziness about the meaning and objectives of ESD is a legitimate concern(;) not only will a definitional murkiness make it difficult to communicate ESD to the public, it will also make it challenging to operationalize objectives, to measure value, and to know what it is that we seek."*[659] To sum up, these are:

1. Definition: How to explain and categorise *DESD* and its components?[660]

---

657 See Matsuura, Koïchiro (01/03/2005) (cf. *footnote 28* op. cit.), p. 2.

658 See López Ospina, Gustavo (2005): Construcción de un futuro sostenible. Década de una educación por un desarrollo sostenible 2005–2014. Volume Primera edición. Quito: UNESCO publishing, p. 169.

659 See Higgitt, David (2009a) (cf. *footnote 103* op. cit.), p. 4; Monroe, Martha C.; Fien, John (2005): The Role Environmental Education Might Play in the Decade for Education for Sustainable Development. In: Applied Environmental Education & Communication, Volume 4, Issue 3, pp. 203–206, p. 204.
Cf. González-Gaudiano, Edgar (2009): The Decade of Education for Sustainable Development: Challenges and Opportunities in México. In: Chalkley, Brian; Haigh, Martin J.; Higgitt, David (eds.): Education for sustainable development. Papers in honour of the United Nations Decade of Education for Sustainable Development (2005–2014). London / New York: Routledge, pp. 273–275, pp. 274–275.

660 Cf. Selby, David (2009) (cf. *footnote 55* op. cit.), pp. 203 et seqq.

2. Conceptualisation: How to arrange different perspectives of understanding within one coherent framework?
3. Communication: How to get the key messages of *DESD* across, institutionally and publicly?
4. *Operationalisation*: How to ensure proper implementation and co-ordination of *DESD*? *"Consequently a major challenge for the Decade is to promote the presence of ESD from words to actions, from concept to reality (...)."*[661]

4 Dimensions

As mentioned earlier, *DESD* carries the burden of having a broad conceptual scope given various modes of understanding and multiple interests.[662] In consequence *DESD* is in danger of being confused with a *catch-all* concept. In order to refrain from definitional arbitrariness *ESD* must be related to certain key dimensions or domains.

The *DESD* vision statement refers to three principal *domains*[663] as well as an additionally and more implicitly mentioned domain of values to be assigned to and conclusively identified as central to *ESD*.[664] These domains of sustainability and sustainable development are:[665]

- Ecology or environment – defining sustainability in terms of the environmental impact of human behaviour;
- Society – defining sustainability in terms of inter- and intra-generational equity,[666] societal transformation and policies in order to *"enable decent living conditions"*;[667]

---

661 See Higgitt, David (2009b) (cf. *footnote 56* op. cit.), p. 99.

662 Cf. UNESCO (2007) (cf. *footnote 52* op. cit.).

663 *Dimension* synonymously expressed as *domain* or *key area*, respectively.
Cf. Deutscher Bundestag (ed.) (1998) (cf. *footnote 52* op. cit.), pp. 17–27; UNESCO (ed.) (2004c) (cf. *footnote 34* op. cit.), p. 12; López Ospina, Gustavo (2005) (cf. *footnote 658* op. cit.), p. 169; Combes, Bernard P. Y. (2009): The United Nations Decade of Education for Sustainable Development (2005–2014): Learning to Live Together Sustainably. In: Chalkley, Brian; Haigh, Martin J.; Higgitt, David (eds.): Education for sustainable development. Papers in honour of the United Nations Decade of Education for Sustainable Development (2005–2014). London / New York: Routledge, pp. 215–219, pp. 215, 217.

664 Cf. UNESCO (ed.) (2005i) (cf. *footnote 216* op. cit.), p. 2; Bartholomäi, Reinhard (1997) (cf. *footnote 98* op. cit.), p. 138.

665 Cf. UNESCO (ed.) (2004c) (cf. *footnote 34* op. cit.), p. 12; UNESCO (ed.) (2005c) (cf. *footnote 23* op. cit.), pp. 8, 17, 36; UNESCO (ed.) (2007c) (cf. *footnote 120* op. cit.), p. 9.
See *Figure 30* in chapter VII 4 *Dimensions* on page 157.

666 Cf. Deutscher Bundestag (ed.) (1998) (cf. *footnote 52* op. cit.), pp. 28–29.

- Economy – defining sustainability in terms of responsibility for an enduring resource base, efficient economic structures and the possibility for economic development; and additionally
- Culture – defining sustainability in terms of preserving cultural heritage and diversity management.[668]

A controversy arises in scientific and institutional discourse in the matter of how to deal purposefully with culture as a proper *DESD* dimension.[669] It has been unanimously agreed upon that there is *"[...] the need to incorporate culture as a strategic element in national and international development policies, as well as in international development cooperation (...)".*[670] This notwithstanding, divergent paradigms lead to programmatic contradictions.[671] Two alternative arguments are generally evinced in the matter of how to integrate cultural provision:

- Regarding culture as a separate, independent and single dimension out of four.[672] The pledge for integrating culture into the set of variables is reinforced, with justification: *"Will it suffice to confine ourselves to the UNESCO mission statement (vis-à-vis DESD) of 'ecological, economic and social' alone? To what extent must this mission statement be extended to incorporate culture?"*[673] This argument receives scant support, most probably due to reluctance, and to the recognition that cultural issues are a politically tough domain.
- Claiming that culture serves a holistic purpose as an 'embedded' dimension. This diplomatically convenient approach,[674] referred to as 'culture as *underlying dimension*',[675] is widely recognised because it allows sufficient freedom of interpretation to integrate culture as a highly politicised domain. *"Culture is an underlying dimension (...) but it is acknowledged more tacitly than overtly."*[676]

---

667 Cf. UNESCO (ed.) (2005i) (cf. *footnote 216* op. cit.), p. 2.
668 Cf. Kono, Toshiyuki (2007) (cf. *footnote 83* op. cit.), p. 259.
669 Cf. Kuhn, Katina (März 2006) (cf. *footnote 88* op. cit.), pp. 30–34.
670 See digit 6 UNESCO (ed.) (2005a) (cf. *footnote 42* op. cit.), p. 2.
671 Cf. UNESCO (ed.) (2008b) (cf. *footnote 74* op. cit.), p. 3.
672 Cf. UNESCO (ed.) (2005c) (cf. *footnote 23* op. cit.), p. 36; Kono, Toshiyuki (2007) (cf. *footnote 83* op. cit.), p. 265.
673 Translation from German into English: *„Reicht es aber aus, sich nur auf das Leitbild der UNESCO ‚ökologisch, ökonomisch und sozial' zu beschränken? Inwiefern ist dieses Leitbild um ‚kulturell' zu erweitern?".*
See Leicht, Alexander; Plum, Jacqueline; Fuchs, Max (2007) (cf. *footnote 19* op. cit.), p. 6.
674 Cf. Combes, Bernard P. Y. (2009) (cf. *footnote 663* op. cit.).
675 Cf. UNESCO (ed.) (2005c) (cf. *footnote 23* op. cit.), p. 8.
676 See Gough, Annette (2009): Towards a Synthesis. In: Maclean, Rupert; Fien, John; Park, Man-Gon (eds.): Work, Learning and Sustainable Development. Opportunities

Meanwhile, taking into account the *renaissance* of holistic approaches,[677] culture is no longer regarded justifiably as a merely *underlying dimension.*[678] Culture represents, in fact, an embedded dimension and complementary *asset*[679] of sustainable development.[680] *"Today the notion of sustainable development includes ecological, economic, social and cultural sustainability."*[681] However, there is an ongoing debate on how to *"bring(...) the cultural dimensions of development together with economic and environmental objectives within a sustainability framework"*.[682]

Despite the frequent observation that culture is mentioned only implicitly when referring to *ESD*; culture increasingly influences and enriches the dis-

---

and Challenges. Dordrecht: Springer Netherlands (Springer-11648 [Dig. Serial], 8), pp. 71–74, p. 71.

677 Cf. UNESCO (ed.) (2008b) (cf. *footnote 74* op. cit.), pp. 3, 5.
E.g., *Convention on the Protection and Promotion of the Diversity of Cultural Expressions* (2005); *UNESCO Universal Declaration on Cultural Diversity* (2002).
Cf. UNESCO (ed.) (2005a) (cf. *footnote 42* op. cit.), p. 5; UNESCO (2007n) (cf. *footnote 79* op. cit.), pp. 326 et seqq; UNESCO (ed.) (2001) (cf. *footnote 77* op. cit.), p. 5; UNESCO (2007n) (cf. *footnote 79* op. cit.), pp. 707 et seqq.

678 See Organización de Estados Iberoamericanos para la Educación, la Ciencia y la Cultura (OEI) (ed.) (2006a): Educación para el desarrollo sostenible I. Década de la Educación para un Futuro Sostenible (2005–2014): un punto de inflexión necesario en la atención a la situación del planeta. Edited by José Gutiérrez Pérez; Teresa Pozo Llorente; Eloísa Tréllez Solís. Madrid: Servicio de Publicaciones (Revista Iberoamericana de Educación, N° 40 I), p. 103; UNESCO (2007) (cf. *footnote 52* op. cit.).

679 E.g., *Convention on the Protection and Promotion of the Diversity of Cultural Expressions* (2005), Article 2 – Guiding principles:
"5. Principle of the complementarity of economic and cultural aspects of development: Since culture is one of the mainsprings of development, the cultural aspects of development are as important as its economic aspects, which individuals and peoples have the fundamental right to participate in and enjoy.", and
"6. Principle of sustainable development: Cultural diversity is a rich asset for individuals and societies. The protection, promotion and maintenance of cultural diversity are an essential requirement for sustainable development for the benefit of present and future generations".
See UNESCO (ed.) (2005a) (cf. *footnote 42* op. cit.), p. 5; UNESCO (2007n) (cf. *footnote 79* op. cit.), pp. 326 et seqq.

680 E.g., *Convention on the Protection and Promotion of the Diversity of Cultural Expressions* (2005), Article 14 – Cooperation for development:
"Parties shall endeavour to support cooperation for sustainable development (...)".
See UNESCO (ed.) (2005a) (cf. *footnote 42* op. cit.), p. 9; UNESCO (2007n) (cf. *footnote 79* op. cit.), pp. 326 et seqq; Bokova, Irina (2009) (cf. *footnote 89* op. cit.).

681 Cf. Lasonen, Johanna (2009) (cf. *footnote 73* op. cit.), p. 187.

682 See UNESCO (ed.) (2008b) (cf. *footnote 74* op. cit.), p. 3.

course on sustainability as an *integrated*,[683] but self-contained dimension.[684] A shift has evidently taken place concerning the understanding of sustainability that leads from a *green orientation* towards a *cultural orientation*[685] in order to *"(...) foster the emergence of a dynamic cultural sector (...)".*[686] This relates above all to *cultural education.*[687] However, some authors of documentation and promotion materials on *DESD* explicitly claim that *"(...) education will have to change so that it addresses the social, economic, cultural and environmental problems that we face in the 21st century".*[688]

To illustrate the programmatic correlation between these four dimensions, different models are proposed, ranging from pillar, egg or pyramids diagrams to *overlapping circles.*[689] In the final balance, the most suitable and most widely

---

683 E.g., *Convention on the Protection and Promotion of the Diversity of Cultural Expressions* (2005), Article 13 – Integration of culture in sustainable development:
"Parties shall endeavour to integrate culture in their development policies at all levels for the creation of conditions conducive to sustainable development and, within this framework, foster aspects relating to the protection and promotion of the diversity of cultural expressions."
See UNESCO (ed.) (2005a) (cf. *footnote 42* op. cit.), p. 9; UNESCO (2007n) (cf. *footnote 79* op. cit.), pp. 326 et seqq.

684 Cf. Kuhn, Katina (März 2006) (cf. *footnote 88* op. cit.), p. iii.

685 See Deutsche UNESCO-Kommission e. V. (DUK) (ed.) (2007) (cf. *footnote 24* op. cit.), p. 13.

686 See UNESCO (ed.) (2005a) (cf. *footnote 42* op. cit.), p. 9.

687 *Cultural education* refers to *"(...) capacity-building through the exchange of information, experience and expertise, as well as the training of human resources in developing countries, in the public and private sector relating to, inter alia, strategic and management capacities, policy development and implementation, promotion and distribution of cultural expressions, small-, medium- and micro-enterprise development, the use of technology, and skills development and transfer (...)".*
See UNESCO (ed.) (2005a) (cf. *footnote 42* op. cit.), p. 10; UNESCO (2007n) (cf. *footnote 79* op. cit.), pp. 326 et seqq.

688 Cf. UNESCO (ed.) (2004c) (cf. *footnote 34* op. cit.), p. 13; UNESCO (ed.) (2005g) (cf. *footnote 16* op. cit.); UNESCO (ed.) (2004c) (cf. *footnote 34* op. cit.), p. 5; UNESCO (ed.) (July 2003) (cf. *footnote 37* op. cit.), p. 4; UNESCO (2007n) (cf. *footnote 79* op. cit.).

689 I.e. Venn diagrams.
Cf. The World Conservation Union (IUCN); University of Cambridge (eds.) (2006): The Future of Sustainability. Re-thinking Environment and Development in the Twenty-first Century. Report of the IUCN Renowned Thinkers Meeting, 29–31 January 2006. Edited by William M. (Bill) Adams. Cambridge: The World Conservation Union (IUCN), p. 2; Centre for Environment Education (CEE); South Asia Youth Environment Network (SAYEN) (eds.) (2007): Sustainable Development: An Introduction. Ahmedabad (Internship Series, Volume 1), pp. 12 et seqq.

accepted is the system of *interlocking circles*.[690] It displays four circles, each of them representing a different *DESD* dimension. Interrelation is depicted by overlapping and incorporating circles according to their definition.[691] The result is comprehensive, and relatively uncomplicated to understand.

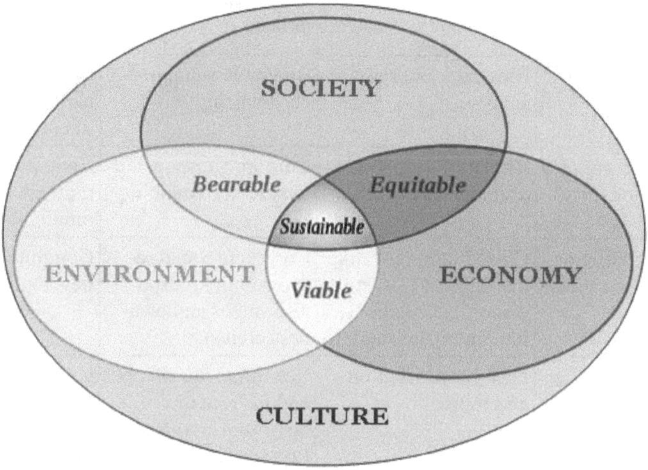

Figure 30: Dimensions of DESD[692]

5 Perspectives

The proposed multi-dimensional model forms the basis for further explanation of *DESD* framework conditions and strategic obstacles in terms of the institutions, procedures and competences involved.[693] There is a strong affiliation vis-

690 See The World Conservation Union (IUCN); University of Cambridge (eds.) (2006) (cf. *footnote 689* op. cit.), p. 2; Centre for Environment Education (CEE); South Asia Youth Environment Network (SAYEN) (eds.) (2007) (cf. *footnote 689* op. cit.), p. 12.

691 Cf. UNESCO (ed.) (2004c) (cf. *footnote 34* op. cit.), p. 13.

692 This chart illustrates the four relevant interdependent dimensions of *DESD* as proposed and defined by UNESCO. Three of them – environment, economy and society – were already recognised from the beginning; the fourth – culture – is in the meantime considered an underlying dimension of *DESD*.
Cf. and based upon The World Conservation Union (IUCN); University of Cambridge (eds.) (2006) (cf. *footnote 689* op. cit.), p. 2; Centre for Environment Education (CEE); South Asia Youth Environment Network (SAYEN) (eds.) (2007) (cf. *footnote 689* op. cit.), pp. 12 et seqq.

693 Cf. Chalkley, Brian; Haigh, Martin J.; Higgitt, David (eds.) (2009): Education for sustainable development. Papers in honour of the United Nations Decade of Education for

à-vis classification in categories between different technical perspectives and respective dimensions. Basic questions and *strategic*[694] *ESD* issues likely to be raised or treated are the following:[695]

Table 20: Examples of relevant DESD issues[696]

Society	*Environment*	*Economy*	*Culture*
Capacity-building	Bioethics and risk analysis	Budget law and deficit financing	Changing cultural patterns and cultures of consumption
Citizenship, commitment and good governance	Climate change and protection	Corporate responsibility and accountability	Civic pluralism, cultural education and multiculturalism
Democratic participation, equity and social justice	Closed loop recycling management (waste disposal regulations, integrated production)	Corporate social responsibility (corporate values and business ethics)	Community cultural development
Family policy	Disaster prevention and mitigation	Economic incentives and instruments of environmental protection (certificates, compensation, public dues, stock exchanges)	Cultural autonomy (self-governance, self management, autodetermination)

Sustainable Development (2005–2014). London / New York: Routledge; UNESCO (ed.) (August 2007): Progress Report by the Director-General on the United Nations Decade of Education for Sustainable Development (2005–2014). 177 EX/9 Annex III. Paris: UNESCO publishing, p. 8; Universität Bayreuth (2009): Ziele der Forschungsstelle for das Recht der Nachhaltigen Entwicklung der Universität Bayreuth (FoRNE). Published by: Rechts- und wirtschaftswissenschaftliche Fakultät / Lehrstuhl Öffentliches Recht I.

694 See UNESCO (ed.) (2005h) (cf. *footnote 539* op. cit.), p. 5.

695 See *Table 20* in chapter VII 5 *Perspectives* on page 158.

696 Cf. UNESCO (05/07/2003) (cf. *footnote 124* op. cit.), pp. 11 et seqq; UNESCO (ed.) (2004c) (cf. *footnote 34* op. cit.), pp. 12–13, 18 et seqq; UNESCO (ed.) (2005h) (cf. *footnote 539* op. cit.), p. 5; UNESCO (ed.) (2005c) (cf. *footnote 23* op. cit.), pp. 22 et seqq; López Ospina, Gustavo (2005) (cf. *footnote 658* op. cit.), p. 315; UNESCO (ed.) (2005c) (cf. *footnote 23* op. cit.), p. 9; United Nations Economic Commission for Europe (UNECE) (ed.) (2006) (cf. *footnote 20* op. cit.), p. 6; UNESCO; Asia-Pacific Centre of Education for International Understanding (APCEIU) (eds.) (2007a): Two Concepts, One Goal: Education for International Understanding (EIU) and Education for Sustainable Development (ESD). TH/2007/PI/H/3. Bangkok / Seoul: UNESCO Asia and Pacific Regional Bureau for Education; Universität Bayreuth (2009) (cf. *footnote 693* op. cit.); Selby, David (2009) (cf. *footnote 55* op. cit.), pp. 200 et seqq.

Society	*Environment*	*Economy*	*Culture*
Food safety	Disaster reduction in agriculture	Financing environmental protection	Cultural relationships
Gender equality	Environmental engineering and innovation	Impacts of public procurement and subsidies	Cultural resources and indigenous or local intellectual property (cultural industries)
Health	Harmonising environmental laws by establishing environmental codes	Inter-generational calculus of investment (cost-benefit analysis)	Ethnicity and cultural affiliation
HIV / AIDS	Land use planning	Legal structures of ownership (private versus public property)	Intercultural dialogue and understanding
Human rights	Natural resources (water, energy, agriculture, biodiversity)	Market economy and fair trade	Making use of cultural diversity and creativity
Indebtedness of developing and threshold countries	Preservation of biological and landscape diversity	Needs, offers and demands	Preserving cultural identity and heritage (arts, language, etc.)
Peace and human security	Principles and instruments of environmental protection	Negotiated environmental agreements	
Population and demographic change	Protection of mountainous areas	Poverty reduction	
Poverty eradication	Protection of oceans and coastal areas	Public-Private-Partnerships	
Social cohesion	Provisions of renewable energies	Risk management	
Sustainability and social welfare systems	Renewable energy supply	Sustainable companies	
Teaching and learning	Rural development	Green Economy	
Urbanisation and human settlement	Soil conservation and land consumption		
	Sustainable urbanisation		
	Traffic, transportation and emissions		

6 Objectives

Ideally, objectives ought to be *SMART* in quality:

- *Specific* in scope;
- *Measurable* in terms of assessment;
- *Attainable* in regard to results;
- *Realistic* in what can be achieved; and
- *Timely* in their realisation.

"At its core, the Decade's goal is that countries achieve sustainable development."[697] In order to perform successfully, *DESD* aims to:

a) Promote education as a basis for a more sustainable human society; and
b) Integrate sustainable development into education systems at all levels.[698]

DESD is meant as a global effort to be reached *in equal measure.*[699] Recalling the vision statement, these objective criteria may be applied to *DESD* accordingly:[700]

Table 21: SMART objectives on DESD

Criteria	Vision statement quotes[701]
Specific in scope	*"The overall goal of DESD is to integrate the values inherent in sustainable development into all aspects of learning...*
Measurable in terms of assessment	*...in order to encourage changes in behaviour...*
Attainable in regard to results	*...that allow for a more sustainable, economically viable and just society for all...*
Realistic in what can be achieved	*...a world where everyone has the opportunity to benefit from education and learn the values, behaviour and lifestyles required for a sustainable future and for positive societal transformation..."*
Timely in their realisation	...within a decade by 2014.

Objectives or goals referring to *DESD* are inconsistently prescribed. The wording differs considerably depending on sources and references.[702] Conse-

697 See Matsuura, Koïchiro (01/03/2005) (cf. *footnote 28* op. cit.), p. 2.
698 Cf. UNESCO (ed.) (2003b) (cf. *footnote 109* op. cit.), p. 2; Richmond, Mark (2010) (cf. *footnote 653* op. cit.), p. 19.
699 Cf. UNESCO (ed.) (2004c) (cf. *footnote 34* op. cit.), p. 24.
700 See *Table 21* in chapter VII 6 *Objectives* on page 160.
701 See UNESCO (ed.) (2005i) (cf. *footnote 216* op. cit.), p. 2; UNESCO (ed.) (2007m) (cf. *footnote 216* op. cit.), p. 1.

quently there are certain objectives being formulated inconsistently due to a work-in-progress approach. The opportunity to develop and present a consolidated version must therefore be seized.

The overall aim of *DESD* translates into four objectives. Accordingly, the mission of *DESD* encompasses:[703]

- Platform for *ESD*:

Providing a space and opportunity for refining and promoting the vision of and transition to sustainable development through all forms of learning and public awareness, especially by facilitating networking, linkages, exchange and interaction among multiple stakeholders in *ESD*;

- Education for *ESD*:

Giving an enhanced profile to the central role of education and learning in the common pursuit of sustainable development by fostering an increased quality of teaching and learning in *ESD*;

- Development for *ESD*:

Helping countries to make progress towards and attain the *Millennium Development Goals* (MDGs), in particular through and combined with *ESD* efforts; and

- Opportunities for *ESD*:

Developing strategies at every level to strengthen capacity in *ESD*, particularly providing countries with new opportunities to incorporate *ESD* into education reform efforts.

702 E.g., ranging from web sites, official documents and extracts to reports, speeches and rather informal data.

703 Cf. UNESCO (ed.) (2004c) (cf. *footnote 34* op. cit.), p. 24; Matsuura, Koïchiro (01/03/2005) (cf. *footnote 28* op. cit.), p. 2; UNESCO (ed.) (2005j) (cf. *footnote 44* op. cit.), pp. 6–7; UNESCO (ed.) (2007k) (cf. *footnote 4* op. cit.), p. 6; UNESCO (ed.) (2007m) (cf. *footnote 216* op. cit.), p. 8.
See *Figure 31* in chapter VII 6 *Objectives* on page 162.

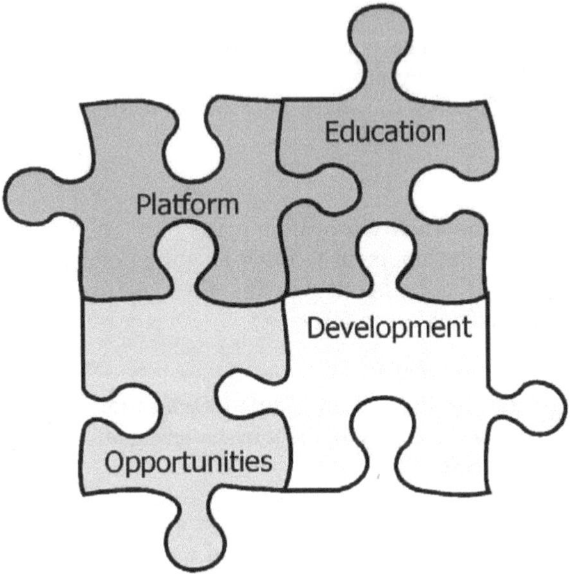

Figure 31: DESD objectives – a consolidated puzzle[704]

Strictly speaking, there is *just* one central issue: *DESD* is all about education. It is unquestionably the main pillar, *"the foundation for all other strategies to promote the concept of sustainable development"*.[705] Education is the basic constitutive and fundamental element for human capacity-building, particularly when attached to questions of resource awareness and sustainability.[706]

Education is regarded as a continuous process. Hence, sustainable development is based upon a life-long learning process aiming towards resource awareness through capacity-building in different fields of action. Accordingly, *"(t)he principles of sustainable development must find their place in children's schooling, higher education, non-formal education and community-based learning activities"*.[707]

704 In brief the four principal objectives of *DESD* are providing the platform for *ESD*, establishing opportunities for *ESD*, emphasising the role of education for *ESD*, and strengthening aspects of development towards *ESD*.

705 See Matsuura, Koïchiro (01/03/2005) (cf. *footnote 28* op. cit.), p. 2.

706 Cf. UNESCO (ed.) (2003b) (cf. *footnote 109* op. cit.), p. 3.
Cf. chapter II 1 *Education* on pages 11 et seqq.

707 See UNESCO (ed.) (2005g) (cf. *footnote 16* op. cit.), p. 9; UNESCO (ed.) (2005c) (cf. *footnote 23* op. cit.), p. 9.

7 Principles

DESD guiding principles can be divided into programmatic and administrative types. Both distinguishable types are built on the basic assumption that *"(t)here is no universal model of education for sustainable development. While there will be overall agreement on the concept, there will be nuanced differences according to local contexts, priorities and approaches. Each country has to define its own priorities and actions. The goals, emphases and processes must, therefore, be locally defined to meet the local environmental, social and economic conditions in culturally appropriate ways. Education for sustainable development is equally relevant and critical for both developed and developing countries".*[708]

Programmatic principles must be clarified prior to administrative questions in order to ensure a common understanding of *DESD* in the first instance. This is particularly applicable to the following considerations:[709]

- Dynamic: *ESD* is considered an evolving and notional concept of interpretation and without fixed presuppositions;
- Normative: value-based strategies are needed to attain substantial (long-term) impacts;
- Holistic: four dimensions of *ESD* are explicitly mentioned to be taken into consideration - environment, society, economy and culture;
- Multi-stakeholder: voluntary *bottom-up*[710] participation from multiple actors is essential in order to make the most use of civic capacities necessary to succeed on a large scale;
- Interdisciplinary: different disciplines contribute to *ESD* by remaining capable of dialogue and exchange;
- Multi-method: various pedagogical techniques are applied to promote participatory learning and advanced thinking skills;
- Inclusive: *ESD* addresses multiple forms and levels of learning contexts and priorities; and
- Subsidiary: *ESD* must meet local or regional needs vis-à-vis global issues.

---

708 See UNESCO (ed.) (2003b) (cf. *footnote 109* op. cit.), p. 3; UNESCO (ed.) (2005j) (cf. *footnote 44* op. cit.), pp. 30–31.

709 Cf. UNESCO (ed.) (2003b) (cf. *footnote 109* op. cit.), p. 4; UNESCO Education Sector (ed.) (2005) (cf. *footnote 21* op. cit.), pp. 4–5; UNESCO (ed.) (2005j) (cf. *footnote 44* op. cit.), pp. 30–31; Leicht, Alexander (2005): Nachhaltigkeit lernen. Die UN-Dekade „Bildung für nachhaltige Entwicklung (2005–2014)" in Deutschland. In: Deutsche UNESCO-Kommission e. V. (DUK) (ed.): forum der unesco-projekt-schulen. Ziel: Zukunftsfähigkeit. Beiträge zur UN-Dekade "Bildung für nachhaltige Entwicklung". Ergebnisse der 40. Jahrestagung der UNESCO-Projektschulen. Zeitschrift der Deutschen UNESCO-Kommission, Sonderheft Nr. 3. Bonn: Bonner Universitäts-Buchdruckerei, pp. 15–17, p. 2.

710 See UNESCO (ed.) (2003b) (cf. *footnote 109* op. cit.), p. 4.

Administrative provisions are, first and foremost, prescribed as a guideline for *DESD* co-ordination and implementation. They are intended to encourage stakeholders to make individual *ESD* efforts consisting of clearly identifiable plans, focal points, strategies and adequate means of monitoring, including periodical reporting and responsibilities for evaluation. Another key to success is to establish modalities for partnerships, technical assistance, guidance and information sharing.[711]

8 Characteristics

Driving features of *DESD* may therefore be listed by taking programmatic and administrative principles into account, accordingly:[712]

- Interdisciplinary and holistic: *ESD* is understood as a cross-cutting, interrelated and open concept to be implemented within educational systems;
- Value-driven: *ESD* is based upon unanimously shared values and principles underpinning sustainable development;
- Critical thinking and problem-solving: *ESD* must lead to a frank address of both the challenges of, and viable solutions for sustainable development;
- Multi-method: *ESD* is neither an *elusive* nor *unidirectional* approach, but pluralist in its consideration of different concepts, levels and pedagogies in modelling processes;
- Participatory decision-making: *ESD* relies upon supporting mechanisms, in particular broad participation and integrative decision-making structures;
- Applicability: *ESD* outcomes - both quantitative and qualitative ones - must prove practical relevance in *day-to-day* contexts in reference to personal and professional life alike;
- Locally relevant: *ESD* is similarly tasked to tackle local, regional and global issues, but must always root itself in the tangible needs in place according to *thinking globally – acting locally*;[713] and
- Culturally appropriate: *"No universal models of ESD exist"*.[714] *ESD* respects cultural diversity and means of expression by encouraging culturally-unique and diverging solutions and approaches at a local and regional level.

711 Cf. UNESCO (ed.) (2006h): Highlights on Progress to Date. September 2006. Paris: UNESCO publishing, p. 2.

712 Cf. UNESCO (ed.) (2004c) (cf. *footnote 34* op. cit.), pp. 17 et seqq; UNESCO Education Sector (ed.) (2005) (cf. *footnote 21* op. cit.), pp. 4–5; UNESCO (ed.) (2005j) (cf. *footnote 44* op. cit.), pp. 7–8; UNESCO (ed.) (2005c) (cf. *footnote 23* op. cit.), p. 9; UNESCO (ed.) (2007k) (cf. *footnote 4* op. cit.), p. 6; UNESCO (2009) (cf. *footnote 579* op. cit.).

713 See Leicht, Alexander (2005) (cf. *footnote 709* op. cit.), p. 2; Schuchardt, Erika; Mbeki, Thabo (eds.) (2005) (cf. *footnote 37* op. cit.), p. 24.

Last but not least, the fundamental, underlying and vital aspect to which *DESD* is dedicated is:

- Communication: *ESD* should be based on exchange. Efficiently communicating *ESD* among its stakeholders is considered most critical in terms of formal and informal exchange of information and ideas.[715] The required framework is provided by a comprehensive *DESD Communication Strategy*.[716]

9 Timeline

ESD is a long-term undertaking. Every component of *ESD* already bears future-oriented aspects:

a) Education represents the prospective investment within society *par excellence* that requires considerable time to yield positive results;
b) Sustainability is, by definition, oriented toward the long term, as more than one generation is concerned; and
c) Development means advancing gradually and must be interpreted dynamically.

As a result, *ESD* combines all components together both by drawing particular attention to consequences in the long run and by cultivating the nexus between present and future generations.[717] Hence, considering the entire evolution illustrated by specific milestones, *DESD* as an institutionalised process of *ESD* covers just part of it. Officially, *DESD* is scheduled from 2005 until 2014.[718] It may roughly be segmented into two stages, marked by a mid-term report, that end

714 See UNESCO (ed.) (2005j) (cf. *footnote 44* op. cit.), p. 30.

715 Cf. UNESCO (ed.) (2006h) (cf. *footnote 711* op. cit.), p. 3.

716 Cf. Krott, Maximilian (2002) (cf. *footnote 203* op. cit.), p. 971; UNESCO (ed.) (2006h) (cf. *footnote 711* op. cit.), p. 3; UNESCO (ed.) (2007d) (cf. *footnote 585* op. cit.), pp. 5 et seqq.

717 Cf. Matsuura, Koïchiro (01/03/2005) (cf. *footnote 28* op. cit.), p. 2.

718 Cf. UNESCO (ed.) (2003b) (cf. *footnote 109* op. cit.); UNESCO (ed.) (2004c) (cf. *footnote 34* op. cit.); Matsuura, Koïchiro (01/03/2005) (cf. *footnote 28* op. cit.), p. 1; UNESCO (ed.) (2005i) (cf. *footnote 216* op. cit.); UNESCO (ed.) (2005d): Education for Sustainable Development. Public information. memobpi. Paris: Bureau of Public Information (BPI), p. 1; UNESCO (ed.) (August 2007) (cf. *footnote 693* op. cit.), p. 2; UNESCO (ed.) (2007l): UN Decade of Education for Sustainable Development 2005–2014. The DESD at a glance. ED/2005/PEQ/ESD/3. Paris: UNESCO publishing, p. 4; UNESCO (2009) (cf. *footnote 597* op. cit.); United Nations (2009) (cf. *footnote 557* op. cit.).

and begin in 2009 and 2010, and an end-of-decade or final report to the United Nations General Assembly by 2015.[719]

10 Thrusts

Based upon the main objectives of *DESD*, four priority areas of *ESD* have been formulated in order to design focused programme activities.[720] Those are both assigned to UNESCO as the mandated organisation and as one which serves as stakeholder assignments.[721] Despite the fact that there is no explicit hierarchy in terms of weighting single priorities, they must be considered consecutive or consequential due to contents and structure:[722]

1. Improving access to basic, quality education and simultaneously addressing *ESD*-related issues;
2. Re-orienting existing education programmes in terms of content, structure and methods towards *ESD*;
3. Developing public understanding and awareness vis-à-vis *ESD* reflected in civic conduct, legislation and consumption; and
4. Providing training measures disseminating *ESD*-relevant knowledge and skills on a large scale.

---

719 Cf. United Nations Economic Commission for Europe (UNECE); United Nations Economic and Social Council (ECOSOC) (eds.) (2004b) (cf. *footnote 391* op. cit.), p. 15; UNESCO (ed.) (2004c) (cf. *footnote 34* op. cit.), p. 44; UNESCO (ed.) (2005j) (cf. *footnote 44* op. cit.), p. 16; UNESCO (ed.) (2006i) (cf. *footnote 579* op. cit.), p. 12.

720 Cf. UNESCO (ed.) (2005j) (cf. *footnote 44* op. cit.), p. 30.

721 Cf. UNESCO (ed.) (2003b) (cf. *footnote 109* op. cit.), p. 2; UNESCO (ed.) (2005j) (cf. *footnote 44* op. cit.), pp. 7, 28–30; UNESCO (2007) (cf. *footnote 52* op. cit.); UNESCO Education Sector (ed.) (2005) (cf. *footnote 21* op. cit.), pp. 5–6.
All four thrusts are sort of *borrowed* and adapted to *ESD*. The last three are originally taken and derived from *Agenda 21*. The first is primarily related to *Education for All* (EFA).
Cf. Chapter 36.2 UN Department of Economic and Social Affairs (ed.) (1992): United Nations Conference on Environment & Development. Agenda 21. Rio de Janeiro, Brazil, 3–14 June 1992. Edited by Division for Sustainable Development. New York: United Nations, pp. 320–328; and No. 7 UNESCO (ed.) (2000) (cf. *footnote 541* op. cit.), p. 8; United Nations Conference on Trade and Development (UNCTAD); UNESCO; United Nations Children's Fund (UNICEF) (eds.) (2001) (cf. *footnote 524* op. cit.), pp. 28–29; UNESCO Education Sector (ed.) (2005) (cf. *footnote 21* op. cit.), p. 2; Yusuf, Abdulqawi A. (ed.) (2007) (cf. *footnote 129* op. cit.), pp. 295 et seqq.

722 See *Figure 32* in chapter VII 11 *Thrusts* on page 167.

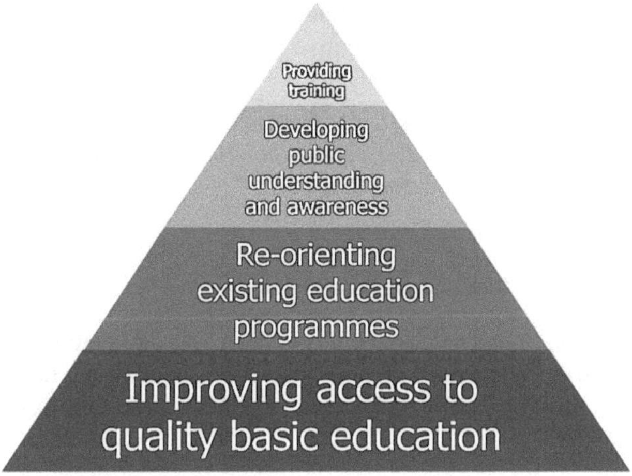

Figure 32: Thrusts and priorities of DESD[723]

11 Stakeholders

DESD has been solidly established as a multi-stakeholder approach. There are consequently many different actors contributing and participating, to varying degrees. In order to obtain a general idea of this plurality, stakeholder commitment may be classified according to several *structural axes* intended to serve as a background reference for enhanced understanding. The variables in relation to *DESD* stakeholders are the following:

a) *Range*, with reference to geography. At what level of involvement is it considered reasonable to participate, predominantly as a local, regional or international stakeholder?
b) *Motivation*, with reference to focal issues. Which topics are prioritised and dealt with, and why?
c) *Institutionalisation*, with reference to formal versus non-formal patterns of participation. How commitment is organised, institution-based or instead loosely embedded within civil society.
d) *Affiliation*, with reference to integration within organisational structures. To what extent parties are, or are not, attached to the United Nations family – UNESCO in particular.

723 This *pyramid of needs* clearly visualises how different thrusts of *DESD* are prioritised. It reflects some typical bottom-up approach that first emphasises access to education before moving to appropriate means of training.

e) *Assignment*, with reference to mandate. Given the distinction between directorial roles (leadership) and executive functions (implementation),[724] which function do stakeholders perform?

The following presentation of *DESD* stakeholders is twofold:[725] a brief, initial introduction to the actor's general profile, followed by a more concise description of the specific role played during *DESD*.[726]

11.1 United Nations affiliation

The *United Nations General Assembly* (UNGA) as the central and democratically-legitimised decision-making body that represents all member states of the United Nations is affiliated in particular with *DESD*, having in common three principal elements:

1. Announcing *DESD*;[727]
2. Delegation of *DESD* leadership responsibilities to UNESCO;[728] and
3. Receipt and analysis of reports on *DESD* implementation and assessment thereof.[729]

The *United Nations Commission on Sustainable Development* (CSD) was brought into effect by *A/RES/47/191*[730] in 1992 as a structural consequence of

---

724 Cf. UNESCO (ed.) (2007k) (cf. *footnote 4* op. cit.), pp. 10, 13.

725 Remark: These two procedural criteria are urgently required in order to keep information straight to the point. There is neither need nor intention to provide any exhaustive list of stakeholders' features, but rather to explain their function within the given context.
Cf. UNESCO (ed.) (2007k) (cf. *footnote 4* op. cit.), pp. 10 et seqq.

726 Due to the challenge of grouping stakeholders according to *multi-faceted* criteria, they are provisionally sorted by *affiliation* related to a) United Nations, b) UNESCO or c) miscellaneous, respectively, followed by a visualised summary.
See *Figure 35* in chapter VII 12.3 *Miscellaneous affiliation* on page 186.

727 Cf. United Nations (ed.) (2002 / 2003) (cf. *footnote 117* op. cit.), p. 1; United Nations (ed.) (2004b): United Nations Decade of Education for Sustainable Development. Resolution adopted by the General Assembly on the report of the Second Committee (A/58/486). A/RES/58/219. New York: United Nations, p. 2.

728 Cf. United Nations (ed.) (2003b): Sustainable development: United Nations Decade of Education for Sustainable Development. Report of the Second Committee. A/58/486. New York: United Nations, p. 2; United Nations (ed.) (2002 / 2003) (cf. *footnote 117* op. cit.), pp. 1–2.

729 Cf. United Nations (ed.) (2005b): United Nations Decade of Education for Sustainable Development. Resolution adopted by the General Assembly on the report of the Second Committee (A/59/483/Add.7). A/RES/59/237. New York: United Nations, p. 3; UNESCO (ed.) (2005i) (cf. *footnote 216* op. cit.), p. 3; UNESCO (ed.) (2008h) (cf. *footnote 219* op. cit.), p. 3.

the *Rio Declaration on Environment and Development*[731] in order to implement the provisions of *Agenda 21.*[732] Addressing a range of issues related to sustainable development, the *United Nations Commission on Sustainable Development* is attached to the *United Nations Economic and Social Council* (ECOSOC) as a functional commission.[733] Although it does draw attention to awareness-raising campaigns in the past,[734] education is not considered *"one of the main themes to be addressed".*[735]

---

730 Cf. United Nations (ed.) (1992 / 1993): Resolution on the report of the second Committee. Institutional arrangements to follow up the United Nations Conference on Environment and Development. A/RES/47/191. New York: United Nations, p. 2.

731 Cf. United Nations (1992): Rio Declaration on Environment and Development. Annex I of the Report of the United Nations Conference on Environment and Development, 12/08/1992, Rio de Janeiro. A/CONF. 151/26 (Vol. I). (1); United Nations Commission for Sustainable Development (CSD); United Nations Economic and Social Council (ECOSOC) (eds.) (2003): Report on the eleventh session (27 January 2003 and 28 April–9 May 2003). Official Records, Supplement No. 9. E/2003/29 / E/CN.17/2003/6. New York: United Nations; Fridtjof Nansens Institutt / The Fridtjof Nansens Institute (ed.) (2005) (cf. *footnote 198* op. cit.).

732 I.e. Chapter 38 of *Agenda 21* containing specific *"international institutional arrangements (...) particularly those on the establishment of a high-level Commission on Sustainable Development".*
See United Nations (ed.) (1992 / 1993) (cf. *footnote 730* op. cit.), p. 1; United Nations (ed.) (1993): Agenda 21. United Nations Conference on Environment and Development (UNCED), 3–14 June 1992, Rio de Janeiro, Brazil. A/CONF.151/26/Rev.1(Vol.I). Volume 1993. New York: UN Department of Public Information (1), pp. 456 et seqq; Beisheim, Marianne; Lode, Birgit; Simon, Nils (2011): Ein Rat für Nachhaltige Entwicklung. Vor der Rio-Konferenz 2012: Optionen zur Reform der VN-Nachhaltigkeitsinstitutionen. In: Stiftung Wissenschaft und Politik (SWP) / Deutsches Institut für Internationale Politik und Sicherheit (ed.): SWP-Aktuell. Berlin: Stiftung Wissenschaft und Politik (SWP), Volume 46, pp. 1–8, p. 1.

733 Cf. United Nations Economic and Social Council (ECOSOC) (ed.) (2003): Future programme, organization and methods of work of the Commission on Sustainable Development. Resolutions 2003/61. E/2003/INF/2/Add.4. New York: United Nations, pp. 159–160; Kaasa, Stine Madland (2007) (cf. *footnote 297* op. cit.), p. 1.

734 E.g., in 1998 *"approving an extensive work programme that calls upon governments to incorporate sustainable development objectives into curricula at all levels of education (...)".*
See United Nations Economic Commission for Europe (UNECE); United Nations Economic and Social Council (ECOSOC) (eds.) (2004e): Draft UNECE Strategy for Education for Sustainable Development. Background. Second regional meeting on education for sustainable development (Rome, 15–16 July 2004). CEP/AC.13/2004/8/Add.1. New York: United Nations, p. 3.

735 See UNESCO (ed.) (2005c) (cf. *footnote 23* op. cit.), p. 39.
Cf. United Nations Economic and Social Council (ECOSOC) (ed.) (2003) (cf. *footnote 733* op. cit.), pp. 159–160.

Therefore, a *Sub-Commission on ESD under CSD* was originally intended that would be dedicated solely to *ESD* in order to ensure *effective*[736] *follow-up*[737] in terms of international co-operation and creating momentum for implementation at a national level.[738] The *United Nations Commission on Sustainable Development* (CSD) connects past and ongoing United Nations processes of sustainable development with *DESD*.[739]

The *United Nations Economic Commission for Europe* (UNECE) is one of five regional commissions of the United Nations and was set up in 1947 by the *United Nations Economic and Social Council* (ECOSOC). The major aim is to promote economic integration through the provision of norms, standards and conventions to facilitate international co-operation within and outside the region. However, it comprises a range of specialisation,[740] notable amongst these being *ESD*.[741] Concerning *DESD*, the *United Nations Economic Commission for Europe* is officially appointed and mandated by UNESCO to carry out regional implementation,[742] supported by proper funding, strategy[743] and by globally-recognised[744] means of evaluation.[745] This will be realised through several sub-

736 For a more in-depth analysis on the effectiveness of the *Commission for Sustainable Development* see and cf. Fridtjof Nansens Institutt / The Fridtjof Nansens Institute (ed.) (2005) (cf. *footnote 198* op. cit.); Andresen, Steinar (2007) (cf. *footnote 320* op. cit.), pp. 15–17; Kaasa, Stine Madland (2007) (cf. *footnote 297* op. cit.), pp. 2 et seqq.

737 See Kaasa, Stine Madland (2007) (cf. *footnote 297* op. cit.), p. 1.

738 Cf. Deutscher Bundestag (ed.) (1998) (cf. *footnote 52* op. cit.), pp. 30 et seqq; United Nations Commission for Sustainable Development (CSD); United Nations Economic and Social Council (ECOSOC) (eds.) (2003) (cf. *footnote 731* op. cit.), p. 30; UNESCO (ed.) (2005c) (cf. *footnote 23* op. cit.), p. 39; UNESCO (ed.) (2005j) (cf. *footnote 44* op. cit.), p. 14.

739 Cf. Mayor, Federico (17/10/1992) (cf. *footnote 41* op. cit.), p. 4; UNESCO (ed.) (2005i) (cf. *footnote 216* op. cit.), p. 3; Beisheim, Marianne; Lode, Birgit; Simon, Nils (2011) (cf. *footnote 732* op. cit.), pp. 1–2; Lode, Birgit (2011): What do you think should be the two or three highest priority political outcomes of the United Nations Conference on Sustainable Development (Rio+20), scheduled for Rio de Janeiro in June 2012? In: Natural Resources Forum, Volume 35, Issue 4, pp. 334–342, p. 338.

740 E.g., economic co-operation and integration, energy, environment, housing and land management, population, statistics, timber, trade and transport.

741 Cf. Linn, Monika; Sochirca, Angela (2010): Learning from each other. In: Witthaus, Michele; McCandless, Karen; Lambert, Rebecca (eds.): Tomorrow today. Leicester, United Kingdom: Tudor Rose; UNESCO publishing, pp. 26–28, p. 27.

742 Cf. United Nations Economic Commission for Europe (UNECE); United Nations Economic and Social Council (ECOSOC) (eds.) (2004b) (cf. *footnote 391* op. cit.), p. 2; UNESCO (ed.) (2007k) (cf. *footnote 4* op. cit.), p. 18.

743 Cf. UNESCO (ed.) (2004c) (cf. *footnote 34* op. cit.), p. 35; UNESCO (ed.) (2005j) (cf. *footnote 44* op. cit.), pp. 13–14; United Nations Economic Commission for Europe (UNECE) (ed.) (2006) (cf. *footnote 20* op. cit.).

744 *"The Strategy will be adopted by interested UNECE member States. States outside the region are also encouraged to follow it."*

commissions, such as the *UNECE Steering Committee on ESD,*[746] the *UNECE Expert Group on ESD indicators*[747] or the *UNECE Committee on Environmental Policy* (CEP).[748]

Moreover, *United Nations Inter-Agency Steering Committees* serve to coordinate the *DESD* activities within the respective regions.[749]

See United Nations Economic Commission for Europe (UNECE); United Nations Economic and Social Council (ECOSOC) (eds.) (2004b) (cf. *footnote 391* op. cit.), p. 3; UNESCO Education Sector (ed.) (2007): Good Practices in the UNECE region. Education for Sustainable Development in Action. ED-2007/WS/31 Good Practices N° 2. Paris: UNESCO workshops.

745 Cf. UNESCO (ed.) (2007f) (cf. *footnote 427* op. cit.), p. 5.

746 Cf. United Nations Economic Commission for Europe (UNECE); United Nations Economic and Social Council (ECOSOC) (eds.) (2004a): Draft Vilnius Framework for the Implementation of the UNECE Strategy for Education for Sustainable Development. High-level meeting of Environment and Education Ministries (Vilnius, 17–18 March 2005). CEP/AC.13/2005/4. New York: United Nations, pp. 3–4; United Nations Economic Commission for Europe (UNECE); United Nations Economic and Social Council (ECOSOC) (eds.) (2005e): UNECE Strategy for Education for Sustainable Development. Report of the High-level meeting of Environment and Education Ministries (Vilnius, 17–18 March 2005). CEP/AC.13/2005/3/Rev.1. New York: United Nations, p. 5; United Nations Economic Commission for Europe (UNECE); United Nations Economic and Social Council (ECOSOC) (eds.) (2005g): Vilnius Framework for the Implementation of the UNECE Strategy for Education for Sustainable Development. High-level meeting of Environment and Education Ministries (Vilnius, 17–18 March 2005). CEP/AC.13/2005/4/Rev.1. New York: United Nations, pp. 5–6.

747 Cf. United Nations Economic Commission for Europe (UNECE); United Nations Economic and Social Council (ECOSOC) (eds.) (2005g) (cf. *footnote 746* op. cit.), p. 7.

748 The *UNECE Committee on Environmental Policy* (CEP) serves as mandated coordinating and implementing platform for *DESD* activities within the *UNECE* region.
Cf. United Nations Economic Commission for Europe (UNECE); United Nations Economic and Social Council (ECOSOC) (eds.) (2003a): Draft Terms of Reference of the Task Force on Education for Sustainable Development. First regional meeting on education for sustainable development. Geneva, 19–20 February 2004. CEP/AC.13/2004/4. New York: United Nations; United Nations Economic Commission for Europe (UNECE); United Nations Economic and Social Council (ECOSOC) (eds.) (2005e) (cf. *footnote 746* op. cit.).

749 E.g., *UNECE Steering Committee on ESD*; *Asia-Pacific UN DESD Interagency Steering Committee.*
Cf. United Nations Economic Commission for Europe (UNECE); United Nations Economic and Social Council (ECOSOC) (eds.) (2004h): Provisional Agenda. High-level meeting of Environment and Education Ministries, Vilnius, 17–18 March 2005. CEP/AC.13/2005/1. New York: United Nations; UNESCO (ed.) (2006h) (cf. *footnote 711* op. cit.), pp. 3, 4–5; UNESCO Bangkok (ed.) (2007): Asia-Pacific UN DESD Interagency Steering Committee. Draft Meeting Report. Eighth Meeting. Bangkok: UNESCO Asia and Pacific Regional Bureau for Education.

Since 1972, the *United Nations Environment Programme* (UNEP) has been the designated United Nations body for effectively addressing environmental issues at global and regional level.[750] Its mandate is to co-ordinate the development of consensus on environmental policy. With regard to *DESD* involvement, the *United Nations Environment Programme* attempts to reconcile the environmental with the economic on a public platform, presenting them as two closely interrelated spheres of sustainability through the initiative *Environment for Development.*[751]

The *UNICEF-United Nations Girls Education Initiative* (UNGEI) was launched in 2000 together with *Education for All* (EFA) at the *World Education Forum in Dakar*[752] by United Nations Secretary-General and is co-ordinated by the *United Nations Children's Fund* (UNICEF). Its goal is to bridge the gender gap in primary and secondary education. By 2015 all children should complete primary schooling. Access to all levels of education must be equal for both girls and boys, but particular efforts are to be made to encourage girls in school to complete their education. On the basis of a multi-stakeholder approach, the *UNICEF-United Nations Girls Education Initiative* focuses on girls' education since girls usually face much greater obstacles. Girls and young women are the future *nucleus* for new life, and *DESD* must therefore be concerned to find forms and ways to address girls' education appropriately.[753]

The *United Nations Human Settlements Programme* (UN Habitat) is the United Nations agency assigned to human settlements. Its global mission is the promotion of socially and environmentally sustainable towns and cities.[754] Particular attention is paid to the provision of adequate shelter for all. As it relates to *DESD*, the *United Nations Habitat Initiative* brings together social, environmental and economic dimensions of sustainability. *Best Practices and Local*

---

750 For a more in-depth analysis on the effectiveness of the *Commission for Sustainable Development* and the *United Nations Environment Programme*, respectively, see and cf. Andresen, Steinar (2007) (cf. *footnote 320* op. cit.).

751 For instance, patterns of sustainable consumption are correlated with *up-to-date* lifestyles of youth as target group. An appropriately-designed and appealing training kit exhorts young people to identify attractive ways *"towards sustainable lifestyles"*.
See UNESCO; United Nations Environment Programme (UNEP); Méta (Media, Ecology and Technology Association), et al. (eds.) (2002 / 2008): www.youthXchange.net – towards sustainable lifestyles. training kit on responsible consumption. THE GUIDE. Paris / New York: United Nations Publications.
Cf. Mayor, Federico (17/10/1992) (cf. *footnote 41* op. cit.), p. 4; UNESCO (ed.) (2005c) (cf. *footnote 23* op. cit.), p. 40.

752 Cf. UNESCO (ed.) (2000) (cf. *footnote 541* op. cit.).

753 Cf. UNESCO (ed.) (2005c) (cf. *footnote 23* op. cit.), p. 39.

754 Cf. UN-HABITAT (2010): Education for sustainable cities. In: Witthaus, Michele; McCandless, Karen; Lambert, Rebecca (eds.): Tomorrow today. Leicester, United Kingdom: Tudor Rose; UNESCO publishing, pp. 42–44.

Leadership Programme(s) (BLP) outline viable solutions prioritising networking in relation to *DESD*.[755]

In a nutshell, there is considerable *DESD* commitment of United Nations affiliated bodies. However, the organisational degree differs. Apart from executing core functions of the international system mainly performed by the *United Nations General Assembly*, other United Nations efforts are less formalised or institutionalised in the way of purposefully pointing at *DESD*. In some cases certain synergy effects between organisational assignments proper and *DESD* appear to be rather coincidental. Probably the most notable exception is the *United Nations Economic Commission for Europe* that formally carries out the regional *DESD* mandate in a distinctive way.

11.2 UNESCO affiliation

UNESCO undoubtedly bears the overall responsibility for fulfilling its United Nations mandate of co-ordinating and implementing *DESD* in its role as the *lead agency*.[756] As a consequence of its *dual role*[757] *UNESCO* combines both leadership and implementation.[758] There are three essential levels of *UNESCO* commitment:

a) At national level *UNESCO national commissions* are *key partners* in promoting and implementing *DESD*. This includes the establishment of national *DESD* committees, first and foremost, but also includes the creation of dialogue and exchange concerning resources and innovative *ESD* policies.[759]
b) At regional level *UNESCO regional offices* work directly under the auspices of the UNESCO's Director-General. This structural requirement at the same time limits the influence of the *DESD secretariat* to some extent. *UNESCO regional offices* are primarily responsible for the regional instigation[760] and strategic promotion of *DESD* taking into consideration region-specific characteristics.[761]

---

755 Cf. UNESCO (ed.) (2005c) (cf. *footnote 23* op. cit.), p. 40.

756 See United Nations (ed.) (2002 / 2003) (cf. *footnote 117* op. cit.), p. 1; Bory-Adams, Aline (2010) (cf. *footnote 37* op. cit.), p. 175.

757 See UNESCO (ed.) (2003b) (cf. *footnote 109* op. cit.), p. 3.

758 Cf. UNESCO (ed.) (2005i) (cf. *footnote 216* op. cit.), p. 1; Dhillon, Sam (2008) (cf. *footnote 609* op. cit.), p. 1.

759 Cf. UNESCO (ed.) (2007k) (cf. *footnote 4* op. cit.), p. 14; Deutsche UNESCO-Kommission e. V. (DUK) (2007): Nachhaltigkeit lernen – Deutsche UNESCO-Kommission. www.bne-portal.de. Supported by: Offenhäußer, Dieter; Schlünkes, Kurt and Möller, Lutz.

760 Cf. Matsuura, Koïchiro (01/03/2005) (cf. *footnote 28* op. cit.), p. 3.

761 Cf. UNESCO (ed.) (2003b) (cf. *footnote 109* op. cit.), p. 7; UNESCO (ed.) (2004c) (cf. *footnote 34* op. cit.), p. 35; UNESCO (ed.) (2007k) (cf. *footnote 4* op. cit.), p. 18;

c) At international level *UNESCO* works in full alignment with its global functional assignments and role.[762] With relation to *DESD*, the most critical tasks are co-ordination, facilitation and implementation.[763]

The *DESD Secretariat* or *Section for DESD Co-ordination* (ED/UNP/DESD) is located in the *Education for Sustainable Development Section of the Division for the Co-ordination of United Nations Priorities in Education* based in Paris.[764] It provides oversight, advice, feedback and supports co-ordination with different programme and thematic areas. Additionally the *DESD Secretariat* acts as interface between further networking bodies.[765] A critical task is to ensure the functional coherence of all *in-house* activities vis-à-vis *DESD*.[766]

Adomßent, Maik; Henze, Christa (eds.) (2007): UN Decade of Education for Sustainable Development – The Contribution from Europe. Conference Report. Documentation of the International Conference in the context of the German Presidency of the Council of the European Union. Berlin, 24–25 May 2007. Bonn: Bonner Universitäts-Buchdruckerei, pp. 55, 97, 112.

762 I.e. to be a *laboratory of ideas*, *standard-setter*, *clearinghouse*, *capacity-builder* and *promoter of international cooperation*, and the formulation of global policies and *policy advice*, *standard-setting* and *monitoring*, respectively.
See UNESCO (ed.) (2007f) (cf. *footnote 427* op. cit.), p. 2; Foreign Office of the Federal Republic of Germany / German Commission for UNESCO (ed.) (2007) (cf. *footnote 21* op. cit.), p. 14; UNESCO (ed.) (2007m) (cf. *footnote 216* op. cit.), p. 2.

763 Cf. UNESCO (ed.) (2005c) (cf. *footnote 23* op. cit.), p. 43; UNESCO (ed.) (2007k) (cf. *footnote 4* op. cit.), pp. 10 et seqq, 13 et seqq.

764 The very fact that *DESD* co-ordination is settled under the auspices of the *UNESCO Education Sector* and *United Nations Priorities* reveals its importance and clear commitment to education as driving issue.
Cf. Michelsen, Gerd (08/05/2007): Interview Talk with Aline Bory-Adams (UNESCO, Paris). Education for Sustainable Development international. Online-Magazine "Education for Sustainable Development". In: BNE-Journal, Volume May 2007, Issue 1, pp. 1–8, p. 1.
See *Figure 33* in chapter VII 12.2 *UNESCO affiliation* on page 175, and *Figure 34* in chapter VII 12.2 *UNESCO affiliation* on page 179.

765 E.g., *Inter-Agency Committee* (IAC), the *DESD Reference Group*, the *Monitoring and Evaluation Expert Group (MEEG)*, the *UNESCO National Commissions* and the *UNESCO Regional Offices and Field Offices*.

766 Cf. UNESCO (ed.) (2007k) (cf. *footnote 4* op. cit.), p. 10; UNESCO (ed.) (August 2007) (cf. *footnote 693* op. cit.), p. 1.

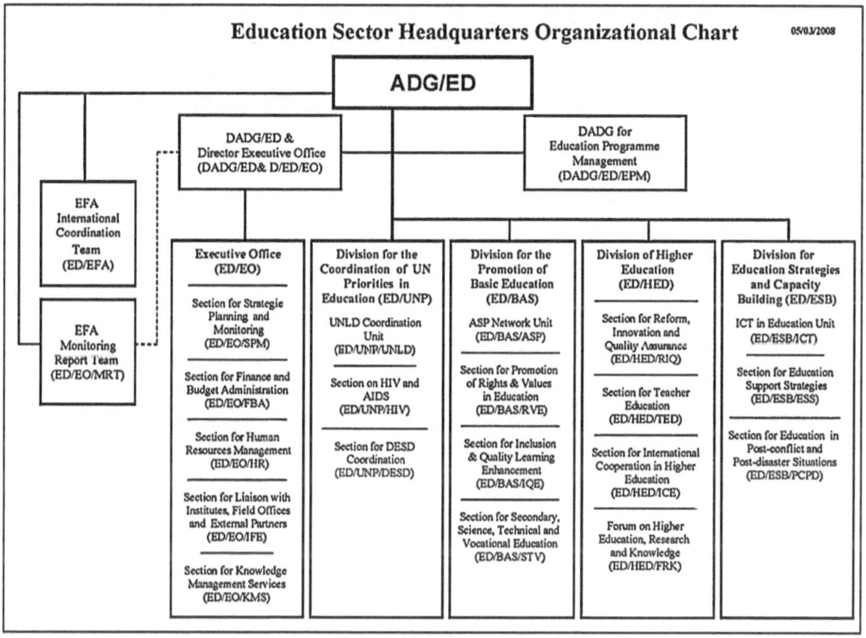

Figure 33: Organisational DESD affiliation[767]

The *UNESCO Executive Board* is elected by the *UNESCO General Conference* and, along with the *UNESCO Secretariat*, is one of the three constitutional organs of UNESCO.[768] It approves the programme of UNESCO work and corresponding budget estimates. Additionally, the *UNESCO Executive Board* ensures the effective and efficient execution of the programme by UNESCO's Director-General. This applies to *DESD* as well: the *UNESCO Executive Board* approves strategic *DESD* programme activities,[769] budgetary planning[770] and provides financing as appropriate.

767 The chart does not only depict the institutional location and setting of *DESD* but does also recall that *DESD* ranges not among the one and exclusive priorities of UNESCO. As shown the *Division for the Co-ordination of United Nations Priorities in Education* comprises of further prioritised realms, too. This certainly impacts the organisation's leadership efforts of *DESD*.
See UNESCO (2008): Education Sector Headquarters Organizational Chart. Slightly adapted and modified version. UNESCO Education Sector.

768 Cf. UNESCO (ed.) (1945) (cf. *footnote 420* op. cit.), pp. 10–17.

769 With particular reference to means of implementation and assessment.
Cf. UNESCO (ed.) (2002f) (cf. *footnote 312* op. cit.); UNESCO (ed.) (2004c) (cf. *footnote 34* op. cit.); UNESCO (ed.) (2005f) (cf. *footnote 37* op. cit.); UNESCO (ed.)

At the *UNESCO General Conference* the representatives of member states meet every two years to discuss and adopt the organisation's focal issues by setting programmes and budget, usually proposed beforehand by the *UNESCO Executive Board.* The *UNESCO General Conference* is similarly involved with *DESD*, but by comparison has much less involvement in operational questions.[771]

The *High-Level Panel on the DESD* (HLP) was set up in 2004, convened by UNESCO's Director-General. It meets occasionally to provide guidance to UNESCO on the implementation of the *DESD*. It is composed of prominent personalities and experts in all fields related to *ESD*. The *High-Level Panel on DESD* is assigned to advise and guide UNESCO with respect to intensifying support for *DESD* at the highest institutional level and assisting UNESCO's partners in mobilising resources for *ESD*.[772]

The *Reference Group for the DESD* began advisory work in 2006. It is comprised of experts in different spheres of *ESD* in order to provide functional assistance to the *DESD Secretariat* and UNESCO, particularly in matters of strategic planning, such as the co-ordination and mobilisation of stakeholders.[773]

Underpinning the interdisciplinary and holistic approach of *DESD*, a *Network of UNESCO focal points* assists in the consolidation of existing programmes and activities hosted by UNESCO sectors. For that purpose *"focal points have been identified within different sectors to maximize participation in the implementation of the DESD (agenda)"*.[774] Those in charge of these focal points are invited to attend regular meetings organised by the *DESD Secretariat*.

Given the fact that *"UNESCO attaches great importance to an intersectoral 'one UNESCO' approach"*[775] as *main advocate*[776] for *DESD*, an *Inter-*

(2005j) (cf. *footnote 44* op. cit.); UNESCO (ed.) (2008h) (cf. *footnote 219* op. cit.); UNESCO (ed.) (2008h) (cf. *footnote 219* op. cit.).

770 Cf. UNESCO (ed.) (2004a) (cf. *footnote 615* op. cit.); UNESCO (ed.) (2006a) (cf. *footnote 616* op. cit.); UNESCO (ed.) (2008a) (cf. *footnote 83* op. cit.); UNESCO (ed.) (2009a) (cf. *footnote 618* op. cit.).

771 Cf. UNESCO (ed.) (2008h) (cf. *footnote 219* op. cit.); UNESCO (ed.) (2007j) (cf. *footnote 39* op. cit.); UNESCO (ed.) (2008f): Report by the Director-General on the development and management of intersectoral platforms. Executive Board. 179 EX/16. Paris: UNESCO publishing; UNESCO (2008): Education Today Newsletter. Education for All by 2015.

772 Cf. UNESCO (ed.) (2007k) (cf. *footnote 4* op. cit.), p. 10; UNESCO (ed.) (2007f) (cf. *footnote 427* op. cit.), p. 3; UNESCO (ed.) (August 2007) (cf. *footnote 693* op. cit.), p. 2.

773 Cf. UNESCO (ed.) (2007k) (cf. *footnote 4* op. cit.), pp. 11–12; UNESCO (ed.) (2007f) (cf. *footnote 427* op. cit.), p. 3.

774 See UNESCO (ed.) (2007k) (cf. *footnote 4* op. cit.), p. 13.

775 See UNESCO (ed.) (2007k) (cf. *footnote 4* op. cit.), p. 13; UNESCO (ed.) (2007f) (cf. *footnote 427* op. cit.), p. 2.

776 See Dhillon, Sam (2008) (cf. *footnote 609* op. cit.).

Sectoral Working Group on ESD (IWG) was set up in 2005 by UNESCO's Director-General.[777] In order to create a broad *enabling environment*,[778] it comprises representatives from all UNESCO programme sectors and offices, including strategic planning and field co-ordination, external relations and co-operation. In addition, UNESCO institutes and regional offices around the globe are also invited to participate. Firstly, the *Inter-Sectoral Working Group* assists the UNESCO in-house Action plan originally contributing to *DESD*.[779] Secondly, it provides recommendations to all UNESCO sectors, divisions and field offices on how to integrate goals and objectives of *DESD* into their assigned activities. Thirdly, settled under the auspices of the *Assistant Director-General for Education*, the *Inter-Sectoral Working Group* fosters inter-sectoral co-ordination amongst the UNESCO headquarters in Paris, regional bureaus, field offices and institutes, with a particular emphasis on linking *DESD* to other *core* initiatives[780] within the educational field.[781]

The *ESD Inter-sectoral Platform* constitutes another biennially scheduled UNESCO *in-house* initiative, led by the *UNESCO Education Sector*, to improve existing mechanisms and frameworks in order to generate increased inter-sectoral *DESD* synergies and enhanced impact. To this end, the *ESD Inter-sectoral Platform* aims above all to involve as many substantial contributions from all *UNESCO sectors*, including field offices, as possible.[782]

The *Inter-Agency Committee for the DESD* (IAC), constituted in 2006, was established to ensure *harmonious international co-ordination*,[783] exchange, support and funding of *DESD* at all levels.[784] It is considered an effective forum in

777 Cf. Blue Note DG/Note/05/34; UNESCO (ed.) (2005i) (cf. *footnote 216* op. cit.), p. 4; UNESCO (ed.) (2006e): Follow-up to 166 EX/DECISION 3.6.1 concerning the proposal for the elaboration of an education programme for the sustainable management of freshwater resources. Report by the Director-General on the development of an intersectoral strategy on education for the management of freshwater resources. 174 EX/INF.13. Paris: UNESCO publishing, p. 4; UNESCO (ed.) (August 2007) (cf. *footnote 693* op. cit.), p. 1.

778 See Dhillon, Sam (2008) (cf. *footnote 609* op. cit.).

779 Cf. UNESCO (ed.) (2007m) (cf. *footnote 216* op. cit.), pp. 4–5.
Cf. *Figure 81* in chapter IX 4.3 *Characteristics* on page 345.

780 E.g., the *Literacy Initiative for Empowerment* (LIFE), the *Teacher Training Initiative for sub-Saharan Africa* (TIISSA) and the *Global Initiative on HIV / AIDS and Education* (EDUCAIDS).

781 Cf. UNESCO (ed.) (2007k) (cf. *footnote 4* op. cit.), p. 13; UNESCO (ed.) (2007f) (cf. *footnote 427* op. cit.), p. 3; Dhillon, Sam (2008) (cf. *footnote 609* op. cit.).

782 *"Given UNESCO's multi-sectoral capacities, UNESCO is well placed to act as the main advocate for ESD in a holistic perspective."*
See Dhillon, Sam (2008) (cf. *footnote 609* op. cit.), p. 1.

783 See UNESCO (ed.) (2006h) (cf. *footnote 711* op. cit.), p. 3; UNESCO (ed.) (2007k) (cf. *footnote 4* op. cit.), p. 15.

784 Cf. UNESCO (ed.) (2007m) (cf. *footnote 216* op. cit.), p. 4.

which to integrate the *ESD* agenda into the work of the United Nations family in a fashion both timely and coherent. This is to be achieved in two ways: promoting dialogue structures between United Nations agencies and beyond for *open-ended*[785] collaboration in favour of *DESD* implementation; and reinforcing and emphasising the crucial role of all forms of education by strategically linking *DESD* to other ongoing international initiatives.[786]

The *Monitoring and Evaluation Expert Group* (MEEG) constituted ad hoc in 2007, constitutes the *clearinghouse* with regard to *DESD* effectiveness by means of self-assessment, or *in-house* evaluation.[787] Convening frequently, the board is instructed to develop an adequate framework of global *DESD* monitoring and evaluation, required to pay attention to any and every *ESD* dimension, to keep up with the multi-stakeholder approach and to appreciate independent regional strategies.[788] In search of sound indicators, the *Monitoring and Evaluation Expert Group* interfaces with systems of monitoring and evaluation already in place and used by other United Nations global initiatives. Both global frameworks and the relevant set of indicators will feed into two reports corresponding with UNESCO's dual and interrelated roles: The findings are to contribute firstly to the regular reports[789] presented by the *DESD Secretariat* to the United Nations General Assembly and secondly to inform the *UNESCO Executive Board* about the progress of implementation and also on the organisation's own contribution to *DESD* by the end of each *biennium*.[790]

---

785 See UNESCO (ed.) (2005i) (cf. *footnote 216* op. cit.), p. 3.

786 E.g., development banks, *Organisation for Economic Co-operation and Development* (OECD), representative regional groupings (*Association of South East Asian Nations* (ASEAN), *African Union* (AU), *European Union* (EU), *Organization of American States* (OAS), *Southern Africa Development Co-ordination Conference* (SADCC), etc.), and NGO.
Cf. UNESCO (ed.) (2005c) (cf. *footnote 23* op. cit.), p. 41; UNESCO (ed.) (2007k) (cf. *footnote 4* op. cit.), p. 11; UNESCO (ed.) (August 2007) (cf. *footnote 693* op. cit.), p. 1.

787 Cf. UNESCO (ed.) (2007f) (cf. *footnote 427* op. cit.), p. 3; UNESCO (ed.) (August 2007) (cf. *footnote 693* op. cit.), p. 17.

788 Cf. United Nations Commission for Sustainable Development (CSD); United Nations Economic and Social Council (ECOSOC) (eds.) (2003) (cf. *footnote 731* op. cit.), p. 36.

789 I.e. in 2010 and 2015.

790 Cf. UNESCO (ed.) (2007k) (cf. *footnote 4* op. cit.), pp. 12–13; UNESCO (ed.) (August 2007) (cf. *footnote 693* op. cit.), pp. 1–2; UNESCO (ed.) (August 2007) (cf. *footnote 693* op. cit.), p. 1; UNESCO (ed.) (2007f) (cf. *footnote 427* op. cit.), p. 3.

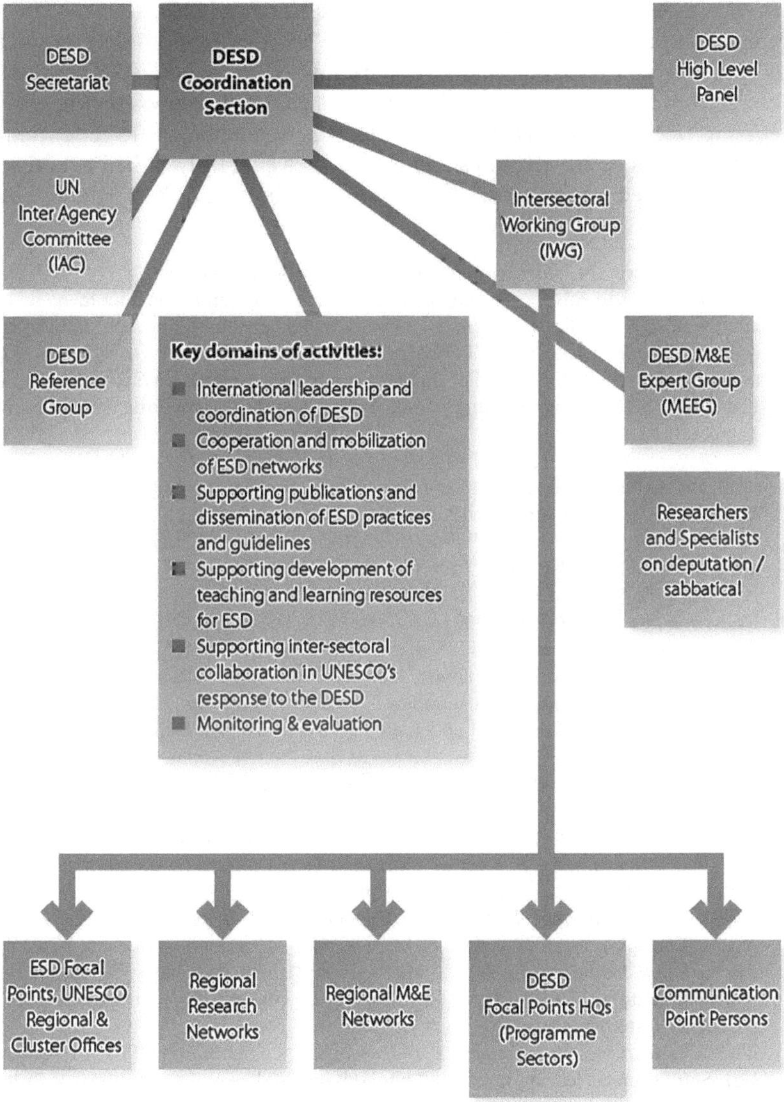

Figure 34: UNESCO DESD co-ordination[791]

791 The *DESD Secretariat* equivalent to the *Section for DESD Co-ordination* (ED/UNP/DESD) mainly provides strategic links to UNESCO-related stakeholders, groups and networks.
See UNESCO (ed.) (2007k) (cf. *footnote 4* op. cit.), p. 59.

UNESCO Chairs reflect the primary activity of the academic *UNITWIN*[792] programme established in 1992.[793] Those *UNESCO Chair* holders around the globe specialising in *ESD*-related issues are invited to assist *DESD* by fostering professional exchange with each other and by arranging *ad-hoc* meetings.[794]

UNESCO scientific institutes are likewise encouraged to contribute to *DESD*, namely those six institutes and two centres expressly linked to and with a specialisation in education work.[795] They are part of *UNESCO's Education Sec-*

792 I.e. abbreviation for *University Twinning and networking scheme.*

793 It is mandated to advance research, training and programme development in higher education by building university networks and encouraging *inter-university* co-operation through transfer of knowledge across borders. The programme is popular and well renowned: At the end of 2009, there are 653 existing *UNESCO Chairs* and 62 *UNITWIN Networks* comprising of some 770 institutions covering 70 disciplines in 126 countries.
Cf. Mayor, Federico (17/10/1992) (cf. *footnote 41* op. cit.), p. 4; UNESCO (ed.) (1992): Resolutions. Records of the General Conference. Twenty-sixth Session Paris, 15 October–7 November 1991. Paris: UNESCO workshops (1), pp. 20, 33; UNESCO (ed.) (2009b): Guidelines and procedures for the UNITWIN/UNESCO Chairs Programme. ED/HED/UNITWIN/2006/PI/1 rev. 4. Paris: UNESCO publishing.

794 E.g., network (pool) of *UNESCO Chairs on ESD* in France.
Cf. Mayor, Federico (17/10/1992) (cf. *footnote 41* op. cit.), p. 4; UNESCO (ed.) (1992) (cf. *footnote 793* op. cit.), pp. 20, 33; UNESCO (ed.) (2009b) (cf. *footnote 793* op. cit.); Institut international de planification de l'éducation (IIPE) (ed.) (2009): Former des acteurs du développement durable. Les défis relevés par le Pôle Développement Durable des Chaires UNESCO en France. Edited by Patrick Blandin. Paris: UNESCO workshops.

795 Cf. UNESCO (ed.) (2005j) (cf. *footnote 44* op. cit.), p. 10; UNESCO (ed.) (2006i) (cf. *footnote 579* op. cit.), p. 6.
These are the following, indicated by scope and registered office:
UNESCO International Bureau of Education (IBE) (Geneva, Switzerland): Concentrating on content and methods of education;
UNESCO International Institute for Capacity-Building in Africa (IICBA) (Addis Ababa, Ethiopia): Developing networks of teacher-education institutes in Africa;
International Institute for Educational Planning (IIEP / IIPE) (Paris, France / Buenos Aires, Argentina): Strengthening the capacity of countries to plan and manage their education systems;
UNESCO Institute for Information Technologies in Education (IITE) (Moscow, Russia): Setting-up a clearing house and undertaking studies on the main trends in the application of Information and Communication Technologies in education;
UNESCO Institute for Lifelong Learning (UIL) (Hamburg, Germany): Focusing particularly on adult, non-formal and lifelong learning;
UNESCO International Institute for Higher Education in Latin America and the Caribbean (IESALC) (Caracas, Venezuela): Implementing a plan of action for the transformation of higher education in the region including university co-operation;
European Centre for Higher Education (CEPES) (Bucharest, Romania): Promoting co-operation and reform in higher education in Europe; and

tor in order to assist countries in solving education problems related to *ESD*, in this case prominently:

a) The *UNESCO International Institute for Educational Planning* (IIEP) dedicates efforts to equity of, quality in and access to education linked to culture. The agenda clearly stresses capacity-building as a prerequisite and as an educational tool for acquiring technical knowledge and skills for development focusing on sustainable structures, organisation and administration of education (*planning*) rather than on implementation;[796] and
b) The *UNESCO Institute for Lifelong Learning* (UIL) carries out research on the interface between literacy and sustainability in education.[797]

To sum up, in terms of stakeholders UNESCO approaches *DESD* in a much more strategic and focused way. Commonly known as *One-UNESCO approach*, due to steering and managerial reasons that concise *DESD* strategy certainly applies to a greater extent to UNESCO bodies proper than to UNESCO-affiliated institutions.

11.3 Miscellaneous affiliation

Civil society is *the* basis and *backbone* of *ESD*. It must be mentioned first, because without the commitment of civil society the whole process of *DESD* becomes obsolete; no institution would be necessary to co-ordinate or implement anything. *Civil society* involvement at national, regional and international scale represented through individuals, associations, foundations,[798] *non-governmental organisations* (NGO),[799] faith-based organisations, *special interest* groups[800] and networks is considered critical for the *bottom-up* approach of *DESD*.[801] This in-

---

International Centre for Technical and Vocational Education and Training (UNEVOC) (Bonn, Germany): Improving education for the world of work.

796 E.g., issues, such as structures for literacy, cultural diversity in educational planning. Cf. Lind, Agneta (2009) (cf. *footnote 480* op. cit.); Inglis, Christine (2008) (cf. *footnote 77* op. cit.).

797 Cf. Bhola, Harbans S.; Valdivielso Gómez, Sofía (eds.) (2008): Signposts to literacy for sustainable development. Complementary studies. Supported by: Ouane, Adama. Hamburg: UNESCO Institute for Lifelong Learning.

798 Cf. Michelsen, Gerd (08/05/2007) (cf. *footnote 764* op. cit.), p. 2.

799 Cf. Blaze Corcoran, Peter; Maathai, Wangari (2005) (cf. *footnote 524* op. cit.); UNESCO; The Earth Charter Initiative (ECI) (eds.) (2007d) (cf. *footnote 585* op. cit.).

800 E.g., such as youth groups and women's groups. Cf. Centre for Environment Education (CEE); South Asia Youth Environment Network (SAYEN) (eds.) (2007) (cf. *footnote 689* op. cit.).

801 Cf. UNESCO (ed.) (2003b) (cf. *footnote 109* op. cit.), p. 4; UNESCO (ed.) (2005c) (cf. *footnote 23* op. cit.), p. 36; UNESCO (ed.) (2005j) (cf. *footnote 44* op. cit.), pp. 11, 12; Haigh, Martin J. (2009) (cf. *footnote 110* op. cit.).

cludes partnerships with national media organisations and companies, too. The media are *lighthouses*[802] in the establishment of contacts amongst stakeholders through communication strategies.[803] As heterogeneous and diversified as *civil society* is, equally manifold are its expressions of its commitment to *ESD*. When looking at educational institutions in the narrow and formal sense, for instance, one can see that much good practice of *ESD* has been implemented, both at schools[804] as well as universities,[805] academic and other research institutions.[806]

Member states are recommended to create national *ESD Hubs* assigned *"to energize and coordinate the implementation of (...) DESD (according to local needs) in each country"*.[807] These *ESD Hubs* may considerably vary in design and function ranging from occasionally-meeting dialogue platforms to *small permanent units*[808] or *task forces*,[809] portals or *self-contained* committees.[810] An-

---

802 See Krott, Maximilian (2002) (cf. *footnote 203* op. cit.), p. 971.

803 Cf. UNESCO (ed.) (2005c) (cf. *footnote 23* op. cit.), p. 36; UNESCO (ed.) (2005j) (cf. *footnote 44* op. cit.), p. 12; UNESCO; Thomson Foundation (eds.) (2008a): Media as partners in education for sustainable development: A Training and Resource Kit. CI/COM/2008/PI/2. Edited by Eleanor Bird; Richard Lutz; Christine Warwick. Paris: UNESCO publishing (UNESCO Series on Journalism Education).

804 E.g., *UNESCO Associated Schools*.
Cf. UNESCO (ed.) (2007e) (cf. *footnote 585* op. cit.); UNESCO; UNESCO Associated Schools (eds.) (2008b) (cf. *footnote 480* op. cit.); UNESCO; UNESCO Associated Schools (eds.) (2009b) (cf. *footnote 585* op. cit.).

805 Cf. United Nations University (UNU); UNESCO; International Association of Universities (IAU) (eds.) (2002): Ubuntu Declaration. On Education and Science and Technology for Sustainable Development. WSSD Johannesburg Summit. New York: United Nations; UNESCO; United Nations University (UNU) (eds.) (2005b): International Conference on Globalization and Education for Sustainable Development. Sustaining the Future. Nagoya, Japan, 28–29 June 2005. Paris: UNESCO publishing.

806 Cf. UNESCO; International Association of Universities (IAU); COPERNICUS-CAMPUS; Association of University Leaders for a Sustainable Future (ULSF) (2001): Global Higher Education for Sustainability Partnership (GHESP). Lüneburg Declaration. Universität Lüneburg / University of Lüneburg; UNESCO; International Association of Universities (IAU); COPERNICUS-CAMPUS; Association of University Leaders for a Sustainable Future (ULSF) (2002): Global Higher Education for Sustainability Partnership (GHESP). Memorandum of Understanding; UNESCO; International Association of Universities (IAU); COPERNICUS-CAMPUS; Association of University Leaders for a Sustainable Future (ULSF) (2004): Global Higher Education for Sustainability Partnership (GHESP). WSSD Type II Partnership. Action Plan; Ginkel, Hans van (2010): For our common future: education for sustainable development. In: Witthaus, Michele; McCandless, Karen; Lambert, Rebecca (eds.): Tomorrow today. Leicester, United Kingdom: Tudor Rose; UNESCO publishing, pp. 29–31, pp. 30–31.

807 See UNESCO (ed.) (2005c) (cf. *footnote 23* op. cit.), p. 35.

808 See UNESCO (ed.) (2005c) (cf. *footnote 23* op. cit.), p. 35.

809 See UNESCO (ed.) (2005j) (cf. *footnote 44* op. cit.), p. 12.

other proposal for an entity envisaged at national level to *"bring all stakeholders together and build momentum"*,[811] the *National ESD Consultative Group*, was withdrawn soon after.[812]

Provisionally termed the *regional ESD Caucus*,[813] stakeholders meet in differently composed groupings at regional level.[814] As far as the *UNECE* region is concerned this refers to meaningful stakeholders, such as the *European Union* (EU)[815] or *Organisation for Economic Co-operation and Development* (OECD).[816]

---

810 E.g., Germany: National (Online) Platform Education for Sustainable Development (BNE).
Cf. Deutsche UNESCO-Kommission e. V. (DUK) (ed.) (2006): UNESCO heute. UN-Dekade "Bildung für nachhaltige Entwicklung". In: Zeitschrift der Deutschen UNESCO-Kommission, Volume 2006, Issue 1. Bonn: Bonner Universitäts-Buchdruckerei, pp. 1–2; Deutsche UNESCO-Kommission e. V. (DUK) (2007): Bildung für Nachhaltige Entwicklung (BNE)-Portal. Supported by: Sobieraj, Anke and Diepenbrock, Freya. Published by: Deutsche UNESCO-Kommission e. V. (DUK) and Bundesministerium für Bildung und Forschung (BMBF). Deutsche UNESCO-Kommission e. V. (DUK); Freie Universität Berlin; Deutsche UNESCO-Kommission e. V. (DUK) (2007) (cf. *footnote 759* op. cit.); Leicht, Alexander; Plum, Jacqueline; Fuchs, Max (2007) (cf. *footnote 19* op. cit.), pp. 7–13; Adomßent, Maik; Henze, Christa (eds.) (2007) (cf. *footnote 761* op. cit.).

811 See UNESCO (ed.) (2005c) (cf. *footnote 23* op. cit.), pp. 35–36.

812 Cf. UNESCO (ed.) (2005c) (cf. *footnote 23* op. cit.), p. 35 with UNESCO (ed.) (2005j) (cf. *footnote 44* op. cit.).

813 See UNESCO (ed.) (2005c) (cf. *footnote 23* op. cit.), p. 38.

814 Cf. UNESCO (ed.) (2005j) (cf. *footnote 44* op. cit.), p. 10.

815 Mainly focusing on aspects of governance and leadership in terms of own initiatives, strategies, etc.
Cf. Council of the European Union (ed.) (2006): Renewed Sustainable Development Strategy. Review of the EU Sustainable Development Strategy (EU SDS) – Renewed Strategy. 10917/06. Brussels: Publications Office of the European Union / Europa Publications Ltd., p. 22; UNESCO (ed.) (2006h) (cf. *footnote 711* op. cit.), pp. 3–4; UNESCO (ed.) (2007k) (cf. *footnote 4* op. cit.), pp. 33 et seqq.

816 Particularly referring to education competencies, skills training and capacity-building.
Cf. Rychen, Dominique Simone; Salganik, Laura Hersh (2001): Defining and selecting key competencies. Seattle: Hogrefe & Huber; Key DeSeCo publications; Rychen, Dominique Simone; Salganik, Laura Hersh (2003): Key competencies for a successful life and a well-functioning society. Cambridge, Massachusetts: Hogrefe & Huber; Key DeSeCo publications; United Nations Economic Commission for Europe (UNECE); United Nations Economic and Social Council (ECOSOC) (eds.) (2005g) (cf. *footnote 746* op. cit.), p. 4; Organization for Economic Cooperation & Development (OECD) (ed.) (2005): The Definition and Selection of Key Competences. Executive Summary. Paris: Key DeSeCo publications, pp. 4, 6; Deutsche UNESCO-Kommission e. V. (DUK) (ed.) (2007) (cf. *footnote 24* op. cit.), p. 18; King, Kenneth (2007) (cf. *footnote 536* op. cit.), p. 382.

The *private sector* is another obstacle to determine *DESD* success: businesses, companies as well as other private associations are encouraged to join *ESD* as broad *Public-Private-Partnerships* (PPP).[817] *Private sector* commitment to *ESD* may be described in two main ways. Both are relatively recent developments. On the one hand, the United Nations initiative of *Global Compact*[818] is mandated to involve business in *DESD* under the assumption that *"(g)ood performance on environmental, social and governance issues in day-to-day business operations contributes directly to the creation of stable and inclusive markets".*[819] On the other hand, *Public-Private-Partnerships* (PPP)[820] illustrate a more general interest in *"enhance(d) cooperation between the United Nations and all relevant partners, in particular the private sector"*[821] and beyond. Ap-

---

817 Cf. Soubbotina, Tatyana P. (2004) (cf. *footnote 86* op. cit.), pp. 61 et seqq; United Nations Economic Commission for Europe (UNECE); United Nations Economic and Social Council (ECOSOC) (eds.) (2004b) (cf. *footnote 391* op. cit.); UNESCO (ed.) (2006j) (cf. *footnote 578* op. cit.); Fien, John (2010): The private sector and education for sustainable development. In: Witthaus, Michele; McCandless, Karen; Lambert, Rebecca (eds.): Tomorrow today. Leicester, United Kingdom: Tudor Rose; UNESCO publishing, pp. 52–53.

818 Cf. UNESCO (ed.) (2005c) (cf. *footnote 23* op. cit.), p. 39; UNESCO (ed.) (2005j) (cf. *footnote 44* op. cit.), p. 10; Pies, Ingo; Winning, Alexandra von (eds.) (2006): Die UN-Dekade "Bildung für eine nachhaltige Entwicklung" und der Beitrag des Global Compact. Eine wirtschaftsethische Perspektive. Halle an der Saale: Lehrstuhl für Wirtschaftsethik an der Martin-Luther-Universität Halle-Wittenberg; Universitäts- und Landesbibliothek Sachsen-Anhalt (Diskussionspapier / Lehrstuhl für Wirtschaftsethik, Martin-Luther-Universität Halle-Wittenberg, 06,5); United Nations Global Compact (ed.) (2007a): Enhancing Partnership Value. A Tool for Assessing Sustainability and Impact. New York: United Nations Global Compact Office; United Nations Global Compact (ed.) (2007b): Joining Forces for Change. Demonstrating innovation and impact through UN-Business Partnerships. New York: United Nations Global Compact Office.

819 See United Nations Global Compact (2007): Issues. Business and Sustainable Development, p. 1.
Global business initiatives of sustainable development beyond United Nations are frequently termed *corporate sustainability*.
See Dow Jones Sustainability Indexes (DJSI) (2009): Corporate sustainability. Published by: SAM Indexes GmbH.

820 Cf. United Nations (ed.) (2002c): Towards global partnerships. A/RES/56/76. New York: United Nations; Nelson, Jane (2002): Building partnerships. Cooperation between the United Nations system and the private sector. New York: UN Department of Public Information; United Nations Publications; UNESCO (ed.) (2005c) (cf. *footnote 23* op. cit.), p. 22; United Nations Global Compact (2007) (cf. *footnote 819* op. cit.), p. 2; United Nations Global Compact (ed.) (2007b) (cf. *footnote 818* op. cit.), p. 2; Hörtreiter, Isabel (2007) (cf. *footnote 510* op. cit.).

821 See United Nations (ed.) (2001): Towards global partnerships. A/RES/55/215. New York: United Nations, p. 1.

plied on a national scale, they are considered promising and full of potential.[822] In this respect, publicly appointed *ESD Champions*[823] or those current tenants of this position may serve as positive examples to clearly *"identify capacity-building needs and the actor best placed to meet them"*[824] in society.

To conclude, all other stakeholders are at best loosely affiliated with *DESD*. Respective platforms are intended to serve as *intensifiers of co-operation* among stakeholders in order to increase goodwill, encourage momentum and instantly support emerging commitment.

Cf. UNESCO (ed.) (2005c) (cf. *footnote 23* op. cit.), p. 22; United Nations (ed.) (2005a): Towards global partnerships. Enhanced cooperation between the United Nations and all relevant partners, in particular the private sector. Report of the Secretary-General. A/60/214. New York: United Nations.

822 Cf. UNESCO (ed.) (2005c) (cf. *footnote 23* op. cit.), p. 36; UNESCO (ed.) (2005j) (cf. *footnote 44* op. cit.), pp. 10, 15, 18, 22; Gerner, Martin (14/09/2009) (cf. *footnote 407* op. cit.).

823 See UNESCO (ed.) (2005c) (cf. *footnote 23* op. cit.), pp. 7, 40.

824 See UNESCO (ed.) (2005j) (cf. *footnote 44* op. cit.), p. 12.

DESD stakeholder	Range	Motivation	Institutionalization	Affiliation	Assignment
United Nations General Assembly	International	Promoting sustainable development	Fully	United Nations	Implementation
United Nations Commission on Sustainable	International	Promoting sustainable development by mandate	Fully	United Nations	Implementation
United Nations Economic Commission for Europe	Regional	Promoting sustainable development by mandate	Fully	United Nations	Leadership
					Implementation
United Nations Inter-Agency Steering	Regional	Coordinating *DESD*	Partly	United Nations	Implementation
United Nations Environment Programme	International	Promoting environmentally sustainable	Fully	United Nations	Implementation
UNICEF-United Nations Girls Education Initiative	International	Promoting gender equity in education	Partly	United Nations	Implementation
United Nations Human Settlements Programme	International	Promoting sustainable urban development	Fully	United Nations	Implementation
UNESCO	International	Promoting *DESD* by mandate	Fully	UNESCO	Leadership
					Implementation
UNESCO national commissions	Local	Promoting and coordinating *DESD*	Fully	UNESCO	Implementation
	Sub-regional				
UNESCO regional offices	Regional	Promoting and coordinating *DESD*	Fully	UNESCO	Implementation
	International				
DESD Secretariat	International	Coordinating *DESD*	Fully	UNESCO	Leadership
UNESCO Executive Board	International	Approving *DESD* strategic planning and financing	Fully	UNESCO	Leadership
UNESCO General Conference	International	Approving *DESD* strategic planning and financing	Fully	UNESCO	Leadership
High-Level Panel on the DESD	International	Guiding UNESCO	Partly	UNESCO	Leadership
Reference Group for the DESD	International	Advising UNESCO	Fully	UNESCO	Leadership
Network of UNESCO focal points	International	Consolidating *DESD* programme activities	Fully	UNESCO	Implementation
Inter-Sectoral Working Group on ESD	International	Integrating *DESD* programme sectors	Fully	UNESCO	Implementation
ESD Inter-sectoral Platform	International	Promoting inter-sectoral synergies	Fully	UNESCO	Implementation
Inter-Agency Committee for the DESD	International	Linking *DESD* structures and programmes	Fully	UNESCO	Leadership
Monitoring and Evaluation Expert Group	International	Assessing *DESD*	Fully	UNESCO	Leadership
					Implementation
UNESCO Chairs	International	Assisting *DESD*	Fully	UNESCO	Implementation
UNESCO scientific institutes	Regional	Advocating *DESD*	Fully	UNESCO	Implementation
	International		Partly		
Civil society	Local	Supporting *DESD*	Fully	Miscellaneous	Implementation
	Regional		Partly		
	International		None		
ESD Hubs	National	Coordinating and assisting *DESD*	Fully	Miscellaneous	Implementation
			Partly		
Private sector	Local	Supporting *DESD*	Fully	Miscellaneous	Implementation
	Regional		Partly		
	International		None		

Figure 35: Overview of DESD stakeholders[825]

12 Milestones

Having examined the fundamentals of *DESD*, a historical contextualisation of the *ESD* process will enhance understanding. Therefore, the global evolution of education combined with sustainable development will be roughly outlined, with reference to particular milestones that have led to *DESD*.[826] This *close-up* perspective of the following *travaux préparatoires* is necessary because otherwise dealing with every single aspect in greater detail is a task both too far-reaching and extensive at this stage.

825 This chart summarises *DESD* involvement by grouping stakeholders according to geographical range, general motivation, level of institutionalisation, mode of affiliation, and functional assignment.

826 See *Table 22* in chapter VII 13 *Milestones* on page 187.

Table 22: Milestones of DESD[827]

Year	*Indication*	*Profile*
1948	*Universal Declaration of Human Rights*[828]	Stating that everyone has the fundamental right to education.
1962	*Silent spring*[829]	Birth of environmental awareness due to ecological degradation.
1968	*UNESCO's Man and the Biosphere Programme* (MAB)[830]	The first intergovernmental conference to reconcile environment and development organised by UNESCO.

827 This table tries to bridge the gap between multiple concerns that correspond to crucial aspects of *DESD*, either directly or indirectly. These are different types and scopes of education, developmental issues, or broadly discussed approaches of sustainability.
Cf. Bartholomäi, Reinhard (1997) (cf. *footnote 98* op. cit.), pp. 52–72; Hartmann, Eva-Maria (2002): 10 Jahre nach Rio. Auf dem Weg zum Weltgipfel für nachhaltige Entwicklung. In: Deutsche UNESCO-Kommission e. V. (DUK) (ed.): forum der unesco-projekt-schulen. Nachhaltigkeit. Zeitschrift der UNESCO-Projektschulen, Sonderheft Nr. 1. Bonn, pp. 4–9; UNESCO (ed.) (July 2003) (cf. *footnote 37* op. cit.), pp. 3–4; United Nations Economic Commission for Europe (UNECE); United Nations Economic and Social Council (ECOSOC) (eds.) (2004e) (cf. *footnote 734* op. cit.); UNESCO (ed.) (2004c) (cf. *footnote 34* op. cit.), pp. 9–12; Leicht, Alexander (2005) (cf. *footnote 709* op. cit.), p. 1; UNESCO (ed.) (2005j) (cf. *footnote 44* op. cit.), pp. 5–7, 25–26; UNESCO (ed.) (2006f) (cf. *footnote 25* op. cit.), pp. 9–11; Organización de Estados Iberoamericanos para la Educación, la Ciencia y la Cultura (OEI) (ed.) (2006a) (cf. *footnote 678* op. cit.), pp. 27 et seqq, 40 et seqq; UNESCO (ed.) (2005d) (cf. *footnote 718* op. cit.), p. 2; Elias, Victoria (2007): Overview of the UNECE Strategy on ESD process. Annex 3. European ECO-Forum, p. 1; UNESCO (2007) (cf. *footnote 52* op. cit.); Kono, Toshiyuki (2007) (cf. *footnote 83* op. cit.), pp. 264–279; Magraw Barstow, Daniel; Hawke, Lisa D. (2007) (cf. *footnote 50* op. cit.), pp. 614–618; UNESCO; Thomson Foundation (eds.) (2008a) (cf. *footnote 803* op. cit.), p. 3; Bhola, Harbans S. (2008) (cf. *footnote 653* op. cit.), pp. 15–25; Fien, John; Goldney, David; Murphy, Tom (2009) (cf. *footnote 47* op. cit.), pp. 23 et seqq; Hopkins, Charles (2010): From Tbilisi to Bonn: an important journey in the historical context of ESD. In: Witthaus, Michele; McCandless, Karen; Lambert, Rebecca (eds.): Tomorrow today. Leicester, United Kingdom: Tudor Rose; UNESCO publishing, pp. 23–25; Vilela, Miriam (2010): Integrating sustainability in teaching and learning: the role of the Earth Charter. In: Witthaus, Michele; McCandless, Karen; Lambert, Rebecca (eds.): Tomorrow today. Leicester, United Kingdom: Tudor Rose; UNESCO publishing, p. 48.

828 See Article 26 United Nations (ed.) (1948) (cf. *footnote 21* op. cit.), p. 76.
Cf. UNESCO Education Sector (ed.) (2005) (cf. *footnote 21* op. cit.), p. 2; Foreign Office of the Federal Republic of Germany / German Commission for UNESCO (ed.) (2007) (cf. *footnote 21* op. cit.), p. 6.

829 Cf. Carson, Rachel (1962 / 2002) (cf. *footnote 57* op. cit.).

830 Cf. UNESCO Natural Sciences (2009): UNESCO's Man and the Biosphere Programme (MAB). UNESCO.

Year	*Indication*	*Profile*
1972	*United Nations Conference on Human Environment*, Stockholm (Sweden)[831]	Raising awareness of global environment and development needs, leading to the establishment of many environmental protection agencies, in particular the *United Nations Environment Programme* (UNEP).
1975	*Belgrade Charter on Environmental Education*, Belgrade (Yugoslavia)[832]	Prioritisation of environmental education through linking environment with development and society by knowledge, skills, attitudes, motivations and commitment.
1977	*Intergovernmental Conference on Environmental Education* (Tbilisi Declaration), Tbilisi (Georgia / USSR)[833]	Attention drawn to environment and related problems through awareness and sensitivity, knowledge and understanding, attitudes of concern, skills, and participation for active involvement.
1986	*Resolution 41/128* and *Declaration on the Right to Development*[834]	Guaranteeing the *unalienable human right* to development.
1987	Report of the World Commission on Sustainable Development *Our Common Future* (Brundtland Report) [835]	Coining and popularisation of the term *sustainable development* - endorsement as an overarching framework for future development policy.
1988	*Magna Charta Universitatum Europaeum*[836]	Advocating for sustainability in value-based independent higher education.
1989	*Convention on the Rights of the Child* (CRC)[837]	Re-affirmation of the right to education irrespective of race, sex, disability or economic status and declaring primary education compulsory and available free to all.

831 Cf. United Nations Environment Programme (UNEP) (ed.) (1972): Stockholm Declaration. Declaration of the United Nations Conference on the Human Environment. The United Nations Conference on the Human Environment, 5–16 June 1972. Stockholm / Nairobi: United Nations.

832 Cf. United Nations Environment Programme (UNEP); UNESCO (eds.) (1975): The Belgrade Charter. A Global Framework for Environmental Education. 13 to 22 October 1975. Belgrade: United Nations.

833 Cf. United Nations Environment Programme (UNEP); UNESCO (eds.) (1977 / 1978): Tbilisi Declaration. Intergovernmental Conference on Environmental Education, 14–26 October 1977. Final Report ED/MD/49. Edited by George Francis. Paris: United Nations.

834 Cf. United Nations (ed.) (1987a) (cf. *footnote 90* op. cit.), pp. 164 et seqq.

835 Cf. United Nations (ed.) (1987c) (cf. *footnote 49* op. cit.); UNESCO (ed.) (2007f) (cf. *footnote 427* op. cit.), p. 1.

836 Cf. The Magna Charta Observatory (September 1988): Magna Charta Universitatum Europaeum.

837 Cf. United Nations (ed.) (1989 / 1990) (cf. *footnote 22* op. cit.).

Year	*Indication*	*Profile*
1990	*World Declaration on Education for All*, Jomtien (Thailand)[838]	Universalisation of access and promotion of equality in education; focusing on learning and broadening the means and scope of basic education; enhancing the environment for learning by strengthening partnerships.
1991	*Caring for the Earth: A Strategy for Sustainable Living*[839]	Formulation of a global strategy for a sustainable society intended to restate current thinking about conservation and development.
1992	*United Nations Conference on Environment and Development* (Earth Summit) and *Agenda 21*, Rio de Janeiro (Brazil)[840]	Leading sustainable development into the 21st century and measurement of both environmental and social progress.
1992	*World Congress for Education and Communication on Environment and Development*, Toronto (Canada)[841]	Training for optimising productivity by encouraging technical progress and by promoting cultural conditions conducive to social and economic change.
1992 / 1993 / 1996 / 1998	*United Nations Commission on Sustainable Development* (CSD)[842]	Facilitation of sustainable development through an international programme of work on education, public awareness and professional training.

838 Cf. UNESCO (ed.) (1990 / 2000) (cf. *footnote 540* op. cit.).

839 Cf. The World Conservation Union (IUCN); United Nations Environment Programme (UNEP); World Wide Fund For Nature (WWF) (1991): Caring for the earth. A strategy for sustainable living. Gland, Switzerland: The World Conservation Union (IUCN) (IUCN Strategies For Sustainable Development Handbook Series); The World Conservation Union (IUCN); University of Cambridge (eds.) (2006) (cf. *footnote 689* op. cit.).

840 Cf. UN Department of Economic and Social Affairs (ed.) (1992) (cf. *footnote 721* op. cit.); United Nations (ed.) (1993) (cf. *footnote 732* op. cit.).

841 Cf. Mayor, Federico (17/10/1992) (cf. *footnote 41* op. cit.), p. 1.

842 Cf. United Nations (ed.) (1992 / 1993) (cf. *footnote 730* op. cit.); United Nations Economic and Social Council (ECOSOC); United Nations Commission for Sustainable Development (CSD) (eds.) (1996): Report on the Fourth Session (18 April–3 May 1996). Official Records, Supplement No. 8. E/CN.17/1996/38. New York: United Nations, pp. 22–24; United Nations Economic and Social Council (ECOSOC); United Nations Commission for Sustainable Development (CSD) (eds.) (1998): Report on the Sixth Session (22 December 1997 and 20 April–1 May 1998). Official Records, Supplement No. 9. E/CN.17/1998/20. New York: United Nations, pp. 29–38; Lode, Birgit (2011) (cf. *footnote 739* op. cit.), p. 338.

Year	*Indication*	*Profile*
1993	*Copernicus University Charter for Sustainable Development*[843]	Strengthening inter-university co-operation on environment by mobilising resources of higher-education institutions to further concept and objective of sustainable development.
1996	Report of the Independent Commission on Education for the 21st Century *Learning: The Treasure Within.* (Delors Report)[844]	Provision of benchmarks required to achieve sustainable development and defining education skills serving the need of education for a democratic and sustained future.
1997	*International Conference on Environment and Society: Education and Public Awareness for Sustainability* (The Declaration of Thessaloniki), Thessaloniki (Greece)[845]	Aiming at embedding skills of sustainability into curricula as a means of ensuring that education for sustainability contributes to education for democracy and peace.
1999	*Bologna Declaration*[846]	Fostering synergies between social-learning and political processes in higher education.
1999	*Global Sustainability Index*[847]	Launch of the first sustainability index tracking corporate commitment and practices.
2000	*Millennium Declaration* and the *Millennium Development Goals* (MDGs)[848]	Adoption of a global 21st-century vision on global progress and development, stimulating truly sustainable development, inter alia.
2000	*Dakar Framework for Action and World Education Forum*, Dakar (Senegal)[849]	Expression of further commitment towards achieving goals and targets of *Education for All* for every citizen and for every society.

843 Cf. Conference of European Rectors (CRE); Centre for Natural Resources (1993 / 1994): Copernicus University Charter for Sustainable Development. Published by: Association of European Universities.

844 Cf. UNESCO (ed.) (1996) (cf. *footnote 29* op. cit.).

845 Cf. UNESCO (1997b) (cf. *footnote 440* op. cit.).

846 Cf. European Commission (ed.) (1999): Bologna Declaration. On the European space for higher education. Bologna / Brussels: Publications Office of the European Union / Europa Publications Ltd.; Adomßent, Maik; Henze, Christa (eds.) (2007) (cf. *footnote 761* op. cit.), pp. 94–95.

847 Cf. SocialFunds.com (2000): The First Global Sustainability Index Turns One. Published by: Social Responsibility Investment Center (SRI World Group Inc.); Dow Jones Sustainability Indexes (DJSI) (2009): Global Sustainability Index. Published by: SAM Indexes GmbH.

848 Cf. United Nations (ed.) (2000): United Nations Millennium Declaration. Resolution adopted by the General Assembly [without reference to a Main Committee (A/55/L.2)]. A/RES/55/2. New York: United Nations.

849 Cf. UNESCO (ed.) (2000) (cf. *footnote 541* op. cit.).

Year	*Indication*	*Profile*
2000	*The Earth Charter*[850]	Longing for sustainable ways of living and some value-based global society.
2001 / 2002	*Global Higher Education for Sustainability Partnership* (GHESP)[851]	Promotion of a global alliance for higher education towards sustainable development.
2002	*Enhancing Global Sustainability*[852]	Positioning of UNESCO's strategic competencies within the supporting framework of sustainable development.
2002	*World Summit on Sustainable Development* (WSSD) (Johannesburg Declaration) and the *Plan of Implementation of the World Summit on Sustainable Development* (Johannesburg Plan of Implementation), Johannesburg (South Africa)[853]	Deepening of commitments towards sustainable development and environmentally sound economic growth at all levels, from the local to the global; adoption of *Decade of Education for Sustainable Development* starting in 2005 considered.

850 Cf. The Earth Charter Initiative (ECI) (ed.) (2000): The Earth Charter. San José, Costa Rica: Earth Charter Center; Blaze Corcoran, Peter; Maathai, Wangari (2005) (cf. *footnote 524* op. cit.).

851 Cf. UNESCO; International Association of Universities (IAU); COPERNICUS-CAMPUS; Association of University Leaders for a Sustainable Future (ULSF) (2001) (cf. *footnote 806* op. cit.); UNESCO; International Association of Universities (IAU); COPERNICUS-CAMPUS; Association of University Leaders for a Sustainable Future (ULSF) (2002) (cf. *footnote 806* op. cit.); UNESCO; International Association of Universities (IAU); COPERNICUS-CAMPUS; Association of University Leaders for a Sustainable Future (ULSF) (2004) (cf. *footnote 806* op. cit.); Altner, Günter; Michelsen, Gerd (eds.) (2005): Baustelle Hochschule. Nachhaltigkeit als neues Fundament für Lehre und Forschung. München: oekom Verlag (Politische Ökologie, 93).

852 Cf. UNESCO (ed.) (2002d) (cf. *footnote 440* op. cit.).

853 Cf. United Nations (ed.) (2002a): Report of the World Summit on Sustainable Development. Johannesburg, South Africa, 26 August–4 September 2002. A/CONF.199/20. New York: United Nations Publications; UN Department of Economic and Social Affairs (ed.) (2002): Plan of Implementation of the World Summit on Sustainable Development. Johannesburg, South Africa, 26 August –4 September 2002. DPI/2305. Edited by Division for Sustainable Development. New York: UN Department of Public Information; United Nations Publications; United Nations University (UNU); UNESCO; International Association of Universities (IAU) (eds.) (2002) (cf. *footnote 805* op. cit.); UNESCO (ed.) (2003b) (cf. *footnote 109* op. cit.), p. 1; UNESCO (ed.) (2004b): Educating for a sustainable future: Commitments and partnerships. Proceedings of the High-Level International Conference on Education for Sustainable Development at the World Summit on Sustainable Development. 2–3 September 2002, Johannesburg. Paris: UNESCO publishing, pp. 75 et seqq; Ginkel, Hans van (2010) (cf. *footnote 806* op. cit.), pp. 30–31.

Year	*Indication*	*Profile*
2002	*From Rio to Johannesburg*[854]	Reporting on the decade between the *United Nations Conference on Environment and Development* in 1992 and the *World Summit on Sustainable Development* (WSSD) in 2002.
2002	Endorsement of the *Johannesburg Declaration* and the *Johannesburg Plan of Implementation*[855]	Adoption of sustainable development as key element of the overarching framework for United Nations activities confirmed.
2002	*Resolution 57/254*[856]	Decision to proclaim *DESD* beginning 1st of January 2005 by consensus.
2004	*Resolution 58/219*[857]	Designation of UNESCO *lead agency* of *DESD*, continuation of global *ESD* momentum and hence call for broad support.
2003–2012	*United Nations Decade of Literacy* (UNLD)[858]	Announcement of the *United Nations Decade of Literacy* (UNLD) with UNESCO taking a co-ordinating role.
2005–2014	*DESD*	International launch of *DESD* with the aim of integrating the principles, values and practices of sustainable development into all aspects of education and learning; comprehensive explanation of sustainable development and encouraging participation in its attainment; embedding culture as fourth dimension of sustainability.
2008	*The Gothenburg Recommendations of Education for Sustainable Development*[859]	Committing stakeholders to prioritise processes that develop and strengthen *ESD*.

854 Cf. UNESCO (ed.) (2002c) (cf. *footnote 440* op. cit.).

855 Cf. General Assembly: Press Release on the endorsement of the Johannesburg Declaration and the Johannesburg Plan of Action and the scheduled adoption of resolution 57/254. Fifty-seventh General Assembly Plenary 78th Meeting (AM). GA/10125. Press release. Issued on 12/12/2002. New York, p. 9.

856 The resolution was introduced and initiated by Japan, subsequently supported and co-sponsored by 46 other countries.
Cf. United Nations (ed.) (2002 / 2003) (cf. *footnote 117* op. cit.); United Nations (20/12/2002): Fifty-seventh session United Nations General Assembly 78th plenary meeting Friday, 20 December 2002, 10 a.m. New York. Official Records. A/57/PV.78. Published by: United Nations. General Assembly. New York.

857 Cf. United Nations (ed.) (2004b) (cf. *footnote 727* op. cit.); United Nations (10/12/2004): Second Committee Summary record of the 14th meeting Held at Headquarters, New York, on Monday, 18 October 2004, at 10 a.m. Official Records. A/C.2/59/SR.14. Published by: United Nations. General Assembly. New York.

858 Cf. United Nations (ed.) (2002b) (cf. *footnote 480* op. cit.), p. 3.

Year	*Indication*	*Profile*
2009	*Bonn Declaration*[860]	Drawing critical conclusion on the first half of *DESD* and stressing the need for accelerated effort and more evenly distributed commitment for 21st century *ESD*.
2012	*United Nations Conference on Sustainable Development* (Rio+12), Rio de Janeiro (Brazil)[861]	Follow-up to the 1992 *United Nations Conference on Environment and Development* (Earth Summit) focussing on economic (business) concepts of sustainable development (*Green Economy*)

13 United Nations decades

Besides *DESD*, there are many more regional and global initiatives in progress. The following compilation depicts chronologically all past and ongoing decades, not by any means intended to disenchant or even discourage efforts made on *DESD*, but rather to obtain a realistic survey of the individual and institutional commitments that have to be managed.[862]

Table 23: International decades designated by the United Nations General Assembly[863]

Period	*Topic*	*Resolution*
2011–2020	United Nations Decade on Biodiversity	A/RES/65/161
2011–2020	Decade of Action for Road Safety	A/RES/64/255
2010–2020	United Nations Decade for Deserts and the Fight against Desertification	A/RES/62/195
2008–2017	Second United Nations Decade for the Eradication of Poverty	A/RES/63/230
2006–2015	Decade of Recovery and Sustainable Development for Communities Affected by 1986 Chernobyl Disaster	A/RES/62/9

859 Cf. Centre for Environment and Sustainability (GMV); Chalmers University of Technology; University of Gothenburg (eds.) (2009) (cf. *footnote 22* op. cit.).

860 Cf. UNESCO; Federal Ministry of Education and Research (BMBF); Deutsche UNESCO-Kommission e. V. (DUK) (eds.) (2009a): Bonn Declaration. UNESCO World Conference on Education for Sustainable Development. 31 March–2 April 2009, Bonn, Germany. Bonn: Deutsche UNESCO-Kommission.

861 Cf. United Nations (ed.) (2012): The future we want. United Nations Conference on Sustainable Development (Rio+12), 20–22 June 2012, Rio de Janeiro, Brazil. A/CONF.216/L.1. Rio de Janeiro; New York: United Nations.

862 See *Table 23* in chapter VII 14 *United Nations decades* on page 193.

863 Cf. United Nations (2009) (cf. *footnote 557* op. cit.); UNESCO (2009) (cf. *footnote 597* op. cit.).

Period	*Topic*	*Resolution*
2005–2014	Second International Decade of the World's Indigenous People	A/RES/59/174
2005–2015	International Decade for Action *Water for Life*	A/RES/58/217
2005–2014	United Nations Decade of Education for Sustainable Development	A/RES/57/254
2003–2012	United Nations Literacy Decade: Education for All	A/RES/56/116
2001–2010	Second International Decade for the Eradication of Colonialism	A/RES/55/146
2001–2010	Decade to Roll Back Malaria in Developing Countries, Particularly in Africa	A/RES/55/284
2001–2010	International Decade for a Culture of Peace and Non-violence for the Children of the World	A/RES/53/25 A/RES/60/3
1997–2006	United Nations Decade for the Eradication of Poverty	A/RES/50/107
1995–2004	United Nations Decade for Human Rights Education	A/RES/49/184
1994–2003	International Decade of the World's Indigenous People	A/RES/48/163
1993–2003	Third Decade to Combat Racism and Racial Discrimination	A/RES/48/91
1993–2002	Asian and Pacific Decade of Disabled Persons	A/RES/48/3
1993–2002	Second Industrial Development Decade for Africa	A/RES/44/237 A/RES/47/177 A/RES/50/94
1991–2000	Fourth United Nations Development Decade	A/RES/45/199
1991–2000	United Nations Decade against Drug Abuse	A/RES/S-17/2
1991–2000	Second Transport and Communications Decade in Africa	A/RES/43/179
1990–2000	International Decade for the Eradication of Colonialism	A/RES/43/47
1990–1999	International Decade for Natural Disaster Reduction	A/RES/42/169 A/RES/44/236
1990–1999	United Nations Decade of International Law	A/RES/44/23
1990's	Third Disarmament Decade	A/RES/43/78 L A/RES/45/62 A
1988–1997	United Nations World Decade for Cultural Development	A/RES/41/187
1983–1993	Second Decade to Combat Racism and Racial Discrimination	A/RES/38/14
1983–1992	United Nations Decade of Disabled Persons	A/RES/37/53
1981–1990	Third United Nations Development Decade	A/RES/35/56
1981–1990	International Drinking Water Supply and Sanitation Decade	A/RES/35/18
1980–1990	Second Disarmament Decade	A/RES/35/46

Period	*Topic*	*Resolution*
1980's	Industrial Development Decade for Africa	A/RES/35/66 B
1978–1988	[First] Transport and Communications Decade in Africa	A/RES/32/160
1976–1985	United Nations Decade for Women: Equality, Development and Peace	A/RES/3520 (XXX)
1973–1983	[First] Decade for Action to Combat Racism and Racial Discrimination	A/RES/2919 (XXVII)
1971–1980	Second United Nations Development Decade	A/RES/2626 (XXV)
1970's	[First] Disarmament Decade	A/RES/2602 E (XXIV)
1960–1970	[First] United Nations Development Decade	A/RES/1710 (XVI)

14 Summary

Two principal conclusions can be drawn from the remarks made above:

1. *DESD* does not *emerge* from nowhere. On the contrary, *DESD* has been deeply rooted and firmly embedded in a global framework dealing with sustainability and the favourable conditions of development for years or even decades. So, the mission itself is not novel at all, but the findings, circumstances and public awareness in relation to issues of sustainable development are. This is proven when comparing past and current legislation or when studying relevant agendas and initiatives, for instance. As a result, *DESD* may be considered a ten-year platform to make best use of extant and nascent momentum by purposefully co-ordinating and channelling stakeholder behaviour; and
2. *DESD* means work in progress and therefore continuous change. Growing concerns correlate with growing responsibilities. What is to some extent original and authentic in *DESD* is the notion of revealing the linkages between education and sustainability. The *DESD* movement therefore logically acquires an enhanced value. Dealing with education issues and sustainability not separately but jointly is one of the main achievements. In addition, *ESD* reflects a *gradual development* that begins with environmental aspects of sustainability at the *Stockholm-Conference* in 1972. Combined with first educational initiatives, this serves as *nucleus* and point of origin for *ESD*. Later social aspects of sustainability become increasingly important, finally expressed at the *Rio-Conference* in 1992. Economic aspects of sustainable development are predominantly raised at the *Johannesburg Summit* in 2002 and

Rio+12 in 2012. Ultimately, during the first millennium decade, cultural facets of sustainability are brought into discussion, particularly with *DESD* in 2005.[864] Along with advanced awareness-raising and capacity-building programmes, culture and cultural education constitute the most recent domain of *ESD*.

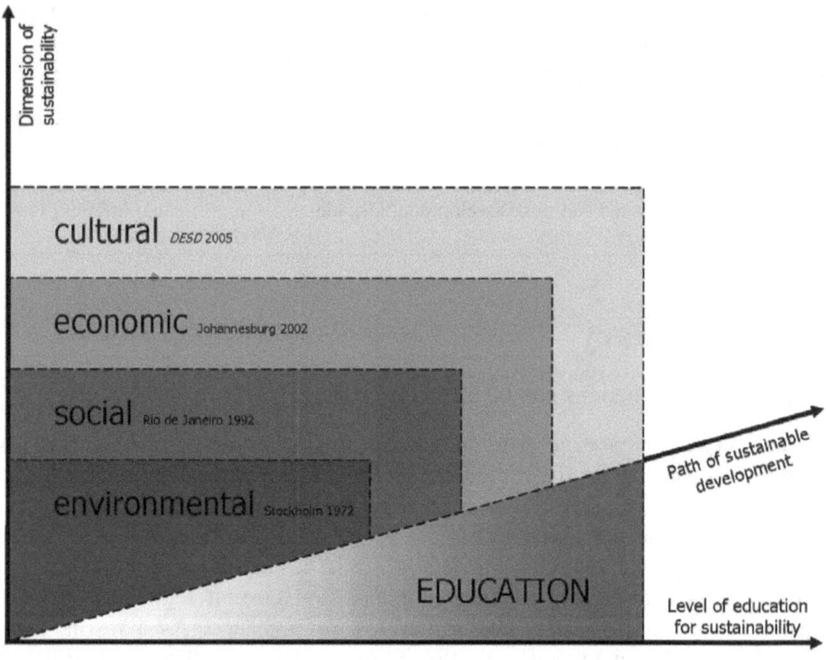

Figure 36: Evolution of DESD[865]

864 See *Figure 36* in chapter VII 15 *Summary* on page 196.

865 This figure claims and considers four principal aspects. First, sustainable development proportionally gains momentum to the extent of education for sustainability. Second, the level of education for sustainability correlates with different dimensions of sustainability. Third, meanwhile four interdependent domains of sustainable development have developed and have been recognised as benchmarks for environmental, social, economic and cultural sustainability. Fourth, education increasingly resorts and responds to those multiple dimensions of sustainability.

VIII Obligation of compliance

Recalling the preliminary findings on the conditions of the DESD framework, the context of DESD mandate as well as the background in which DESD is embedded, the question of how to ensure commitment through respective means of compliance arises. This chapter will examine which means of force and effect does UNESCO employ in order to facilitate effective DESD implementation?

1 Theoretical setting

UNESCO's threefold assignment[866] of standard-setting, policy advice and monitoring is subject to normative action carried out by UNESCO in relation to a range of legally binding decisions, instruments and substantive results. Given that binding adds to human behaviour, by law,[867] an element of the *non-optional*, the overarching system of reference for UNESCO's activities as a specialised agency of the United Nations is constituted through the normative provisions of international public law.

---

866 I.e. *modalities of action*.
See Foreign Office of the Federal Republic of Germany / German Commission for UNESCO (ed.) (2007) (cf. *footnote 21* op. cit.), p. 12.
Cf. chapter V 1.2 *Role* on page 100.

867 Cf. Hoof, G. J. H. (Fried) van (1983): Rethinking the sources of international law. Deventer / Boston / Frankfurt am Main: Kluwer Law and Taxation Publishers, p. 20.

1.1 Sources

The predominant and most conventional sources of international law are stipulated in the *numerus clausus* provisions[868] of the statute of the *International Court of Justice* (ICJ) .[869] Four principal sources are commonly accepted and consistently applied:

> *"1. The Court, whose function is to decide in accordance with international law such disputes as are submitted to it, shall apply:*
>
> *a) international conventions, whether general or particular, establishing rules expressly recognised by the contesting states;*
>
> *b) international custom, as evidence of a general practice accepted as law;*
>
> *c) the general principles of law recognised by civilised nations;*
>
> *d) (...) judicial decisions[870] and the teachings of the most highly qualified publicists of the various nations, as subsidiary means for the determination of rules of law.*
>
> *2. This provision shall not prejudice the power of the Court to decide a case ex aequo et bono (i.e. in justice and fairness), if the parties agree thereto".*[871]

These traditional provisions are inarguably characterised by the imposition of direct legal binding, and the exertion of judicial interpretation and dispute settlement before the court (*hard law*). However, *"(t)here is quite clearly a broad*

---

868 It is indeed debatable whether these provisions constitute an exhaustive list or not. Most items leave enough room for interpretation and further reflection.
Cf. Hörtreiter, Isabel (2007) (cf. *footnote 510* op. cit.), p. 280.

869 I.e. Article 38 paragraph 1 statute of the International Court of Justice (ICJ).
Cf. Hoof, G. J. H. (Fried) van (1983) (cf. *footnote 867* op. cit.), pp. 83 et seqq; Fastenrath, Ulrich (1993): Relative Normativity in International Law. In: European Journal of International Law (EJIL), Volume 4, Issue 3, pp. 305–340, pp. 329–330; Zemanek, Karl (1998): Is the Term 'Soft Law' Convenient? In: Hafner, Gerhard; Seidl-Hohenveldern, Ignaz (eds.): Liber amicorum Professor Ignaz Seidl-Hohenveldern. In honour of his 80th birthday. The Hague: Kluwer Law International, pp. 843–862, p. 844; Hillgenberg, Hartmut (1999): A Fresh Look at Soft Law. In: European Journal of International Law (EJIL), Volume 10, Issue 3, pp. 499–515, p. 499; Novak Talavera, Fabián; García Corrochano Moyano, Luis (2000): Derecho Internacional Público. Introducción y fuentes. Volume 1. edición. Lima: Pontificia Universidad Católica del Perú Fondo Editorial (Derecho internacional público / Fabián Novak Talavera Luis García-Corrochano Moyano, Tomo I); Hörtreiter, Isabel (2007) (cf. *footnote 510* op. cit.), p. 280; Varwick, Johannes (2008): Völkerrecht / Internationales Recht. In: Woyke, Wichard (ed.): Handwörterbuch internationale Politik. 11. überarbeitete und aktualisierte Auflage. Opladen: Budrich (UTB für Wissenschaft, 702), pp. 541–548, p. 542.

870 Relating both to *jurisdiction in contentious cases* and so-called *advisory jurisdiction* as requested by organs of the United Nations or specialised agencies authorised to make such a request.
Cf. International Court of Justice (2009): Statute of the International Court of Justice.

871 See International Court of Justice (2009) (cf. *footnote 870* op. cit.), pp. Article 38.

area of situations in which states enter into commitment without concluding a formal treaty under international law".[872]

This is exactly true in the case of *DESD* whose non-legally binding nature may be determined without difficulty from the statute.[873] *DESD* is based upon resolution and declaration. It therefore does not correspond to any of the categories listed below:[874]

- International conventions, agreements or treaties which establish rules expressly recognised by the contesting states;
- International customary law as evidence of a general practice accepted (or rejected) as law (*opinio iuris sive necessitatis*);
- General *erga-omnes* principles of *preremptory* law recognised by civilised nations according to basic values and convictions (*ius cogens*);[875] or
- Judicial decision of court's jurisdiction.

Strictly speaking, *DESD* does not *eo ipso* produce *any* legal effect or *imperative*[876] in terms of establishing rights and duties. Consequently, treaty-based documents are not applicable in the clarification of any potential obligation in this case.[877] But *"(...) there is ample evidence to show that Article 38 is not ex-*

872 See Hillgenberg, Hartmut (1999) (cf. *footnote 869* op. cit.), p. 500.

873 Cf. Goldmann, Matthias (2009): Inside Relative Normativity: From Sources to Standard Instruments for the Exercise of International Public Authority. In: German Law Journal, Volume 9, Issue 11, pp. 1865–1908, p. 1869.

874 Cf. Verdross, Alfred; Simma, Bruno (1984 / 2010): Universelles Völkerrecht. Theorie und Praxis. Volume 3. Auflage, unveränderter Nachdruck. Berlin: Duncker & Humblot, pp. 328–394; Sloan, Blaine (1987): General Assembly resolutions revisited. Forty years later. In: British year book of international law, Volume 58, Issue 8, pp. 39–150, pp. 46, 68, 78, 95 et seqq; Doehring, Karl (1999): Völkerrecht. Ein Lehrbuch. Heidelberg: C. F. Müller Verlag, pp. 131 et seqq; Novak Talavera, Fabián; García Corrochano Moyano, Luis (2001): Derecho Internacional Público. Sujetos de derecho internacional. Volume 1. edición. Lima: Pontificia Universidad Católica del Perú Fondo Editorial (Derecho internacional público / Fabián Novak Talavera Luis García-Corrochano Moyano, Tomo II, Volumen I), p. 19; Doehring, Karl (2004): Völkerrecht. Ein Lehrbuch. Volume 2. neubearbeitete Auflage. Heidelberg: C. F. Müller Verlag (Großes Lehrbuch), pp. 121 et seqq.

875 Cf. Weil, Prosper (1982 / 1983): Vers une normativité relative en droit international? / Towards Relative Normativity in International Law. In: Revue General de Droit International Public (RGDIP) / American Journal of International Law, Volume 86 / 77, 1 / 3, pp. 5–47 / 413–442, p. 421; Shelton, Dinah (2006d): International Law and 'Relative Normativity'. In: Evans, Malcolm David (ed.): International Law. 2. edition. Oxford: Oxford University Press, pp. 159–185, p. 162; Hörtreiter, Isabel (2007) (cf. *footnote 510* op. cit.), p. 281.

876 See Abi-Saab, Georges (2007) (cf. *footnote 488* op. cit.), p. 420.

877 I.e. Vienna Convention on the Law of Treaties.
Cf. United Nations (ed.) (1969): Vienna Convention on the Law of Treaties. Vienna: United Nations Publications (Treaty Series, 2); Hillgenberg, Hartmut (1999) (cf. *foot-*

haustive. That is clearly demonstrated by authoritative acts of international organs or unilateral acts. (...) (Hence), (t)hese examples support the submission that Article 38 (...) does not describe a closed system of law-making".[878]

1.2 Challenges

Since its inception there has been ongoing debate about *new sources of international law*[879] in terms of whether to extend the catalogue of internationally binding instruments *ex professo*[880] or not.[881] There is no unambiguous doctrine: *"New areas of international law are developing and much of this expansion is of recent origin".*[882] Both parties of opinion receive extensive representation.[883] Regardless of the *factual* impact effected,[884] particular attention is drawn to the still pending question of *legal* binding force and to the other legal effects of resolutions.[885] This controversial discussion of *normative* or *law-declaring resolutions*[886] is directly applicable within the present context of *DESD*.

Two major challenges of general scope can frequently be observed in practical law making:

---

note 869 op. cit.), pp. 499, 503; D'Amato, Anthony (2008): International Soft Law, Hard Law, and Coherence. In: Northwestern Public Law Research Paper, 08–01, p. 13.

878 See Zemanek, Karl (1998) (cf. *footnote 869* op. cit.), p. 844.

879 E.g., based upon consensus, acceptance and recognition to meet community expectations through manifest community law permitted to serve in a representative capacity (vacuum filling).
See Sloan, Blaine (1987) (cf. *footnote 874* op. cit.), pp. 90 et seqq.

880 See Francioni, Francesco (1996 / 2008): International 'soft law': a contemporary assessment. In: Lowe, Vaughan; Fitzmaurice, Malgosia (eds.): Fifty years of the International Court of Justice. Essays in honour of Sir Robert Jennings. Cambridge: Cambridge University Press; Grotius Publications, pp. 167–180, p. 168.

881 Cf. Hillgenberg, Hartmut (1999) (cf. *footnote 869* op. cit.), p. 502; Mazuelos Bellido, Ángeles (2004): Soft Law: ¿Mucho ruido y pocas nueces? In: Revista Electrónica de Estudios Internacionales, Issue 8, pp. 1–40, p. 2.

882 See Burgstaller, Markus (2005) (cf. *footnote 445* op. cit.), p. 22.

883 Cf. Kälin, Walter; Baldegger, Mirjam (eds.) (2006) (cf. *footnote 510* op. cit.), pp. 222–223.

884 Agreement and respective commitment is, to all intents and purposes, known as fact and subsequent practice beyond treaty-based law.
Cf. Article 31, paragraph 3 b United Nations (ed.) (1969) (cf. *footnote 877* op. cit.); Hillgenberg, Hartmut (1999) (cf. *footnote 869* op. cit.), pp. 513–514.

885 Cf. Hoof, G. J. H. (Fried) van (1983) (cf. *footnote 867* op. cit.), pp. 139 et seqq; Sloan, Blaine (1987) (cf. *footnote 874* op. cit.), p. 45; Mazuelos Bellido, Ángeles (2004) (cf. *footnote 881* op. cit.), pp. 2–3; Hörtreiter, Isabel (2007) (cf. *footnote 510* op. cit.), p. 281.

886 See Hillgenberg, Hartmut (1999) (cf. *footnote 869* op. cit.), p. 514; Kiss, Alexandre (2003) (cf. *footnote 297* op. cit.), p. 224.

1. No more treaties:[887] The phenomenon of the failure, for various reasons, of *hard-law* approaches.[888]
2. The application of alternative sources and instruments which do not impose any obligation of legal compliance *sensu stricto*, but which do, of course, either exert or intend certain binding effects:[889] *"The fact that law is not the only system of social rules determining human behaviour is well known to legal theory".*[890]

Declarations and resolutions pertain predominantly to the two above issues. Generally speaking, conclusions of international conferences based on established practice (*declarations of intent*[891]) and resolutions are not binding on member states as subjects being addressed by international law,[892] even though they demonstrate a high rate of acceptance as evidenced, for example, by majority vote.[893] *"Resolutions (of the United Nations) are not legally binding, and it is evident that those content-based provisions can only achieve binding force when they are turned into international customs."*[894]

---

887 E.g., since 1945 more than 40.000 treaties between state parties have been adopted, signed and implemented. Even more legislation must be considered taking into account the growing importance of law making with international organisations additionally.
Cf. Varwick, Johannes (2008) (cf. *footnote 869* op. cit.), p. 541; Gerner, Martin (14/09/2009) (cf. *footnote 407* op. cit.).

888 Due, for example, to a lack of momentum and commitment, a preference for extra-legal and usually more flexible arrangements, the avoidance of hard choices given justiciable consequences (*lip services*), etc.
Cf. Kirton, John J.; Trebilcock, Michael J. (eds.) (2004): Hard choices, soft law. Voluntary standards in global trade, environment, and social governance. Aldershot / Burlington, Vermont: Ashgate Dartmouth (Global environmental governance), p. 4.

889 For example, in order to foster decision-making processes directed to create opinio iuris.
Cf. Bleckmann, Albert (1982): Grundprobleme und Methoden des Völkerrechts. Freiburg im Breisgau / München: Alber Verlag (Kolleg Rechtstheorie, Sonderband 1), p. 340; Dupuy, Pierre-Marie (2007) (cf. *footnote 485* op. cit.), p. 383.

890 See Bothe, Michael (1980) (cf. *footnote 510* op. cit.), p. 65.

891 Cf. Sloan, Blaine (1987) (cf. *footnote 874* op. cit.), p. 140; Hillgenberg, Hartmut (1999) (cf. *footnote 869* op. cit.), p. 507.

892 Cf. Novak Talavera, Fabián; García Corrochano Moyano, Luis (2001) (cf. *footnote 874* op. cit.), pp. 30 et seqq.

893 Cf. Jabloner, Clemens; Okresek, Wolf (1983) (cf. *footnote 525* op. cit.), p. 220; Frowein, Jochen Abraham (1989) (cf. *footnote 203* op. cit.), pp. 783 et seqq; Brownlie, Ian (2002) (cf. *footnote 510* op. cit.); Doehring, Karl (2004) (cf. *footnote 874* op. cit.), p. 122; Kälin, Walter; Baldegger, Mirjam (eds.) (2006) (cf. *footnote 510* op. cit.), p. 218; Hörtreiter, Isabel (2007) (cf. *footnote 510* op. cit.), pp. 282–283.

894 Translation from Italian into English: *"Risoluzioni (delle Nazione Unite) non hanno forza vincolante, ed è chiaro che le norme in esse contenute possono acquistare tale forza solo se vengono trasformate in consuetudini internazionali".*

According to the *Charter of the United Nations*,[895] resolutions cannot serve as an independent source of international law,[896] because at present the *United Nations General Assembly* is not fully legitimised as a universal legislative body.[897] Certain activities may result in legal consequences which are beyond the organisation's power (*ultra vires*).[898] The *General Assembly* nonetheless serves, to a certain extent, a *quasi-legislative*[899] function in the interpretation and formal emendation of separate treaties, establishing an *opinio iuris* by acceptance, acquiescence or rejection of customary rules, or transforming customary norms into general principles of law.[900] In this respect resolutions can have more implicit potential considering:[901]

a) *Soft-law* effects with the *twilight existence*[902] between law and politics of non-binding and the difficulty of assessment of international agreements;[903]

See Conforti, Benedetto (1995) (cf. *footnote 510* op. cit.), p. 40.

895 In particular Articles 10 to 14 referring to functions and power. Cf. United Nations (ed.) (1945) (cf. *footnote 420* op. cit.), pp. 4–5.

896 Cf. Verdross, Alfred; Simma, Bruno (1984 / 2010) (cf. *footnote 874* op. cit.), pp. 405–412; Heusel, Wolfgang (1991): "Weiches" Völkerrecht. Eine vergleichende Untersuchung typischer Erscheinungsformen. Volume 1. Auflage. Baden-Baden: Nomos Verlagsgesellschaft, p. 20; Vitzthum, Wolfgang Graf; Bothe, Michael (eds.) (2007) (cf. *footnote 505* op. cit.), p. 32.

897 Cf. Sloan, Blaine (1987) (cf. *footnote 874* op. cit.), p. 95; Klabbers, Jan (1996a): The Redundancy of Soft Law. In: Nordic Journal of International Law, Volume 65, Issue 2, pp. 167–182(16), p. 171; Mazuelos Bellido, Ángeles (2004) (cf. *footnote 881* op. cit.), pp. 4–6; Hobe, Stephan; Kimminich, Otto (2004) (cf. *footnote 511* op. cit.), p. 196; Schweisfurth, Theodor (2006): Völkerrecht. Tübingen: Mohr Siebeck, p. 95; Klabbers, Jan (2007): The redundancy of soft law. In: Koskenniemi, Martti (ed.): Sources of international law. Reprinted. Aldershot: Ashgate Dartmouth (The Library of Essays in International Law, 5), Volume Nordic Journal of International Law 65: 167–182, 1996, pp. 189–204, p. 193.

898 Cf. Hillgenberg, Hartmut (1999) (cf. *footnote 869* op. cit.), p. 515; Doehring, Karl (1999) (cf. *footnote 874* op. cit.), pp. 131 et seqq; Doehring, Karl (2004) (cf. *footnote 874* op. cit.), p. 136; Krajewski, Markus (2006) (cf. *footnote 510* op. cit.), pp. 25–26; Aust, Anthony (2006) (cf. *footnote 200* op. cit.), p. 198.

899 See Hoof, G. J. H. (Fried) van (1983) (cf. *footnote 867* op. cit.), p. 14.

900 Cf. Sloan, Blaine (1987) (cf. *footnote 874* op. cit.), p. 102.

901 Cf. Simma, Bruno (1981): Zur völkerrechtlichen Bedeutung von Resolutionen der UN-Generalversammlung. In: Skubiszewski, Krzysztof; Bernhardt, Rudolf (eds.): Die Bedeutung der Resolutionen der Generalversammlung der Vereinten Nationen. 1. Auflage. Baden-Baden: Nomos Verlagsgesellschaft. Fünftes Deutsch-Polnisches Juristen-Kolloquium, Volume 2, pp. 45–76, pp. 53, 55; Sloan, Blaine (1987) (cf. *footnote 874* op. cit.), pp. 107, 108, 112, 114, 121; Kälin, Walter; Baldegger, Mirjam (eds.) (2006) (cf. *footnote 510* op. cit.), pp. 223–225. See *Figure 37* in chapter VIII 1.2 *Challenges* on page 203.

902 See Sloan, Blaine (1987) (cf. *footnote 874* op. cit.), p. 107; Skjærseth, Jon Birger; Stokke, Olav Schram; Wettestad, Jørgen (2006) (cf. *footnote 294* op. cit.), p. 104.

b) Quasi-judicial or constitutive effects in terms of reliance and codes of conduct (*pouvoir constituant*);[904]
c) Operative effects concerning territorial administration or other operational organs and activities;
d) Effects on basic actions of states and organisations (*immediate formless member states' consensus*);[905] or
e) Persuasive effects concerning questions of good faith and *estoppel*.[906]

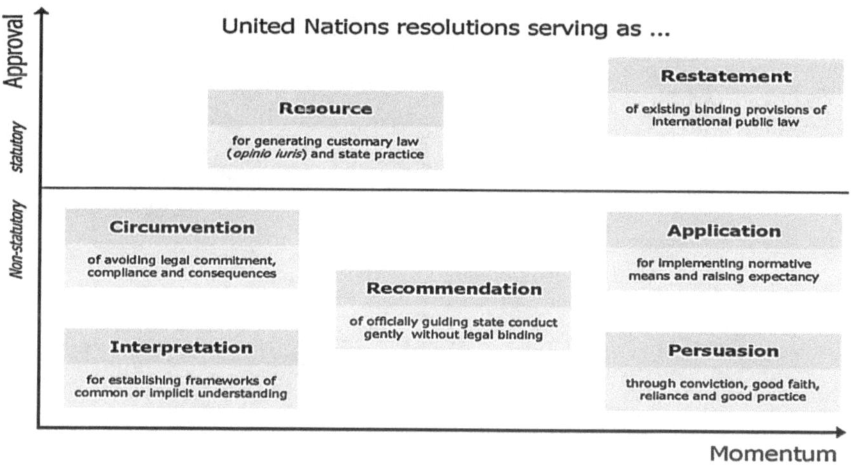

Figure 37: Functional profiles of United Nations resolutions[907]

Due to their quasi-legal nature, the effect (particularly the legal effect for compliance) of *General Assembly* resolutions is not defined *a priori*, but deter-

903 Cf. Weil, Prosper (1982 / 1983) (cf. *footnote 875* op. cit.), pp. 416–417; Heusel, Wolfgang (1991) (cf. *footnote 896* op. cit.), p. 275.

904 Cf. Heusel, Wolfgang (1991) (cf. *footnote 896* op. cit.), p. 33; Hörtreiter, Isabel (2007) (cf. *footnote 510* op. cit.), pp. 280–293.

905 For example, the basis for implementation or enforcement, the basis for diplomatic judicial and other proceedings (advocacy, etc.), the basis for incorporation into municipal law and treaties, permissive or authorising resolutions, basis for self-defense, or basis for excusable cessation of performance.
Cf. Heusel, Wolfgang (1991) (cf. *footnote 896* op. cit.), p. 34.

906 I.e. the principle of *venire contra factum proprium*. For instance, agreeing and taking resolutions' decisions, but acting differently in reality.
Cf. Heusel, Wolfgang (1991) (cf. *footnote 896* op. cit.), p. 276; Doehring, Karl (2004) (cf. *footnote 874* op. cit.), p. 137.

907 This chart offers an overview of divergent functional perceptions of United Nations resolutions in practice. It is important to note that apparently momentum does not necessarily depend on the level of approval, neither statutory nor non-statutory.
Cf. Hörtreiter, Isabel (2007) (cf. *footnote 510* op. cit.), pp. 283–294.

mined by case-specific interpretations of individual factors.[908] The decisive question is whether the particular resolution or declaration is constitutive of *opinio iuris*.[909]

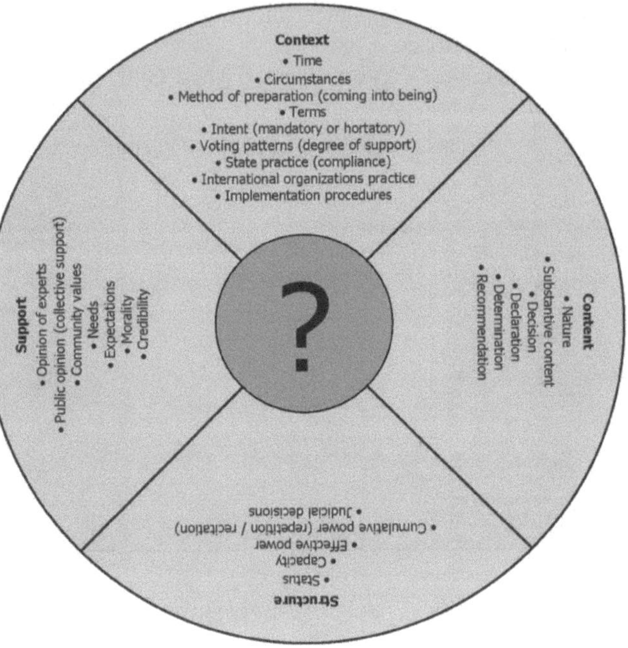

Figure 38: Factors determining the legal effect of General Assembly resolutions[910]

The way in which resolutions are dealt with reveals changes in the perception of them. The importance of resolutions increases as the sources of international law are extended.[911] In this regard, resolutions constitute expressions of legal convictions as indispensably supportive and complementary elements of

908 See *Figure 38* in chapter VIII 1.2 *Challenges* on page 204.

909 Cf. Sloan, Blaine (1987) (cf. *footnote 874* op. cit.), p. 140; Heusel, Wolfgang (1991) (cf. *footnote 896* op. cit.), p. 279; Vitzthum, Wolfgang Graf; Bothe, Michael (eds.) (2007) (cf. *footnote 505* op. cit.), p. 32.

910 Most notable factors influencing compliance with respective resolutions can be related to content, structure, support and context.
Cf. Sloan, Blaine (1987) (cf. *footnote 874* op. cit.), pp. 126 et seqq; Sloan, Blaine (1991): United Nations General Assembly resolutions in our changing world. Ardsley-on-Hudson, New York: Transnational Publishers; Brill Academic Publishers.

911 See Hoof, G. J. H. (Fried) van (1983) (cf. *footnote 867* op. cit.), pp. 65–71.

international customary law (*opinio iuris*).[912] They unquestionably form part of the international legal framework irrespective of their lack of legal authority. Due to the diversity of driving factors, the transitions between binding and non-binding force are undefined.[913] However, their *declaratory effect*[914] and *recommendatory character*[915] prevails and is therefore notable. Nascent debates at international level on legitimacy, conformity and reputation of resolutions are typically the first step in their presentation and gradual internalisation (*norm cascade*).[916] This coincides with the current shift from an international law of co-existence towards an international law of co-operation. The latter emphasises the positive (voluntary) obligation to act rather than to adhere to fixed patterns.[917] When applied to UNESCO and *DESD*, the distinction between non-binding recommendations and other binding UNESCO resolutions and decisions remains relevant, and a preference for instruments that express norms, principles and general rules aiming at the adoption of legislations, framework documents or administrative means by member states therefore becomes apparent.[918] The normative content is ultimately decisive given the fact that *"(r)ules and norms formulate shared or community expectations as to how those to whom a norm is addressed will behave"*.[919]

---

912 Cf. Krajewski, Markus (2006) (cf. *footnote 510* op. cit.), pp. 25–26; Kälin, Walter; Baldegger, Mirjam (eds.) (2006) (cf. *footnote 510* op. cit.), pp. 223–225; Vitzthum, Wolfgang Graf; Bothe, Michael (eds.) (2007) (cf. *footnote 505* op. cit.), p. 12; Hörtreiter, Isabel (2007) (cf. *footnote 510* op. cit.), pp. 285–287; Shaw, Malcolm N. (2008): International Law. Volume 6th edition. Cambridge UK / New York: Cambridge University Press, pp. 117–119.

913 Cf. Heusel, Wolfgang (1991) (cf. *footnote 896* op. cit.), pp. 287–289; Vitzthum, Wolfgang Graf; Bothe, Michael (eds.) (2007) (cf. *footnote 505* op. cit.), pp. 12, 148.

914 Cf. Hobe, Stephan; Kimminich, Otto (2004) (cf. *footnote 511* op. cit.), p. 196; Kälin, Walter; Baldegger, Mirjam (eds.) (2006) (cf. *footnote 510* op. cit.), p. 218; Hörtreiter, Isabel (2007) (cf. *footnote 510* op. cit.), p. 281.

915 Cf. Schweisfurth, Theodor (2006) (cf. *footnote 897* op. cit.), p. 95.

916 Cf. Schemmann, Michael (2009): Das unausgeschöpfte Potential des Neo-Institutionalismus – Die Verknüpfung der analytischen Ebenen als zukünftiger Forschungsfokus. In: Koch, Sascha; Schemmann, Michael; Göhlich, Michael (eds.): Neo-Institutionalismus in der Erziehungswissenschaft. Grundlegende Texte und empirische Studien. Organisation und Pädagogik 6. 1. Auflage. Wiesbaden: VS Verlag für Sozialwissenschaften, pp. 347–358, pp. 353 et seqq.

917 Cf. Abi-Saab, Georges (2007) (cf. *footnote 488* op. cit.), pp. 418–421.

918 Cf. Yusuf, Abdulqawi A. (2007b) (cf. *footnote 129* op. cit.), p. 36.

919 See Bothe, Michael (1980) (cf. *footnote 510* op. cit.), p. 66; ff. Kremser, Holger (1996): "Soft Law" der UNESCO und Grundgesetz. Dargestellt am Beispiel der Mediendeklaration. Frankfurt am Main / New York: Peter Lang GmbH (Schriften zum internationalen und zum öffentlichen Recht, 10), pp. 127–128.

See *Table 24* in chapter VIII 1.2 *Challenges* on page 206.

Cf. *Figure 37* in chapter VIII 1.2 *Challenges* on page 203.

Table 24: Organisational modes of binding[920]

Mode	Content
Force d'applicabilité[921]	Building momentum through application
Factual effectiveness[922]	Creating *faits accomplis*
New haven approach[923]	Considering law as process of authoritative and controlling decisions
Statement of intent[924]	Achieving effectiveness through adding written statements of intent
Continuing codification[925]	Codifying and furthering normative content
Soft law[926]	Encouraging morally binding character

1.3 Gradual normativity

At this stage the formal distinction between binding and non-binding provisions does not purposefully serve an analysis of the context of *DESD*, and in particular the question of compliance, for two obvious reasons:

1. According to the choice, definition and application of sources of international law *DESD* is neither designed nor qualified to commit state parties to unquestioned compliance; and
2. Presuming an *opinio iuris* in the case of *DESD* in order to subsume *DESD* under the binding provisions of international customary law is highly theoretical.[927]

Disregarding the question of compliance for a moment, the issue of normativity must first be clarified. Norms are intended to affect human behaviour irrespective of their being *soft* or *hard law*.[928]

920 There are a number of modes of binding that can be fostered by organisations. Apart from the most common mode of codifying normative content and its application, some more subtle modes of *soft enforcement* do exist, too.
Cf. Kremser, Holger (1996) (cf. *footnote 919* op. cit.), pp. 114 et seqq.

921 See Kremser, Holger (1996) (cf. *footnote 919* op. cit.), pp. 116–117.

922 Cf. Kremser, Holger (1996) (cf. *footnote 919* op. cit.), pp. 117–118.

923 See Kremser, Holger (1996) (cf. *footnote 919* op. cit.), pp. 118–119.

924 Cf. Kremser, Holger (1996) (cf. *footnote 919* op. cit.), p. 120.

925 Cf. Kremser, Holger (1996) (cf. *footnote 919* op. cit.), pp. 121–122.

926 See Kremser, Holger (1996) (cf. *footnote 919* op. cit.), pp. 123–125.

927 It is even more than questionable given the unascertained and legally unreliable fact of member states' voting behaviour while formally adopting DESD, let alone any substantive practical commitment.
Cf. United Nations (20/12/2002) (cf. *footnote 856* op. cit.), p. 8.

Normativity is therefore defined as the description or setting of standards and rules of behaviour. *DESD* may apply to the concept of *normative resolutions* by:[929]

- Ordering conduct in a specific manner; and
- Declaring principles of a general scope.

Does UNESCO address *DESD* issues normatively, so that they might be subject to any degree of compliance? Recalling briefly the wording of the vision of *DESD* to envisage *"(t)he overall goal (...) to integrate the values (...) into all aspects of learning (...) in order to encourage changes in behaviour that allow for a more sustainable, economically viable and just society for all (...)"*,[930] the *normative intent*[931] can indeed be assumed.

Furthermore, *DESD* is mandatorily oriented towards the provision of principles for changing behaviour, ideally by setting global standards in favour of *ESD*: *"Sustainable development can properly claim a normative status as an element of the process of judicial reasoning. It is a meta-principle, acting upon other rules and principles – a legal concept exercising a kind of interstitial normativity, pushing and pulling the boundaries of true primary norms when they threaten to overlap or conflict with each other"*.[932]

928 Cf. Bilder, Richard B. (2003): Beyond Compliance: Helping Nations Cooperate. In: Shelton, Dinah (ed.): Commitment and Compliance. The Role of Non-Binding Norms in the International Legal System. Published new in paperback. Oxford / New York: Oxford University Press, pp. 65–73, p. 67.

929 See Kiss, Alexandre (2003) (cf. *footnote 297* op. cit.), p. 224.

930 See UNESCO (ed.) (2005i) (cf. *footnote 216* op. cit.), p. 2.

931 See Shelton, Dinah (2003c) (cf. *footnote 357* op. cit.), p. 4.
See *Figure 39* in chapter VIII 1.3 *Gradual normativity* on page 208.

932 See Boyle, Alan E. (2006): Soft Law in International Law-Making. In: Evans, Malcolm David (ed.): International Law. 2. edition. Oxford: Oxford University Press, pp. 141–158, p. 152.

Content	Form	
	Legal instrument	Non-binding instrument
normative	*Law*	*Commitment*
promotional	*Hortatory language*	*Freedom of action*

Figure 39: Normative intent[933]

Once normativity is established as an abiding principle, matters of compliance can also be addressed alternatively. The following approach can be considered a *workaround* strategy: avoidance of being dependent on the exclusive *knock-out criterion* of *hard-law*, as is often preferable – a unique but hardly goal-oriented feature; and reconciliation of the *hard-* versus *soft-law* dichotomy towards gradual approaches.[934]

The distinction between *hard law* and *soft law* is already a *hot-potato issue* because *"(hard law) is not the only means of seeking to prevent or resolve social problems"*.[935] The nature of this distinction, along with its impact, is not subject to consensus from all theorists involved in the debate.[936] *"Regimes of public legislation and regulation, contract and treaty, and, indeed, the conduct of personal affairs, rest in good part on maintaining the integrity of this law-non-law distinction. Much of the work of lawyers and judges in fact relates to administering and policing the law-non-law-boundary and arguing or deciding on which side of it various alleged norms and conduct fall."*[937] Recognition is due principally to the scientific perspectives on the following:[938]

933 Normative content may equally apply to legal instruments, considered as *law*, and non-binding instruments, considered as *commitment*, accordingly.
Cf. Shelton, Dinah (2003c) (cf. *footnote 357* op. cit.), p. 4.

934 Cf. D'Aspremont, Jean (2008): Softness in International Law: A Self-Serving Quest for New Legal Materials. In: European Journal of International Law (EJIL), Volume 19, Issue 9, pp. 1075–1093, p. 1.

935 Other alternatives are, for instance: market mechanisms, private charity, education, information, negotiations, morality, courtesy, or social custom.
See Shelton, Dinah (2003c) (cf. *footnote 357* op. cit.), p. 8.

936 Cf. Heusel, Wolfgang (1991) (cf. *footnote 896* op. cit.), p. 315; Klabbers, Jan (1996 / 1998): The concept of treaty in international law. The Hague: Kluwer Law International; Evans, Malcolm David (ed.) (2006): International Law. Volume 2. edition. Oxford: Oxford University Press; Klabbers, Jan (2007) (cf. *footnote 897* op. cit.); Shaffer, Gregory; Pollack, Mark A. (2008): How Hard and Soft Law Interact in International Regulatory Governance: Alternatives, Complements and Antagonists. Inaugural Conference 2008 Paper. In: Society of International Economic Law (SIEL), Issue 45, pp. 1–68, p. 2.

937 See Bilder, Richard B. (2003) (cf. *footnote 928* op. cit.), p. 71.

938 Cf. Shaffer, Gregory; Pollack, Mark A. (2008) (cf. *footnote 936* op. cit.), p. 2.
See *Table 25* in chapter VIII 1.3 *Gradual normativity* on page 209.

Table 25: Scholarly doctrine and soft- versus hard-law choices[939]

Approach	Positions
Legal positivist	• Questioning whether *soft law* is law at all because it is not legally binding • Conceding *soft law* the significance of an instrument inferior to (real) *hard law*
Rationalist	• Choosing freely between *hard-* and *soft-law* instruments depending on the intended level of commitment • Deciding rationally the advantages offered in different circumstances and settings (*calculus approach*)[940] • Making judgments on, and applying law-making instruments in equal measure • Contending the evolution from *soft law* to *hard law* in progressive cycles of law-making which lead to greater regulatory co-operation
Constructivist	• Maintaining state interests and facilitating interstate interaction through processes of socialisation and fostered by *soft law* • Favouring *soft-law* instruments due to the ability to generate shared norms, a sense of common purpose and identity • Focusing on *soft-law* dependent, non-state actors to effect change in international law and in national regulatory practice • Contending the evolution from *soft law* to *hard law* in progressive cycles of law-making leading to greater regulatory co-operation

The need to define alternative sources of compliance can be explained as result of changing global contexts:[941] *"International law is undergoing a transformation affecting both constituent parts of its essence: the role of States as sole authors of international norms, and the binding nature of norms."*[942]

Increasing awareness affects the complexity of the international legal order tremendously.[943] *"There is real doubt whether this nineteenth-century invention*

939 The formal ascription to either soft- or hard-law choices differs in legal positivist, rationalist or constructivist perspectives.
Cf. Hoof, G. J. H. (Fried) van (1983) (cf. *footnote 867* op. cit.), pp. 34 et seqq; Fastenrath, Ulrich (1993) (cf. *footnote 869* op. cit.), pp. 307 et seqq; Hörtreiter, Isabel (2007) (cf. *footnote 510* op. cit.), p. 289; Shaffer, Gregory; Pollack, Mark A. (2008) (cf. *footnote 936* op. cit.), p. 2.

940 Economically speaking, *soft law* is more probable in situations of uncertainty, less costly for states to negotiate, and less costly to their sovereignty.
Cf. Shaffer, Gregory; Pollack, Mark A. (2008) (cf. *footnote 936* op. cit.), p. 2.

941 Cf. Burgstaller, Markus (2005) (cf. *footnote 445* op. cit.), pp. 9 et seqq.

942 See Heyvaert, Veerle (2009): Hybrid Norms in International Law. In: London School of Economics & Political Science (LSE) Legal Studies Working Papers, Volume 6, pp. 1–26, p. 1.

943 Cf. Kiss, Alexandre (2003) (cf. *footnote 297* op. cit.), p. 227.

and inheritance of heavily legalised, bureaucratically heavy, hard law intergovernmental organizations, centred on the United Nations system, can adequately address the pressing needs of the new age. The UN still is grounded in, and in some ways imprisoned by, a fixed, formal constitution-like legal charter that lacks proper recognition of the value, or even the existence, of the natural environment, not to speak of non-state actors."[944]

New *decision-takers*[945] and regimes emerged demanding regulatory order. The appearance of globalised regimes dealing with various issues leads to an increase need for co-ordination.[946] *"With new actors and new issues, the developing international order (...) utilises numerous methods to express expectations of behaviour."*[947]

New institutionalism provides the relevant theoretical background in positivism, mainly through re-defining, re-locating and emphasising the autonomous role of institutions.[948] Start-up (non-governmental) organisations and emerging institutional bodies have not been adequately represented yet within the post-war international legal order.[949] However, these corporate bodies of authority have been constantly producing ideas, visions and normative instruments.[950]

Binding implementation requires either an internationally valid mandate (*legitimisation*) or any recognised affiliation with the approved sources of international law. Thus, *"soft law is the sole alternative to non-state actors given the fact that they do not have the capacity to create norms and legally-binding international obligations"*.[951] That extra-legal, *soft-law* alternatives should be preferred to *hard-law* approaches is frequently due to one of these barriers.

Although frequently mentioned, how are *hard law* and *soft law* defined? Given the different scholarly approaches controversy is inevitable:[952] *"The very*

---

944 See Kirton, John J.; Trebilcock, Michael J. (eds.) (2004) (cf. *footnote 888* op. cit.), p. 4.

945 See Burgstaller, Markus (2005) (cf. *footnote 445* op. cit.), p. 9.

946 Cf. Hoof, G. J. H. (Fried) van (1983) (cf. *footnote 867* op. cit.), pp. 65–71; Burgstaller, Markus (2005) (cf. *footnote 445* op. cit.), p. 9.

947 See Shelton, Dinah (2003b): Editor's Concluding Note. The Role of Non-binding Norms in the International Legal System. In: Shelton, Dinah (ed.): Commitment and Compliance. The Role of Non-Binding Norms in the International Legal System. Published new in paperback. Oxford / New York: Oxford University Press, pp. 554–556, p. 554.

948 Cf. Burgstaller, Markus (2005) (cf. *footnote 445* op. cit.), p. 9.

949 Cf. Mazuelos Bellido, Ángeles (2004) (cf. *footnote 881* op. cit.), pp. 13–14.

950 Cf. Shaffer, Gregory; Pollack, Mark A. (2008) (cf. *footnote 936* op. cit.), p. 9.

951 Translation from Spanish into English: *"El soft law es también la única alternativa para los actores no estatales dado que no tienen capacidad para crear normas y obligaciones jurídicas internacionales"*.
See Mazuelos Bellido, Ángeles (2004) (cf. *footnote 881* op. cit.), p. 13.

952 Cf. Shaffer, Gregory; Pollack, Mark A. (2008) (cf. *footnote 936* op. cit.), p. 5.
See *Table 26* in chapter VIII 1.3 *Gradual normativity* on page 213.

term soft law has given rise to a lot of confusion: some writers use it to denote everything that falls short of being hard law, others include non-legal phenomena in their definition, whereas yet others use the term predominantly to refer to politically or morally binding agreements".[953]

In order to avoid elaboration on the *minutiae* of notional differences in definition, a brief and consolidated version is suggested: *hard law* or, alternatively, *strict law*[954] is *"(...) the legislative and regulatory context put in place by the government to meet certain objectives".*[955] It may be composed of three sub-features: precision, obligation and delegation.[956] *Hard law* is characterised by the *legal imperative*[957] of *pacta sunt servanda* prescribing an instrument of rules which is *a priori* legally binding – classically, treaties and formal agreements.[958]

Conversely, *soft law*, or sometimes pejoratively referred to as *junk law*,[959] is an implicit instrument of descriptive principles with normative content that is not *sui generis* legally binding,[960] unless turned into legally binding *a posteriori* (alternation) through processes of recognition, legitimisation or any other *cross reference*.[961] Therefore, *"(s)oft law (...) (is) defined as an agreement that is nei-*

953 See Klabbers, Jan (1996a) (cf. *footnote 897* op. cit.), p. 168; Klabbers, Jan (2007) (cf. *footnote 897* op. cit.), p. 190.

954 See Jabloner, Clemens; Okresek, Wolf (1983) (cf. *footnote 525* op. cit.), p. 221.

955 See Kirton, John J.; Trebilcock, Michael J. (eds.) (2004) (cf. *footnote 888* op. cit.), p. 324.

956 Cf. Kirton, John J.; Trebilcock, Michael J. (eds.) (2004) (cf. *footnote 888* op. cit.), p. 8; Kirton, John J.; Trebilcock, Michael J. (2004): Introduction: Hard Choices and Soft Law in Sustainable Governance. In: Kirton, John J.; Trebilcock, Michael J. (eds.): Hard choices, soft law. Voluntary standards in global trade, environment, and social governance. Aldershot / Burlington, Vermont: Ashgate Dartmouth (Global environmental governance), pp. 3–30, p. 8; Mörth, Ulrika (ed.) (2004): Soft law in governance and regulation. An interdisciplinary analysis. Cheltenham / Northampton: Edward Elgar Publishing, p. 6.

957 See Abi-Saab, Georges (2007) (cf. *footnote 488* op. cit.), p. 420.

958 Cf. Hillgenberg, Hartmut (1998): Soft Law im Völkerrecht. In: Zeitschrift für Europarechtliche Studien (ZEUS), Volume Vol. 1, Issue 1, pp. 81–102, p. 100; Abi-Saab, Georges (2007) (cf. *footnote 488* op. cit.), p. 420.

959 See Shaffer, Gregory; Pollack, Mark A. (2008) (cf. *footnote 936* op. cit.), p. 13.

960 Cf. Klabbers, Jan (1998b): The Undesirability of Soft Law. In: Nordic Journal of International Law, Volume 67, Issue 4, pp. 381–391(11), p. 386; Chinkin, Christine (2003) (cf. *footnote 444* op. cit.), p. 30; Ipsen, Knut; Menzel, Eberhard; Epping, Volker (2004): Völkerrecht. Volume 5. völlig neu bearbeitete Auflage. München: Verlag C. H. Beck, p. 251.

961 Cf. Boyle, Alan E. (1999): Some Reflections on the Relationship of Treaties and Soft Law. In: International and Comparative Law Quarterly, Volume 48, October 1999, pp. 901–913, p. 901; Shelton, Dinah (ed.) (2000) (cf. *footnote 357* op. cit.), p. 17; Kiss, Alexandre (2003) (cf. *footnote 297* op. cit.), p. 225; Hörtreiter, Isabel (2007) (cf. *footnote 510* op. cit.), pp. 276–277; Shaffer, Gregory; Pollack, Mark A. (2008) (cf. *foot-*

ther a formal treaty nor customary law".[962] Prominent examples are resolutions, declarations and recommendations,[963] or *"(...) other measures such as voluntary programmes, covenants, or bi-lateral agreements between a government and a company (or the civil society)"*.[964]

Soft-soft law combines both non-binding content and a non-binding instrumentality.[965] *Soft law* may also serve as a *precursor*[966] part of the multilateral, treaty-making process when it comes to defining instruments and mechanisms, standards and procedures of implementation, or an *ex-ante* agreed-upon understanding of terms (*opinio iuris*).[967] Analogously speaking, *"(h)ard law is like marriage; soft law is like courtship or cohabitation"*.[968]

Undoubtedly, *"(t)he hard law / soft law distinction has energised the analysis of international law in its richness and diversity. Moreover, understanding the relative pros and cons of soft and hard law options has given policy makers a broader and potentially more effective arsenal of tools to pursue international policy objectives (...)"*:[969]

---

note 936 op. cit.), p. 1; Guzman, Andrew T. (2008): How international law works. A rational choice theory. New York: Oxford University Press, p. 59.

962 See Guzman, Andrew T. (2008) (cf. *footnote 961* op. cit.), p. 59.

963 Cf. Kälin, Walter; Baldegger, Mirjam (eds.) (2006) (cf. *footnote 510* op. cit.), p. 218; Vitzthum, Wolfgang Graf; Bothe, Michael (eds.) (2007) (cf. *footnote 505* op. cit.), p. 12.

964 See Kirton, John J.; Trebilcock, Michael J. (eds.) (2004) (cf. *footnote 888* op. cit.), p. 324.

965 Cf. Mazuelos Bellido, Ángeles (2004) (cf. *footnote 881* op. cit.), pp. 2, 29; Abi-Saab, Georges (2007) (cf. *footnote 488* op. cit.), p. 420.

966 See Heyvaert, Veerle (2009) (cf. *footnote 942* op. cit.), p. 3.

967 Cf. Zemanek, Karl (1998) (cf. *footnote 869* op. cit.), pp. 858–859; Boyle, Alan E. (1999) (cf. *footnote 961* op. cit.), pp. 904–906; Ipsen, Knut; Menzel, Eberhard; Epping, Volker (2004) (cf. *footnote 960* op. cit.), p. 250.

968 See Kirton, John J.; Trebilcock, Michael J. (eds.) (2004) (cf. *footnote 888* op. cit.), p. 351.

969 See Heyvaert, Veerle (2009) (cf. *footnote 942* op. cit.), p. 3.

Table 26: Advantages and disadvantages of hard law and soft law[970]

	Hard law	*Soft law*
Advantages	• More credible commitment (*integrated* compliance) and conformity • Less uncertainty • Direct legal effects (self-executing or legal enactment) • Ease of monitoring, reporting, follow-up, assessing performance and dispute settlement (courts' decisions) • Creation of mechanisms to interpret or elaborate specific legal commitments (guidelines) • Internal consistency • Effectiveness (explicit pressure) • Existence of authoritative, material and sanctioning power	• Dynamic, de-formalised, highly intentional and adaptive • Pursuit of common goals (implicit pressure) and giving information about legislative preferences • Easier and less costly to reach agreement (contracting costs) • Gaining consensus step-by-step (inclusion) and bottom-up • Flexible to adopt, amend, change, adapt and replace • More participation, representation, diversity and support (fall-back provisions) • Easier to adhere to implementing instruments (compliance, soft enforcement and dispute avoidance)

970 Still, opinion-making on *advantages* and *disadvantages* of hard law and soft law, respectively, are highly biased.
Cf. Jabloner, Clemens; Okresek, Wolf (1983) (cf. *footnote 525* op. cit.), pp. 220–229; Hillgenberg, Hartmut (1998) (cf. *footnote 958* op. cit.), pp. 84 et seqq; Hillgenberg, Hartmut (1999) (cf. *footnote 869* op. cit.), p. 501; Klabbers, Jan (1996 / 1998) (cf. *footnote 936* op. cit.); Boyle, Alan E. (1999) (cf. *footnote 961* op. cit.), pp. 902–912; Shelton, Dinah (ed.) (2000) (cf. *footnote 357* op. cit.), pp. 12–13; Abbott, Kenneth W.; Snidal, Duncan (2000): Hard Law and Soft Law in International Governance. In: International Organization, Volume 54, Issue 3, pp. 421–456, pp. 424 et seqq, 434 et seqq; Shelton, Dinah (ed.) (2003): Commitment and Compliance. The Role of Non-Binding Norms in the International Legal System. Volume Published new in paperback. Oxford / New York: Oxford University Press; Shelton, Dinah (2003c) (cf. *footnote 357* op. cit.), pp. 11–13; Chinkin, Christine (2003) (cf. *footnote 444* op. cit.), pp. 30 et seqq; Kiss, Alexandre (2003) (cf. *footnote 297* op. cit.), pp. 237–238; Kirton, John J.; Trebilcock, Michael J. (eds.) (2004) (cf. *footnote 888* op. cit.), p. 5; Skjærseth, Jon Birger; Stokke, Olav Schram; Wettestad, Jørgen (2006) (cf. *footnote 294* op. cit.), pp. 105–106; Boyle, Alan E. (2006) (cf. *footnote 932* op. cit.), pp. 143 et seqq; Abi-Saab, Georges (2007) (cf. *footnote 488* op. cit.), p. 420; Klabbers, Jan (2007) (cf. *footnote 897* op. cit.); Hörtreiter, Isabel (2007) (cf. *footnote 510* op. cit.), pp. 295–311; Shaffer, Gregory; Pollack, Mark A. (2008) (cf. *footnote 936* op. cit.), pp. 8–14; Gersen, Jacob E.; Posner, Eric A. (2008): Soft Law. In: Stanford Law Review / University of Chicago, Public Law and Legal Theory Working Paper, Volume March 2008, Issue 213, pp. 2–50, pp. 18–22; Heyvaert, Veerle (2009) (cf. *footnote 942* op. cit.), p. 2.

	Hard law	*Soft law*
Disadvantages	• Fixed and interpretative • Costly (contracting costs) • Bureaucracy • Time- and energy-consuming • Principle of exclusion • Limiting enforceability and coercion • Less transparency	• Incompleteness and uncertainty • Difficult monitoring and appropriate assessment (surveillance) • Not readily enforceable through binding dispute resolution • Non-enforceable dispute settlement mechanisms (authority)

"All this seems to drive us inevitably into the embrace of the binary code, which thinks only in terms of legal and illegal, binding and non-binding, black and white."[971] The *binary mode*[972] distinction between *hard law* and *soft law* cannot serve as an end in itself but must be target-oriented instead. Within a fragmented international system of differently legally-binding instruments, *hard law* and *soft law* do not only interact complementarily but also antagonistically.[973] *"For these reasons, a growing number of scholars in law and political science have advocated a pragmatic approach, selecting alternative hard and soft law approaches depending on the characteristics of the issue and the negotiating and institutional context in question. Scholars have noted, in particular, how hard and soft law instruments may be effectively combined to lead to greater cooperation."*[974]

In consequence, a *new approach* has been in development that reconciles both elements of law-making. It is the evolution of *"'hybrid norms', a new category of international norm that is situated between our conventional conceptions of 'hard law' and 'soft law'"*.[975]

Table 27: Benefits and challenges of hybrid norms[976]

Benefits	*Challenges*
Avoiding distortions and discrimination	Ensuring equity and comparability
Creating context-dependent momentum	Providing incentives of adherence
Promising flexibility in enforcement	Establishing accountability and transparency

971 See Klabbers, Jan (1996a) (cf. *footnote 897* op. cit.), p. 179; Klabbers, Jan (2007) (cf. *footnote 897* op. cit.), p. 201.

972 See Klabbers, Jan (1996a) (cf. *footnote 897* op. cit.), p. 181; Klabbers, Jan (2007) (cf. *footnote 897* op. cit.), p. 203.

973 Cf. Shaffer, Gregory; Pollack, Mark A. (2008) (cf. *footnote 936* op. cit.), p. 3.

974 See Shaffer, Gregory; Pollack, Mark A. (2008) (cf. *footnote 936* op. cit.), p. 14.

975 See Heyvaert, Veerle (2009) (cf. *footnote 942* op. cit.), p. 2.
See *Table 27* in chapter VIII 1.3 *Gradual normativity* on page 214.

976 Illustrated by the Stockholm Convention on Persistent Organic Pollutants (2001).
Cf. Heyvaert, Veerle (2009) (cf. *footnote 942* op. cit.), pp. 4 et seqq.

Pragmatically speaking, the category to which an instrument of law-making belongs is not as telling as the effect it ultimately has on certain issues. This may *"result(...) in a complex hybrid of hard and soft law instruments"*[977] oscillating to varying degrees between *de-jure* and *de-facto* binding.[978] *Hybrid* forms of complex, soft international law-making are characterised by their *relative*[979] or *gradual normativity*[980] as a *blended* theoretical construct.[981] For instance, *"(s)ome (...) (soft-law) instruments operate in the shadow of binding instruments"*.[982] As a consequence, inside *hard-soft law continuum*[983] from *"legal obligation to complete freedom of action"*[984] the binding force is subject to change according to the conditions of context.[985]

Figure 40: Gradual normativity in law-making[986]

The most prominent *soft-law* and best-practice example for *gradual normativity*, or the *"blurring of the normativity threshold"*,[987] can be witnessed in international human rights law.[988] Human rights guarantees and obligations result

977 See Shaffer, Gregory; Pollack, Mark A. (2008) (cf. *footnote 936* op. cit.), p. 9.

978 Cf. Yusuf, Abdulqawi A. (2007a) (cf. *footnote 129* op. cit.), p. 369.

979 See Kälin, Walter; Baldegger, Mirjam (eds.) (2006) (cf. *footnote 510* op. cit.), p. 218.

980 See Yusuf, Abdulqawi A. (2007a) (cf. *footnote 129* op. cit.), p. 369.

981 Cf. Heusel, Wolfgang (1991) (cf. *footnote 896* op. cit.), p. 317; Mazuelos Bellido, Ángeles (2004) (cf. *footnote 881* op. cit.), pp. 36–37.

982 See Goldmann, Matthias (2009) (cf. *footnote 873* op. cit.), p. 1866.

983 See Shelton, Dinah (2006d) (cf. *footnote 875* op. cit.), pp. 180–181; Shaffer, Gregory; Pollack, Mark A. (2008) (cf. *footnote 936* op. cit.), p. 1; Guzman, Andrew T. (2008) (cf. *footnote 961* op. cit.), p. 142.
See *Figure 40* in chapter VIII 1.3 *Gradual normativity* on page 215.

984 See Shelton, Dinah (2006d) (cf. *footnote 875* op. cit.), pp. 180–181.

985 Cf. Weil, Prosper (1982 / 1983) (cf. *footnote 875* op. cit.), p. 415; Mazuelos Bellido, Ángeles (2004) (cf. *footnote 881* op. cit.), p. 16; Vitzthum, Wolfgang Graf; Bothe, Michael (eds.) (2007) (cf. *footnote 505* op. cit.), p. 148; Goldmann, Matthias (2009) (cf. *footnote 873* op. cit.), p. 1872.

986 This figure argues for *gradual normativity* to serve as first-hand concept of building bridges between soft- and hard-law approaches.

987 See Weil, Prosper (1982 / 1983) (cf. *footnote 875* op. cit.), pp. 415, 430–431.

988 Cf. Frowein, Jochen Abraham (1989) (cf. *footnote 203* op. cit.), p. 779; Mutua, Makau (ed.) (2007): Standard Setting in Human Rights: Critique and Prognosis. Volume Paper No. 2007–013. New York: BUFFALO Legal Studies Research Paper Series (Human Rights Quarterly, Vol. 29), pp. 560, 603, 613, 619.

from the combination of binding and non-binding instruments.[989] More precisely, the *Universal Declaration of Human Rights* (UDHR) of 1948 turned from a non-binding United Nations resolution into a common standard of realisation through incorporating abstract rights into the concision of binding international agreements.[990] Due to these *dynamic cross references* the *Universal Declaration of Human Rights* (UDHR) is considered to be binding customary international law (*opinio iuris*).[991]

1.4 Soft law

"Soft law is manifestly a multi-faceted concept, whose relationship to treaties is both subtle and diverse. It presents alternatives to treaties in certain circumstances, at other times it complements them, while also providing different ways of understanding the legal effect of different kinds of treaty. (...) It is simply another tool in the professional lawyer's armoury."[992]

Although *soft law* has always been applied knowingly or unconsciously, it has only recently developed into a proper mainstream subject. As a result, early definitions omit to interpret *soft law* as a theoretical concept of its own. Instead, theorists tend to define *soft law* imprecisely alongside conventional categories of law-making, namely norm-based *hard law*: *soft law* is typically defined as *"[...] (a)ny international instrument other than a treaty containing principles, norms, standards, or other statements of expected behaviour"*.[993] For instance, *soft law* may be related to *"(a) norms whose status is uncertain or whose content is vague and scope imprecise, to (b) obligations considered real but not enforceable in a court, to (c) various levels of obligation where the difference is not one of kind of degree – weak and strong, hard and soft, grey rather black or white"*.[994] Hard-line opponents of *soft-law* would refuse any proximity to the term *norm*.[995]

---

989 Cf. Shelton, Dinah (2003a): Commentary and Conclusions. In: Shelton, Dinah (ed.): Commitment and Compliance. The Role of Non-Binding Norms in the International Legal System. Published new in paperback. Oxford / New York: Oxford University Press, pp. 449–463, p. 449.

990 Cf. Symonides, Janusz; Volodin, Vladimir (1996): UNESCO and Human Rights. Standard-Setting Instruments Major Meetings Publications. Selection of documents and introduction SHS-96/WS/8. Supported by: Rivet, Sophie. Paris: UNESCO workshops.

991 Cf. Zemanek, Karl (1998) (cf. *footnote 869* op. cit.), p. 853.

992 See Boyle, Alan E. (1999) (cf. *footnote 961* op. cit.), p. 913.

993 See Shelton, Dinah (2006d) (cf. *footnote 875* op. cit.), p. 180.

994 See Sloan, Blaine (1987) (cf. *footnote 874* op. cit.), p. 107.

995 Cf. Verdross, Alfred; Simma, Bruno (1984 / 2010) (cf. *footnote 874* op. cit.), pp. 419–422.

Soft law has since gained increasing importance and independence in both theory and practice. This is due to the fact that *"soft law instruments (...) can provide an experimental response to new challenges as they continually arise".*[996] The recognised wording clearly documents and evidences the *raison d'être* and development of *soft law.*[997] Moreover, *"(t)he concept of soft law which rests on the idea that the binary nature of law is ill-suited to accommodate the growing complexity of contemporary international relations (...)".*[998]

"The ubiquity of soft international law is due to the absence of an authoritative interpreter that takes care to distinguish communications that comply with formalities and those that do not. States comply with soft law when they have an interest in cooperating, just as they do for hard law."[999] *Soft law* results from two consecutive steps that are similar to *hard-law* making:[1000]

- Mutual consent on particular rules of conduct combined with;
- Extra-legal tools defined, confirmed or regulated by international law.

Without wishing to enter again into the loop of dichotomised definitions,[1001] what are the constitutive elements of *soft law*?[1002]

996 See O'Connell, Mary Ellen (2003): The Role of Soft Law in a Global Order. In: Shelton, Dinah (ed.): Commitment and Compliance. The Role of Non-Binding Norms in the International Legal System. Published new in paperback. Oxford / New York: Oxford University Press, pp. 100–114, p. 110.

997 Identifying and defining *soft law*, *droit mou* or *droit indicatif*, *diritto morbido*, etc. in the context of and even as a complementary source of *European Union* law-making. See Conforti, Benedetto (1995) (cf. *footnote 510* op. cit.), p. 40; Chinkin, Christine (2003) (cf. *footnote 444* op. cit.), p. 30; Senden, Linda (2004): Soft law in European Community law. Oxford: Hart Publishing (Modern studies in European law, 1), pp. 107 et seqq.

998 See D'Aspremont, Jean (2008) (cf. *footnote 934* op. cit.), p. 1.

999 See Gersen, Jacob E.; Posner, Eric A. (2008) (cf. *footnote 970* op. cit.), p. 44.

1000 Cf. Schweisfurth, Theodor (2006) (cf. *footnote 897* op. cit.), p. 93.

1001 Cf. Zemanek, Karl (1998) (cf. *footnote 869* op. cit.), p. 858.

1002 See *Figure 41* in chapter VIII 1.4 *Soft law* on page 218.

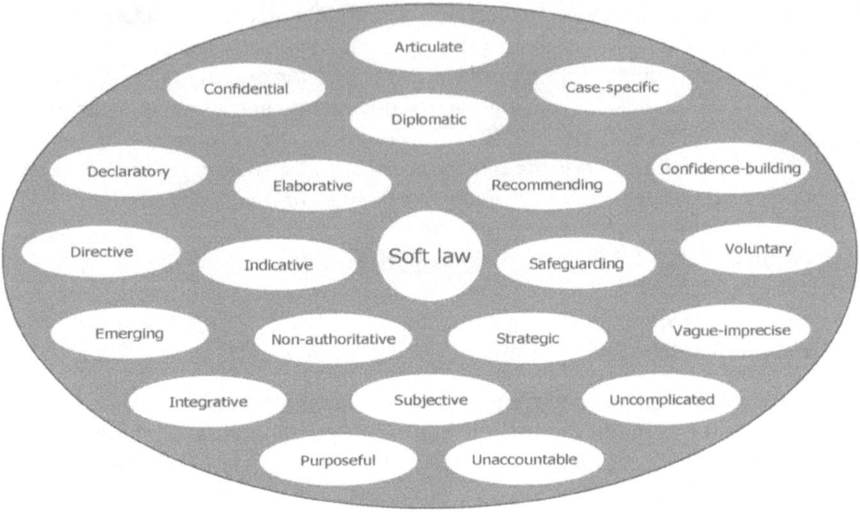

Figure 41: Basic characteristics of soft law[1003]

Given that non-binding norms have a complex and unquantifiable impact in the development of international law,[1004] different types of *soft law* can be distinguished on an international scale and in accordance with both horizontal and vertical structuring.[1005] The first applies to changing structural modes of expression, which include:

- Simple and only weakly-binding recommendations, such as codes of conduct; via
- Recommendation combined with an institutionalised follow-up, such as guidelines of reporting, monitoring, national-level enactment and implementation, consultation and co-operation;[1006] and
- Declarations of intent as sets of flexible mechanisms for co-ordinated co-operation, like notification, ratification or approval; and

1003 Given the plurality of characteristics soft law may appropriately meet contextual requirements serving as sources to compliance and commitment.
Cf. Hillgenberg, Hartmut (1998) (cf. *footnote 958* op. cit.), pp. 84 et seqq; Jabloner, Clemens; Okresek, Wolf (1983) (cf. *footnote 525* op. cit.), p. 218; Chinkin, Christine (2003) (cf. *footnote 444* op. cit.), pp. 30 et seqq.

1004 Cf. Zemanek, Karl (1998) (cf. *footnote 869* op. cit.), pp. 860–861; Shelton, Dinah (ed.) (2000) (cf. *footnote 357* op. cit.), p. 1.

1005 Cf. Jabloner, Clemens; Okresek, Wolf (1983) (cf. *footnote 525* op. cit.), pp. 223 et seqq; Zemanek, Karl (1998) (cf. *footnote 869* op. cit.), p. 856; Shelton, Dinah (ed.) (2000) (cf. *footnote 357* op. cit.), pp. 12–13.

1006 See Jabloner, Clemens; Okresek, Wolf (1983) (cf. *footnote 525* op. cit.), p. 223.

- *Strict law* in the shape of *soft law* through the generation of contractual agreements, such as non-committing appendices to international treaties, and so-called *framework agreements*.

The latter concerns the substance of *soft law*:

- *Primary soft law* relates to normative texts which are not adopted in treaty form but addressed to the international community, either on the whole or to the entire membership of the adoptive institution or organisation.[1007]
- *Secondary soft law* relates to recommendations and general comments on the supervisory organs of international human rights, the jurisprudence of courts and commissions, the decisions of rapporteurs and other *ad-hoc* bodies, and the resolutions of political organs of international organisations which apply primary norms.[1008] It is established through *dynamic cross references* by binding treaties, and ensured by monitoring the mechanisms of appointed individuals, working groups, thematic mandates and particular rapporteurs.[1009]

Reference to *soft law* is certainly more than *cheap talk*:[1010] Moral consensus (*opinio iuris*) and its application (*usus)*[1011] may lead to *mutual confidence-building*[1012] and normative authority (compliance) of its own kind. *Soft law* supports accountability through influencing the establishment of international institutions. It creates promising and stimulating alternatives to the adoption of more progressive decisions through *hard law*, *least-common-denominator* norms.[1013] It establishes continuing debate suitable to the expression of *opinio iuris*.[1014] It provides opportunity for different levels of commitment representing the increased strength, catalytic effects and maturity of the forms of international law.[1015] It adds flexible mechanisms for dynamic interaction, expedient adoption, amendment or replacement.[1016] It enables effective decision-making in

1007 Cf. Shelton, Dinah (2003a) (cf. *footnote 989* op. cit.), pp. 449–451.

1008 Cf. Mazuelos Bellido, Ángeles (2004) (cf. *footnote 881* op. cit.), p. 26; Fischer-Lescano, Andreas; Teubner, Gunther (2006) (cf. *footnote 140* op. cit.), p. 55.

1009 Cf. Shelton, Dinah (2003a) (cf. *footnote 989* op. cit.), pp. 451–453; Mazuelos Bellido, Ángeles (2004) (cf. *footnote 881* op. cit.), p. 7.

1010 See Gersen, Jacob E.; Posner, Eric A. (2008) (cf. *footnote 970* op. cit.), p. 14.

1011 Cf. Hoof, G. J. H. (Fried) van (1983) (cf. *footnote 867* op. cit.), p. 91; Shelton, Dinah (2003c) (cf. *footnote 357* op. cit.), p. 1; Gersen, Jacob E.; Posner, Eric A. (2008) (cf. *footnote 970* op. cit.), p. 16.

1012 See Hillgenberg, Hartmut (1999) (cf. *footnote 869* op. cit.), p. 501.

1013 Cf. Abbott, Kenneth W.; Snidal, Duncan (2000) (cf. *footnote 970* op. cit.), pp. 444 et seqq.

1014 Cf. Ipsen, Knut; Menzel, Eberhard; Epping, Volker (2004) (cf. *footnote 960* op. cit.), p. 250; Shelton, Dinah (2006d) (cf. *footnote 875* op. cit.), p. 182; Gerner, Martin (14/09/2009) (cf. *footnote 407* op. cit.).

1015 Cf. Boyle, Alan E. (2006) (cf. *footnote 932* op. cit.), p. 155.

1016 Cf. Shelton, Dinah (2006d) (cf. *footnote 875* op. cit.), p. 182.

cases of uncertainty or other urgent cases requiring action.[1017] Lastly, it allows more direct participation and awareness-raising by opening access to the processes of legislation for parties which do not have the legal power to conclude treaties under international law.[1018] There is, in conclusion, a public interest in and a demand for *soft law*.[1019]

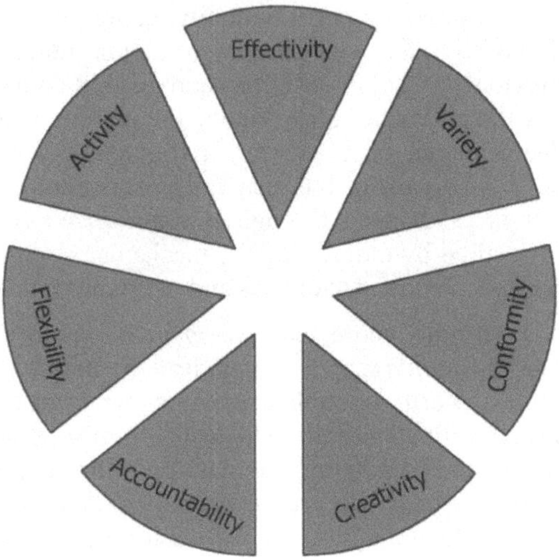

Figure 42: Benefits of soft law[1020]

Despite the demonstrable benefits of *soft law*, fundamental critique is nonetheless levelled at it. Critical activities range from interrogation of its effects to

1017 Cf. Bleckmann, Albert (1982) (cf. *footnote 889* op. cit.), p. 340.

1018 Non-state actors, usually.
Cf. Hillgenberg, Hartmut (1999) (cf. *footnote 869* op. cit.), p. 501; Kiss, Alexandre (2003) (cf. *footnote 297* op. cit.), pp. 226–227; Mazuelos Bellido, Ángeles (2004) (cf. *footnote 881* op. cit.), pp. 13–14; Ebbesson, Jonas (2007): Public Participation. In: Bodansky, Daniel; Brunée, Jutta; Hey, Ellen (eds.): The Oxford handbook of international environmental law. Oxford: Oxford University Press (Oxford handbooks), pp. 681–703, pp. 693–696.
See *Figure 42* in chapter VIII 1.4 *Soft law* on page 220.
Cf. *Figure 41* in chapter VIII 1.4 *Soft law* on page 218.

1019 Cf. Francioni, Francesco (1996 / 2008) (cf. *footnote 880* op. cit.), p. 174.

1020 Despite of occasionally harsh criticism major advantages of *soft law* are its effectivity, variety, conformity, creativity, accountability, flexibility and activity.
Cf. Hillgenberg, Hartmut (1999) (cf. *footnote 869* op. cit.), p. 501; Shelton, Dinah (2003c) (cf. *footnote 357* op. cit.), pp. 11–13; Kiss, Alexandre (2003) (cf. *footnote 297* op. cit.), p. 239; Kirton, John J.; Trebilcock, Michael J. (eds.) (2004) (cf. *footnote 888* op. cit.), p. 9.

proclamations that it is wholly redundant and undesirable. Is it just *"much ado about nothing"*,[1021] apart from which objections are justified and truly valid? Main arguments consider *"(...) both a practical and theoretical nature: (soft law) lacks plausible theoretical underpinnings, and it finds little support in both state practice and judicial practice (...)"*.[1022] These three controversial arguments about *soft-law* can briefly be summarised as follows:[1023]

1. Lack of theory:

Is the theoretical basis of *soft law under-conceptualised*[1024] or limited, deficient or inconsistent, usually claiming that *soft law* serves interpretative purposes only? Language is generally interpretative and highly indeterminate in the case of both *soft law* and *hard law* alike. International law is by definition regarded interpretatively. Thus, *soft law* cannot serve as the exclusive domain for the realisation of political commitment. Conversely, *hard law* can only be created as a result of political agreement. Consequently, a self-contained theory of *soft-law* cannot exist. Applying and implementing *soft law* suggests a *turning point* between binding, pre-stage and interim law, or non-binding, non-law.[1025]

2. Ambiguous state practice:

"(...) (I)t is not all that obvious that states can conclude agreements yet at the same time deny that such agreements would amount to hard law (...)".[1026] State practice questions *soft-law* approaches, because there is no proper reason why agreements are negotiated if they are not subject to legal compliance.[1027] Put differently, *"(...) (do) not worry, as our solution is only soft law (...)"*[1028] cannot serve as *leitmotiv* of action, either in international politics or law.

3. Redundant in legal practice:

1021 Translation from Spanish into English: *"¿Mucho ruido y pocas nueces?"* See Mazuelos Bellido, Ángeles (2004) (cf. *footnote 881* op. cit.), p. 1.

1022 See Klabbers, Jan (1996a) (cf. *footnote 897* op. cit.), p. 168; Klabbers, Jan (2007) (cf. *footnote 897* op. cit.), p. 190.

1023 Cf. Klabbers, Jan (1996a) (cf. *footnote 897* op. cit.), pp. 172–174, 177 et seqq; Klabbers, Jan (1998b) (cf. *footnote 960* op. cit.), pp. 382 et seqq; Hillgenberg, Hartmut (1999) (cf. *footnote 869* op. cit.), pp. 514–515; Klabbers, Jan (2007) (cf. *footnote 897* op. cit.), pp. 194–196, 199 et seqq; Goldmann, Matthias (2009) (cf. *footnote 873* op. cit.), p. 1876.

1024 See Goldmann, Matthias (2009) (cf. *footnote 873* op. cit.), p. 1869.

1025 That is, *non-legal* obligations, e.g., moral, pre-legal, para-legal, moral, political commitment.
Cf. Bothe, Michael (1980) (cf. *footnote 510* op. cit.), p. 65; Hobe, Stephan; Kimminich, Otto (2004) (cf. *footnote 511* op. cit.), pp. 198–201.

1026 See Klabbers, Jan (1996a) (cf. *footnote 897* op. cit.), p. 172; Klabbers, Jan (2007) (cf. *footnote 897* op. cit.), p. 194.

1027 Cf. Shelton, Dinah (ed.) (2000) (cf. *footnote 357* op. cit.), p. 461.

1028 See Klabbers, Jan (1998b) (cf. *footnote 960* op. cit.), p. 384.

Firstly, there is in legal reality little support for *soft law* because it does not produce decisive legal effects that can be validated empirically.[1029] Consequently, most *"(...) (decisions based on soft law) are somehow recast into the more accepted sources of international law: treaties and custom (...) they are typically applied in a binary fashion. Soft law instruments turn out to be either violated or not, either complied with or not (...)".*[1030] Secondly, *soft law* does not manage to deal with rules of conflict. In case of conflict between instruments of *soft-law* and *hard-law*, the application of *lex posterior* or *lex specialis* is not possible, because this implies that *soft* and *hard law* are of equal weight. In this case the *hard-law* instrument is interpreted in the light of the later *soft-law* instrument. S*oft law* therefore contributes an interpretative rather than an autonomous element of law.[1031] Essentially, *"(the) binary (hard versus soft) law is well capable of handling all kinds of subtleties and sensitivities; within the binary mode, law can be more or less specific, more or less exact, more or less determinate, more or less wide in scope, more or less pressing, more or less serious, more or less far-reaching; the only thing it cannot be is more or less binding".*[1032]

How can the polarity of the *soft versus hard law* debate be transformed into constructive momentum? In summation of the critical voices, the mere distinction between the non-coercive, non-legally binding (*soft law*) and the coercive, legally binding (*hard law*) leads to pure irresolution, since it does not satisfactorily answer the question of compliance.

Firstly, clarification is needed on the intent of normative *constructs*:[1033] such constructs are largely indispensable in fostering common understanding and, as a result, making behaviour predictable.[1034] That refers to both treaty-based and

---

1029 Cf. Klabbers, Jan (1998b) (cf. *footnote 960* op. cit.), p. 382.

1030 See Klabbers, Jan (1996a) (cf. *footnote 897* op. cit.), p. 174; Klabbers, Jan (2007) (cf. *footnote 897* op. cit.), p. 196; Koskenniemi, Martti (ed.) (2007): Sources of international law. Volume Reprinted. Aldershot: Ashgate Dartmouth (The Library of Essays in International Law, 5), pp. 189 et seqq.

1031 Cf. Ipsen, Knut; Menzel, Eberhard; Epping, Volker (2004) (cf. *footnote 960* op. cit.), p. 250.

1032 See Klabbers, Jan (1996a) (cf. *footnote 897* op. cit.), p. 181; Klabbers, Jan (2007) (cf. *footnote 897* op. cit.), p. 203; Koskenniemi, Martti (ed.) (2007) (cf. *footnote 1030* op. cit.), pp. 189 et seqq.
To take an example: by considering non-legal obligations as obligations of good faith the case occurs that faith is already regarded as a legal conception according to the doctrine of estoppel. The difficulty already lies in grounding respect for non-legal obligations in a legal concept. This is not appropriate.
Cf. Bothe, Michael (1980) (cf. *footnote 510* op. cit.), p. 95.

1033 E.g., norms, rules, agreements, decisions, etc.

1034 Cf. Bothe, Michael (1980) (cf. *footnote 510* op. cit.), p. 66; Fastenrath, Ulrich (1993) (cf. *footnote 869* op. cit.), p. 332.

other instruments being adopted either between non-state parties[1035] or state parties[1036] *inter se*. *"As law is given the general task of influencing human behaviour, (it) must be judged according to how effectively (it) fulfil(ls) this task. In this context, limited effectiveness of a legal theory implies limited normativity."*[1037]

Secondly, another insight achieved is the acknowledgement of varying degrees of binding;[1038] acceptance notwithstanding, ranging forms of commitment may apply alike.[1039] This is due to the assumption that law is generally imperfect, containing certain gaps of understanding that must be compensated for through (con-)textual interpretation.[1040] These so called *lacunae*[1041] are an immanent though truly positive feature within the framework of international law, influencing not only the exegesis of treaties but also the sense of justice beyond.[1042] They originate from subjective creativity in interpretation and in ex-

1035 A non-exhaustive list of possible forms includes gentlemen's agreements, codes of conduct, memorandum of understanding, etc.
Cf. Hillgenberg, Hartmut (1998) (cf. *footnote 958* op. cit.); Mazuelos Bellido, Ángeles (2004) (cf. *footnote 881* op. cit.), pp. 19–20; Doehring, Karl (2004) (cf. *footnote 874* op. cit.), p. 124; Shaw, Malcolm N. (2008) (cf. *footnote 912* op. cit.), pp. 117–119.

1036 A non-exhaustive list of possible forms includes resolutions, declarations, agendas, summit diplomacy, programmes, platforms of action, comity, good faith, drafts, travaux préparatoires, etc.
Cf. Bothe, Michael (1980) (cf. *footnote 510* op. cit.), p. 70; Conforti, Benedetto (1995) (cf. *footnote 510* op. cit.), p. 40; Chinkin, Christine (2003) (cf. *footnote 444* op. cit.), pp. 30 et seqq; Schweisfurth, Theodor (2006) (cf. *footnote 897* op. cit.), p. 93; Hörtreiter, Isabel (2007) (cf. *footnote 510* op. cit.), p. 252.

1037 See Fastenrath, Ulrich (1993) (cf. *footnote 869* op. cit.), p. 332.

1038 So called *zebra codes*, for instance, combine legally binding with non-binding documents aiming at first to reach legally binding agreements and later to achieve non-binding, more extensive or further reaching standards beyond the legally binding with the consent of member states. Certainly the most prominent example is the 1992 *Rio Declaration on Environment and Development* consisting of five interdependent documents: two international (legally binding) treaties, two legally non-binding declarations and the political programme of action (implementation) (Agenda 21).
Cf. United Nations (1992) (cf. *footnote 733*op. cit.); United Nations (ed.) (1993) (cf. *footnote 732* op. cit.); Hobe, Stephan; Kimminich, Otto (2004) (cf. *footnote 511* op. cit.), p. 200.

1039 Cf. Brownlie, Ian (2002) (cf. *footnote 510* op. cit.); Shaffer, Gregory; Pollack, Mark A. (2008) (cf. *footnote 936* op. cit.), pp. 6–7.

1040 This includes cultural predispositions, intellectual backgrounds and specific use of language, for instance.

1041 See Fastenrath, Ulrich (1993) (cf. *footnote 869* op. cit.), pp. 329, 330; Koskenniemi, Martti (ed.) (2007) (cf. *footnote 1030* op. cit.), pp. 153 et seqq.

1042 For example, the development of customary law, general principles (*ius cogens*) or obligations *erga omnes*.
Cf. Fastenrath, Ulrich (1993) (cf. *footnote 869* op. cit.), pp. 338–341; Koskenniemi, Martti (ed.) (2007) (cf. *footnote 1030* op. cit.), pp. 153 et seqq.

pression. *"The interpretative regress reinforces what we know anyway about treaties: that they have gaps in their coverage and in any event cannot cover every subject matter that might be relevant to their object and purpose. By contrast, customary law is gap-free and theoretically unlimited."*[1043] As a consequence *relative* or *graduated normativity*[1044] of law is unavoidable in practice and actually desired. Normative instruments are designed accordingly,[1045] likewise calling for *"instrumental pluralism in the post-national constellation"*.[1046]

Thirdly, determining the dividing line between legal and other kinds of norms is under significant theoretical debate.[1047] It is ultimately the practical implication and functional facilitation that really matter.[1048] Meanwhile, due to rising *interdisciplinary engagement*,[1049] jurisprudence appears to offer gradually increasing support to multi-legal arrangements through case-specific jurisdiction.[1050] In this respect and regardless of pejorative dimensions, it is fairly true *"that soft law is a good thing because a soft agreement is always better than no agreement at all"*.[1051] Following this argument, *relative normativity*[1052] should

---

1043 See D'Amato, Anthony (2008) (cf. *footnote 877* op. cit.), p. 13.

1044 See Weil, Prosper (1982 / 1983) (cf. *footnote 875* op. cit.), p. 423; Fastenrath, Ulrich (1993) (cf. *footnote 869* op. cit.), pp. 330, 331; Koskenniemi, Martti (ed.) (2007) (cf. *footnote 1030* op. cit.), pp. 153 et seqq; Goldmann, Matthias (2009) (cf. *footnote 873* op. cit.), p. 1871.

1045 Cf. Shelton, Dinah (ed.) (2000) (cf. *footnote 357* op. cit.), p. 461; Eisemann, Pierre Michel (2007) (cf. *footnote 478* op. cit.), p. 26; Shelton, Dinah; Jonge Oudraat, Chantal de; Simmons, P. J. (1999 / 2009): Commitment and Compliance: What Role for International Soft Law? Presentation review. Supported by: Blavin, Jonathan. Carnegie Endowment for International Peace, p. 4.

1046 See Goldmann, Matthias (2009) (cf. *footnote 873* op. cit.), p. 1870.

1047 Cf. Lowe, Vaughan; Fitzmaurice, Malgosia (eds.) (1996 / 2008): Fifty years of the International Court of Justice. Essays in honour of Sir Robert Jennings. Cambridge: Cambridge University Press; Grotius Publications, p. xxii.

1048 Cf. Hillgenberg, Hartmut (1999) (cf. *footnote 869* op. cit.), pp. 505, 515; Goldmann, Matthias (2009) (cf. *footnote 873* op. cit.), p. 1877; Gerner, Martin (14/09/2009) (cf. *footnote 407* op. cit.).

1049 See Armstrong, David; Brunée, Jutta (eds.) (2009): Routledge Handbook of International Law. London: Routledge (Routledge International Handbooks), p. 2.

1050 A non-exhaustive list of concerns: peace, environmental protection and sustainability, international human rights, economic (trade) relations, nuclear proliferation, drug traffic, control of biotechnologies, preservation of the world cultural heritage, prevention of international terrorism, punishment of international crimes, etc.
Cf. Kiss, Alexandre (2003) (cf. *footnote 297* op. cit.), p. 223; Francioni, Francesco (1996 / 2008) (cf. *footnote 880* op. cit.), pp. 168–173, 174; Shaw, Malcolm N. (2008) (cf. *footnote 912* op. cit.), pp. 117–119.

1051 See Klabbers, Jan (1996a) (cf. *footnote 897* op. cit.), p. 178; Klabbers, Jan (2007) (cf. *footnote 897* op. cit.), p. 200.

1052 See Verdross, Alfred; Simma, Bruno (1984 / 2010) (cf. *footnote 874* op. cit.), p. 422; Shelton, Dinah (2006d) (cf. *footnote 875* op. cit.), p. 159.

be interpreted as a differentiated,[1053] outcome-oriented and *free-floating continuum* unless expressly directed towards the production of effects, the facilitation of inherent commitment[1054] and the creation of tangible *repercussions*.[1055]

"Although soft norms may not be binding per se, they can indicate the likely direction in which formally binding legal obligations will develop."[1056] They are an important source of legal evolution.[1057] Adopting and complying with non-binding instruments proves that novel modes of law-making are acceptable.[1058] Assessing norm-creation is rather difficult, since a long-term perspective is necessary. Even though desirable for decision-making, the potential of emerging legal provisions (*lex in status nascendi*[1059]) can hardly be calculated in advance.[1060] Considerations *ex ante* are challenging because they are highly notional and often diffuse. Judgments on processes of norm-creation are only feasible from an *ex-post* perspective.[1061] Waiting for some (non-)fulfilling evidence is certainly not the preferable option.

Therefore, proponents of more constructivist approaches argue for considering *soft law* as part of the regime of governance from the very outset, and with good reasons:

1. Given its advantageous profile, *soft law* meets the challenge of globalisation particularly well. The irreversible increase in internationalisation, interdependence and trans-nationalism calls for commonly shared global interests in many fields of action. *Soft law* does not *per se* provide legal solutions, but it fosters the making and initiating of arrangements amongst multiple stake-

---

1053 See Weil, Prosper (1982 / 1983) (cf. *footnote 875* op. cit.), p. 424.

1054 This forms part of the subsequent state practice of avoiding treaties that are too costly and time-consuming or otherwise unnecessary.
Cf. Hillgenberg, Hartmut (1999) (cf. *footnote 869* op. cit.), p. 511; Shelton, Dinah (2006d) (cf. *footnote 875* op. cit.), p. 182.

1055 See Goldmann, Matthias (2009) (cf. *footnote 873* op. cit.), p. 1866.

1056 See Kiss, Alexandre (2003) (cf. *footnote 297* op. cit.), pp. 229–239.

1057 Cf. Kremser, Holger (1996) (cf. *footnote 919* op. cit.); Kiss, Alexandre (2003) (cf. *footnote 297* op. cit.), pp. 223–229; Kirton, John J.; Trebilcock, Michael J. (2004) (cf. *footnote 956* op. cit.), pp. 10–11; Mörth, Ulrika (ed.) (2004) (cf. *footnote 956* op. cit.); Skjærseth, Jon Birger; Stokke, Olav Schram; Wettestad, Jørgen (2006) (cf. *footnote 294* op. cit.), p. 118; Hörtreiter, Isabel (2007) (cf. *footnote 510* op. cit.), pp. 252 et seqq; Shaw, Malcolm N. (2008) (cf. *footnote 912* op. cit.), pp. 117–119; Shaffer, Gregory; Pollack, Mark A. (2008) (cf. *footnote 936* op. cit.), p. 52.

1058 Cf. Shelton, Dinah (ed.) (2000) (cf. *footnote 357* op. cit.), pp. 5 et seqq.

1059 Cf. Mazuelos Bellido, Ángeles (2004) (cf. *footnote 881* op. cit.), p. 11; Hobe, Stephan; Kimminich, Otto (2004) (cf. *footnote 511* op. cit.), pp. 198–201; Kälin, Walter; Baldegger, Mirjam (eds.) (2006) (cf. *footnote 510* op. cit.), pp. 223–225; Krajewski, Markus (2006) (cf. *footnote 510* op. cit.), pp. 25–26.

1060 Cf. Goldmann, Matthias (2009) (cf. *footnote 873* op. cit.), p. 1879.

1061 Cf. Ipsen, Knut; Menzel, Eberhard; Epping, Volker (2004) (cf. *footnote 960* op. cit.), p. 250.

holders. Moreover, the entirety of international society is invited to actively shape global governance through new *soft-law* making, pleading accordingly for *experimental soft law.*[1062]

2. Recalling the definition of *"(i)nternational regimes (that) are (...) anarchical in the sense that it lacks a centralised public authority or a government (...)"*,[1063] it reflects exactly the referential framework into which *soft law* fits perfectly. Why should *soft law* be linked with regime theory and governance? From a structural perspective, because of low thresholds, de-centralised informal institutions and greater flexibility.[1064] From a strategic perspective, because of the global need to achieve voluntary standards and thus to adequately address interdependent issues of economic, ecological-sustainable, social or cultural governance.
3. *Regime formation*[1065] is inextricably linked with the evolution of *soft law.* Regimes may be regarded as institutionalised patterns of directing behaviour through methods of varying normativity,[1066] thus including *soft-law* instruments. *Soft-law governance*[1067] refers to the international multi-level coordination of self-contained regimes.[1068] This relates to *soft-law regimes*[1069] as an alternative, more easily attainable and broadly preferable method of global legislation.[1070]

To sum up, *"(s)oft law most certainly has a place in international law, law for an ever-more-globalised society".*[1071] Non-binding norms may have a complex and potentially large impact on the development of international law.[1072]

However, *soft enforcement*[1073] is a *fait accompli. "(S)oft law may be used precisely because compliance is expected to be difficult; it begins a dynamic process over time that may lead to hard law or the norm may remain soft at the international level but become hard law internally (or regionally)."*[1074] How-

1062 Cf. O'Connell, Mary Ellen (2003) (cf. *footnote 996* op. cit.), p. 114.
1063 See Breitmeier, Helmut; Young, Oran R.; Zürn, Michael (2006) (cf. *footnote 158* op. cit.), p. 3.
1064 Cf. Gallopin, Gilberto (ed.) (March 2003) (cf. *footnote 60* op. cit.), pp. 17–18; Kirton, John J.; Trebilcock, Michael J. (2004) (cf. *footnote 956* op. cit.), pp. 6–8.
1065 Cf. Breitmeier, Helmut; Young, Oran R.; Zürn, Michael (2006) (cf. *footnote 158* op. cit.), p. 25.
1066 Cf. Peters, Brainard Guy (2005) (cf. *footnote 142* op. cit.), p. 130; Hasenclever, Andreas; Mayer, Peter (2007) (cf. *footnote 131* op. cit.), p. 14.
1067 See Shaffer, Gregory; Pollack, Mark A. (2008) (cf. *footnote 936* op. cit.), p. 18.
1068 Cf. Hillgenberg, Hartmut (1999) (cf. *footnote 869* op. cit.), p. 510.
1069 See Kirton, John J.; Trebilcock, Michael J. (2004) (cf. *footnote 956* op. cit.), p. 9.
1070 Cf. Abbott, Kenneth W.; Snidal, Duncan (2000) (cf. *footnote 970* op. cit.), p. 456.
1071 See O'Connell, Mary Ellen (2003) (cf. *footnote 996* op. cit.), p. 114.
1072 Cf. Shelton, Dinah (ed.) (2000) (cf. *footnote 357* op. cit.), p. 1.
1073 See Francioni, Francesco (1996 / 2008) (cf. *footnote 880* op. cit.), p. 176.
1074 See Shelton, Dinah (ed.) (2000) (cf. *footnote 357* op. cit.), p. 17.

ever, *"no conclusions may (a priori) be drawn (...) about the binding or non-binding character of rules of conduct which are generated in a different way".*[1075] *Hence, given the conception of relative normativity, it is more than advisable to sustain "(t)he (e)lusive (q)uest for (b)indingness".*[1076] To this end, *soft law* must be disconnected and dealt with separately from issues of compliance and legal binding: non-binding instruments do not necessarily imply non-compliance.[1077]

1.5 Compliance

The preliminary result of dealing with normativity in terms of international law is expressible through the following conclusive, general principle: If there is no legal obligation, legal compliance cannot be called for. However, it is indeed acceptable and consistent to assume that compliance does not necessarily depend on force and effect, first and foremost. *"If the (notion of normativity) is once understood, the good sense of compliance with it becomes self-evident."*[1078] This is due to the fact that *"(i)n this consent-based system, declarations, resolutions, memoranda of understanding, and other non-binding instruments are not adopted as law, soft or hard, although they frequently are intended to alter the behavio(u)r of their targets".*[1079]

Consequently, as long as compliance does affect behavioural change of stakeholders (*rule targets*),[1080] it must to a certain extent be regarded as means *eo ipso*, irrespective of legal binding and driven by the basic assumption that *"(g)enerally, (stakeholders) that have voluntarily negotiated, drafted, and adopted an international (soft-law) instrument comply with the agreement which is the final product of their efforts. Thus functionally, such instruments often approximate international treaties".*[1081] What is more, compliance may serve independently and therefore be subtly distinct from what is legally binding: *"The beauty of law is, that it is able to capture all those different moods and sentiments, and is able to translate them into a workable mode of analysis: it can translate all the various political or moral subtleties and nuances in simple dichotomies such as binding / non-binding, legal / illegal, and do justice to those*

1075 See Zemanek, Karl (1998) (cf. *footnote 869* op. cit.), p. 844.
1076 See Goldmann, Matthias (2009) (cf. *footnote 873* op. cit.), p. 1906.
1077 Cf. Shelton, Dinah (2003a) (cf. *footnote 989* op. cit.), p. 462; Gerner, Martin (14/09/2009) (cf. *footnote 407* op. cit.).
1078 See Lowe, Vaughan; Fitzmaurice, Malgosia (eds.) (1996 / 2008) (cf. *footnote 1047* op. cit.), p. xxiii.
1079 See Shelton, Dinah (2003b) (cf. *footnote 947* op. cit.), p. 554.
1080 See Börzel, Tanja; Risse, Thomas (2002) (cf. *footnote 336* op. cit.), p. 143.
1081 See Kiss, Alexandre (2003) (cf. *footnote 297* op. cit.), p. 242.

subtleties and nuances by determining exactly what it is that is binding, or legal".[1082]

Thus, compliance can have manifold sources and motivations reflected in both theory[1083] and practice. In this context, *deliberate or intentional compliance*[1084] must be distinguished from the addressee's *serendipitous compliance.*[1085] Such *conforming acts* can be subject to:[1086]

- Individual Habit;
- Motivated self-interested decision;
- Imposed sanctions and other forms of coercion, and / or
- Managerial incentives.

In the same way, compliance is hypothetically influenced and determined by multiple factors, most notably the following:[1087]

1. Institutional settings – infrastructure, hierarchy, transparency and responsiveness, reputation, responsibilities and accountability, welfare orientation, increasing efficiency, flexibility;
2. Context of norm-creation – general frameworks, consensus on the underlying norm, legitimacy shared by communities in relation to regional diversity and cultural differences;[1088]
3. Content of the norm – the degree of legalisation or type of obligation in terms of abstention versus adoption;
4. Targets of the norm – continuing voluntary relationship among participants, generality versus specificity; and
5. Miscellaneous – time (*window of opportunity*), place or agenda.

1082 Cf. Klabbers, Jan (1996a) (cf. *footnote 897* op. cit.), p. 182; Klabbers, Jan (2007) (cf. *footnote 897* op. cit.), p. 204.

1083 Cf. Burgstaller, Markus (2005) (cf. *footnote 445* op. cit.), pp. 104–164 et seqq.

1084 E.g., *Liberal Theory* by Anne-Marie Slaughter and Andrew Moravcsik: Social identity based on liberal states is source to comply.
Cf. Burgstaller, Markus (2005) (cf. *footnote 445* op. cit.), pp. 165 et seqq.

1085 States' actions fit international obligations without deliberately expressed choice.
Cf. Hass, Peter M. (2003): Compliance Theories. Choosing to Comply: Theorizing from International Relations and Comparative Politics. In: Shelton, Dinah (ed.): Commitment and Compliance. The Role of Non-Binding Norms in the International Legal System. Published new in paperback. Oxford / New York: Oxford University Press, pp. 43–64, p. 45.

1086 Cf. Börzel, Tanja; Risse, Thomas (2002) (cf. *footnote 336* op. cit.), pp. 145–149; Shelton, Dinah (2003c) (cf. *footnote 357* op. cit.), pp. 1–2.

1087 Cf. Bothe, Michael (1980) (cf. *footnote 510* op. cit.), p. 75; Shelton, Dinah (2003c) (cf. *footnote 357* op. cit.), pp. 3–5; Shelton, Dinah (2003b) (cf. *footnote 947* op. cit.), pp. 454–456; Weiss, Edith Brown (2003) (cf. *footnote 520* op. cit.), pp. 539–546; Breitmeier, Helmut; Young, Oran R.; Zürn, Michael (2006) (cf. *footnote 158* op. cit.), p. 72.

1088 Cf. Alkoby, Asher (2008) (cf. *footnote 77* op. cit.), pp. 153 et seqq.

"(W)hile it is essential to use compliance strategies that are tailored to the intent and capacity of the individual states and other relevant actors to comply with particular instruments, it is also essential to develop and maintain the processes joining the participants and to elaborate mechanisms of accountability among states and other relevant actors."[1089]

Different *modes* of compliance *"address [...] the gap between the law-in-the-books and the law-in-action"*:[1090]

a) *De-jure* compliance is related to *substantive* changes in both domestic and international legal frameworks; whereas
b) *De-facto* compliance is related to the question of *binding* effectiveness as an *operational* concept by using significant indicators.[1091]

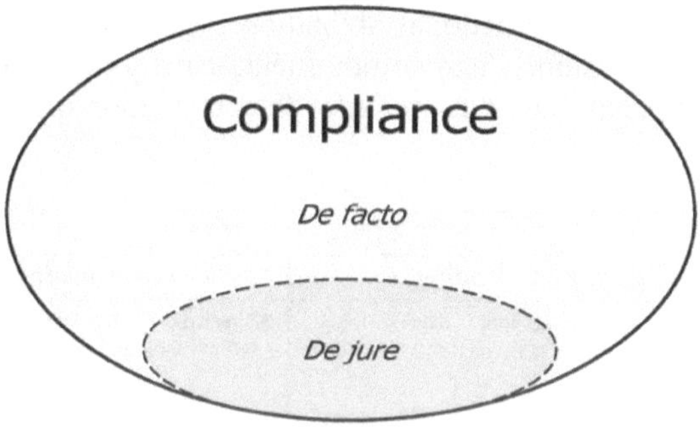

Figure 43: Compliance – de jure versus de facto[1092]

Compliance relates to different aspects of enforcement, implementation, monitoring, supervision and effectiveness simultaneously.[1093] There are similarities and differences between legally and non-legally binding instruments:[1094]

1089 See Weiss, Edith Brown (2003) (cf. *footnote 520* op. cit.), p. 553.

1090 See Shaffer, Gregory; Pollack, Mark A. (2008) (cf. *footnote 936* op. cit.), p. 6. See *Figure 43* in chapter VIII 1.5 *Compliance* on page 229.

1091 Without concealing all related methodological problems, such as reporting, monitoring, policy surveillance, verification, evaluation, etc. Cf. Shelton, Dinah (2003a) (cf. *footnote 989* op. cit.), pp. 451–453; Hass, Peter M. (2003) (cf. *footnote 1085* op. cit.), pp. 53–58.

1092 The figure illustrates two modes compliance and openly argues that *de-jure compliance* must be considered as one but by far not the only source of compliance. In terms of effective commitment *de-facto compliance* must be taken into account, too.

1093 Cf. Bothe, Michael (1980) (cf. *footnote 510* op. cit.), p. 75; Shelton, Dinah (2003c) (cf. *footnote 357* op. cit.), pp. 3–5.

1094 Cf. Bothe, Michael (1980) (cf. *footnote 510* op. cit.), pp. 85–90. See *Figure 44* in chapter VIII 1.5 *Compliance* on page 230.

- Expressing a shared certainty of expectations (*favor seriositatis*[1095]) by taking into account the conditions of tentative content analysis and document wording. Non-legal obligations are characterised by the advantage of greater flexibility in interpretation.
- Providing different measures to secure compliance, either formal dispute settlement and sanctions (*value depriviations*[1096]) or flexible procedures of implementation. *"Compliance includes implementation, but is broader, concerned with factual matching of state behaviour and international norms (...).*"[1097]
- Emergent possibilities of termination or withdrawal. The thresholds and procedural requirements are most likely lower and it is easier to quit clauses with non-legal obligations.
- Dealing with questions of national law: There is no obligation to introduce or to incorporate non-legal international obligations. Internalisation remains an issue of political responsibility and commitment, usually dependent upon the actions of any competent national organ for the acquisition of relevancy in a national sphere.

CONTENT	STRUCTURE / FORM	
	Legally Binding Instrument	Non-Legally Binding Instrument
Normative	**Law** - An instrument that is binding--legal action may be taken if there is non-compliance.	**Commitment** - A political or moral obligation that not legally binding.
Promotional Inspiration	**Hortatory** - Law with normative elements but with very weak obligations.	**Freedom of Action** - No commitment at all.

Figure 44: Content, structure and form of compliance[1098]

The range of reasons for compliance can be elaborated from perspectives of legal positivism, normativity and political economy.[1099]

1095 See Bothe, Michael (1980) (cf. *footnote 510* op. cit.), p. 85.

1096 See Bothe, Michael (1980) (cf. *footnote 510* op. cit.), p. 88.

1097 See Shelton, Dinah (2003c) (cf. *footnote 357* op. cit.), p. 5.

1098 The normative reach of compliance ultimately depends on content (normative versus promotional) and structural (legally binding versus non-legally binding) prerequisites. See Shelton, Dinah; Jonge Oudraat, Chantal de; Simmons, P. J. (1999 / 2009) (cf. *footnote 1045* op. cit.), p. 1.
Cf. *Figure 39* in chapter VIII 1.3 *Gradual normativity* on page 208.

1099 Cf. Shaffer, Gregory; Pollack, Mark A. (2008) (cf. *footnote 936* op. cit.), pp. 1–2.

1.5.1 Positivist perspective

In the legal positivist or institutionalist[1100] perspective, compliance is explained as the result of formally approved decisions made by empowered legislative or governmental bodies in the regulation of particular areas of society and human conduct (*social facts*).[1101] According to theorists of new institutionalism, regimes claim the competence themselves to set up formal rules of organisation that guide strategic behaviour.[1102] Distinctive mechanisms such as these typically characterise regime activities:[1103]

a) Coercing and ensuring compliance through institutional design,[1104] in the first instance;
b) Enmeshing states through launching programmatic activities;
c) Shaping expectations of national concerns;[1105]
d) Promoting stepwise processes through capacity-building; and
e) Including new forms of *dispute settlement*[1106] and prevention.

The only way to examine and assess legal positivist mechanisms of enforcement in a state of evolution is to compare methods of compliance *ex ante* and *ex-post*, respectively. This is, however, a long-term and somehow rather reactionary undertaking.

1100 See Burgstaller, Markus (2005) (cf. *footnote 445* op. cit.), p. 99.

1101 E.g., *The power of legitimacy among nations* by Thomas Franck: Compliance is achieved through legitimacy. Hence, United Nations' approaches largely fail.
Cf. Burgstaller, Markus (2005) (cf. *footnote 445* op. cit.), pp. 113 et seqq.

1102 Also including, for instance, compliance explained by theories of informal social norms that create commitment through not *explicit* but *implicit* coercion.
Cf. Hass, Peter M. (2003) (cf. *footnote 1085* op. cit.), pp. 50 et seqq; Weiss, Edith Brown (2003) (cf. *footnote 520* op. cit.), pp. 539–546.

1103 Cf. Young, Oran R. (1999a) (cf. *footnote 344* op. cit.), pp. 265–268; Young, Oran R. (ed.) (1999a) (cf. *footnote 140* op. cit.), p. 1; Shelton, Dinah (2003c) (cf. *footnote 357* op. cit.), p. 2; Hass, Peter M. (2003) (cf. *footnote 1085* op. cit.), pp. 53–58; Hörtreiter, Isabel (2007) (cf. *footnote 510* op. cit.), pp. 290–291.

1104 I.e. *horizontal* linkages: dense networks of institutional factors; *vertical* linkages (nesting): array of hierarchical influences and information on state compliance with international obligations both conceptual and legal in nature.

1105 E.g., *Fairness in international law and institutions* by Thomas Franck.
Cf. Burgstaller, Markus (2005) (cf. *footnote 445* op. cit.), pp. 122 et seqq.

1106 Cf. Schorlemer, Sabine von (2007): Elaborating and Implementing UNESCO's Standard-setting Instruments. UNESCO Dispute Settlement. In: Yusuf, Abdulqawi A. (ed.): Normative action in education, science and culture. Essays in commemoration of the sixtieth anniversary of UNESCO. French edition. Paris / Leiden / Boston: UNESCO publishing; Martinus Nijhoff Publishers (UNESCO reference works series, 1), pp. 75–105.

1.5.2 Normative perspective

From a normative perspective the *duty to obey* forms part of the social constructivist understanding: compliance arises out of the common understanding, amongst the majority of citizens, that eventually shapes, influences and induces state behaviour through norms.[1107] Thus, *"(c)ivil society has an especially important role in furthering compliance with soft law, or building the consensus needed for negotiating binding legal instruments"*.[1108]

Form	Purpose	
Binding	*Modifying behaviour*	*Encouraging specified behaviour*
Non-binding	*Modifying behaviour*	*Permitting stakeholder desired behaviour*

Figure 45: Relationship between form and purpose of binding and non-binding instruments[1109]

Legitimacy is achieved by norms *qua* norms or law *qua* law.[1110] Compliance is therefore regarded as a function of national intent considering priorities and conditions as well as capacities to succeed (in terms of effective bureaucracy) economic resources and sufficient public support.[1111] Compliance is thus based upon knowledge, ethical and moral sensibility, or causal belief.[1112] The relative-normative *rate of compliance*[1113] depends on a *web of factors*.[1114]

1107 E.g., *The new sovereignty: Compliance with international regulatory agreements* by Chayes and Chayes: Based upon interpreting treaty language and reporting mechanisms.
Cf. Burgstaller, Markus (2005) (cf. *footnote 445* op. cit.), pp. 141 et seqq.

1108 See Weiss, Edith Brown (2003) (cf. *footnote 520* op. cit.), p. 553.
See *Figure 45* in chapter VIII 1.5.2 *Normative perspective* on page 232.
Cf. *Figure 44* in chapter VIII 1.5 *Compliance* on page 230.

1109 Normatively speaking, compliance is always directed towards changing or modifying behaviour. However, even if the purpose is similar or the same, impacts are different: Binding instruments are encouraging some specified behaviour whereas non-binding instruments rather permit stakeholder-centred behaviour.
Cf. Weiss, Edith Brown (2003) (cf. *footnote 520* op. cit.), p. 535.

1110 Such as the legitimacy of procedure, institutional legitimacy, legitimacy of legal internalisation, and legitimacy of social *internalisation.*
Cf. Börzel, Tanja; Risse, Thomas (2002) (cf. *footnote 336* op. cit.), pp. 142–143; Burgstaller, Markus (2005) (cf. *footnote 445* op. cit.), pp. 101–102.

1111 Cf. Weiss, Edith Brown (2003) (cf. *footnote 520* op. cit.), pp. 550–553; Mitchell, Ronald B. (2007): Compliance Theory. Compliance, Effectiveness, and Behaviour Change in International Environmental Law. In: Bodansky, Daniel; Brunée, Jutta; Hey, Ellen (eds.): The Oxford handbook of international environmental law. Oxford: Oxford University Press (Oxford handbooks), pp. 893–921, p. 901.

1112 E.g., following the principle of *pacta sunt servanda* (made in good faith).

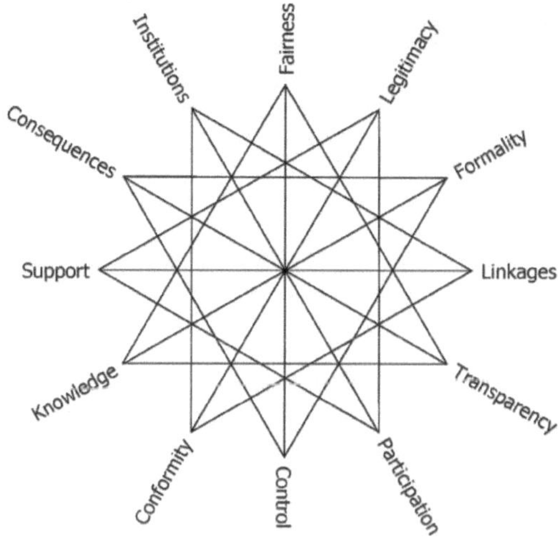

Linkages	between *soft-law* norms, *hard law*, amongst *soft-law* norms, and practices
Transparency	of *soft-law* norms in terms of verification and implementation
Participation	vis-à-vis stakeholders' involvement and support for *soft-law*
Control	over *soft-law* regulation, i.e. governance structures
Conformity	of behaviour with *soft law* both structural, economic and legal capabilities
Knowledge	of existing *epistemic* communities and stakeholders
Support	for *soft-law* norms, particularly utilitarian interests of norm targets
Consequences	of non-compliance, e.g., sanctions, dispute settlement procedures
Institutions	linking *soft-law* norms with established international institutions
Fairness	in terms of perceived moral and ethical aspects of *soft-law* norms
Legitimacy	of the norm-creating process
Formality	of acceptance by target group

Figure 46: Interdependence of factors of compliance[1115]

Cf. Hass, Peter M. (2003) (cf. *footnote 1085* op. cit.), p. 62.

1113 See Charney, Jonathan L. (2003): Compliance With International Soft Law. In: Shelton, Dinah (ed.): Commitment and Compliance. The Role of Non-Binding Norms in the International Legal System. Published new in paperback. Oxford / New York: Oxford University Press, pp. 115–118, p. 117.

1114 See *Figure 46* in chapter VIII 1.5.2 *Normative perspective* on page 233, and *Figure 47* in chapter VIII 1.5.2 *Normative perspective* on page 234.

1115 Compliance can effectively be interpreted as *web* of interdependent characteristics. Cf. Charney, Jonathan L. (2003) (cf. *footnote 1113* op. cit.), p. 117; Shelton, Dinah (2003c) (cf. *footnote 357* op. cit.), p. 9; Magraw Barstow, Daniel; Hawke, Lisa D. (2007) (cf. *footnote 50* op. cit.), pp. 632–637.

	Verification
+	Participation
+	Institutionalization
+	Juridification
+	Enforcement
=	Rate of compliance

Figure 47: Success of compliance[1116]

1.5.3 Rationalist perspective

In the rationalist or realist perspective the approach of questioning how international law affects state behaviour despite the lack of coercive enforcement mechanisms is more pragmatic. The answer is astonishingly simple: Compliance is achieved as long as benefits exceed the costs of compliance.[1117] According to (neo-) realists, compliance is a matter of systemic distribution of material capabilities in order to create *interstate leverage.*[1118] Operational mechanisms work similarly, irrespective of *soft* or *hard* law. However, (*hard*) law is considered to generate only marginal increase in compliance.[1119] Conversely, *soft-law* provisions may create some cost-efficient *modus vivendi*[1120] preferring non-legal commitments, because difficult law-making processes may be circumvented and

1116 In normative perspective, the rate of compliance can be expressed as formula consisting of five elements: verification of the purpose, participation of relevant stakeholders, institutionalisation of opinion-making, juridification of decisions, and finally, enforcement of agreed-upon codes of conduct.
Cf. Breitmeier, Helmut; Young, Oran R.; Zürn, Michael (2006) (cf. *footnote 158* op. cit.), p. 112.

1117 For example: costs of non-compliance (*legalisation hypothesis*), costs of non-transfers of administrative and political resources (*management hypothesis*), costs of non-autonomy of enforcement (*liberal-institution-centrist hypothesis*), and costs of institutional opportunities (*liberal-stakeholder-centrist hypothesis*).
Cf. Börzel, Tanja; Risse, Thomas (2002) (cf. *footnote 336* op. cit.), p. 142; Burgstaller, Markus (2005) (cf. *footnote 445* op. cit.), p. 96; Mitchell, Ronald B. (2007) (cf. *footnote 1111* op. cit.), p. 901; Guzman, Andrew T. (2008) (cf. *footnote 961* op. cit.), p. 9.

1118 See Hass, Peter M. (2003) (cf. *footnote 1085* op. cit.), pp. 50 et seqq.

1119 Cf. Guzman, Andrew T. (2008) (cf. *footnote 961* op. cit.), pp. 22–23.

1120 See Bothe, Michael (1980) (cf. *footnote 510* op. cit.), p. 91.

increases in status and moral or political prestige may be possible.[1121] In this respect, compliance becomes a principle of political economy in that parties maximise their payoffs. As a result, competitive incentives dominate compliance, particularly with *soft law*.[1122]

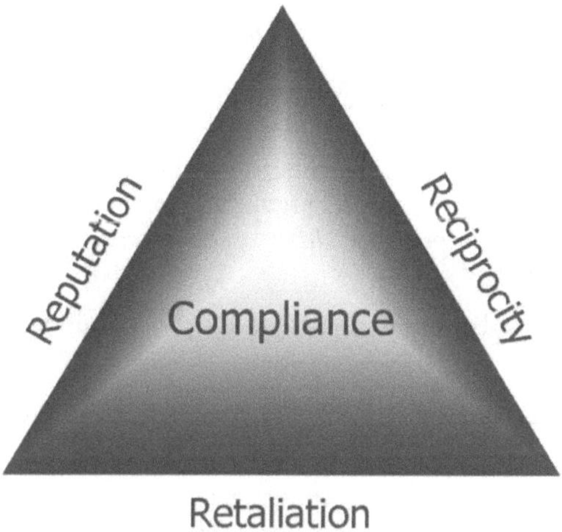

Figure 48: The three R's of compliance[1123]

The comparative economic advantage of rational choices can be expressed in two different ways:

a) *Tit-for-tat*, derived from *do ut des*,[1124] exemplifies the *symbiosis* between treaties and social behaviour:[1125] you comply because others do. Put differently, you expect compliance in accordance with your own principle. Clauses involving this principle are driving factors in international co-operation and compliance; or alternatively,

1121 Cf. Bothe, Michael (1980) (cf. *footnote 510* op. cit.), pp. 92, 94; Goldmann, Matthias (2009) (cf. *footnote 873* op. cit.), p. 1875.

1122 See *Figure 48* in chapter VIII 1.5.3 *Rationalist perspective* on page 235.

1123 In rationalist perspective, compliance is primarily subject to economic principles, such as reciprocity, reputation and retaliation of individual actors' relations.
See and cf. Guzman, Andrew T. (2008) (cf. *footnote 961* op. cit.), p. 9.

1124 Latin origin: *I give so that you may give.*
Cf. Hillgenberg, Hartmut (1999) (cf. *footnote 869* op. cit.), p. 512.

1125 Cf. Burgstaller, Markus (2005) (cf. *footnote 445* op. cit.), pp. 89–90.

b) *Prisoner's dilemma* opens up a game-theoretic perspective that is related to aspects of reputation and retaliation.[1126] Compliance is considered a gamble in which parties could maximise their total joint payoff through mutual co-operation; however each player thinks he can do better by defecting or not complying.

Now, the assumption is that violating provisions of international law imposes costs.[1127] Non-compliance increases costs due to the loss of reputation and *international prestige*[1128] that weakens the bargaining position.[1129] Strategically thinking, state parties want to avoid these *costs of (neglected) opportunity*. The rationale behind complying with agreements is maximisation of the joint surplus[1130] by avoiding transaction costs of bargaining, for instance.[1131] Additionally, there is an *"opportunity to pool activities, assets or risks"*[1132] and therefore an active incentive to comply.[1133]

To sum up, the rationalist *calculus of compliance*[1134] is subject to three cost-related variables:[1135]

1. Treating compliance as function of *will* and *capacity* essentially focusing on the structure of incentives:[1136]

1126 Cf. Burgstaller, Markus (2005) (cf. *footnote 445* op. cit.), pp. 90, 96; Guzman, Andrew T. (2008) (cf. *footnote 961* op. cit.), p. 9; Shaffer, Gregory; Pollack, Mark A. (2008) (cf. *footnote 936* op. cit.), pp. 23–24.

1127 E.g., negotiation costs, transaction costs, implementation costs (*bureaucracy*), etc.

1128 See Burgstaller, Markus (2005) (cf. *footnote 445* op. cit.), p. 106.

1129 Cf. Skjærseth, Jon Birger; Stokke, Olav Schram; Wettestad, Jørgen (2006) (cf. *footnote 294* op. cit.), p. 119.

1130 *Pareto-efficiency* or *-improvement* by Vilfredo Pareto: Making some parties better off without necessarily making any other party worse off, and avoiding *ex-parte* disadvantages, for example through *most-favouring* agreements.
Cf. Shaffer, Gregory; Pollack, Mark A. (2008) (cf. *footnote 936* op. cit.), p. 25.

1131 I.e. *Coase theorem* by Ronald Coase (1937 / 1966): Eliminating external distortions of market-based allocation of resources through defining property rights and reducing costs of transaction, for example by complying with commonly shared treaty provisions.
Cf. Guzman, Andrew T. (2008) (cf. *footnote 961* op. cit.), p. 121.

1132 See Alvarez, José Enrique (2006) (cf. *footnote 141* op. cit.), p. 346.

1133 For example, *The foreign policy cost-benefit analysis* by Hanspeter Neuhold.
Cf. Hass, Peter M. (2003) (cf. *footnote 1085* op. cit.), pp. 50 et seqq; Burgstaller, Markus (2005) (cf. *footnote 445* op. cit.), pp. 104 et seqq; Breitmeier, Helmut; Young, Oran R.; Zürn, Michael (2006) (cf. *footnote 158* op. cit.), p. 72.
See *Figure 49* in chapter VIII 1.5.3 *Rationalist perspective* on page 237.

1134 See Underdal, Arild (1998) (cf. *footnote 358* op. cit.), p. 7.

1135 Cf. Underdal, Arild (1998) (cf. *footnote 358* op. cit.), pp. 7 et seqq; Börzel, Tanja; Risse, Thomas (2002) (cf. *footnote 336* op. cit.), pp. 145–149.

1136 Cf. Underdal, Arild (1998) (cf. *footnote 358* op. cit.), pp. 7–12.

2. Defining political success or failure in view of effective *implementation*;[1137] and
3. Achieving and promoting *social learning*[1138] and policy diffusion.

Stakeholder capability and willingness		Costs of compliance	
		High	Low or None
a)	capable and willing	*possible*	*most likely*
b)	capable and unwilling	*unlikely*	*unlikely*
c)	incapable and willing	*rather unlikely*	*possible*
d)	incapable and unwilling	*highly unlikely*	*unlikely*

Figure 49: Likelihood of compliance[1139]

1.6 Summary

There is good news: commitment is a question of compliance rather than of legal, customary or treaty binding. Ensuring compliance is far more promising than becoming stuck with controversial debates: *"The considerable recourse to and compliance with non-binding norms appears to represent a maturing of the international system. The on-going relationships among states and other actors, deepening and changing with globalisation, create a climate that may require that fewer expectations of behavio(u)r be set forth in formal legal obligations. Formally non-binding norms or informal social norms can be effective and offer a flexible and efficient way to order responses to common problems. While they are not law, such norms have an indispensable place in the modern legal system".*[1140]

1137 Cf. Underdal, Arild (1998) (cf. *footnote 358* op. cit.), pp. 12–20; Kiss, Alexandre (2003) (cf. *footnote 297* op. cit.), pp. 231, 240.

1138 For instance, processes of trans-national learning and formation (beliefs, convictions, ideas, etc.).
Cf. Underdal, Arild (1998) (cf. *footnote 358* op. cit.), pp. 20–23.

1139 The figure shows the *trade-off* between the attempt to comply and the expectation to fail in order to attract resources from international institutions to improve performance and capacity. Costs of compliance include financial and material resources as well as political consequences (consequences, sanctions, etc.). Stakeholders are both state parties and non-state parties, including non-governmental organisations and international governmental organisations, professional associations, transnational corporations, mixed entities, etc.
Cf. Hass, Peter M. (2003) (cf. *footnote 1085* op. cit.), p. 47; Shelton, Dinah (2003c) (cf. *footnote 357* op. cit.), pp. 5–6.

1140 See Shelton, Dinah (2003b) (cf. *footnote 947* op. cit.), p. 556.

Conducive conditions and frameworks must be provided in order to transform compliance into active commitment. *"Poor compliance (...) often occurred because of lack of leadership and commitment amongst treaty members."*[1141] Selected case studies confirm effective mechanisms of compliance.[1142]

At international level guidelines are first formulated as *jointly honoured principles*;[1143] these internationally adopted guidelines are then applied as *soft law*; thirdly, gradual *opinio iuris* develops as customary law; fourthly, *soft-law* norms are eventually re-introduced as legally binding instruments (*hard law*).[1144]

At national level appropriate regulatory measures are introduced within domestic legal orders in order to meet international requirements (harmonisation),[1145] and, secondly, the appropriate institutional arrangements for participation (the framework) are provided.[1146]

1141 See Shelton, Dinah; Jonge Oudraat, Chantal de; Simmons, P. J. (1999 / 2009) (cf. *footnote 1045* op. cit.), p. 3.

1142 Cf. Shelton, Dinah; Jonge Oudraat, Chantal de; Simmons, P. J. (1999 / 2009) (cf. *footnote 1045* op. cit.), p. 2; Kiss, Alexandre (2003) (cf. *footnote 297* op. cit.), pp. 228–236; Shaw, Malcolm N. (2008) (cf. *footnote 912* op. cit.), pp. 117–119.

1143 Cf. Kiss, Alexandre (2003) (cf. *footnote 297* op. cit.), p. 228.

1144 Depending on the authority of the text, content (language), monitoring (pressure); e.g., so called *Rio-principles*.
Cf. United Nations (1992) (cf. *footnote 731* op. cit.); United Nations (ed.) (1993) (cf. *footnote 732* op. cit.); Kiss, Alexandre (2003) (cf. *footnote 297* op. cit.), p. 239.

1145 Pure implementation (endorsement and ratification) does not ensure compliance, but may serve as an incentive, e.g., the incorporation of the so called *Rio-principles* by states and the *Organisation for Economic Co-operation and Development* (OECD) by implementing the *Agenda 21* into national strategies and regional agendas.
Cf. United Nations (1992) (cf. *footnote 731* op. cit.); United Nations (ed.) (1993) (cf. *footnote 732* op. cit.); Kiss, Alexandre (2003) (cf. *footnote 297* op. cit.), pp. 231, 235, 240.

1146 See *Figure 50* in chapter VIII 1.6 *Summary* on page 239.

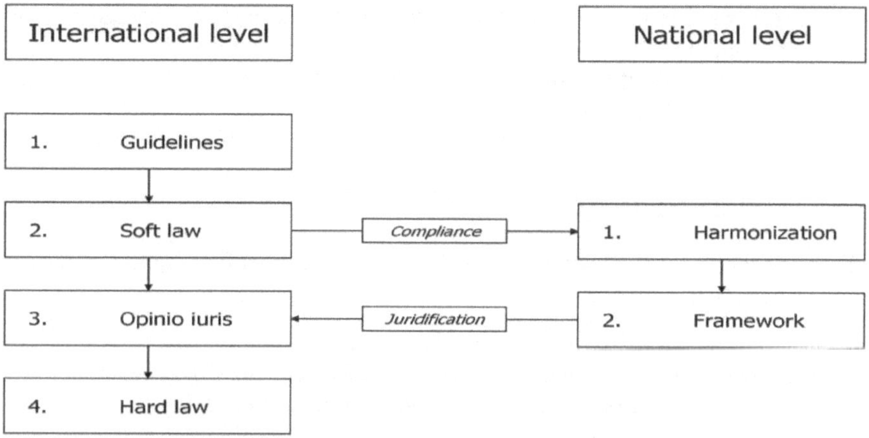

Figure 50: Institutionalising compliance[1147]

"International regimes vary in the extent of their legalisation along these dimensions, which can give them a 'harder' or 'softer' legal character."[1148] Coming back to the theoretical context of *DESD*, contrary to *hard-law regimes*,[1149] *DESD* may be typically considered a *soft-law regime*:

1. *DESD* shares several regime characteristics;
2. *DESD* is not legally binding *eo ipso* although it is undoubtedly directed towards changing social behaviour (*soft law*);
3. *DESD* claims *normative intent* of approved normativity including compliance;[1150]
4. *DESD* is internationally adopted and to be nationally implemented; and
5. *DESD* develops dynamically and depends largely on commitment.

Ultimately, the success of *DESD* qua *soft-law regime* depends on:[1151]

- Binding in order to achieve compliance through consistent and concise communication which avoids ambivalence and ambiguity, and through effective monitoring and assessment also;

1147 In a nutshell, institutionalising compliance is a matter of organising commitment or binding force between different interrelated levels at international, regional, subregional and local scale.
Cf. Shelton, Dinah; Jonge Oudraat, Chantal de; Simmons, P. J. (1999 / 2009) (cf. *footnote 1045* op. cit.), p. 2; Kiss, Alexandre (2003) (cf. *footnote 297* op. cit.), pp. 228–236; Shaw, Malcolm N. (2008) (cf. *footnote 912* op. cit.), pp. 117–119.

1148 See Shaffer, Gregory; Pollack, Mark A. (2008) (cf. *footnote 936* op. cit.), p. 6.

1149 Cf. Shaffer, Gregory; Pollack, Mark A. (2008) (cf. *footnote 936* op. cit.), p. 3.

1150 Cf. Boyle, Alan E. (2006) (cf. *footnote 932* op. cit.), p. 152.

1151 Cf. Hörtreiter, Isabel (2007) (cf. *footnote 510* op. cit.), pp. 306–311.

- Managing skills in order to achieve collective learning and change through flexible and dynamic mechanisms of soft implementation; and
- Strategic cost-benefit thinking in order to achieve *added value*, avoid negative effects, and increase the notional fair market value.

2 Application

Applying the theoretical settings of *soft law* to *DESD* confirms some of the hypotheses made in advance:[1152]

- Accepting the normative character and binding nature of *DESD*;
- Establishing mechanisms of monitoring and assessment of *DESD*; and
- Recommending particular codes of conduct in relation to *DESD*.

Given this definition, *soft law* is applicable to *DESD*: *Primary soft law* relates to normative texts which are not adopted in treaty form but addressed to the international community, either on the whole or to the entire membership of the adopting institution or organisation.[1153] Both criteria correlate well with *DESD*: *DESD* has been approved as declaratory document and *DESD* addresses the international community, and UNESCO member states in particular.[1154]

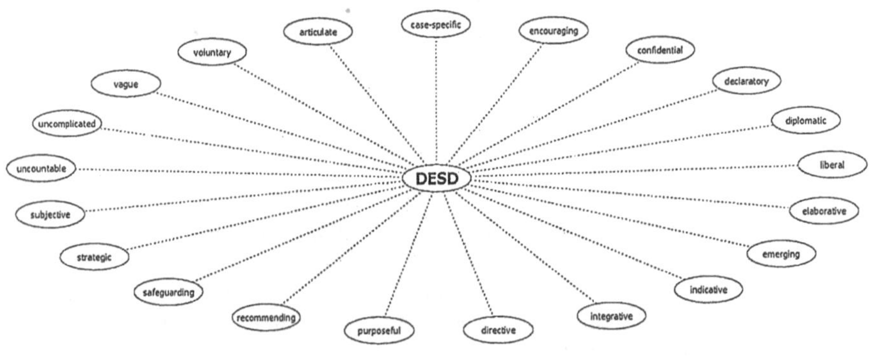

Figure 51: DESD as soft-law regime – a mind map[1155]

It will be seen in the course of implementation and evaluation whether *DESD* may serve as a *tool* to reach moral consensus on *ESD* (*opinio iuris*)[1156]

1152 Cf. Hörtreiter, Isabel (2007) (cf. *footnote 510* op. cit.), pp. 295–305.
1153 Cf. Shelton, Dinah (2003a) (cf. *footnote 989* op. cit.), pp. 449–451.
1154 See *Figure 51* in chapter VIII 2 *Application* on page 240.
1155 Approaching *DESD* as *soft-law regime*, calls for combining characteristics of soft law with those of regime theory.
1156 Cf. Shelton, Dinah (2003a) (cf. *footnote 989* op. cit.), p. 461.

with UNESCO as a normative authority (*lead agency*) promoting implementation and compliance,[1157] and a clearly-marked ambit of application (*usus*).

In the case of *DESD*, to what extent does compliance influence commitment? More precisely speaking, how can *ESD* be conceptualised as a self-contained *performance standard*,[1158] as a policy and monitoring framework? Which means or instruments are viable and applicable to *DESD*?

2.1 Standard-setting

Accepting the normative character and binding nature of *DESD* in any way may hypothetically lead to the establishment of *de-facto standards*.[1159]

A *standard* is *"(...) a predominantly indirectly binding instrument of (specific) regulation formulated by organisations or structures instituted for this particular purpose"*.[1160] Moreover, given the definition of standard-setting as *"the proper following of a prescribed, rational system of rules or procedures resulting in the assignment of a number to differentiate between two or more states or degrees of performance"*,[1161] standards carry out several functions, sometimes simultaneously, and, amongst others:

a) Expressing the *lowest common denominator* of structural regulation and coordination;
b) Constituting rules of procedure as means of enhancing competition and efficiency;[1162] and
c) Contributing to performance orientation and momentum-building as a consequence of one's individual capabilities.[1163]

1157 Cf. Goldmann, Matthias (2009) (cf. *footnote 873* op. cit.), p. 1868.

1158 Cf. Cizek, Gregory J. (2001): Setting performance standards. Concepts, methods, and perspectives. Mahwah, New Jersey: Lawrence Erlbaum Associates; Cizek, Gregory J.; Bunch, Michael B. (2006) (cf. *footnote 455* op. cit.).

1159 See Shelton, Dinah (2003a) (cf. *footnote 989* op. cit.), pp. 451–453.

1160 Translation from German into English: Ein Standard ist ein *„(...) in der Regel nicht unmittelbar verbindliche (Detail-)Regelung, die von speziell zu diesem Zweck errichteten Organisationen oder Strukturen formuliert wird"*.
See Röhl, Hans Christian (2007) (cf. *footnote 452* op. cit.), p. 319; Möllers, Christoph; Vosskuhle, Andreas; Walter, Christian (eds.) (2007): Internationales Verwaltungsrecht. Tübingen: Mohr Siebeck (Jus internationale et Europaeum, 16).

1161 See Cizek, Gregory J.; Bunch, Michael B. (2006) (cf. *footnote 455* op. cit.), p. 15.

1162 Standard-setting provides *"incalculable social, economic, and personal benefits"*, e.g., through channeling behaviour and resource allocation.
See Cizek, Gregory J. (2001) (cf. *footnote 1158* op. cit.), p. 14.
Cf. Gellhorn, Ernest (15/04/2002): Standard-Setting. George Mason University. Manuscript. Officially released and issued on 15/04/2002, Fairfax, Virginia, p. 1.

The process of standard-setting relates principally to (legal) norms and (non-legal) standards.

Reference to multi-level analysis of the model of *life cycles*[1164] explains norm- and standard-creation in line with the social theory of institutionalism:[1165]

1. *Forming*: firstly, *norm entrepreneurs*[1166] express a desire for certain advantageous modes of behaviour by proposing appropriate terminology and framework conditions. Secondly, the normative basis is disseminated at organisational level and instantly exposed to influences and critique. Thirdly, in the case of broad acceptance and consensus, norms or standards enter into the cascading phase by passing the crucial *tipping point*;
2. *Cascading*: Due to the internal pressure of legitimacy, conformity and reputation, norms or standards are gradually introduced and adopted; and
3. *Internalising*: Broad norm or standard acceptance leads to internalisation by stakeholders, either enforced by law (*de jure* = norm) or fostered by other mechanisms of compliance (*de facto* = standard).

Institutions are significant facilitators of norm and standard creation. Given the persistently changing conditions of society, institutions must be flexible enough to meet the need for appropriate *transformation*. In the philosophy of new institutionalism, this *institutional entrepreneurship* is emphasised as integral component of institutional change.[1167] Ultimately, standard-setting and norm-creation relies on strong proponents and *advocates*.[1168]

Internationally, resolutions may serve as the initial step to building and initiating momentum up to the *tipping point*. Subsequently, lead signatories are pioneers in the course of cascading, advocating and promoting following. Norms and standards are subject to varying levels of implementation, taking into account specific contexts and conditions.

1163 Norms and standards in particular are highly contextual: there are no uniform but *conditioned* (legal) standards.
Cf. Francioni, Francesco (1996 / 2008) (cf. *footnote 880* op. cit.), p. 175; Goldmann, Matthias (2009) (cf. *footnote 873* op. cit.), pp. 1868, 1879 et seqq; Heyvaert, Veerle (2009) (cf. *footnote 942* op. cit.), pp. 10 et seqq, 16.

1164 See Schemmann, Michael (2009) (cf. *footnote 916* op. cit.), p. 352.

1165 Cf. Schemmann, Michael (2009) (cf. *footnote 916* op. cit.), pp. 352–254.
See *Figure 52* in chapter VIII 2.1 *Standard-setting* on page 243.

1166 See Schemmann, Michael (2009) (cf. *footnote 916* op. cit.), p. 352.

1167 Cf. Schemmann, Michael (2009) (cf. *footnote 916* op. cit.), p. 353.

1168 E.g., UNESCO's pro-active role during the *United Nations Week of Adult Learning* in 1997.
Cf. Schemmann, Michael (2009) (cf. *footnote 916* op. cit.), p. 354.

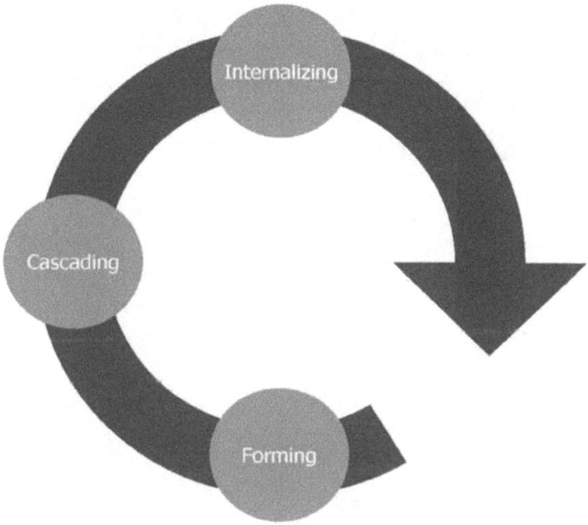

Figure 52: Evolution and life cycles of standards[1169]

Just as the evolution of norms is related to institutional structures, so is standard-setting:[1170] *"(s)tandard instruments (may) constitute the backbone of international institutional law (...)"*.[1171] Depending on intent, two types of standards can, *grosso modo*, be distinguished:[1172]

- *Performance* versus *content* standard

Performance standards set down certain levels or categories of accomplishments in relation to a given instrument and are assessed via specific benchmarks (*cut scores*) or indicators;[1173] conversely, *content standards* consider the prescribed or acquired substance only;[1174] and

- *De-facto* versus *de-jure* standard

1169 The evolution of *de-facto* or *de-jure* standards can be characterised as circular process consisting of forming, cascading and internalising periods.
Cf. Schemmann, Michael (2009) (cf. *footnote 916* op. cit.), pp. 352 et seqq.

1170 Cf. Kirton, John J.; Trebilcock, Michael J. (eds.) (2004) (cf. *footnote 888* op. cit.), pp. 4 et seqq; Schemmann, Michael (2009) (cf. *footnote 916* op. cit.), pp. 352 et seqq.

1171 See Goldmann, Matthias (2009) (cf. *footnote 873* op. cit.), p. 1871.

1172 See *Figure 53* in chapter VIII 2.1 *Standard-setting* on page 244.

1173 I.e. so called *path-goal theory*.
Cf. Cizek, Gregory J. (2001) (cf. *footnote 1158* op. cit.), p. 159; Cizek, Gregory J.; Bunch, Michael B. (2006) (cf. *footnote 455* op. cit.), pp. 5, 60.

1174 Cf. Cizek, Gregory J.; Bunch, Michael B. (2006) (cf. *footnote 455* op. cit.), pp. 5 et seqq.

De-facto standards are verifiably observable substantive changes of behaviour in real life (*bottom- up*); conversely, *de-jure standards* are changes prescribed in the legal order (*top-down*). Because membership is by choice, both *de-facto* and *de-jure* standards occur in regime theory. However, *de-facto standards* provide the most self-enforcing and intentional incentives.[1175]

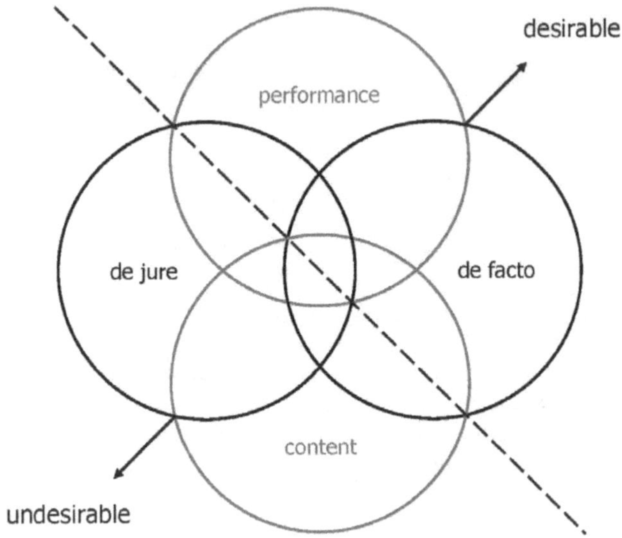

Figure 53: Desirability of setting respective standards[1176]

Common elements in setting *de-facto-performance* standards are:[1177]

a) Defining purpose and objectives;
b) Addressing adequate methods (*format*) in terms of purpose orientation, knowledge, skills and abilities, available resources, and integration of results;
c) Conceptualising *dynamic* levels and descriptions of performance (*labels*);
d) Providing training in facilitation and participation; and

1175 Cf. Shaffer, Gregory; Pollack, Mark A. (2008) (cf. *footnote 936* op. cit.), pp. 25, 27.

1176 With respect to effectively promoting behavioural changes, *DESD* is advocating, for instance, *de-facto* and *performance* standards can be considered more preferable for the following reason. Unlike this particular set of standards, *de-jure* and *content* standards do not sufficiently reflect to the notion of *DESD* with regard to its non-binding set-up, structural *soft-law* arrangement and process-related subject matter.

1177 Cf. Cizek, Gregory J.; Bunch, Michael B. (2006) (cf. *footnote 455* op. cit.), pp. 5 et seqq, 60.
See *Figure 54* in chapter VIII 2.1 *Standard-setting* on page 245.

e) Actively seeking feedback and evaluation mechanisms, considering procedural,[1178] internal,[1179] as well as external criteria (*cut scores*).[1180]

As noted, the conditions for successful standard-setting are manifold: *"(r)ecent experience (...) with controversial and complicated topics has underlined the importance of selecting a subject for standard setting 'only when the necessary research and preparatory work has been carried out and the subject can reasonably be considered to be 'ripe' for standard setting'"*.[1181]

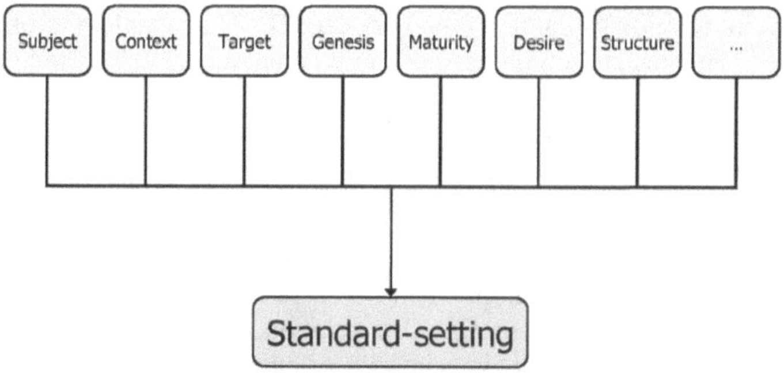

Figure 54: Criteria of success for standard-setting – towards a synthesis[1182]

In general, UNESCO normative action and standard-setting is based predominantly upon *de-jure* and *content* standards (*legal commitments*).[1183] Both may be implemented and assessed with far greater ease. It is however more difficult to reach a consensus.

Assessing standard-setting is a difficult business and often controversial. This is due to the methodological problem of referring exclusively to either *de-jure* or *de-facto* standards. Depending on the relevant standpoint, significant voids in standard-setting can be discovered.[1184] Professional scientific guidelines

1178 Explicitness, practicability, implementation, feedback, documentation.

1179 Methodological consistency, intra-participant consistency, inter-participant consistency, and consistency of decision.

1180 I.e. comparisons to other standard-setting methods, comparisons to other sources of information, reasonableness of cut scores.

1181 See Kirton, John J.; Trebilcock, Michael J. (eds.) (2004) (cf. *footnote 888* op. cit.), p. 147.

1182 Ultimately succesful standard-setting depends on a non-quantifiable multitude of criteria that, *grosso modo*, largely coincide with regime-theoretic assumptions.

1183 Cf. Yusuf, Abdulqawi A. (ed.) (2007) (cf. *footnote 129* op. cit.), pp. 51 et seqq.

1184 For instance, assessment of compliance with human rights is highly debated. Does it suffice to comply *de jure* by making substantive changes in domestic legal frameworks or to comply *de facto*, as may be proven by significant indicators?
Cf. Shelton, Dinah (2003a) (cf. *footnote 989* op. cit.), pp. 454 et seqq.

for assessing standard-setting require reliability, validity and replicability.[1185] As concerns procedural requirements, standards need to be systematically, rationally, substantively and consistently implemented.[1186] The very same challenge equally applies to *DESD*.

"Soft law is used regularly for international (...) norm-setting, either as an ultimate or an intermediate expression of international consensus."[1187] Taking into account *primary soft law* as a main source for developing new standards, *DESD* may well form the basis vis-à-vis *ESD* for UNESCO and beyond.[1188] Thus, points of reference are criteria-based standards provided by a catalogue of criteria in relation to and applied to *DESD*. This catalogue of criteria for *DESD*[1189] enables and combines both implementation *ex ante* and evaluation *ex post*.[1190]

For various reasons it corresponds both to the nature of *de-jure* standards and standards of *content* to preferably regard *DESD* as a *de-facto* standard of *performance*:[1191]

1. Genesis of *DESD* in terms of legal crafting: there has from the outset been no intention to technically implement *DESD* as a legally-binding instrument;[1192]
2. Structural arrangement of *DESD* in relation to legal effects: considering the *soft-law* notion of *DESD* is primarily oriented towards performance and *de-facto* binding;[1193] and
3. Subject matter: given its distinct process-related and future-oriented conceptions,[1194] the very substance of *DESD* is related more to strategies of performance than to the setting of contents.

1185 Cf. Cizek, Gregory J.; Bunch, Michael B. (2006) (cf. *footnote 455* op. cit.), p. 60.

1186 Cf. Cizek, Gregory J.; Bunch, Michael B. (2006) (cf. *footnote 455* op. cit.), p. 15.

1187 See Shelton, Dinah (2003a) (cf. *footnote 989* op. cit.), p. 461.

1188 Cf. Shelton, Dinah (2003a) (cf. *footnote 989* op. cit.), pp. 449–451.

1189 That *DESD* should be interdisciplinary and holistic, values-driven, multi-method, capable of critical thinking, problem-solving and participatory decision-making, locally relevant, and culturally appropriate.
See Becker, Egon; Jahn, Thomas; Stieß, Immanuel, et al. (eds.) (1997) (cf. *footnote 53* op. cit.); UNESCO (2007) (cf. *footnote 52* op. cit.); UNESCO (2009) (cf. *footnote 579* op. cit.).

1190 Cf. Eisemann, Pierre Michel (2007) (cf. *footnote 478* op. cit.), pp. 27–28.

1191 See *Figure 55* in chapter VIII 2.1 *Standard-setting* on page 247.

1192 Cf. UNESCO (05/07/2003) (cf. *footnote 124* op. cit.), p. 24; Gerner, Martin (14/09/2009) (cf. *footnote 407* op. cit.).

1193 I.e. declaratory adoption practice, de-centralised steering and regional strategies, long-term duration, definable wording, recommending guidelines and schedules, committed financing, etc.
Cf. Heusel, Wolfgang (1991) (cf. *footnote 896* op. cit.), p. 275.
Cf. chapter V 3 *Standard-setting* on pages 104 et seqq.

1194 I.e. development, sustainability and education.

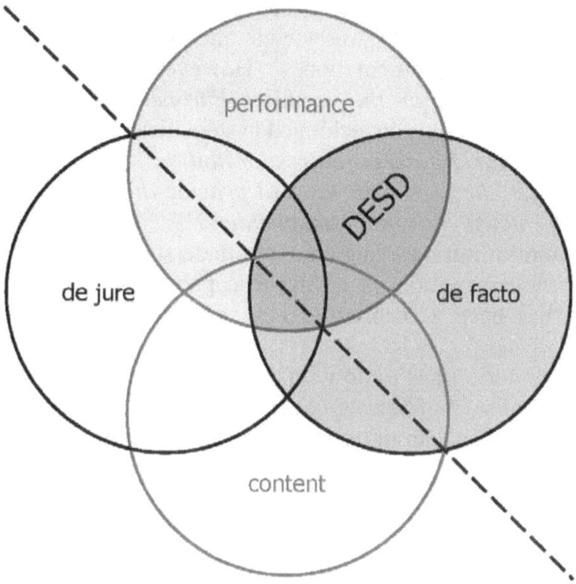

Figure 55: DESD standard-setting[1195]

2.2 Monitoring

Hypothetically speaking, establishing mechanisms of monitoring and assessment of *DESD* may lead to mutual understanding, enhanced communication and compliance.[1196]

Firstly, institutional mechanisms of monitoring enable a common understanding of agreed-upon standard-setting procedures to be established.[1197] In other words, monitoring and standard-setting are inextricably linked: monitoring can only take place if standards have been defined beforehand. Moreover, *"(n)ot everything that counts can be counted, and not everything that can be counted counts".*[1198] Given the growing importance of promoting *polycentric*[1199] norma-

1195 For various reasons this figure recommends to approach *DESD*, due to its notion, as *de-facto* and *performance*-oriented regime of standard-setting.

1196 Cf. chapter V 4 *Monitoring* on pages 115 et seqq.

1197 Cf. Weiss, Edith Brown (2003) (cf. *footnote 520* op. cit.), p. 538; Yusuf, Abdulqawi A. (ed.) (2007) (cf. *footnote 129* op. cit.), pp. 51 et seqq; UNESCO (ed.) (2008h) (cf. *footnote 219* op. cit.); Gerner, Martin (30/07/2009) (cf. *footnote 407* op. cit.).

1198 Albert Einstein. Sign hanging in his office at Princeton.
Cf. UNESCO (ed.) (2008h) (cf. *footnote 219* op. cit.), p. 2.

1199 Cf. Boisson de Chazournes, Laurence (2007) (cf. *footnote 496* op. cit.), p. 52.

tive instruments and implementation, the distribution of necessary information,[1200] criteria or indicators,[1201] knowledge and skills is an indispensable prerequisite of monitoring implementation.[1202] However, *"[...] it (is) important not to base ESD exclusively upon the dominant European knowledge system".*[1203] Effective monitoring can only be achieved systematically[1204] by taking into consideration *common but differentiated responsibilities*[1205] *"or differential treatment, refer(ring) to 'the use of norms that provide different, presumably more advantageous, treatment to some (stakeholders)'".*[1206] Since 1992[1207] this particular idea of monitoring, fostering common understanding on the one hand and differentiating implementation according to capabilities and responsibilities on the other hand has been a recognised key principle of the entire *DESD* discourse.[1208]

Secondly, monitoring has to do with communication, since effective and efficient communication[1209] enhances understanding and reduces certain costs of decision-making.[1210] This can only be achieved through interactive partnerships and a multi-lateral approach of integrative consultation. Two ways of communicating *DESD* can be distinguished:

1200 Cf. Boisson de Chazournes, Laurence (2007) (cf. *footnote 496* op. cit.), pp. 72–73; Foreign Office of the Federal Republic of Germany / German Commission for UNESCO (ed.) (2007) (cf. *footnote 21* op. cit.), pp. 30 et seqq.

1201 Cf. Tilbury, Daniella (2007) (cf. *footnote 219* op. cit.), pp. 241–242.

1202 Cf. Eisemann, Pierre Michel (2007) (cf. *footnote 478* op. cit.), pp. 27–28.

1203 See Deutsche UNESCO-Kommission e. V. (DUK) (ed.) (2007) (cf. *footnote 24* op. cit.), p. 20.

1204 Cf. Cizek, Gregory J.; Bunch, Michael B. (2006) (cf. *footnote 455* op. cit.), p. 15.

1205 See Principle 7 United Nations (1992) (cf. *footnote 731* op. cit.); Heyvaert, Veerle (2009) (cf. *footnote 942* op. cit.), p. 4.

1206 See Shelton, Dinah (2007e) (cf. *footnote 62* op. cit.), pp. 656–658; Heyvaert, Veerle (2009) (cf. *footnote 942* op. cit.), p. 4.

1207 Cf. United Nations (1992) (cf. *footnote 731* op. cit.); UN Department of Economic and Social Affairs (ed.) (2002) (cf. *footnote 853* op. cit.), p. 2.

1208 Cf. Tilbury, Daniella (2007) (cf. *footnote 219* op. cit.), p. 239; UNESCO (ed.) (2008h) (cf. *footnote 219* op. cit.), p. 15; Adomßent, Maik; Henze, Christa (eds.) (2007) (cf. *footnote 761* op. cit.), pp. 54 et seqq, 110 et seqq; Matsuura, Koïchiro (2007) (cf. *footnote 427* op. cit.), p. 13; UNESCO Section for DESD Coordination (ed.) (2009) (cf. *footnote 116* op. cit.), pp. 25 et seqq.

1209 Cf. Foreign Office of the Federal Republic of Germany / German Commission for UNESCO (ed.) (2007) (cf. *footnote 21* op. cit.), pp. 6 et seqq, 10 et seqq; Combes, Bernard P. Y. (2009) (cf. *footnote 663* op. cit.), pp. 216 et seqq.

1210 Cf. DiMaggio, Paul Joseph; Powell, Walter Woody (1991 / 2004 / 2008) (cf. *footnote 134* op. cit.), p. 7; United Nations Economic Commission for Europe (UNECE); United Nations Economic and Social Council (ECOSOC) (eds.) (2005f) (cf. *footnote 391* op. cit.), p. 5; UNESCO (ed.) (2008h) (cf. *footnote 219* op. cit.), p. 9.

- *External*: Making *DESD* publicly visible is a crucial strategy and key concern[1211] for the success of *DESD*. Considered as a self-contained framework,[1212] *DESD* communication is based upon culturally appropriate communication according to regionally differentiated responsibilities,[1213] and includes multiple and in each case available communication technologies;[1214] and
- *Internal*: *DESD* communication is also about stakeholder-driven or internal communication[1215] given the sheer number of regional communication platforms and the multitude of cross-cutting *DESD* issues.[1216] For instance, education is a matter of communication.[1217]

1211 Cf. UNESCO (ed.) (July 2003) (cf. *footnote 37* op. cit.), pp. 14–15; UNESCO (ed.) (2004c) (cf. *footnote 34* op. cit.), pp. 30 et seqq; Foreign Office of the Federal Republic of Germany / German Commission for UNESCO (ed.) (2007) (cf. *footnote 21* op. cit.), pp. 10 et seqq; Michelsen, Gerd (08/05/2007) (cf. *footnote 764* op. cit.), p. 5; UNESCO (ed.) (2007k) (cf. *footnote 4* op. cit.), pp. 53 et seqq; Gerner, Martin (10/08/2009) (cf. *footnote 407* op. cit.).

1212 Cf. UNESCO (ed.) (2007d) (cf. *footnote 585* op. cit.); UNESCO (ed.) (2008h) (cf. *footnote 219* op. cit.), pp. 8 et seqq; Heyvaert, Veerle (2009) (cf. *footnote 942* op. cit.), pp. 4–5; UNESCO (2009) (cf. *footnote 579* op. cit.).

1213 Cf. United Nations Economic Commission for Europe (UNECE); United Nations Economic and Social Council (ECOSOC) (eds.) (2005f) (cf. *footnote 391* op. cit.), p. 5; Oficina Regional de Educación de la UNESCO para América Latina y el Caribe (OREALC) (2008b): Marco Mundial de Monitoreo y la Evaluación de la Ejecución de las Actividades del DEDS. Glosario para la untilización del cuestionario. Published by: UNESCO. Oficina Regional de Educación de la UNESCO para América Latina y el Caribe (OREALC). Santiago de Chile; Oficina Regional de Educación de la UNESCO para América Latina y el Caribe (OREALC) (2008c): Marco Mundial de Monitoreo y la Evaluación de la Ejecución de las Actividades del DEDS. Contexto y Estructura del la Educación para el Desrrollo Sostenible (EDS) en los estados miembros. Cuestionario 1. Published by: UNESCO. Oficina Regional de Educación de la UNESCO para América Latina y el Caribe (OREALC). Santiago de Chile; UNESCO Section for DESD Coordination (ed.) (2009) (cf. *footnote 116* op. cit.), pp. 16 et seqq.

1214 Cf. UNESCO (ed.) (2003b) (cf. *footnote 109* op. cit.), p. 5.

1215 Cf. North, Douglass Cecil (1997) (cf. *footnote 68* op. cit.), p. 117; Boisson de Chazournes, Laurence (2007) (cf. *footnote 496* op. cit.), p. 61.

1216 E.g., *European Union* (EU), *United Nations Economic Commission for Europe* (UNECE), etc.
Cf. United Nations Economic Commission for Europe (UNECE); United Nations Economic and Social Council (ECOSOC) (eds.) (2004b) (cf. *footnote 391* op. cit.), pp. 3 et seqq; European Commission; Secretariat-General (eds.) (2008b): Progress on EU Sustainable Development Strategy. Final Report. Brussels / Rotterdam: ECORYS Nederland BV, pp. 123 et seqq.

1217 For many years environmental education has been counting as *prototype* of regime communication.

Thirdly, and lastly, compliance can be considered as the aggregation of mutual understanding and effective communication.[1218] *"Whether norms are binding or non-binding, compliance seems most directly linked to the existence of effective monitoring and independent supervision."*[1219]

Unlike many prevalent discussions, the monitoring of regime activities, such as *DESD*, can be interpreted as a matter of instituting communication rather than *coercion* or any *excessive control*.[1220]

2.3 Policy advice

Hypothetically speaking, recommending particular codes of conduct in relation to *DESD* may result in increased commitment.[1221]

There is no uniform concept of policy advice. In business practice as well as in politics policy advice applies individually and flexibly according to context and preferences of the contracting parties involved. Likewise, policy advice on *DESD* is de-centralised, case-dependent, issue-related and stakeholder-oriented. Aiming to provide guidance, to address decision-makers and to transfer commitment into all spheres,[1222] policy advice is offered both:

a) Pro-actively through *DESD* planning strategies,[1223] position or policy papers[1224], tool kits and manuals for implementing *DESD* into respective frameworks;[1225] and

---

Cf. UNESCO (1997b) (cf. *footnote 440* op. cit.), p. 1; Monroe, Martha C.; Fien, John (2005) (cf. *footnote 659* op. cit.); Chalkley, Brian; Haigh, Martin J.; Higgitt, David (eds.) (2009) (cf. *footnote 693* op. cit.).

1218 Cf. Shelton, Dinah (ed.) (2000) (cf. *footnote 357* op. cit.), p. 5; Shelton, Dinah (2003c) (cf. *footnote 357* op. cit.), pp. 3–5; Abi-Saab, Georges (2007) (cf. *footnote 488* op. cit.), p. 420; Heyvaert, Veerle (2009) (cf. *footnote 942* op. cit.), p. 6.

1219 See Shelton, Dinah (2003a) (cf. *footnote 989* op. cit.), p. 462.

1220 Cf. Jepperson, Ronald L. (1991 / 2004 / 2008) (cf. *footnote 144* op. cit.), p. 150; Kiss, Alexandre (2003) (cf. *footnote 297* op. cit.), p. 239.

1221 Cf. Shelton, Dinah (ed.) (2000) (cf. *footnote 357* op. cit.), pp. 14–17; Gerner, Martin (10/08/2009) (cf. *footnote 407* op. cit.).
Cf. chapter V 2 *Formulation of global policies and policy advice* on pages 101 et seqq.

1222 Cf. Foreign Office of the Federal Republic of Germany / German Commission for UNESCO (ed.) (2007) (cf. *footnote 21* op. cit.), pp. 12 et seqq; Young, Oran R.; King, Leslie A; Schroeder, Heike (eds.) (2008) (cf. *footnote 320* op. cit.).

1223 Cf. United Nations Economic Commission for Europe (UNECE); United Nations Economic and Social Council (ECOSOC) (eds.) (2005f) (cf. *footnote 391* op. cit.); Organización de Estados Iberoamericanos para la Educación, la Ciencia y la Cultura (OEI) (ed.) (2007): Construyendo una Educación para el Desarrollo Sostenible en América Latina y el Caribe. Estrategia Regional. Madrid / San José / Paris: UNESCO Santiago; Servicio de Publicaciones; Oficina Regional de Educación de la UNESCO

b) On demand through *ad-hoc* consultation and translation of *DESD* into recognised applicability (*good* or *best practices*).

3 Conclusion

The aim of this chapter was to examine the character of *DESD* in relation to specific (legal) effects in creating commitment to *DESD* through various means of compliance. From a theoretical perspective, UNESCO's threefold functional predisposition towards normative actions was briefly recalled: standard-setting, monitoring and policy advice. Considering the approved sources of international law it soon becomes obvious that *DESD* is not applicable in the case of any of them. Forming part of the highly debatable category of resolutions and declarations, it had to be openly stated that *DESD* is not legally (*de jure*) binding at all. Despite the fact that for quite some time structures in international law have been subject to change, not a single *hard-law* reference can be made in the case of *DESD*, failing for two reasons: *DESD* neither reflects international customary law,[1226] assuming *opinio iuris* and *usus*, nor a general principle, assuming recognised practice adhered to by all states.

Approaching compliance as a matter of gradual or relative normativity shows the way out of the *hard-law* versus *soft-law* dichotomy. The reasoning is plausible: Changing international order requires new institutional patterns of international law-making. On the one hand, it is true that *"we need to insist on a*

---

para América Latina y el Caribe (OREALC) (ed.) (2008): Estrategias de comunicación y educación para el desarrollo sostenible. Edited by David Solano. Santiago de Chile; UNESCO Education Sector (ed.) (March 2009): UNESCO Strategy for the Second Half of the United Nations Decade of Education for Sustainable Development. Supporting Member States and other stakeholders in addressing global sustainable development challenges through ESD. Education for Sustainable Development in Action / 2010/ED/UNP/DESD/PI/1. Paris: UNESCO workshops.

1224 Cf. Tilbury, Daniella (2007) (cf. *footnote 219* op. cit.).

1225 Cf. UNESCO (ed.) (2003b) (cf. *footnote 109* op. cit.); United Nations Economic Commission for Europe (UNECE); United Nations Economic and Social Council (ECOSOC) (eds.) (2004g) (cf. *footnote 391* op. cit.); UNESCO (ed.) (2006f) (cf. *footnote 25* op. cit.); Federal Ministry of Education and Research (BMBF) (ed.) (2006): Research for Sustainability. Framework programme of the German Federal Ministry of Education and Research (BMBF) for a sustainable, innovative society. Berlin: BMBF Publik; UNESCO (ed.) (2007d) (cf. *footnote 585* op. cit.); UNESCO (ed.) (2008h) (cf. *footnote 219* op. cit.); Oficina Regional de Educación de la UNESCO para América Latina y el Caribe (OREALC) (2008b) (cf. *footnote 1213* op. cit.); Oficina Regional de Educación de la UNESCO para América Latina y el Caribe (OREALC) (2008c) (cf. *footnote 1213* op. cit.).

1226 Cf. Magraw Barstow, Daniel; Hawke, Lisa D. (2007) (cf. *footnote 50* op. cit.), pp. 623–625.

degree of formalism, because it is precisely this formalism that protects us from arbitrariness on the part of the powers that be";[1227] on the other hand, a certain *permeability* in applying legal instruments is essential. Legal binding does not *eo ipso* represent the *via regia* or *silver bullet* to obtain ultimate commitment and compliance. It is therefore reasonable to apply *soft law* to *DESD*. Stakeholders may comply with proper self-interest and good will, either following some *me-too-strategy* in terms of *tit-for-tat* or calculating their own benefits, prestige or opportunity costs as part of the *rational-choice game* considering the classic *prisoner's dilemma.*

Applying the theoretical settings of *soft law* to *DESD* is promising, because it confirms some of the hypotheses made in advance:[1228]

- Standard-setting: possibly, accepting the normative character and binding nature of *DESD*;
- Monitoring: probably, establishing mechanisms of monitoring and assessment of *DESD*; and
- Policy advice: desirably, recommending particular codes of conduct in relation to *DESD*.

1227 See Klabbers, Jan (1998b) (cf. *footnote 960* op. cit.), p. 391.

1228 Cf. Hörtreiter, Isabel (2007) (cf. *footnote 510* op. cit.), pp. 295–305.
Cf. chapter V 5 *Conclusion* on pages 119 et seqq.
See *Figure 56* in chapter VIII 3 *Conclusion* on page 253.

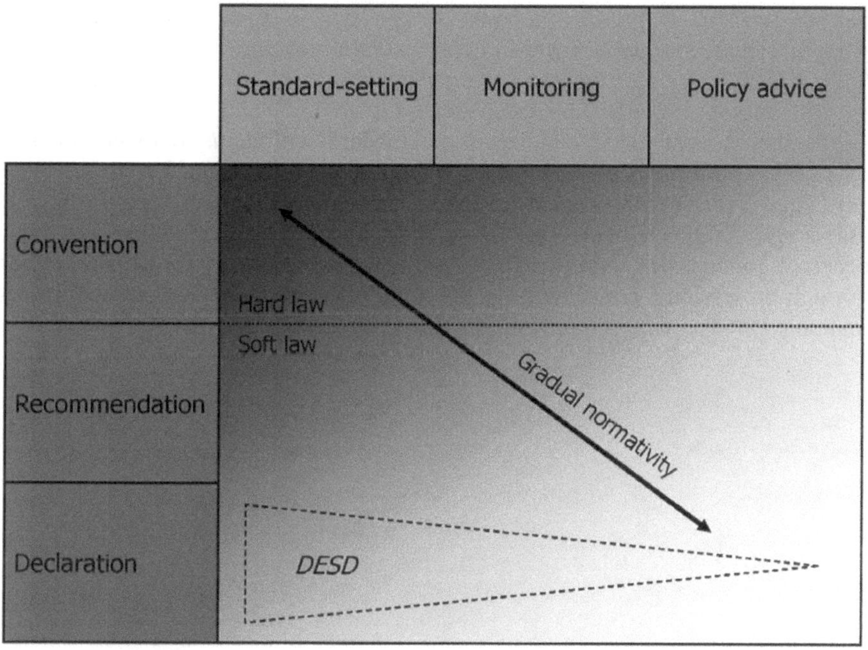

Figure 56: Matrix of UNESCO instruments, assignments[1229] *and DESD practices*[1230] *in place*[1231]

Soft law must be regarded as *grey zone*[1232] that may be difficult to handle due to qualitative and quantitative validation.[1233] However, it should, fairly, be appreciated as an approach through which *"(...) to conclude agreements with one another, create institutions, foster cooperation. The world may be anarchic,*

1229 Cf. Hüfner, Klaus; Reuther, Wolfgang (eds.) (2005) (cf. *footnote 412* op. cit.), p. 29; UNESCO (ed.) (2006b) (cf. *footnote 21* op. cit.); UNESCO (2007) (cf. *footnote 474* op. cit.); Foreign Office of the Federal Republic of Germany / German Commission for UNESCO (ed.) (2007) (cf. *footnote 21* op. cit.), pp. 12 et seqq.

1230 E.g., right to education, human rights and human rights education. Cf. Symonides, Janusz; Volodin, Vladimir (1996) (cf. *footnote 990* op. cit.); Hüfner, Klaus; Reuther, Wolfgang (eds.) (2005) (cf. *footnote 412* op. cit.), pp. 302 et seqq; UNESCO (ed.) (2006b) (cf. *footnote 21* op. cit.); Mutua, Makau (ed.) (2007) (cf. *footnote 988* op. cit.), pp. 550 et seqq.

1231 Generally, referring to the international law system as *umbrella*, *DESD* binding is low and not attached to legal provisions. However, according the functional assignment UNESCO still aims to address *DESD* by each part of normative action, though mainly focusing on the standard-setting perspective.

1232 Cf. Mazuelos Bellido, Ángeles (2004) (cf. *footnote 881* op. cit.), p. 21.

1233 Cf. Hoof, G. J. H. (Fried) van (1983) (cf. *footnote 867* op. cit.), pp. 65–71, 83, 91, 139 et seqq.

but then we will simply have to save the world from itself. And on this line of thought, any institution is better than no institution whatsoever; any form of co-operation is better than no form of cooperation at all; and any agreement, no matter how soft, is better than no agreement at all".[1234]

In the case of *DESD*, in terms of standard-setting, *de-facto* compliance based upon performance standards is preferable to paying some *lip service*[1235] to any normative binding. Regarding monitoring, mechanisms of monitoring and assessing *DESD* have been established. With respect to policy advice, particular codes of conduct pertaining to *DESD* are provided primarily on demand either through professional consultation or through other means of instructional information.

1234 See Klabbers, Jan (1998b) (cf. *footnote 960* op. cit.), p. 383.
1235 Cf. chapter VIII 1.2 *Challenges* on page 200.

IX Implementation practices

Implementation is without doubt the heart of DESD. It constitutes the core process of translating ESD from concept into reality, or, put differently, from theory into practice. This chapter will cover two critical aspects of DESD implementation: the actual putting into effect (implementation) as well as the integration of reporting and evaluation (monitoring). Both elements, structures of implementation and feedback alike, are key to answering the question of how does UNESCO co-ordinate and monitor the implementation of DESD?

1 Principles of implementation

Implementing *DESD* requires considerable effort on the part of UNESCO. Of course, it does not take place arbitrarily but is strategically organised and based upon certain guiding principles.[1236] These can be derived from two different sources:

1. *Good governance* in international organisations is regime-based and oriented towards general principles, such as *participation* in decision-making and implementation in accordance with the active ownership concept, *accountability* in the flow of information and effectiveness, and *fairness* in procedural and substantive aspects of representation or decision-making;[1237] and

1236 Most of the principles of implementation and monitoring are very much in line with the 2002 *Johannesburg World Summit on Sustainable Development* intended to enter into implementation by 2005 and later substituted by *DESD*.
Cf. United Nations (ed.) (2003c): The Road from Johannesburg. World Summit on Sustainable Development. What Was Achieved and the Way Forward. New York: United Nations, pp. 2–3, 9.

1237 Cf. Woods, Ngaire (2004 / 2006): Good Governance in International Organizations. In: Sinclair, Timothy J. (ed.): Global Governance: Critical Concepts in Political Science. London / New York / London: Taylor & Francis, Inc.; Routledge (Critical Concepts in Political Science, Volume II), Volume Global Governance 5 (1) (1999): 39–61, pp. 361–383, pp. 362–363, 365 et seqq; Breitmeier, Helmut; Young, Oran R.; Zürn, Michael (2006) (cf. *footnote 158* op. cit.), p. 3; Gerner, Martin (2008) (cf. *footnote 259* op. cit.), pp. 15, 21, 28.

2. *Self-perception* in terms of declared tasks and working methods of UNESCO as an international organisation,[1238] considering in particular relevant interconnected normative approaches.[1239]

1.1 Regional strategies

The fundamental principle of implementation of *DESD* was set out by Koïchiro Matsuura (Director-General of the *United Nations Educational, Scientific and Cultural Organization* (UNESCO)) in his speech on 1st March 2005 to mark the international launch of the *United Nations Decade of Education for Sustainable Development* (2005–2014). At the United Nations Headquarters in New York he announced the introduction of the *International Implementation Scheme* (IIS) of *DESD*[1240] in pursuit of a framework of international co-ordination. It thus serves primarily to provide a dynamic but common understanding of *DESD*.[1241]

"Following this international launch, there will be a series of regional, sub-regional and national launches that will give the DESD partnership opportunities to stimulate public interest and mobilise action. Regional ESD strategies are being formulated, for example in the Europe-North America and Asia-Pacific Regions, and UNESCO has been an active partner in these processes. UNESCO is facilitating the development of regional strategies in the other regions and the processes are well under way."[1242]

Koïchiro Matsuura explicitly encouraged different regional *ESD* strategies that would follow the international launch on a regional, sub-regional and national level. UNESCO is therefore making an active effort to support regional diversity throughout the implementation process. That is to say, "(t)*he objectives for each education and training system stem from each country's culture, economic and environmental context*".[1243]

Although *DESD* unquestionably follows a universal approach regarding overall aims and objectives, regional strategies of *ESD* represent a necessary step towards appropriate implementation.[1244] However, the question to be tack-

1238 Cf. Foreign Office of the Federal Republic of Germany / German Commission for UNESCO (ed.) (2007) (cf. *footnote 21* op. cit.), pp. 12 et seqq; UNESCO (ed.) (2007c) (cf. *footnote 120* op. cit.), pp. 7, 14.

1239 Cf. Yusuf, Abdulqawi A. (ed.) (2007) (cf. *footnote 129* op. cit.); UNESCO (2009) (cf. *footnote 579* op. cit.), pp. 25 et seqq.

1240 Cf. UNESCO (ed.) (2005j) (cf. *footnote 44* op. cit.).

1241 Cf. Matsuura, Koïchiro (01/03/2005) (cf. *footnote 28* op. cit.).

1242 See Matsuura, Koïchiro (01/03/2005) (cf. *footnote 28* op. cit.), p. 4.

1243 See Lasonen, Johanna (2009) (cf. *footnote 73* op. cit.), p. 187.

1244 Cf. UNESCO (ed.) (2003b) (cf. *footnote 109* op. cit.), p. 3; UNESCO (ed.) (2004c) (cf. *footnote 34* op. cit.), p. 35; UNESCO Education Sector (ed.) (March 2009) (cf. *footnote 1223* op. cit.), p. 12.
See *Figure 57* in chapter IX 1.1 *Regional strategies* on page 258.

led is how to meet sufficiently the specific needs and *nuanced differences*[1245] of any specific region or area.[1246]

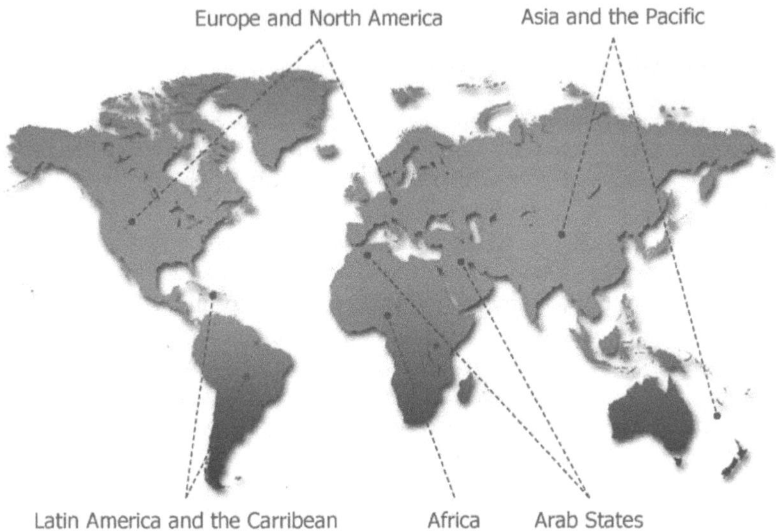

Figure 57: UNESCO regions worldwide[1247]

1.2 Synergy effects

Making efficient use of and drawing benefit from existing programmes, platforms, institutions and partners is a crucial and necessary UNESCO principle of *DESD* implementation. Essentially, the sharing of resources and expertise is essential for the organisation's efficiency and participatory success. Here follow examples of how synergy effects are intended to be strengthened on *DESD*-related issues.

1245 Cf. UNESCO (ed.) (2003b) (cf. *footnote 109* op. cit.), p. 2; Deutsche UNESCO-Kommission e. V. (DUK) (ed.) (2007) (cf. *footnote 24* op. cit.), p. 27.

1246 Cf. Adomßent, Maik; Henze, Christa (eds.) (2007) (cf. *footnote 761* op. cit.), pp. 54 et seqq, 110 et seqq.

1247 See UNESCO (2010b): UNESCO regions. Worldwide. Map. Published by: UNESCO. Considering the five UNESCO world regions in terms of *DESD* implementation: Africa, Arab States, Asia and the Pacific, Europe and North America, Latin America and the Caribbean.
Cf. UNESCO Education Sector (ed.) (March 2009) (cf. *footnote 1223* op. cit.), pp. 4 et seqq.

1.2.1 Programmes

There are a number of United Nations programmes aligned with *DESD*, both in a temporary and topical perspective.[1248] *"Although distinctive in significant respects, these initiatives share much in common in terms of their underlying values and ideals as well as their goals and target dates."*[1249] Together with *DESD*, the following are also in progress: *Education for All* (EFA), the *Millennium Development Goals* (MDG), the *International Decade for Action "Water for Life"* and the *United Nations Literacy Decade* (UNLD). Even though each has a different and distinctive focus, they all form part of efforts being made within a United Nations framework. The implication is of synergy effects and genuine alignment amongst each other rather than rivalry and competition.[1250]

Two facts must be mentioned: firstly, there is apparently no principle of subordination in terms of priority areas.[1251] Secondly, content, context and target group relations between certain programmes may inevitably vary according to their intended purpose.[1252] The following example illustrates these two aspects: Both *Education for All* (EFA) and *DESD* are in progress with a different focus on education.[1253] These programmes are independent with respect to aims and objectives but are nonetheless interrelated. While *EFA* focuses on access[1254] to quality education and organised learning in general, *DESD "addresses all levels and modalities of education, including quality media and corporate training programmes"*.[1255] Contexts are diverse yet interdisciplinary. *EFA* favours *DESD* through institutionalised education. *DESD* primarily refers to an extended educational concept, including so-called *non-quality education*, such as informal or non-formal education. Content-wise *DESD* refers to sustainable development. Consequently, synergy effects in support of *DESD* may evolve in the field of quality education, which is usually fostered through educational plans and applied learning through national politics.

Therefore, UNESCO proposes seven strategies to transfer the concept of sustainable development into the quality education sector, namely through plans of national education:[1256]

- Advocacy and vision-building;

1248 Cf. UNESCO (2006) (cf. *footnote 44* op. cit.), p. 2.
1249 See UNESCO (ed.) (2005g) (cf. *footnote 16* op. cit.), p. 4.
1250 Cf. UNESCO (ed.) (2005i) (cf. *footnote 216* op. cit.), p. 3.
1251 Cf. UNESCO (ed.) (2005g) (cf. *footnote 16* op. cit.), p. 4.
1252 Cf. UNESCO (ed.) (2005g) (cf. *footnote 16* op. cit.), p. 11.
1253 Cf. for details Wade, Ros; Parker, Jenneth (eds.) (2008) (cf. *footnote 480* op. cit.); Bhola, Harbans S. (2008) (cf. *footnote 653* op. cit.).
1254 Cf. Faundez, Julio (2007) (cf. *footnote 419* op. cit.), p. 334.
1255 See UNESCO (ed.) (2005i) (cf. *footnote 216* op. cit.), p. 3.
1256 Cf. UNESCO (ed.) (2005i) (cf. *footnote 216* op. cit.), p. 3.

- Consultation and ownership;
- Partnership and networks;
- Capacity-building and training;
- Research and innovation;
- Information and communication technologies; and
- Monitoring and evaluation.

DESD may be regarded as both a coherent *umbrella concept*[1257] and an integral part of United Nations educational programmes. Undoubtedly *education* is the essential *glue* and nexus that links together four substantial challenges:[1258]

Table 28: Cross-cutting DESD-related programmes and initiatives

Programme or initiative	Focal issues or strategic objectives
United Nations Decade on ESD (*DESD*)[1259] (2005–2014)	Transforming societies into sustainable ones referring to knowledge through professional education systems;
Education for All (EFA)[1260]	Ensuring the equal opportunity of access to quality education – six goals with a target date of 2015;

1257 Cf. UNESCO (ed.) (2005g) (cf. *footnote 16* op. cit.), p. 9; Combes, Bernard P. Y. (2009) (cf. *footnote 663* op. cit.), p. 216.
"The outreach of the DESD is broader than the other initiatives as it tackles more than just education [...]."
See UNESCO (ed.) (2007k) (cf. *footnote 4* op. cit.), p. 7.

1258 Cf. UNESCO (05/07/2003) (cf. *footnote 124* op. cit.), pp. 8–10; UNESCO (ed.) (2005c) (cf. *footnote 23* op. cit.), pp. 14–15; UNESCO (ed.) (2005i) (cf. *footnote 216* op. cit.), p. 3; UNESCO (ed.) (2005g) (cf. *footnote 16* op. cit.), pp. 4 et seqq; Valdivielso Gómez, Sofía (2008): Luggage for a Journey: From Functional Literacy and Development to Integral Literacy and Sustainable Development. In: Bhola, Harbans S.; Valdivielso Gómez, Sofía (eds.): Signposts to literacy for sustainable development. Complementary studies. Hamburg: UNESCO Institute for Lifelong Learning, pp. 79–171.
See *Table 28* in chapter IX 1.2.1 *Programmes* on page 260.

1259 Characteristics: the 1980s ideas on sustainability have been picked up by a United Nations initiative on education for sustainable development, reconciling two initially contrasting concepts of development and sustainability with educational, behavioural and valuable goals, such as making people aware that education is a good basis for a sustainable way of life; making sure that ideas about sustainable development are part of schools, colleges, universities and other ways of learning; making sure that organisations and governments worldwide work together, so that they can learn from new experiences and from activities in different parts of the world. *DESD* reaches far beyond education as it broadens horizons towards ways of life, values and behaviour; education functions as a necessary mediator for a sustainable knowledge base; education establishes further links through a multi-target group approach.
Cf. UNESCO (ed.) (2005g) (cf. *footnote 16* op. cit.), p. 9.

Programme or initiative	Focal issues or strategic objectives
International Decade for Action 'Water for Life'[1261] (2005–2015)	Contributing to the effective management of water resources;
United Nations Literacy Decade (UNLD)[1262] (2003–2012)	Promoting literacy as a key tool for all learning types and levels; and

1260 Characteristics: aiming at good basic education *Education for All* (EFA) had already been initiated in 1990, and implemented through a follow-up conference in 2000 setting up the *Dakar Framework for Action* on six educational goals: 1. Giving more pre-school children the chance of good care and early learning; 2. Making sure that all children complete a good primary education, free of charge, by 2015; 3. Giving young people and adults the chance to learn the skills they need; 4. Making sure that fifty per cent more people are literate before 2015; 5. Making sure that boys and girls are enrolled in school in equal numbers by 2005, and that they have all enrolled and have equal opportunities in school, by 2015; and 6. Improving the quality of education and ensuring full reference with education, particularly interconnecting education with development.
Cf. UNESCO (ed.) (2000) (cf. *footnote 541* op. cit.); UNESCO (ed.) (2005g) (cf. *footnote 16* op. cit.), pp. 7–8; Benedek, Wolfgang (2007) (cf. *footnote 22* op. cit.).

1261 Characteristics: dealing with important water-related issues, such as scarcity, access to sanitation and health, water and gender, capacity-building, financing, valuation, integrated water resources management, trans-boundary water issues, environment and biodiversity, disaster prevention, food and agriculture, pollution and energy, the *International Decade for Action 'Water for Life'* aims at achieving the following goals: 1. Promoting efforts to fulfill international commitments made on water and water-related issues by 2015; 2. Stopping unsustainable exploitation of water resources; 3. Developing integrated water resource management and water efficiency plans by 2005; 4.) Providing access to basic sanitation; and 5. Ensuring the participation and involvement of women in these development efforts.
Cf. United Nations (ed.) (2003a): International Decade for Action, "Water for Life", 2005–2015. Resolution adopted by the General Assembly. A/RES/58/217. New York: United Nations; UNESCO (ed.) (2007i): Natural Disaster Preparedness and Education for Sustainable Development. APE/ESD/07/OP/006–2000. Bangkok: UNESCO Asia and Pacific Regional Bureau for Education, p. 59.

1262 Characteristics: tackling the vision of *literacy for all*, the United Nations General Assembly in 2003 launched a universally accessible Decade of Action on illiteracy as a crucial *"tool for learning and a means to take part in society"*, aiming to achieve the following goals: 1. Making sure that 50 per cent more people can use reading and writing by 2015, giving special attention to women; 2. Making a considerable contribution to the other EFA goals for 2015 helping all learners to read, write and calculate well, to think critically, to have positive values as citizens and to acquire other skills they need; 3. Helping to ensure that people use their literacy in creative ways, in school and in the community; 4. Making life better through less poverty, more income, better health, taking part more in political life, knowing what one's rights and duties are in one's own country, and taking account of the equal rights of men and women; direct contribution to education and EFA goals as literacy works as a prerequisite *"for the full range of education and learning possibilities"*. All contexts, ranging from institution-

Programme or initiative	Focal issues or strategic objectives
Millennium Development Goals (MDG)[1263]	Measuring development progress by eight goals with a target date of 2015 based upon education as one significant input and indicator.

With the intention of enabling a comprehensive understanding of cross-cutting programmes with *DESD*, UNESCO provides technical guidance through a paper on education-related issues,[1264] briefly introducing the four global initiatives and listing similarities, overlaps and differences between them, explaining in particular how they work together.

All four international initiatives have the following aspects in common:[1265]

- Aiming at improving the quality of life by reducing poverty and improving health and health care conditions;
- Promoting human rights, gender equity and fair access to education;
- Committing multiple efforts to education as *key to development*;
- Appreciating the fundamental role of primary education; and
- Involving multi-party stakeholders, e.g., governments, non-governmental organisations, civil society, the private sector, communities and individuals.

Some initiatives share different aspects with each other, which might be called *topical overlaps*:[1266]

---

alised to non-formal, and target groups, ranging from industrialised to developing, are being addressed.
Cf. UNESCO (ed.) (2005g) (cf. *footnote 16* op. cit.), pp. 8–9; Lind, Agneta (2009) (cf. *footnote 480* op. cit.).

1263 Characteristics: eight priorities adopted as *Millennium Declaration* by the United Nations General Assembly in 2000 with a target date of 2015 *"expressing common worldwide priorities in development"*: Goal 1: Eradicate extreme poverty and hunger; Goal 2: Achieve universal primary education; Goal 3: Promote gender equality and empower women; Goal 4: Reduce child mortality; Goal 5: Improve maternal health; Goal 6: Combat HIV / AIDS, malaria and other diseases; Goal 7: Ensure environmental sustainability; and Goal 8: Develop a global partnership for development; direct linkage through education related issues: Goal 2 and 3.
Cf. UNESCO (ed.) (2005g) (cf. *footnote 16* op. cit.), pp. 6–7; UNESCO (2006) (cf. *footnote 44* op. cit.), pp. 2–3; Maclean, Rupert; Fien, John; Park, Man-Gon (eds.) (2009) (cf. *footnote 42* op. cit.).

1264 UN Decade of Education for Sustainable Development: *Links between the Global Initiatives in Education. Education for Sustainable Development in Action*: Technical Paper N 1.
See UNESCO (ed.) (2005g) (cf. *footnote 16* op. cit.).

1265 Cf. UNESCO (ed.) (2003b) (cf. *footnote 109* op. cit.), pp. 2–3; UNESCO (ed.) (2005g) (cf. *footnote 16* op. cit.), pp. 9–10; UNESCO (ed.) (2007k) (cf. *footnote 4* op. cit.), p. 7; Fien, John (2010) (cf. *footnote 817* op. cit.).

- Focusing equally on quality education (*EFA* and *DESD*), particularly how to be taught and learned;
- Integrating non-formal or informal ways of learning outside institutional contexts (*EFA*, *DESD* and *UNLD*);[1267] and
- Dedicating efforts to literacy as a foundational principle of learning and educational access (*UNLD* and *EFA* as prerequisite of *DESD*).

Differences in programmes relate to either structure or content. Structural differences are evident and primarily due to target group orientation. For instance, the framework of international co-operation on *Millennium Development Goals* (MDG) is to be applied differently in developing and industrialised countries. Differences in content result from issues of purpose and focus. There is common ground in that questions of formal and non-formal, quality and informal, primary and higher education, literacy, and equitable access to education, either formal or informal, have to be dealt with differently in terms of adjusting programmes.[1268] However, a more general difference between *DESD* and *EFA*, educational goals two and three of *MDG* and *UNLD*, may be observed with respect to both target group and content orientation: whereas *DESD* reflects a *content-driven* approach (that is, to address the necessity and relevance of education for sustainable development for all, irrespective of *"whether (...) within or outside of (any) planned learning activities"*[1269]) *EFA*, *MDG* and *UNLD* refer instead to a *structure-driven* approach[1270] oriented towards the needs and conditions of learning processes.[1271]

Apart from the *Millennium Development Goals* (MDG), UNESCO has been given a co-ordination mandate by the United Nations General Assembly for three of four global initiatives on education, namely *EFA*, *UNLD* and *DESD*.[1272]

1266 Cf. UNESCO (ed.) (2005g) (cf. *footnote 16* op. cit.), p. 10.
Various *topical overlaps*, common interests and synergies are intended to be pursued according to the four domains of ecology, economy, society and culture with respect to: overcoming poverty, attainment of gender equality, health promotion, environmental conservation and protection, rural transformation, human rights, intercultural understanding and peace, sustainable production and consumption, cultural diversity, information and communication technologies.
Cf. UNESCO (ed.) (July 2003) (cf. *footnote 37* op. cit.), pp. 7–9.

1267 Cf. UNESCO (ed.) (2007k) (cf. *footnote 4* op. cit.), p. 8.

1268 Cf. UNESCO (ed.) (2005g) (cf. *footnote 16* op. cit.), pp. 10–11.

1269 Cf. UNESCO (ed.) (2005g) (cf. *footnote 16* op. cit.), p. 11.

1270 I.e. education in terms of rights, access, equity, quality, learners' needs.

1271 Cf. UNESCO (ed.) (2005g) (cf. *footnote 16* op. cit.), p. 11.

1272 The *Millennium Development Goals* (MDG) are being co-ordinated by the *United Nations Development Programme* (UNDP) together with international taskforces, one for each goal and, additionally, with an independent advisory panel to the United Nations Secretary-General in charge of recommendations with respect to the *Millennium Project* through *"A Global Plan to Achieve the Millennium Development Goals"*.

Appreciating the advantageous *turnkey situation*, UNESCO acts as major facilitator, developing and fostering activities to promote international co-operation for each programme. For instance, such linkages concern:[1273]

- *Education for All* (EFA):
  - *EFA Working Group* to discuss technical and professional matters on reaching EFA;
  - *EFA High-Level Group* to provide a platform for meetings of ministers, agency heads and leaders of *non-governmental organisations* (NGO) to examine EFA priorities and create political will for EFA;
  - Publishing a *Global EFA Monitoring Report* on countries' progress;
- *United Nations Literacy Decade* (UNLD):
  - *Inter-agency group* to co-ordinate approaches and share experience in promoting literacy;
  - Annual *International Literacy Day* highlighting different literacy themes;
- *United Nations Decade of Education for Sustainable Development* (DESD):[1274]
  - UNESCO mechanisms for co-ordinating and promoting the Decade;
  - *High-Level Advisory Panel.*

Cf. UNESCO (ed.) (2005g) (cf. *footnote 16* op. cit.), p. 12.

1273 See *Figure 58* in chapter IX 1.2.1 *Programmes* on page 265.

1274 Subsuming and including the *International Decade for Action "Water for Life"* 2005–2015 (A/RES/58/217) taking place simultaneously.
Cf. Combes, Bernard P. Y. (2009) (cf. *footnote 663* op. cit.), p. 216.

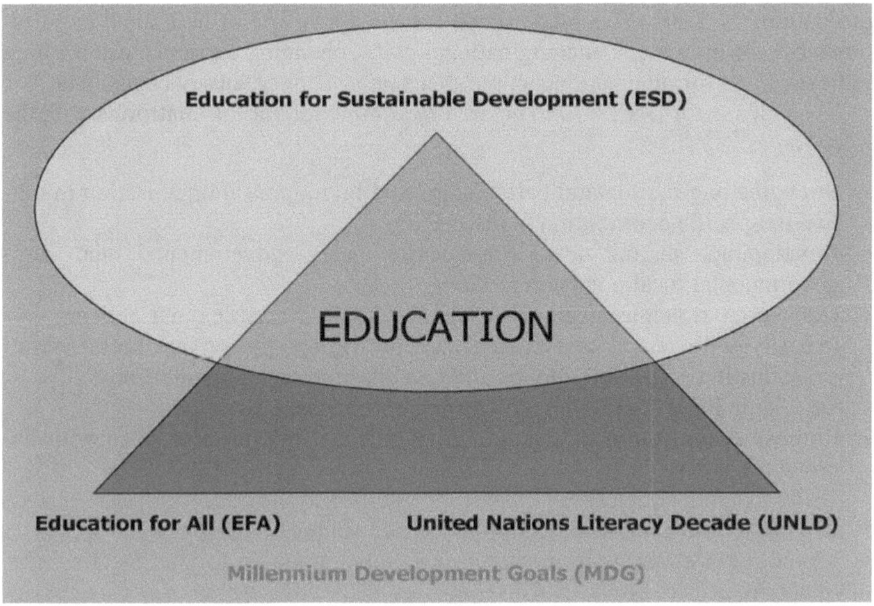

Figure 58: Education as central strategy for ESD-interlinked United Nations concepts[1275]

The fact of UNESCO's programme co-ordination is widely regarded as highly beneficial in terms of synergy effects. These are achieved through joint or complementary efforts which are likely to avoid inefficient *overlaps*,[1276] and above all the knowledge, experience and core expertise in education of UNESCO. However, this approach of dealing with three *construction sites* at the very same time requires considerable means of resources.

1.2.2 Platforms

UNESCO welcomes initiatives developed by countries and organisations on *DESD*-related issues. Even though UNESCO holds a strong leading mandate which prescribes its proactive role of international leadership and co-

1275 This figure relates major United Nations concerns, activities and programmes that are linked with *DESD* to some extent. All of them are based on *education* as principal strategy. Thus, *ESD* is directly connected with *Education for All* (EFA) and the *United Nations Literacy Decade* (UNLD). However, *ESD* is further reaching in scope since *DESD* addresses issues on development and sustainability, too. With this respect, *ESD* additionally ties up with objectives of the *Millennium Development Goals* (MDG) as rather underlying global concern.
See UNESCO (ed.) (2003b) (cf. *footnote 109* op. cit.), pp. 3–4.

1276 See UNESCO (ed.) (2005g) (cf. *footnote 16* op. cit.), p. 12.

ordination,[1277] it strives to retain scope for the dynamism of individual opportunities by, for instance, launching national plans, changing curricula, establishing indicators and forming national committees on *ESD* or advocacy campaigns.

The idea is for UNESCO to act as a *facilitator* for various platforms with the intention of:[1278]

- Strengthening multilateral partnerships and inviting each organisation to outline its specific contribution to the *DESD*;
- Developing, sharing and strategically using governmental and non-governmental focal points on *DESD*;
- Convening strategic meetings to engage key partnerships and actions, particularly with regard to research and innovation, the private sector, faith-based institutions, youth groups and non-governmental organisations;[1279]
- Developing and distributing key *technical assistance packages*;
- Proposing and introducing monitoring mechanisms in accordance with national priorities;
- Using existing structures;
- Creating some kind of leadership index as a source of advocacy and support;
- Promoting a *DESD* platform to ensure global attention to UNESCO's fields of action.

As a result of the process of open and dynamic facilitation that UNESCO sets in motion (in accordance with the *International Implementation Scheme* (IIS)[1280]) an *Inter-Agency Committee for the DESD* has been set up which serves as *"a multilateral forum with open-ended collaboration bringing international agencies together to:*

- *Share programmes and plans in order to encourage mutual reinforcement and avoid duplication or overlap;*
- *Harmonise approaches to ESD and sustainable development practices within each institution; and*
- *Provide a forum for agencies to integrate the insights and perspectives of other international actors into their ESD agendas".*[1281]

Apart from establishing and facilitating a dynamic platform on *DESD* this *Inter-Agency Committee* provides additional support towards UNESCO in the fields of:[1282]

1277 Cf. UNESCO (ed.) (2005i) (cf. *footnote 216* op. cit.), p. 3.

1278 Cf. UNESCO (ed.) (2005i) (cf. *footnote 216* op. cit.), p. 4.

1279 Cf. UNESCO; Asia-Pacific Centre of Education for International Understanding (APCEIU) (eds.) (2007a) (cf. *footnote 696* op. cit.); Fien, John (2010) (cf. *footnote 817* op. cit.).

1280 Cf. UNESCO (ed.) (2005j) (cf. *footnote 44* op. cit.), p. 14.

1281 See UNESCO (ed.) (2005i) (cf. *footnote 216* op. cit.), p. 4.

1. Planning and promoting *DESD*;
2. Mobilising financial resources;
3. Co-ordinating multi-stakeholder implementation;
4. Assessing and reporting.[1283]

UNESCO functions with reference to an *open-access approach* of co-operation, leaving results to some extent *open-ended*, at least in the first instance.[1284]

1.2.3 Communities

"During the Decade and beyond, all parts of UNESCO will work together",[1285] in terms of both *horizontal* and *vertical* organisation: burden sharing means expertise sharing. This might be an appropriate motto for joint collaboration amongst all UNESCO sectors and partners. Horizontally, the following organisation's entities are obliged to work together:

1. UNESCO headquarters and sectors providing support and technical backstopping;
2. UNESCO programme sectors developing short-, medium- and long-term plans for *DESD*; and
3. UNESCO institutes contributing through expertise in education, statistics and sciences.

In a vertical perspective tasks are arranged with reference to a country-region approach:

a) National offices play proactive roles by promoting *ESD* and *DESD* by initiating dialogues among stakeholders;
b) Cluster offices working closely with both national and regional offices in order to integrate elements of *ESD* into education systems; and
c) Regional offices (*bureaux*) facilitate regional strategies.

The crucial prerequisites of community collaboration are efficient means through which to communicate, report and provide technical assistance.

1282 Cf. UNESCO (ed.) (2005i) (cf. *footnote 216* op. cit.), p. 4.

1283 Entities charged with assessment and reporting are: UNESCO, the United Nations General Assembly, the *Commission for Sustainable Development* (CSD) and other stakeholders and partners.
Cf. UNESCO (ed.) (2005i) (cf. *footnote 216* op. cit.), p. 4.

1284 Cf. Deutsche UNESCO-Kommission e. V. (DUK) (ed.) (2007) (cf. *footnote 24* op. cit.), p. 26.

1285 See UNESCO (ed.) (2005i) (cf. *footnote 216* op. cit.), p. 5.

1.3 Bottom-up

Instead of top-down implementation, UNESCO explicitly favours the promising bottom-up approach of creating commitment to *DESD from below*,[1286] including and emphasising field perspectives and challenges.[1287] The intention is to create flexibility of content and the utmost freedom of application while implementing.[1288] Bottom-up initiatives may confer upon an enterprise additional legitimacy, expertise, and other innovative resources for making and enforcing new norms and standards.[1289]

1.4 Participatory

UNESCO seeks broad, voluntary and multi-stakeholder participation, not only in preparing *DESD* implementation, but as a general principle in the course of the whole decade.[1290] The vision is to provide an opportunity for contributions at the very beginning in order to build *momentum*[1291] and to achieve optimal rates of *DESD* acceptance and compliance.[1292] *"The value of the wider picture provides the global view of the problems associated with sustainable development, and which not only teachers need to be aware of but all humankind as well."*[1293] *"Getting people on board"*[1294] requires service-oriented policies and effective

---

1286 Cf. Cox, Robert W. (2004 / 2006) (cf. *footnote 546* op. cit.), p. 207; Deutsche UNESCO-Kommission e. V. (DUK) (ed.) (2007) (cf. *footnote 24* op. cit.), pp. 23, 26.

1287 Cf. UNESCO (ed.) (2003b) (cf. *footnote 109* op. cit.), p. 4.

1288 Cf. UNESCO (2007) (cf. *footnote 52* op. cit.).

1289 Cf. Kirton, John J.; Trebilcock, Michael J. (eds.) (2004) (cf. *footnote 888* op. cit.), p. 5; Deutsche UNESCO-Kommission e. V. (DUK) (ed.) (2007) (cf. *footnote 24* op. cit.), pp. 23, 26.

1290 Cf. López Ospina, Gustavo (2005) (cf. *footnote 658* op. cit.), p. 73; Gerner, Martin (10/08/2009) (cf. *footnote 407* op. cit.).

1291 See UNESCO (ed.) (2003b) (cf. *footnote 109* op. cit.), p. 6; Bory-Adams, Aline (2010) (cf. *footnote 37* op. cit.), pp. 176, 178.
Aiming at broad participation, commitment and ownership in favour of *DESD*, UNESCO must necessarily tackle the integration of potential stakeholders at the very beginning, i.e. at the planning and preparatory stage.

1292 Cf. Kiss, Alexandre (2003) (cf. *footnote 297* op. cit.), pp. 237–238; Mutua, Makau (ed.) (2007) (cf. *footnote 988* op. cit.), pp. 548, 555.

1293 See Thomas, Elwyn (2009) (cf. *footnote 48* op. cit.), p. 91.

1294 See Gerner, Martin (14/09/2009) (cf. *footnote 407* op. cit.).

management and consultation structures.[1295] Thus, the following players are involved in the development of an implementation scheme:[1296]

- Academic and other research institutions;
- Non-governmental organisations and civil society organisations at the local, national and international level;[1297]
- Special interest groups, such as youth groups and women's groups;
- Faith-based organisations;
- Private sector,[1298] including *Public-Private-Partnerships* (PPP); and
- Media groups.

1.5 Multi-sphere

The call for participation does not necessarily address all relevant groups of stakeholders. Therefore, *"(t)his great endeavour calls for cooperation and collaboration from the grassroots level upward, as well as for new creative forms of partnership. UNESCO is eager to work with educators, policymakers, governments, academia, associations, NGOs, and civil society groups to develop national action plans and to fill out (the organisation's mandate)".*[1299] UNESCO therefore favours a *qualitative approach* in the sense of involving the *horizontal* representation of stakeholders in different, but *interrelated spheres*[1300] of participation, experience and influence.[1301]

1295 Cf. Adomßent, Maik; Henze, Christa (eds.) (2007) (cf. *footnote 761* op. cit.), pp. 54 et seqq, 110 et seqq; Mutua, Makau (ed.) (2007) (cf. *footnote 988* op. cit.), p. 629; UNESCO (ed.) (2008h) (cf. *footnote 219* op. cit.), p. 6.

1296 Cf. UNESCO (ed.) (2005i) (cf. *footnote 216* op. cit.), p. 5; Combes, Bernard P. Y. (2009) (cf. *footnote 663* op. cit.), p. 216; Lasonen, Johanna (2009) (cf. *footnote 73* op. cit.), p. 187.

1297 Cf. Ebbesson, Jonas (2007) (cf. *footnote 1018* op. cit.), pp. 682–685.

1298 Cf. Higgitt, David (2009b) (cf. *footnote 56* op. cit.); Fien, John (2010) (cf. *footnote 817* op. cit.).

1299 See Combes, Bernard P. Y. (2009) (cf. *footnote 663* op. cit.), p. 218.

1300 See UNESCO (ed.) (2003b) (cf. *footnote 109* op. cit.), p. 5; UNESCO (ed.) (2005j) (cf. *footnote 44* op. cit.), pp. 9–10.

1301 For instance, increasing co-operation between the United Nations system and the private sector as an example of good-practice.
Cf. Nelson, Jane (2002) (cf. *footnote 820* op. cit.), pp. 133 et seqq, 307; UNESCO (ed.) (2007f) (cf. *footnote 427* op. cit.), p. 2; Fien, John (2010) (cf. *footnote 817* op. cit.).

1.6 Multi-level

Different regional strategies of implementation and multiple subjects of participation both require differentiated means and approaches for commitment on a geographical scale.[1302]

Accordingly, UNESCO's stakeholder strategy is arranged in line with its partners' specific needs on four levels: sub-national,[1303] national, regional[1304] and international.[1305] *"Promoting co-operation and sustainable development involves a wider assessment and monitoring of the global environment. This includes the policies and actions of international and regional organisations, for example, the UN environmental agencies, the EU, the World Bank and the WWF."*[1306]

1302 I.e. guiding principle of implementation of the Johannesburg *World Summit of Sustainable Development* in 2002.
Cf. Shelton, Dinah (ed.) (2000) (cf. *footnote 357* op. cit.), pp. 12–13; United Nations (ed.) (2003c) (cf. *footnote 1236* op. cit.), p. 9; Kiss, Alexandre (2003) (cf. *footnote 297* op. cit.), pp. 228 et seqq.

1303 Namely, local or community level.

1304 For example: *United Nations Economic Commission for Europe* (UNECE).
Cf. United Nations Economic Commission for Europe (UNECE); United Nations Economic and Social Council (ECOSOC) (eds.) (2004b) (cf. *footnote 391* op. cit.).

1305 Cf. UNESCO (ed.) (2003b) (cf. *footnote 109* op. cit.), pp. 6–7.
See *Figure 59* in chapter IX 1.6 *Multi-level* on page 271.

1306 See Thomas, Elwyn (2009) (cf. *footnote 48* op. cit.), p. 91.

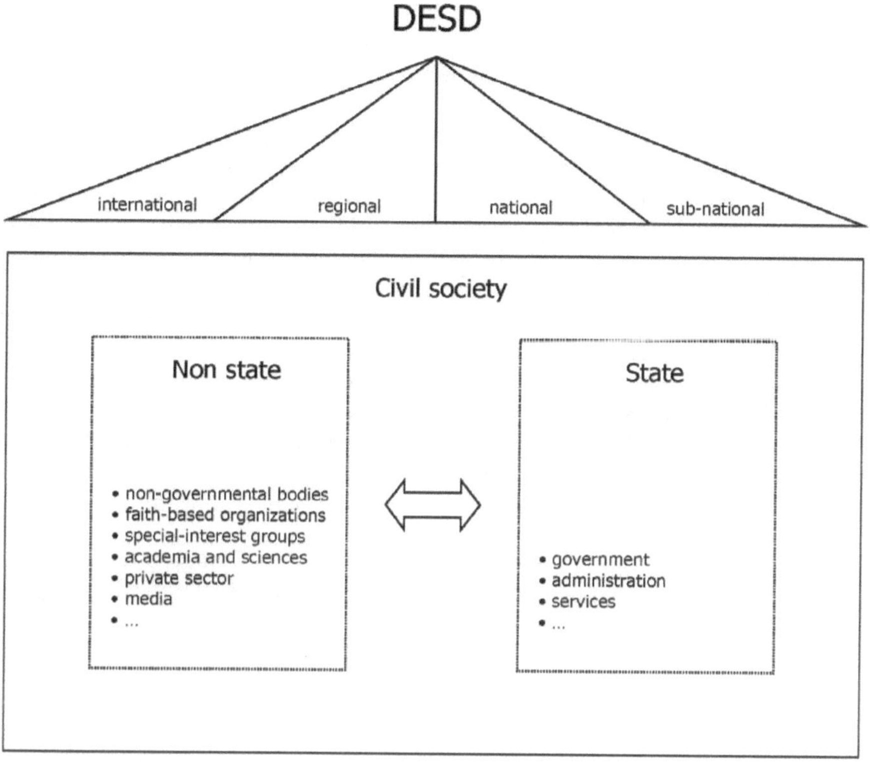

Figure 59: Multi-sphere and multi-level interplay of DESD[1307]

1.7 Cross-cutting

Synonyms like *inter-sectoral*, *inter-disciplinary*, *transverse*, *cross-cutting*, *cross-sectoral* or *trans-disciplinary* all point at an important UNESCO principle of *DESD* implementation.[1308] *"Addressing sustainability requires a holistic, in-*

1307 Principally *DESD* involves stakeholders of multiple spheres and on different levels. With respect to spheres *DESD* should be regarded as an effort directed to civil society, first and foremost. This refers to actors that are both non-state *and* state-affiliated. As to levels *DESD* takes place in different geographical settings: international, regional, national and sub-national.
Cf. UNESCO (ed.) (2003b) (cf. *footnote 109* op. cit.), pp. 6–7.

1308 Frequently, these terms are applied and used interchangeably, for an obvious reason. They are all directed towards overcoming frontiers between disciplines in science and professional practice. Two different forms of bridging disciplines can be distinguished

terdisciplinary approach which brings together the different disciplines and institutions while retaining their distinct identities."[1309] Unlike many declarations in the theory and practice of interdisciplinary approaches, UNESCO firmly believes in it.

In this respect, *DESD* constitutes an *inter-sectoral pursuit.*[1310] What slowly becomes a noticeable tendency in science has already been a staple UNESCO practice for more than sixty years.[1311] It is the organisation's conviction and continuing *comparative advantage*[1312] that the world is neither black nor white and thus, cannot be reduced to the approach of a single discipline. Cross-cutting or interdisciplinary solutions to multi-layer problems are in great demand.[1313]

With reference to education as its core competence, UNESCO has to tackle a multi-disciplinary approach encompassing *"economic, social, cultural, demographic and environmental issues".*[1314] What originated in the science sector ought to become a viable inter-sectoral method of dealing with sustainable development and education for sustainable development as an initiative adopted by the whole of UNESCO.[1315] In the case of *DESD*, the cross-cutting principle can be observed in relation to three different aspects; namely, institutions, dimensions and programme activities.

As far as institutions are concerned, interdisciplinary approaches essentially form part of UNESCO's institutional practices and those of UNESCO communi-

according to the degree of qualitative exchange: *Multi-disciplinary* approaches mean *"looking at an issue from many knowledge or practical disciplinary perspectives, but not integrating them (in practice). The multidisciplinary approach involves different subjects of study in one activity, without changes in disciplinary and theoretical structures (...)"*; and *inter-disciplinary or cross-cutting approaches* emphasise *"the interconnections between different perspectives. Interdisciplinary approach (...) involving two or more different subjects (are characterised by practical) cooperation within a common framework shared by the disciplines involved [...]".*
See United Nations Economic Commission for Europe (UNECE); United Nations Economic and Social Council (ECOSOC) (eds.) (2004f) (cf. *footnote 27* op. cit.), p. 5.

1309 See UNESCO (1997b) (cf. *footnote 440* op. cit.), p. 2.

1310 See UNESCO (ed.) (2006e) (cf. *footnote 777* op. cit.), p. 4.

1311 Cf. UNESCO (ed.) (2006a) (cf. *footnote 616* op. cit.); Matsuura, Koïchiro (2007) (cf. *footnote 427* op. cit.), p. 13.

1312 See UNESCO (ed.) (2005i) (cf. *footnote 216* op. cit.), p. 5.

1313 Cf. UNESCO; International Association of Universities (IAU); COPERNICUS-CAMPUS; Association of University Leaders for a Sustainable Future (ULSF) (2002) (cf. *footnote 806* op. cit.), p. 1; López Ospina, Gustavo (2005) (cf. *footnote 658* op. cit.), p. 73; Ginkel, Hans van (2010) (cf. *footnote 806* op. cit.), pp. 30–31.

1314 See UNESCO (ed.) (2005i) (cf. *footnote 216* op. cit.), p. 5.
Cf. *Figure 30* in chapter VII 4 *Dimensions* on page 157.

1315 See UNESCO (ed.) (July 2003) (cf. *footnote 37* op. cit.), p. 16.

ties.[1316] All sectors and offices are vertically and horizontally linked, working hand in hand with respect to *DESD* on all levels of competence. These are *"education, the social and human sciences, science, culture and communication"*.[1317] Furthermore, inter-institutional co-operation is fostered by UNESCO, among United Nations stakeholder organisations.[1318]

By definition, *DESD* involves multiple dimensions. UNESCO is therefore necessarily tasked with the promotion of inter-sectoral collaboration and co-ordination for the purpose of meeting its own responsibilities for *"planning and implementing UNESCO's own substantive contribution"*[1319] to *DESD*.[1320]

To draw benefit from diverse programmes and platforms, both technical and content-based co-ordination is required. This will only be possible if there is a common ground of interdisciplinary respect and appreciation. Without close attention to inter-sectoral understanding it will be impossible to make use of synergy effects and benefits from existing programme activities.

In order to carry out cross-cutting analyses and to facilitate joint actions, UNESCO has set up an *Inter-sectoral Working Group* (IWG)[1321] intended and tasked to *"provide advice, monitor activities and ensure inter-sectoral co-ordination"*[1322] among stakeholders and programmes relating to *ESD* according to the following criteria:[1323]

- Broad base of representation and participation;
- Efficiency and effectiveness in advisory functions, communication and monitoring; and
- Expertise and awareness of UNESCO's priorities, project and programme variety.[1324]

1316 Cf. Foreign Office of the Federal Republic of Germany / German Commission for UNESCO (ed.) (2007) (cf. *footnote 21* op. cit.), p. 10.

1317 See UNESCO (ed.) (2005i) (cf. *footnote 216* op. cit.), p. 5.

1318 For example: *United Nations Development Programme* (UNDP), *Economic Commission for Latin America and the Caribbean* (ECLAC / CEPAL), *United Nations Economic Commission for Europe* (UNECE), etc.

1319 See UNESCO (ed.) (2005i) (cf. *footnote 216* op. cit.), p. 5.

1320 Cf. United Nations Economic Commission for Europe (UNECE); United Nations Economic and Social Council (ECOSOC) (eds.) (2004a) (cf. *footnote 746* op. cit.), p. 1.

1321 See UNESCO (ed.) (2005i) (cf. *footnote 216* op. cit.), p. 5.

1322 See UNESCO (ed.) (2005i) (cf. *footnote 216* op. cit.), p. 5.
Cf. *Figure 81* in chapter IX 4.3 *Characteristics* on page 345.

1323 Cf. UNESCO (ed.) (2005i) (cf. *footnote 216* op. cit.), p. 5.

1324 For example: *United Nations Decade on ESD (DESD)*; *Education for All* (EFA); *Millennium Development Goals* (MDG); *United Nations Literacy Decade* (UNLD), i.e. the *Literacy Initiative for Empowerment (LIFE)*, the *Teacher Training Initiative for sub-Saharan Africa* and the *Global Initiative on HIV / AIDS and Education* (EDUCAIDS).
Cf. UNESCO (ed.) (2005i) (cf. *footnote 216* op. cit.), p. 5.

The *Inter-sectoral Working Group* (IWG) therefore independently envisages its contribution through:[1325]

1. Developing a fully fledged in-house action plan;
2. Making recommendations to all UNESCO sectors, divisions and field offices to integrate the goals and objectives of *DESD* in their activities;
3. Approving a monitoring and assessment framework; and
4. Developing reporting mechanisms.

1.8 Evidence-based

Furthermore, UNESCO dedicates *DESD* implementation efforts towards evidence-based principles which involve *"the use of case studies of good practice"* as well as *"new approaches combining the results of research and field experiences"*.[1326] Displaying more immediate empirical evidence is considered essential to international support and consensus.[1327] Compliance and momentum can be achieved primarily through effectively communicating activities of good- or best practice.[1328] That is what sound practices of international *DESD* commitment clearly show.[1329]

1325 Cf. UNESCO (ed.) (2005i) (cf. *footnote 216* op. cit.), p. 5.
Cf. *Figure 81* in chapter IX 4.3 *Characteristics* on page 345.

1326 See UNESCO (ed.) (2003b) (cf. *footnote 109* op. cit.), p. 5.
Cf. chapter IV 4.1 *Qualitative approach* on page 88.

1327 Cf. Miles, Edward L. (ed.) (2002) (cf. *footnote 294* op. cit.); Boyle, Alan E. (2006) (cf. *footnote 932* op. cit.), p. 144.

1328 Cf. examples of evidence-based *ESD* communication and critical reflections of Germany: Deutsche UNESCO-Kommission e. V. (DUK) (ed.) (2002): forum der unesco-projekt-schulen. Nachhaltigkeit. In: Zeitschrift der UNESCO-Projektschulen, Volume 2002, Issue 1. Bonn; Federal Ministry of Education and Research (BMBF) (ed.) (2002): Report of the Federal Government on education for a sustainable development. Translation of Bundestag document No. 14/7971 from January 3, 2002. Bonn: BMBF Publik; Merkel, Christine; Gördel, Bettina (2002): Die vergessene Priorität von Rio. Bildung für nachhaltige Entwicklung. In: Deutsche UNESCO-Kommission e. V. (DUK) (ed.): forum der unesco-projekt-schulen. Nachhaltigkeit. Zeitschrift der UNESCO-Projektschulen, Sonderheft Nr. 1. Bonn, pp. 13–19; Pötter, Bernhard (2002): Was wurde aus der Agenda 21. Bilanz der Halbherzigkeiten. In: Deutsche UNESCO-Kommission e. V. (DUK) (ed.): forum der unesco-projekt-schulen. Nachhaltigkeit. Zeitschrift der UNESCO-Projektschulen, Sonderheft Nr. 1. Bonn, pp. 10–12; Deutsche UNESCO-Kommission e. V. (DUK) (ed.) (2005b): forum der unesco-projekt-schulen. Nachhaltigkeit. In: Zeitschrift der UNESCO-Projektschulen, Volume 2005, Issue 1. Bonn: Bonner Universitäts-Buchdruckerei; Deutsche UNESCO-Kommission e. V. (DUK) (ed.) (2005a): forum der unesco-projekt-schulen. Ziel: Zukunftsfähigkeit. Beiträge zur UN-Dekade "Bildung für nachhaltige Entwicklung". Ergebnisse der 40. Jahrestagung der UNESCO-Projektschulen. In: Zeitschrift der Deut-

1.9 Innovative

DESD stakeholders are expressly encouraged to find flexible and creative solutions[1330] that *"will (...) strengthen international cooperation towards the development and sharing of innovative education for sustainable development programmes, practices and policies"*.[1331] For example, innovative conceptions of education concern specific holistic approaches of *cross-border* and *multi-channel* learning.[1332] Another example involves interactive tool kits for implementing, facilitating and assessing *DESD*.[1333]

schen UNESCO-Kommission, Volume 2005, Issue 3. Bonn: Bonner Universitäts-Buchdruckerei; Köhler, Karl-Heinz (2005): Nachhaltigkeit lernen. Zur UN-Dekade und möglichen Beiträgen der unesco-projekt-schulen. In: Deutsche UNESCO-Kommission e. V. (DUK) (ed.): forum der unesco-projekt-schulen. Nachhaltigkeit. Zeitschrift der UNESCO-Projektschulen, Sonderheft Nr. 1. Bonn: Bonner Universitäts-Buchdruckerei, pp. 5–7; Minsch, Jürg (2005): Nachhaltigkeit: Aufforderung zur Weiterentwicklung der offenen Gesellschaft. Essay mit ökologisch-ökonomischem Repertoire. In: Deutsche UNESCO-Kommission e. V. (DUK) (ed.): forum der unesco-projekt-schulen. Ziel: Zukunftsfähigkeit. Beiträge zur UN-Dekade "Bildung für nachhaltige Entwicklung". Ergebnisse der 40. Jahrestagung der UNESCO-Projektschulen. Zeitschrift der Deutschen UNESCO-Kommission, Sonderheft Nr. 3. Bonn: Bonner Universitäts-Buchdruckerei, pp. 6–14; Federal Ministry of Education and Research (BMBF) (ed.) (2006) (cf. *footnote 1225* op. cit.).

1329 Cf. Sloan, Blaine (1987) (cf. *footnote 874* op. cit.), p. 68; UNESCO (ed.) (2003b) (cf. *footnote 109* op. cit.), p. 4; UNESCO (ed.) (2008h) (cf. *footnote 219* op. cit.), p. 7.

1330 See Leicht, Alexander; Plum, Jacqueline; Fuchs, Max (2007) (cf. *footnote 19* op. cit.), p. 8; Gallopin, Gilberto (ed.) (March 2003) (cf. *footnote 60* op. cit.), pp. 17–18.

1331 See UNESCO (ed.) (2003b) (cf. *footnote 109* op. cit.), p. 2.

1332 Cf. United Nations Economic Commission for Europe (UNECE); United Nations Economic and Social Council (ECOSOC) (eds.) (2005f) (cf. *footnote 391* op. cit.), p. 6; Hüfner, Klaus; Reuther, Wolfgang (eds.) (2005) (cf. *footnote 412* op. cit.), pp. 65–67; UNESCO (2009) (cf. *footnote 579* op. cit.).

1333 Cf. Forum for the Future; Higher Education Partnership for Sustainability (HEPS) (eds.) (2004) (cf. *footnote 652* op. cit.); UNESCO (ed.) (2006d): Education for Sustainable Development Toolkit. Education for Sustainable Development in Action. Learning & Training Tools N°1. Edited by Rosalyn McKeown; Charles Hopkins; Regina Rizzi; Marianne Chrystalbride. Paris: UNESCO workshops; UNESCO (2006): Teaching and Learning for a Sustainable Future. A multimedia teacher education programme. CD-ROM. Published by: UNESCO. (Educating for a Sustainable Future).

1.10 Summary

UNESCO's self-claimed principles for *DESD* implementation are related in two ways to general codes of good governance in international organisations and the organisation's self-image proper.[1334]

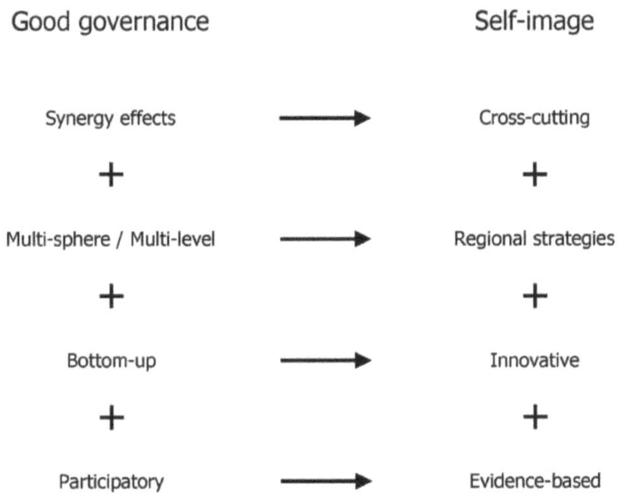

Figure 60: Principles of DESD implementation[1335]

2 UNESCO's contributions

As already noted, UNESCO follows an inter-sectoral or cross-cutting approach in order to define the specific aims of *DESD*. This suggests the integration of major issues and priorities of the organisation's educational work, and among those the realisation of the goals of the programme *Education for All* (EFA) and the *Millennium Development Goals* (MDG). UNESCO fosters the integration of those key elements into all education work, including *DESD*.[1336]

1334 Cf. chapter IX 1 *Principles of implementation* on page 256.
See *Figure 60* in chapter IX 1.10 *Summary* on page 276.

1335 This figure shows how principles of good governance can equally be correlated with those affiliated to UNESCO's approach towards *DESD*.

1336 Cf. UNESCO (ed.) (2005i) (cf. *footnote 216* op. cit.), p. 6; UNESCO (ed.) (2006a) (cf. *footnote 616* op. cit.), pp. 223, 228; UNESCO (ed.) (2008a) (cf. *footnote 83* op. cit.), pp. 190, 285; UNESCO (ed.) (2008f) (cf. *footnote 771* op. cit.).

UNESCO is *"not starting from scratch"*.[1337] The advantage for *DESD* is obvious and rational: UNESCO already relies on deep expertise and key competences relating to the management of knowledge, materials and, above all, broad programme infrastructure.[1338] There is actually no need to start from the very beginning, as *"all sectors are already working in support of ESD, as well as for sustainable development"*.[1339]

In light of this fact, UNESCO's education sector started to set up a proprietary *road map*[1340] both in accordance with and addition to an *International Implementation Scheme* (IIS), in order to define the organisation's contribution to *DESD* in terms of co-ordination and facilitation.

A key element of the *UNESCO action plan* is to provide a concise answer to the question of how UNESCO substantially contributes to implement *DESD* as proper stakeholder organisation, taking into account both the overall *DESD* goals and the diversity of audiences.

2.1 Functions

As part of its leadership mandate *"UNESCO has a dual role to play"*:[1341] One as *international co-ordinator and facilitator* of *DESD*; one as *substantive implementer*[1342] of *DESD*.[1343] There is no doubt that both roles deal with issues of implementation, but each role has a different focus.

The core element in the fulfilment of its first role, co-ordination and facilitation as *lead agency* for the decade,[1344] is the *International Implementation Scheme* (IIS) as the appropriate *tool* in order to:

- *"Lead the global process to re-orient education in support of sustainable development in national policies and education systems"*;[1345]
- Build awareness among various actors and potential *DESD* stakeholders;
- Facilitate consultation and participation processes; and

1337 See UNESCO (ed.) (2005i) (cf. *footnote 216* op. cit.), p. 6.
1338 Cf. chapter V 1.2 *Role* on page 100, and chapter VI 2.2 *Expertise* on pages 131 et seqq.
1339 See UNESCO (ed.) (2005i) (cf. *footnote 216* op. cit.), p. 6.
1340 See UNESCO (ed.) (2005i) (cf. *footnote 216* op. cit.), p. 6.
1341 See UNESCO (ed.) (2005i) (cf. *footnote 216* op. cit.), p. 2.
Cf. Matsuura, Koïchiro (01/03/2005) (cf. *footnote 28* op. cit.), p. 2.
1342 See UNESCO (ed.) (2005i) (cf. *footnote 216* op. cit.), p. 2.
1343 Cf. UNESCO (05/07/2003) (cf. *footnote 124* op. cit.), p. 4; UNESCO (ed.) (2007k) (cf. *footnote 4* op. cit.), p. 10.
Cf. *Figure 63* in chapter IX 2.3 *Summary* on page 289.
1344 Cf. UNESCO (ed.) (2003b) (cf. *footnote 109* op. cit.), p. 4; Bory-Adams, Aline (2010) (cf. *footnote 37* op. cit.), p. 178.
Cf. chapter VI 2.1 *Lead agency* on page 125.
1345 See UNESCO (ed.) (2005i) (cf. *footnote 216* op. cit.), p. 2.

- Play *"a catalytic role in dialogue and consensus-building to make recommendations on the draft implementation scheme and to facilitate the work […]"*.[1346]

The focal point is UNESCO's leadership role in relation to *"the myriad potential actors striving to implement its goals"*.[1347]

Living up to expectations of its second role as a substantive force of implementation of *DESD*, UNESCO pursues a *"broad-based inter-sectoral action plan"*[1348] in accordance with the *International Implementation Scheme* (IIS). Additionally, UNESCO has to determine *"how best to contribute to the fulfilment"*[1349] of those educational objectives for sustainable development that are already on track globally. Consequently, UNESCO must work throughout the process of implementation towards a *puzzle-like* harmonisation by *"selecting strategic projects, programmes, activities and efforts to maximise quality and impact with available human and financial resources"*.[1350]

As preliminary result, UNESCO is highly qualified both to promote its *genuine*, organisational focal issues based upon education and capacity-building in the context of sustainability; and to foster globally the integration of *"sustainable development issues and practices, including local knowledge and culture, into education systems"*.[1351]

2.2 Domains

The UNESCO priority plan is structured according to the four major domains of education for sustainable development. It provides a systematic solution by which activities and initiatives are co-ordinated and carried out at different levels, in different spheres and by the different UNESCO programme sectors, field offices and institutes.[1352]

Substantial contributions are considered to be made within the following four domains or *thrusts*[1353] of interest:[1354]

1346 See UNESCO (ed.) (2003b) (cf. *footnote 109* op. cit.), p. 4.
1347 See UNESCO (ed.) (2006e) (cf. *footnote 777* op. cit.), p. 3.
1348 See UNESCO (ed.) (2005i) (cf. *footnote 216* op. cit.), p. 2.
1349 See UNESCO (ed.) (2003b) (cf. *footnote 109* op. cit.), p. 4.
1350 See UNESCO (ed.) (2003b) (cf. *footnote 109* op. cit.), p. 4.
1351 See UNESCO (ed.) (2005i) (cf. *footnote 216* op. cit.), p. 2.
1352 Cf. chapter IX 2.2.3 *Developing public awareness of sustainability* on page 282.
1353 These domains are originally derived from chapter 36 of *Agenda 21* on education to support a sustainable future.
See UN Department of Economic and Social Affairs (ed.) (1992) (cf. *footnote 721* op. cit.), pp. 320–328; UNESCO (ed.) (2003b) (cf. *footnote 109* op. cit.); UNESCO (ed.) (2005j) (cf. *footnote 44* op. cit.), p. 28.

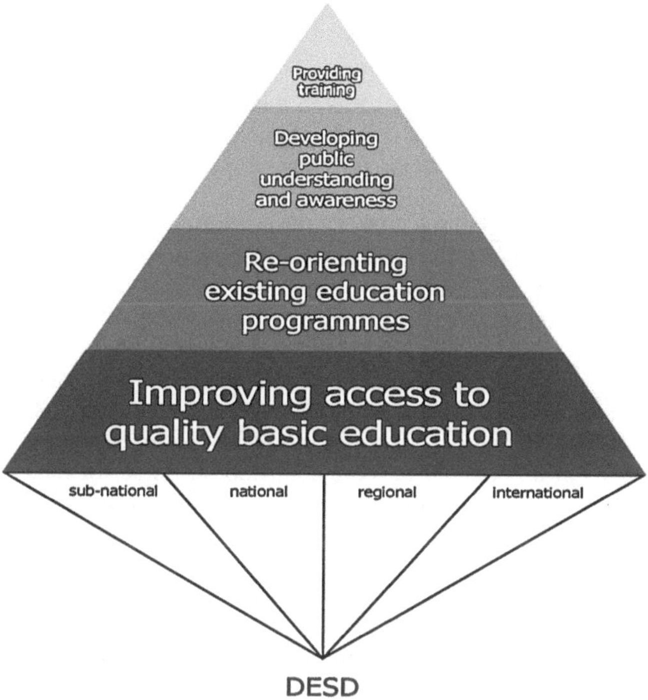

Figure 61: Domains or thrusts of DESD in multi-level perspective[1355]

2.2.1 Promoting and improving basic education

There are many people who participate neither in formal nor in non-formal education due to deficiencies in *access.*[1356] UNESCO aims to provide quality basic education, including literacy, as an initial part of a lifelong process of learning. The intention in terms of sustainability is to link basic education directly with

1354 See *Figure 61* in chapter IX 2.2 *Domains* on page 279.

1355 Built on multiple levels *DESD* is organised and implemented according to set priorities. The pyramid illustrates the four prioritised *thrusts* of *DESD* starting with promoting and improving basic education, followed by re-orienting existing education programmes, towards developing public awareness, and finally providing means of training.
Cf. UNESCO (05/07/2003) (cf. *footnote 124* op. cit.), p. 5; UNESCO (ed.) (2003b) (cf. *footnote 109* op. cit.); UNESCO (ed.) (2005i) (cf. *footnote 216* op. cit.), pp. 6 et seqq; UNESCO (ed.) (2005j) (cf. *footnote 44* op. cit.), pp. 28–30; UNESCO (ed.) (2007c) (cf. *footnote 120* op. cit.), p. 12; UNESCO (ed.) (2007k) (cf. *footnote 4* op. cit.), p. 6.

1356 Cf. UNESCO (ed.) (2003b) (cf. *footnote 109* op. cit.), p. 3.

the knowledge, skills, values and perspectives relevant to sustainable livelihoods.

Basic education is therefore the key to helping citizens to lead sustainable lives. A multi-method approach helps to meet the different needs people have. Moreover, this domain is most closely aligned with the programmes *Education for All* (EFA), the *United Nations Literacy Decade* (UNLD) and the *Millennium Development Goals*.

From the very beginning, UNESCO has issued educational materials and tool kits directed mainly towards environmental protection at primary-school level. At the secondary level, education modules have been introduced, aiming at a more comprehensive understanding and awareness of sustainable development.[1357]

Subsequently, in the field of formal education, it was necessary to institutionalise the topic of sustainable development at a national or state level. That is why UNESCO encouraged the adaptation of national education legislation to implant issues of sustainable development into curricula, to establish networks of information and think-tanks through educational institutions and to promote research programmes at medium term in higher education centres, such as universities or research institutions.

Promoting and improving basic education involves lifelong learning for sustainable livelihoods in formal, non-formal or informal settings. It is primarily based on access, literacy, opportunity and quality. This domain relates to children, youth and adults alike.[1358]

2.2.2 Re-orienting existing education programmes

UNESCO strongly favours the re-thinking and revision of existing education programmes and organisational structures according to the principle of *intergenerational equity*, so *"from nursery school through university"*.[1359] By using a holistic and interdisciplinary approach the idea is to develop a knowledge platform that includes aspects of sustainability from the very beginning and in all necessary dimensions – economic, social, environmental,[1360] and eventually cultural. Existing curricula therefore have to be reviewed and the compatibility of

1357 There are numerous examples for this type of *awareness building*, e.g., pedagogical science kits on dry lands, posters displaying issues of biodiversity, educational materials on combating desertification, the role of wetlands ecosystems, etc. Following the idea of catching and stimulating interest topics of sustainability, like earth's resources and outer space, are elaborated according to the age level and distributed as booklets. Cf. UNESCO (ed.) (2005i) (cf. *footnote 216* op. cit.), p. 7.

1358 Cf. UNESCO (ed.) (2007m) (cf. *footnote 216* op. cit.), pp. 7–8.

1359 See UNESCO (ed.) (2005i) (cf. *footnote 216* op. cit.), p. 7.

1360 Cf. UNESCO (ed.) (2003b) (cf. *footnote 109* op. cit.), p. 3.

their content examined in order to develop a trans-disciplinary understanding of sustainability. The skills of *lifelong learning* for sustainable development require new ways of thinking and distributing knowledge.[1361] For this reason a review and update of recommended and mandated teaching, learning and assessment must also be integrated into the re-orientation of education programmes.

The focal issues backed by UNESCO are education policies and strategies as well as processes of capacity-building. Globalisation demands new programmatic answers in the field of skills in order to meet demands appropriately which are, inter alia, needed in relation to *"expansion of technology, rapid social changes, increasing interdependence between countries, more international migration, and changes in consumption patterns and production processes"*.[1362]

Three issues are considered critical in terms of education policies and strategies:

- Re-examination of national policies from the perspective of sustainable development;
- Re-orientation of education systems and training process; and
- Integration of education and information within strategies and national plans of sustainable development.

Covering both conceptual elaboration on *ESD*-related topics in reality and its transfer into society, UNESCO proposes to provide *University Twinning and network scheme* (UNITWIN) and UNESCO Chairs as think tanks and networks as transfer agencies, especially dedicated to sustainability issues.[1363] Consultancy should be provided by those chairs in the medium or long term perspectives developing recommendations to policy-makers and other stakeholders. This involves comprehensive research plans on trends, feasibility and specific strategies both on teaching and learning *ESD*. For instance, there is a need to introduce new or at least adapted curricula on sustainable development in primary and secondary school education.[1364]

Short term activities consist of a variety of teaching modules in sustainable development at all levels of the education system, train-the-trainer programmes aiming to enhance teachers' skills as well as cross-sectional plans to connect

1361 For example: teacher education and professional formation.
Cf. UNESCO (ed.) (2005e): Guidelines and Recommendations for Reorienting Teacher Education to Address Sustainability. Education for Sustainable Development in Action. ED-2005/WS/66 Technical Paper N° 2 – 2005. Paris: UNESCO workshops.

1362 See UNESCO (ed.) (2005i) (cf. *footnote 216* op. cit.), p. 7.

1363 Cf. UNESCO (ed.) (1992) (cf. *footnote 793* op. cit.), pp. 20, 33; UNESCO (ed.) (2006c): Drivers and Barriers for Implementing Sustainable Development in Higher Education. Education for Sustainable Development in Action. Göteborg Workshop December 7–9, 2005. ED-2006/WS/63 Technical Paper N° 3. Edited by John Holmberg; Bo E. Samuelsson. Paris: UNESCO publishing, p. 7.

1364 Cf. UNESCO (ed.) (2007b) (cf. *footnote 46* op. cit.), pp. 16–17.

DESD with existing programmes and initiatives. The central task might be seen in a systematic dissemination of methodological information regarding *DESD* for teachers *and* students.

Issues in sustainable development will have to be further integrated into science education whilst also strengthening a cultural profile of *DESD*. Cases of best practice may serve in particular to strengthen criteria of cultural sustainability.[1365]

In summary, revisiting educational programmes at all levels serves the purpose of incorporating social, environmental, cultural and economic knowledge, skills, perspectives and values of sustainability into the processes of education.[1366]

2.2.3 Developing public awareness of sustainability

More sustainable societies require people to be well-informed and committed on different levels of action: local, national and global. Beside the important issues of high-quality information, the issue of communicating sustainable development must play a role in society.[1367] The media must therefore be involved as well as institutions which promote community education. Finally, effectively embedding issues of sustainability into societal discourse requires an informed, committed and active citizenry.[1368]

In support of public awareness-raising for *DESD*, all *four* UNESCO sectors (education, culture, science and communication) operate in close collaboration, from the very earliest conception onwards.[1369]

1365 Best-practice examples and intentions:
UNESCO Associated Schools Project Network (ASPnet): development of bilingual and intercultural methods profiling indigenous knowledge and practice in the classroom, launch of an environmental encyclopaedia in local schools to develop teacher manuals and methods, Youth Visioning Projects;
Local and Indigenous Knowledge Systems (LINKS): integrating knowledge of local knowledge-holders into pedagogical concepts, providing opportunities for learning outside of the classroom in meaningful natural settings, fostering an active role played by indigenous groups creating and participating in networks in order to share experiences and examples of best-practice.
Cf. UNESCO (ed.) (2005i) (cf. *footnote 216* op. cit.), p. 7; Schuchardt, Erika; Mbeki, Thabo (eds.) (2005) (cf. *footnote 37* op. cit.), pp. 18, 57 et seqq, 241 et seqq; UNESCO; UNESCO Associated Schools (eds.) (2008b) (cf. *footnote 480* op. cit.); UNESCO; UNESCO Associated Schools (eds.) (2009b) (cf. *footnote 585* op. cit.).
Cf. chapter II 2.4 *Cultural sustainability* on page 24.

1366 Cf. UNESCO (ed.) (2007m) (cf. *footnote 216* op. cit.), p. 8.

1367 Cf. UNESCO (ed.) (2003b) (cf. *footnote 109* op. cit.), p. 3.

1368 Cf. UNESCO (ed.) (2007m) (cf. *footnote 216* op. cit.), p. 8.

1369 Cf. UNESCO (05/07/2003) (cf. *footnote 124* op. cit.), pp. 4, 16.

UNESCO's education sector, in co-operation with other programme sectors, takes the role as *major facilitator*[1370] of consolidation in order to disseminate the concept of sustainable development across different levels of communication:

- Fostering dialogue between educational stakeholders for the exchange of experience and information on education and sustainable development;
- Establishing closer links between educational institutions and local communities in order to benefit from the use of knowledge by communities and to generate knowledge for sustainable development;
- Organising contests and awards within and among schools on *ESD*-related projects;[1371]
- Supporting joint school and community initiatives;[1372] and
- Providing regular reports and updates on the work accomplished by UNESCO as *lead agency*[1373] in the implementation of *DESD*.[1374]

UNESCO's culture sector contributes to *DESD* implementation in a more indirect way which is fully in line with the idea and interpretation of *culture* as an *underlying dimension*. Consequently, the organisational assignment is less mandatory and concise when compared to other UNESCO sectors:[1375]

- Fostering values and attitudes of respect for cultural diversity and pluralism in education;[1376]

Cf. *Figure 25* in chapter VI 2.3.2 *Financing* on page 139, and *Figure 82* in chapter IX 4.3 *Characteristics* on page 348.

1370 Cf. UNESCO (ed.) (2002f) (cf. *footnote 312* op. cit.), pp. 20–23; UNESCO (ed.) (2002a) (cf. *footnote 614* op. cit.), p. 281; UNESCO (ed.) (2004a) (cf. *footnote 615* op. cit.), pp. 359–379; UNESCO (ed.) (2005i) (cf. *footnote 216* op. cit.), p. 8; UNESCO (ed.) (2006a) (cf. *footnote 616* op. cit.), pp. 36–54; UNESCO (ed.) (2008a) (cf. *footnote 83* op. cit.), pp. 30–36; UNESCO (ed.) (2009a) (cf. *footnote 618* op. cit.), pp. 10–11, 24–53.

1371 For example: essays, debates, working group sessions, small-income-generating projects.
Cf. UNESCO (ed.) (2005i) (cf. *footnote 216* op. cit.), p. 8.

1372 For example: reforestation, recycling, conferences and debates, internships at local businesses, input from local actors for introduction of local contents.
Cf. UNESCO (ed.) (2005i) (cf. *footnote 216* op. cit.), p. 8.

1373 See UNESCO (ed.) (2005i) (cf. *footnote 216* op. cit.), p. 1; Bory-Adams, Aline (2010) (cf. *footnote 37* op. cit.), p. 178.

1374 For example: *Connect*: UNESCO's International Newsletter for Science, Technology and Environmental Education; UNESCO internet portal on *DESD*.
Cf. UNESCO (ed.) (2005i) (cf. *footnote 216* op. cit.), p. 8.

1375 Cf. UNESCO (ed.) (2002f) (cf. *footnote 312* op. cit.), pp. 38–43; UNESCO (ed.) (2004a) (cf. *footnote 615* op. cit.), pp. 430–444; UNESCO (ed.) (2006a) (cf. *footnote 616* op. cit.), p. 156.

1376 Cf. UNESCO (ed.) (2007j) (cf. *footnote 39* op. cit.), p. 27.

- Recognising cultural diversity and the variety of socio-cultural contexts in the world;
- Promoting dialogue and social interaction;
- Acknowledging local indigenous knowledge and sustainable traditional practices;
- Fostering support of practices and traditions which build sustainability;
- Recognising and working with culturally-specific views of nature, society and the world; and
- Employing local patterns of development, including the use of local languages as reference points of interaction and cultural identity.

Aspects of cultural development entered into debate mainly through the *Declaration on the Right to Development*.[1377] Shortly afterward, the *World Decade for Cultural Development* (1988–1997) emphasised *culture* as a critical parameter of sustainable development. This is due to the fact that endogenous development in relation to sustainability requires the cultural basis of consciousness and awareness.[1378] What is more, *culture* is considered an essential resource for any kind of successful movement.

Taking into account the importance of UNESCO's cultural sector in terms of heritage and responsibility,[1379] sustainable development can be strengthened through capacity-building and training activities in relation to the conservation and promotion of cultural diversity. This increase in awareness-raising is also reflected in UNESCO's standard-setting activities, notably through the 2005 *Convention on the Protection and Promotion of the Diversity of Cultural Expressions*.[1380]

UNESCO's science sector[1381] continues to work closely with UNESCO's education sector on numerous programmes,[1382] such as:

- Promoting approaches of linking ecosystem management and local community needs;[1383]

1377 Cf. United Nations (ed.) (1987a) (cf. *footnote 90* op. cit.), pp. 164 et seqq.

1378 Cf. Goncalves G., María Paola (ed.) (1998) (cf. *footnote 566* op. cit.), pp. 6, 7, 16, 17, 18.

1379 Cf. UNESCO Culture Sector (ed.) (1997) (cf. *footnote 88* op. cit.), pp. 3–4.

1380 For example: Article 2 paragraph 6 – *Principle of Sustainable Development*, Article 13 – *Integration of culture in sustainable development*, and Article 14 – *Cooperation for development*.
Cf. UNESCO (ed.) (2005a) (cf. *footnote 42* op. cit.), pp. 4, 8.

1381 Including natural, social and human sciences.

1382 Cf. UNESCO (ed.) (2002f) (cf. *footnote 312* op. cit.), pp. 27–34; UNESCO (ed.) (2004a) (cf. *footnote 615* op. cit.), pp. 381–418; UNESCO (ed.) (2006a) (cf. *footnote 616* op. cit.), pp. 82–107; UNESCO (ed.) (2008a) (cf. *footnote 83* op. cit.), pp. 82–84; UNESCO (ed.) (2009a) (cf. *footnote 618* op. cit.), p. 27; UNESCO (ed.) (2009a) (cf. *footnote 618* op. cit.), pp. 81–82.

- Encouraging partnership between all sectors of society through awareness and training actions;
- Appreciating traditional and indigenous values in managing cultural and biological diversity;
- Reinforcing concepts of *learning by doing*;[1384]
- Publishing training and awareness-raising materials;[1385]
- Focusing on education, research, capacity-building and policy advice;[1386]
- Contributing to the enhancement of knowledge and awareness of earth sciences and the management of natural resources;[1387]
- Promoting forms of *creative space* as an educational and research tool in science and technology to achieve sustainable development and meet the *Millennium Development Goals* (MDG);[1388]
- Establishing partnerships with science museums and, more generally, mobilising science networking in relation to *ESD* concepts, mainly in Latin America; and
- Proposing awareness programmes at various hierarchical levels in developing countries.[1389]

UNESCO's communication sector[1390] regards sustainable development as the core of an overall strategy in knowledge societies. Linked through new patterns of growth and wealth creation determined by knowledge and information, new possibilities are being generated for more effective poverty reduction and sustainable development.[1391]

1383 For example: *Man and the Biosphere Programme* (MAB).
Cf. UNESCO (ed.) (2005i) (cf. *footnote 216* op. cit.), p. 8.

1384 For example: further contribution to the sustainable development of small islands: *Coastal Regions and Small Islands* (CSI).
Cf. UNESCO (ed.) (2005i) (cf. *footnote 216* op. cit.), p. 8; UNESCO (ed.) (2007c) (cf. *footnote 120* op. cit.), p. 12.

1385 For example: for urban planners and managers, water managers and the public in Iran.
Cf. UNESCO (ed.) (2005i) (cf. *footnote 216* op. cit.), p. 8.

1386 For example: UNESCO-IHE Institute for Water Education (Delft).
Cf. UNESCO (ed.) (2005i) (cf. *footnote 216* op. cit.), p. 8.

1387 For example: *International Geoscience Programme* (IGCP).
Cf. UNESCO (ed.) (2005i) (cf. *footnote 216* op. cit.), p. 8.

1388 For example: *Space Education Programme* (SEP).
Cf. UNESCO (ed.) (2005i) (cf. *footnote 216* op. cit.), p. 8.

1389 For example: *Inter-parliamentary Conference* (IOC) on sustainable development issues in the Mediterranean region.
Cf. UNESCO (ed.) (2005i) (cf. *footnote 216* op. cit.), p. 8.

1390 Including communication and information.

1391 Cf. UNESCO (ed.) (2002f) (cf. *footnote 312* op. cit.), p. 45; UNESCO (ed.) (2004a) (cf. *footnote 615* op. cit.), p. 460; UNESCO (ed.) (2009a) (cf. *footnote 618* op. cit.), pp. 161–167.

Communication plays an important role in raising awareness amongst media professionals of the various dimensions of sustainable development.[1392] Promoting broad knowledge of sustainable development and relevant practices is the fundamental basis, after all, of public attention, visibility and awareness. As a consequence, there has to be appropriate training for media professionals as well as networking opportunities in the field of sustainable development topics, including knowledge exchanges designed for different target groups.[1393]

Communication is structured in a *dual* mode, including both traditional and new communication means. The strategy presented in 2007 is to change communication behaviour from a traditional approach, usually based on a vertical perception of communication with limited resources and unilateral direction, to a *new communication framework.*[1394] This enables people to adopt and apply their tools of communication in order to develop horizontal networks with an infinite range of information sources, through awareness-raising, capacity-building and partnership with the private sector.[1395]

UNESCO regards private sector commitment in the field of raising awareness and producing consciousness to be at least as important as public sector initiatives, declaring that *"the private sector can be real players for sustainable development, in accordance with the ethical principles expressed through their corporate social responsibility programmes, is another vital sphere of activity"*.[1396]

Remarkably, UNESCO sets its *DESD* communication strategy in a far broader context, using various linkages with different programmes and techniques to create a certain *culture of prevention.*[1397]

1392 Cf. UNESCO (ed.) (July 2003) (cf. *footnote 37* op. cit.), p. 14; UNESCO (ed.) (2005j) (cf. *footnote 44* op. cit.), p. 15; UNESCO (ed.) (2008h) (cf. *footnote 219* op. cit.), pp. 8 et seqq; Gerner, Martin (10/08/2009) (cf. *footnote 407* op. cit.).

1393 For example: policy-makers, practitioners and advocacy groups.
Cf. UNESCO (ed.) (2005i) (cf. *footnote 216* op. cit.), p. 9.
See *Figure 62* in chapter IX 2.2.3 *Developing public awareness of sustainability* on page 287.

1394 Cf. UNESCO (ed.) (2005i) (cf. *footnote 216* op. cit.), p. 8; UNESCO (ed.) (2007d) (cf. *footnote 585* op. cit.), pp. 5, 14.

1395 I.e. *Public-Private-Partnerships* (PPP).

1396 See UNESCO (ed.) (2005i) (cf. *footnote 216* op. cit.), p. 9.

1397 This fact can be stressed and exemplified in regard to UNESCO efforts to incorporate the issue of disaster risk reduction into educational programmes, for instance. This is certainly an important issue in the matter of *DESD*, taking into consideration the fact that it might serve well in the context of *"wider public understanding of the risks and vulnerabilities"*. Ultimately, the question of *"how human action may increase or reduce them"* addresses the whole *DESD* debate.
One example of how this communication strategy may be related to a suitable topic is the use of renewable energy. Through awareness-raising campaigns, educational and training initiatives, UNESCO is able both to advocate and promote topics.

2006	2007	2008	2009	2010
Consensus	building			
		Lobbying	Mobilizing	
				Visibility of the mid-term review

2006	2007	2008	2009	2010
Visibility of the Decade				
		Strengthening capabilities		
		Visibility of UNESCO		

Figure 62: DESD topicality and visibility – trade-off relations?[1398]

2.2.4 Training

Specialised and vocational training programmes, skills labs and tool kits are designed for professionals working with *DESD*. UNESCO points out that knowledge and skills are essential for all sectors to perform their work properly.[1399] This applies not only to UNESCO staff working in programme sectors but also to regional bureaux, field offices, institutes and networks.

All UNESCO-related actors are involved in assisting with capacity-building in *ESD* at national levels in policy formulation and decision making[1400] and to *"advocate for the recognition of the value and impact of non-formal and informal learning and continuing education for sustainable development"*.[1401] Capacity-development is primarily based on an approach of *learning by doing*.[1402]

At the level of higher education UNESCO aims to promote *ESD* globally through building inclusive and sustainable systems and institutions of education. Two objectives must be met in this field of action:

Cf. UNESCO (ed.) (2005i) (cf. *footnote 216* op. cit.), p. 9; UNESCO (ed.) (2007d) (cf. *footnote 585* op. cit.), pp. 5, 14; UNESCO (ed.) (2007i) (cf. *footnote 1261* op. cit.), pp. 24, 59.

1398 Advocating *DESD* involves consciousness and broad support in public. This implies that *DESD* is generally appreciated. On the one hand there will be any public interest without any visibility of *DESD*. On the other hand, visible results can hardly be accomplished if *DESD* lacks topical impetus or momentum.
See UNESCO (ed.) (2007d) (cf. *footnote 585* op. cit.), p. 6.

1399 Cf. UNESCO (ed.) (2005i) (cf. *footnote 216* op. cit.), p. 9.

1400 Cf. UNESCO (ed.) (2003b) (cf. *footnote 109* op. cit.), p. 3.

1401 Cf. UNESCO (ed.) (2005i) (cf. *footnote 216* op. cit.), p. 9.

1402 Examples of de-centralised *ESD* initiatives following the concept of *learning by doing*: communities planning their own future development; groups sharing eco-friendly practices; youth promoting local languages; school children adopting a hands-on approach to addressing environmental issues.
Cf. UNESCO (ed.) (2005i) (cf. *footnote 216* op. cit.), p. 9; UNESCO (ed.) (2007c) (cf. *footnote 120* op. cit.), p. 12.

1. That of enhancing the central role of education and training in the common pursuit of sustainable development; and
2. That of facilitating collaboration and networking, exchange and interaction in *ESD* in a *multi-stakeholder approach.*[1403]

Above all, UNESCO considers itself to be a facilitator for training activities in science education, both in the area of specific ecosystem-related activities[1404] as well as in that of conflict prevention and management.

2.3 Summary

In summary, UNESCO's contribution to the implementation of *DESD* has two important and distinct aspects. Designated the *lead agency* for *DESD*, UNESCO aims to fulfil a *dual function.* The mandate is twofold and comprises of interrelated roles both as:[1405]

1. The leading organisation for *DESD* as a global process; and
2. The implementing organisation for *DESD* at the agency level (amongst other *DESD* stakeholders).

Each function is affiliated with specific assignments. These are dealt with in detail by specific programmes and strategic documents.

1403 Examples for comprehensive networking and multi-party co-operation through support of: inter-university co-operation, e.g.; *UNITWIN*; networking to facilitate experience-sharing; development of interdisciplinary and trans-disciplinary innovative approaches to sustainability in educational institutions; and North-South and South-South co-operation in the areas of training and research.
Cf. UNESCO (ed.) (2005i) (cf. *footnote 216* op. cit.), p. 9; Altner, Günter; Michelsen, Gerd (eds.) (2005) (cf. *footnote 851* op. cit.).

1404 For example: aspects of marine, mountain or desert biodiversity as well as approaches in the field of sustainable water resource management: reinforcing capacity-building and water education and training within the framework of action of the *International Hydrological Programme* (IHP); carrying out training and technology transfer in the area of urban water to improve integrated planning and development; strengthening support through training and capacity-building networks related to integrated water resource management, for example: through the *Framework Programme for Research Education and Training in Water* (FETWater) in South Africa.

1405 Cf. UNESCO (ed.) (August 2007) (cf. *footnote 693* op. cit.), p. 2.
See *Figure 63* in chapter IX 2.3 *Summary* on page 289.

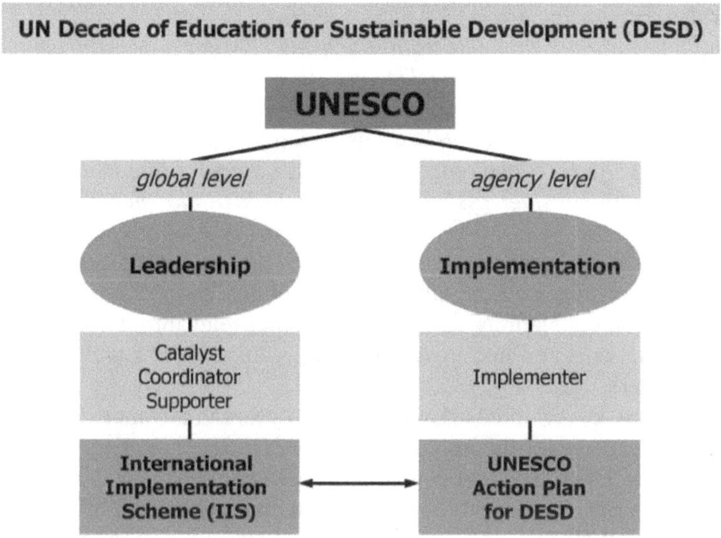

Figure 63: UNESCO's dual contribution to the implementation of DESD[1406]

3 International Implementation Scheme

The initial point of implementation of *DESD* is marked by the United Nations General Assembly resolution of 2003 which announces the *United Nations Educational, Scientific and Cultural Organization* (UNESCO) as the *lead agency*[1407] for the promotion of *DESD. "The (UN-Resolution 57/254) itself is the culmination of a long and winding journey through high level international commissions that can ultimately be traced back more than a quarter of a century (...).*"[1408]

At the same time the organisation is explicitly requested *"to develop a draft international implementation scheme"* in order *"to provid(e) recommendations for Governments on how to promote and improve the integration of education*

1406 UNESCO's role in the course of *DESD* is divided into two separate but linked aspects. First, globally leading *DESD* as catalyst, co-ordinator and supporter driven by an international agenda of implementation. Second, institutionally contributing to *DESD* as substantive implementer guided through an international action plan.
Cf. UNESCO (ed.) (2007k) (cf. *footnote 4* op. cit.), p. 10.

1407 See UNESCO (ed.) (2005i) (cf. *footnote 216* op. cit.), p. 1; UNESCO (ed.) (2003b) (cf. *footnote 109* op. cit.), p. 1.

1408 See Higgitt, David (2009a) (cf. *footnote 103* op. cit.), p. 1.

for sustainable development in their respective educational strategies and action plans at the appropriate level".[1409]

"The International Implementation Scheme sets out a broad framework for all partners to contribute to the Decade. It is not prescriptive, but provides overall guidance and shows why, how, when and where the enormous range of partners can develop their contributions based on their particular contexts. It briefly presents the ESD challenge and outlines the kind of education that, collectively, partners consider essential in order to facilitate sustainable development."[1410]

The *International Implementation Scheme* (IIS) must be drafted both in accordance with existing and ongoing educational processes[1411] and in close consultation with United Nations' organisations, other relevant international organisations, governments and non-governmental organisations as well as other relevant stakeholders.[1412]

Furthermore, governments are invited, two years in advance, to consider the inclusion of measures for the implementation of *DESD* in their respective education systems by 2005. Signatories explicitly take into account the *International Implementation Scheme* (IIS) to be created and institutionalised by UNESCO.

UNESCO initially favoured an open-access approach sharing expertise and experience to clarify key elements of a universal implementation scheme which ultimately serves as a worldwide framework on *DESD* implementation.[1413] Thus, consultation among United Nations partners started in 2003, shortly after the approval of *DESD* by United Nations General Assembly in February 2003. More than two thousand contributions had to be integrated into the crafting process, and, presumably, *"many of these represent (...) the consolidation of opinions of hundreds".*[1414] The organisation's mandate can be described as a relatively binding, highly participatory, cross-sectional, multi-party and multi-level approach.

1409 See UNESCO (ed.) (2003b) (cf. *footnote 109* op. cit.), p. 1.

1410 See UNESCO (2005): International Implementation Scheme for the UN Decade of Education for Sustainable Development (2005–2014). In: Connect, Volume 30, Issue 1, pp. 1–28, p. 1.

1411 I.e. Dakar Framework for Action (*Education for All* / EFA) (1990 / 2000), *United Nations Literacy Decade* (UNLD) (2003–2012).

1412 For example: civil society, companies, media, etc.
Cf. chapter VII 11 *Stakeholders* on pages 167 et seqq.

1413 Cf. *Figure 63* in chapter IX 2.3 *Summary* on page 289.

1414 See UNESCO (2005) (cf. *footnote 1410* op. cit.), p. 1.
Cf. UNESCO (ed.) (2005j) (cf. *footnote 44* op. cit.), p. 5.

3.1 Objectives

In the course of implementation UNESCO aims to address a *"wide range of stakeholders"* outlining *five objectives* for implementation:[1415]

1. Giving an enhanced profile to the central role of education and learning in the common pursuit of sustainable development;
2. Facilitating links, networking, exchange and interaction among stakeholders in *ESD*;
3. Providing a space and an opportunity for refining and promoting the vision of, and transition to, sustainable development – through all forms of learning and public awareness;
4. Fostering increased quality of teaching and learning in *ESD*; and
5. Developing strategies at every level to strengthen capacity in *ESD*.

3.2 Drafting history

Before dealing with *DESD* implementation in any depth, attention must be paid to its genesis. This timeline is not intended to cover every detail nor does it represent the evolution of *DESD* itself. What is instead sketched is a reflection of only one aspect of *DESD*.

DESD originated in the adoption of resolution *A/RES/57/254*[1416] on 20 December 2002, published 21 February 2003, by the United Nations General Assembly. What primarily served as the *DESD* founding document also paved the way for its simultaneous implementation. It *"requests (UNESCO) to develop a draft international implementation scheme, clarifying its relationship with the existing educational processes"*.[1417] The UNESCO implementation mandate was expressed more explicitly by requesting governments to integrate *DESD* into their educational strategies and plans, *"taking into account the international implementation scheme to be prepared by the United Nations Educational, Scientific and Cultural Organization"*.[1418] Interestingly, UNESCO's mandate to coordinate implementation is timed from the very beginning of *DESD*, namely by 2005.[1419]

Starting from scratch with multiple versions of position papers,[1420] by July 2003 the first guidelines on *DESD* implementation were expressed through a draft version of a *Framework for a Draft International Implementation*

1415 Cf. No. 8 UNESCO (ed.) (2005c) (cf. *footnote 23* op. cit.), p. 2.
1416 Cf. United Nations (ed.) (2002 / 2003) (cf. *footnote 117* op. cit.).
1417 See No. 2 United Nations (ed.) (2002 / 2003) (cf. *footnote 117* op. cit.), p. 1.
1418 See No. 3 United Nations (ed.) (2002 / 2003) (cf. *footnote 117* op. cit.), p. 1.
1419 Cf. No. 3 United Nations (ed.) (2002 / 2003) (cf. *footnote 117* op. cit.), p. 1.
1420 Cf. UNESCO (05/07/2003) (cf. *footnote 124* op. cit.).

Scheme.[1421] This *double-draft* fixed both conceptual ideas of *DESD* and the *partnership approach* to its implementation.

Shortly after, on 26 August 2003, UNESCO presented the *framework* document *32 C/INF.9*[1422] containing *"elements for developing a draft international implementation scheme with a timetable for activities up to December 2005"*.[1423]

By September 2003, as requested, and based on the *framework* timeline, (informal) consultations *"with the United Nations and other relevant international organisations, Governments, non-governmental organisations and other stakeholders"* were started.[1424]

Throughout the course of the 2nd plenary meeting of United Nations General Assembly 58th session on 19 and 23 September 2003, all *DESD*-related items – including implementation – were re-allocated in the adoption of *A/58/PV.2*[1425] and *A/C.2/58/1*[1426] by the General Committee of United Nations General Assembly and were transferred to its Second Committee. Ever since, the decade has been officially entitled *DESD*.

Document *A/C.2/58/SR.15*[1427] contains official records of the 15th meeting of United Nations Second Committee on 20 October 2003, published 27 May 2004. Agenda item 96 paved the ground for *DESD* itself, recognising preceding or parallel processes, such as the implementation of *Agenda 21*, the *Programme for the Further Implementation of Agenda 21* and the outcomes of the *World Summit on Sustainable Development* (WSSD) in 2002[1428] and stating *"a consensus regarding the key role of education in sustainable development"*.[1429] Simultaneously, it serves as preparation for its (draft) implementation by mentioning the main objective of an implementation scheme to be pursued *"to mobilise governments and help them promote education for sustainable development by*

1421 Cf. UNESCO (ed.) (July 2003) (cf. *footnote 37* op. cit.).

1422 Cf. UNESCO (ed.) (2003b) (cf. *footnote 109* op. cit.).
This shorter version of the draft framework has been especially designed to serve at the 32nd session of the General Conference.
Cf. UNESCO (ed.) (2005b): Decisions adopted by the Executive Board at its 171st session. Draft international implementation scheme for the United Nations Decade of Education for Sustainable Development. 171 EX/Decisions. Paris: UNESCO publishing, p. 7.

1423 See document outline UNESCO (ed.) (2003b) (cf. *footnote 109* op. cit.), p. 1.

1424 See No. 2 United Nations (ed.) (2002 / 2003) (cf. *footnote 117* op. cit.), p. 1.

1425 Cf. United Nations (19/09/2003): 2nd plenary meeting. Official Records. A/58/PV.2. Published by: United Nations. General Assembly. New York.

1426 Cf. No. 6 United Nations (2003): Fifty-eighth session Second Committee. Allocation of agenda items to the Second Committee. A/C.2/58/1. General Assembly. New York.

1427 Cf. United Nations (20/10/2003): Second Committee Summary record of the 15th meeting. Official Records. A/C.2/58/SR.15. General Assembly. New York.

1428 Cf. United Nations (20/10/2003) (cf. *footnote 1427* op. cit.), p. 1.

1429 See United Nations (20/10/2003) (cf. *footnote 1427* op. cit.), p. 3.

integrating it, at the appropriate level, into their educational strategies and plans of action".[1430] In addition, interdisciplinary consultation *"with the United Nations and other relevant international organisations, governments, non-governmental organisations and other stakeholders"*[1431] in the developed and developing countries receives particular emphasis.

On 15 December 2003 the Second Committee of United Nations General Assembly adopted resolution proposal *A/58/486*[1432] entitled *"United Nations Decade of Education for Sustainable Development"*[1433] repeatedly stressing UNESCO's role as *DESD* implementer. Furthermore, *DESD* was included *"in the provisional agenda of (United Nation's) fifty-ninth (General Assembly) session".*[1434]

The Second Committee of the United Nations General Assembly subsequently recommended the adoption of *A/58/486*[1435] to the General Assembly in report *A/58/PV.78.*[1436]

The United Nations General Assembly actively followed the Second Committee's recommendation by approving resolution proposal *A/RES/58/219*[1437] on 23 December 2003, published 9 February 2004. Its formal adoption designated UNESCO as the *DESD* implementation agency acknowledging all efforts made so far, namely by recognising *"the Framework for a Draft International Implementation Scheme prepared"*[1438] by UNESCO, and UNESCO's role as agenda setter for *DESD*-related issues.[1439] In addition this resolution *"further requests (UNESCO) to finalise the international implementation scheme".*[1440]

By May 2004 the first draft *International Implementation Scheme* (IIS) had already been developed, taking into account the *"the comments received from the different stakeholders and partners into the Framework"* and *"the outcomes of conferences and workshops on ESD worldwide as well as regional and national strategies".*[1441] Over the course of this time the draft is being discussed

1430 See United Nations (20/10/2003) (cf. *footnote 1427* op. cit.), p. 3.

1431 See United Nations (20/10/2003) (cf. *footnote 1427* op. cit.), p. 4.
For example: consultations with nine United Nations agencies, World Bank, governments, the academic community, associations, non-governmental organisations and civil society groups.

1432 Cf. United Nations (ed.) (2003b) (cf. *footnote 728* op. cit.).

1433 See II No. 5 United Nations (ed.) (2003b) (cf. *footnote 728* op. cit.), p. 2.

1434 See III No. 4 United Nations (ed.) (2003b) (cf. *footnote 728* op. cit.), p. 2.

1435 Cf. United Nations (ed.) (2003b) (cf. *footnote 728* op. cit.).

1436 Cf. United Nations (23/12/2003): 78th plenary meeting. Official Records. A/58/PV.78. General Assembly. New York.

1437 Cf. United Nations (ed.) (2004b) (cf. *footnote 727* op. cit.).

1438 See No. 1 United Nations (ed.) (2004b) (cf. *footnote 727* op. cit.), p. 2.

1439 Cf. No. 1 United Nations (ed.) (2004b) (cf. *footnote 727* op. cit.), p. 4.

1440 See No. 1 United Nations (ed.) (2004b) (cf. *footnote 727* op. cit.), p. 2.

1441 See UNESCO (ed.) (2005c) (cf. *footnote 23* op. cit.), p. 2.

and reviewed by all UNESCO sectors on various regional levels as well as leading experts in field and academics, before eventually being submitted to the High-Level Panel on *DESD*.

On 20 July 2004 the High-Level Panel on *DESD*[1442] met, composed of leading experts in the field and convened by UNESCO's Director-General Koïchiro Matsuura with the objective of giving professional guidance to UNESCO on *DESD*, its draft implementation scheme and the launch of activities of the decade. The panel regarded UNESCO as *"uniquely positioned to play the leadership and co-ordination role for the Decade"* and *DESD* itself as *"a golden opportunity for everyone involved in education"*.[1443]

UNESCO stressed the links between *DESD* and other international UNESCO-driven frameworks which pay particular attention to quality education. Key issues and technical questions raised in *"a frank, wide-ranging and constructive exchange of views"*[1444] were:

1. Transferring the concept of *in-situ* or *ex-situ* environmental education[1445] to the notion of education for sustainable development *ESD*;
2. Generating a concept of sustainable development based upon the *Johannesburg Summit* definition of sustainability in 2002;
3. Learning and benefiting from experiences of other decades through transfer of know-how;
4. Building on proven strengths and anticipating the necessary follow-up mechanisms;
5. Linking *DESD* to other frameworks of international action, notably *Education for All* (EFA), the *Millennium Development Goals* (MDG) and the *United Nations Literacy Decade* (UNLD);
6. Transmitting key values, particularly through faith communities, pertaining to *ESD*;
7. Stressing the importance of culture;
8. Drawing attention towards quality education, the need for sound indicators, effective monitoring and reporting; and
9. Launching *DESD* on international, regional and national levels.

1442 Cf. UNESCO (20/07/2004): High-Level Panel on the United Nations Decade of Education for Sustainable Development. Paris.

1443 See UNESCO (20/07/2004) (cf. *footnote 1442* op. cit.).

1444 See UNESCO (20/07/2004) (cf. *footnote 1442* op. cit.).

1445 I.e. establishing field study centres and learning stations, or launching official outreach programmes for schools, universities, etc.
Cf. Lim, Gary; Zach Abdullah, Khaeril (2009): Sustainable Development by Instinct, Challenges, and Opportunities in the Decade. In: Chalkley, Brian; Haigh, Martin J.; Higgitt, David (eds.): Education for sustainable development. Papers in honour of the United Nations Decade of Education for Sustainable Development (2005–2014). London / New York: Routledge, pp. 269–272, p. 270.

The panel members expressly committed themselves to *DESD* in declaring their continuing participation in the High-Level Panel and recommending the extension of its membership in the case of gender and a more pronounced representation of society.

Sharing experiences and advice with the High-Level Panel on strategy and substance regarding *DESD*, UNESCO presented the final draft of an *International Implementation Scheme*[1446] in October 2004. This draft was to be considered compliant with the requirements of resolution *A/RES/57/254*.[1447] It was presented at the 59th session of the United Nations General Assembly in New York on 18 and 19 October 2004.

In order to formally embed rights and obligations of UNESCO in the matter of *DESD* implementation, Japan proposed draft resolution *A/C.2/59/L.9*[1448] on 21 October 2004 to the Second Committee of the United Nations General Assembly. A few weeks later, on 5 November 2004, this version was finally withdrawn by Japan and its sponsors by the adoption of draft resolution *A/C.2/59/L.24*[1449] orally corrected in the course of informal consultations. Substantial changes are made particularly with respect to abstaining from a fixed timeline for implementation into national education plans and programmes, to the incorporation of aspects of equal access to all levels education and risk management into the *DESD* priority list, to the issue of explicit reference to the needs of developing countries and to the clarification of relationships with existing educational processes. *A/C.2/59/L.24*[1450] appears to be more demanding, explicit[1451] and UNESCO-centred in terms of member state contribution and participation.[1452]

1446 Cf. UNESCO (ed.) (2004c) (cf. *footnote 34* op. cit.).

1447 Cf. United Nations (ed.) (2002 / 2003) (cf. *footnote 117* op. cit.).

1448 Cf. United Nations (ed.) (2004c): United Nations Decade of Education for Sustainable Development. Fifty-ninth session Second Committee. Japan: draft resolution. A/C.2/59/L.9. Paris: United Nations.

1449 Cf. United Nations (ed.) (2004d): United Nations Decade of Education for Sustainable Development. Fifty-ninth session Second Committee. Draft resolution on the basis of informal consultations held on draft resolution A/C.2/59/L.9. A/C.2/59/L.24. Paris: United Nations.

1450 Cf. United Nations (ed.) (2004d) (cf. *footnote 1449* op. cit.).

1451 In, for example, directly addressing persons and functions, such as United Nations Secretary-General or UNESCO's Director-General.

1452 For instance, *A/C.2/59/L.24* requests UNESCO's Director-General *"to submit the draft International Implementation Scheme to the governing bodies of the United Nations Educational, Scientific and Cultural Organisation for their final consideration and adoption"*.
See No. 4 United Nations (ed.) (2004d) (cf. *footnote 1449* op. cit.), p. 2.
By contrast, the original draft version *A/C.2/59/L.9* intends the distribution of the *International Implementation Scheme* (IIS) to *all* member states for commenting.
Cf. No. 3 United Nations (ed.) (2004c) (cf. *footnote 1448* op. cit.), p. 2.

Based upon the draft resolution introduced by Japan, the Second Committee of the United Nations General Assembly considered the same draft resolution to be recommended for adoption to United Nations General Assembly by *A/59/483/Add.7*[1453] on 15 December 2004. UNESCO was mentioned as a critical promoter of *DESD* making mention of its responsibility for co-ordination, implementation, monitoring and evaluation.[1454]

During its 75th plenary meeting on 22 December 2004 the United Nations General Assembly adopted the decisive resolution *A/RES/59/237*,[1455] published 24 February 2005, formulating the foundational requirements and requests regarding UNESCO's role in *DESD* implementation. The United Nations General Assembly requested its Secretary-General to call on UNESCO to:

- Finalise the draft *International Implementation Scheme* (IIS) for *DESD* in stakeholder consultation before its launch;
- Submit the draft *International Implementation Scheme* (IIS) to the governing bodies of UNESCO for final edition and adoption; and
- Prepare a mid-term report of the implementation of *DESD* to be submitted to United Nations General Assembly[1456] by 2010.[1457]

The final draft version of the *International Implementation Scheme* (IIS) was presented as an appended document for approval in the run-up to the 171st UNESCO Executive Board's session in January 2005.[1458] *"While this document reflects the agreement of many partners and stakeholders, it is awaiting formal recognition by the Executive Board of UNESCO in April 2005."*[1459]

In accordance with *171 EX/Decisions*[1460] and *A/RES/59/237*[1461], UNESCO's Director-General in *171 EX/7*[1462] officially *"submit(ted) the draft International Implementation Scheme for the United Nations Decade of Education for Sustainable Development (DESD) to the Executive Board for its final consideration and adoption"*[1463] on 31 March 2005.

1453 Cf. United Nations (ed.) (2004a): Sustainable development: United Nations Decade of Education for Sustainable Development. Report of the Second Committee. A/59/483/Add.7. New York: United Nations.

1454 Cf. Nos. 1–7 United Nations (ed.) (2004a) (cf. *footnote 1453* op. cit.), p. 5.

1455 Cf. United Nations (ed.) (2005b) (cf. *footnote 729* op. cit.).

1456 I.e. *"at its sixty-fifth session under the sub-item entitled 'United Nations Decade of Education for Sustainable Development'".*
See No. 7 United Nations (ed.) (2005b) (cf. *footnote 729* op. cit.), p. 3.

1457 Cf. Nos. 3, 4, 7 United Nations (ed.) (2005b) (cf. *footnote 729* op. cit.), pp. 2–3.

1458 Cf. UNESCO (ed.) (2005c) (cf. *footnote 23* op. cit.), pp. 4 et seqq.

1459 See UNESCO (ed.) (2005c) (cf. *footnote 23* op. cit.), p. 5.

1460 Cf. UNESCO (ed.) (2005b) (cf. *footnote 1422* op. cit.), pp. 7–8.

1461 Cf. United Nations (ed.) (2005b) (cf. *footnote 729* op. cit.).

1462 Cf. UNESCO (ed.) (2005c) (cf. *footnote 23* op. cit.).

1463 See UNESCO (ed.) (2005c) (cf. *footnote 23* op. cit.), p. 1.

Finally, the text of the *International Implementation Scheme* (IIS) was given formal recognition by the Executive Board of UNESCO in March and April 2005 adopting *171 EX/7.*[1464]

On 25 May 2005 UNESCO's Executive Board took note of the organisations' efforts towards *DESD* implementation by *171 EX/Decisions,*[1465] showing appreciation of, in particular, the text of the draft *International Implementation Scheme* (IIS). The Board further requested UNESCO's Director-General to:

1. *"(T)ake all necessary measures to ensure UNESCO's (appropriate) response to United Nations General Assembly resolutions";*[1466]
2. *"(P)ursue (...) consultations with other United Nations agencies, with Member States and with civil society";*[1467]
3. Consider how best to *"(enable) UNESCO to play a major and visible role in the effective implementation (...)";*[1468]
4. Foster *"a more strategically focused, consolidated version"*[1469] of the *International Implementation Scheme* (IIS);
5. *"(E)nsure wide dissemination of the consolidated international implementation scheme to Member States, to United Nations Member States, other United Nations agencies, civil society organisations and (non-governmental organisations)";*[1470]
6. *"(E)stablish a clear and focused plan based on a holistic and interdisciplinary approach to UNESCO's involvement in the Decade";*[1471] and
7. *"(S)pecify the precise contributions of UNESCO to the implementation of the Decade".*[1472]

Report *172 EX/11*[1473] aims to meet the request made by the UNESCO Executive Board's *171 EX/Decisions*[1474] asking for *"a more strategically focused, consolidated version"*[1475] of the *International Implementation Scheme* (IIS). On 11 August 2005 the Executive Board *"consider(ed) and adopt(ed) the consolidated text"* and simultaneously introduced the former draft version as *Draft Consolidated International Implementation Scheme* (IIS).[1476]

1464 See UNESCO (ed.) (2005c) (cf. *footnote 23* op. cit.), pp. 1, 5.
1465 Cf. UNESCO (ed.) (2005b) (cf. *footnote 1422* op. cit.), pp. 7–8.
1466 See No. 5 UNESCO (ed.) (2005b) (cf. *footnote 1422* op. cit.), p. 8.
1467 See No. 6 UNESCO (ed.) (2005b) (cf. *footnote 1422* op. cit.), p. 8.
1468 See No. 6 UNESCO (ed.) (2005b) (cf. *footnote 1422* op. cit.), p. 8.
1469 See No. 7 UNESCO (ed.) (2005b) (cf. *footnote 1422* op. cit.), p. 8.
1470 See No. 8 UNESCO (ed.) (2005b) (cf. *footnote 1422* op. cit.), p. 8.
1471 See No. 9 UNESCO (ed.) (2005b) (cf. *footnote 1422* op. cit.), p. 8.
1472 See No. 9 UNESCO (ed.) (2005b) (cf. *footnote 1422* op. cit.), p. 8.
1473 Cf. UNESCO (ed.) (2005f) (cf. *footnote 37* op. cit.).
1474 Cf. UNESCO (ed.) (2005b) (cf. *footnote 1422* op. cit.), pp. 7–8.
1475 See No. 7 UNESCO (ed.) (2005b) (cf. *footnote 1422* op. cit.), p. 8.
1476 See No. 4 UNESCO (ed.) (2005f) (cf. *footnote 37* op. cit.), p. 3.

UNESCO Executive Board's report *172 EX/INF.4*,[1477] published 19 August 2005, both clarifies UNESCO's role as *lead agency* for *DESD* and, in parallel, outlines its coming into effect in preparatory work for the development of the *"fully fledged UNESCO Action Plan for the Decade"*.[1478]

On 14 October 2005, resulting from an intense and comprehensive consultation process, the *International Implementation Scheme* (IIS)[1479] took effect, after almost two years of intense discussion and ten months after launching *DESD*.

Document *174 EX/INF.13*[1480] refers to the proposal of a *UNESCO Action Plan for the DESD*,[1481] published 5 April 2006, as UNESCO's own and original contribution to *DESD* implementation. Considering the drafting process, different key elements are singled out for essential consideration in order to *"to develop its own programme of implementation for the DESD"*.[1482]

Interestingly, one year after passing the *International Implementation Scheme* (IIS)[1483], on 10 December 2006 the UNESCO Education Sector published an additional document, confusingly called *Framework for the UN DESD International Implementation Scheme.*[1484] It is more far-reaching in terms of defining key concepts and approaches. Besides, all other relevant aspects of the 2005 *International Implementation Scheme* (IIS) are also carefully covered.[1485]

As a comprehensive and far-reaching *road map* the final draft and summary of the *UNESCO Action Plan for DESD*[1486] was introduced in January 2007.[1487] It represents a *"broad-based inter-sectoral action plan in line with the IIS"*[1488] and aims primarily to clarify the strategic focus of UNESCO's own initiatives and activities.[1489] The action plan responds in particular to the UNESCO cross-

1477 Cf. UNESCO (ed.) (2005i) (cf. *footnote 216* op. cit.).
1478 See UNESCO (ed.) (2005i) (cf. *footnote 216* op. cit.), p. 1.
1479 Cf. UNESCO (ed.) (2005j) (cf. *footnote 44* op. cit.).
1480 Cf. UNESCO (ed.) (2006e) (cf. *footnote 777* op. cit.), pp. 3–4.
1481 Cf. UNESCO (ed.) (2006e) (cf. *footnote 777* op. cit.).
1482 See UNESCO (ed.) (2006e) (cf. *footnote 777* op. cit.), p. 3.
1483 Cf. UNESCO (ed.) (2005j) (cf. *footnote 44* op. cit.).
1484 Cf. UNESCO (ed.) (2006f) (cf. *footnote 25* op. cit.).
1485 It may be considered wholly legitimate to raise the question of this additional *International Implementation Scheme* (IIS) publication by UNESCO's education sector. One assumption made is that it is a revised, updated or consolidated edition based upon more detailed background information referring to the 2004 *Draft International Implementation Scheme*. Both documents are astonishingly similar with regard to content and structure. Another reason probably can be seen in a more reader- and publisher-friendly version.
Cf. UNESCO (ed.) (2004c) (cf. *footnote 34* op. cit.).
1486 Cf. UNESCO (ed.) (2007f) (cf. *footnote 427* op. cit.), p. 2; UNESCO (ed.) (2007k) (cf. *footnote 4* op. cit.), pp. 14 et seqq.
1487 Cf. UNESCO (ed.) (2007m) (cf. *footnote 216* op. cit.).
1488 See UNESCO (ed.) (2005i) (cf. *footnote 216* op. cit.), p. 2.
1489 Cf. UNESCO (ed.) (2007m) (cf. *footnote 216* op. cit.), p. 2.

cutting request *176 EX/5* and fulfils the *key function* of providing cross- or inter-sectoral capacity-building programmes.[1490]

The UNESCO *DESD* High-Level Panel met on 8 February 2007 to debate the UNESCO implementation of *DESD*, providing strategic advice on how to intensify support to *DESD* at the highest level and how to assist partners in mobilising resources for *ESD*.[1491]

In his report *177 EX/9 Annex III*[1492] on 3 August 2007 the UNESCO Director-General outlined the progress made with regard to the implementation of *DESD* both internationally and within UNESCO. Annex III provides an overview of thematic programmes of the *UNESCO Action Plan for the DESD* that altogether serve as the organisation's own programme of implementation for *DESD*.

Mayor achievements, milestones and steps of *DESD* implementation are visualised systematically in the following chart.[1493]

Table 29: Timeline of DESD implementation[1494]

Date	*Document*	*Comment and catch word*
20 December 2002	A/RES/57/254	UNESCO *DESD* implementation mandate
5 July 2003	Position paper	UNESCO strategies as *lead agency*
July 2003	Framework for a Draft International Implementation Scheme	Guidelines on *DESD* implementation
26 August 2003	32 C/INF.9	Activities timetable
September 2003		Informal consultations
19 / 23 September 2003	A/58/PV.2; A/C.2/58/1	*DESD* entitlement; Responsibility of Second Committee of United Nations General Assembly

1490 Cf. UNESCO (ed.) (2007j) (cf. *footnote 39* op. cit.), pp. 17 et seqq.

1491 Cf. UNESCO (ed.) (2007f) (cf. *footnote 427* op. cit.), p. 3.

1492 Cf. UNESCO (ed.) (August 2007) (cf. *footnote 693* op. cit.), pp. 12 et seqq.

1493 See *Table 29* in chapter IX 3.2 *Drafting history* on page 299.

1494 Note: What eventually pretends to reflect a linear development, in reality shows the result of several parallel multi-level processes. This can be best explained by taking the example of the dual character of UNESCO, representing both a substantial *DESD* implementer – as requested by United Nations General Assembly – and a *genuine* implementation agency at the same time. Efforts made upon the *International Implementation Scheme* (IIS) and the *UNESCO Action Plan for DESD* are directed towards different ends: facilitating *DESD* versus actively contributing to *DESD* by coming up with genuine initiatives. Both conceptual designs are on the one hand separate but on the other hand inextricably intertwined.

Date	*Document*	*Comment and catch word*
20 October 2003	A/C.2/58/SR.15	*DESD* networking; Implementation objectives; Interdisciplinary consultation
15 December 2003	Second Committee Proposal A/58/486	*DESD* agenda-setting; UNESCO as *DESD* implementer
	A/58/PV.78	Recommendation for the adoption of A/58/486
23 December 2003	A/Res/58/219	Approval of UNESCO as *DESD* implementation agency; UNESCO as agenda setter for *DESD*
May 2004	1st Draft International Implementation Scheme	Inter-sectoral discussion; Submission to UNESCO High-Level Panel on *DESD*
20 July 2004		UNESCO High-Level Panel on *DESD*; Professional guidance; Linking UNESCO frameworks; Formulating key issues
October 2004	Final Draft International Implementation Scheme	Introduction
18 / 19 October	Final Draft International Implementation Scheme	Presentation to United Nations General Assembly by UNESCO High-Level Panel
21 October 2004	A/C.2/59/L.9	Guideline on rights and obligations on *DESD* implementation
5 November 2004	A/C.2/59/L.24	Clarifying UNESCO member state contribution and participation on *DESD*
15 December 2004	Draft resolution A/59/237	United Nations General Assembly requests UNESCO's role in *DESD* implementation
January 2005	Final draft version of International Implementation Scheme	Presentation for approval by UNESCO Executive Board
31 March 2005	171 EX/7	Submission of draft International Implementation Scheme to UNESCO Executive Board; Final considerations
March / April 2005	171 EX/7	Adoption of International Implementation Scheme by UNESCO Executive Board

Date	*Document*	*Comment and catch word*
25 May 2005	171 EX/Decisions	Assessing progress on *DESD* implementation; Specifying requests
11 August 2005	172 EX/11; Draft Consolidated International Implementations Scheme	Presentation
19 August 2005	172 EX/INF.4	Clarifying UNESCO's role as the *lead agency* for *DESD*; Development of UNESCO Action Plan for *DESD*
14 October 2005	International Implementation Scheme	Launch
5 April 2006	174 EX/INF.13; Draft UNESCO Action Plan	Key elements
10 December 2006	Framework of the United Nations *DESD* International Implementation Scheme	In-depth-definition of key concepts and approaches
January 2007	UNESCO Action Plan for *DESD*	Strategic focus on UNESCO's genuine initiatives and activities
8 February 2007		UNESCO High-Level Panel on *DESD*; Strategic advice on *DESD* implementation
3 August 2007	177 EX/9 Annex III	Progress on *DESD*; UNESCO's own implementation programme

3.3 Framework

Almost two years in advance, dating back to July and August 2003, UNESCO had started its ambitious programme of preparation for *DESD*. Long before the official launch of the decade in 2005 the UNESCO General Conference had adopted detailed proposals on how to implement *DESD* effectively and efficiently.[1495] It therefore set up a framework intended to serve as a structural and topical background leading up to what is later officially recognised as *International Implementation Scheme* (IIS).

A framework generally serves as a structure providing shape and support through a set of principles. In particular the *"Framework for the International*

1495 Cf. UNESCO (ed.) (2003b) (cf. *footnote 109* op. cit.).

Implementation Scheme" provides introduction and guidance both in terms of content and time.

First of all, the *framework* serves to develop a draft implementation scheme for *DESD*. It demands close consultations, starting in September 2003, with relevant partners – potential stakeholders – at local, national, regional and international levels.[1496] All of them are invited to actively contribute to the contextualisation of *sustainable development* as prescribed and approved at the *World Summit on Sustainable Development* (WSSD) in Johannesburg in 2002.[1497] *"More than 2,000 contributions, many of these representing the consolidation of opinions of hundreds, were received."*[1498] Furthermore, the *framework* aims at clarifying interrelationships between existing education-related UNESCO initiatives, namely *DESD*, *Education for All* (EFA), the *United Nations Literacy Decade* (UNLD) and the *Millennium Development Goals* (MDG).

The draft *Framework for a Draft International Implementation Scheme*, published in July 2003, briefly points out the main guidelines necessary to fulfil a prospective implementation scheme. Section I serves as analysis to highlight the background and synergistic embeddings of *DESD "with other major international educational processes and priorities"*.[1499] The role of education is emphasised primarily by mentioning a *new vision*[1500] of education towards sustainability through:

- Providing scientific and technical skills;
- Fostering values, behaviour and lifestyles through awareness and capacity-building;[1501]

1496 Cf. UNESCO (ed.) (2005c) (cf. *footnote 23* op. cit.), p. 2.

1497 Cf. United Nations (ed.) (2002a) (cf. *footnote 853* op. cit.).

1498 See UNESCO (ed.) (2005c) (cf. *footnote 23* op. cit.), p. 2.

1499 See UNESCO (ed.) (July 2003) (cf. *footnote 37* op. cit.), p. 3.

1500 See UNESCO (ed.) (July 2003) (cf. *footnote 37* op. cit.), p. 5.

1501 The 2002 *World Summit for Sustainable Development* in Johannesburg links four principles for achieving sustainable human development with the four UNESCO pillars of education:

Achieving sustainable development requires:	*Education provides the skills for:*
Recognition of the challenge	Learning to know
Collective responsibility and constructive partnership	Learning to live together
Acting with determination	Learning to do
The indivisibility of human dignity	Learning to be

See UNESCO (ed.) (1996) (cf. *footnote 29* op. cit.), pp. 9, 22 et seqq, 57.

Cf. UNESCO (ed.) (July 2003) (cf. *footnote 37* op. cit.), p. 5.

These directly translate into the respective four *domains* of *ESD*: Providing basic education; re-orienting existing education programmes; developing public awareness and understanding of sustainability; and training.

Cf. UNESCO (ed.) (July 2003) (cf. *footnote 37* op. cit.), pp. 5–6; Maclean, Rupert; Fien, John; Park, Man-Gon (eds.) (2009) (cf. *footnote 42* op. cit.), p. xxii.

- Integrating long-term factors and dimensions; and
- Introducing a *futures-oriented*[1502] inter-generational perspective.

Section II expressly refers to the wide-ranging and all-level partnership approach intended to ensure that all *DESD* implementation activities *"have maximum impact upon education policy, programmes and practice around the world".*[1503] *"With such an enormous and diverse group of potential partners"*[1504] UNESCO suggests a guided process for developing partnerships. These guiding principles are:[1505]

1. *Vision*: Developing an overall and a particular partner-shaped vision for *ESD*;
2. *Demonstration activities*: Adapting to different learning situations to be locally relevant and culturally appropriate; and
3. *Networking*: Addressing all kinds of educational structures and learning situations.

Section III indicates a timeline proposing activities *"aimed at catalysing world society in preparation for the DESD"*[1506] before its final launch in 2005. These activities are divided into two strategies directed towards a) communication and advocacy and b) building momentum, partnerships and *DESD* support. Accordingly a number of technical questions are raised referring to text production, publishing, distribution and vocational training.

After recalling the genesis of *DESD* dating back to the *Johannesburg Summit* in 2002 the framework document *32 C/INF.9*[1507] points out UNESCO's leadership role requesting the organisation to develop a draft international implementation scheme, specifying above all domains, objects and targets.

Highly relevant for *DESD* implementation is the foundational concept of education: UNESCO regards education as dynamic, particularly in the context of sustainable development, because *"(t)here is no universal model of education for sustainable development. While there will be overall agreement on the concept, there will be nuanced differences according to local contexts, priorities and approaches. Each country has to define its own priorities and actions. The goals, emphases and processes must, therefore, be locally defined to meet the local environmental, social and economic conditions in culturally appropriate ways. Education for sustainable development is equally relevant and critical for both developed and developing countries."*[1508]

1502 See UNESCO (ed.) (July 2003) (cf. *footnote 37* op. cit.), p. 5.
1503 See UNESCO (ed.) (July 2003) (cf. *footnote 37* op. cit.), p. 3.
1504 See UNESCO (ed.) (July 2003) (cf. *footnote 37* op. cit.), p. 11.
1505 Cf. UNESCO (ed.) (July 2003) (cf. *footnote 37* op. cit.), p. 10.
1506 See UNESCO (ed.) (July 2003) (cf. *footnote 37* op. cit.), p. 3.
1507 Cf. UNESCO (ed.) (2003b) (cf. *footnote 109* op. cit.).
1508 See UNESCO (ed.) (2003b) (cf. *footnote 109* op. cit.), p. 3.

The implications for implementing *DESD* are evident: regional plans are the only viable way to address *DESD* according to specific contexts. In this respect, UNESCO clearly works as a standard-setter institution using its key role as *DESD lead agency*. *"UNESCO must play a key role in setting quality standards in education for sustainable development."*[1509]

As regards working towards professional *DESD* preparation and implementation, UNESCO has a double role to fulfil, implementing and leading the decade simultaneously. The list of tasks and strategies assigned to those engaged in drafting a *DESD* implementation scheme appears vast, diverse and challenging:[1510]

- Showing ways of integrating the education for sustainable development perspective into national education;
- Providing guidance to member states;
- Developing and integrating quantitative and qualitative indicators for measuring progress on education for sustainable development;
- Addressing new partners;
- Involving information, communication technologies and the media for implementation; and
- Generating national capacities for education in sustainable development.

Special attention must be paid to the ambitious framework timeline proposed by UNESCO, with *DESD* implementation taking effect at the very launch of *DESD* by 2005. Two facts are remarkable: in the long run, *DESD* is structured in two-year periods, or *biennium*.[1511] In the short or mid-term period, timings and durations are divided in detail into three-month segments.[1512]

1509 See UNESCO (ed.) (2003b) (cf. *footnote 109* op. cit.), p. 3.
1510 Cf. UNESCO (ed.) (2003b) (cf. *footnote 109* op. cit.), pp. 5–6.
1511 This structure becomes especially evident with the launch of *DESD* beginning in 2005. Still, already two years in advance this pattern has been approved viable during preparation and implementation.
1512 Cf. UNESCO (ed.) (2003b) (cf. *footnote 109* op. cit.), p. 10.
See *Figure 64* in chapter IX 3.3 *Framework* on page 305, and *Figure 65* in chapter IX 3.3 *Framework* on page 305.

	2003 July – Sept.	2003 Oct. – Dec.	2004 Jan. – March	2004 April – June	2004 July – Sept.	2004 Oct. – Dec.	2005 Jan. – March	2005 April – June	2005 July – Sept.	2005 Oct.– Dec.
Communication and advocacy	Promotion and capacity-building for ESD and the Decade within and across all UNESCO sectors, field offices and centres, including:· • internal capacity-building within UNESCO so that the organization as a whole is mobilized to fulfil its role as lead agency; • dissemination of information on the Decade to all UNESCO staff so that they can include appropriate reference to and discussion of it in papers and presentations that they make in international forums.									
	Extensive consultation on framework of implementation scheme	Formation of international ad hoc working group	Meeting of international ad hoc working group	Develop and distribute the vision statement	Develop and distribute guidelines and multi-media package to support national planning and launches		International and national launches	Sustainable development theme in Global EFA Week	International Experts' Consultation Meeting on education for sustainable development (30 years after Belgrade, to prepare for Intergovernmental Conference in 2007 (30 years after Tbilisi)	
	Design Communication and advocacy strategy	Presentation of the Framework to the General Conference	Decade website launch	Acceptance of International Implementation Scheme by international partners						
	Design UNESCO's Decade website	Presentation of report to United Nations General Assembly		Develop, maintain and disseminate a calendar of international, regional, subregional and national activities						
				Develop and maintain website as major international vehicle for news and networking on activities and discussion						

Figure 64: Proposed framework timeline I[1513]

	2003 July – Sept.	2003 Oct. – Dec.	2004 Jan. – March	2004 April – June	2004 July – Sept.	2004 Oct. – Dec.	2005 Jan. – March	2005 April – June	2005 July – Sept.	2005 Oct. – Dec.
Building momentum and participation	Consultation on and development of the framework of the draft implementation scheme with: • EFA Working Group • Meeting of the Heads of United Nations Agencies • Member States • International NGOs and specialist ESD community	Presentation of a proposal for a framework of a draft International Implementation Scheme to: • UNESCO General Conference • EFA High-Level Group (Nov.)		CSD 12	EFA Working Group inter-agency ESD Task Force	EFA High-Level Group	•	CSD 13	EFA Working Group	EFA High-Level Group
			UNESCO leads regional/subregional workshops to build awareness and regional and country-level commitment to planning of activities for the Decade				Governments host subnational/local stakeholder consultations Meetings of national Decade working groups			
			UNESCO facilitates consultations with regional/subregional organizations, and national governments, where appropriate, to build awareness and regional and country-level commitment to planning of activities for the Decade							
			UNESCO develops and disseminates guidelines and multi-media package to support national planning and launch of programmes and activities							
			Planning of support structures and strategies for managing the Decade by: governments, international agencies, regional organizations, civil society organizations and professional bodies							

Figure 65: Proposed framework timeline II[1514]

The United Nations General Assembly has appreciatively taken note of UNESCO's framework initiative and positively requested the organisation to

1513 Detailed schedule of pre-planning communication and advocacy prior to launching *DESD*.
See UNESCO (ed.) (2003b) (cf. *footnote 109* op. cit.), p. 11.

1514 Detailed schedule of pre-planning momentum-building and participation prior to launching *DESD*.
See UNESCO (ed.) (2003b) (cf. *footnote 109* op. cit.), p. 12.

continue finalising the *International Implementation Scheme* (IIS), focusing in particular on its relationship with ongoing educational processes.[1515] Simultaneously, resolution *A/RES/58/219* calls for active governmental support in favour of UNESCO's efforts on *DESD*.[1516]

By 2005 the framework had dealt with the most critical questions relating to *DESD* and had in fact moved far beyond implementation. It must be regarded as a comprehensive attempt to embed *DESD* into its appropriate context: Literally speaking, the framework concept encloses or *frames* the current *status quo* situation –established networks, decisions, institutions and societal, economic, environmental, political and cultural background – with prospection towards desired outcomes in the field of sustainable development and *DESD*. As requested, the published framework tackles all the relevant topics necessary for the production of a dynamic picture of *DESD*:[1517]

- Starting with the nature of *Education for Sustainable Development per se*, elaborating on links between education and sustainable development, the different perspectives and its objectives;
- Referring to *Stakeholders and Strategies* for the attainment of objectives;
- Mentioning *Implementation and Evaluation* processes from local to international levels, explaining modes of stakeholder participation, possible outcomes as well as ways of monitoring and finally evaluating *DESD*; and
- Focusing on *Programming the Decade* with respect to necessary resources and timings.

The framework may be regarded as a continuous process directed towards a draft and final version of an *International Implementation Scheme* (IIS). It is consistently characterised by the same patterns requested for implementing *DESD*: participatory, bottom-up, dynamic and goal-oriented. The framework ultimately directly paves the way to the *International Implementation Scheme* (IIS). Boundaries between framework and implementation scheme are free-floating. In other words, the framework forms an integral part of the implementation[1518] – an eminent example of how UNESCO aims to efficiently use synergy effects.

1515 Cf. No. 1 United Nations (ed.) (2004b) (cf. *footnote 727* op. cit.), p. 2.

1516 E.g., implementing *DESD* into respective educational strategies and national development plans by 2005, promoting public awareness on *DESD*, strengthening participation through co-operation and initiatives, etc.
Cf. Nos. 2 and 3 United Nations (ed.) (2004b) (cf. *footnote 727* op. cit.), p. 2.

1517 Cf. Table of Contents UNESCO (ed.) (2005c) (cf. *footnote 23* op. cit.), p. 6; UNESCO (ed.) (2006f) (cf. *footnote 25* op. cit.), p. 8.

1518 The relevant documents prove this fact: Expressions like *framework* and *draft* used synonymously for almost the same document clearly show topical proximity.
Cf. UNESCO (ed.) (2005c) (cf. *footnote 23* op. cit.); UNESCO (ed.) (2006f) (cf. *footnote 25* op. cit.).

3.4 International Implementation Scheme

"The International Implementation Scheme sets out a broad framework for all partners to contribute to the Decade."[1519]

As mentioned previously, the *framework* and draft versions are closely linked: they go hand in hand. Outcomes of the framework consultation process amongst prospective stakeholders are directly integrated into implementation. In contrast to the *UNESCO Action plan*, the *International Implementation Scheme* (IIS) constitutes an integrated approach of implementation involving multiple external stakeholders besides UNESCO.

It is impossible to distinguish clearly between the components of the framework and the draft implementation scheme. Both are developed in sequence: the framework started up in August 2003[1520] because the first approved draft version dealing with implementation was to be presented only one year later, in October 2004.[1521]

Benefiting from the multi-party, -level and -stakeholder framework approach, the first (informal) draft version for an *International Implementation Scheme* (IIS) on *DESD* was developed by May 2004. There was in advance of publication a broad consensus base shared among different stakeholders and partners thanks to active incorporation of comments, conference and workshop outcomes on a global, regional and national level.

Participation is not a dispensable fad, but rather a guiding principle in commenting and reviewing at all levels: stakeholders, prospective partners, academics, experts and, of course, UNESCO staff. The best evidence for the advantages of such an approach to consultation is the fact of the submission of the first draft version to the UNESCO High-Level Panel on *DESD* in July 2004, followed directly by its presentation at the 59th United Nations General Assembly in October the same year.[1522]

The draft *International Implementation Scheme* (IIS) relates mainly to the same document structure as applied with the related framework documents.[1523] It consists of five chapters intended to provide not prescription but *overall guidance.*[1524] The purpose is to *"show why, how, when and where the enormous range of partners can develop their contributions based on their particular contexts."*[1525] In a systematic way, the challenge of *ESD* is addressed, followed by

1519 See UNESCO (ed.) (2005c) (cf. *footnote 23* op. cit.), p. 2.
1520 Cf. UNESCO (ed.) (2003b) (cf. *footnote 109* op. cit.).
1521 Cf. UNESCO (ed.) (2004c) (cf. *footnote 34* op. cit.).
1522 Cf. UNESCO (ed.) (2005c) (cf. *footnote 23* op. cit.), p. 2.
1523 Cf. Table of Contents UNESCO (ed.) (July 2003) (cf. *footnote 37* op. cit.), p. 2; UNESCO (ed.) (2005c) (cf. *footnote 23* op. cit.), p. 6; UNESCO (ed.) (2006f) (cf. *footnote 25* op. cit.), p. 8.
1524 See UNESCO (ed.) (2005c) (cf. *footnote 23* op. cit.), p. 11.
1525 See UNESCO (ed.) (2005c) (cf. *footnote 23* op. cit.), p. 11.

an *ESD* specific educational proposal of how collectively to facilitate sustainable development among partners. Thus, the emphasis expressly lies on implementation as an activating approach.[1526]

3.4.1 Introduction

Making *DESD* interesting, accessible and imaginable for everyone from the very beginning must be the core concern of an implementation document like the *International Implementation Scheme* (IIS). Three main items are covered in the introductory chapter.

First of all, an executive summary provides basic orientation on *DESD* implementation 'at a glance', referring to fundamental concepts such as vision, objectives, dimensions, characteristics, applied strategies, expected outcomes and estimated timetable.

Secondly, the nature and context of this draft *International Implementation Scheme* (IIS) are clarified and updated by briefly summarising its legislative and institutional provisions (namely United Nations 2002 General Assembly Resolution 57/254 appointing UNESCO as *DESD lead agency*), the process of partner participation, and the formal adoption by the UNESCO High-Level Panel on *DESD*.

Thirdly, the issues of *ESD* and *DESD* themselves are dealt with in an attempt to build personal momentum by emblematically linking the question of sustainable development to everybody's spheres of existence. Aiming at a topical acquaintance, the whole process of the genesis of *DESD* is briefly sketched according to important milestones. In addition, a major paragraph is dedicated to explaining the relevance and necessity of coping with issues of sustainability. Sustainable development denotes a topic of *growing concern*[1527] which is intertwined with multiple aspects of economic growth. These are related to production and consumption alike. The fact of interrelating problems and causal structures demands an appropriate approach in response. As a consequence, cross-sectional perspectives are favoured, based on a fairly broad definition concept of sustainability. In order to avoid *empty shells* of catch-all statements on sustainability, areas of priority have to be identified. Education is considered a key element of *DESD* as a fruitful means of raising awareness on sustainable issues. Being in charge of *DESD* implementation, UNESCO fosters a programme-

1526 Cf. UNESCO (ed.) (2005c) (cf. *footnote 23* op. cit.), pp. 8 et seqq.
Given the fact that the UNESCO *International Implementation Scheme* (IIS) on *DESD* represents a holistic rather than a specific concept, i.e. not particularly dedicated to implementation issues exclusively, it is necessary to explain that matters of implementation constitute the main focal point in the following sections. General *DESD* issues are discussed in-depth within the respective chapters.

1527 See UNESCO (ed.) (2005c) (cf. *footnote 23* op. cit.), p. 12.

integrated approach benefiting from synergy effects related to international initiatives already in place.

In discussing *DESD* implementation this introduction refers to the background in which *DESD* is embedded, to justify dealing with *DESD* through its technical and topical relevance. Thus, it corresponds to the founding basis that enables further considerations.

3.4.2 Section I: Education for Sustainable Development

The introduction to the *International Implementation Scheme* (IIS) delivers two crucial presumptive messages: firstly, sustainability is a topic of growing importance that affects all of us; secondly, education is considered to be sufficiently well-suited to tackling the large issue of sustainable development. The explanatory link between education and sustainable development is missing.

Historical references to sustainable development are outlined briefly at the beginning. It is noted clearly that sustainable development is a relatively recent concept. The document emphasises the two directions of *DESD*, rooted in the present and directed towards the future. Since the 1970s the amount of discourse on sustainability has steadily grown. Sustainable development is described as a dynamic and colourful concept which ranges from environmental issues to questions of inter-generational justice and socio-economic development. Consequently, four interlinked key areas or dimensions of sustainable development with specific *strategic perspectives*[1528] are defined: society, environment, economy and culture as underlying dimensions.[1529]

All different connotations and derived models have one important aspect in common: there is no sustainable development without popular commitment. As a result all considerations pertaining to sustainability must be needs-based and concerned with the *human element*[1530] in order to achieve the broad compliance necessary for change.

Most critically, education is considered the core element and *driving force*[1531] for sustainable development, for the following reasons and convictions:[1532]

- Education provides a base of knowledge and communication.
- Education promotes and improves capacity-building processes.
- Education enables reasoning, decision-making and involvement.

1528 Cf. UNESCO (ed.) (2005c) (cf. *footnote 23* op. cit.), p. 22.
1529 Cf. UNESCO (ed.) (2005c) (cf. *footnote 23* op. cit.), p. 17.
1530 See UNESCO (ed.) (2005c) (cf. *footnote 23* op. cit.), p. 19.
1531 See UNESCO (ed.) (2005c) (cf. *footnote 23* op. cit.), p. 16.
1532 Cf. UNESCO (ed.) (2005c) (cf. *footnote 23* op. cit.), p. 20.

- Education enhances self-reflection, vision-building and future-oriented thinking.
- Education paves the way for active participation.
- Education may set standards and values.
- Education can change attitudes and behaviours.

Awareness of sustainable development must be raised through quality education. Without adequate education, there is no opportunity. Although labelled *DESD*, stressing the word *education*, efforts towards sustainable development cannot be restricted to this specific form of institutionalised learning alone.[1533] One must also consider significant places of learning apart from education systems. Learning encompasses education, life-skills, expertise and experience.

Because sustainable development is *multi-faceted*,[1534] the catalogue helps to identify relevant features which serve as criteria for the successful translation of projects into practice.[1535] Moreover, strategic perspectives and learning spaces which might support the planning and implementation of *DESD* are also proposed.[1536]

As far as *DESD* implementation is concerned, this chapter contributes considerably to clarification of the nexus between learning concepts and sustainable development: education is a precondition of future-oriented thinking and performance. As a result, different forms of education are deemed feasible for the fulfilment of certain objectives and for strengthening strategic perspectives grounded in human needs.

3.4.3 Section II: Stakeholders and Strategies

Not every institution, organisation or private entity affected by *DESD* is a potential stakeholder. Stakeholder participation is organised in a multi-dimensional and systematic way. Partners and stakeholders in *DESD* implementation are identified according to:

- Targeted focal issues which match *DESD* dimensions and strategic perspectives;[1537]
- Complementary functions, represented by either governmental bodies, civil society organisations or private sector entities;[1538] and

---

1533 Cf. UNESCO (ed.) (2005c) (cf. *footnote 23* op. cit.), p. 20.
1534 See UNESCO (ed.) (2005c) (cf. *footnote 23* op. cit.), p. 20.
1535 Cf. UNESCO (ed.) (2005c) (cf. *footnote 23* op. cit.), p. 21.
1536 Cf. UNESCO (ed.) (2005c) (cf. *footnote 23* op. cit.), pp. 22 et seqq, 25 et seqq.
1537 Cf. UNESCO (ed.) (2005c) (cf. *footnote 23* op. cit.), p. 22.
1538 Cf. UNESCO (ed.) (2005c) (cf. *footnote 23* op. cit.), p. 30; Fien, John (2010) (cf. *footnote 817* op. cit.).

- Level and radius of action: local (sub-national), national, regional or international.[1539]

Implementing such a complex *DESD* initiative in a joint multi-stakeholder approach requires both guidelines and powerful management tools. These have to be universally applicable independently of contexts, stakeholders and levels. For more than a decade UNESCO has relied on a decentralised network of partners and stakeholders.

In order to ensure effectiveness and orientation towards a common goal, individual initiatives are linked by *seven* strategies to be applied either within proper institutional frameworks or in the appropriate networks and alliances. These are:[1540]

1. Advocacy and vision-building: raising global awareness of social, economic, environmental and cultural issues; developing local, national and global visions of sustainability; generating global commitment; lobbying and advocacy; and focusing on a *theme of the year*[1541] as topic of particular interest.
2. Consultation and ownership: comprehensible publishing; fostering integrative stakeholder processes; ensuring multi-level consultations; debating; campaigning; commissioning research and *evidence-based policy making*;[1542]
3. Partnership and networks: *Outward-looking*[1543] orientation of *DESD* partners; aiming at focused partnerships; making use of multiplier and synergy effects; regular and systematic exchange of information and experience;
4. Capacity-building and training: communication and awareness-raising; planning, management and evaluation; training and train-the-trainer programmes; developing analytical tools, instructional contents and innovative, target group-specific materials; the provision of appropriate instructional methodologies;
5. Research and innovation: progress markers through baseline studies; evidence-based action; interdisciplinary, conceptual and practical links; impact analysis of stakeholders through longitudinal studies; scenario development; identification, documentation and dissemination of examples of good-

1539 Cf. UNESCO (ed.) (2005c) (cf. *footnote 23* op. cit.), pp. 30–31.

1540 Cf. UNESCO (ed.) (2005c) (cf. *footnote 23* op. cit.), pp. 31 et seqq.
See *Figure 66* in chapter IX 3.4.3 *Section II: Stakeholders and Strategies* on page 312.

1541 For example: sustainable consumption; cultural diversity; health and quality of life; water and energy; biosphere reserves as places of learning; world heritage sites as places of learning; *ESD* in the knowledge society; citizen participation and good governance; poverty reduction and sustainable development projects; inter-generational justice and ethics.
Cf. UNESCO (ed.) (2005c) (cf. *footnote 23* op. cit.), p. 49; Gerner, Martin (2008) (cf. *footnote 259* op. cit.), p. 21.

1542 See UNESCO (ed.) (2005c) (cf. *footnote 23* op. cit.), p. 32.

1543 See UNESCO (ed.) (2005c) (cf. *footnote 23* op. cit.), p. 33.

practice in regard to institutional arrangements, modes of partnership relations and *DESD* managerial approaches;
6. Use of *information and communication technologies* (ICT):[1544] transfer and interactive use of information; establishing a *knowledge economy*[1545] through global dialogue by linking distant partners; storing data; sharing information and news real-time; offering new modes and spaces of learning; and
7. Monitoring and evaluation: Identifying significant changes, differences and impact of *DESD*.

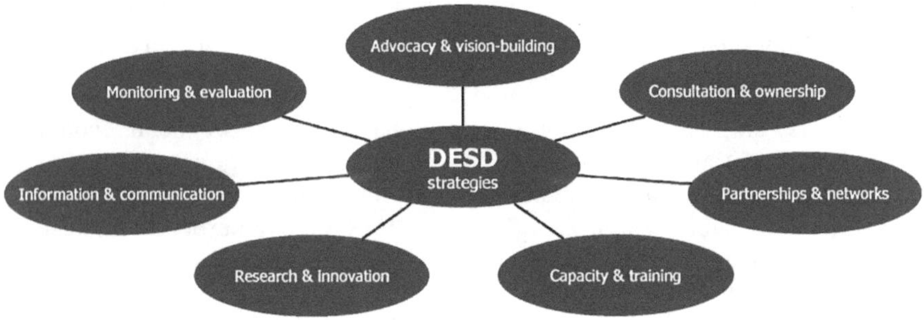

Figure 66: DESD strategies[1546]

Due to the complexity of *DESD* implementation UNESCO favours a multi-stakeholder approach binding partners and stakeholders to commonly shared or desired *DESD* values. This *knot* is represented by a set of certain strategies of implementation that serve as a pronounced expectation of *DESD* of specific stakeholder participation. The overall implementation approach combines elements of *open access*, *bottom-up* and *top-down* strategies:

- *Open access*, meaning the ability to allow multiple stakeholders to develop their own concepts, programmes, theories, initiatives, etc;
- *Bottom-up*, in the sense of decisions taken at the best and most relevant level according to the principle of *subsidiarity*; and
- *Top-down*, referring to basic key issues on *DESD* represented by UNESCO in order to ensure global goal orientation and a programmatic lead.

1544 Cf. Makrakis, Vassilio (2010): Strategies to reinforce the role of ICT in teaching and learning for sustainability. In: Witthaus, Michele; McCandless, Karen; Lambert, Rebecca (eds.): Tomorrow today. Leicester, United Kingdom: Tudor Rose; UNESCO publishing, pp. 169–171.

1545 See UNESCO (ed.) (2005c) (cf. *footnote 23* op. cit.), p. 35.

1546 Seven self-contained strategies are applied in order to address *DESD*.

3.4.4 Section III: Implementation and Evaluation

This is *DESD* implementation in close-up: how does *DESD* enter into practice, what results can be expected and how is *DESD* monitored and evaluated?

The overall idea is to implement *ESD* at all community levels, starting from local commitment, realising national aims, encompassing regional perspectives and finally envisioning global assets. Therefore *"the four elements of sustainable development – society, environment, economy and culture – are in focus at local and global levels and at all levels in between".*[1547] Particular attention is paid to initiatives, co-operations and plans made by stakeholders at the local level, *"starting from and aiming to address grassroots realities".*[1548]

With regard to *local-level implementation*, *"(t)he local level is the primary place at which lessons for better practice in sustainable development can be learnt, shared and applied".*[1549] The central element of *DESD* implementation is strengthening local-level[1550] or community commitment. S*upport networks*[1551] are composed of local institutions and groups, such as education systems, *non-governmental organisations* (NGO) and community associations, as well as local governments. The overall objective is to provide appropriate solutions adapted to the local educational context.[1552] There are some crucial prerequisites to ensuring that *ESD* is successful in local – *community-based*[1553] – institutions and groups which represent particular *"places where sustainable development practices can be modelled and learnt"*:[1554]

- Understanding values, relationships and reciprocal effects related to *ESD*;[1555]
- Identifying relevant areas and *real causes*[1556] where *ESD* can be learned, modelled and applied;[1557]

1547 See UNESCO (ed.) (2005c) (cf. *footnote 23* op. cit.), p. 36.
1548 See UNESCO (ed.) (2005c) (cf. *footnote 23* op. cit.), p. 36.
1549 See UNESCO (ed.) (2005c) (cf. *footnote 23* op. cit.), p. 37.
1550 With regard to wording: UNESCO uses the term *sub-national* where appropriate, although this terminology appears to be far too diffuse and remote from the real point of embedding *DESD locally*.
1551 See UNESCO (ed.) (2005c) (cf. *footnote 23* op. cit.), p. 36.
1552 In the case of the most likely educational context of implementation at the local level, schools are highly capable of creating momentum on *DESD* through new content knowledge, innovative pedagogical concepts and through administrative support by co-ordinating programme logistics and community support.
Cf. UNESCO (ed.) (2005c) (cf. *footnote 23* op. cit.), p. 36.
See *Figure 67* in chapter IX 3.4.4 *Section III: Implementation and Evaluation* on page 315.
1553 See UNESCO (ed.) (2005c) (cf. *footnote 23* op. cit.), p. 37.
1554 See UNESCO (ed.) (2005c) (cf. *footnote 23* op. cit.), p. 36.
1555 Cf. UNESCO; Asia-Pacific Centre of Education for International Understanding (APCEIU) (eds.) (2007a) (cf. *footnote 696* op. cit.), pp. 2 et seqq.

- Co-operating and learning about *ESD* in basic and in adult education;
- Forming consortia aimed at inter-institutional collaboration in research, teaching and training;[1558] and
- Applying relevant findings to local education plans, policies and local agenda as appropriate.

Local governments play a pivotal role as they represent the *"closest level of government to the people"*.[1559] As suppliers of public goods, services and programmes, local governments are in the best position to promote initiatives in relation to *DESD*. In order to carry out their *active* mandate on *ESD* effectively, following a priority list, local governments are in need of:

- Effective management and co-ordination capacity;
- De-centralised and strong structures of local governance; and
- Up-to-date resources in communication, information technology and finance.

Two modes of local-level commitment, either *community-based* or in local government, are conceivable:[1560]

a) Integrating *ESD* into their respective institutions' and organisations' agendas and programmes, including the target group-specific, locally relevant and identifiable implementation of *ESD*; or
b) Co-operating in *local groupings*[1561] and formally setting up (*ad-hoc*) networks, involving local challenges in *ESD* and the exchange of experiences.

UNESCO as a *catalyst* and significant *DESD* implementer is thus tasked with leading the process of identifying and activating prospective local partners. It is necessary to ensure the broadest representation and most active participation as possible at grass-root level. Non-exclusion is one of the key premises. Hence, UNESCO must effectively manage to both reach and integrate marginalised groups[1562] and enable them to take part in *ESD*.

1556 See UNESCO (ed.) (2005c) (cf. *footnote 23* op. cit.), p. 36.

1557 For example: energy use, waste disposal, recycling, ways of production and consumption, etc.

1558 A desirable example would be co-operation between primary and secondary schools on a project base with universities or research institutions both conducting topical research on *ESD* and, effectively, teaching the subject.
Cf. UNESCO (ed.) (2005c) (cf. *footnote 23* op. cit.), p. 36.

1559 See UNESCO (ed.) (2005c) (cf. *footnote 23* op. cit.), p. 37.

1560 Cf. UNESCO (ed.) (2005c) (cf. *footnote 23* op. cit.), p. 37.

1561 See UNESCO (ed.) (2005c) (cf. *footnote 23* op. cit.), p. 37.

1562 For example: the disabled, the very poor, nomads and migrants, ethnic and linguistic minorities, the aged and the chronically ill.

Community-based institutions and organisations such as:	Working individually to:	Cooperating in ad hoc or formal local groupings to:
▶ schools and school support groups, cultural associations, youth organisations, cooperatives, faith-based groupings, self-help groups, development committees, local government	▶ integrate ESD into regular learning activities and programmes ▶ identify and reach marginalised groups ▶ identify and implement learning strategies	▶ identify local sustainable development challenges ▶ integrate local knowledge and skills into ESD ▶ exchange ESD experiences and learn lessons for better practice

Figure 67: Local-level co-operation in ESD[1563]

In terms of *national-level implementation*, representing an *inter-national* organisation, the member state or national level is the primary point of reference and the addressee for UNESCO. With respect to *DESD* implementation, the United Nations General Assembly in resolution *A/RES/57/254* clearly calls upon governments *"to consider the inclusion of measures to implement the Decade in their respective educational strategies and action plans by 2005, taking into account th(is) international implementation scheme".*[1564] In other words, governments are held expressly responsible for:[1565]

- *"(S)etting parameters for effective cooperation and action in DESD"*;[1566]
- Launching *DESD* nationally;
- Promoting consultation and vision-building at local and national level;
- Interactively developing national *DESD* strategies with all relevant stakeholders involved with education;
- Elaborating on a *policy framework* to provide guidance *"in mobilising political will, resources and effort"*;[1567]
- Formulating policies for local action and responsibility;

1563 Local-level involvement aims to create the platform of community-based institutions and organisations working towards *DESD*.
See UNESCO (ed.) (2005c) (cf. *footnote 23* op. cit.), p. 37.

1564 See United Nations (ed.) (2002 / 2003) (cf. *footnote 117* op. cit.), p. 2.

1565 Cf. UNESCO (ed.) (2005c) (cf. *footnote 23* op. cit.), p. 38.
See *Figure 68* in chapter IX 3.4.4 *Section III: Implementation and Evaluation* on page 317.

1566 See UNESCO (ed.) (2005c) (cf. *footnote 23* op. cit.), p. 38.

1567 A *policy framework* is *"an over-arching framework for national policy and how to promote ownership of it"*. It is primarily directed to identify and analyse each member state's individual contribution to *DESD*, with regards to areas of policy, communication, science and research.
See and cf. UNESCO (ed.) (2005c) (cf. *footnote 23* op. cit.), p. 39.

- Exploring and strengthening potential value-based partnerships and promising networks *"with institutions of educational research, curriculum reform and development and teacher training"*;[1568]
- Co-ordinating stakeholder engagement and involvement in order to avoid duplication and overlap of effort;
- Establishing coherence in regard to the documentation of policy papers and strategies;
- Focused communication in order to achieve broad public support;
- Providing institutional arrangements, such as an appropriate *ESD Hub* and an *ESD Consultative Group*[1569] at national level;
- Mobilising financial resources and allocating *DESD* spending within the ordinary budgetary process;[1570]
- Directing and linking civil society and non-governmental organisations through specific networks *"to ensure a strong and coherent voice"*;[1571]
- Highlighting critical issues, stimulating debate and disseminating in-depth information by media organisations and companies; and
- Involving private sector commitment for local educational initiatives through relevant task forces and platforms.[1572]

National implementation of *DESD* is an ambitious and demanding multi-faceted undertaking. Due to the complexity of various stakeholder-driven approaches, effective and resource-efficient means of co-ordination and leadership are required. In the case of measurable *DESD* success at national level what is even more important is the member state's reliance on its stakeholders and partners operating both in favour of and in compliance with *DESD* principles and values.

1568 See UNESCO (ed.) (2005c) (cf. *footnote 23* op. cit.), p. 38.

1569 See UNESCO (ed.) (2005c) (cf. *footnote 23* op. cit.), p. 38.

1570 It must be mentioned that *ESD* spending should not reflect any *opportunity cost* for any member state. Given the fact that, since the Rio Declaration *Agenda 21* in 1992, sustainable development has constituted a key goal of co-operation in international development, *"ESD should have a prominent place in long-term development strategies and national development planning"*. As a result, countries receiving international development aid are requested to publish their *ESD* components as costs or spending as part of the *Poverty Reduction Strategy Papers* (PRSP). Essentially, there is no excuse not to participate in *DESD* due to a budgetary lack of financial resources.
See and cf. UNESCO (ed.) (2005c) (cf. *footnote 23* op. cit.), p. 39.
Cf. *Agenda 21*, chapter 2, no. 2.1 on *International Cooperation to accelerate sustainable development in developing countries and related domestic policies*: *"sustainable development should become a priority item on the agenda of the international community. [...] It is equally important to strengthen national and international policies and multinational cooperation to adapt to the new realities."*
See UN Department of Economic and Social Affairs (ed.) (1992) (cf. *footnote 721* op. cit.), p. 4.

1571 See UNESCO (ed.) (2005c) (cf. *footnote 23* op. cit.), p. 39.

1572 For example: *Public-Private-Partnerships* (PPP).

Actors at national level	Working to:
Government (education ministry, universities, other relevant ministries and departments)	▶ provide a national policy framework for ESD ▶ budget and mobilise resources ▶ support sub-national departments ▶ foster public awareness of ESD and sustainable development
NGOs, NGO and civil society networks and alliances	▶ link local experience to national policy-making ▶ advocate and lobby on ESD ▶ facilitate exchange and information sharing among their members about ESD practices and experiences
Media groups and agencies	▶ integrate ESD and SD awareness building into media strategies
Private sector companies and trade associations	▶ provide a forum to identify SD challenges they face, identify and address necessary learning needs

Figure 68: Contributions to ESD achieved by stakeholders at national level[1573]

Additionally, a detailed checklist is provided to guide *DESD* implementation at national level. When considering stakeholder collaboration to be an essential element of this process, the *starter kit* must provide guidance *"given the wide variety of national situations"*.[1574] All questions raised must therefore lead to concrete action in the fields of:[1575]

- Initiating partnership and action;
- Implementing *ESD*; and
- Evaluating *ESD*.

1573 National *DESD* efforts are mainly expected from joint strategic partnerships between non-state and state stakeholders of civil society.
See UNESCO (ed.) (2005c) (cf. *footnote 23* op. cit.), p. 40.

1574 See UNESCO (ed.) (2005c) (cf. *footnote 23* op. cit.), p. 54.

1575 See *Table 30* in chapter IX 3.4.4 *Section III: Implementation and Evaluation* on page 318.

Table 30: Checklist of national DESD implementation[1576]

Stage	*Questions and suggestions*
Initiating partnership and action on:	Identifying prospective stakeholders
	Establishing initial consultations
	Nominating the multi-stakeholder body at national level to co-ordinate, promote and facilitate *DESD*
	Assessing financial needs of *DESD* implementation
	Identifying potential sources of funding
	Setting up financial mechanisms
	Reviewing existing education plans to reflect *ESD* commitment
	Identifying key national issues in sustainable development
	Formulating key messages for public awareness-raising on *ESD*
	Setting up a plan of national *ESD* objectives
	Drawing up a target group-related advocacy and communication plan
	Undertaking baseline studies on status-quo *ESD* integration into educational initiatives
	Examining the national legal and institutional framework
	Assessing the potential of local governance structures and processes in support of *DESD*
	Developing a framework for co-operation at national and local levels
Implementing	Developing plans on public awareness and participation
	Providing communication through media, materials and messages
	Launching public awareness campaigns
	Facilitating regular contact with media
	Initiating scenario development for different contexts
	Adapting and examining initial and in-service training for educators, facilitators and teachers (*multipliers*) on *ESD*
	Examining and adapting curricula in formal and non-formal educational settings to include *ESD* approaches
	Providing framework for local, non-formal groups in support of *ESD* practice
	Initiating project planning at city, municipal or district level[1577]

1576 Cf. UNESCO (ed.) (2005c) (cf. *footnote 23* op. cit.), pp. 54–55.

1577 Projects have to be related to *ESD*, limited in duration and target group-specific. Contents have to be in line with *DESD* dimensions – environmental, economic, social and cultural – including, for example: cleanup, *greening*, improving and preserving the environment for wild animals, preservation of old town streets, protection of cultural

Stage	*Questions and suggestions*
Evaluating	Determining aspects of *DESD* monitoring in co-operation with stakeholder groups
	Decision-taking upon analysis and use of resulting information
	Establishing *smart* indicators and monitoring processes according to national *DESD* objectives
	Managing data collection at national and local level
	Clarifying responsibilities at all levels

Concerning *regional-level implementation*, UNESCO considers regional-level co-operation to be *"particularly enriching and stimulating, since experiences (...) are often similar enough to be comparable, but different enough to provide new perspectives and ideas"*.[1578] In this case region might be defined as an area without fixed limits but nevertheless linked to certain commonly shared aspects. Depending on similar backgrounds, such as geo-physical and environmental conditions, culture, history, language and politics, for instance, sharing expertise can produce valuable synergy effects, reciprocal understanding and learning. Given these specifics, co-operation and commitment at regional level is, for this reason, considered more effective and *"more useful in directly applicable terms"*[1579] than isolated international efforts.

The sharing and exchange of experiences, concerted policies, challenges and progress is considered to be the leading function at regional level. The purpose is, firstly, to provide mutual support between countries forming part of the region and, secondly, to establish contact and facilitate communication between regional counterparts.[1580]

Networks of regional co-operation are already well-established. As a consequence these *umbrella bodies*[1581] do not have to be created anew. They may just serve as *ESD programme carriers*, and as such are endowed with great potential for the integration of *DESD* within the respective region.[1582]

heritage, promotion of clean energy, the reuse and recycling of products, securing biodiversity, promoting environmental education, etc.

1578 See UNESCO (ed.) (2005c) (cf. *footnote 23* op. cit.), p. 40.

1579 See UNESCO (ed.) (2005c) (cf. *footnote 23* op. cit.), p. 40.

1580 Cf. UNESCO (ed.) (2005c) (cf. *footnote 23* op. cit.), p. 40.

1581 See UNESCO (ed.) (2005c) (cf. *footnote 23* op. cit.), p. 40.

1582 *United Nations Economic Commission for Europe* (UNECC) is a sound and successful example of *"how an ESD strategy can be developed and espoused within existing co-operative frameworks"*.
See and cf. UNESCO (ed.) (2005c) (cf. *footnote 23* op. cit.), p. 40.
See *Figure 69* in chapter IX 3.4.4 *Section III: Implementation and Evaluation* on page 320.

Actors at regional level	Working individually to:
Regional intergovernmental organisations	▶ support national-level policy-making ▶ foster exchange of experience and information
Regional civil society and NGO networks, coalitions and alliances	▶ foster exchange and learning among member networks and organisations
Regional media groupings	▶ share media strategies for SD and ESD
Regional private sector associations	▶ promote cooperation of private sector with other actors in ESD
Regional representatives of international agencies	▶ learn and communicate common lessons from cross-national experience ▶ facilitate cross-national exchange on ESD
Regional representatives of bilateral cooperation	▶ assess ways to support national and regional ESD initiatives

Figure 69: Regional groupings and their respective functions at regional level[1583]

In parallel with ongoing processes of national implementation UNESCO recommends accordingly the creation of an equivalent *ESD Hub*[1584] at regional level. A *regional ESD Caucus*[1585] serves as a platform in a flexible arrangement not only to facilitate communication between counterparts and co-operation amongst organisations and groupings in other countries of the region, but also to build *regional momentum* through concerted efforts.

With respect to *international-level implementation*, UNESCO has to comply with the strategic mandate of fostering *DESD* by facilitating awareness-raising, incorporating *ESD* into agendas, monitoring compliance and evaluating outcomes. The means required to meet these objectives are typically attached to technical aspects of implementation:[1586]

- Mobilising political will and relevant resources (funding);
- Strengthening common public commitment;
- Providing international platforms and forums to create high visibility for *ESD* challenges, progress and impacts;
- Fostering global exchange of practice, policy and progress;
- Forging strategic international partnerships on crucial *DESD* issues;
- Integrating and strategically linking *ESD* with respective agendas;[1587] and

1583 The range of stakeholders is similar to the range of actors listed at national level, and only functions change due to making use of synergies and addressing new points of reference at regional level.
See UNESCO (ed.) (2005c) (cf. *footnote 23* op. cit.), p. 40.

1584 Cf. UNESCO (ed.) (2005c) (cf. *footnote 23* op. cit.), p. 38.

1585 See UNESCO (ed.) (2005c) (cf. *footnote 23* op. cit.), p. 41.

1586 Cf. UNESCO (ed.) (2005c) (cf. *footnote 23* op. cit.), p. 41.

1587 For example: keeping education high on the agenda of the United Nations Commission for Sustainable Development; integrating *DESD* into the *Education for All* (EFA) agendas.

- Monitoring and evaluating *DESD*.

Opportunities for dialogue, consultation and the exchange of experiences are provided or created at international level in patterns similar to national- and regional-level implementation. In addition to international forums and conferences, inter-governmental agencies and committees are created in order to connect key international agencies in charge of *DESD*-related issues as part of their respective mandates.[1588]

Apart from the technical aspect of platform-building, *"the expansion of international exchange and cooperation between educational institutions will also enhance the impact of DESD".*[1589] The intention is to make practical synergetic use of established structures of networking in defining new cultures and spaces for learning in *ESD*. As a result, networks and platforms no longer serve only as purely technical arrangements,[1590] but rather as a comprehensive *"global learning space on education and sustainability that promotes cooperation and exchange between institutions at all levels and in all sectors of education around the world".*[1591]

A similar strategic approach is used in the case of international private sector involvement. Since 1999, the *Global Compact* has served as a forum of voluntary learning and dialogue around the issue of corporate citizenship between privately owned companies and civil society organisations on the international

---

Cf. UNESCO (ed.) (2005c) (cf. *footnote 23* op. cit.), p. 41.

1588 A prominent example of such *DESD hot-spot creating* institution is the *Inter-Agency Committee for the DESD* tasked to bring together international agencies of the United Nations System and different stakeholder groups (development banks, non-governmental organisations, and relevant regional groupings) in order to provide updated information and consultation.
Cf. UNESCO (ed.) (2005c) (cf. *footnote 23* op. cit.), pp. 41, 43.
See *Figure 70* in chapter IX 3.4.4 *Section III: Implementation and Evaluation* on page 322.

1589 See UNESCO (ed.) (2005c) (cf. *footnote 23* op. cit.), p. 41.

1590 There is no *non-learning*, as far as sustainable issues are concerned. For instance, launching *DESD*-related events, such as national or international assemblies of educators, multipliers, youth and children, or *practical learning-by-doing events* at local level, in itself constitutes a means of learning.
Cf. UNESCO (ed.) (2005c) (cf. *footnote 23* op. cit.), p. 49.

1591 As an international educational initiative on *DESD* the *Ubuntu Declaration*, signed in 2002 at the *Johannesburg World Summit on Sustainable Development* (WSSD), aims to strengthen spaces of *"science and technology education for sustainable development". "This space must be developed on the basis of international networks of institutions and the creation of regional centers of excellence, which bring together universities, polytechnics, and institutions of secondary education and primary schools."*
See United Nations University (UNU); UNESCO; International Association of Universities (IAU) (eds.) (2002) (cf. *footnote 805* op. cit.), pp. 1–2.

stage.[1592] Although not among the focal issues, the stakeholders in *Global Compact* proclaim themselves to be part of a joint *alliance on learning sustainability.*[1593] As far as *ESD* is concerned UNESCO expressly welcomes *Global Compact* corporations joining in with partnerships to contribute to the raising of public awareness and to workforce training. UNESCO is in favour of, ideally, a tripartite network consisting of the private sector, the organisation itself and other international agencies for the following reason: addressing bodies of both production and consumption is advantageous, because it simultaneously enables standard-setting via dialogue. In the same way, performance indicators in sustainable development can easily be used as benchmarks of quality by private-sector institutions.[1594]

International-level implementation of *DESD* is comparable to an *umbrella concept.* On the one hand it has a unifying *roof function* in dealing with multiple stakeholders and partners all of whom are different in their functions and objectives. On the other hand it has to serve as a grounded and value-driven *framework* in order to provide objective-oriented guidance.

Actors at international level	Roles and functions
Intergovernmental agencies (UN and others)	► promote ESD and integrate ESD planning into relevant work plans and initiatives ► facilitate and participate in international and regional fora
UNESCO (DESD Lead Agency)	► (see below)
Civil society and NGO networks	► promote inter-regional exchange and learning ► inform members of ESD developments ► advocate and lobby with international bodies
Bilateral agencies	► integrate ESD into programmes and budgets ► promote research in ESD
Private sector	► public awareness ► standard setting and indicator development

Figure 70: Summary on DESD co-operation at international level[1595]

As far as specific *DESD*-related initiatives and programmes of United Nations organisations or agencies are concerned, programmatic guidance has to be offered in order to make use of synergy effects.[1596]

1592 Cf. UNESCO (ed.) (2005c) (cf. *footnote 23* op. cit.), p. 42; Pies, Ingo; Winning, Alexandra von (eds.) (2006) (cf. *footnote 818* op. cit.), pp. 7–8.

1593 Cf. Pies, Ingo; Winning, Alexandra von (eds.) (2006) (cf. *footnote 818* op. cit.), p. 8; United Nations Global Compact (2007) (cf. *footnote 819* op. cit.).

1594 Cf. UNESCO (ed.) (2005c) (cf. *footnote 23* op. cit.), p. 42.

1595 The international level of *DESD* co-operation serves as *umbrella* of both roofing stakeholders and providing guidance through framework structures.
See UNESCO (ed.) (2005c) (cf. *footnote 23* op. cit.), p. 42.

In the course of implementation, UNESCO, as designated *lead agency*, must negotiate a number of obstacles posed by *DESD* co-ordination:[1597]

- Ensuring continued international energy and momentum;
- Co-ordinating cross-cutting programmes in parallel with other initiatives;
- Keeping abreast of progress in other related international agendas;
- Ensuring goal-oriented partnerships as well as concerted and targeted action;
- Providing outlines of and perspectives on *DESD* implementation: strategies, expected outcomes, evaluation indicators and schedules;
- Fostering stakeholder dialogue, strategic and goal-oriented partnerships among United Nations organisations and agencies, other international bodies, member states, private sector and civil society;
- Encouraging partners and stakeholders of joint planning, implementation and evaluation; and
- Staying in permanent contact with media and broadcasting agencies in order to provide advocacy and awareness-raising through documentation and dissemination of *DESD*-related issues.

Implementing such a complex issue as *DESD* requires a multi-level approach. This is achieved through an extensive and comprehensive scheme of implementation, not as a list for cross-checking but in a manner that affords the delegation of responsibilities. Each proposed group or body is exhorted to create coherence and powerful momentum reliably and in support of *DESD* at the appropriate level:[1598]

1596 Examples being, for instance: *United Nations International Children's Emergency Fund* (UNICEF): *UN Girls Education Initiative* (UNGEI) on gender parity and equality in education; *United Nations Environment Programme* (UNEP): Environment for Development on environmental aspects of *DESD* and environmental education; and UN Habitat: *Best Practices and Local Leadership Programme* (BLP) on the identification and exchange of successful solutions for sustainable development.
Cf. UNESCO (ed.) (2005c) (cf. *footnote 23* op. cit.), pp. 42–43; UNESCO; Asia-Pacific Centre of Education for International Understanding (APCEIU) (eds.) (2007a) (cf. *footnote 696* op. cit.); UN-HABITAT (2010) (cf. *footnote 754* op. cit.).

1597 Cf. UNESCO (ed.) (2005c) (cf. *footnote 23* op. cit.), p. 43.

1598 See *Figure 71* in chapter IX 3.4.4 *Section III: Implementation and Evaluation* on page 324.

Level	Grouping	Main purposes
Local (sub-national) level	Stakeholder consultations	identify challenges, integrate local knowledge and skills into ESD, exchange experience
National level	ESD Hub	energise, facilitate connections, coordinate
	ESD Consultative Group	bring stakeholders together for policy input, debate, exchange, planning
Regional level	ESD Caucus	build common understandings, give mutual support, plan joint actions and research
International level	UNESCO	energise, facilitate connections, coordinate, monitor progress
	Inter-Agency Committee on DESD	foster political commitment, identify key global priorities, exchange, consult and update

Figure 71: Levels, stakeholder groups and tasks of DESD implementation[1599]

Essentially, the critical question is whether the implementation of *DESD* has been successful in inspiring decisions and actions based upon attitudes and values created anew in order to make sustainable development a realistic and *more attainable ideal.*[1600] In line with the multi-level *umbrella concept* this main objective translates into five sub-objectives. These constitute the globally normative basis necessary for the evaluation of *outcomes*.

The outcomes of learning processes can be categorised as cognitive, emotional and behavioural. Despite the fact that cognitive results are usually directly measurable against certain *ex-ante* criteria, emotional and behavioural outcomes are far more difficult to be evaluated.

It is important to note that outcomes are *high-level*: they will be applied at the appropriate level depending on *"the extent to which the kinds of energy and inputs (...) are available"*[1601] and measured according to the *DESD* implementation scheme. The envisaged outcomes are not *loose* but are instead flexible enough to be adapted to specific contexts.[1602]

1599 *DESD* implementation is painstakingly *grounded* on the specific prerequisites of each level. The principle of regional strategies is coherently exercised in the way that needs and interests are expressed bottom up in order to be delegated to the next level of steering and management. In other words, ideally local implementing commitment leads to political commitment at international level.
See UNESCO (ed.) (2005c) (cf. *footnote 23* op. cit.), p. 44.

1600 Cf. UNESCO (ed.) (2005c) (cf. *footnote 23* op. cit.), p. 44.

1601 See UNESCO (ed.) (2005c) (cf. *footnote 23* op. cit.), p. 44.

1602 See *Figure 72* in chapter IX 3.4.4 *Section III: Implementation and Evaluation* on page 325.

Objective	Expected outcomes
1. Give an enhanced profile to the central role of education and learning in the common pursuit of sustainable development	► Integration of educational components into plans for sustainable development ► Assessment of the need for and role of ESD in all development planning
2. Facilitate links and networking, exchange and interaction among stakeholders in ESD	► Through consultations and fora of all kinds and at all levels – ➢ growing consensus on the strategic importance of ESD ➢ growing cooperation and mutual reinforcement among ESD initiatives
3. Provide a space and opportunity for refining and promoting the vision of, and transition to sustainable development – through all forms of learning and public awareness	► Broad public awareness of the nature and principles of sustainable development ► Regular and substantial media presence for sustainable development issues
4. Foster increased quality of teaching and learning in education for sustainable development	► The thread of sustainable development woven into EFA efforts to raise educational quality ► ESD-specific approaches increasingly adopted in learning situations of all kinds
5. Develop strategies at every level to strengthen capacity in ESD	► ESD as part of educator training ► High-quality materials and methodologies in ESD ► Adequate management capacity to maintain ESD

Figure 72: Expected cognitive outcomes against DESD sub-objectives[1603]

Value-driven processes, such as *ESD*, gain momentum and are successful when the basic message trickles down effectively to the individual level. Knowledge and awareness are a useful basis, but may not be secure indicators of achievement. Promising outcomes are only achievable as long as people feel individually addressed, personally involved in or even directly affected by the necessity of dealing with issues of sustainability. In other words, emotional involvement is crucial to fulfil challenging objectives.

Yet more is required to change behavioural patterns of, for instance, consumption or production. Understanding alone is not sufficient. Commitment starts where affection alone ends. Usually thresholds are significantly high. Indeed, the process that leads to adopting certain changes in behavioural dispositions lasts for a long period of time.[1604]

1603 This figure of expected outcomes of *DESD* once again underpins the principle of regional strategies since sub-objectives are related to different levels.
See UNESCO (ed.) (2005c) (cf. *footnote 23* op. cit.), p. 45.

1604 See *Table 31* in chapter IX 3.4.4 *Section III: Implementation and Evaluation* on page 326.

Table 31: Potential emotional and behavioural outcomes[1605]

Category	Outcome	Description
Emotional	Respect	*Respect for other people of current and future generations, recognising their right to a life of quality and to equitable sharing in the world's resources;*
	Humility	*Respect for the natural world, based on an understanding of how it works, of how we can steward its resources and of the devastating effects of not respecting it;*
	Decision-making	*Knowing how to make choices and decisions, individually and collectively, which take into account the long-term future of social equity, ecological viability and economic progress;*
Behavioural	Commitment	*Committed and aware individuals with a global view, but also with the capacity to envisage alternative futures and create change within their societies; (and)*
	Multiplying effect	*Capacity to work with others to bring about structural or institutional change within society so that efforts can be embedded within the mainstream. ESD must go beyond self-development to promote structural social change.*[1606]

Issues of implementation are closely related to aspects of monitoring and evaluating *DESD*; indeed, these two stages of the project go hand in hand and are inextricably linked. In line with UNESCO's functions and *DESD* strategies, *DESD* is being monitored and evaluated in order to assess and, if necessary, to re-orient programmes in the course of implementation.[1607] *"Without that, it will be impossible to know if the Decade is making any difference and what that difference is."*[1608] From the very beginning of *DESD*, appropriate mechanisms have been planned and scheduled, primarily in order to avoid *end-of-pipe* adjustments. Indeed, *smart* indicators must be developed *ex ante* and serve thereafter as mandatory benchmarks which are sufficiently suitable, measurable, achievable, realistic and timely (*SMART*) to identify progress and change at every level of *DESD* – local, national, regional and international – and for each initiative and programme. Monitoring and evaluation results are intended to be employed in assessment, advocacy and publication.

Given that *DESD* implementation is principally based on a de-centralised and stakeholder-driven approach *"through the integration of ESD concerns into*

1605 This table demonstrates how different qualities of outcomes may be correlated with *DESD*.
Cf. modified version UNESCO (ed.) (2005c) (cf. *footnote 23* op. cit.), p. 45.
1606 See UNESCO (ed.) (2005c) (cf. *footnote 23* op. cit.), p. 45.
1607 Cf. Boisson de Chazournes, Laurence (2007) (cf. *footnote 496* op. cit.), pp. 72–73.
1608 See UNESCO (ed.) (2005c) (cf. *footnote 23* op. cit.), p. 45.

existing networks and alliances and through the creation of new ones",[1609] it is reasonable and conceivable for each grouping to develop and manage its own objectives, expected outcomes and indicators in line with the focal issues of UNESCO.[1610]

As a result of the different natures of *DESD* outcomes – cognitive, emotional and behavioural – instruments of monitoring and evaluating must be suitably applied. For this reason, exclusive reference to quantitative indicators, given the ease of data collection, omits valuable information and feedback. Not every type of data can be obtained in such a systematic way.[1611] Consequently, a qualitatively-oriented evaluative approach must be integrated.[1612]

1609 See UNESCO (ed.) (2005c) (cf. *footnote 23* op. cit.), p. 46.

1610 Cf. UNESCO (ed.) (2008h) (cf. *footnote 219* op. cit.).

1611 Let us take, for instance, the indicator of success at local level: successful implementation depends on the *"extent to which ESD becomes part of the development dialogue at community level"*. In this case there are at least two aspects to be dealt with: how often does *ESD* play a substantial role at community-level communication (quantitative)? And, how and which topics are relevant to discussions (qualitative)?
Cf. UNESCO (ed.) (2005c) (cf. *footnote 23* op. cit.), p. 36.

1612 For example: qualitative empirical analysis, case-studies, field research, ethnographic studies, participatory observation, longitudinal studies, comparative approaches between country groups and *ESD* initiatives, etc.
Cf. UNESCO (ed.) (2005c) (cf. *footnote 23* op. cit.), p. 47.
See *Figure 73* in chapter IX 3.4.4 *Section III: Implementation and Evaluation* on page 328.

Expected outcomes	Potential indicators	Data for use in verification
► Integration of educational components into plans for sustainable development	Education on regular agenda of CSD, regional, national and local sustainable development fora	Frequency of ESD in proceedings, minutes and other meeting outputs
► Assessment of the need for and role of ESD in all development planning	ESD factored into PRSPs, regional plans (eg NEPAD), and national planning cycles	Number of PRSPs with ESD component; number of specific ESD sections in development planning documents
► Growing consensus on the strategic importance of ESD	Incorporation of ESD into Education Ministry structures and plans, and into CS and NGO actions	Numbers of countries, CSOs and NGOs including specific ESD provision in their programmes
► Growing cooperation and mutual reinforcement among ESD initiatives	Creation of ESD networks and alliances	Numbers and membership of ESD networks and alliances
	Joint programming between government, CS and NGOs at all levels	Numbers of joint initiatives and numbers of bodies participating in them
► Broad public awareness of the nature and principles of sustainable development	Popular participation in sustainable development events, campaigns, fora	Level of unsolicited feedback from the public on sustainable development issues
	Participation in local, practical sustainable development initiatives	Numbers of initiatives and levels of participation
► Regular and substantial media presence for sustainable development issues	TV, radio and press coverage of sustainable development and ESD	Numbers of reports, editorials and articles on sustainable development

Expected outcomes	Potential indicators	Data for use in verification
► The thread of sustainable development woven into EFA efforts to raise educational quality	Use of sustainable development themes in basic education	Numbers of countries with sustainable development in basic education curricula
	Sustainable development a key indicator in EFA monitoring	Regular sustainable development monitoring in national and international EFA reports
► ESD-specific approaches increasingly adopted in learning situations of all kinds	Modelling of sustainable development learning processes and in formal and non-formal settings	Number of schools and non-formal programmes modelling sustainable development approaches
► ESD as part of educator training	Integration of sustainable development principles into teacher and educator/ facilitator training	Numbers of teacher training courses with integrated sustainable development theme; numbers of NFE educators/facilitators using sustainable development approaches
► High-quality materials and methodologies in ESD	Relevant, stimulating, practical print, electronic, audio-visual materials available in learning situations and in use	Numbers of materials, distribution and rates of adoption
	Learning/teaching methodologies reflecting sustainable development principles and modelling them	Numbers of schools adopting sustainable development principles; number of in-service teacher/ educator training courses
► Adequate management capacity to maintain ESD	ESD integrated into education management training (head teachers, inspectors, administrators, planners, etc)	Numbers of trained managers; numbers of educational institutions where sustainable development approaches are active

Figure 73: Evaluation based on quantitative DESD indicators[1613]

1613 This is the ambitious attempt of quantifying and verifying outcomes of *DESD* by adequate sets of indicators.

As part of its role as *DESD lead agency*, UNESCO will be tasked to set up a database or pool of meaningful indicators and tools for assessment at international level. Furthermore, expertise will be shared accordingly in a cross-cutting manner amongst other international monitoring initiatives.[1614]

3.4.5 Section IV: Programming the Decade

Both, providing financial and human *resources*, and developing a *timeline*, are fundamental elements of programming *DESD*.

As to *resources*, *DESD* is a global initiative shared between United Nations and UNESCO member states. Together with the member states it will bc implemented both within member states and internationally. In order to build international momentum effectively, followed by national and local action, it is important that both human and material resources are *"available for the appropriate (stakeholder) role at each level"*.[1615]

In general, UNESCO expects that financing *DESD "will be a matter of strengthening or re-orienting existing work using existing resources"*.[1616] In other words, *DESD* implementation depends mainly on synergy effects. It has been estimated that only *"modest (...) extra resources (...) will be required in order to ensure that the extra energy for promoting, facilitating and coordinating the Decade is available"*.[1617]

Table 32: Financing DESD implementation[1618]

Level	*Sources / Resources*	*Requirements*
national	• Regular budgets or other existing financing mechanisms; • Existing programmes and projects; • Extra resources.	• Adjustments of priorities towards *ESD*; • Additional personnel and finances for the *ESD Hub* and its work in awareness-raising.

See UNESCO (ed.) (2005c) (cf. *footnote 23* op. cit.), pp. 46–47.
1614 For example: EFA (*Education for All*) *Global Monitoring Report*, *UN Literacy Decade* (UNLD) monitoring initiatives, MDG (*Millennium Development Goals*) monitoring, etc.
Cf. UNESCO (ed.) (2005c) (cf. *footnote 23* op. cit.), pp. 46–47.
1615 See UNESCO (ed.) (2005c) (cf. *footnote 23* op. cit.), p. 48.
See *Table 32* in chapter IX 3.4.5 *Section IV: Programming the Decade* on page 329.
Cf. chapter VI 2.3 *Resources* on pages 133 et seqq.
1616 See UNESCO (ed.) (2005c) (cf. *footnote 23* op. cit.), p. 48.
1617 See UNESCO (ed.) (2005c) (cf. *footnote 23* op. cit.), p. 48.
1618 Cf. UNESCO (ed.) (2005c) (cf. *footnote 23* op. cit.), p. 48.

Level	*Sources / Resources*	*Requirements*
regional	• Existing programmes; • Exchange through university networks and *Education for All* (EFA) events; • Extra resources.	• Re-orientation towards *ESD*; • Additional resources for interaction in an *ESD Caucus* and for work in capacity-building.
international	• UNESCO: personnel and some financial support for *DESD* co-ordination, an inter-sectoral *ESD Task Force* and funding of *ESD*-related programmes; • Existing budgets and programmes; • Extra resources.	• Re-orientation towards *ESD*; • Additional resources for facilitating targeted interaction between stakeholders in the *Inter-Agency Committee for the DESD*.

As to *timeline*, *DESD* is scheduled over a ten-year period, subdivided into a first half (2005–2009), at the end of which is a *mid-term review*, and a second half (2010–2014), immediately followed by an *international conference*.[1619] The first half of the decade is treated in much greater detail than the second half, because: a) preparatory work has to be done at the launch of *DESD*; b) initiatives must have been implemented by the very beginning of *DESD*; and c) planning for the second half depends to a large extent on the outcomes of the first.[1620] At this stage of planning implementation, indications of time are genuinely set out, but are also to a certain extent provisional, particularly with regards to the second half of *DESD*.

In line with *DESD* objectives and strategies, the timeline follows the *five poles of activity:*

- Advocacy and vision-building;
- Partnerships and networks;
- Capacity-building and training;
- Research and innovation; and

1619 As proposed, an international conference at the beginning of 2015 aims to integrate data and reports from national and regional conferences, as well as the evaluation report on *DESD* as a whole.
Cf. UNESCO (ed.) (2005c) (cf. *footnote 23* op. cit.), p. 49; Witthaus, Michele; McCandless, Karen; Lambert, Rebecca (eds.) (2010): Tomorrow today. Supported by: Nicklin, Sean and Cornwell, Ben. Leicester, United Kingdom: Tudor Rose; UNESCO publishing.
See *Figure 74* in chapter IX 3.4.5 *Section IV: Programming the Decade* on page 332, and *Figure 75* in chapter IX 3.4.5 *Section IV: Programming the Decade* on page 332.

1620 Cf. UNESCO Education Sector (ed.) (March 2009) (cf. *footnote 1222* op. cit.), pp. 3, 18–19.

- Monitoring and evaluation.[1621]

Together with chronological indications they form a particular planning segment of *DESD* implementation.

	(2004)	2005		2006		2007		2008		2009	
Advocacy and vision-building	Launch DESD website; Slogan competition (young people)	International and national DESD launches									
		SD theme in Global EFA Week (April)	Development of media networking and plan for media coverage at national level								
	Develop and disseminate a calendar of DESD activities at all levels										
Partnership and networks		Establish national ESD Consultative Groups Governments host sub-national/ local stakeholder consultations Set up national ESD Hubs				National ESD Consultative Group	Sub-national/ local stakeholder consultations	National ESD Consultative Group	Sub-national/ local stakeholder consultations	National ESD Consultative Group	Sub-national/ local stakeholder consultations
			Establish regional ESD Caucuses				Regional ESD Caucuses		Regional ESD Caucuses		Regional ESD Caucuses
	(2004)	2005		2006		2007		2008		2009	
	Formation of Inter-Agency Committee on DESD		Inter-Agency Committee on DESD		Inter-Agency Committee on DESD		Inter-Agency Committee on DESD		Inter-Agency Committee on DESD		Inter-Agency Committee on DESD
	EFA HLG 4	CSD 13 EFA Working Group 6	EFA HLG 5	CSD 14 EFA Working Group 7	EFA HLG 6	CSD 15 EFA Working Group 8	EFA HLG 7	CSD 16 EFA Working Group 9	EFA HLG 8	CSD 17 EFA Working Group 10	EFA HLG 9
			International Experts' Consultation (prepare Intergovt Conf 2007)				Intergovernmental Conference (30 years after Tbilisi)				
Capacity-building and training	UNESCO leads regional/sub-regional workshops to build DESD awareness and region and country level commitment to planning of activities for DESD		Series of workshops – regional or national as negotiated between UNESCO and member states – on: communication and awareness-raising; planning management and evaluation; training and retraining of educators; tools for analysis; instructional content and materials; instructional methodologies (see Section 6.4)								
	UNESCO develops and disseminates guidelines and multi-media package to support national planning and launch of DESD programmes and activities										

1621 See UNESCO (ed.) (2005c) (cf. *footnote 23* op. cit.), p. 48.

	(2004)	2005	2006	2007	2008	2009
Research and Innovation		Baseline studies as basis for longitudinal impact assessment				
		Regional conferences on ESD research issues		launch of cooperative regional research projects		
		Develop and publish ESD scenarios				
Monitoring and evaluation		Indicator development at national and sub-national levels	Ongoing national monitoring with annual review meeting			
		Establishment of monitoring and data collection mechanisms at national level				
		UNESCO establishes indicators and a database to track DESD progress internationally				

Figure 74: Planned timeline for the first half of DESD (2005–2009)[1622]

	2010	2011	2012	2013	2014	(2015)
	Regional mid-term research conferences			Evaluation of DESD at national level		
	International DESD mid-term review				Evaluation of DESD at regional and international levels	End-of-Decade international conference

Figure 75: Planned timeline for the second half of DESD (2010–2014)[1623]

In the case of platforms and forums as decisive places of *DESD* implementation, UNESCO needs to establish an official and *"regular cycle of local, national, regional and international consultations".*[1624] Such groupings, each composed of sub-national and local stakeholders, and among them national *ESD Consultative Groups*, the *Regional ESD Caucus* or the *Inter-Agency Committee for the DESD*, will meet periodically throughout the year.

3.4.6 Launch

The *International Implementation Scheme* (IIS) on *DESD* is shaped by an institutional process of consultation.[1625] Permanent changes and adjustments have been made, and all relevant draft versions serve as meaningful and comprehen-

1622 The first half of *DESD* is mainly characterised by preparatory work, implementing work of initiatives, and further planning for the second half of *DESD*. See UNESCO (ed.) (2005c) (cf. *footnote 23* op. cit.), pp. 50–52.

1623 The second half of *DESD* is mainly characterised by reporting and evaluation. See UNESCO (ed.) (2005c) (cf. *footnote 23* op. cit.), p. 52; UNESCO Education Sector (ed.) (March 2009) (cf. *footnote 1223* op. cit.), p. 12.

1624 See UNESCO (ed.) (2005c) (cf. *footnote 23* op. cit.), p. 48.

1625 Cf. Combes, Bernard P. Y. (2009) (cf. *footnote 663* op. cit.).

sive sources for the versions which are ultimately adopted. Similarities between draft and officially adopted versions clearly outweigh the differences, even though such differences can be substantial.

As far as structure and volume are concerned, drafts are further-reaching, more detailed and descriptive. The officially adopted *International Implementation Scheme* (IIS) is shorter, more direct and stronger on strategic perspective.

As regards content, it is more advisable to point out major differences and changes than to list aspects which they have in common. The most striking fact that distinguishes the draft from the adopted version lies in its focal strategic role: whereas the draft versions are non-binding and more inclined towards recommendation in character, the adopted *International Implementation Scheme* (IIS) changes from a non-prescriptive into a normative document that exerts a binding force on its adherents.

Furthermore, the *International Implementation Scheme* (IIS) more expressly stresses the nature of the partnership approach of *DESD*. Coherence is strengthened through appropriate wording and the avoidance of doubling. With regard to levels of implementation, the terminology used is more precise. Instead of referring to a diffuse concept of local or sub-national level implementation, community-level implementation tends to be far more inclusive. Following the structure of national, regional and international implementation, community generally stands for *"those who share a common milieu and therefore face an interlocking set of challenges in sustainable development"*.[1626]

The *International Implementation Scheme* (IIS) renders *partnership* more precisely through an *integrated approach*[1627] of *strengthened implementation*,[1628] and, in particular, inter-connection and co-operation at all levels in the use of synergy effects. More precisely speaking:

- At national level, structures and terminology are simplified. A *national ESD taskforce* integrates both the *ESD Hub* and the national *ESD Consultative Group*. In addition, the concept of building *national plan(s)*[1629] for *DESD* is introduced;[1630]

1626 See UNESCO (ed.) (2005j) (cf. *footnote 44* op. cit.), p. 11.

1627 See UNESCO (ed.) (2005j) (cf. *footnote 44* op. cit.), p. 12.

1628 See Weiss, Edith Brown (2000): Engaging countries. Strengthening compliance with international environmental accords. Volume 1. paperback edition. Cambridge, Massachusetts: MIT Press, p. 512.

1629 See UNESCO (ed.) (2005j) (cf. *footnote 44* op. cit.), p. 12.

1630 See *Figure 76* in chapter IX 3.4.6 *Launch* on page 334.

Actors at national level	Working individually to:	Working together as an national ESD task force to:
Education ministry and other relevant ministries	▸ provide a national policy framework for ESD ▸ budget and mobilise resources ▸ support sub-national departments ▸ foster public awareness on ESD and SD	▸ debate and recommend ESD policy options which reflect local-level experience and challenges ▸ integrate ESD into EFA and UNLD planning in the context of the EFA forum ▸ provide a forum for exchange of experience, positive and negative, in ESD ▸ identify research issues in ESD and plan cooperative research projects ▸ identify capacity-building needs and the actor best placed to meet them ▸ develop relevant monitoring indicators for ESD
NGOs, NGO and civil society networks and alliances	▸ facilitate exchange and information sharing among their members about ESD practices and experiences	
Media groups and agencies	▸ integrate ESD and SD awareness building into media strategies	
Private sector companies and trade associations	▸ provide a forum to identify SD challenges they face, and identify necessary learning needs	

Figure 76: Strengthening partnerships among stakeholders at national-level[1631]

- At regional level, *cross-sectoral links*[1632] are fostered. In parallel with national-level implementation, a *regional ESD group* replaces the *regional ESD Caucus*. Regional strategies and individual representation are highly appreciated and welcome.[1633]

1631 This figure illustrates how *DESD* assignments are concisely attributed to single actors or stakeholder groups at national level.
See UNESCO (ed.) (2005j) (cf. *footnote 44* op. cit.), p. 12.
Cf. *Figure 68* in chapter IX 3.4.4 *Section III: Implementation and Evaluation* on page 317.

1632 See UNESCO (ed.) (2005j) (cf. *footnote 44* op. cit.), p. 12.

1633 Cf. Matsuura, Koïchiro (01/03/2005) (cf. *footnote 28* op. cit.), p. 3; Adomßent, Maik; Henze, Christa (eds.) (2007) (cf. *footnote 761* op. cit.), pp. 54 et seqq, 110 et seqq; UNESCO (ed.) (2007k) (cf. *footnote 4* op. cit.), p. 5; Gerner, Martin (14/09/2009) (cf. *footnote 407* op. cit.); UNESCO Education Sector (ed.) (March 2009) (cf. *footnote 1223* op. cit.), pp. 4 et seqq.
See *Figure 77* in chapter IX 3.4.6 *Launch* on page 335.

<table>
<tr><th>Actors at regional level</th><th>Working individually to:</th><th>Working together as a regional ESD group to:</th></tr>
<tr><td>National government representatives</td><td>(see national level)</td><td rowspan="7">▸ conduct regional consultations on priorities for DESD
▸ share policies, practices, knowledge and progress
▸ identify common challenges
▸ learn from diverse strategies
▸ forge consensus on regional challenges and action
▸ organise cross-national training and capacity-building</td></tr>
<tr><td>Regional intergovernmental organisations</td><td>▸ support national-level policy-making
▸ foster exchange of experience and information</td></tr>
<tr><td>Regional civil society and NGO networks, coalitions and alliances</td><td>▸ foster exchange and learning among member networks and organisations</td></tr>
<tr><td>Regional media groupings</td><td>▸ share media strategies for SD and ESD</td></tr>
<tr><td>Regional private sector associations</td><td>▸ promote cooperation of private sector with other actors in ESD</td></tr>
<tr><td>Regional representatives of international agencies</td><td>▸ learn and communicate common lessons from cross-national experience
▸ facilitate cross-national exchange on ESD</td></tr>
<tr><td>Regional representatives of bilateral cooperation</td><td>▸ assess ways to support national and regional ESD initiatives</td></tr>
</table>

Figure 77: Providing institutional opportunity for co-ordination at regional level[1634]

- International-level implementation, on the other hand, requires more specific *profiling* in terms of task-lists and network patterns of international actors in order to assist and advice *DESD*. Therefore, *effective* mechanisms of reporting must be established.[1635]

1634 This figure illustrates how *DESD* assignments concisely attributed to national actors or stakeholder groups are going to be pursued at regional level.
See UNESCO (ed.) (2005j) (cf. *footnote 44* op. cit.), p. 13.
Cf. *Figure 69* in chapter IX 3.4.4 *Section III: Implementation and Evaluation* on page 320.

1635 See *Figure 78* in chapter IX 3.4.6 *Launch* on page 336.

<table>
<tr><th>Actors at international level</th><th>Working individually to:</th><th>Working together in various forums to:</th></tr>
<tr><td>International Ad hoc Working Group</td><td>▶gather information on developments in ESD and emerging priorities
▶promoting DESD</td><td>▶advise UNESCO on developments and emerging priorities in ESD
▶assist UNESCO in forming partnerships and developing projects in support of DESD</td></tr>
<tr><td>Intergovernmental agencies (United Nations and others)</td><td>▶contribute to Inter-Agency Task Force
▶integrate ESD planning into relevant work plans and initiatives
▶participate in international and regional forums</td><td rowspan="4">▶keep ESD high on the CSD agenda
▶mobilize political will and strengthen mutual commitment, through CSD, or an Inter-Agency Task Force
▶integrate ESD into EFA agendas (Monitoring Report, High-Level and Working Groups)
▶foster global exchange of practice, policy and progress
▶organize international, regional and subregional capacity-building workshops, and conferences to advance DESD and ESD</td></tr>
<tr><td>UNESCO[2]
(DESD Lead Agency)</td><td>▶promotion and capacity-building for ESD and DESD within and across UNESCO sectors
▶advocacy and communication with international community
▶building partnerships and collective momentum</td></tr>
<tr><td>Civil society and NGO networks</td><td>▶promote interregional exchange and learning
▶inform members of ESD developments</td></tr>
<tr><td>Bilateral and multilateral development agencies</td><td>▶integrate ESD into programmes and budgets
▶promote research in ESD</td></tr>
</table>

Figure 78: Burden-sharing through detailed networks of co-operation at international level[1636]

In the case of *DESD* strategies, more emphasis is given to the objectives of *ownership* and *development* forming a now integral part of *research, development and innovation.*[1637]

1636 This figure illustrates how institutional responsibilities and synergies are distributed by sharing respective networks of co-operation at international level.
See UNESCO (ed.) (2005f) (cf. *footnote 37* op. cit.), p. 12; UNESCO (ed.) (2005j) (cf. *footnote 44* op. cit.), pp. 14–15.
Cf. *Figure 70* in chapter IX 3.4.4 *Section III: Implementation and Evaluation* on page 322.

1637 See *Figure 79* in chapter IX 3.4.6 *Launch* on page 337.

Strategy	Examples
Vision-Building and Advocacy	• Lobby to embed ESD in government policies and development plans. • Establish a need for ESD by promoting the benefits of ESD.
Consultation and Ownership	• Model transparency and inclusivity in conducting public participation events. • Open the DESD consultation processes to all interested organizations and individuals. • Identify roles and responsibilities for stakeholders.
Partnership and Networks	• Actively seek a wide range of stakeholders. • Identify existing advocates and work in unison. • Identify partners and networks in all four thrusts of ESD.
Capacity-building and Training	• Address professional development needs at all levels including leadership. • Build upon existing actors and expertise including NGOs, private sector, and civil society. • Link to ongoing local and national sustainability initiatives.
Research, Development and Innovation	• Develop ESD materials to fill curricular gaps and develop associated assessment instruments. • Create research and development agendas for all four thrusts of ESD. • Disseminate ESD research, development and innovative practices to practitioners.
Information & Communication Technologies	• Explore how sustainable development messages can be infused in games and popular culture through ICTs. • Use ICTs in training and in-service professional development activities. • Use ICTs to reach geographically isolated populations.
Monitoring and Evaluation	• Develop indicators to assess the impact of the DESD. • Gather baseline data and set up longitudinal studies. • Use data from EFA and other initiatives to track progress.

Figure 79: Profiling DESD strategies[1638]

UNESCO's leadership role is indicated more expressly:[1639] *DESD* is fully in line with UNESCO's international functions *"as (a) laboratory of ideas, standard-setter, clearing house, capacity-builder and promoter of international co-operation"*.[1640] The organisation claims its pro-active and inter-sectoral approach to be wholly suited to a role of strong leadership and co-ordination: *"UNESCO can and will play (its part) to ensure efficiency and success to the Decade"*.[1641]

It is noteworthy that the adopted *International Implementation Scheme* (IIS) contains no estimated outcome, no part concerning monitoring and evaluation, nor any proposition of chronology or scheduling. This may be the case in order to keep the aspects of monitoring and evaluation separate from issues of imple-

1638 The table exemplifies which and how *DESD* strategies are collocated with multi-level stakeholder assignments.
See UNESCO (ed.) (2005f) (cf. *footnote 37* op. cit.), p. 19; UNESCO (ed.) (2005j) (cf. *footnote 44* op. cit.), pp. 22–23.
Cf. *Figure 66* in chapter IX 3.4.3 *Section II: Stakeholders and Strategies* on page 312.
1639 Cf. UNESCO (ed.) (2005j) (cf. *footnote 44* op. cit.), pp. 15–16.
1640 See UNESCO (ed.) (2005j) (cf. *footnote 44* op. cit.), p. 15.
1641 See UNESCO (ed.) (2005j) (cf. *footnote 44* op. cit.), p. 15.
Cf. *Figure 81* in chapter IX 4.3 *Characteristics* on page 345.

mentation. Another possible explanation is that relevant aspects of outcomes and timelines are covered at different places in order to avoid stakeholders being officially bound or obliged.

Also in support of *DESD* a detailed *infrastructure* is proposed referring to the planning of resources, governance and leadership, as well as to procedures.[1642]

Infrastructure elements	**Examples**
Leadership	• Chair or Co-Chairs elected by the committee members or appointed by government. • Transparent decision-making processes. • Articulate leader with ESD experience.
Governance structures	• Bylaws and charters that are open to the public. • Democratic processes of governance. • Representation of the breadth of ESD.
Administrative support	• Office and equipment to support the staff. • Responsive to public needs. • Adequate staffing.
Human resources	• Balanced representation of environment, society, and economy. • Capable of influencing leaders, media, private sector, etc. • Sufficient staff to coordinate volunteers
Financial resources	• To hire paid staff. • For travel to engage partners and present a case for DESD. • To monitor progress and publish reports.
Material resources	• Access to Internet, DESD publications, etc. • Information on national and local sustainability issues. • Office equipped to accept paid staff and volunteers.
Operating procedures	• Clear mandate regarding the scope of the work. • Clear understanding of roles, rights and responsibilities. • Due process for partner disagreements.
Accountability	• Ensuring delivery of funded projects. • Solid fiscal accounting practices. • To partners and stakeholders.
Evaluation, tracking and reporting	• System for recording DESD activities. • Monitoring and evaluating the impact of DESD activities. • Liaison with national and international monitoring units.
Vision-building	• Input from a wide range of civil society. • Access to accurate sustainability issue research and information in all three spheres. • Address all four thrusts of ESD.
Engagement and retention	• Actively seek members from all sectors of civil society. • Celebrate and thank members for successes. • Manage volunteers to consider their available time in assigning realistic workloads.

Figure 80: Paving the way for DESD effectively and efficiently[1643]

As appendages, the *International Implementation Scheme* (IIS) provides detailed background references on *DESD*-related issues covering origins, key con-

1642 See *Figure 80* in chapter IX 3.4.6 *Launch* on page 338.

1643 *DESD* strategies are attributed to infrastructural elements complemented by potential examples of realisation.
See UNESCO (ed.) (2005f) (cf. *footnote 37* op. cit.), p. 20; UNESCO (ed.) (2005j) (cf. *footnote 44* op. cit.), pp. 23–24.
Cf. *Figure 60* in chapter IX 1.10 *Summary* on page 276.

cepts (such as quality education, *ESD* and its cross-cutting *thrusts*) as well as a refined and updated list of the key characteristics of *DESD*.[1644]

3.5 Summary

Consideration of the development of the *DESD International Implementation Scheme* (IIS) reveals a dynamic and interactive process over a period of roughly two years.[1645]

Table 33: Overview of development stages of DESD implementation

DESD International Implementation Scheme		
Draft versions	*Official versions*	*Framework*
October 2004[1646]		
January 2005[1647]		
	August 2005[1648]	
	October 2005[1649]	
		December 2006[1650]

The following guiding principles are critical in the matter of *DESD* implementation:

1. UNESCO clearly favours a *bottom-up* instead of *top-down* approach. This turns the hierarchical pyramid upside-down: *"Before addressing the national level, and higher levels, it is important therefore to place them in the context of sub-national, local initiative"*.[1651] *DESD* must first be locally-rooted in order to achieve global momentum.
2. UNESCO definitively commits itself to supporting *qualitative* instead of *quantitative* approaches. *"It is not the number and nature of coordinating and facilitating activities which will count in the end, but changing patterns of development and progress towards more sustainable models and im-*

1644 Cf. UNESCO (ed.) (2005j) (cf. *footnote 44* op. cit.), pp. 30–31.
1645 See *Table 33* in chapter VII 12.2 *UNESCO affiliation* on page 339.
1646 Cf. UNESCO (ed.) (2004c) (cf. *footnote 34* op. cit.).
1647 Cf. UNESCO (ed.) (2005c) (cf. *footnote 23* op. cit.).
1648 Cf. UNESCO (ed.) (2005f) (cf. *footnote 37* op. cit.).
1649 Cf. UNESCO (ed.) (2005j) (cf. *footnote 44* op. cit.).
1650 Cf. UNESCO (ed.) (2006f) (cf. *footnote 25* op. cit.).
1651 See UNESCO (ed.) (2005c) (cf. *footnote 23* op. cit.), p. 36.

provements in the quality of life."[1652] As far as monitoring and evaluation is concerned, a combination of both is intended.
3. UNESCO focuses on the *de-centralisation* of decision-making processes. Apart from basic strategic decisions on *DESD* most considerations are, in practice, left to the appropriate level and body.
4. UNESCO carefully aims at the *cross-sectoral* representation of society. Visibility is the key word for *DESD* as a holistic approach that also draws attention to marginalised groups.
5. Ultimately, *DESD* translates into the provision of meaningful *platforms* and the creation of powerful *partnerships* in support of sustainable development.

4 UNESCO Action plan

4.1 Objectives

Besides the leadership mandate of worldwide *DESD* implementation, UNESCO runs an original programme of action, too. The organisation thus acts both as a leading implementing body and programmatic implementer.[1653] In other words, UNESCO embodies a functional duality by carrying out this interrelated, *dual role*.

UNESCO's *genuine DESD* implementation initiative is expressed and defined in the *UNESCO Action plan*. Unlike global action plans,[1654] it is *"a result of in-house consultation (...) devised to guide the organisation's programmatic contribution to the (d)ecade"*.[1655] Considered a *working document*,[1656] this comprehensive and inter-sectoral plan outlines UNESCO's own programme with approved budget for the implementation of *DESD*.[1657] An action plan aims to

1652 See UNESCO (ed.) (2005c) (cf. *footnote 23* op. cit.), p. 36.

1653 Cf. UNESCO (ed.) (2007k) (cf. *footnote 4* op. cit.), p. 10.
Cf. *Figure 63* in chapter IX 2.3 *Summary* on page 289.

1654 For example: *Agenda 21* to the most prominent example in the field of sustainable development.
Cf. United Nations (ed.) (1993) (cf. *footnote 732* op. cit.).

1655 See Dhillon, Sam (2008) (cf. *footnote 609* op. cit.), p. 1.

1656 See UNESCO (ed.) (2007m) (cf. *footnote 216* op. cit.), p. 3; UNESCO (ed.) (2007k) (cf. *footnote 4* op. cit.), p. 15.
A *working document* refers to its development as being in a *state of flux*. Continuous change is due to the evolution of subsequent programmes and budgetary plans.
Cf. UNESCO (ed.) (2007m) (cf. *footnote 216* op. cit.), p. 4; UNESCO (ed.) (August 2007) (cf. *footnote 693* op. cit.), pp. 3 et seqq.

1657 Cf. UNESCO (ed.) (2006a) (cf. *footnote 616* op. cit.), p. 43; UNESCO (ed.) (2008a) (cf. *footnote 83* op. cit.), p. 190; UNESCO (ed.) (2009a) (cf. *footnote 618* op. cit.), pp. 45, 166.

guide the organisation's efforts in the *pro-active*[1658] and *concerted*[1659] implementation of initiatives. It covers detailed biennium goals with which UNESCO places itself strategically as an example of best-practice intended to generate *spillover effects*.

4.2 Drafting history

Dealing with *DESD*-related issues in an inter-sectoral way is a crucial element of developing the *UNESCO Action plan.*[1660] *166 EX/Decision 3.6.1*[1661] of 14 May 2003 marks one of the first initiatives to incorporate inter-sectoral co-operation into *DESD*. Referring initially to *"the elaboration of an education programme for the sustainable management of freshwater resources"*, the UNESCO Executive Board calls for improved co-operation with respect to the implementation of inter-sectoral policies (and in this particular case formal and non-formal water education).[1662] Accordingly, *"all [...] human and financial resources required for the realisation of such inter-sectoral cooperation (will have to be applied effectively), including mobilising the expanded participation of the international community and civil society and of the public and private sectors in Member States in order to obtain the human and financial resources required to achieve the desired impact at the global level"*.[1663]

In line with the launch of *DESD*, *171 EX/Decisions*[1664] of 25 May 2005 encourages UNESCO *"to establish a clear and focused plan based on a holistic and interdisciplinary approach to UNESCO's (genuine) involvement (...) to specify the precise contributions (...) to the implementation of the Decade [...]"*.[1665]

On 29 July 2005 the *Inter-sectoral Working Group* (IWG) on *ESD* was installed by a blue note of the Director-General (*DG/Note/05/34*).[1666]

1658 Cf. UNESCO (ed.) (2002b) (cf. *footnote 80* op. cit.); Kiss, Alexandre (2003) (cf. *footnote 297* op. cit.), pp. 237–238; UNESCO (ed.) (2005i) (cf. *footnote 216* op. cit.), p. 2; Fridtjof Nansens Institutt / The Fridtjof Nansens Institute (ed.) (2005) (cf. *footnote 198* op. cit.), pp. 1–2.

1659 See UNESCO (ed.) (2007j) (cf. *footnote 39* op. cit.), p. 17.

1660 See *Table 34* in chapter VII 12.2 *UNESCO affiliation* on page 343.

1661 Cf. UNESCO (ed.) (2003a): Decisions adopted by the Executive Board at its 166th session. Executive Board. 166 EX/Decisions. Paris: UNESCO publishing; UNESCO (ed.) (2006e) (cf. *footnote 777* op. cit.), p. 3.

1662 I.e. The UNESCO-IHE Institute for Water Education.
Cf. UNESCO (ed.) (2008a) (cf. *footnote 83* op. cit.).

1663 See UNESCO (ed.) (2003a) (cf. *footnote 1661* op. cit.), p. 34.

1664 Cf. UNESCO (ed.) (2005b) (cf. *footnote 1422* op. cit.).

1665 Cf. No. 9 UNESCO (ed.) (2005b) (cf. *footnote 1422* op. cit.), p. 14.

1666 Cf. UNESCO (ed.) (2007k) (cf. *footnote 4* op. cit.), p. 15.

At its 172nd session on 19 August 2005 the UNESCO Executive Board outlined the organisation's role *"as a laboratory of ideas, standard-setter, clearing-house, capacity-builder and promoter of international co-operation".*[1667] Document *172 EX/INF.4*[1668] clearly indicates the inter-sectoral approach: *"(A)ll of the parts of the Organisation will work together in an inter-sectoral manner so that it plays the strong leadership and co-ordination role at international level [...]".*[1669]

Once a consensus on the basic element of inter-sectoral co-operation was reached, *"a fully-fledged UNESCO Action plan"*[1670] was well under way. In order to develop a first draft of a plan of action, all UNESCO sectors were asked for substantial contributions. The importance of setting up a proprietary UNESCO-wide programme of action on *DESD* was expressly outlined by document *174 EX/INF.13*[1671] on 5 April 2006:

- To provide *"the substantive and operational framework for reinforcing and broadening the inter-sectoral cooperation"*;[1672] and
- To consider *DESD*-related issues as *"an inter-sectoral pursuit".*[1673]

Shortly after, as a result of *"intensive inter-sectoral collaboration and extensive consultative process between all the UNESCO programme sectors, bureaux, regional, cluster and national offices and institutes"*,[1674] the final draft of the *UNESCO Action plan* was submitted to the *Inter-sectoral Working Group* (IWG) on 30 April 2006.

The final draft of *UNESCO Action plan* was released in January 2007.[1675] It was approved by the *Inter-sectoral Working Group* (IWG) in March 2007.[1676]

On 16 April 2007 UNESCO Executive Board referring to *176 EX/5 Add.2*[1677] appreciated efforts made by both the Culture Sector and Education Sector to finalise the *UNESCO Action plan for DESD.*

In addition to a framework of global monitoring and evaluation to be realised by a *DESD Monitoring and Evaluation Expert Group* (MEEG),[1678] nine

1667 See UNESCO (ed.) (2005i) (cf. *footnote 216* op. cit.), p. 2.
1668 Cf. UNESCO (ed.) (2005i) (cf. *footnote 216* op. cit.).
1669 Cf. UNESCO (ed.) (2005i) (cf. *footnote 216* op. cit.), p. 3. Cf. *Figure 81* in chapter IX 4.3 *Characteristics* on page 345.
1670 See UNESCO (ed.) (2006e) (cf. *footnote 777* op. cit.), p. 3.
1671 Cf. UNESCO (ed.) (2006e) (cf. *footnote 777* op. cit.).
1672 See UNESCO (ed.) (2006e) (cf. *footnote 777* op. cit.), p. 3.
1673 See UNESCO (ed.) (2006e) (cf. *footnote 777* op. cit.), p. 4.
1674 See UNESCO (ed.) (2007f) (cf. *footnote 427* op. cit.), p. 2.
1675 Cf. UNESCO (ed.) (2007m) (cf. *footnote 216* op. cit.).
1676 Cf. UNESCO (ed.) (August 2007) (cf. *footnote 693* op. cit.), p. 3.
1677 Cf. UNESCO (ed.) (2007j) (cf. *footnote 39* op. cit.), p. 4.
1678 See UNESCO (ed.) (August 2007) (cf. *footnote 693* op. cit.), p. 4.

thematic programmes were proposed as focal issues of the *UNESCO Action plan* on 3 August 2007 by *177 EX/9 Annex III*:[1679]

1. International leadership and advocacy of the *DESD*;
2. Integrating *ESD* into basic education;
3. Re-orienting general secondary education for *ESD*;
4. Integrating *ESD* into *Technical and Vocational Education and Training* (TVET);
5. Integrating *ESD* into higher education;[1680]
6. Teacher education for *ESD*;
7. Mainstreaming cultural diversity and intercultural dialogue in *ESD*;
8. Education for sustainable water management; and
9. Education for sustainable ecosystems and livelihoods.

Document *34 C/5*[1681] marks the technical and budgetary approval of *UNESCO Action plan for DESD* in March 2008. It provides a biennial programme and budget (2008–2009)[1682] as part of the organisation's medium-term strategy (2008–2013) forwarded for consideration by the member states.[1683] *"Education for sustainable development"* is explicitly listed as an inter-sectoral platform *"with inputs from all sectors"*.[1684]

Table 34: UNESCO Action plan for DESD – drafting timeline

Date	*Document*	*Key Elements*
14 May 2003	166 EX/Decision 3.6.1	Integrating inter-sectoral co-operation into *DESD*-related issues
25 May 2005	171 EX/Decisions	Demand for focused plan pointing out UNESCO's own contributions to *DESD*
29 July 2005	DG/Note/05/34	Installation of Inter-sectoral Working Group (IWG)
19 August 2005	172 EX/INF.4	Executive Board outlines UNESCO's role and emphasises inter-sectoral approaches

1679 Cf. UNESCO (ed.) (August 2007) (cf. *footnote 693* op. cit.), p. 3; UNESCO (ed.) (2007k) (cf. *footnote 4* op. cit.), p. 15; UNESCO (ed.) (2007g): Highlights on DESD Progress to Date. April 2007. Paris: UNESCO publishing, p. 3.
See *Table 35* in chapterIX 4.3 *Characteristics* on page 353.

1680 Cf. Altner, Günter; Michelsen, Gerd (eds.) (2005) (cf. *footnote 851* op. cit.); Ginkel, Hans van (2010) (cf. *footnote 806* op. cit.), p. 30.

1681 Cf. UNESCO (ed.) (2008a) (cf. *footnote 83* op. cit.).

1682 So called *biennial work plans*.
Cf. UNESCO (ed.) (2006h) (cf. *footnote 711* op. cit.), p. 2.

1683 Cf. UNESCO (ed.) (2008a) (cf. *footnote 83* op. cit.), p. 195; UNESCO (ed.) (2006h) (cf. *footnote 711* op. cit.), p. 2.

1684 See No. 3, paragraph 08004 UNESCO (ed.) (2008a) (cf. *footnote 83* op. cit.), p. 195.

Date	*Document*	*Key Elements*
5 April 2006	174 EX/INF.13	Designing UNESCO Action plan for *DESD*
30 April 2006	Final draft version of UNESCO Action plan for *DESD*	Submission to the Inter-sectoral Working Group (IWG)
January 2007	Final draft version of UNESCO Action plan for *DESD*	Official release / publication
March 2007	Final draft version of UNESCO Action plan for *DESD*	Approval by Inter-sectoral Working Group (IWG)
16 April 2007	176 EX/5 Add.2	Executive Board's appreciation of inter-sectoral designing UNESCO Action plan
3 August 2007	177 EX/9 Annex III	Integrating concepts of global monitoring and evaluation; establishing focal issues
March 2008	34 C/5	Final approval (as part of UNESCO's medium-term strategy)

4.3 Characteristics

Developing the *UNESCO Action plan for DESD* involved contributions from all UNESCO sectors from the very beginning. *"(It) is a result of intensive inter-sectoral collaboration and extensive consultative process between all the UNESCO programme sectors, bureaux, regional, cluster and national offices and institutes."*[1685] The process of coming into being may be described as inter-sectoral and dynamic. UNESCO's Education Sector is responsible for co-ordinating all inter-connected UNESCO activities, such as thematic programmes and their respective projects. The *Inter-sectoral Working Group on ESD* (IWG) provides active support through guidance accordingly.[1686]

1685 See UNESCO (ed.) (2006h) (cf. *footnote 711* op. cit.), p. 2.
1686 Cf. UNESCO (ed.) (2008a) (cf. *footnote 83* op. cit.), p. 199.
See *Figure 81* in chapter IX 4.3 *Characteristics* on page 345.

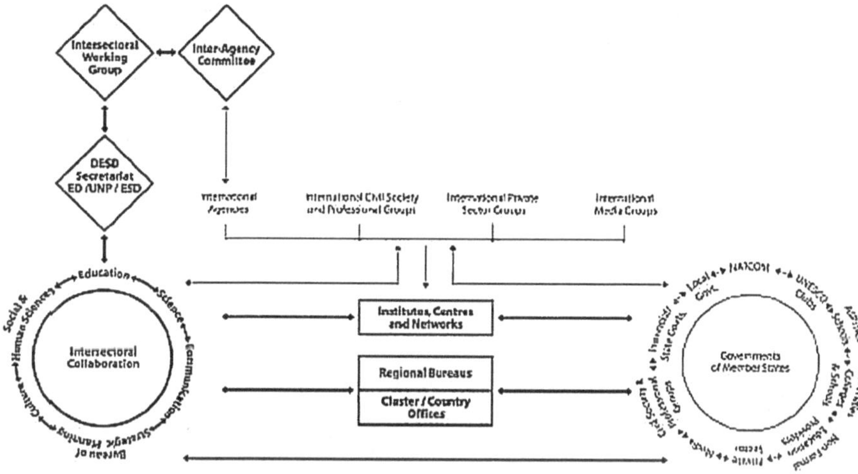

Figure 81: The inter-sectoral basis of the DESD Action plan for DESD[1687]

A comprehensive profile of the *UNESCO Action plan* may be obtained from a catalogue of criteria. These are its elements:[1688]

1687 See UNESCO (ed.) (2007m) (cf. *footnote 216* op. cit.), p. 6.
The diagram shows the dynamics of: a) *ESD*-related activities of member states; b) *in-house* inter-sectoral collaboration between UNESCO sectors in *ESD*-related issues; c) functional linkages between UNESCO sectors and *ESD*-co-ordinating bodies; d) intermediary relations between member states and UNESCO; e) *Inter-sectoral Working Group* (IWG) tasked with *"the scope, management and review of all programmes and activities conducted by UNESCO"* during *DESD*; f) *ED/UNP/ESD* providing the *DESD Secretariat "for the day-to-day co-ordination of UNESCO's DESD programmes and activities"*; g) *Inter-Agency Committee* (IAC) convened and chaired by UNESCO in order to mobilise *"funds and resources to coordinate strategic interventions at all levels"*; h) catalysing partnerships between UNESCO, private sector groups, media and non-governmental organisations in favour of multi-level *DESD* implementation; and i) *National Commissions for UNESCO, UNESCO's Regional, Country and Cluster Offices* and *UNESCO Institutes, Centres and Networks* catalysing member states' commitment *and "assisting them with processes of policy re-orientation, capacity-building (and DESD funding)".*
Cf. UNESCO (ed.) (2007m) (cf. *footnote 216* op. cit.), p. 5; UNESCO (ed.) (2007f) (cf. *footnote 427* op. cit.), p. 2; Fien, John (2010) (cf. *footnote 817* op. cit.).
Cf. *Figure 25* in chapter VI 2.3.2 *Financing* on page 139.

1688 Cf. UNESCO (ed.) (2006e) (cf. *footnote 777* op. cit.), pp. 3–4.
See *Figure 82* in chapter IX 4.3 *Characteristics* on page 348.

- Focusing on a clear and agreed vision and mission directed towards capacity development and integration of values, principles and content of sustainable development into processes of learning and teaching;[1689]
- Defining specific key audiences or target groups of *ESD*, namely *"senior education decision-makers and planners in formal and non-formal education, curriculum and syllabus development officers, teacher education institutions, and providers of continuing professional development and adult and non-formal learning opportunities"*;[1690]
- Specifying *thrusts* of *Education for Sustainable Development* (*ESD*) in order to activate resources and broaden participation in economic, environmental, social and cultural contexts;
- Envisaging output orientation through *results-based management*[1691] linked to objectives, targets and expected outcomes[1692] to be achieved by member states through this *Action Plan*;[1693]
- Translating objectives and thrusts of the *DESD International Implementation Scheme* (IIS) into manageable targets and sub-objectives;
- Publishing examples of good practice;
- Making use of guiding principles for the development, implementation and communication of programmes under the *Action plan*;
- Communicating topical relevance through particular *thematic programmes* which enable UNESCO to create the *"enabling environment and capacity-building for member states"*[1694] and other stakeholders to achieve *DESD*-related objectives;[1695]
- Installing *milestones* or *areas of focus* specified at biennial level;[1696]
- Providing appropriate organisational structures to catalyse inter-sectoral co-ordination and collaboration in line with the *One-UNESCO approach*;[1697]

1689 Cf. UNESCO (ed.) (2008a) (cf. *footnote 83* op. cit.), p. 199.

1690 See UNESCO (ed.) (2008a) (cf. *footnote 83* op. cit.), p. 199.

1691 See UNESCO (ed.) (2007m) (cf. *footnote 216* op. cit.), p. 5.

1692 For example, expected *ESD*-outcomes of the 2008–2009 biennium are:
Public policies, plans and programmes in support of *ESD* will have to be developed;
Capacities of member states and stakeholders will have to be enhanced in order to integrate sustainable development issues and practices into all types and levels of education, with a view to improving its quality; and
Knowledge on *ESD* will have to be enhanced through the exchange of innovative experiences, the documentation and dissemination of lessons learned.
Cf. Dhillon, Sam (2008) (cf. *footnote 609* op. cit.), p. 2.

1693 Cf. UNESCO (ed.) (2008a) (cf. *footnote 83* op. cit.), p. 200.

1694 See UNESCO (ed.) (2007m) (cf. *footnote 216* op. cit.), p. 4.

1695 Cf. UNESCO (ed.) (August 2007) (cf. *footnote 693* op. cit.), pp. 12–16.

1696 Cf. UNESCO (ed.) (August 2007) (cf. *footnote 693* op. cit.), pp. 12–16.

1697 See UNESCO (ed.) (2007f) (cf. *footnote 427* op. cit.), p. 2.

- Making substantive use of an *inter-sectoral platform*[1698] that is almost independent in terms of the *"strategies and objectives to be pursued"*, *"expected results"*, *"efforts by the concerned sectors"* as well as *"indicative financial allocations identified for the (respective) platforms"*;[1699]
- Guiding *DESD*-networks of partners to participate in and to support thematic programmes which may *"harness and improve existing mechanisms and frameworks in order to generate increased inter-sectoral synergies and enhanced impact"*;[1700]
- Enabling research and impact analysis that provides the knowledge upon which continued programme planning can take place; and lastly
- Monitoring and evaluating *DESD qua* continuous and institutionalised process oriented towards a mid-term review in 2009–2010 and a final evaluation in 2014.[1701]

1698 See UNESCO (ed.) (2008f) (cf. *footnote 771* op. cit.), pp. 3–5.

1699 See UNESCO (ed.) (2008a) (cf. *footnote 83* op. cit.), p. 195.
For instance, twelve major inter-sectoral platforms are approved for implementation throughout the 2008–2009 biennium, such as the *ESD Inter-sectoral Platform* with input required from all UNESCO sectors.
See Dhillon, Sam (2008) (cf. *footnote 609* op. cit.), p. 2.
Cf. No. 3, paragraph 08004 UNESCO (ed.) (2008a) (cf. *footnote 83* op. cit.), p. 195.

1700 See Dhillon, Sam (2008) (cf. *footnote 609* op. cit.), p. 1.

1701 Cf. UNESCO (ed.) (August 2007) (cf. *footnote 693* op. cit.), pp. 17–18; Gerner, Martin (30/07/2009) (cf. *footnote 407* op. cit.).

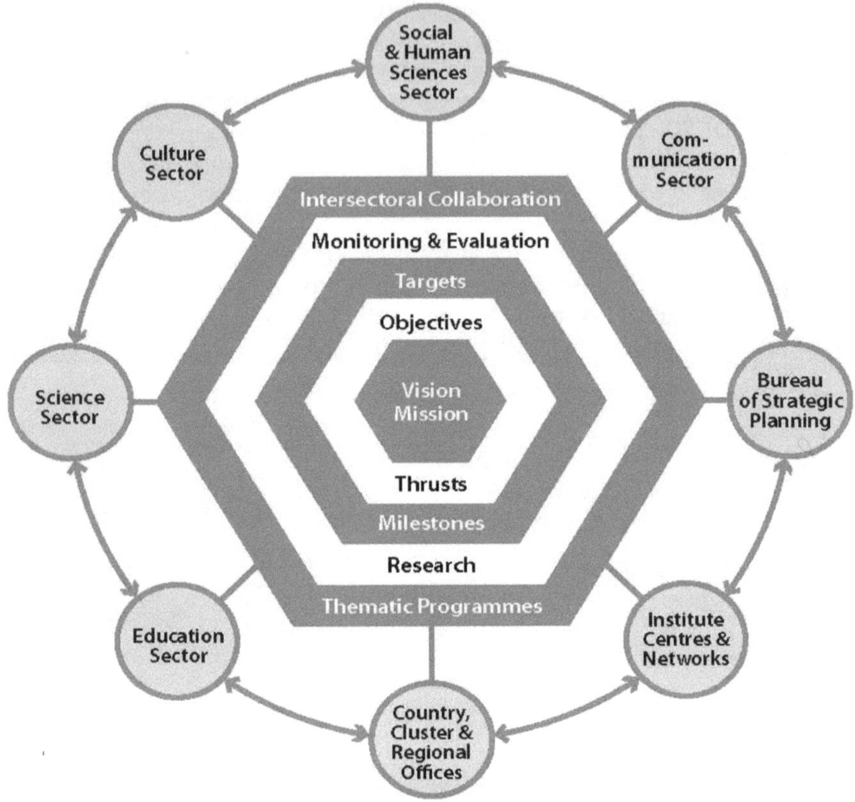

Figure 82: Critical elements of UNESCO Action plan for DESD[1702]

In fact, the general *vision* of *DESD* corresponds to the *UNESCO Action plan*: *"The overall goal of DESD is to integrate the values inherent in sustainable development into all aspects of learning in order to encourage changes in behaviour that allow for a more sustainable, economically viable and just society for all, a world where everyone has the opportunity to benefit from education and learn the values, behaviour and lifestyles required for a sustainable future and for positive societal transformation".*[1703]

1702 Emphasising the role of UNESCO as substantial implementer, the *UNESCO Action plan for DESD* integrates both institutional structures and contents in favour of *DESD* and in line with the organisation's functional capacities.
See UNESCO (ed.) (2007m) (cf. *footnote 216* op. cit.), p. 7; UNESCO (ed.) (2007k) (cf. *footnote 4* op. cit.), p. 14.

1703 See UNESCO (ed.) (2007m) (cf. *footnote 216* op. cit.), p. 7.
Cf. UNESCO (ed.) (2005i) (cf. *footnote 216* op. cit.), p. 2.

The *mission* of the *UNESCO Action Plan* is *"(t)o create the enabling environment and capacity for Member States and other stakeholders to successfully play their roles in working towards the vision and objectives of the DESD"*.[1704]

Given that the *UNESCO Action plan* is consistently installed in line with the *International Implementation Scheme* (IIS), *thrusts* do equally apply where appropriate.[1705]

What applies to domains or thrusts of *DESD* may also be referred to as *DESD objectives*: those of the *UNESCO Action plan* go hand in hand with those of the *International Implementation Scheme* (IIS):[1706]

1. Facilitating networking, linkages, exchange and interaction among stakeholders in *ESD*;
2. Fostering an increased quality of teaching and learning in education for sustainable development;
3. Helping countries to make progress towards and attain the *Millennium Development Goals* (MDG) through efforts in *ESD*; and
4. Providing countries with new opportunities to incorporate *ESD* into efforts towards reform in education.

The underlying *principles* of the *UNESCO Action plan* can be summarised as follows:[1707]

- Stressing the nature of *DESD* as a campaign for *processes of* education and capacity-building which promote sustainable development and not for sustainable development *per se*;
- Aligning all *DESD*-related educational programmes with implementation provisions of the 2002 *World Summit on Sustainable Development* (WSSD) in Johannesburg;[1708]
- Keeping a balanced focus of *DESD*-related programmes, activities and initiatives between the dimensions concerned: economy, society, environment and culture;
- Creating favourable momentum for member states' *own DESD* implementation strategies through an enabling environment and through capacity-building;
- Positioning *DESD*-related activities for results and evaluation at national, regional and international levels;

Cf. chapter VII 1 *Vision* on page 149.

1704 See UNESCO (ed.) (2007m) (cf. *footnote 216* op. cit.), p. 7.

1705 Cf. domains or thrusts of *DESD* in chapter VII 10 *Thrusts* on page 166.

1706 Cf. UNESCO (ed.) (2007m) (cf. *footnote 216* op. cit.), p. 8; Combes, Bernard P. Y. (2009) (cf. *footnote 663* op. cit.), p. 216.

1707 Cf. UNESCO (ed.) (2007m) (cf. *footnote 216* op. cit.), p. 8.

1708 Cf. United Nations (ed.) (2002a) (cf. *footnote 853* op. cit.).

- Promoting a broad-based, multi-level and participatory platform of stakeholders, including member states, civil society, private sector, the media and professional educational associations;[1709]
- Working in accordance with a co-ordinated inter-sectoral *DESD* approach across UNESCO;
- Following a *One-UNESCO approach*[1710] relying on UNESCO institutions, such as UNESCO sectors, divisions and sections, research institutes and centres, and regional, cluster and country offices as resourceful contributors to the implementation of *DESD* and the *Action Plan*;[1711]
- Subsuming *DESD*-related activities under co-ordinated thematic programmes of the *UNESCO Action plan* in order to create high involvement in accordance with areas of responsibilities and expertise;
- Fostering the autonomous, flexible and needs-based solutions of implementing the *UNESCO Action plan* by UNESCO sectors, divisions and sections, research institutes and centres, and regional, cluster and country offices in relation to the different thematic programmes;
- Embedding inter-sectoral and inter-office programmes and activities through strong and co-ordinated management processes;
- Developing a unanimous understanding of the essentials of *DESD*;
- Strengthening both external and internal communications;
- Sharing of experiences and good-practice examples; and
- Reinforcing inter-sectoral collaboration through beneficial organisational structures and budget planning processes.

Strategic objectives are directed to achieve a specific purpose. With regard to the *UNESCO Action plan* they provide focus and programmatic drive.

The four strategic targets to be achieved are to establish *"(a)n enabling environment and capacity-building opportunities available for all Member States:*

a) (T)o develop policies and plans for achieving a high quality of education provision and outcomes by integrating ESD principles and priorities in all sectors and levels of education in contextually relevant ways;

1709 Cf. UNESCO; International Association of Universities (IAU); COPERNICUS-CAMPUS; Association of University Leaders for a Sustainable Future (ULSF) (2002) (cf. *footnote 806* op. cit.); UNESCO; International Association of Universities (IAU); COPERNICUS-CAMPUS; Association of University Leaders for a Sustainable Future (ULSF) (2004) (cf. *footnote 806* op. cit.), p. 1; Ginkel, Hans van (2010) (cf. *footnote 806* op. cit.), pp. 30–31; Fien, John (2010) (cf. *footnote 817* op. cit.).

1710 See UNESCO (ed.) (2007f) (cf. *footnote 427* op. cit.), p. 2; UNESCO (ed.) (2007m) (cf. *footnote 216* op. cit.), p. 8.

1711 Cf. Combes, Bernard P. Y. (2009) (cf. *footnote 663* op. cit.), p. 218; Gerner, Martin (14/09/2009) (cf. *footnote 407* op. cit.).

b) (T)o integrate educational processes as key tools in strategies for sustainable development (especially for attaining and exceeding the (Millennium Development Goals) MDG;

c) (T)o support educational institutions, the media, business and industry and civil society groups in the use of education to promote widespread awareness and understanding of sustainable development issues and priorities; (and)

d) (T)o integrate sustainable development issues and priorities into policies and programmes for workforce development across schools, (technical and vocational education and training) TVET, higher education and lifelong learning".[1712]

Organised at biennial intervals, *outcome estimates* are important in two ways: firstly because expected outcomes determine the *"work plans (of the Action plan) by progressively developing the targeted elements"*;[1713] and secondly because well-structured outcome analysis eventually facilitates the means of monitoring and evaluation.[1714]

1712 See UNESCO (ed.) (2007m) (cf. *footnote 216* op. cit.), p. 9.

1713 See UNESCO (ed.) (2007m) (cf. *footnote 216* op. cit.), p. 9.

1714 See *Figure 83* in chapter IX 4.3 *Characteristics* on page 352.

Biennium	Key actions	Expected outcomes	Expected results
2006–07	Review and planning	The scoping and development of detailed plans for the Thematic Programme as part of planning the 2008-2013 Medium-Term Strategy and 34/C5	Thematic Programme plan: • Approved by Intersectoral Working Group, and • Integrated into 2008-2013 Medium-Term Strategy and 34/C5
2008–09 (34/C5)	"Research-Policy Dialogue": • document and analyse case studies of good practice and develop guidelines from them • advocacy and institutional capacity development with senior decision-makers in all countries • Mid-Decade Review	Review, development and dissemination of case studies of innovative and effective practice related to the theme	• Regional and/or International Experts' Meeting(s) held • Meta-analysis completed • Book of case studies published • Guidelines and Briefing Papers published
		Building commitment and capacity of senior decision-makers to the theme	• Advocacy and capacity-building materials for senior decision makers prepared • Delivery of advocacy and capacity-building activities in each region
2010–11 (35/C5)	Policy review and reorientation - development of guidelines and capacity-building materials Capacity-building and demonstration projects in 5-8 countries in each region	Policy review and reorientation for ESD related to the theme	• Guidelines and capacity-building materials to support policy review and reorientation prepared • Delivery of guidelines and capacity-building activities in each region • Demonstration Projects conducted in each region
		Capacity-building for planners and educators on the theme	• Capacity-building activities prepared for planners and educators • Delivery of capacity-building activities for planners and educators in each region • Demonstration Projects conducted in each region
		Consolidating and widening innovative programmes and practice around the theme	• Delivery of capacity-building activities in each region • Demonstration Projects conducted in each region
2012–13 (36/C5)	Scaling up – up to 5-8 more countries in each region	Extending and scaling-up the Thematic Programme to other countries	• Delivery of capacity-building activities in each region • New projects conducted in each region
2014 (37/C5)	End-of-Decade Review	Review and evaluation of outcomes related to the theme.	• Regional evaluations and international synthesis completed • Results of synthesis integrated into overall evaluation of DESD

Figure 83: Expected biennial outcomes of UNESCO Action plan for DESD[1715]

Thematic programmes are long-term inter-sectoral strategies that constitute *"a suite of interconnected projects and activities that seek to promote all relevant aspects of an enabling environment and capacity-building for member states"*.[1716] These programmes are related to a particular facet of DESD, be that a specific aspect, objective, *thrust* (dimension) or topic. They are strategically designed, planned and run primarily by a designated UNESCO programme sector, division or section. In addition, these institutional bodies are supported by other offices and institutions as contributing partners in accordance with their own focal issues.

At first, nine focal issues are regarded as *thematic programmes*. This list is not exhaustive, and further aspects may be added as thematic programmes as *DESD* advances. They are not based upon project or topic areas, as one might assume, but upon organisational units of UNESCO headed by team leaders.[1717]

1715 Targets and expected outcomes of *DESD* are divided into small (biennial) sections primarily in order to ensure and facilitate evaluation.
See UNESCO (ed.) (2007m) (cf. *footnote 216* op. cit.), p. 12.
Cf. *Figure 73* in chapter IX 3.4.4 *Section III: Implementation and Evaluation* on page 328.

1716 See UNESCO (ed.) (2007m) (cf. *footnote 216* op. cit.), p. 10.

1717 Cf. UNESCO (ed.) (2008f) (cf. *footnote 771* op. cit.), p. 5.

The reason for this is to profit effectively from already existing resources, long-termed focal issues and programmes or organisational structures.[1718]

Proposed as an integral part of the *UNESCO Action plan*, these are the current thematic programmes including the relevant UNESCO bodies held responsible for:[1719]

Table 35: UNESCO in-house thematic programmes and responsibilities[1720]

Thematic programme	*UNESCO responsibility*
International Leadership and Advocacy of the *DESD*	*United Nations Decade of Education for Sustainable Development* (ED/*DESD*) secretariat
Integrating *ESD* into Basic Education	*Division for the Promotion of Basic Education* (ED/BAS)
Re-orienting General Secondary Education for *ESD*	*Division for the Promotion of Basic Education* (ED/BAS)
Integrating *ESD* into *Technical and Vocational Education and Training* (TVET)	*International Centre for Technical and Vocational Education and Training* (UNESCO/UNEVOC)
Integrating *ESD* into Higher Education	*Division of Higher Education* (ED/HED)
Teacher Education for *ESD* (ED/HED)	*Division of Higher Education* (ED/HED)
Mainstreaming Cultural Diversity and Intercultural Dialogue through *ESD*	Culture Sector
Education for Sustainable Water Management	*Division of Water Sciences* (Science Sector/HYD)
Education for Sustainable Ecosystems and Livelihoods	*Inter-governmental Oceanographic Commission Electronic Scanning Sensor+ Social and Human Sciences Sector / Management of Social Transformations Programme* (Science Sector / ESS+SHS / MOST)

Integrating member state commitment and broad stakeholder participation into the *UNESCO Action plan* programmes requires catalytic processes or *mechanisms* of co-ordination. It is ultimately the relevant team leaders who have full *"leadership and management responsibility"*[1721] on each single thematic

1718 *"Existing areas which (still) focus on different aspects of ESD are seen as important contributors (...) and need to be integrated (...) to the extent that resources allow."* See UNESCO (ed.) (2007m) (cf. *footnote 216* op. cit.), p. 10.

1719 Cf. UNESCO (ed.) (2007m) (cf. *footnote 216* op. cit.), p. 10; UNESCO (ed.) (August 2007) (cf. *footnote 693* op. cit.), pp. 12–16.
See *Table 35* in chapter IX 4.3 *Characteristics* on page 353.

1720 Cf. *Figure 82* in chapter IX 4.3 *Characteristics* on page 348.

1721 See UNESCO (ed.) (2007m) (cf. *footnote 216* op. cit.), p. 10.

programme executed under the *UNESCO Action plan*. This suggests that UNESCO has the final say on partners, both in UNESCO and in international agencies, and on whatever substantial contributions they make. Each thematic programme section is therefore requested *"to develop a coordinated approach (...) needed for attaining the objectives of the DESD in the particular thematic area"*.[1722]

Prospective *partners* in co-operation and inter-sectoral collaboration are proposed according to the scope of their work. The first and foremost criterion is their compatibility with the relevant focal issues or thematic programmes of the *Action plan*.

Perceived to be a fundamental component of all thematic programmes, *research* is considered to be an indispensable resource base *"for providing the knowledge needed to plan and implement programmes effectively"*.[1723] Research ought preferably to meet the requirements of being both useful and applicable in a direct way. Relevant fields of *DESD*-related investigation are, for instance:[1724]

- Developing strategies for inter-sectoral and international collaboration in processes of educational change;
- Examining changes in the ways in which education is conceptualised and practised in different parts of the world;
- Elaborating on factors contributing to different interpretations and practices of *ESD* in different regions of the world;
- Commenting on universal strategies of establishing common understanding of *ESD*;
- Communicating the core dimensions of *ESD* in different cultural contexts;
- Evaluating the effectiveness of capacity-building and training on the subject of *ESD*; and
- Analysing effects of implementing innovative *ESD* practices in different educational settings.

In order to have information available on time, research tasks are scheduled in alignment with the biennial cycles of outcome analysis.[1725] In consequence, research is considered to be a dynamic instrument appropriate for influencing *"different phases in the implementation of the Action Plan across (DESD)"*.[1726]

1722 See UNESCO (ed.) (2007m) (cf. *footnote 216* op. cit.), p. 10.
1723 See UNESCO (ed.) (2007m) (cf. *footnote 216* op. cit.), p. 13.
Cf. *Figure 79* in chapter IX 3.4.6 *Launch* on page 337.
1724 See UNESCO (ed.) (2007m) (cf. *footnote 216* op. cit.), p. 13.
1725 Cf. expected outcomes in chapter IX 4.3 *Characteristics* on pages 351 et seqq.
1726 See UNESCO (ed.) (2007m) (cf. *footnote 216* op. cit.), p. 13.
See *Figure 84* in chapter IX 4.3 *Characteristics* on page 355.

2006–07	• Benchmarking studies of the attitudes (comprising knowledge, beliefs and actions) to sustainable development and sustainable ways of living held by the general public as well as special groups such as youth, scientists, teachers, business and industry leaders, etc. • Research on the factors underpinning different interpretations and practices in ESD around the world and strategies for building consensus on, and communicating, the core dimensions of ESD in different cultural contexts.
2008–09	• Research on the attitudes (comprising knowledge, beliefs and actions) of senior decision-makers to ESD and ways of successfully communicating with them about the importance of ESD. • Research on factors and processes that facilitate the successful review and reorientation of education policies and plans in order to embed ESD in them. • Research on factors and processes that promote effective capacity-building and training in ESD in different education sectors. • Research on factors and processes that facilitate the adoption and effective implementation of ESD in different education sectors.
2010–14	• Factors and processes that facilitate the scaling-up of innovative ESD practices and their wider adoption and embedding as 'normal' practice in different education settings. • Strategies for identifying and evaluating the results of education programmes such as ESD whose impacts are likely to be realised in the longer, rather than shorter term, i.e. beyond the period of the DESD itself.

Figure 84: Research objectives of UNESCO Action plan for DESD[1727]

In the case of *monitoring and evaluating DESD*, the *UNESCO Action Plan* plays a particular role as a reference document. The fact that the *UNESCO Action Plan* establishes specific obligations to be fulfilled by the end of *DESD* facilitates its evaluation towards the fixed targets. Results will be monitored at least once and evaluated at least twice through a mid-term review in 2009 and a final evaluation in 2014. These outcomes will then again form the basis of a mid-term report on *DESD* in 2010 and a final report in 2015 to United Nations General Assembly.[1728]

In order to properly monitor and evaluate activities proposed by the *in-house UNESCO Action plan*[1729] two different sets of evidence-based indicators will be applied:

1727 Research on *ESD* is considered one major strategy of *DESD*, particularly in the realm of UNESCO's competencies.
See UNESCO (ed.) (2007m) (cf. *footnote 216* op. cit.), p. 13.
Cf. *Figure 82* in chapter IX 4.3 *Characteristics* on page 348.

1728 Cf. UNESCO (ed.) (2007m) (cf. *footnote 216* op. cit.), p. 13.

1729 See UNESCO (ed.) (2007m) (cf. *footnote 216* op. cit.), p. 13.

1. *Whole-of-House*[1730] indicators to evaluate the commitment of UNESCO to the *Action plan* internally; and
2. Results of UNESCO *DESD*-activities to evaluate effects externally.[1731]

Table 36: Benchmarks for monitoring and evaluating UNESCO Action plan for DESD

UNESCO Action plan for DESD	
Internal benchmark[1732]	External benchmark[1733]
Development of operational plans for nine thematic programmes and their integration into the (UNESCO topical and budgetary strategies)	*Increased number of senior decision-makers in Member States committed to DESD*
Funding and related mechanisms in place to encourage inter-sectoral collaboration	*Countries in each region undertake demonstration projects on policy review and re-development for ESD by 2010 and up to ten more in each region by 2013*
Development of a common understanding of the key messages of ESD	*Completion of mid-decade review and end-of-decade final evaluation reveals countries are addressing the objectives and thrusts of ESD*
Achievement of common expected outcomes in each biennium	
Integration of outcomes of thematic programmes into a co-ordinated set of publications (e.g., book series, briefing papers, capacity-building materials, etc.)	
Coherence of DESD activities between UNESCO headquarters and field offices	
Coherence of DESD activities between UNESCO and international agencies	

4.4 Illustration

The cross-sectoral capacity-building programmes may serve as examples of good practice which soundly underpin the character of the *UNESCO Action Plan.*[1734] Designed to raise capacity-building in UNESCO member states, these programmes clearly prove the necessity of inter-sectoral co-operation. In the field of building capacities for sustainable development, water education, for

1730 See UNESCO (ed.) (2007m) (cf. *footnote 216* op. cit.), p. 13.
1731 See *Table 36* in chapter IX 4.3 *Characteristics* on page 356.
1732 Cf. UNESCO (ed.) (2007m) (cf. *footnote 216* op. cit.), p. 14.
1733 Cf. UNESCO (ed.) (2007m) (cf. *footnote 216* op. cit.), p. 14.
1734 Cf. UNESCO (ed.) (2007j) (cf. *footnote 39* op. cit.), pp. 17 et seqq.

instance, plays an important role, as mentioned at the beginning.[1735] The following examples illustrate collaboration between different UNESCO programmes for the furtherance of *DESD*-related issues:[1736]

Table 37: Inter-sectoral co-operation of programme sectors in line with UNESCO Action plan[1737]

Programme	Project	UNESCO programme sectors
Area	*Building capacities for sustainable development in coastal regions and small islands*	
Coastal regions and Small Islands (CSI) *Platform*	*Sandwatch* *Youth Visioning for Island Living* (YVIL) *Small Islands Voice* (SIV)	Natural Sciences, Education, Communication and Information
Area	*Building capacities to utilise local and indigenous knowledge systems for sustainable development*	
Local and Indigenous Knowledge Systems (LINKS)	*Learning Resource Pack*	Natural, Social and Human Sciences, Education, Culture, Communication and Information
Area	*South-South collaboration for sustainable development*	
UNESCO Chair; *UNESCO Institute for Lifelong Learning* (UIL)	*South-South Cooperation for Sustainable Development*	Education
Area	*Building capacities in urban water management, with a focus on the provision of safe drinking water*	
International Hydrological Programme (IHP); Urban Water Management Programme	*SWITCH Managing Water for the City of the Future* *Water and civilisation*	Natural, Social and Human Sciences
Area	*Capacity-building in marine sciences*	
Intergovernmental Oceanographic Commission (IOC)	*UNITWIN Chairs and Participation Programme* *UNESCO-IHE Institute for Water Education*	Natural Sciences, Education

1735 Cf. (viii) Education for sustainable water management UNESCO (ed.) (August 2007) (cf. *footnote 693* op. cit.), p. 3.

1736 See *Table 37* in chapter IX 4.4 *Illustration* on page 357.

1737 Cf. UNESCO (ed.) (2007j) (cf. *footnote 39* op. cit.), pp. 25–28; UNESCO (ed.) (2009b) (cf. *footnote 793* op. cit.), pp. 9, 12.
Cf. *Table 35* in chapter IX 4.3 *Characteristics* on page 353.

Programme	Project	UNESCO programme sectors
Area	*Cultural diversity and education for sustainable development*	
Mainstreaming cultural diversity and intercultural dialogue in *DESD*	*Communications, Education and Public Awareness* (CEPA) *Convention on Biological Diversity* (CBD)	Natural Sciences, Culture, Education
Area	*Water education for sustainable development*	
International Hydrological Programme (IHP)	*Water Education and Capacity-Building Working Group*	Natural Sciences, Education

4.5 Summary

"In summary, the (UNESCO Action plan) is structured to identify a practical, realistic and achievable role for UNESCO

- *(I)n supporting Member States and their partners in their efforts to achieve the objectives of the DESD*
- *(B)y drawing upon the strategic comparative strengths and capacities of UNESCO as:*
  - *(...) catalyst for innovation,*
  - *(...) generator of knowledge sharing, -management, -building,*
  - *(...) mobiliser of partners, and*
  - *(...) builder of capacity through training, policy review, -development and institutional, -system reform."*[1738]

5 Monitoring

"On-going monitoring is (the) prerequisite for a purposeful and well-organised Decade."[1739]

Monitoring is comprised of reporting and evaluation. Implementation and monitoring are inextricably linked: monitoring is instrumental to implementation, because monitoring aims to check the performance and progress of implementation processes. However, monitoring activities are usually not carried out *ex post*. They are dynamic and based upon an interdependent circular model.[1740]

1738 See UNESCO (ed.) (2007m) (cf. *footnote 216* op. cit.), p. 6.
1739 See UNESCO (ed.) (July 2003) (cf. *footnote 37* op. cit.), p. 114.
1740 Cf. Bothe, Michael (1980) (cf. *footnote 510* op. cit.), p. 75; Boyle, Alan E. (1999) (cf. *footnote 961* op. cit.), pp. 904–906; Chinkin, Christine (2003) (cf. *footnote 444* op. cit.), pp. 37 et seqq.

The need to monitor *DESD* implementation coincides with UNESCO's functional mandate: in terms of monitoring and supervision it can be summarised as:[1741]

- Initiative function for norm respect;
- Control function; and
- Informative function for norm-compliant communication

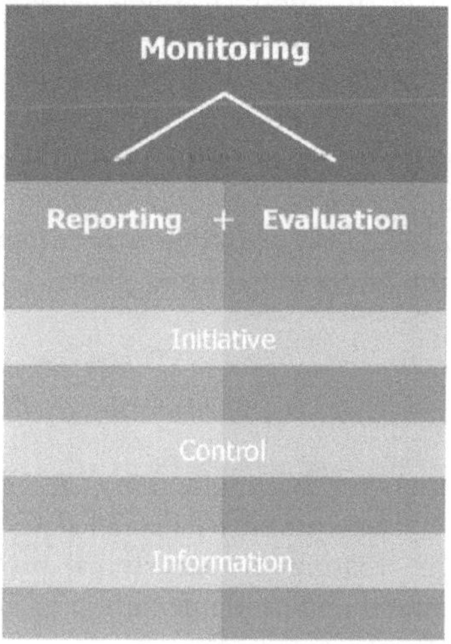

Figure 85: Components and UNESCO functions of monitoring[1742]

5.1 Drafting history

The necessity of appropriate mechanisms of monitoring has, strictly speaking, already been established by the proclamation of *DESD* through resolution *A/RES/57/254*.[1743]

1741 Cf. Boisson de Chazournes, Laurence (2007) (cf. *footnote 496* op. cit.), pp. 52, 72–73; UNESCO (ed.) (2007f) (cf. *footnote 427* op. cit.), p. 2.
Cf. chapter V 4 *Monitoring* on pages 115 et seqq.
See *Figure 85* in chapter IX 5 *Monitoring* on page 359.

1742 Monitoring is composed of two critical elements: reporting and evaluation. Both are interdependent means to initiate, control and inform *DESD* stakeholders.

1743 Cf. United Nations (ed.) (2002 / 2003) (cf. *footnote 117* op. cit.).
See *Table 38* in chapter IX 5.1 *Drafting history* on page 361.

UNESCO's implementation and monitoring activities go hand in hand. Thus, requirements of monitoring are mentioned shortly after *DESD* adoption as part of the *Framework for a Draft International Implementation Scheme.*[1744]

The *International Implementation Scheme* (IIS) highlights the importance of effective monitoring: *"An initiative as long and complex as a Decade must benefit from adequate processes of monitoring and evaluation from the start. Without that, it will be impossible to know if the Decade is making a difference and what that difference is. A key aspect of monitoring and evaluation will be the identification of suitable and relevant indicators at every level – local, national, regional and international and for each initiative and programme".*[1745]

Results of the *DESD Monitoring and Evaluation Expert Group* (MEEG),[1746] which was formally established in 2007,[1747] led to the first institutionalised provisions of monitoring given in the comprehensive *UN DESD Global Monitoring and Evaluation Framework* (GMEF).[1748] The document was commissioned to assist in the formalisation of monitoring and evaluation at global level through, mainly, an accompanying operational plan.[1749]

The *UNESCO Strategy for the Second Half of DESD* stresses the need for international strategies and practices as well as the importance of visible and concrete *DESD* outcomes.[1750]

The first *DESD* monitoring results are highlighted by the 2009 *DESD Global Report*. This mid-decade review was primarily designed to identify obstacles and challenges encountered in creating the structures, provisions and conditions which facilitate the development and implementation of *ESD.*[1751]

1744 Cf. UNESCO (ed.) (July 2003) (cf. *footnote 37* op. cit.), pp. 12, 14.

1745 See UNESCO (ed.) (2005j) (cf. *footnote 44* op. cit.), p. 21; UNESCO (ed.) (2008h) (cf. *footnote 219* op. cit.), p. 3.

1746 Cf. Gerner, Martin (30/07/2009) (cf. *footnote 407* op. cit.).

1747 Cf. UNESCO (ed.) (August 2007) (cf. *footnote 693* op. cit.), pp. 2, 6, 17; Tilbury, Daniella (2007) (cf. *footnote 219* op. cit.), p. 252.

1748 Cf. UNESCO (ed.) (2008h) (cf. *footnote 219* op. cit.).

1749 Cf. UNESCO (ed.) (2008h) (cf. *footnote 219* op. cit.), p. 3; UNESCO (ed.) (2008c): DESD Quarterly Highlights. December 2008. Paris: UNESCO publishing, p. 3; Gerner, Martin (30/07/2009) (cf. *footnote 407* op. cit.); Gerner, Martin (14/09/2009) (cf. *footnote 407* op. cit.).

1750 Cf. UNESCO Education Sector (ed.) (March 2009) (cf. *footnote 1223* op. cit.), pp. 8, 12, 21.

1751 Cf. UNESCO Section for DESD Coordination (ed.) (2009) (cf. *footnote 116* op. cit.), pp. 6, 10.

Table 38: Timeline of DESD monitoring[1752]

Date	*Document*	*Comment and catch word*
20 December 2002	A/RES/57/254	UNESCO *DESD* implementation mandate
July 2003	Framework for a Draft International Implementation Scheme	Stating need and providing guidelines for *DESD* monitoring
October 2005	International Implementation Scheme (IIS)	Building momentum for monitoring and creating commitment
August 2007	177 EX/9 Annex III	Introducing the *DESD Monitoring and Evaluation Expert Group* (MEEG)
May 2008	UN DESD Global Monitoring and Evaluation Framework (GMEF)	Operationalising *DESD* monitoring by providing methods and structures for data collection, analysis and global reporting processes
March 2009	UNESCO Strategy for the Second Half of DESD	Furthering the development of the global monitoring and evaluation system to evaluate *ESD* and presenting international strategies and practices leading to successful conclusions of *DESD* with visible and concrete outcomes
July 2009	DESD Global Report	Presenting results of the first phase of the *DESD* Monitoring and Evaluation process: 2007–2009 guided by the *Global Monitoring and Evaluation Framework*

5.2 Indicators

Monitoring cannot be performed without indicators. An indicator consists of *"the ability to point to an issue or condition and identify how well a system is working"*.[1753] Sound indicators are instrumental to measuring *ESD* performance

1752 Cf. United Nations (ed.) (2002 / 2003) (cf. *footnote 117* op. cit.), p. 2; UNESCO (ed.) (July 2003) (cf. *footnote 37* op. cit.), pp. 12, 14 et seqq; UNESCO (ed.) (2005j) (cf. *footnote 44* op. cit.), pp. 12, 21 et seqq; UNESCO (ed.) (August 2007) (cf. *footnote 693* op. cit.), pp. 17–18; UNESCO (ed.) (2008h) (cf. *footnote 219* op. cit.); UNESCO Education Sector (ed.) (March 2009) (cf. *footnote 1223* op. cit.), pp. 8, 12, 21; UNESCO Section for DESD Coordination (ed.) (2009) (cf. *footnote 116* op. cit.).

1753 See Australian Research Institute in Education for Sustainability (ARIES); Macquarie University Sydney; Australian Government Department of the Environment and Water Resources (eds.) (2006): Development of a National Approach to Monitoring, Assessment and Reporting on the Decade of Education for Sustainable Development. Summarising Documented Experiences on the Development of ESD Indicators and Networking with Expert Groups on ESD Indicators. Sydney: Photospin, p. 8.

and competences through proving or disapproving *evidence*[1754] of regime effectiveness.[1755]

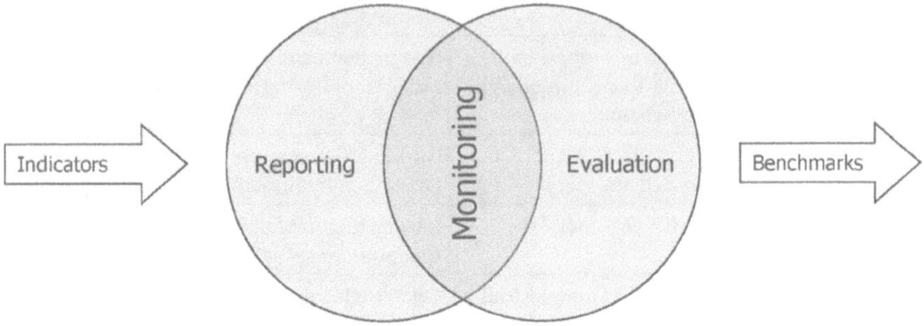

Figure 86: Indicators as baseline for effecting monitoring[1756]

"Reviewing (the) UN Decade in progress is highly complex when considering

- *the geographical scope (the globe),*
- *the time-frame (10 years),*
- *its ambition to affect multiple levels of governance and to bring in multiple stakeholders and marginalised groups and voices in society and, finally,*
- *the different meanings attributed to its focus: Education for Sustainable Development (ESD)."*[1757]

1754 Cf. Miles, Edward L. (ed.) (2002) (cf. *footnote 294* op. cit.).

1755 Cf. Andresen, Steinar (2007) (cf. *footnote 320* op. cit.), p. 10; UNESCO (2009) (cf. *footnote 579* op. cit.); Wals, Arjen E. J. (13/05/2009): Towards non-prescriptive and emergent indicator frameworks for self-determined sustainability with a planetary conscience. Fourth International RCE Conference 2009. Volume United Nations University. Montreal: Wageningen University, p. 3.
See *Figure 86* in chapter IX 5.2 *Indicators* on page 362, *Figure 87* in chapter IX 5.2 *Indicators* on page 363, and *Figure 88* in chapter IX 5.2 *Indicators* on page 364.

1756 Indicators constitute the normative *input* for reporting. These are then checked and evaluated on the basis of pre-defined criteria. Altogether reporting and evaluation form the monitoring process. This can result in formulating *output*-like benchmarks which once again may influence the quality or choice of indicators.
Cf. Wals, Arjen E. J. (13/05/2009) (cf. *footnote 1755* op. cit.), p. 2.

1757 See UNESCO Section for DESD Coordination (ed.) (2009) (cf. *footnote 116* op. cit.), p. 10; Wals, Arjen E. J. (July 2009) (cf. *footnote 533* op. cit.), p. 196.

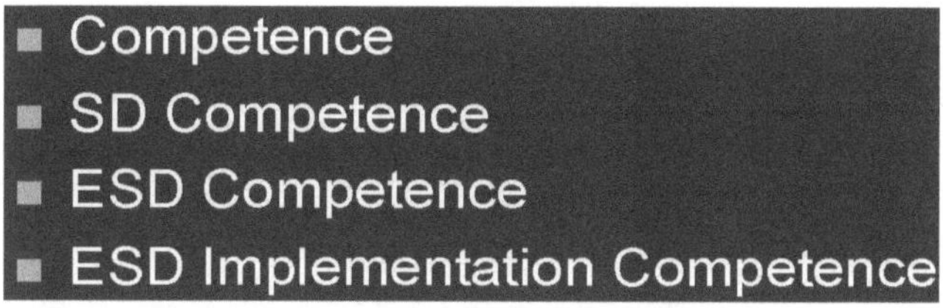

Figure 87: ESD-related competencies[1758]

The development of indicators constitutes a complex undertaking. Indicators are the *affidavit of means*, because they represent condensed conceptions which ultimately encapsulate all difficulties, incompatibilities and challenges related to an issue.[1759]

Given these additional obstacles, UNESCO must address the issue of finding significant and meaningful indicators of *DESD* performance.[1760] This is generally done by specially appointed individuals, particular *rapporteurs* or working groups in accordance with respective thematic mandates.[1761]

1758 See Wals, Arjen E. J. (13/05/2009) (cf. *footnote 1755* op. cit.), p. 9.
Competencies that are directed and may possibly lead to trans-cultural, trans-generational, trans-disciplinary and trans-geographical shifts in behaviour.

1759 Cf. Gerner, Martin (14/09/2009) (cf. *footnote 407* op. cit.).

1760 I.e. considering priorities of methodology and delivery, and competencies to be dealt with by an expert group.
Cf. Rychen, Dominique Simone; Salganik, Laura Hersh (2003) (cf. *footnote 816* op. cit.); Organization for Economic Cooperation & Development (OECD) (ed.) (2005) (cf. *footnote 816* op. cit.), pp. 4, 7, 13; Deutsche UNESCO-Kommission e. V. (DUK) (ed.) (2007) (cf. *footnote 24* op. cit.), p. 25; Foreign Office of the Federal Republic of Germany / German Commission for UNESCO (ed.) (2007) (cf. *footnote 21* op. cit.), p. 16; Gerner, Martin (14/09/2009) (cf. *footnote 407* op. cit.).

1761 Cf. Shelton, Dinah (2003a) (cf. *footnote 989* op. cit.), pp. 451–453.

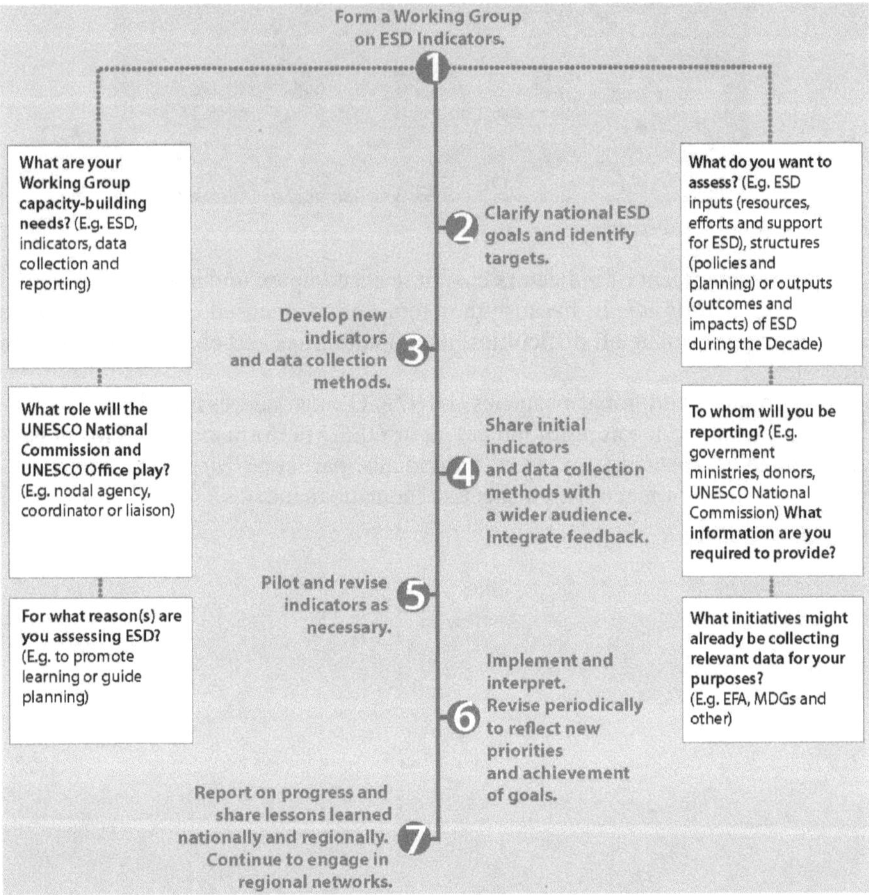

Figure 88: Procedural rules for the development of ESD indicators[1762]

Pioneering work on different kinds of indicators has been carried out in a de-centralised and case-specific way, mostly at project scale, bringing together different visions of what indicators should ideally look like.[1763]

1762 The scheme depicts how *ESD* indicators are developed in order to support the stage of reporting on *ESD*.
See UNESCO (ed.) (2007h): Monitoring and assessing progress during the UNDESD in the Asia-Pacific Region: A quick guide to developing national ESD indicators. APE/ESD/07/OP/022–1500. Edited by Daniella Tilbury; Sonja Janousek; Leanne Denby; Derek Elias; Joel E. Bacha. Bangkok: UNESCO Asia and Pacific Regional Bureau for Education, p. 12.
Cf. *Figure 86* in chapter IX 5.2 *Indicators* on page 362.

Figure 89: Jungle of multi-directional indicators[1764]

Quantitative and qualitative indicators for measuring *ESD* are considered equally important, but differ both in concept and application.[1765] Thus, interpret-

---

1763 For example: co-operation with independent institutes, universities, governments or experts.
Cf. Australian Research Institute in Education for Sustainability (ARIES); Macquarie University Sydney; Australian Government Department of the Environment and Water Resources (eds.) (2006) (cf. *footnote 1753* op. cit.), p. 5; UNESCO (ed.) (August 2007) (cf. *footnote 693* op. cit.), pp. 5, 17; Centre for Environment Education (CEE); South Asia Youth Environment Network (SAYEN) (eds.) (2007) (cf. *footnote 689* op. cit.), pp. 16 et seqq; UNESCO (ed.) (2008h) (cf. *footnote 219* op. cit.), pp. 8–9.
See *Figure 89* in chapter IX 5.2 *Indicators* on page 365.

1764 This figure alludes to the problem of properly choosing the adequate type of indicator in a rather self-deprecating manner.
See United Nations Economic Commission for Europe (UNECE); United Nations Economic and Social Council (ECOSOC) (eds.) (2005c) (cf. *footnote 411* op. cit.), pp. 2–3; UNESCO (ed.) (2007a): Asia-Pacific Guidelines for the Development of National ESD Indicators. APE/ESD/07/OP/022–1000. Edited by Daniella Tilbury; Sonja Janousek; Leanne Denby; Derek Elias; Joel E. Bacha. Bangkok: UNESCO Asia and Pacific Regional Bureau for Education, p. i; UNESCO (ed.) (2007h) (cf. *footnote 1762* op. cit.), p. i; Tilbury, Daniella (2010): Change for a better world: assessing the contribution of the DESD. In: Witthaus, Michele; McCandless, Karen; Lambert, Rebecca (eds.): Tomorrow today. Leicester, United Kingdom: Tudor Rose; UNESCO publishing, pp. 146–148.

1765 Cf. UNESCO (ed.) (2003b) (cf. *footnote 109* op. cit.), p. 5; United Nations Economic Commission for Europe (UNECE); United Nations Economic and Social Council (ECOSOC) (eds.) (2004b) (cf. *footnote 391* op. cit.), p. 15; United Nations Economic Commission for Europe (UNECE); United Nations Economic and Social Council

ing them can best be related to the type and functional assignment of the indicator.[1766]

	Indicator Type	Function	Indicator Example
Status	***Baseline***	To identify the status of the overall ESD picture	*Percentage of new teachers currently receiving preservice training in ESD.*
Facilitative	***Context***	To identify the existence of ESD support systems	*A national mandatory policy exists in requiring preservice teacher education courses to provide training in ESD to all students.*
	Process	To identify the existence of ESD processes and activities	*All preservice teacher education courses provide training on the content and pedagogy underpinning ESD.*
	Learning	To promote learning and reflection on ESD	*Lessons learnt in the process of training preservice teachers in ESD are captured.*
Effect	***Output***	To assess outputs such as tools and learning resources	*Percentage of new teachers certified as having received preservice training in ESD.*
	Outcome	To assess outcomes related to changes or improvements that result from ESD efforts	*All new teachers have new or improved skills and understanding in ESD.*
	Impact	To assess impacts that result from ESD efforts	*All new teachers are practicing ESD in the classroom*
	Performance	To assess the change in the status of the overall ESD picture in a region or country	*Increase in numbers of new teachers receiving preservice training*

Figure 90: Proposed types and examples of ESD indicators[1767]

Moreover, according to the very nature of *DESD*, indicators may vary considerably in spatial and structural scope.[1768] Conceptually speaking, some *trade-off* relationship or *conflict of interest* does exist between *region-specific* and *universal* approaches. Taking into account the aspect of assessment alone, *universal* indicators would be preferable because they ensure standards for comparison. However, given regional strategies of implementation, developing *region-specific* indicators is wholly mandatory.

(ECOSOC) (eds.) (2005c) (cf. *footnote 411* op. cit.), p. 2; Tilbury, Daniella (2007) (cf. *footnote 219* op. cit.), p. 241.

1766 See *Figure 90* in chapter IX 5.2 *Indicators* on page 366.

1767 This table serves as introduction to different sets and types of indicators that particularly match the nature of *DESD* and its specific regime requirements.
See Tilbury, Daniella (2007) (cf. *footnote 219* op. cit.), p. 251 (originally published in the Journal of Education for Sustainable Development, Vol. 1, No. 2. Copyright © 2007 Centre for Environment Education, Ahmedabad, Gujarat. All rights reserved. Reproduced with the permission of the copyright holders and the publishers, Sage Publications India Pvt. Ltd, New Delhi.); Wals, Arjen E. J. (13/05/2009) (cf. *footnote 1755* op. cit.), pp. 5–7.

1768 Cf. United Nations Economic Commission for Europe (UNECE); United Nations Economic and Social Council (ECOSOC) (eds.) (2004b) (cf. *footnote 391* op. cit.), p. 15.

Universal indicators are considered a *foundation*[1769] for furthering regional implementation and monitoring. They are intended to be a *global conceptual blueprint* and they are hence proposed as worldwide monitoring standards.[1770] In order to achieve comparability of monitoring there is a continuing quest for uniform and globally-valid indicators. The set of global indicators must be consistent with the *International Implementation Scheme* (IIS) and other contributing regional approaches;[1771] this may be done by assessing progress in *ESD* and addressing the following:

- Contexts and structures,
- Processes and learning, and
- Impacts and outcomes.[1772]

Region-specific indicators are proposed and accredited, namely for North America and Europe (UNECE) as well as Asia and the Pacific.[1773] It has been among the priorities of UNECE to independently provide a scheduled, prioritised and timely approach for implementing *ESD* into regional practice.[1774] UNECE ac-

1769 Cf. United Nations Economic Commission for Europe (UNECE); United Nations Economic and Social Council (ECOSOC) (eds.) (2004b) (cf. *footnote 391* op. cit.), p. 2; United Nations Economic Commission for Europe (UNECE); United Nations Economic and Social Council (ECOSOC) (eds.) (2005f) (cf. *footnote 391* op. cit.), p. 2.

1770 For example: working on a common collection and dissemination of regional best practices on *ESD*.
Cf. UNESCO (ed.) (2006h) (cf. *footnote 711* op. cit.), p. 3; Tilbury, Daniella (2007) (cf. *footnote 219* op. cit.), p. 252; Gerner, Martin (14/09/2009) (cf. *footnote 407* op. cit.).

1771 I.e. UNECE and UNESCO-IUCN Asia-Pacific efforts.
Cf. Tilbury, Daniella (2007) (cf. *footnote 219* op. cit.), p. 239; UNESCO (ed.) (August 2007) (cf. *footnote 693* op. cit.).

1772 Cf. Tilbury, Daniella (2007) (cf. *footnote 219* op. cit.), p. 240; UNESCO (ed.) (2008h) (cf. *footnote 219* op. cit.), p. 18.
See *Figure 97* in chapter IX 5.5 *Summary* on page 382.

1773 Cf. UNESCO (ed.) (August 2007) (cf. *footnote 693* op. cit.).
See *Figure 93* in chapter IX 5.2 *Indicators* on page 373.

1774 Cf. United Nations Economic Commission for Europe (UNECE); United Nations Economic and Social Council (ECOSOC) (eds.) (2005c) (cf. *footnote 411* op. cit.), p. 1; United Nations Economic Commission for Europe (UNECE); United Nations Economic and Social Council (ECOSOC) (eds.) (2005f) (cf. *footnote 391* op. cit.), pp. 11, 14; United Nations Economic Commission for Europe (UNECE); United Nations Economic and Social Council (ECOSOC) (eds.) (2005e) (cf. *footnote 746* op. cit.), pp. 4, 5; United Nations Economic Commission for Europe (UNECE); United Nations Economic and Social Council (ECOSOC) (eds.) (2006): Report of the Meeting. First meeting, Geneva, 13–14 December 2005. CEP/AC.13/2005/7. New York: United Nations, p. 4; United Nations Economic Commission for Europe (UNECE) (ed.) (2006) (cf. *footnote 20* op. cit.), pp. 3–6; United Nations Economic Commission for Europe (UNECE); United Nations Economic and Social Council (ECOSOC) (eds.) (2007d): Sixth

tivities in *DESD* replace UNESCO actions on *DESD* within the UNECE region, which encompasses Europe and North America. The catalogue of *ESD* indicators proposed by UNECE, though not particularly designed as a consistent worldwide approach, has been offered to UNESCO for global use as standard-setting indicators.[1775] For instance, UNECE uses an alternative definitional basis for the range of indicators, distinguishing between:[1776]

- *Checklist indicators*: providing information on initial policy, legislation, regulatory and governance measures taken by a government in the course of *DESD* implementation;
- *Input indicators*: providing information on a broader spectrum of activities taking place in the implementation of *DESD*;[1777]
- *Output indicators*: providing information on the results of these activities;[1778]
- *Outcome indicators*: providing information on the possible impact of *DESD* implementation, in particular its qualitative aspect in terms of values, attitudes and choices relating to *ESD*.[1779]

Ministerial Conference "Environment for Europe" Belgrade, 10–12 October 2007. Declaration "Building Bridges to the Future" by Ministers of the region of the United Nations Economic Commission for Europe (UNECE). ECE/BELGRADE.CONF/2007/8. New York: United Nations, p. 4; United Nations Economic Commission for Europe (UNECE); United Nations Economic and Social Council (ECOSOC) (eds.) (2007a): Environment for Europe – Chair's Summary. Sixth Ministerial Conference "Environment for Europe" Belgrade, 10–12 October 2007. ECE/BELGRADE.CONF/2007/9. Edited by Saša Dragin. New York: United Nations, p. 5; United Nations Economic Commission for Europe (UNECE); United Nations Economic and Social Council (ECOSOC) (eds.) (2007c): Report of the Meeting. Second meeting, Geneva, 4–5 December 2006. ECE/CEP/AC.13/2006/3. New York: United Nations, p. 3; UNESCO (ed.) (August 2007) (cf. *footnote 693* op. cit.), p. 6; UNESCO (ed.) (2007k) (cf. *footnote 4* op. cit.), p. 32; UNESCO (ed.) (2007f) (cf. *footnote 427* op. cit.), pp. 5 et seqq.

1775 Cf. United Nations Economic Commission for Europe (UNECE); United Nations Economic and Social Council (ECOSOC) (eds.) (2005e) (cf. *footnote 746* op. cit.), p. 2; Gerner, Martin (14/09/2009) (cf. *footnote 407* op. cit.); Gerner, Martin (30/07/2009) (cf. *footnote 407* op. cit.).
See *Figure 91* in chapter IX 5.2 *Indicators* on page 370.

1776 Cf. United Nations Economic Commission for Europe (UNECE); United Nations Economic and Social Council (ECOSOC) (eds.) (2005c) (cf. *footnote 411* op. cit.), pp. 2–3.

1777 For example: amount of public authority money invested and materials spent on *DESD*, or proportion of publicly supported research on *DESD*.

1778 For example: performance of trained teachers, number of businesses involved in *ESD* projects, proportion of educators who received training on *ESD* issues, etc.

1779 For example: learning outcomes resulting from *ESD* partnerships, community-based projects and business involvement).

	Indicators / sub-indicators	Type	Source of verification
OBJECTIVE 1[1]. ENSURE THAT POLICY, REGULATORY AND OPERATIONAL FRAMEWORKS SUPPORT THE PROMOTION OF ESD			
Indicator 1.1.	**Prerequisite measures are taken to support the promotion of ESD**		
Sub-indicator 1.1.1	Is the UNECE Strategy for ESD available in your national[2] language(s)?	Qualitative; "Checklist"	Government reports
Sub-indicator 1.1.2	Have you appointed a national focal point to deal with the UNECE Strategy for ESD?	Qualitative; "Checklist"	Government reports
Sub-indicator 1.1.3	Do you have a coordinating body for implementation of ESD?	Qualitative; "Checklist"	Government reports
Sub-indicator 1.1.4	Do you have a national implementation plan for ESD?	Qualitative; "Checklist"	Government reports
Sub-indicator 1.1.5	Are there any synergies at the national level between UNECE ESD process, the UNESCO global process on the UN Decade of ESD[4], and other policy processes relevant to ESD?	Qualitative; "Checklist"	Government reports; Reports of relevant Ministries
Indicator 1.2	**Policy, regulatory and operational frameworks support the promotion of ESD**		
Sub-indicator 1.2.1	Is ESD reflected in any national policy[5] document(s)?	Qualitative; "Checklist"	Government reports
Sub-indicator 1.2.2	Is ESD: (a) addressed in relevant national education legislation/regulatory document(s); and (b) included in your national curricula and/or national standards/ ordinances/ requirements; at all levels of formal education, as understood by your education system in accordance with ISCED[6]?	Qualitative; "Input"	Reports of relevant Ministries
Sub-indicator 1.2.3	Is non-formal and informal ESD addressed in your relevant national policy and/or regulatory document(s) and operational frameworks?	Qualitative; "Checklist"	Government reports
Sub-indicator 1.2.4	Is public awareness in relation to ESD addressed in relevant national document(s)?	Qualitative; "Checklist"	Government reports
Sub-indicator 1.2.5	Does a formal structure for interdepartmental[7] cooperation relevant to ESD exist in your government?	Qualitative; "Checklist"	Government reports
Sub-indicator 1.2.6	Does a mechanism for multi-stakeholder cooperation on ESD exist with the involvement of your government[8]?	Qualitative; "Checklist"	Government reports
Sub-indicator 1.2.7	Are public budgets and/or economic incentives available specifically to support ESD?	Qualitative; "Input"	Government reports
Indicator 1.3	**National policies support synergies between processes related to SD and ESD**		
Sub-indicator 1.3.1	Is ESD part of SD policy(s) if such exist in your country?	Qualitative; "Checklist"	Government reports; Reports of relevant Ministries
OBJECTIVE 2. PROMOTE SD THROUGH FORMAL, NON-FORMAL AND INFORMAL LEARNING			
Indicator 2.1	**SD key themes are addressed in formal education**		
Sub-indicator 2.1.1	Are key themes of SD[9] addressed explicitly in the curriculum[10]/programme of study at various levels of formal education?	Qualitative; "Input"	Education institutions and Ministries responsible for Education
Sub-indicator 2.1.2	Are learning outcomes (skills, attitudes and values) that support ESD addressed explicitly in the curriculum[11]/programme of study at various levels of formal education?	Qualitative; "Input"	Education institutions and Ministries responsible for Education
Indicator 2.2	**Strategies to implement ESD are clearly identified**		
Sub-indicator 2.2.1	Is ESD addressed through[12]: (a) Existing subjects[13] only? ; (b) A cross-curriculum approach? ; (c) The provision of specific subject programmes and courses?; (d) A stand-alone project[14]?	Qualitative; "Input"	Education institutions and Ministries responsible for Education
Indicator 2.3	**A whole institution approach[15] to ESD/SD is promoted**		
Sub-indicator 2.3.1	Do educational institutions[16] adopt a "whole institution approach" to SD/ESD?	Qualitative; "Output"	Education institutions, funding agencies
Sub-indicator 2.3.2	Are there any incentives (guidelines, award scheme, funding, technical support) that support "a whole institution approach to SD/ESD"?	Quantitative; "Output"	Education institutions, funding agencies
Sub-indicator 2.3.3	Do institutions/learners develop their own SD indicators for their institution/organisation?	Qualitative; "Output"	Education institutions, funding agencies
Indicator 2.4	**ESD is addressed by quality assessment / enhancement systems**		
Sub-indicator 2.4.1	Are there any education quality assessment/enhancement systems that include criteria on ESD [17] in: (a) National systems and (b) Other?	Qualitative; "Input"	Education institutions and Ministries responsible for Education
Indicator 2.5	**ESD methods and instruments for non-formal and informal learning are in place to assess changes in knowledge, attitude and practice**		
Sub-indicator 2.5.1	Are SD issues addressed in informal and public awareness raising activities?	Qualitative; "Input"	Reports by the trade unions and professional associations, relevant Ministries
Sub-indicator 2.5.2	Is there any support for work-based learning (e.g. for small companies, farmers, trade unions, associations, etc.), which addresses SD issues?	Quantitative; "Input"	Reports by the trade unions and professional associations, relevant Ministries
Sub-indicator 2.5.3	Are there any instruments (e.g. research, survey, etc.) in place to assess the outcomes of ESD as a result of non-formal and informal learning?	Qualitative; "Input" / "Outcome"	Reports by the trade unions and professional associations, relevant Ministries
Indicator 2.6	**ESD implementation is a multi-stakeholder process[18]**		
Sub-indicator 2.6.1	Is ESD implementation a multi-stakeholder process?	Qualitative; "Input"	Reports by the trade unions and professional associations, relevant Ministries
OBJECTIVE 3. EQUIP EDUCATORS WITH THE COMPETENCE TO INCLUDE SD IN THEIR TEACHING			
Indicator 3.1	**ESD is included in the training[19] of educators**		
Sub-indicator 3.1.1	Is ESD a part of the initial educators' training[20]?	Qualitative; "Input"	Educational institutions, Ministry of Education
Sub-indicator 3.1.2	Is ESD a part of the educators' in-service training?[21]	Qualitative; "Input"	Educational institutions, Ministry of Education
Sub-indicator 3.1.3	Is ESD a part of training of leaders and administrators of educational institutions?	Qualitative; "Input"	Educational institutions, Ministry of Education

	Indicators / sub-indicators	Type	Source of verification
Indicator 3.2	**Opportunities exist for educators to cooperate on ESD**		
Sub-indicator 3.2.1	Are there any networks / platforms of educators and/or leaders/administrators who are involved in ESD in your country?	Qualitative; "Output"	Educational institutions, relevant Ministries
Sub-indicator 3.2.2	Are ESD networks/platforms supported by the government in any way[22]?	Qualitative; "Input"	Educational institutions, relevant Ministries
OBJECTIVE 4. ENSURE THAT ADEQUATE TOOLS AND MATERIALS FOR ESD ARE ACCESSIBLE			
Indicator 4.1	**Teaching tools and materials for ESD are produced**		
Sub-indicator 4.1.1	Does a national strategy/ mechanism for encouragement of development and production of ESD tools and materials exist?	Qualitative "Input"	Relevant ministries / public authorities
Sub-indicator 4.1.2	Is public (national, sub-national, local) authority money invested in this activity?	Qualitative "Input"	Relevant ministries / public authorities
Indicator 4.2	**Quality control mechanisms for teaching tools and materials for ESD exist**		
Sub-indicator 4.2.1	Do you have quality criteria and/or quality guidelines for ESD-related teaching tools and materials that are: (a) Supported by public authorities?; (b) Approved by public authorities?; (c) Tested and recommended for selection by educational institutions?	Qualitative "Input"	Relevant ministries / public authorities
Sub-indicator 4.2.2	Are ESD teaching tools / materials available: (a) In national languages?; (b) For all levels of education according to ISCED?	Qualitative "Input"	Relevant ministries / public authorities
Indicator 4.3	**Teaching tools and materials for ESD are accessible**		
Sub-indicator 4.3.1	Does a national strategy/mechanism for dissemination of ESD tools and materials exist?	Qualitative "Input"	Relevant ministries / public authorities
Sub-indicator 4.3.2	Is public authority money invested in this activity?	Qualitative "Input"	Relevant ministries / public authorities
Sub-indicator 4.3.3	Are approved ESD teaching materials available through the Internet?	Qualitative "Input"	Relevant ministries / public authorities
Sub-indicator 4.3.4	Is a register or database of ESD teaching tools and materials in national language(s): (a) accessible through the Internet?; (b) provided through other channels?	Qualitative "Input"	Relevant ministries / public authorities
OBJECTIVE 5. PROMOTE RESEARCH ON AND DEVELOPMENT OF ESD			
Indicator 5.1	**Research[23] on ESD is promoted**		
Sub-indicator 5.1.1	Is research that addresses content and methods for ESD[24] supported?	Qualitative; "Input"	Relevant Ministries
Sub-indicator 5.1.2	Does any research evaluate the outcome of the implementation of the UNECE Strategy for ESD?	Qualitative/ Quantitative; "Input"	Relevant Ministries
Sub-indicator 5.1.3	Are post-graduate programmes available: (1) on ESD[25]: (a) for Masters level?; (b) for Doctorate level? (2) addressing ESD: (a) for Masters level?; (b) for Doctorate level?	Qualitative; "Input"	Ministry of Education; Institutions of Higher Education
Sub-indicator 5.1.4	Are there any scholarships supported by public authorities for post-graduate research in ESD: (a) for Masters level; (b) for Doctorate level?	Qualitative; "Input"	Ministry of Education; Institutions of Higher Education
Indicator 5.2	**Development of ESD is promoted**		
Sub-indicator 5.2.1	Is there any support for innovation and capacity building in ESD practice[26]?	Qualitative; "Input"	Ministry of Education; Institutions of Education
Indicator 5.3	**Dissemination of research results on ESD is promoted**		
Sub-indicator 5.3.1	Is there any public authority support for mechanisms[27] to share the results of research and examples of good practices in ESD[28] among authorities and stakeholders?	Qualitative/ Quantitative; "Input"	Ministry of Education; Governmental agencies outside education system; Institutions of Higher Education, NGOs
Sub-indicator 5.3.2	Are there any scientific publications: (a) specifically on ESD?; (b) addressing ESD?	Quantitative; "Output"	Education and research institutions; relevant Ministries; NGOs; publishers
OBJECTIVE 6. STRENGTHEN COOPERATION ON ESD AT ALL LEVELS WITHIN THE UNECE REGION			
Indicator 6.1	**International cooperation on ESD is strengthened within the UNECE region and beyond**		
Sub-indicator 6.1.1	Do your public authorities cooperate in/support international[29] networks on ESD?	Qualitative / Quantitative; "Input"	Report of relevant authorities
Sub-indicator 6.1.2	Do educational institutions/organisations (formal and non-formal) in your country participate in international networks related to ESD?	Qualitative / Quantitative; "Output"	Report of relevant authorities
Sub-indicator 6.1.3	Are there any state, bilateral and/or multilateral cooperation mechanisms/agreements that include an explicit ESD component?	Qualitative / Quantitative; "Output"	Report of relevant authorities
Sub-indicator 6.1.4	Does your Government take any steps to promote ESD in international forums outside the UNECE region?	Qualitative; "Output"	Report of relevant authorities

Figure 91: UNECE ESD indicators[1780]

1780 Sample of region-specific *ESD* indicators applied to North America and Europe (UN-ECE), in this very context.
See United Nations Economic Commission for Europe (UNECE); United Nations Economic and Social Council (ECOSOC) (eds.) (2007b) (cf. *footnote 385* op. cit.), pp. 5–10.

In the case of Asia, the *Asia-Pacific DESD Indicators Project* was initiated by an agreement in 2004 between UNESCO Bangkok in collaboration with other stakeholders to produce a set of specific guidelines that might assist UNESCO member states in the region with the development of national *ESD* indicators.[1781]

There are indeed operational similarities with the UNECE-region indicators, notwithstanding, conceptual differences do prevail.[1782]

1781 Cf. Haddad, Caroline (ed.) (2005): A Situational Analysis of Education for Sustainable Development in the Asia-Pacific Region. ESD/05/OP/396–1000. Volume Revised Edition. Supported by: Elias, Derek; Nakayama, Shuichi and Hargreaves, Lucy. Bangkok: UNESCO publishing; Australian Research Institute in Education for Sustainability (ARIES); Macquarie University Sydney; Australian Government Department of the Environment and Water Resources (eds.) (2006) (cf. *footnote 1753* op. cit.), pp. 33–34; UNESCO (ed.) (2007a) (cf. *footnote 1764* op. cit.), p. iv; Tilbury, Daniella (2007) (cf. *footnote 219* op. cit.); Elias, Derek; Sachathep, Karampreet (eds.) (2009): ESD Currents: Changing Perspectives from the Asia-Pacific. ESD/09/OS/002–1000. Bangkok: UNESCO publishing.
See *Figure 92* in chapter IX 5.2 *Indicators* on page 372.

1782 For example: referring to the UNESCO *structural hierarchy* of types of indicators. Cf. UNESCO (ed.) (2007h) (cf. *footnote 1762* op. cit.), pp. 4, 6.

Categories:	Status Indicators*	Facilitative Indicators**			Effect Indicators***			
Indicator Type:	Baseline	Context	Process	Learning	Output	Outcome	Impact	Performance
Why would this indicator type be used?	• To identify the current status of ESD in a region	• To identify the existence of ESD support systems	• To identify the existence of ESD processes, activities and opportunities	• To ensure the validity and improve effectiveness of ESD development, implementation and assessment • To promote learning and reflection on ESD progress	• To identify the existence of products, resources and tools that assist with implementation and integration of ESD	• To identify increased ESD awareness, understanding and skills	• To identify the existence of medium to long-term effects of ESD efforts that correspond to different ways of making decisions and taking action	• To identify change in the status of the overall ESD picture
What ESD elements does this indicator type assess? (specifics depend on goal & target identified)	• The overall ESD picture	• ESD governance mechanisms • Institutional support systems • Public opinions on ESD	• ESD processes, activities and opportunities for engagement	• Learning during ESD development and assessment processes • Learning from the indicators themselves	• ESD outputs often come in the form of materials such as tools and learning resources or show immediate results	• ESD outcomes or changes that result from ESD efforts provide the context for longer-term achievement • These assist persons to address SD in their daily lives so they are now capable of making change	• ESD impacts or lasting changes resulting from ESD efforts, goes beyond targets to show how goals are reached and decision-making and actions change	• Change in the overall ESD picture
What are the benefits of the indicator type?****	• Easy to identify areas that require improvement • Provides a practical way to design impact indicators • Helps to determine quantitative change relating to the overall ESD picture • Relatively simple to develop and monitor indicators as well as to collect, interpret, and communicate data • More likely to be comparable across regions	• Provides a 'snap shot' of the ESD governance and support structures in place • Easy to identify ESD support systems not in place • Relatively simple to develop and monitor indicators as well as to collect, interpret and communicate data; however, it can depend on the quantitative or qualitative nature of the indicator • Comparable at times, particularly if quantitative	• Provides a 'snap shot' of the ESD processes and activities • Easy to identify areas that require improvement • Comparable at times, particularly if quantitative	• Provides info on genuine ESD progress (quality) rather than existence or status • Promotes learning for change (or higher level learning) • Promotes multi-stakeholder involvement and ownership of processes • Contributes to the continual improvement of development and monitoring processes • Learning can be shared across regions through case studies	• Provides a 'snap shot' of ESD tools and resources available • Easy to identify areas that require attention • Simple to communicate and understand	• Provides a 'snap shot' of improvements resulting from ESD efforts • Simple to communicate and understand 'improvement' • Comparable when explicitly defined	• Provides a 'snap shot' of achievement in ESD (actions that are being taken as a result of efforts) • Relatively simple to communicate (for example when increase or decrease in numbers or ratios) • May be comparable depending on contexts	• Easy to identify areas that require improvement • Helps to determine quantitative change in the overall ESD picture relating to efforts undertaken • Relatively simple to develop and monitor indicators as well as to collect, interpret, and communicate data • More likely to be comparable across regions
What are the limitations of the indicator type?	• Unable to provide relatively detailed information on ESD efforts • Potential for an indicator set to become too large and impractical, limiting the ability to communicate change (*large numbers of indicators are a challenge among all indicator types*) • Explicit criteria must be developed to define what constitutes the overall ESD picture	• Details about the quality of the support structures may be challenging to attain or qualify • Explicit criteria must be developed to define what constitutes a support structure	• Often difficult to define a process • Details about the quality of processes and approaches in place may be challenging to attain or qualify • Challenging to compare as it is context-specific • Explicit criteria must be developed to define what constitutes an ESD activity or process as well engagement with ESD	• Details about learning may be challenging to attain or qualify • This data has not been traditionally gathered and therefore may present some challenges • Explicit criteria must be developed to define what constitutes learning and reflection • Not comparable	• Unable to provide information on details of the tools and resources • Explicit criteria must be developed to define what constitutes an ESD tool or resource • Challenging to compare due to context specific needs	• More work might be required to measure knowledge and competency • Improvement can be challenging to qualify • Explicit criteria must be developed to define the boundaries of improvement as well as make the indicators comparable	• Difficult to establish clear cause and effect relationships (i.e. how ESD leads to sustainable practices) • Difficult to identify source of change (i.e. whether results stem from increased awareness, understanding, capacity-building or legislation, for example) • Few programmes include funding for long-term assessment • Difficult to know when it is realistic to expect an impact to occur • Difficult to ensure that the impacts are lasting	• Unable to provide detailed information on ESD efforts • Potential for an indicator set to become too large and impractical, limiting the ability to communicate change (*large numbers of indicators are a challenge among all indicator types*) • Explicit criteria must be developed to define what constitutes the overall ESD picture

Figure 92: Asia-Pacific ESD indicators[1783]

1783 Region-specific *ESD* indicators and categories applied to Asia and the Pacific. See UNESCO (ed.) (2007a) (cf. *footnote 1764* op. cit.), pp. 36–37.

In line with the indicators of the Asia-Pacific framework, the UNECE strategy on monitoring *DESD* is considered more targeted to carrying out advocacy for *DESD* in the UNECE region.[1784]

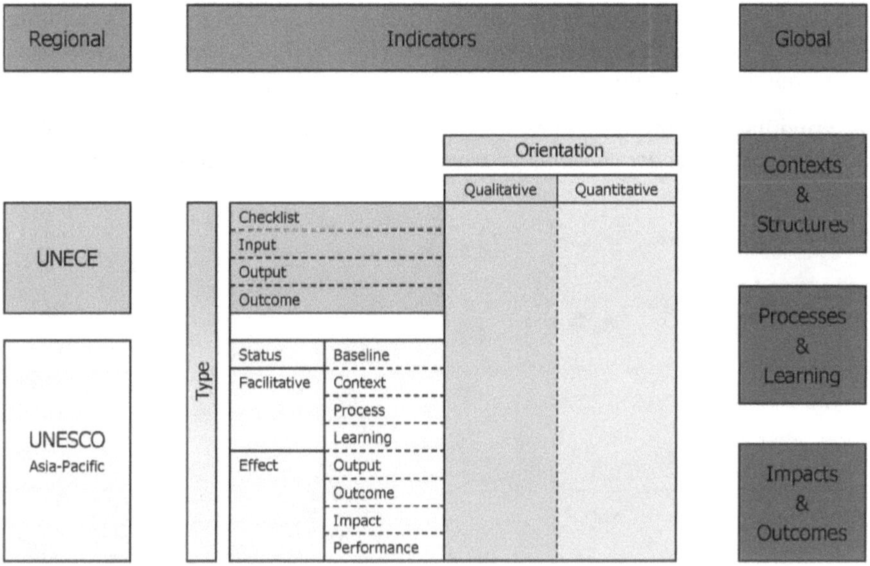

Figure 93: Summary of ESD indicators[1785]

5.3 Reporting

Reporting is the process of providing written accounts showing the result of an event, experiment, investigation, action or inquiry carried out. Reporting is specific in scope and provided exclusively for a particular audience. This *channelled* reporting is both prior and instrumental to evaluation. As regards *DESD*, progress is reported twice: in the first instance by 2009 or 2010 as appropriate in order to generate the mid-term review to be presented before the United Nations General Assembly, and in the second instance by the end of 2014 in order to

---

1784 Cf. Gerner, Martin (14/09/2009) (cf. *footnote 407* op. cit.); Gerner, Martin (30/07/2009) (cf. *footnote 407* op. cit.).

1785 The chart serves as summary of *ESD* indicators. Despite the fact that these are proclaimed at global level, too, according to the principles of *DESD* they comprise of a clearly marked regional scope. Irrespective of the regional requirements the type of indicator is exclusively determined by its definitional basis. Additionally, *ESD* indicators can rather consist of qualitative or quantitative orientations.

prepare the final *DESD* report in 2015 to be presented before the United Nations General Assembly as well.[1786] General reporting relies entirely upon decentralised, region-specific reporting.[1787]

As elsewhere, UNECE has pioneered the regional reporting process that is wholly in line with the structure of UNESCO global reporting, and in addition UNECE offers guidance at the global level. This *implicit* leadership function can be accomplished in two ways:

1. Providing guiding principles for reporting:[1788] recommendation of templates for reporting (*report format*)[1789] based on appropriate indicators;[1790] and

1786 Cf. UNESCO (ed.) (2008d): DESD Quarterly Highlights. July 2008. Paris: UNESCO publishing, p. 2; Gerner, Martin (10/08/2009) (cf. *footnote 407* op. cit.).

1787 Cf. Gerner, Martin (14/09/2009) (cf. *footnote 407* op. cit.).

1788 Cf. United Nations Economic Commission for Europe (UNECE) (ed.) (2006) (cf. *footnote 20* op. cit.), pp. 2, 3–6.

1789 See United Nations Economic Commission for Europe (UNECE); United Nations Economic and Social Council (ECOSOC) (eds.) (2005b): Draft work plan for the implementation of the UNECE Strategy for Education for Sustainable Development, 2005–2007 (Geneva, 13–14 December 2005). For adoption by the Steering Committee UNECE Steering Committee on Education for Sustainable Development. CEP/AC.13/2005/8. New York: United Nations, pp. 4, 8–9; United Nations Economic Commission for Europe (UNECE) (26/10/2006) (cf. *footnote 413* op. cit.); United Nations Economic Commission for Europe (UNECE) (ed.) (2009): Learning from each other. The UNECE Strategy for Education for Sustainable Development. ECE/CEP/159. Geneva / New York: United Nations Publications, pp. 51–69.

1790 Cf. Gerner, Martin (14/09/2009) (cf. *footnote 407* op. cit.).
See *Figure 94* in chapter IX 5.3 *Reporting* on page 375.

If necessary, provide relevant information on your country situation regarding this specific objective. (up to 1,500 characters with spaces)	
Indicator 4.1 Teaching tools and materials for ESD are produced.	
Sub-indicator 4.1.1	Does a national strategy/ mechanism for encouragement of development and production of ESD tools and materials exist?
Yes ☐ No ☐	*Please describe.*
Sub-indicator 4.1.2	Is public (national, subnational, local) authority money invested in this activity?
Yes ☐ No ☐	*Phase II: Please specify to what extent public authority money is invested in this activity, by providing an indication of the amount (in USD) referring to the amount of ESD-related research and development expenditures, annually.*
Indicator 4.2 Quality control mechanisms for teaching tools and materials for ESD exist.	
Sub-indicator 4.2.1	Do you have quality criteria and/or quality guidelines for ESD-related teaching tools and materials that are: (a) supported by public authorities? (b) approved by public authorities? (c) tested and recommended for selection by educational institutions?
(a) Yes ☐ No ☐ (b) Yes ☐ No ☐ (c) Yes ☐ No ☐	*Phase I: for (a) and (b) please describe.* *Phase II: Please specify for (a), (b) and (c) for formal, informal and non-formal education. For (c) please also describe.*
Sub-indicator 4.2.2	Are ESD teaching tools / materials available: (a) in national languages? (b) for all levels of education according to ISCED?
(a) Yes ☐ No ☐ (b) Yes ☐ No ☐	*Phase I: For (a) please specify.* *Phase II: For (b) please specify in the table by ticking (V) as appropriate.*
Indicator 4.3 Teaching tools and materials for ESD are accessible.	
Sub-indicator 4.3.1	Does a national strategy/mechanism for dissemination of ESD tools and materials exist?
Yes ☐ No ☐	*Phase II: Please describe.*
Sub-indicator 4.3.2	Is public authority money invested in this activity?
Yes ☐ No ☐	*Please specify to what extent by providing an indication of the amount in USD referring to the amount of ESD related R&D expenditures, annually.*

ISCED levels	(b)	
	Yes	*No*
0		
1		
2		
3		
4		
5		
6		
Teacher education		

Figure 94: UNECE template for reporting on ESD[1791]

2. Proving good practice of reporting: submitting timely reports, advisory and binding alike, on the assessment of indicators which have the potential to be of use to both UNESCO at the region-specific level *and* UNECE at the nation-specific level, and which include focal points pertaining to education and the environment.[1792]

1791 Sample page for reporting that is in accordance with the UNECE indicators. See United Nations Economic Commission for Europe (UNECE) (26/10/2006) (cf. *footnote 413* op. cit.), p. 8.
Cf. *Figure 91* in chapter IX 5.2 *Indicators* on page 370.

1792 Cf. Council of Ministers of Education, Canada; Environment Canada; Canadian Commission for UNESCO (eds.) (2007): Report to UNECE and UNESCO on Indicators of Education for Sustainable Development. Report for Canada. Prepared by the Council of Ministers of Education, Canada in collaboration with Environment Canada and The Canadian Commission for UNESCO. Ottawa: UNESCO Canada, pp. 4, 7; COMHAR Sustainable Development Council; ECO-UNESCO (eds.) (2007): Education for Sustainable Development in Ireland. Research Project compiled by ECO-UNESCO. Research Project on ESD commissioned by COMHAR SDC and undertaken by ECO-UNESCO. Edited by Elaine Nevin; Derek Ginnetty. Dublin: ECO-UNESCO, pp. 8 et seqq; UNESCO Section for DESD Coordination (ed.) (2009) (cf. *footnote 116* op. cit.), p. 79; United Nations Economic Commission for Europe (UNECE) (ed.) (2009) (cf. *footnote 1789* op. cit.), pp. 49–50.
See *Figure 95* in chapter IX 5.3 *Reporting* on page 376.

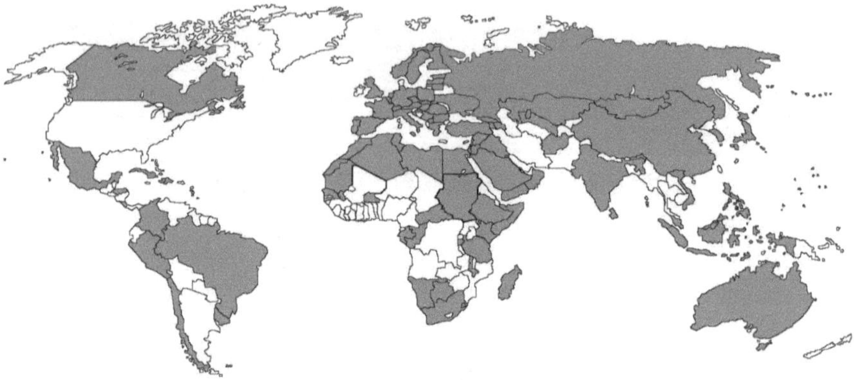

Figure 95: Countries responded to the 2009 mid-term DESD monitoring and evaluation call[1793]

Four principal components ought to constitute the reporting on *DESD*:[1794]

a) *Questionnaire* of binding reporting arranged according to the *DESD* objectives or trusts and based upon the UNECE-indicators;
b) *Complementary* data and *research* provided through reports given by regional experts;
c) *Multi-stakeholder* consultation process on networks and *engagement*; and
d) *UNESCO self-evaluating portfolio*[1795] based on interviews with the *DESD* thematic programme leaders and showcases on UNESCO's own contribution on *ESD*.[1796]

1793 The figure illustrates the return questionnaires to the 2009 mid-term *DESD* monitoring and evaluation call. Due to the fact that information is presented graphically, any valid conclusion can be drawn in respect of the quality of responses.
See UNESCO Section for DESD Coordination (ed.) (2009) (cf. *footnote 116* op. cit.), p. 79.

1794 Cf. UNESCO (ed.) (2008d) (cf. *footnote 1786* op. cit.), p. 3; Gerner, Martin (30/07/2009) (cf. *footnote 407* op. cit.); UNESCO Section for DESD Coordination (ed.) (2009) (cf. *footnote 116* op. cit.), p. 13.

1795 See UNESCO (ed.) (2008c) (cf. *footnote 1749* op. cit.), p. 3.

1796 This component underpins the *DESD Action Plan* that is fully in line with the *one-UNESCO* approach to *DESD*.

Successful projects at local level are collected for use at national level. These national (sub-regional) reports are collated in regional reports. All regional reports are than consolidated into one global report by the *global report coordinator* (GRC).[1797]

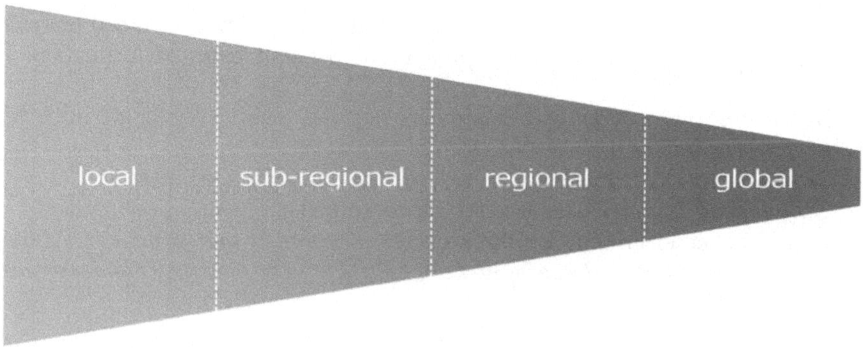

Figure 96: Focusing and channelling DESD reporting[1798]

5.4 Evaluation

The essence of evaluation is to determine systematically the significance, performance, accomplishment and *consequences* of relevant developments or actions, and in the course of this process apply performance criteria against predefined sets of standards or procedures.[1799] Evaluation must be based on meaningful and reliable reporting data.[1800] Dealing with aspects of explicitness, prac-

1797 The co-ordinator for the 2009 and 2010 *DESD* mid-term review is Arjen E. J. Wals. See Gerner, Martin (30/07/2009) (cf. *footnote 407* op. cit.); UNESCO Section for DESD Coordination (ed.) (2009) (cf. *footnote 116* op. cit.), p. 14; Witthaus, Michele; McCandless, Karen; Lambert, Rebecca (eds.) (2010) (cf. *footnote 1619* op. cit.). See *Figure 96* in chapter IX 5.3 *Reporting* on page 377.

1798 *DESD* reporting ought to reflect the principle of regional implementation, since both evaluation criteria and respective mechanisms are to be regionally grounded.

1799 Cf. Jabloner, Clemens; Okresek, Wolf (1983) (cf. *footnote 525* op. cit.), p. 222; Boyle, Bill; Christie, Tom (1996) (cf. *footnote 433* op. cit.), p. 33; Krott, Maximilian (2002) (cf. *footnote 203* op. cit.), p. 965; UNESCO (2003): UNESCO and The International Decade of Education for Sustainable Development (2005–2015). In: Connect, Volume 28, Issue 1, pp. 1–28, p. 6; Underdal, Arild; Young, Oran R. (eds.) (2004) (cf. *footnote 338* op. cit.), pp. 1–2.

1800 Cf. Mayring, Philipp (2002) (cf. *footnote 377* op. cit.), pp. 63–64; Wals, Arjen E. J. (13/05/2009) (cf. *footnote 1755* op. cit.), p. 3.

ticability, implementation, feedback and documentation, such evaluation may be conducted internally or externally.[1801]

The salient aspects of evaluation in the context of *DESD* are derived, in principle, from the *UN DESD Global Monitoring and Evaluation Framework* (GMEF).[1802] Consequently, *DESD* evaluation can be described as:

- *In-house*: despite the fact that UNESCO makes use of an outsourced *external advisory capacity*, there is no proper independent external evaluation of *DESD*;[1803]
- *Non-exhaustive*: covering gradual changes rather than every single initiative or action under the umbrella of *DESD*;[1804]
- *Trans-disciplinary*: involving at least four disciplinary perspectives;[1805]
- *Uniform*: relying upon standardised report formats;[1806] and
- *Threefold*: concentrating on three cycles of *contexts and structures* (2008–2009), *processes and learning* (2009–2011), and *outcomes and impacts* (2011–2013).[1807]

The *DESD Global Report*[1808] of 2009 represents the completion of the first phase of the *DESD* monitoring and evaluation process related to contexts and structures of *ESD*. With the assumption that successful developments have taken place in *ESD*, this report identifies major contextual and structural challenges in implementation.

These observations can be briefly summarised as follows:[1809]

1801 Cf. Boyle, Bill; Christie, Tom (1996) (cf. *footnote 433* op. cit.), p. 60; Bohnsack, Ralf; Marotzki, Winfried; Meuser, Michael (eds.) (2006) (cf. *footnote 306* op. cit.), pp. 55–57; Foreign Office of the Federal Republic of Germany / German Commission for UNESCO (ed.) (2007) (cf. *footnote 21* op. cit.), p. 24.

1802 Cf. UNESCO (ed.) (2008h) (cf. *footnote 219* op. cit.); Tilbury, Daniella (2010) (cf. *footnote 1764* op. cit.), pp. 146 et seqq.

1803 Cf. Gerner, Martin (14/09/2009) (cf. *footnote 407* op. cit.); Gerner, Martin (30/07/2009) (cf. *footnote 407* op. cit.).

1804 Cf. Wals, Arjen E. J. (July 2009) (cf. *footnote 533* op. cit.), pp. 196–197.

1805 Economics, ecology, social sciences and cultural studies, for example. Steps suggested for *trans-disciplinary* evaluation are: a) *scientific-community* evaluation, b) *meta-scientific* evaluation, and c) *political* evaluation.
Cf. Krott, Maximilian (2002) (cf. *footnote 203* op. cit.), pp. 966–970.

1806 Cf. Wals, Arjen E. J. (July 2009) (cf. *footnote 533* op. cit.), p. 197.

1807 Cf. Tilbury, Daniella (July 2009): Tracking Our Progress: A Global Monitoring and Evaluation Framework for the UN DESD. In: Journal of Education for Sustainable Development, Volume 3, Issue 2, pp. 189–193; Gerner, Martin (30/07/2009) (cf. *footnote 407* op. cit.); Bory-Adams, Aline (2010) (cf. *footnote 37* op. cit.), p. 177.

1808 Cf. UNESCO Section for DESD Coordination (ed.) (2009) (cf. *footnote 116* op. cit.).

1809 Cf. Bory-Adams, Aline; Wals, Arjen E. J. (14/05/2009): DESD Global Monitoring and Evaluation process. Fourth International RCE Conference 2009. Volume United Nations University. Montreal: UNESCO DESD Coordination Section, pp. 6, 9; Bory-

- Lack of commitment: not all countries participated reporting on *DESD*;[1810]
- Conceptual ambiguity of meanings: *DESD* is an elusive and diffuse concept; *ESD* is neither easily nor fully understood;[1811]
- Lack of resources: *ESD* receives insufficient financial support due to the minimal availability of public budgets, or non-existent economic incentives;
- Limited collaboration: *DESD* lacks efficient regional, inter-sectoral, inter-departmental and governmental co-operation. At United Nations level, for instance, there is no *one concerted UN response*[1812] to *ESD*;
- Many-voiced co-ordination bodies: Particularly at national level, co-ordination boards vary considerably in quantity and quality leading, in all likelihood, to dispersed responsibilities;
- Lack of specific *ESD* policies or strategies: *DESD* often lacks distinct commitment and the support of institutions, particularly at national level;
- Under-represented categories of learning: educational settings tend to be limited to *formal* education alone;
- Disintegration of stakeholders: non-governmental organisations, faith-based groups or other civil society organisations wishing to contribute to *ESD* in semi-structured learning environments are excluded from or are the object of disfavour in participation due to policies of funds distribution;
- Deficient conceptual background: more long-term research on, development of and dissemination of information about *ESD* is required;[1813] and
- Lack of facilitating momentum: *ESD* networks are intended to facilitate *DESD* implementation rather than publicise their existence.

Adams, Aline; Wals, Arjen E. J. (14/05/2009) (cf. *footnote 1809* op. cit.); UNESCO Section for DESD Coordination (ed.) (2009) (cf. *footnote 116* op. cit.), pp. 69–73; Wals, Arjen E. J. (July 2009) (cf. *footnote 533* op. cit.), pp. 197–200; Bory-Adams, Aline (2010) (cf. *footnote 37* op. cit.).

1810 Cf. Hollander, Astrid; Salgado, Carol (23/07/2008): UNESCO y la Década de las Naciones Unidas "Educación para el desarrollo sostenible" en América Latina. Oficina Regional de Educación para América Latina y el Caribe (OREALC). Interview. Format: doc (Questionnaire). Santiago de Chile.

1811 Cf. Wals, Arjen E. J. (13/05/2009) (cf. *footnote 1755* op. cit.), p. 3.

1812 See Wals, Arjen E. J. (July 2009) (cf. *footnote 533* op. cit.), p. 198.

1813 For instance, longitudinal analysis was initially intended for assessment, but was obviously skipped later on. Particular emphasis might also be placed on the evaluation of trans-disciplinary research.
Cf. Krott, Maximilian (2002) (cf. *footnote 203* op. cit.), pp. 966–970; UNESCO (ed.) (2008h) (cf. *footnote 219* op. cit.), p. 7; UNESCO (ed.) (2008d) (cf. *footnote 1786* op. cit.), p. 3; Bory-Adams, Aline; Wals, Arjen E. J. (14/05/2009) (cf. *footnote 1809* op. cit.), p. 5; UNESCO Section for DESD Coordination (ed.) (2009) (cf. *footnote 116* op. cit.), pp. 69–73; Bory-Adams, Aline (2010) (cf. *footnote 37* op. cit.).

Given these aspects of operational implementation and reporting tools,[1814] mid-term reviews of *DESD* are directed towards both critical appraisal and the provision of specific suggestions for improvements or changes.[1815]

5.5 Summary

Monitoring forms a crucial part of the implementation process. It is far more than an *end-of-pipe* assessment that might draw conclusions of success or failure. Moreover, monitoring must be understood as an integrated element which reflects the symbiotic relationship between procedures of implementation and monitoring. The entire process of monitoring consists of reporting and evaluation alike.

The *DESD* monitoring process is structured in exactly the same way. According to the twofold pattern of reporting and evaluation, the first phase of implementing *contexts and structures* leads to the provisional mid-term reporting (2009 and 2010) as a result of which recommendations are provided for the second phase of implementing *processes and learning*, which leads to the final reporting on *outcomes and impacts* (2014 and 2015).[1816] Paradoxically, the entire process aims to reconcile two conflicting strands:

- Meta-scientific monitoring of *DESD*, because it integrates certain axiomatic, institution-related *rationales*[1817] into the analytical framework, while simultaneously excluding inherent values and judgments from analysis;[1818] and
- Political monitoring of *DESD*, because it is driven by certain facts, attitudes and values serving the expectations and interests of stakeholders within the international political system.[1819]

Grosso modo, implementing and monitoring *DESD* are closely related to UNESCO's commitment as *lead agency*. There is in fact no means of independent, external evaluation, and to some extent this absence constitutes a monopoly

1814 Cf. United Nations Economic Commission for Europe (UNECE) (26/10/2006) (cf. *footnote 413* op. cit.); UNESCO (ed.) (2008h) (cf. *footnote 219* op. cit.), pp. 4 et seqq; UNESCO Section for DESD Coordination (ed.) (2009) (cf. *footnote 116* op. cit.).

1815 Cf. Wals, Arjen E. J. (July 2009) (cf. *footnote 533* op. cit.), pp. 200–203; Witthaus, Michele; McCandless, Karen; Lambert, Rebecca (eds.) (2010) (cf. *footnote 1619* op. cit.).

1816 See *Figure 97* in chapter IX 5.5 *Summary* on page 382.

1817 For example: leadership performance, schedule, cost-benefit-calculus, cost effectiveness (efficiency), etc.

1818 Cf. Krott, Maximilian (2002) (cf. *footnote 203* op. cit.), pp. 966, 969.

1819 I.e. market- or target-group oriented evaluation.
Cf. Krott, Maximilian (2002) (cf. *footnote 203* op. cit.), p. 970.

on the judgement of *DESD* success. Experience shows that monitoring is preferably carried out independently by third-party bodies.

On the one hand, the advantage of the *one-UNESCO approach* is its close relation to *DESD* implementation procedures, but on the other hand the problem appears to be that *"[...] compliance seems most directly linked to the existence of effective monitoring and independent supervision".*[1820] The issue of *DESD* compliance internationally is complex, since the objective is to assess the progress of *DESD* in its global implementation rather than through regional or institutional perspectives,[1821] and any assessment of success is therefore more difficult if conducted exclusively *in-house.*[1822] Unless this point is addressed, stakeholder acceptance and commitment towards *DESD* may gradually decline.

DESD monitoring is partly carried out on behalf of UNESCO by external experts affiliated to and explicitly tasked by the organisation.[1823] An illusion of independence is thereby sustained, but *in-house* monitoring is much more reflective of the reality. The question therefore immediately arises of how to then qualify the common disclaimer that *"(t)he author is responsible for the choice and presentation of the facts contained in this document and for the opinions expressed therein, which are not necessarily those of UNESCO and do not commit the Organisation".*[1824] At any rate, there are different experts, albeit affiliated to and even collaborating with UNESCO, in charge of carrying out different aspects of the process, such as:

a) Establishing the *UN DESD Global Monitoring and Evaluation Framework* (GMEF)[1825] in fulfillment of the *initiative* function; and
b) Reviewing conducted by means of the *DESD Global Report*[1826] in fulfillment of the *control* and *informative* function of UNESCO monitoring.

1820 See Shelton, Dinah (2003a) (cf. *footnote 989* op. cit.), p. 462.

1821 Cf. Hoof, G. J. H. (Fried) van (1983) (cf. *footnote 867* op. cit.), p. 91.

1822 Cf. Gerner, Martin (14/09/2009) (cf. *footnote 407* op. cit.). Cf. chapter IX 5.4 *Evaluation* on page 378.

1823 Cf. Gerner, Martin (14/09/2009) (cf. *footnote 407* op. cit.); Gerner, Martin (30/07/2009) (cf. *footnote 407* op. cit.).

1824 Cf. UNESCO Section for DESD Coordination (ed.) (2009) (cf. *footnote 116* op. cit.), p. 2.

1825 Such evaluation has been conducted by Daniella Tilbury and others. She holds the Chair of the UNESCO *Global Monitoring and Evaluation Expert Group* (MEEG) for the UN Decade in Education for Sustainable Development at the University of Gloucestershire, United Kingdom, and is a member of the *ESD Indicators Working Group* of the *UNESCO UK National Commission.* Cf. Tilbury, Daniella (2007) (cf. *footnote 219* op. cit.); UNESCO (ed.) (2008h) (cf. *footnote 219* op. cit.); Tilbury, Daniella (July 2009) (cf. *footnote 1807* op. cit.).

1826 Examples include that conducted by Arjen E. J. Wals and others. He holds the *UNESCO Chair of Social Learning and Sustainable Development* at *Wageningen University* in the Netherlands.

However, neither critical thinking nor honest indication of existing problems and deficits can outweigh or resolve this inconsistent *structural* dilemma.[1827]

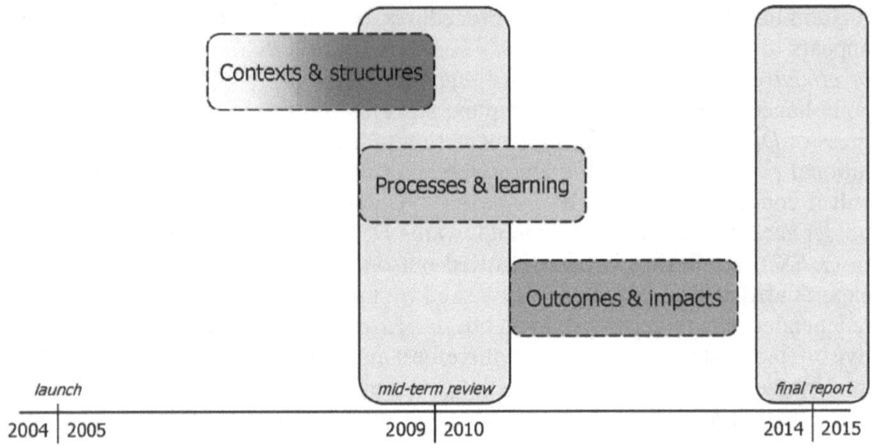

Figure 97: DESD monitoring[1828]

6 Regional implementation

6.1 Introduction

Effective implementation of *DESD* is not possible without the commitment of member states. Neither UNESCO's nor any other organisation's efforts will succeed if *DESD* does not gain momentum at grassroots level. For this reason member states are explicitly requested to *"[...] (develop) regional plans or strategies. These may also be present at sub-regional levels [...]"*.[1829] In other words, UNESCO reservedly delegates its mandatory responsibility of global leadership. *"These United Nations Regional Strategies take into account the overarching goals of the Decade and build regionally relevant approaches to*

Cf. UNESCO Section for DESD Coordination (ed.) (2009) (cf. *footnote 116* op. cit.).

1827 Cf. Wals, Arjen E. J. (July 2009) (cf. *footnote 533* op. cit.).

1828 *Two* stages of mid-term reviewing and final reporting determine and correlate with *three* phases focussing on contexts and structures, processes and learning, and outcomes and impacts of *DESD*.
Cf. Tilbury, Daniella (July 2009) (cf. *footnote 1807* op. cit.); Gerner, Martin (30/07/2009) (cf. *footnote 407* op. cit.); Tilbury, Daniella (2010) (cf. *footnote 1764* op. cit.), p. 546.

1829 See UNESCO (ed.) (2006h) (cf. *footnote 711* op. cit.), p. 2.

address the realities of needs, priorities, and resources in their respective regions."[1830]

Regional implementation of *DESD* is characterised by a cluster- and decentralised country-region approach[1831] in a flat organisational hierarchy, as *"(a)ll educational development efforts, beginning with planning and capacity-building, can only succeed through robust, diverse and multiple partnerships that respond to the articulated needs of the countries involved.*"[1832]

UNESCO's conceptual frameworks make an active contribution to this country-region approach because they relate primarily to the commitment of member states:[1833] both documents relevant for leadership and implementation, namely the *International Implementation Scheme* (IIS) and the *UNESCO Action plan for DESD*, show member states and regional platforms to be the principal addressees.

6.2 Specifics

Regional solutions are neither a new concept nor specifically designed for *DESD* implementation; regional approaches are common and accepted United Nations principles. To take an example from a similar, albeit slightly different context, in accordance with the *Johannesburg Plan of Implementation* (adopted at the *World Summit on Sustainable Development* in Johannesburg, South Africa, 26 August to 4 September 2002), the *United Nations Commission for Sustainable Development* (CSD) is in charge of monitoring the implementation of conference outcomes (stressing the importance of regional and sub-regional approaches).[1834]

To that end, responsibility is delegated to regional implementation forums addressing their particular needs and priorities. There are five regional forums that play a role in *DESD* implementation:

a) *Economic Commission for Latin America and the Caribbean* (ECLAC);
b) *Economic Commission for Europe* (ECE);

1830 See UNESCO (ed.) (2005f) (cf. *footnote 37* op. cit.), p. 11.

1831 In this context, *regional* is broadly defined both as national implementation and as the consultation and co-ordination platform on a regional scale.
Cf. chapter IX 1.1 *Regional strategies* on pages 257 et seqq.

1832 See UNESCO (ed.) (2005i) (cf. *footnote 216* op. cit.), p. 3.

1833 Not to underestimate efforts made in terms of non-state stakeholder involvement, such as civil society, non-governmental organisations or private business sector.

1834 Cf. General Assembly (cf. *footnote 855* op. cit.); United Nations Economic and Social Council (ECOSOC) (ed.) (2003) (cf. *footnote 733* op. cit.); Beisheim, Marianne; Lode, Birgit; Simon, Nils (2011) (cf. *footnote 732* op. cit.), p. 7; Lode, Birgit (2011) (cf. *footnote 739* op. cit.), p. 338.

c) *Economic Commission for Africa* (ECA);
d) *Economic and Social Commission for Western Asia* (ESCWA);
e) *Economic and Social Commission for Asia and the Pacific* (ESCAP).[1835]

A guiding principle of regional implementation of *DESD* is UNESCO's fundamental conviction that decisions have to be taken *"(...) according to (member states') priorities and approaches (...)"*.[1836] Context exerts a determinative influence on outcomes, and consequently *DESD* must be locally relevant in order to be successfully implemented. Therefore, *"the importance of sustainable development strategies at the regional, sub-regional and local levels (...) (is) strongly emphasised."*[1837]

At country level, UNESCO national commissions of member states undoubtedly play the key role *"as actors, initiators and catalysts"*[1838] in the implementation of *DESD* on a national scale. There is a substantial and varied normative mandate to be performed in compliance with UNESCO requirements:[1839]

- Initiating the establishment of national commissions on *DESD*;
- Promoting *DESD* goals at national level;
- Integrating *ESD* into national educational policies, strategies and plans;
- Implementing initiatives, organising training programmes and campaigns;
- Commissioning studies on *DESD*;
- Contributing to the mobilisation of civil society by acting as facilitators and reliable brokers;
- Linking UNESCO programmes with national institutions and civil society at large on the subject of various issues related to *ESD*;
- Acting as advisory and advocatory stakeholders;
- Providing links or interfaces with governments, informing and influencing decision-makers, such as ministries of education, environment, science, culture, environment, trade and finance; and
- Strengthening international co-operation by innovation and exchange of ideas.

1835 Cf. United Nations Commission for Sustainable Development (CSD); United Nations Economic and Social Council (ECOSOC) (eds.) (2003) (cf. *footnote 731* op. cit.), pp. 35–37.
1836 See UNESCO (ed.) (2006h) (cf. *footnote 711* op. cit.), p. 2.
1837 See United Nations Commission for Sustainable Development (CSD); United Nations Economic and Social Council (ECOSOC) (eds.) (2003) (cf. *footnote 731* op. cit.), p. 36.
1838 See UNESCO (ed.) (2005i) (cf. *footnote 216* op. cit.), p. 5.
1839 Cf. UNESCO (ed.) (2005i) (cf. *footnote 216* op. cit.), pp. 5–6.

Regional UNESCO offices are working towards a joint regional approach on *DESD* through:[1840]

- Facilitating the development of regional strategies for *DESD*;
- Exploring possibilities of organising regional exchanges and sharing experiences on *ESD*;
- Providing technical and professional support to *cluster* and national offices to assist the member states;
- Strengthening regional networks, partnerships and frameworks by stakeholder participation and co-ordination; and
- Generating programmes and initiatives.

Due to conferred competences on *DESD* implementation, member states and regions decide independently on, in particular, how and when to launch *DESD*.[1841] There are therefore several regional and national strategies and launches to be considered.

The following catalogue has to be regarded as a collation which aims to name the most important ones according to criteria such as:[1842]

- Name of *DESD* implementation strategy (by region or member state);
- Place, date and occasion of launch;
- Institutional bodies involved;
- Objectives to be pursued;
- Target groups and stakeholders; and
- Focal issues and activities.

1840 Cf. UNESCO (ed.) (2005i) (cf. *footnote 216* op. cit.), p. 5.

1841 In most cases regional and national launches of *DESD* tend to take place in close proximity to the international launch of *DESD* announced on 1st March 2005 by UNESCO's Director-General Koïchiro Matsuura. Proposed occasions of official regional launches are conferences on *ESD* or *DESD*.

1842 See *Table 39* in chapter IX 6.2 *Specifics* on page 386, and *Figure 98* in chapter IX 6.2 *Specifics* on page 394.

Table 39: Summary of regional strategies of DESD implementation[1843]

Strategy	*Europe and North America region*
Launch	Vilnius, Lithuania; 17–18 March 2005 at *High-Level Meeting of Environment and Education Ministries*
Institutions	*United Nations Economic Commission for Europe* (UNECE)
Objectives	• Clearly defining *ESD* • Promoting a comprehensive approach • Facilitating the introduction and promotion of *ESD* in the UNECE region (*UNECE Strategy for ESD*) • Ensuring that policy, regulatory and operational frameworks support *ESD* • Promoting sustainable development through formal, non formal and informal education • Equipping educators with the skills to include sustainable development into teaching • Making tools and materials appropriate for *ESD* accessible • Promoting research and development on *ESD*-related issues • Strengthening co-operation on *ESD* at all levels within the region • Making *ESD* heard in the political arena, nationally and internationally
Stakeholders	• Governments of 55 UNECE member states • United Nations agencies • (Non-governmental) International organisations • Universities

1843 Cf. UNESCO (ed.) (2006g): Highlights on Progress to Date. January 2006. Paris: UNESCO publishing; UNESCO (ed.) (2006h) (cf. *footnote 711* op. cit.), pp. 3 et seqq; UNESCO (ed.) (2007f) (cf. *footnote 427* op. cit.), pp. 5 et seqq; UNESCO (ed.) (August 2007) (cf. *footnote 693* op. cit.), pp. 4–7, 9; UNESCO (ed.) (2007k) (cf. *footnote 4* op. cit.), pp. 18 et seqq; UNESCO (ed.) (2010a): Youth Poverty Alleviation Through Tourism and Heritage An Educational Tool for Sustainable Development Youth PATH. Introduction to Youth Poverty Alleviation Tourism and Heritage. An Educational Tool for Sustainable Development. Kingston: Pear Tree Press; Vilela, Miriam (2010) (cf. *footnote 827* op. cit.); Fien, John (2010) (cf. *footnote 817* op. cit.).

Issues	• Mobilising and supporting governments to integrate *ESD* at respective levels • Setting up appropriate and workable indicators in order to measure effectiveness of *DESD* implementation • Collecting and disseminating regional best practices on *ESD* • Integrating *ESD* into the European Union Education Council • Acknowledging *ESD* as an integral part of the revised EU strategy on Sustainable Development • *Conference on Education for Sustainable Development towards Responsible Global Citizenship* (Vienna; 13–15 March 2006) • *International Symposium on Progress and proposals regarding ESD* (Paris; 14–16 June 2006) • *Nordic Conference on Sustainable Social Development* (Oslo, Norway; 26–27 October 2006) • *US Partnership for Education for Sustainable Development* (Washington, D. C., USA; 9–10 November 2006) as think-tank and expertise sharing platform • *International Workshop on the UN Decade of Education for Sustainable Development on Education for Sustainable Development Worldwide – Commonalities and Differences* (Bonn, Germany; 27–28 November 2006) • *European regions for sustainable development education seminar* organised by the *Network of European Regions on Education for Sustainability* (RES) (Brussels, Belgium; 27 November 2006) • *International Conference on Education for Sustainable Development – Heading for the Future – Goals and Strategies of ESD* (Lisbon, Portugal; 14–15 December 2006) • *First international meeting of the Task Force on Education for Sustainable Consumption* (Genova, Italy; 16–17 April 2007) to accelerate the shift towards sustainable consumption and production patterns • *EU Conference on the UN DESD* (Berlin, Germany; 24–25 May 2007) in the context of the *German Presidency of the European Council on the UN Decade of Education for Sustainable Development* • *Report on progress of implementing the UNECE strategy at the Sixth Ministerial Conference on Environment for Europe* (Belgrade; 10–12 October 2007)
Strategy	*Commonwealth of Independent States (CIS) region*
Launch	Minsk, Belarus; 5–6 April 2005 at CIS Education Minister's Conference
Institutions	Ministry of Education of the Republic of Belarus, Council on Co-operation in Education of the Commonwealth of Independent States (CIS), UNESCO Moscow Office and IFESCCO, Minsk
Objectives	• Developing an *ESD* framework, strategy and action plans • Brainstorming on *ESD*-related issues • Establishing dialogues and networks on *ESD* and *Technical and Vocational Education and Training* (TVET)

Stakeholders	• Youth • Officials • Politicians • Civil society (experts) • Media • Private sector • Educators • Universities
Issues	• Transition from school to university to professional work • Youth unemployment and poverty reduction • Entrepreneurship education for the world of work • *Technical and Vocational Education and Training* (TVET) and sustainable development • Developing professional education at all levels of education • Establishing high level co-ordination among stakeholders
Strategy	*Asia and Pacific region*
Launch	Nagoya, Japan; 28 June 2005 at *United Nations University (UNU) / UNESCO International Conference*
Institutions	UNESCO Office in Bangkok and Regional Bureau for Education
Objectives	• Integrating *ESD* into various educational settings • Moving from environmental education towards a holistic concept of *ESD* • Fostering inter-sectoral mandates • Establishing platforms for sharing information and local knowledge • Developing sound regional *ESD* indicators • Promoting the idea of think global and act local
Stakeholders	• Youth • Rural and indigenous communities (community leaders) • Civil society (experts) • Media • Private sector • UNESCO national commissions • Educators • Universities

Issues	• *Situational Analysis of Education for Sustainable Development in the Asia-Pacific Region* • Working Paper: *Asia-Pacific Regional Strategy for Education for Sustainable Development* as open document adaptable for revision according to changing needs and emerging issues • *DESD* co-ordination through *Asia-Pacific Regional UN Inter Agency Steering Committee* • *Young Minds in Action: Youth ESD Envisioning Contest* launched through the *UNESCO Associated Schools Project Network* (ASPnet) • Media workshop on *ESD* in order to enhance knowledge and dissemination of information • *Pacific Consultative Meeting on the UN Decade of Education for Sustainable Development* (Apia, Samoa; March 2006) for developing collaborative mechanisms for *DESD* in the Pacific islands region • *ESD-NET – Asia-Pacific Network of Teacher Education Institutions* (TEIs) (May 2006) • *1st Pacific Youth Festival* focusing on *DESD* (*Pacific Youth Charter*) (Tahiti, French Polynesia; 17–22 July 2006) • *UNESCO-IUCN CEC Asia-Pacific DESD Indicators Project / Regional ESD Monitoring and Evaluation Project: Review Meeting of the Asia-Pacific Guidelines for National DESD indicators* (Hiroshima, Japan; 10–11 August 2006) • *Pacific Framework for Action on the DESD* endorsed by the *Pacific Education Ministers Meeting* (Nadi, Fiji; 21–22 September 2006) as co-ordinating mechanism for specific goals of *DESD* implementation for the Pacific region • *10th UNESCO-APEID International Conference on Learning Together for Tomorrow: Education for Sustainable Development* (Bangkok, Thailand; 6–8 December 2006) • Capacity-building workshops in Bangkok (February 2005), Hiroshima (August 2006) and Bangkok (April 2007) on Asia-Pacific *ESD* indicators • Establishing mechanisms of monitoring and evaluation • Initiative of *Youth Visioning for Island Living* • *International Workshop on Engineering Education for Sustainable Development* (Tsinghua, China; 31 October-2 November, 2006)
Strategy	*Latin America region*
Launch	Rio de Janeiro, Brazil; 31 May-2 June 2005 at *Ibero-American Conference on Sustainable Development*
Institutions	*Brazilian Business Council for Sustainable Development* (CEBDS); UNESCO
Objectives	• Integrating *ESD* as a new, multidimensional and interdisciplinary concept into the region • Debating and exchanging experiences • Mobilising prospective stakeholders • Assessing needed regional educational and training resources

Stakeholders	• Governments of Ibero-American member states • Representatives of public and private institutions • Business people • International organisations (OREALC / UNESCO) • Non-governmental organisations • Academic and educational communities
Issues	• Encouraging joint actions by the government, civil society and corporations • Promoting actions among individuals, groups and institutions by *Centro de Educación y Capacitación para el Desarrollo Sustentable* (CECADSU) in Mexico • *International Seminar on Education for Sustainable Development: A Contribution from Science Education* (Buenos Aires, Argentina; July 2004) in preparation for *DESD* • *Latin America Regional Mobilisation Meeting* (San José, Costa Rica; 31 October-2 November 2006) for stressing linkages with the *UN Literacy Decade* (UNLD) and the need to prevent the spread of *HIV-AIDS* through education • Draft regional strategy on *Building Education for Sustainable Development in Latin America and the Caribbean* • Sharing the use of the *Earth Charter* • *International Seminar on Education for Sustainable Development* (Santiago de Chile; January 2005) • *International Seminar on Environmental Education for Sustainable Development* (Lima, Peru; November 2005) launching *DESD* within the Andean-Amazon region (PANACEA)
Strategy	*Arab region*
Launch	Bahrain; 17–18th September 2005
Institutions	UNESCO Associated Schools Project Network; UNESCO
Objectives	• Installing co-ordination bodies • Elaborating a medium-term work-plan for 2007–2010 • Implementing an *Arab Agenda on DESD* as regional strategy
Stakeholders	• Universities • UNESCO national commissions • Agencies

Issues	• *Third Arab Conference on Education on Education and Sustainable Development* (Beirut, Lebanon; 24–26 April 2006) as first regional forum on *DESD* • *Launching of the First Regional Flagship Protect on Water for ASPnet schools* (Abu Dhabi, United Arab Emirates) for three-level activities at six schools • Focusing on *Fresh Water Quality and Quantity* • *Workshop on Enhancing Teachers' Competencies in Sustainable Development* (Alexandria University, Egypt; 7–9 May 2007)
Strategy	*Caribbean region*
Launch	Kingston, Jamaica; 18–20 October 2005 at *Caribbean Regional Conference on Education for Sustainable Development: New Approaches for the Future*
Institutions	University of the West Indies; UNESCO
Objectives	• Providing a forum to discuss and address the issues of *ESD* • Launching *DESD* in the Caribbean • Preparing action plans for implementing *ESD* in the region • Building partnerships among formal and non-formal educators within the region • Re-orienting teachers' education to address *ESD*
Stakeholders	• Teachers, educators and administrators from pre-primary, primary, secondary and tertiary institutions in the Caribbean • Universities • Youth representatives from *Youth-Path* and other organisations • Non-governmental organisations • Government ministries • UNESCO, UNDP, ILO and other organisations • Private sector
Issues	• Extending *ESD* understanding from physical and biological terms to physical, biological, social, cultural and economic aspects • Making use of existing environmental educational activities in order to further integrate social, cultural and economic aspects • *UNESCO Guidelines and Recommendations to Address Sustainability* • *Teachers Colleges meeting on ESD* (Montego Bay, Jamaica; 28–29 June 2006) • *Northern Caribbean workshop of the Re-orienting Teacher Education for Sustainable Development in the Caribbean project* (Kingston, Jamaica; 22–23 August 2006) • *Electronic discussion list for teacher educators on ESD* • *Youth Poverty Alleviation through Tourism and Heritage* (YouthPATH) training programme
Strategy	*Mediterranean region*
Launch	Athens, Greece; 26–27 November 2005 at an International Conference

Institutions	Hellenic Ministry of National Education & Religious Affairs; Italian Ministry for Environment & Territory, *United Nations Environment Programme* (UNEP / MAP) and *The Mediterranean Information Office for Environment, Culture and Sustainable Development* (MIO-ECSDE); UNESCO; UNECE
Objectives	• Linking *DESD* with two major regional initiatives: the *UNECE Strategy of ESD* and the *Mediterranean Strategy for Sustainable Development* (MSSD) • Presenting the state-of-the-art *ESD* in the national formal educational systems • Raising awareness on various national non-formal and informal initiatives on *ESD* • Raising and assuring political commitment in support of *ESD* • Providing the dialogue in the Mediterranean region
Stakeholders	• Schools and universities • Youth • Non-governmental organisations • Government ministries • UNESCO, UNECE • Private sector
Issues	• Environment and development • Use of freshwater resources in all forms (sanitation, health, floods, agriculture, etc.) • Waste pollution and management • Development in coastal areas, mass tourism and intensive agriculture
Strategy	*Africa region*
Launch	Libreville, Gabon; 27–31 March 2006 at the *Association for the Development of Education in Africa (ADEA) Biennial meeting*
Institutions	*Association for the Development of Education in Africa* (ADEA); UNESCO
Objectives	• Disseminating information and providing training on *DESD* • Integrating *DESD* into local community contexts • Taking into account multiple and diverse indigenous knowledge systems and cultural perspectives • Implementing the regional *Strategy of Education for Sustainable Development for Sub-Saharan Africa* (SSAESD) • Working on *DESD*-related curriculum development, materials production, teacher training and policy making • Facilitating ownership and advocacy • Establishing a clearing-house of documentation • Compiling and sharing databases • Facilitating exchanges, cross-border dialogue and linkages to the global *DESD* learning space • Developing *ESD* curricula and introducing *transformative education*

Stakeholders	• Governments of cluster member states • International organisations (UNEP, UNESCO) • Association of African Universities • Civil society initiatives • Environmental networks and local initiatives
Issues	• *Mainstreaming Environmental Education in Francophone Sub-Saharan Africa* (MESA) (Nairobi, Kenya; 4–9 May 2006) • Train-the trainer workshops on *ESD* • Developing appropriate training material (tool kit) • *Eastern Africa Education for Sustainable Development* (*ESD*) *Network for creating an Eastern Africa Learning Space for Sustainable Development* by translating the objectives of *DESD* into the context of local communities of sub-regions • *Windhoek Southern Africa ESD Sub-regional Meeting* • *Southern African Development Community and Regional Environmental Education Programme* • Preparing national and sub-regional action plans • Addressing challenges in the socio-economic (poverty), environmental (degradation, desertification, climate change) and cultural (erosion of languages, traditional faiths and heritages) spheres • Proposal for a *Kenya Regional Centre of Excellence* (RCE) as pivotal platform for consultation • Strengthening complementary synergies between the *Millennium Development Goals* (MDG), *Education for All* (EFA), *United Nations Literacy Decade* (UNLD), *Education for HIV & AIDS* (EDUCAIDS) and the *African Union 2nd Decades of Education in Africa* • Fostering linkages between objectives of a) the *New Partnership for Africa's Development* (NEPAD) and *DESD*; and b) *DESD* and the *Second Decade of Education in Africa* launched by the *African Union* (AU) (Maputo, Mozambique; 2006) • *Eastern Africa Education for Sustainable Development* (*ESD*) *Network for creating an Eastern Africa Learning Space* • *Regional Centres of Expertise* (RCE) on *DESD* (January 2007)
Strategy	*Central Asia region*
Launch	Almaty, Kazakhstan; 21–22 September 2005 at *4th Sub-regional Conference on Environmental Education / Education for Sustainable Development in Central Asia*
Institutions	*United Nations Economic Commission for Europe* (UNECE)
Objectives	• Providing opportunity for active participation in *ESD* processes • Guiding through co-ordination and integration of national and sub-regional programmes with global and regional initiatives

Stakeholders	• Governments and diplomatic corps • Education and science sector (high schools and universities) • Media • Non-governmental organisations • International organisations (UNESCO, OSCE)
Issues	• *Joint Central Asian Working Group on Implementation of EE and ESD* • *Regional Environment Centre for Central Asia* (CAREC) • Launching the project on *Promotion of Education for sustainable development into formal, non-formal and informal education* (30 May 2006) • *Central Asian Workshop on Education for Sustainable Development (ESD): Innovative Approaches in In-service Teacher Training* (TT) *Systems* (Almaty; 3–5 July 2007)

Some national / sub-national launches

- Germany (Mainz, Germany - 13 January 2005)
- Chile (Santiago – 12-14 January 2005), organization of the *"II Seminario Internacional Educacion para el desarrollo sostenible"* for the national launch
- New Zealand (Auckland - 5 March 2005) at Ecoshow 2005, Waitakere City, Auckland
- Japan (6 March 2005) launching event organized by ESD-J (Japan Council on the DESD)
- Canada (Toronto - 10-12 March 2005) at the Annual General Meeting of the Canadian National Commission on the theme of 'Sustainable Development: Learning to Live Together'
- Mexico (Mexico City – 11 March 2005), national launch and signature of a National Commitment for DESD, in the presence of President Vicente Fox and representatives of all sectors of society.
- Norway (Hamar – 15 March 2005) on the theme of 'YouthXchange and the DESD national and global challenges for sustainable consumption'
- The Netherlands (The Hague - 5 April 2005)
- Quebec Province, Canada (Quebec City, 19-20 May 2005) at the 'Carrefour de la citoyenneté responsable'
- French-speaking community, Belgium (Mons–Frameries - 1 June 2005), during the 'Forum de lancement de la Décennie de l'Education vers un Développement Durable en Communauté française de Belgique'
- Scotland, UK (Stirling - 3 June 2005)
- China (Tongji University, in collaboration with the Chinese National Commission for UNESCO – 10 September 2005)
- UK (London – 13 December 2005), UK Launch Conference for the Decade on Education for Sustainable Development at the University of London Institute of Education hosted by the UK National Commission for UNESCO
- Pakistan (Islamabad – 29 December 2005)
- Viet Nam (Hanoi – 5 January 2006), national launch and installation of a national committee

Figure 98: National strategies of DESD implementation at a glance[1844]

1844 This list evidences that a considerable number of national of *DESD* initiatives was launched almost simultaneously with the international proclamation of *DESD* in March 2005.
See UNESCO (ed.) (2007k) (cf. *footnote 4* op. cit.), p. 19.

6.3 Close-up

Case studies are a workable means of illustrating respective processes of implementing *DESD*. They are intended to:

- Provide a comprehensive and more detailed understanding of *DESD* in close-up;
- Consider *DESD* in theory and in practice, especially in terms of regional differences and UNESCO's role and leadership performance; and
- Illustrate different methodological approaches in addressing qualitative and quantitative means of research.

Case-oriented research requires the judicious selection of cases. Why, therefore, have the cases of Europe and North America been represented by the *United Nations Economic Commission for Europe* (UNECE) and Latin America been chosen?

The region of Europe and North America is an interesting and internally heterogeneous region with varying levels of consciousness of *ESD* and variation in both the level and nature of implementation.[1845] This region is considered to have rich experience and *leadership* in *ESD*-related issues. For instance, there has been a relatively strong but nonetheless diffuse commitment towards environmental issues in education. Taking into account different priorities, the question arises of the possibility of achieving a consolidated and accepted strategy towards *DESD*. Contributing factors are a certain cultural proximity within the region additionally coupled with a reasonable availability of qualitative information and far more *quantitative* resources.

Latin America is an attention-grabbing choice of region with an internal heterogeneity composed simultaneously of industrialised, emerging and developing nations. Due to diverging priorities, needs and compulsions, differing levels of experience and commitment towards *DESD* may be discerned. The critical question remains of whether these divergences can be integrated sufficiently and simultaneously into processes of development and *ESD* alike. The access to and availability of officially published information on *DESD* constitutes in itself an issue of some complexity. One may, however, depend on *qualitative* sources of information provided by experts and interviewees.

1845 Cf. Gerner, Martin (14/09/2009) (cf. *footnote 407* op. cit.); Gerner, Martin (30/07/2009) (cf. *footnote 407* op. cit.).

6.4 Europe and North America

Europe and North America's[1846] major agency of *DESD* implementation is the *United Nations Economic Commission for Europe* (UNECE).[1847] The point of departure is again the *International Implementation Scheme* (IIS) which prescribes not only regional representation itself, but refers explicitly to the UN-ECE region's *genuine* implementation agenda: *"(r)ecognising that education is a fundamental tool for (...) sustainable development (UNECE) invited all countries to integrate sustainable development into their education systems at all levels (...) in order to promote education as a key agent for change. (UNECE) also welcomed the proclamation (...) of the United Nations Decade of Education for Sustainable Development starting in 2005, and agreed to take the lead in promoting it regionally".*[1848]

In order to ensure alignment with its *DESD* mandate UNESCO maintains close links with UNECE, which may be described in four ways:[1849]

1. Contributing to and actively participating in the preparation of the UNECE regional *DESD* implementation strategy for Europe and North America;
2. Jointly implementing the UNECE strategy, supporting governments in the promotion of *ESD* by integrating its principles into respective educational strategies and plans of action in particular;
3. Developing appropriate indicators to measure the effectiveness of implementing the UNECE strategy; and
4. Collecting and disseminating examples of regional best practice in *ESD*.

1846 As far as Europe's involvement on sustainable issues is concerned one has to distinguish between three different initiatives being under way: European contribution to the *Rio Declaration* expressed in *Agenda 21*; EU Sustainable Development Strategy as an independent approach; and *UNECE Strategy for ESD* as a joint effort of *DESD* implementation.
These differ in background, scope, objectives, means of implementation and methods of their assessment. Each single effort may be regarded as unique but also as interrelated, fully or partly, either institutionally, topically or historically, and are all subject to the common goal of sustainable development. Considering primarily the *DESD* perspective the following remarks may only scratch the surface of linking the UNECE strategy with the EU strategy.

1847 UNECE consists of all European countries with the addition of the United States of America and Canada.
Cf. *Figure 57* in chapter IX 1.1 *Regional strategies* on page 258.

1848 Cf. United Nations Economic Commission for Europe (UNECE); United Nations Economic and Social Council (ECOSOC) (eds.) (2003e): Framework for the Post-Kiev Work on Education for Sustainable Development. CEP/2003/22. New York: United Nations, p. 1.

1849 Cf. UNESCO (ed.) (2006h) (cf. *footnote 711* op. cit.), pp. 3 et seqq; United Nations Economic Commission for Europe (UNECE) (ed.) (2009) (cf. *footnote 1789* op. cit.), p. 8.

All institutional efforts within the UNECE region that are directed towards *DESD* can be subsumed under the *UNECE Strategy for ESD. "The aim of this Strategy is to encourage UNECE member States to develop and incorporate ESD into their formal education systems, in all relevant subjects, and in non-formal and informal education".*[1850]

The *United Nations Economic Commission for Europe* (UNECE) works with relative autonomy within the region considering that *DESD* is a politically sensitive issue, particularly in the matter of outside application within the UN-ECE region.[1851] Neither the UNECE framework nor the indicators are legally binding and adoption and compliance is voluntary.[1852] In addition there are limited possibilities to promote the *UNECE Strategy for ESD*[1853] across and beyond the region, as there exists neither the mandate nor the necessary resources. The concern is with attitudinal change in a broader context.

Given this, there is less permissibly applicable pressure, fewer resources and funding is more difficult to obtain; on the other hand, there are to this the advantages of greater flexibility, greater adaptability to differences and more scope for promoting processes that centre on participation, such as bringing together different stakeholders or *"getting people on board"*.[1854] The implicit intention of UNECE implementation and of the monitoring of *DESD* is to serve as a foundation (and example) for further regional implementation of *DESD* worldwide.[1855]

6.4.1 Drafting history

UNECE development of *DESD* began with the issue of environmental education discussed at the *Belgrade Conference* in 1975.[1856] Followed by the *Kiev Decla-*

1850 See UNESCO (ed.) (2005j) (cf. *footnote 44* op. cit.), p. 14.

1851 Cf. Gerner, Martin (14/09/2009) (cf. *footnote 407* op. cit.).

1852 Practical experience shows that obviously more *hard-law* provisions are needed in eastern countries, whereas good results in compliance with non-binding instruments have been evidenced throughout the western hemisphere. This may be subject to socio-cultural orientations towards the centralisation of strategy.
Cf. Gerner, Martin (14/09/2009) (cf. *footnote 407* op. cit.); Gerner, Martin (30/07/2009) (cf. *footnote 407* op. cit.).

1853 Cf. United Nations Economic Commission for Europe (UNECE); United Nations Economic and Social Council (ECOSOC) (eds.) (2005f) (cf. *footnote 391* op. cit.); United Nations Economic Commission for Europe (UNECE) (ed.) (2009) (cf. *footnote 1789* op. cit.).

1854 Cf. Linn, Monika; Sochirca, Angela (2010) (cf. *footnote 741* op. cit.).

1855 Cf. UNESCO (2009) (cf. *footnote 579* op. cit.); Gerner, Martin (14/09/2009) (cf. *footnote 407* op. cit.).

1856 Cf. United Nations Environment Programme (UNEP); UNESCO (eds.) (1975) (cf. *footnote 832* op. cit.).

ration 2003,[1857] the *Vilnius Framework* was established in 2005, setting the starting point for UNESCO *DESD* co-operation.[1858] UNECE implementation of *DESD* is considered to be iterative and twofold, comprising guidance and materials for national action plans, as well as implementation and assessment.[1859]

Instead of proclaiming an ad-hoc regional *DESD* implementation strategy by mandate, the UNECE strategy originates mainly from a non-mandatory background. With this respect the 2003 conference held by the environmental ministers of the UNECE region[1860] paved the way to a future UNECE strategy almost en passant.[1861] It was endorsed as the *Statement on Education for Sustainable Development by the UNECE Ministers of the Environment*[1862] in which member states invite UNECE to work on a regional implementation strategy both according to its mandate and together with UNESCO, the *Council of Europe* and other stakeholders.[1863] Dedicated initially to environmental protection only, the final declaration reveals crucial elements of *DESD*. For instance:

1857 Cf. United Nations Economic Commission for Europe (UNECE); United Nations Economic and Social Council (ECOSOC) (eds.) (2003c): Fifth Ministerial Conference "Environment for Europe" Kiev, Ukraine, 21–23 May 2003. Declaration by the Environment Ministers of the region of the United Nations Economic Commission for Europe (UNECE). ECE/CEP/94/Rev.1. New York: United Nations.

1858 Cf. United Nations Economic Commission for Europe (UNECE); United Nations Economic and Social Council (ECOSOC) (eds.) (2005g) (cf. *footnote 746* op. cit.), pp. 2, 5, 7.

1859 Cf. Gerner, Martin (14/09/2009) (cf. *footnote 407* op. cit.); United Nations Economic Commission for Europe (UNECE) (ed.) (2009) (cf. *footnote 1789* op. cit.), p. 10. See *Table 40* in chapter IX 6.4.1 *Drafting history* on page 408.

1860 These *Environment for Europe* conferences serve as follow-ups which comply with the implementational requirements of both the *Agenda 21* and the *Johannesburg Plan of Implementation*.
Cf. United Nations Commission for Sustainable Development (CSD); United Nations Economic and Social Council (ECOSOC) (eds.) (2003) (cf. *footnote 731* op. cit.), pp. 35–36.

1861 Cf. United Nations Economic Commission for Europe (UNECE); United Nations Economic and Social Council (ECOSOC) (eds.) (2003c) (cf. *footnote 1857* op. cit.).

1862 Cf. United Nations Economic Commission for Europe (UNECE); United Nations Economic and Social Council (ECOSOC) (eds.) (2003d): Fifth Ministerial Conference "Environment for Europe", Kiev, Ukraine, 21–23 May 2003. Statement on Education for Sustainable Development by the UNECE Ministers of the Environment. ECE/CEP/102/Rev.1. New York: United Nations; United Nations Economic Commission for Europe (UNECE) (ed.) (2009) (cf. *footnote 1789* op. cit.), pp. 27–28.

1863 Cf. United Nations Economic Commission for Europe (UNECE); United Nations Economic and Social Council (ECOSOC) (eds.) (2004e) (cf. *footnote 734* op. cit.), p. 5.

- It recalls all relevant conference outcomes and documents related to sustainable development;[1864]
- It recognises the multi-dimensional characteristics of sustainability,[1865] emphasising in particular the promising nexus between environmental issues and socio-economic development;[1866]
- It identifies education as *"a fundamental tool for environmental protection and sustainable development"*[1867] at all levels of the educational system;[1868]
- It welcomes the proclamation and launch of *DESD*;
- It declares that UNECE takes *"the lead in promoting (DESD) regionally in cooperation with (UNESCO)"*;[1869] and
- It contributes to *"UNECE regional implementation of global sustainable development process"*.[1870]

This so-called *Kiev Declaration* represents the unilaterally affirmed point of departure of the UNECE mandate and its commitment to regional *DESD* implementation.[1871]

In addition to the provisions of the *Kiev Declaration* a statement was released relating to *ESD* which unanimously declared that:

1864 Cf. United Nations Economic Commission for Europe (UNECE); United Nations Economic and Social Council (ECOSOC) (eds.) (2003c) (cf. *footnote 1857* op. cit.), pp. 4–5.

1865 *"Education for sustainable development should address environmental protection, social development and economic development."*
See United Nations Economic Commission for Europe (UNECE); United Nations Economic and Social Council (ECOSOC) (eds.) (2003e) (cf. *footnote 1848* op. cit.), p. 1.

1866 Cf. United Nations Economic Commission for Europe (UNECE); United Nations Economic and Social Council (ECOSOC) (eds.) (2003c) (cf. *footnote 1857* op. cit.), pp. 7, 9.

1867 See United Nations Economic Commission for Europe (UNECE); United Nations Economic and Social Council (ECOSOC) (eds.) (2003c) (cf. *footnote 1857* op. cit.), p. 15.

1868 Cf. United Nations Economic Commission for Europe (UNECE) (ed.) (2009) (cf. *footnote 1789* op. cit.), p. 15.

1869 See United Nations Economic Commission for Europe (UNECE); United Nations Economic and Social Council (ECOSOC) (eds.) (2003c) (cf. *footnote 1857* op. cit.), p. 15.

1870 See United Nations Economic Commission for Europe (UNECE); United Nations Economic and Social Council (ECOSOC) (eds.) (2003c) (cf. *footnote 1857* op. cit.), p. 18.

1871 Cf. United Nations Economic Commission for Europe (UNECE); United Nations Economic and Social Council (ECOSOC) (eds.) (2004i): Report on the Tenth Session 20–22 October 2003. ECE/CEP/116. New York: United Nations, p. 11.

- *ESD* has to be regarded as a cross-sectoral and multi-dimensional issue which encompasses economy, environment and society and which requires a holistic and participatory approach;
- *ESD* should be addressed at all educational levels and programmes, including formal, non-formal and informal educational contexts, referring also to vocational and continuing education; and
- Both state and non-state actors have to be encouraged in order to create broad momentum for citizen empowerment.[1872]

UNECE highlights its ambitious role *"in the (regional) promotion of education for sustainable development"*.[1873] As regional promoter of *ESD*, UNECE invites member states to participate actively in finalising the UNECE strategy for *ESD*, establishing focal state issues and reporting on progress being made. In the question of finance UNECE calls for appropriate resources to be made available, arguing for *ESD* as *"an investment in our future"*,[1874] either supported by governments, ensured through donations or funded by bilateral or multilateral donors. Most importantly, the statement concludes with the reaffirmed intention of UNECE to *"work in accordance with its mandate, with UNESCO and the Council of Europe on a regional strategy for education for sustainable development"*.[1875] UNECE states that it is part of the *DESD* multi-stakeholder network that is led by UNESCO.

Following the *Kiev Declaration* adopted at the conference in May 2003 the UNECE Committee on Environmental Policy set up an open and *open-ended task force*[1876] jointly and voluntarily led by the Russian Federation and Sweden

1872 Cf. United Nations Economic Commission for Europe (UNECE); United Nations Economic and Social Council (ECOSOC) (eds.) (2003d) (cf. *footnote 1862* op. cit.), p. 5.

1873 See United Nations Economic Commission for Europe (UNECE); United Nations Economic and Social Council (ECOSOC) (eds.) (2003d) (cf. *footnote 1862* op. cit.), p. 5.

1874 See United Nations Economic Commission for Europe (UNECE); United Nations Economic and Social Council (ECOSOC) (eds.) (2003d) (cf. *footnote 1862* op. cit.), p. 5.

1875 See United Nations Economic Commission for Europe (UNECE); United Nations Economic and Social Council (ECOSOC) (eds.) (2003d) (cf. *footnote 1862* op. cit.), p. 6; United Nations Economic Commission for Europe (UNECE); United Nations Economic and Social Council (ECOSOC) (eds.) (2003e) (cf. *footnote 1848* op. cit.), p. 1.

1876 See United Nations Economic Commission for Europe (UNECE); United Nations Economic and Social Council (ECOSOC) (eds.) (2003a) (cf. *footnote 748* op. cit.), p. 1.
Essential elements of the UNECE task force on *DESD* are: a) an *ad-hoc* foundation; b) its nature as an open-ended process; c) equity in terms of geographical representation; d) an obligation to welcome comments and report; and e) compliance with United Nations practice.

to draft a UNECE strategy.[1877] The *task force* serves *"as an instrument for UN-ECE member states to develop and finalise a (regional DESD) strategy"* due *"to report [...] on its work"*.[1878] It is composed of UNECE member states and other relevant stakeholders have observer status.[1879]

Emphasising its commitment to regional leadership UNECE introduces a framework document that provides detailed and strategic elaboration.[1880] It provides suggestions on topics such as stakeholders, structures, communication mechanisms, phases, budgetary planning and funding.

Developed through a participatory process that includes representatives from both environmental and educational sectors, UNESCO, the *Council of Europe*, non-governmental organisations and other stakeholders,[1881] the UNECE regional strategy serves as a flexible framework to be adapted to national contexts. Ideally, the member states serve as *national focal points*.[1882] Furthermore, this strategy constitutes a consolidated framework which is built on consensus and through the participation of UNECE member states.

The UNECE strategy has been the subject of particular discussion from the perspective of links between different initiatives already in place, and namely between the UNECE implementation and the *Johannesburg Plan of Implementation*.[1883] As a result, UNECE leaves sufficient strategic space for carefully introducing its strategy involving *"a steering committee of representatives of the environment and education sectors (...) with a view to ensuring equal opportu-*

Cf. United Nations Economic Commission for Europe (UNECE); United Nations Economic and Social Council (ECOSOC) (eds.) (2004i) (cf. *footnote 1871* op. cit.), pp. 11–12.

1877 Cf. United Nations Economic Commission for Europe (UNECE); United Nations Economic and Social Council (ECOSOC) (eds.) (2004i) (cf. *footnote 1871* op. cit.), pp. 11 et seqq.

1878 See United Nations Economic Commission for Europe (UNECE); United Nations Economic and Social Council (ECOSOC) (eds.) (2003a) (cf. *footnote 748* op. cit.), p. 1.

1879 For example: UNESCO, the Council of Europe, (non-governmental) organisations, etc. The *task force* may be subdivided into a smaller drafting unit with *"equitable geographical representation"* in order to *"help prepare the strategy"*.
Cf. United Nations Economic Commission for Europe (UNECE); United Nations Economic and Social Council (ECOSOC) (eds.) (2003a) (cf. *footnote 748* op. cit.), p. 2.

1880 Cf. United Nations Economic Commission for Europe (UNECE); United Nations Economic and Social Council (ECOSOC) (eds.) (2003e) (cf. *footnote 1848* op. cit.).

1881 Cf. United Nations Economic Commission for Europe (UNECE); United Nations Economic and Social Council (ECOSOC) (eds.) (2003a) (cf. *footnote 748* op. cit.), p. 2.

1882 See United Nations Economic Commission for Europe (UNECE); United Nations Economic and Social Council (ECOSOC) (eds.) (2003a) (cf. *footnote 748* op. cit.), p. 2.

1883 Cf. UN Department of Economic and Social Affairs (ed.) (2002) (cf. *footnote 853* op. cit.).

nities for representation and input from both sectors"[1884] and key stakeholders as observers:[1885]

1. Ensuring that policy, regulatory and operational frameworks support *ESD*;
2. Promoting sustainable development through formal, non-formal and informal learning;
3. Equipping educators with the competence to include sustainable development in their teaching curricula;
4. Ensuring access to adequate tools and materials for *ESD*; and
5. Promoting research on and development of *ESD*.

Particular attention is drawn to the implementation framework of the UNECE strategy in terms of:[1886]

- Activities;
- Co-ordination and review;
- Financial arrangements;
- Establishing a steering committee; and
- Setting up an expert group on *ESD* performance indicators.

In line with the framework on the commitment of UNECE to *DESD*, the task force set up a work programme concerning several pre-scheduled meetings before the final approval and regional launch. The adoption of the UNECE strategy on *DESD* has been scheduled to take place in February 2005, its national implementation by March 2005 and its assessment from October 2006 onwards.[1887]

Shortly after its nomination as the regional implementation agency, the UNECE secretariat provided the first proposal of a draft UNECE strategy.[1888] This

1884 See United Nations Economic Commission for Europe (UNECE); United Nations Economic and Social Council (ECOSOC) (eds.) (2004h) (cf. *footnote 749* op. cit.), p. 4.

1885 Cf. United Nations Economic Commission for Europe (UNECE); United Nations Economic and Social Council (ECOSOC) (eds.) (2004h) (cf. *footnote 749* op. cit.), p. 4; United Nations Economic Commission for Europe (UNECE) (ed.) (2009) (cf. *footnote 1789* op. cit.), p. 16.

1886 Cf. United Nations Economic Commission for Europe (UNECE); United Nations Economic and Social Council (ECOSOC) (eds.) (2004h) (cf. *footnote 749* op. cit.), p. 4.

1887 Cf. United Nations Economic Commission for Europe (UNECE); United Nations Economic and Social Council (ECOSOC) (eds.) (2003f): Work Programme of the Task Force on Education for Sustainable Development. First regional meeting on education for sustainable development. Geneva, 19–20 February 2004. CEP/AC.13/2004/5. New York: United Nations, pp. 2–4.

1888 Cf. No. 3 United Nations Economic Commission for Europe (UNECE); United Nations Economic and Social Council (ECOSOC) (eds.) (2003f) (cf. *footnote 1887* op. cit.), p. 1.

document serves as a reference point and as a *blueprint* for further debate. The first draft UNECE strategy had therefore already been published before the first meeting of the task force on 17 December 2003.[1889] Based on similar official documents it is evident that the draft strategy draws on the UNESCO *International Implementation Scheme* (IIS), although the UNECE strategy appears to be far more focused on the creation of specific momentum. Additionally, it reveals through its very nature a more *Eurocentric* perspective.[1890]

The first draft of the UNECE strategy was officially adopted on 13–15 October 2004 by the *task force*. A driving factor in the adoption was the coherence established between the UNECE strategy and existing global processes on the subject of education. Since the first draft proposal expressly mentions European initiatives and efforts towards *ESD*-related issues it is remarkable that this aspect should be omitted entirely from the draft version.[1891] At the same time, the *task force* agreed upon the collaborative means of implementing UNECE strategy sketched in a framework document. It consists of, amongst other things, areas of national priority, the scheduled phases of implementation, demands for the collation of examples of good practice and of appropriate indicators as well as of reporting mechanisms, means of process management, budgetary planning and assessment.[1892]

A consolidated draft version of the UNECE strategy was communicated to the public on 7 December 2004. In contrast to previous drafts this document points out an important difference with regard to the scope of the UNECE strat-

1889 Cf. United Nations Economic Commission for Europe (UNECE); United Nations Economic and Social Council (ECOSOC) (eds.) (2003b): Draft UNECE Strategy for Education for Sustainable Development. First regional meeting on education for sustainable development. Geneva, 19–20 February 2004. CEP/AC.13/2004/3. New York: United Nations.

1890 A strong European dimension is reflected in the explicit references to respective legal frameworks of sustainability within the UNECE region. These are primarily: *Baltic 21E*, an Agenda 21 for *ESD* in the Baltic Sea Region; *Thessaloniki Declaration*, UNESCO, 1997; *The Sixth Environmental Action Programme of the European Union*, 2001–2010; *Magna Charter Universitatum Europaeum*, Bologna, Italy, 1988; *Copernicus University Charter for Sustainable Development*, Rio de Janeiro, Brazil, 1992; *Statement on Education for Sustainable Development*; *Basic Elements for a UNECE Strategy for Education for Sustainable Development*, *Fifth Ministerial Conference "Environment for Europe"*, Kiev, 2003.
Cf. United Nations Economic Commission for Europe (UNECE); United Nations Economic and Social Council (ECOSOC) (eds.) (2003b) (cf. *footnote 1889* op. cit.), p. 2.

1891 Cf. United Nations Economic Commission for Europe (UNECE); United Nations Economic and Social Council (ECOSOC) (eds.) (2004c): Draft UNECE Strategy for Education for Sustainable Development. Eleventh session (Geneva, 13–15 October 2004). CEP/2004/15 / CEP/AC.13/2004/8/Rev.1. New York: United Nations, pp. 3–4.

1892 Cf. United Nations Economic Commission for Europe (UNECE); United Nations Economic and Social Council (ECOSOC) (eds.) (2004g) (cf. *footnote 391* op. cit.).

egy: according to the text the UNECE strategy *"will be adopted by (only) interested UNECE member states".*[1893] In other words, the document suggests that implementation will be based exclusively on the goodwill of participants, or rather, those who are not interested are not obliged to comply with the UNECE strategy.

Since the UNECE strategy covers the basic aspects of regional *DESD* implementation only, but not the process itself, the *task force* provides the strategic assistance necessary by developing a framework for implementing the strategy. The so called *Vilnius Framework for Implementation*[1894] is instrumental in responding to the most critical questions concerning particular activities within the implementation, co-ordination and the review of implementation as well as the financing of implementation.[1895] Both the UNECE strategy and the framework for implementation are placed on the agenda for adoption at the Vilnius conference on 17–18 March 2005, a follow-up to the Kiev conference in 2003.[1896]

"In Vilnius on 17–18 March 2005, UNECE Ministers, Vice-Ministers and other representatives of Environment and Education Ministries adopted the UNECE Strategy for Education for Sustainable Development. They also adopted the Vilnius Framework for Implementation, setting up a steering committee and an expert group on indicators in order to facilitate the co-ordination and review of the Strategy's implementation."[1897] The fact of established and well-functioning education systems, guaranteed access to basic education and equal rights to education for all gave cause for optimism. Despite considerable political, social and economic differences, *"the (UNECE) region as a whole is considered to have a good basis for implementing ESD".*[1898] At the same time concerns were raised about the possible negative impact on the quality of education through regional under-development and poverty. Furthermore *"education sys-*

1893 Cf. United Nations Economic Commission for Europe (UNECE); United Nations Economic and Social Council (ECOSOC) (eds.) (2004b) (cf. *footnote 391* op. cit.), p. 3.

1894 Cf. United Nations Economic Commission for Europe (UNECE); United Nations Economic and Social Council (ECOSOC) (eds.) (2004g) (cf. *footnote 391* op. cit.).

1895 Cf. United Nations Economic Commission for Europe (UNECE); United Nations Economic and Social Council (ECOSOC) (eds.) (2004a) (cf. *footnote 746* op. cit.); United Nations Economic Commission for Europe (UNECE) (ed.) (2009) (cf. *footnote 1789* op. cit.), p. 4.

1896 Cf. United Nations Economic Commission for Europe (UNECE); United Nations Economic and Social Council (ECOSOC) (eds.) (2004h) (cf. *footnote 749* op. cit.), pp. 2, 4.

1897 See United Nations Economic Commission for Europe (UNECE); United Nations Economic and Social Council (ECOSOC) (eds.) (2005a): Chair's Summary. High-level meeting of Environment and Education Ministries, Vilnius, 17–18 March 2005. CEP/AC.13/2005/5. New York: United Nations, p. 1.

1898 Cf. United Nations Economic Commission for Europe (UNECE); United Nations Economic and Social Council (ECOSOC) (eds.) (2005a) (cf. *footnote 1897* op. cit.), p. 2.

tems must become more flexible in view of the cross-cutting nature of (ESD)".[1899]

Both the adopted *UNECE Strategy for ESD* and the *Vilnius Framework for Implementation* were officially confirmed and released on 23 and 25 March 2005 respectively.[1900]

DESD was formally launched within the UNECE region at the Vilnius conference in March 2005. As prescribed in the founding documents UNECE member states were requested to submit their candidates for the:[1901]

a) *UNECE Steering Committee on ESD*[1902] mandated to supervise the implementing process; and
b) The *Expert group on indicators for DESD* according to *"equitable regional representation".*[1903]

Once established, both the *UNECE Steering Committee on ESD* and the *UNECE Expert Group on ESD indicators* jointly decided upon a draft *work plan*[1904] that *"presents activities that aim at facilitating the start of the implementation".*[1905]

1899 See United Nations Economic Commission for Europe (UNECE); United Nations Economic and Social Council (ECOSOC) (eds.) (2005a) (cf. *footnote 1897* op. cit.), p. 2.

1900 Cf. United Nations Economic Commission for Europe (UNECE); United Nations Economic and Social Council (ECOSOC) (eds.) (2005f) (cf. *footnote 391* op. cit.); United Nations Economic Commission for Europe (UNECE); United Nations Economic and Social Council (ECOSOC) (eds.) (2005g) (cf. *footnote 746* op. cit.).

1901 Cf. United Nations Economic Commission for Europe (UNECE); United Nations Economic and Social Council (ECOSOC) (eds.) (2005e) (cf. *footnote 746* op. cit.), p. 5; United Nations Economic Commission for Europe (UNECE); United Nations Economic and Social Council (ECOSOC) (eds.) (2005d): Report of the Meeting. High-level meeting of Environment and Education Ministries, Vilnius, 17–18 March 2005. CEP/AC.13/2005/2. New York: United Nations; UNESCO (ed.) (2007k) (cf. *footnote 4* op. cit.), p. 31.

1902 Apart from the representatives of member states the committee consists of *interested stakeholders*, such as international organisations, regional environmental centres, non-governmental organisations and business representatives in the capacity of observers. Accordingly, this also applies to UNESCO since the organisation *"was invited to be a permanent observer".*
See United Nations Economic Commission for Europe (UNECE); United Nations Economic and Social Council (ECOSOC) (eds.) (2005e) (cf. *footnote 746* op. cit.), p. 5.

1903 See United Nations Economic Commission for Europe (UNECE) (ed.) (2009) (cf. *footnote 1789* op. cit.), p. 4.

1904 Cf. United Nations Economic Commission for Europe (UNECE) (ed.) (2009) (cf. *footnote 1789* op. cit.), pp. 4–5.

1905 Cf. United Nations Economic Commission for Europe (UNECE); United Nations Economic and Social Council (ECOSOC) (eds.) (2005b) (cf. *footnote 1789* op. cit.), p. 1.

In preparation for the first meeting of the *UNECE Steering Committee on ESD* on 14–15 December 2005, the *UNECE Expert Group on ESD indicators* presented a draft outline of appropriate indicators on 23 November 2005.[1906]

Accompanied by intense discussion, remarks and comments, the work plan for the *Vilnius Framework for Implementation* was adopted on 27 January 2006.[1907] The draft work done by the *UNECE Expert Group on ESD indicators* on measuring the effectiveness of *DESD* implementation within the UNECE region was widely appreciated as *"both substantive and innovative"*.[1908]

Further strengthening the process of UNECE implementation, the European Union declared explicit conformity and compliance with the *UNECE strategy for ESD*. In the context of an EU presidency conference in Vienna on 13–15 March 2006 all member states unanimously recommended to the European Union that it should:

1. *"Tak(e)(...) concrete steps towards acceptance, support and facilitation of the implementation of ESD, as stated in the UNECE Strategy for (ESD) across the EU and its neighbourhood, with the involvement of all relevant sectors and stakeholders;*
2. *Confirm(...) this commitment through relevant statements by the EU Council and other relevant bodies; (and)*
3. *Support(...) the inclusion of a joint (m)inisterial (s)egment on ESD (...)"*.[1909]

Moreover, as part of a revised EU sustainable development strategy member states *"should also implement the UNECE Strategy for Education for Sustainable Development adopted in Vilnius in 2005. Education for sustainable development should also be promoted at EU level"*.[1910]

On 4–5 December 2006, the *UNECE Steering Committee on ESD* endorsed the set of indicators finalised by the respective UNECE Expert Group on *ESD*

1906 Cf. United Nations Economic Commission for Europe (UNECE); United Nations Economic and Social Council (ECOSOC) (eds.) (2005c) (cf. *footnote 411* op. cit.); United Nations Economic Commission for Europe (UNECE) (ed.) (2009) (cf. *footnote 1789* op. cit.), p. 4.

1907 Cf. No. 26 United Nations Economic Commission for Europe (UNECE); United Nations Economic and Social Council (ECOSOC) (eds.) (2006) (cf. *footnote 1774* op. cit.), p. 6.

1908 See United Nations Economic Commission for Europe (UNECE); United Nations Economic and Social Council (ECOSOC) (eds.) (2006) (cf. *footnote 1774* op. cit.), p. 4.

1909 See Austrian Federal Ministry for Education, the Arts and Culture (BMUKK) (ed.) (2006): Resolution adopted by the participants of the EU Presidency Conference on "ESD towards responsible Global Citizenship". Vienna, 13–15 March 2006. Vienna.

1910 See UNESCO (ed.) (2007k) (cf. *footnote 4* op. cit.), p. 33.

indicators.[1911] Due to the excellent work done and the extension of the mandate of the *UNECE Steering Committee on ESD* the mandate of the expert group was a) extended and b) provided with a supplementary task profile in which it was directed to:

- *"(R)evise (...) the set of indicators, following the pilot reporting exercise and the feedback received from countries on the workability and feasibility of the indicators and requested information for reporting; (and)*
- *(E)xplore the possibility of developing criteria to assess success in implementation of the UNECE Strategy for ESD in the countries of the UNECE region, based on the indicators as well as on the examples submitted by the countries (...)".*[1912]

A thoroughly positive conclusion on the implementation of the UNECE strategy was drawn at the UNECE conference jointly led by ministers of education and the environment as well as other major stakeholders in *ESD*. The process is *"well under way; (since) most countries were showing commitment to establishing the necessary policies and institutional structures to implement the (s)trategy".*[1913]

The essence of the Belgrade conference on 10–12 October 2007 was the adoption of a programmatic declaration entitled *"Building Bridges to the Future"* . As far as *ESD* is concerned considerable improvement had been made since the Kiev conference in 2003. Substantive contributions were warmly welcomed from all member states in order *"to further strengthen efforts for the implementation of the UNECE Strategy for ESD at all levels by the end of the United Nations Decade of Education for Sustainable Development (in 2015)".*[1914]

1911 Cf. No. 18 United Nations Economic Commission for Europe (UNECE); United Nations Economic and Social Council (ECOSOC) (eds.) (2007c) (cf. *footnote 1774* op. cit.), p. 4; United Nations Economic Commission for Europe (UNECE); United Nations Economic and Social Council (ECOSOC) (eds.) (2007b) (cf. *footnote 385* op. cit.); UNESCO (ed.) (2007f) (cf. *footnote 427* op. cit.), p. 5; United Nations Economic Commission for Europe (UNECE) (26/10/2006) (cf. *footnote 413* op. cit.).

1912 See UNESCO (ed.) (2007k) (cf. *footnote 4* op. cit.), p. 32; United Nations Economic Commission for Europe (UNECE); United Nations Economic and Social Council (ECOSOC) (eds.) (2007c) (cf. *footnote 1774* op. cit.), p. 4.

1913 See United Nations Economic Commission for Europe (UNECE); United Nations Economic and Social Council (ECOSOC) (eds.) (2007a) (cf. *footnote 1774* op. cit.), p. 7.

1914 See United Nations Economic Commission for Europe (UNECE); United Nations Economic and Social Council (ECOSOC) (eds.) (2007d) (cf. *footnote 1774* op. cit.), p. 6; Elias, Victoria (2007) (cf. *footnote 827* op. cit.); UNESCO (2007) (cf. *footnote 52* op. cit.).

Table 40: Development of the UNECE strategy and the Vilnius Framework for Implementation

Date	*Document*	*Content*
11 June 2003	ECE/CEP/94/Rev.1 (Kiev Declaration)	Appreciating *DESD*; declaring UNECE regional leadership
	ECE/CEP/102/Rev.1 (Statement on *ESD*)	UNECE promoting *DESD* at regional scale
11 August 2003	CEP/2003/22	Framework on *DESD* within the UNECE region
20–22 October 2003 / 18 November 2003	ECE/CEP/116 / CEP/AC.13/2004/4	Task force and working programme on UNECE strategy
17 December 2003	CEP/AC.13/2004/3	First draft UNECE strategy
19–20 February 2004		First UNECE task force meeting
4 August 2004 / 13–15 October 2004	CEP/2004/15 / CEP/AC.13/2004/8/Rev.1	Adoption of the draft UNECE strategy and decision upon the implementation framework
	CEP/2004/17 / CEP/AC.13/2004/10	Decision upon the UNECE implementation framework
7 December 2004	CEP/AC.13/2005/3	Draft UNECE strategy
16 December 2004	CEP/AC.13/2005/4	Draft Vilnius Framework for Implementation
30 November 2004	CEP/AC.13/2005/1	Presentation of the UNECE strategy for *ESD* and implementation framework
17–18 March 2005	CEP/AC.13/2005/5	Adoption of the UNECE strategy and the Vilnius Framework for Implementation
23 / 25 March 2005	CEP/AC.13/2005/3/Rev.1 CEP/AC.13/2005/4/Rev.1	Adoption of the UNECE strategy and the Vilnius Framework for Implementation at the High-level Meeting
2 May 2005	CEP/AC.13/2005/2	Launching the UNECE strategy and the Vilnius Framework for Implementation
21 September 2005	CEP/AC.13/2005/8	Draft work plan for UNECE strategy implementation under UNECE Steering Committee on *ESD*
23 November 2005	CEP/AC.13/2005/9	Draft on UNECE indicators for *ESD*

Date	*Document*	*Content*
14–15 December 2005		First meeting of the UNECE Steering Committee on *ESD*
27 January 2006	CEP/AC.13/2005/7	Adoption of the work plan for the Vilnius Framework for Implementation
13–15 March 2006	Resolution adopted by the participants of the EU Presidency Conference on *ESD towards responsible Global Citisenship*	EU officially supports UNECE strategy and the Vilnius Framework for Implementation
4–5 December 2006	ECE/CEP/AC.13/2006/5 / ECE/CEP/AC.13/2006/3 / ECE/CEP/AC.13/2006/5/Add.1	Endorsement of UNECE indicators for *ESD* and the reporting template (format)
10–12 October 2007	ECE/BELGRADE.CONF/2007/9 / ECE/BELGRADE.CONF/2007/8	Joint UNECE session on *ESD* and Belgrade Declaration *Building Bridges to the Future*

6.4.2 Contents

Referring to *stakeholders*, all addressees of both the *UNECE strategy for ESD* and the *Vilnius Framework for Implementation* are institutions or organisations within the UNECE region. Since UNECE promotes the UNESCO multi-stakeholder, cross-cutting and participatory approach to *DESD* they are affiliated with diverse aspects of sustainability and focus either on educational or environmental issues.[1915]

Particular attention can be attributed to the *commitment of the European Union* vis-à-vis *DESD*. So far, the *UNECE strategy for ESD* and the *Vilnius Framework for Implementation* constitute only procedural recommendations for UNECE member states. However, bearing similarity in this case to *DESD* on an international scale, it does not produce any legal effects in terms of compliance. A remarkable attempt at integrating *DESD* into a legally-binding regional framework was undertaken at European level by the Austrian Presidency in March and May 2006: during a conference held on *ESD* from March 13 to 15 2006 in Vienna, the Austrian Presidency aimed to highlight the importance of *ESD* and tried to build momentum in order to achieve a consensus on binding

1915 Cf. United Nations Economic Commission for Europe (UNECE); United Nations Economic and Social Council (ECOSOC) (eds.) (2003e) (cf. *footnote 1848* op. cit.), p. 2; United Nations Economic Commission for Europe (UNECE); United Nations Economic and Social Council (ECOSOC) (eds.) (2005f) (cf. *footnote 391* op. cit.), p. 13; Fien, John (2010) (cf. *footnote 817* op. cit.).
See *Table 41* in chapter IX 6.4.2 *Contents* on page 410.

commitment and integration of the UNECE principles on *DESD* into the revised strategy of the European Union on sustainable development.[1916]

This *"strategic text on the role of education as a basis and a precondition for sustainable development"* was adopted as a result of the *European Union Education Council* on 19 May 2006. Apart from more general declarations *"(stressing) the importance of including education in the revised EU sustainable development strategy"*,[1917] the *Council of the European Union* recommends that:

- EU Member states *"should also implement the UNECE Strategy for Education for Sustainable Development adopted in Vilnius in2005 [...]"*; and
- *"Education for sustainable development should also be promoted at EU level"*.[1918]

The *Council of the European Union* finally endorsed this linkage between UNECE and EU strategy as part of the relevant sustainable development strategy.[1919] Although officially institutionalised, the fully binding nature of its implementation is not made clear in recommendations to member states of the European Union.[1920]

Table 41: UNECE stakeholders for DESD

Stakeholders	Characteristics
Member states	Representation of UNECE membership
	Governments (delegates)
	Communities and indigenous people
	Local authorities and institutions
UNECE	Committee on Environmental Policy
UNESCO	Observer and consultative status
Council of Europe	EU membership representation

1916 Cf. Council of the European Union (ed.) (2006) (cf. *footnote 815* op. cit.), p. 3.

1917 See UNESCO (ed.) (2006h) (cf. *footnote 711* op. cit.), p. 3.

1918 See UNESCO (ed.) (2006h) (cf. *footnote 711* op. cit.), pp. 3–4.

1919 Cf. Council of the European Union (ed.) (2006) (cf. *footnote 815* op. cit.), p. 22; European Commission; Secretariat-General (eds.) (2008a): A sustainable future in our hands. A Guide to the EU's Sustainable Development Strategy. Brussels: Publications Office of the European Union / Europa Publications Ltd., pp. 7–8; European Commission; Secretariat-General (eds.) (2008b) (cf. *footnote 1216* op. cit.), p. 117.

1920 This is mainly due to the weak and reluctant wording in conditional moods, expressing for instance that *"(m)ember (s)tates could further develop their national action plans"*, that *"(t)hey should also implement the UNECE Strategy"* and that *"(e)ducation for sustainable development should also be promoted at EU level"*.
See No. 17 Council of the European Union (ed.) (2006) (cf. *footnote 815* op. cit.), p. 22.

Stakeholders	Characteristics
World Health Organisation (WHO)	Experts in education on sustainable social development (gender, human rights, democracy, health)
Centre for Educational Research and Innovation of the *Organisation for Economic Co-operation and Development* (OECD)	Experts on education in sustainable economic development
Regional Environmental Centres (RECs)	Experts in informal education and in environmental education
Non-governmental organisations	
Private sector	Representatives of industry, transport and agriculture, trade and labour unions
Media	Mass media

Regional *implementation* is co-ordinated by UNECE in its secretarial capacity. The *umbrella framework* and the institutional point of reference is the *UNECE Committee on Environmental Policy.*[1921] The same also applies to the conceptual basis of *DESD* within the UNECE region. On the one hand, other efforts being made in terms of environmental education are expressly acknowledged. On the other hand, the UNECE strategy clearly states the major differences between *ESD* and pure environment-oriented education. Unlike common practices of equating issues of sustainability with environmental questions, UNECE implementation provides a distinctive, more comprehensive view in a multi-dimensional context: there will be no environmentally acceptable situation without recognition that people need to *"have a decent social and economic situation, and* (also) *that a healthy environment is a prerequisite for a vital economy in the long term. Thus environmental, social and economic aspects are interwoven in ESD".*[1922]

UNECE implementation is considered to be a process that *"benefit(s) from experience gained both within the region and globally (...). [...] It is also a contribution to and in line with the Framework for a draft implementation scheme for the Decade of Education for Sustainable Development developed by UNESCO and should be used as a foundation for the regional implementation of the Decade".*[1923] The *UNECE strategy for ESD* and the *Vilnius Framework for*

1921 Cf. United Nations Economic Commission for Europe (UNECE); United Nations Economic and Social Council (ECOSOC) (eds.) (2003e) (cf. *footnote 1848* op. cit.), p. 2.

1922 See United Nations Economic Commission for Europe (UNECE); United Nations Economic and Social Council (ECOSOC) (eds.) (2004f) (cf. *footnote 27* op. cit.), p. 7.

1923 See United Nations Economic Commission for Europe (UNECE); United Nations Economic and Social Council (ECOSOC) (eds.) (2004e) (cf. *footnote 734* op. cit.), p. 5.

Implementation are therefore wholly complementary and to a certain extent supplementary to global implementation of *DESD*.[1924]

Table 42: Issues of sustainability and education on global and regional (UNECE) agendas[1925]

Year	Commitment for education and sustainability		Mainly concerned with:
	Global level	*European / UNECE level*	
1971		North American Association for Environmental Education	Networking professionals and students in the field of promoting environmental education
1972	United Nations Conference on the Human Environment		Establishing an international, interdisciplinary, multi-level and multi-stakeholder programme in environmental education
1975	Belgrade Charter		Creating the global framework for environmental education
1977	Tbilisi Declaration		Formulating the commonly shared aims and objectives on environmental education
1988		Magna Charta Universitatum Europaeum	Ensuring the maintenance of a natural environment and life in equilibrium through education and training by contributing universities
1990	World Conference on Education for All		Defining basic learning tools and learning content

1924 See *Table 42* in chapter IX 6.4.2 *Contents* on page 412.

1925 This table shows the interplay between global and regional commitment for education and sustainability. On the one hand, activities on European or UNECE level are embedded into and linked with international processes. On the other hand, in addition to the global trends, there are numerous self-contained regional developments to be taken into consideration, too.
Cf. Hartmann, Eva-Maria (2002) (cf. *footnote 827* op. cit.), p. 9; United Nations Economic Commission for Europe (UNECE); United Nations Economic and Social Council (ECOSOC) (eds.) (2004e) (cf. *footnote 734* op. cit.); Hopkins, Charles (2010) (cf. *footnote 827* op. cit.); Vilela, Miriam (2010) (cf. *footnote 827* op. cit.).

Year	Commitment for education and sustainability		Mainly concerned with:
	Global level	*European / UNECE level*	
1992	Rio Declaration on Environment and Development		Rating sustainable development as common concern and *ESD* as cross-cutting and multi-dimensional concept
	Programme of Action for Sustainable Development *Agenda 21*		Defining education in a holistic, participatory and process-oriented way and as critical driving-force
	World Congress for Education and Communication on Environment and Development		Relating development to economic growth with environment as input factor and referring to sustainable development as a compromise
1993	United Nations Commission on Sustainable Development		Implementing *Agenda 21* effectively and incorporating sustainable development objectives into educational curricula
		Copernicus University Charter for Sustainable Development	Involving committed European universities into the European network to share the knowledge and expertise in the field of sustainable development
	United Nations Conference on Human Rights		Building international consensus on sustainable development as learning process and stressing the critical role of education
1994	United Nations Conference on Population and Development		
	United Nations Conference on Small Island Developing States		
1995	United Nations Conference on Social Development		
	United Nations Conference on Women		
1996	United Nations Conference on Food Security		

Year	Commitment for education and sustainability		Mainly concerned with:
	Global level	*European / UNECE level*	
	United Nations Conference on Human Settlements		
	UNESCO-led International Commission on Education for the Twenty-first Century *Learning: the treasure within*		Extracting four pillars of education: learning to live together, learning to know, learning to do and learning to be
		Baltic 21: An Agenda 21 for the Baltic Sea Region	Implementing *Agenda 21* within the Baltic Sea Region
1997	International Conference on Environment and Society: Education and Public Awareness for Sustainability		Expressing alternative visions of development encompassing sustainability as state of natural equilibrium
1998		UNECE Aarhus Convention on Access to Information, Public Participation in Decision-making and Access to Justice in Environmental Matters	Providing public access to environmental information; promoting public participation in environmental decision-making; ensuring access to justice
1999		Bologna Declaration	Supporting a *Europe of Knowledge* as a driving factor of social and human growth and development
2000	Education for All		Providing quality education, equitable access and standards for all
	Dakar Framework for Action		Categorising education as a fundamental human right and key to sustainable development
	Earth Charter		Disseminating values and principles for a sustainable future and promoting the transition to more sustainable ways of life

Year	Commitment for education and sustainability		Mainly concerned with:
	Global level	*European / UNECE level*	
	Millennium Development Goals (MDG) / United Nations Millennium Declaration		Reducing poverty and substantially improving standards of living in eight specific fields of action
2001		Regional Ministerial Meeting for the World Summit on Sustainable Development	Improving education systems and the design of learning programmes on sustainable development and implementing and promoting *ESD* in practice
2002	UNESCO Report on Education for Sustainability. From Rio to Johannesburg: Lessons learnt from a decade of commitment		Providing a new vision of education dealing with sustainable development
	World Summit on Sustainable Development in Johannesburg		Integrating *ESD* into education systems at all levels; proposal of launching *DESD* in 2005
2003		Fifth Ministerial Conference *Environment for Europe*	Inviting member states to integrate sustainable development into education systems and proclaiming regional UNECE leadership for *DESD*
	Quality Education: Member States Ministers of Education Joint Communiqué, 32nd General Conference of UNESCO		Defining and discussing ways of achieving quality education

Based upon the *Vilnius Framework for Implementation* a working plan was drafted in order to prepare its strategic translation into practice. This document concentrates on three priority areas:[1926]

- Co-ordination;
- Capacity-building and sharing experiences; and
- Review of implementation.

1926 Cf. United Nations Economic Commission for Europe (UNECE); United Nations Economic and Social Council (ECOSOC) (eds.) (2005b) (cf. *footnote 1789* op. cit.), p. 2.

Co-ordinating activities must take place at both national and international-regional UNECE level. The first major decision was to charge a UNECE Steering Committee on *ESD* with overseeing the implementation of the strategy. The second programmatic decision was to make effective use of the existing *"Environment for Europe process as a platform for regional high-level promotion of the implementation of the Strategy".*[1927] At national level member states were requested to establish a network of national focal points which might facilitate contacts and regional co-ordination between relevant stakeholders. Furthermore, by 2007 member states were invited to develop national implementation plans, to establish consultative mechanisms for implementation and to translate the UNECE strategy into their respective languages.

With respect to capacity-building and sharing experiences the work plan suggests the following methods:

a) Offering sub-regional workshops to meet the specific needs sufficiently;
b) Compiling examples of good practice nationally to be collected, translated and published, digitally and in print;
c) Using electronic tools which *"facilitate the sharing of good practices, innovative approaches, experience, projects and other information"*;[1928] and
d) Encouraging the application of case studies and qualitatively calibrated models *"for illustrating in a practical way achievements and challenges in the implementation of the Strategy".*[1929]

A comprehensive review of UNECE implementation requires three subsequent steps in order to set up *"a region wide reporting mechanism".*[1930] It requires:

- Appropriate sets of indicators to be developed by 2006;
- Applicable formats for reporting to be adopted and jointly *streamlined* by UNESCO and UNECE; and
- Binding procedural rules for reporting.

1927 Cf. United Nations Economic Commission for Europe (UNECE); United Nations Economic and Social Council (ECOSOC) (eds.) (2005b) (cf. *footnote 1789* op. cit.), p. 2; United Nations Economic Commission for Europe (UNECE); United Nations Economic and Social Council (ECOSOC) (eds.) (2005g) (cf. *footnote 746* op. cit.), p. 4.

1928 E. g., web portals, tool kits, forums, etc.
See United Nations Economic Commission for Europe (UNECE); United Nations Economic and Social Council (ECOSOC) (eds.) (2005b) (cf. *footnote 1789* op. cit.), p. 3.

1929 See United Nations Economic Commission for Europe (UNECE); United Nations Economic and Social Council (ECOSOC) (eds.) (2005b) (cf. *footnote 1789* op. cit.), p. 3.

1930 See United Nations Economic Commission for Europe (UNECE); United Nations Economic and Social Council (ECOSOC) (eds.) (2005b) (cf. *footnote 1789* op. cit.), p. 3.

The UNECE strategy[1931] serves two purposes: as a conceptual basis which facilitates the introduction and promotion of *ESD* throughout the UNECE region and additionally as an example of good practice for regional implementation of *DESD* worldwide.[1932]

Taking into account the pluralistic structure of the UNECE region the implementation of *DESD* is addressed in two ways:

1. A *participatory approach* ensures the involvement of governments, educational institutions, *non-governmental organisations* (NGO), stakeholders in the UNECE region and international organisations; and
2. An *integrative approach* brings together different countries of the UNECE region in full awareness of their cultural heterogeneity and difference in socio-economic and political conditions.

It is commonly agreed that the UNECE region has the needs and preconditions and the prerequisites for the successful implementation of *DESD*:[1933]

- Systems of professional education;
- Access to basic education and equal rights to education for all;
- High levels of literacy;
- Scientific potential and resources; and
- The participation of the civil society.

There are also challenges to be faced, namely those of how to:

- Appropriately address the interdisciplinary nature of *ESD* through education systems;
- Open up *DESD* implementation for greater involvement and commitment on the part of civil society; and
- Ensure the mobilisation of appropriate institutional and material provisions.

As to *objectives*, the primary issue is to encourage UNECE member states to develop and incorporate *ESD* into their respective systems of formal education, within all relevant subjects as well as in the settings of non-formal and informal education. Both information and capacity-building must therefore be provided in order to achieve knowledge of and skills in sustainable development; and to attain the competence and confidence to seize new opportunities with regard to nature, social values, cultural diversity and gender equality; essentially, to raise awareness of issues related to sustainability and development through education.

1931 Cf. United Nations Economic Commission for Europe (UNECE); United Nations Economic and Social Council (ECOSOC) (eds.) (2005f) (cf. *footnote 391* op. cit.).

1932 Cf. Gerner, Martin (14/09/2009) (cf. *footnote 407* op. cit.).

1933 Cf. United Nations Economic Commission for Europe (UNECE); United Nations Economic and Social Council (ECOSOC) (eds.) (2005f) (cf. *footnote 391* op. cit.), p. 2.

With education as the decisive driving factor, this guiding principle translates into six objectives:[1934]

1. To ensure that policy, regulatory and operational frameworks support *ESD*;
2. Promoting through formal, non-formal and informal channels of learning;
3. Building educators' competence to include issues of sustainable development in their teaching appropriately;
4. Making sure that adequate tools and materials for *ESD* are accessible;
5. Promoting substantive research on and development of *ESD*; and
6. Strengthen co-operation on *ESD* at all levels within the UNECE region.

In terms of *scope*, the co-ordinated and strategic approach to the regional implementation of *DESD* within the UNECE region has been adopted by UNECE member states,[1935] and the addressees of policy statements are therefore governments in power. Being the executive branch elected by the sovereign – the people – decisions on how to incorporate *ESD* principles into education and learning systems therefore rest with the government. In order to succeed, broad support given by various stakeholders is necessary. Consequently, the UNECE strategy has been defined as a flexible framework directed to meet specific needs and circumstances according to the priorities and initiatives of the countries concerned.[1936]

The UNECE strategy aims to promote inter-departmental and multi-stakeholder co-operation and partnerships in the spheres of both participation and funding. Economically speaking, *DESD* implementation is comparable to an investment made with both material and human resources. The *International Implementation Scheme* (IIS) provided by UNESCO explicitly encourages synergies with existing programmes and initiatives. Likewise, the UNECE strategy expresses theoretical concordance with and support of all major activities in the field of education and sustainability. Coherently transparent, inclusive and ac-

---

1934 Cf. United Nations Economic Commission for Europe (UNECE); United Nations Economic and Social Council (ECOSOC) (eds.) (2005f) (cf. *footnote 391* op. cit.), p. 3; United Nations Economic Commission for Europe (UNECE) (ed.) (2009) (cf. *footnote 1789* op. cit.), pp. 18–20.

1935 Interestingly, the final endorsed version of the UNECE strategy contains the phrase *"interested UNECE member States"* which entices one towards the conclusion that implementing *DESD* at a regional stage is, from the beginning, no more than a voluntary commitment. The regional focus is notably non-exclusive. This means that external states from outside the UNECE region are more than welcome to join the initiative. See United Nations Economic Commission for Europe (UNECE); United Nations Economic and Social Council (ECOSOC) (eds.) (2005f) (cf. *footnote 391* op. cit.), p. 3.

1936 Cf. United Nations Economic Commission for Europe (UNECE) (ed.) (2009) (cf. *footnote 1789* op. cit.), p. 17.

countable decision-making as well as people's empowerment can be seen as such concordance in practice.

The UNECE strategy *grosso modo* recalls the basic *principles* of implementation of the *International Implementation Scheme* (IIS) at the global stage.[1937] Indeed, within that particular document, no specific regional focus is discernible. However, a review of certain paragraphs helps to ensure a common understanding and provides the programmatic basis required for further considerations:[1938]

- Sustainable development is a continuous and imperfect learning process. Learning targets for *ESD* should include knowledge, skills, understanding, attitudes and values;
- *ESD* is developing as a broad and comprehensive conceptualisation of interdisciplinarity. It is based on four thematic pillars – environment, culture, society and economy;
- Due to its multi-dimensional nature, *ESD* requires a holistic approach covering key themes, such as the alleviation of poverty, citizenship, peace, ethics, responsibility in local and global contexts, democracy and governance, justice, security, human rights, health, gender equity, cultural diversity, rural and urban development, the economy, patterns of production and consumption, corporate responsibility, environmental protection, natural resource management and biological and landscape diversity;
- The basic areas of implementation are derived from *Agenda 21* and should address improvements in basic education, thereby re-orienting education towards sustainable development, increasing public awareness and promoting training;
- *ESD* should foster cultural understanding by recognising the role of indigenous peoples, preserving cultural diversity and valuating culture-bound knowledge as a useful resource base;
- *ESD* ought to enable systemic, critical and creative thinking and relational reflection in both local and global contexts;
- *ESD* represents a lifelong learning process from early childhood to higher and adult education and goes beyond the boundaries of formal education;
- Higher education is requested to contribute significantly to *ESD* in terms of developing appropriate, applicable knowledge as well as methodological competences;

1937 Cf. chapter IX 1 *Principles of implementation* on pages 256 et seqq.

1938 Cf. United Nations Economic Commission for Europe (UNECE); United Nations Economic and Social Council (ECOSOC) (eds.) (2005f) (cf. *footnote 391* op. cit.), pp. 4–6; United Nations Economic Commission for Europe (UNECE) (ed.) (2009) (cf. *footnote 1789* op. cit.), pp. 17–18.
Cf. chapter IX 3.4 *International Implementation Scheme* on pages 307 et seqq, and chapter IX 3.4.4 *Section III: Implementation and Evaluation* on page 313.

- *ESD* should be context- or case-sensitive, taking into account diverse local, national and regional circumstances as well as the global context. In accordance with the motto of thinking global and acting local *ESD* has to achieve a balance between global and local interests;
- *ESD* supports initiatives towards equal access to education in both rural and urban areas.
- *ESD* raises various ethical questions to be given a practical application, among such questions are issues of equity, inter-generational justice or wealth distribution;
- *ESD* should open horizons by facilitating dialogue through an experience of life and work far beyond the classroom among pupils, students, authorities and civil society: *"In this way, ESD presents an opportunity for education to overcome its isolation vis-à-vis society"*;[1939]
- *ESD* should be seen as a process of facilitation and as a factor contributing to interactive and integrated policy- and decision-making; and
- *ESD* follows a cross-sectoral and multi-stakeholder approach.[1940]

"ESD demands a re-orientation away from focusing entirely on providing knowledge towards dealing with problems and identifying possible solutions."[1941] As a consequence, individuals in real-life situations are the first and foremost *points of reference*. This means that *ESD* must adjust learning programmes and teaching methods to different structures and include therein an interactive, collaborative understanding between educators and learners. Formal, non-formal, informal education and educator training are all equally important. Sharing experiences and establishing close links with research groups in relation to *ESD* subject matter, methods, structures and outcomes are considered to be crucial for the effectiveness of *DESD*. There are a number of contributing factors that have immediate influence on the effectiveness of measures.[1942]

1939 See United Nations Economic Commission for Europe (UNECE); United Nations Economic and Social Council (ECOSOC) (eds.) (2005f) (cf. *footnote 391* op. cit.), p. 5.

1940 Such approaches involve the main actors, such as governments and local authorities, the education and science sectors, the health sector, the private sector, industry, transport and agriculture, trade and labour, unions, the mass media, non-governmental organisations, various communities, indigenous peoples and international organisations. Cf. United Nations Economic Commission for Europe (UNECE); United Nations Economic and Social Council (ECOSOC) (eds.) (2005f) (cf. *footnote 391* op. cit.), pp. 5–6.

1941 See United Nations Economic Commission for Europe (UNECE); United Nations Economic and Social Council (ECOSOC) (eds.) (2005f) (cf. *footnote 391* op. cit.), p. 6.

1942 See *Table 43* in chapter IX 6.4.2 *Contents* on page 421.

Table 43: Determinants on effectiveness of DESD implementation[1943]

Determinants	Description
Theory	Degree of integration of *ESD*-related topics across all relevant subjects, programmes and courses
Methodology	Degree of provision of appropriate instruments according to an interdisciplinary and multi-method approach[1944]
Training	Degree at which *ESD*-specific training programmes and courses are offered
Materials	Degree of provision of *ESD*-relevant and locally affordable instruction materials[1945]
Context	Degree of consideration of different circumstances and multiple contexts[1946]
Communication	Degree of internal and external *ESD*-related interaction[1947]
Partnerships	Degree of increase in partnerships and cross-sectoral co-operation[1948]
Experiences	Degree at which *ESD*-related *multi-channel* learning experiences are enabled[1949]

1943 Cf. United Nations Economic Commission for Europe (UNECE); United Nations Economic and Social Council (ECOSOC) (eds.) (2005f) (cf. *footnote 391* op. cit.), pp. 6–7.

1944 The *ESD*-approach is characterised by *"participatory, process- and solution-oriented educational methods (such as) discussions, conceptual and perceptual mapping, philosophical inquiry, value clarification, simulations, scenarios, modeling, role playing, games, information and communication technology (ICT), surveys, case studies, excursions and outdoor learning, learner-driven projects, good practice analyses, workplace experience and problem solving".*
See United Nations Economic Commission for Europe (UNECE); United Nations Economic and Social Council (ECOSOC) (eds.) (2005f) (cf. *footnote 391* op. cit.), p. 7.

1945 For example: methodological, pedagogic and didactic publications, textbooks, visual aids, brochures, cases studies and good practices, electronic, audio and video resources (tool kits, websites).

1946 For example: time, range (local, regional, global), rules, links between social, cultural and economic and environmental issues.

1947 For example: professional communication strategies (press releases); role of mass-media in mobilising *"know-how and distribution channels to pass reliable information and key messages on SD-related issues".*
See United Nations Economic Commission for Europe (UNECE); United Nations Economic and Social Council (ECOSOC) (eds.) (2005f) (cf. *footnote 391* op. cit.), p. 7.

1948 One might consider *Public-Private-Partnerships* (PPP); co-operative vocational training, training programmes *on the job* and continuing education in order to upgrade knowledge and skills and to provide new competencies.

1949 *Multi-channel* refers to different but topically intertwined contexts. The issue of sustainable consumption, for example, may gain importance both in educational institu-

Determinants	Description
Support	Degree of stakeholder support and commitment[1950]
Exchange	Degree of exchange of information and experiences[1951]

Structural implementation *requirements* are expressed in the *Framework for Implementation*[1952] being part of the *UNECE strategy for ESD*. As a complement to the *Vilnius Framework for Implementation*, it briefly sketches issues of competence, areas for action, international co-operation, roles and responsibilities, financial matters and timing.

As far as competence is concerned, UNECE member states are fully accountable for *ESD* implementation and are driven by strong political support. Three initial steps are proposed: translating the text of the strategy into the member state's respective language, distributing the strategy to the relevant authorities and designating national focal points.

The provisions of the UNECE strategy then need to be integrated into national and local strategies of planning, investment and management for all levels of education and for all educational institutions and organisations. This requires flexibility as measures must accord with the legislations, policies and other existing operational frameworks of member states. Based on the principle of co-operation, subsidiarity, shared responsibility and leadership of all relevant state bodies, both environment and education ministries take the lead. The education sector holds a vital managerial function, serving as a *drop-in centre*, creating an enabling environment of inclusion and encouraging self-evaluation. The UNECE strategy suggests establishing nationally specific mechanisms for the implementation of *DESD*, by setting up proper *national ESD platforms*, for example. Designed as participatory plans of national implementation they represent context-appropriate ways of implementation with reference to objectives, activi-

tions, at the workplace or in the family. The topic stays the same but aspects and relations are different.

1950 For example: governments being in charge of formal education (*informed citizens*); non-governmental organisations as a) providers of informal and non-formal learning, b) resourceful knowledge base and c) mediators between the public and government; private sector.

1951 How, for example, the permeability of experience and practice with research and development worldwide might be assessed.

1952 Cf. United Nations Economic Commission for Europe (UNECE); United Nations Economic and Social Council (ECOSOC) (eds.) (2004b) (cf. *footnote 391* op. cit.), pp. 9 et seqq; United Nations Economic Commission for Europe (UNECE); United Nations Economic and Social Council (ECOSOC) (eds.) (2005f) (cf. *footnote 391* op. cit.), pp. 8 et seqq; United Nations Economic Commission for Europe (UNECE); United Nations Economic and Social Council (ECOSOC) (eds.) (2005e) (cf. *footnote 746* op. cit.), pp. 3 et seqq.

ties, measures, provisional timetables, and relevant means of implementation and instruments of evaluation. In view of this background and the associated principles, five consecutive areas for actions are therefore proposed by the UN-ECE strategy:[1953]

1. Ensuring that frameworks of policy, regulation and operation support the promotion of *ESD*;
2. Promoting *ESD* through formal, non-formal and informal learning including raising public awareness, professional skills and knowledge;
3. Building competences to engage, support and guide *ESD* processes;
4. Developing and providing access to *ESD*-related materials and tools; and
5. Promoting continuing research on and development of *ESD*.

International co-operation aims to enhance both general understanding of *ESD* and intercultural dialogue, and regional-level reviews contribute to global perspectives.[1954] The UNECE strategy makes regional and sub-regional forums a high priority. Particular attention is drawn to the development of multi-disciplinary forms of education, such as national and sub-regional networks, education, working groups, networks and associations of universities, programmes and partnerships.

The strategy furthermore stresses the need for joint efforts in difficult regions, in countries with economies in transition, for instance, the *Eastern Europe, the Caucasus and Central Asia region* (EECCA), and the South-Eastern region.[1955] Providing capacity-building, financial assistance and support to education as well as programmes of research and public awareness relating to *ESD* are a major concern. Considering the individual needs of each single member state, UNECE calls for appropriate *ESD* focal points in all UNECE member states and relevant international organisations.[1956]

1953 Cf. United Nations Economic Commission for Europe (UNECE); United Nations Economic and Social Council (ECOSOC) (eds.) (2005f) (cf. *footnote 391* op. cit.), pp. 10–11; United Nations Economic Commission for Europe (UNECE) (ed.) (2009) (cf. *footnote 1789* op. cit.), p. 21.

1954 Cf. United Nations Economic Commission for Europe (UNECE) (ed.) (2009) (cf. *footnote 1789* op. cit.), p. 22.

1955 Cf. United Nations Economic Commission for Europe (UNECE); United Nations Economic and Social Council (ECOSOC) (eds.) (2005f) (cf. *footnote 391* op. cit.), p. 12.

1956 Cf. United Nations Economic Commission for Europe (UNECE) (ed.) (2009) (cf. *footnote 1789* op. cit.), p. 23.
See *Figure 99* in chapter IX 6.4.2 *Contents* on page 424.

Indicator	Sub-indicator	Number of the responded countries	Fulfilled (percentage)
Prerequisite measures are taken to support the promotion of ESD	Strategy has been translated in the national language of the country	44	79.5
	A national focal point has been appointed	34	73.5
	A coordinating body is established	38	72.6
	A national implementation plan has been developed	40	35.0
	There are synergies between the UNECE process and other processes relevant to ESD	37	69.9
Policy, regultory and operational frameworks support the promotion of ESD	The ESD is addressed in national policy documents	36	86.1
	Public budgets to support ESD are available	36	56
	There is a formal structure for interdepartmental cooperation	39	79.5
	A mechanism for multi-stakeholder cooperation on ESD exists	37	70.3
National policies support synergies between processes related to SD and ESD		29	75

Figure 99: UNECE requirements and accomplishments of DESD implementation[1957]

The most important and *proactive*[1958] *role* in promoting, facilitating and assessing *DESD* implementation within the UNECE region is played by governments as the principal agents.[1959] In accordance with their constitutional mandate, local educational authorities and institutions of formal education are also invited to take responsibility for implementing and monitoring. Other stakeholders are encouraged to participate in accordance with their defined priorities.

With regard to budgetary planning, education should, to sound an initial note of optimism, always be regarded as an investment that will pay off in the

1957 Guidance and precise feedback structures provided within the UNECE region represent important means in order to both appropriately set requirements and measure accomplishments of *DESD* implementation at national level.
See United Nations Economic Commission for Europe (UNECE) (ed.) (2009) (cf. *footnote 1789* op. cit.), p. 45.

1958 See United Nations Economic Commission for Europe (UNECE); United Nations Economic and Social Council (ECOSOC) (eds.) (2005f) (cf. *footnote 391* op. cit.), p. 13.

1959 Cf. Gerner, Martin (14/09/2009) (cf. *footnote 407* op. cit.).

long run. *ESD* is likewise supposed to have both an *original* and *derivative* added value. Implementation costs are usually covered by each country or through sub-regional or region-wide projects. There is no supplementary UNECE budget available for implementation carried out by member states.[1960]

UNECE activities depend exclusively upon the following:[1961]

a) *Core*-funding only through the budget by the United Nations secretariat *via* the United Nations General Assembly;
b) *Co*- or trust-funding by agencies and associations, to a limited extent; or
c) *Extra*-budgetary funding which is considered difficult to obtain since it is easier to raise funds with legally-binding documents for official policy frameworks rather than by schemes of voluntary contribution.

Further commitment is subject to the financial assistance offered by miscellaneous agencies, funding or private donors. It is dedicated primarily to partnerships. Organisational expenses and international exchange may be granted in particular cases, especially for member states with economies in transition.[1962] Few private-sector donations or extra-budgetary contributions are made to the UNECE implementation of *DESD*. There is in general a high potential for public-private initiatives.[1963]

As far as *timing* is concerned, the UNECE strategy is a continuous process which favours *process-oriented evaluation and benchmarking*.[1964] Statements on the results of implementation are only expected after a long period of time. In order to retain an orientation towards long-term evaluation, the strategy suggests a combination of pre-scheduled tasks, report mechanisms and their respective indicators. Explicitly incorporated within the *Vilnius Framework for Implementation* are three phases of *DESD* implementation at UNECE level:[1965]

1960 Cf. Gerner, Martin (14/09/2009) (cf. *footnote 407* op. cit.).

1961 Cf. Gerner, Martin (14/09/2009) (cf. *footnote 407* op. cit.).

1962 Cf. United Nations Economic Commission for Europe (UNECE); United Nations Economic and Social Council (ECOSOC) (eds.) (2005f) (cf. *footnote 391* op. cit.), pp. 13–14; United Nations Economic Commission for Europe (UNECE); United Nations Economic and Social Council (ECOSOC) (eds.) (2005g) (cf. *footnote 746* op. cit.), p. 3.

1963 Examples might include *public-private-partnerships* (PPP) at national level, such as the Air France emissions calculator, car pooling, etc.
Cf. Gerner, Martin (14/09/2009) (cf. *footnote 407* op. cit.); Fien, John (2010) (cf. *footnote 817* op. cit.).

1964 See United Nations Economic Commission for Europe (UNECE); United Nations Economic and Social Council (ECOSOC) (eds.) (2005f) (cf. *footnote 391* op. cit.), p. 14.

1965 See *Table 44* in chapter IX 6.4.2 *Contents* on page 426, and *Figure 100* in chapter IX 6.4.2 *Contents* on page 429.

Table 44: Phases of UNECE DESD implementation[1966]

Phase	*Time frame*	*Targets*
Phase I	by 2007	Identification; review of current policies, legal and operational frameworks, financial mechanisms, and educational activities; development of (qualitative) indicators and evaluation methods
Phase II	by 2010	National and regional progress reviews and revision, if necessary
Phase III	by 2015 and beyond	Considerable progress in the implementation of *ESD*

Prepared by the *task force*, the *Vilnius Framework for Implementation*[1967] complements the *UNECE Strategy for ESD*.[1968] Although both documents contain procedural provisions, the framework document furthers strategic UNECE implementation in two particular ways:

1. Proposing specific activities linked to specific time frames and *"focused on co-ordination, sharing experience and good practices; capacity-building; raising public awareness; and strengthening sub-regional cooperation"*;[1969] and
2. Establishing mechanisms of reporting, monitoring and assessing the implementation process.

The framework contains clear recommendations of sub-regional meetings in order to facilitate work on driving issues and to strengthen sub-regional cooperation. These meetings should be co-ordinated in accordance with ongoing UNECE processes. The next step is to compile and publish examples of good practice on *ESD* collected by member state authorities. Additionally, a web portal is considered an important, efficient and effective tool to promote the *"shar-*

1966 Cf. United Nations Economic Commission for Europe (UNECE); United Nations Economic and Social Council (ECOSOC) (eds.) (2005f) (cf. *footnote 391* op. cit.), p. 14; United Nations Economic Commission for Europe (UNECE); United Nations Economic and Social Council (ECOSOC) (eds.) (2005g) (cf. *footnote 746* op. cit.), p. 2; Linn, Monika; Sochirca, Angela (2010) (cf. *footnote 741* op. cit.), p. 26.

1967 Cf. United Nations Economic Commission for Europe (UNECE); United Nations Economic and Social Council (ECOSOC) (eds.) (2005g) (cf. *footnote 746* op. cit.).

1968 Cf. United Nations Economic Commission for Europe (UNECE); United Nations Economic and Social Council (ECOSOC) (eds.) (2005f) (cf. *footnote 391* op. cit.).

1969 See United Nations Economic Commission for Europe (UNECE); United Nations Economic and Social Council (ECOSOC) (eds.) (2005g) (cf. *footnote 746* op. cit.), p. 2.

ing of good practices, innovative approaches, experiences, projects and other information"[1970] quickly and at lower cost.

Two bodies are introduced to contribute to the measurement of the effectiveness of implementing the UNECE strategy:

- *UNECE Steering Committee on ESD*; and
- *UNECE Expert Group on ESD indicators.*

The *UNECE Steering Committee on ESD* has been installed in order to make strategic decisions on the implementation of the UNECE strategy, and also to guide and review the process simultaneously.[1971] The committee is supported by the UNECE secretariat and includes representatives from the educational and environmental sectors of member states as well as other relevant stakeholders with observer status.

In order to maintain continuity of contact, *"UNESCO will be a permanent observer".*[1972] Constituting *"the principal decision-making body for the activities on the Strategy for education for sustainable development in the UNECE region"*,[1973] the task list in its entirety is as follows:

- *"Promote and coordinate the implementation of the Strategy with other international activities, seeking synergies and avoiding overlaps;*
- *Monitor the progress of the implementation of the Strategy; prepare assessments of progress made and propose priorities for actions, identify issues and propose corrective measures, where appropriate;*
- *Liaise and cooperate closely with relevant intergovernmental organisations and nongovernmental organisations that are active in education, the environment and sustainable development;*
- *Facilitate cross-sectoral co-ordination and international cooperation of public and private institutions;*
- *Establish ad hoc working groups, task forces and other bodies as needed to implement the activities;*

1970 See United Nations Economic Commission for Europe (UNECE); United Nations Economic and Social Council (ECOSOC) (eds.) (2005g) (cf. *footnote 746* op. cit.), p. 3.

1971 Cf. United Nations Economic Commission for Europe (UNECE); United Nations Economic and Social Council (ECOSOC) (eds.) (2005g) (cf. *footnote 746* op. cit.), pp. 4, 5.

1972 See United Nations Economic Commission for Europe (UNECE); United Nations Economic and Social Council (ECOSOC) (eds.) (2005g) (cf. *footnote 746* op. cit.), p. 5; UNESCO (ed.) (2006h) (cf. *footnote 711* op. cit.), p. 3.

1973 See United Nations Economic Commission for Europe (UNECE); United Nations Economic and Social Council (ECOSOC) (eds.) (2005g) (cf. *footnote 746* op. cit.), p. 5.

- *Provide guidance on the need for possible new instruments promoting education for sustainable development;*
- *Serve as a forum for the consideration of issues related to education for sustainable development at regional and international level;*
- *Prepare ESD-related inputs for the Commission for Sustainable Development and other relevant processes;*
- *Liaise, as required, with the other United Nations regional commissions for matters related to its competence; (and)*
- *Keep the UNECE Committee on Environmental Policy informed about its activities, unless it is decided otherwise".*[1974]

The *UNECE Expert Group on ESD indicators* has been set up as a *peripatetic* group of experts linked with the UNECE secretariat. Pursuant to the adoption of the UNECE strategy it is assigned the task of *"develop(ing) (sound) indicators to measure the effectiveness of the implementation".*[1975] These will be presented as a report to the *UNECE Steering Committee on ESD.*

1974 See United Nations Economic Commission for Europe (UNECE); United Nations Economic and Social Council (ECOSOC) (eds.) (2005g) (cf. *footnote 746* op. cit.), pp. 5–6.

1975 See United Nations Economic Commission for Europe (UNECE); United Nations Economic and Social Council (ECOSOC) (eds.) (2005g) (cf. *footnote 746* op. cit.), p. 7.

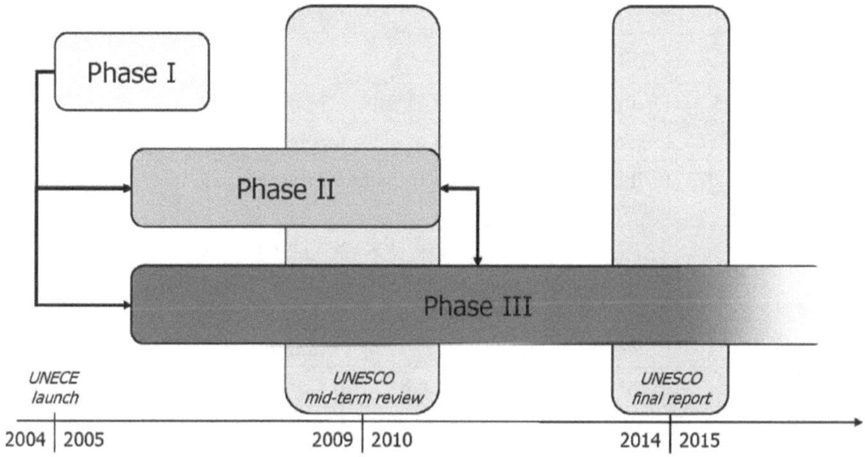

Figure 100: UNECE DESD implementation and UNESCO monitoring[1976]

6.4.3 Indicators

"Indicators are key to improving decision-making during the DESD and provide an important avenue through which to engage stakeholders in ESD."[1977]

The starting point for UNECE indicators of *DESD* implementation is the draft work plan which refers to the *UNECE Expert Group on ESD indicators* tasked with developing appropriate indicators within a defined and ambitious time frame. *"[...] (Its continuing) efforts can help us navigate through the potentially complex territory of choosing appropriate ESD indicators and guiding the involvement of stakeholders in the process."*[1978]

1976 This figure demonstrates how UNECE *DESD* implementation is affiliated with UNESCO global monitoring of *DESD*. Two strands can be observed. In first place, the UNECE implementation and monitoring agenda fully coincides with UNESCO's reviewing and final reporting stages. In second place, however, the UNECE timeline is independent to certain extent and thus differs from the global approach of UNESCO. To give two sound examples: all relevant phases are launched prior to the officially introduced *DESD* schedule. The implementation and monitoring process is continuing and reaches beyond the decade's temporal scope.
Cf. United Nations Economic Commission for Europe (UNECE) (ed.) (2009) (cf. *footnote 1789* op. cit.), pp. 23, 31; Linn, Monika; Sochirca, Angela (2010) (cf. *footnote 741* op. cit.), p. 26.
Cf. *Figure 97* in chapter IX 5.5 *Summary* on page 382.

1977 See Tilbury, Daniella (2007) (cf. *footnote 219* op. cit.), p. 3.

1978 See Tilbury, Daniella (2007) (cf. *footnote 219* op. cit.), p. 2.
See *Table 45* in chapter IX 6.4.3 *Indicators* on page 430.

Table 45: Development of UNECE indicators on DESD implementation[1979]

Period	*Progress*
September 2005	First meeting of the UNECE Expert Group on *ESD*
	Preparation of a first draft of indicators based on a background paper
October 2005	First draft for comments by national focal points and relevant stakeholders
November 2005	Second meeting of the UNECE Expert Group on *ESD*
	Preparation of a third draft submitted to the UNECE Steering Committee on *ESD* for commenting
December 2005	Commenting by UNECE Steering Committee on *ESD*
March 2006	Third meeting of the UNECE Expert Group on *ESD*
	Preparation of a fourth draft
April 2006	Draft for commenting by national focal points and key stakeholders
May 2006	Fourth meeting of the UNECE Expert Group on *ESD*
	Finalising the draft indicators
December 2006	Endorsement of a set of indicators by UNECE Steering Committee on *ESD*
	Agreement of using UNECE indicators for assessing implementation
October 2007	End of pilot reporting to learn about UNECE implementation and to test workability
	Urging governments to use indicators and to submit timely reports

Different indicators *"valued as tools in monitoring and assessment"*[1980] ought to reflect the relevant objectives of the UNECE strategy.[1981] Thus, there

1979 Cf. United Nations Economic Commission for Europe (UNECE); United Nations Economic and Social Council (ECOSOC) (eds.) (2005c) (cf. *footnote 411* op. cit.), p. 3; UNESCO (ed.) (2007f) (cf. *footnote 427* op. cit.), p. 5; UNESCO (ed.) (August 2007) (cf. *footnote 693* op. cit.), p. 6; UNESCO (ed.) (2007k) (cf. *footnote 4* op. cit.), pp. 31 et seqq.

1980 See Tilbury, Daniella (2007) (cf. *footnote 219* op. cit.), p. 2.

1981 Taking into consideration, for instance, quantitative versus qualitative approaches, numerous specific indicators versus aggregated indicators, national validity versus comparability, etc.
Cf. United Nations Economic Commission for Europe (UNECE) (ed.) (2009) (cf. *footnote 1789* op. cit.), pp. 5–6.

are areas of action to be considered under each objective *"with the view of ensuring that indicators address all the key issues"*.[1982]

6.4.4 Reporting

"In order to carry out a comprehensive review of the implementation of the Strategy, a region wide reporting mechanism should be set up."[1983] Procedural provisions for reporting are again raised within the draft work plan for implementing the UNECE strategy. Reporting connects directly with implementation since performance indicators are involved.[1984] Particular reporting requirements and procedures are to be developed as standard templates through a joint effort by UNESCO and UNECE for the reason that these *"would also serve as a report on the implementation of the Decade on ESD"*[1985] as a whole.[1986] Above all, this refers to the following catalogue of *synchronised* reporting:[1987]

1. *Questionnaire*;
2. Complementary *research reports*;
3. Reports based on *stakeholder engagement*;
4. Optional *longitudinal assessment*; and
5. UNESCO *self-reporting process* and *portfolio of evidence.*[1988]

Pursuant to the approval of the *UNECE strategy for ESD* and the *Vilnius Framework for Implementation* in May 2005 the first draft reporting format was presented in October the same year[1989] and followed by the final template[1990] just

1982 See United Nations Economic Commission for Europe (UNECE); United Nations Economic and Social Council (ECOSOC) (eds.) (2005c) (cf. *footnote 411* op. cit.), p. 1.

1983 See United Nations Economic Commission for Europe (UNECE); United Nations Economic and Social Council (ECOSOC) (eds.) (2005c) (cf. *footnote 411* op. cit.), p. 3.

1984 Cf. United Nations Economic Commission for Europe (UNECE); United Nations Economic and Social Council (ECOSOC) (eds.) (2005b) (cf. *footnote 1789* op. cit.), p. 3.

1985 See United Nations Economic Commission for Europe (UNECE); United Nations Economic and Social Council (ECOSOC) (eds.) (2005b) (cf. *footnote 1789* op. cit.), p. 4.

1986 Cf. Gerner, Martin (30/07/2009) (cf. *footnote 407* op. cit.).

1987 Cf. Tilbury, Daniella (July 2009) (cf. *footnote 1807* op. cit.), p. 191; Tilbury, Daniella (2010) (cf. *footnote 1764* op. cit.), pp. 146–147.

1988 According to the *UNESCO Action plan on DESD.*

1989 Cf. United Nations Economic Commission for Europe (UNECE); United Nations Economic and Social Council (ECOSOC) (eds.) (2005b) (cf. *footnote 1789* op. cit.), pp. 8–9.

1990 Cf. United Nations Economic Commission for Europe (UNECE) (26/10/2006) (cf. *footnote 413* op. cit.), pp. 2 et seqq; United Nations Economic Commission for Europe (UNECE) (ed.) (2009) (cf. *footnote 1789* op. cit.), pp. 6–7.

one year later in 2006; *"(t)he reporting format (...) (is) a tool to facilitate the review of the implementation of the UNECE Strategy for Education for Sustainable Development (ESD)."*[1991]

Standardised reporting is based on sound criteria and sub-divided into several categories:[1992]

- Objective 1) Ensuring that policy, regulatory and operational frameworks support the promotion of *ESD*;
- Objective 2) Promoting sustainable development through formal, non-formal and informal learning;
- Objective 3) Equipping educators with the competence to include sustainable development in their teaching;
- Objective 4) Ensuring that sufficient tools and materials for *ESD* are accessible;
- Objective 5) Promoting research on and development of *ESD*;
- Objective 6) Strengthening co-operation on *ESD* at all levels within the UNECE region;
- Objective 7) Fostering conservation, use and promotion of knowledge of indigenous peoples in *ESD*;
- Objective 8) Describing any challenges and obstacles encountered in the implementation of the strategy; and
- Objective 9) Describing any assistance needed to improve implementation.

The template is accompanied by informal *guidance material*[1993] aiming to *"facilitat(e) the completion of the (respective) reporting format"*.[1994] It contains a compilation of all relevant document links attached to the implementation of the UNECE strategy,[1995] and it provides guidance in terms of *"information on the*

1991 See United Nations Economic Commission for Europe (UNECE) (ed.) (2006) (cf. *footnote 20* op. cit.), p. 1.

1992 Objectives one to six are directly in accordance with the objectives of the UNECE strategy, whereas objectives seven to nine are added for the purpose of indication.
Cf. United Nations Economic Commission for Europe (UNECE); United Nations Economic and Social Council (ECOSOC) (eds.) (2007b) (cf. *footnote 385* op. cit.), pp. 5 et seqq; United Nations Economic Commission for Europe (UNECE) (26/10/2006) (cf. *footnote 413* op. cit.), pp. 2 et seqq.

1993 See United Nations Economic Commission for Europe (UNECE) (ed.) (2009) (cf. *footnote 1789* op. cit.), p. 73.

1994 See United Nations Economic Commission for Europe (UNECE) (ed.) (2006) (cf. *footnote 20* op. cit.), p. 1.

1995 Cf. United Nations Economic Commission for Europe (UNECE) (ed.) (2009) (cf. *footnote 1789* op. cit.), pp. 7–8, 74–142.

methodology, suggestions for sources and data collecting, and on procedures relevant to the reporting".[1996]

Compiling and disseminating examples of good and best practice in implementing *DESD* is another essential element of the UNECE strategy.[1997] *"UNECE and UNESCO are (...) collaborating on a common collection and dissemination of regional best practices on ESD."*[1998] Best practices are published both digitally and in print as collections of specific case studies,[1999] or they are compiled as country reports.[2000]

6.4.5 Summary

Recalling that the overall aim is *"(...) to encourage UNECE member States to develop and incorporate ESD into their formal education systems, in all relevant subjects, and in non-formal and informal education",*[2001] there can be no doubt that the process of UNECE implementation constitutes in itself a considerable contribution to the implementation of *DESD* for the following reasons:

1. It provides an independent and comprehensive regional perspective on *DESD*;
2. It is well aligned with international *DESD* principles, procedures and ongoing processes;

1996 See United Nations Economic Commission for Europe (UNECE) (ed.) (2006) (cf. *footnote 20* op. cit.), p. 1.
A sound and comprehensive example of reporting was presented by the Canadian government in October 2007.
Cf. Canada Council of Ministers of Education, Canada; Environment Canada; Canadian Commission for UNESCO (eds.) (2007) (cf. *footnote 1792* op. cit.); United Nations Economic Commission for Europe (UNECE) (ed.) (2009) (cf. *footnote 1789* op. cit.), pp. 145–150 or Ireland COMHAR Sustainable Development Council; ECO-UNESCO (eds.) (2007) (cf. *footnote 1792* op. cit.).

1997 Cf. United Nations Economic Commission for Europe (UNECE); United Nations Economic and Social Council (ECOSOC) (eds.) (2005f) (cf. *footnote 391* op. cit.), pp. 7, 12, 13; United Nations Economic Commission for Europe (UNECE); United Nations Economic and Social Council (ECOSOC) (eds.) (2005g) (cf. *footnote 746* op. cit.), p. 3; United Nations Economic Commission for Europe (UNECE); United Nations Economic and Social Council (ECOSOC) (eds.) (2005c) (cf. *footnote 411* op. cit.), p. 17; United Nations Economic Commission for Europe (UNECE) (ed.) (2009) (cf. *footnote 1789* op. cit.), pp. 39–44, 46.

1998 See UNESCO (ed.) (2006h) (cf. *footnote 711* op. cit.), p. 3.

1999 Cf. UNESCO (ed.) (2007e) (cf. *footnote 585* op. cit.); UNESCO; The Earth Charter Initiative (ECI) (eds.) (2007d) (cf. *footnote 585* op. cit.); UNESCO; UNESCO Associated Schools (eds.) (2008b) (cf. *footnote 480* op. cit.); UNESCO; UNESCO Associated Schools (eds.) (2009b) (cf. *footnote 585* op. cit.).

2000 Cf. UNESCO Education Sector (ed.) (2007) (cf. *footnote 744* op. cit.).

2001 See UNESCO (ed.) (2005j) (cf. *footnote 44* op. cit.), p. 14.

3. It provides programmatic and professional guidance intended to fulfil the desire to create *spillover effects* on an international scale; and
4. It integrates features of both implementation and evaluation from a long-term perspective.[2002]

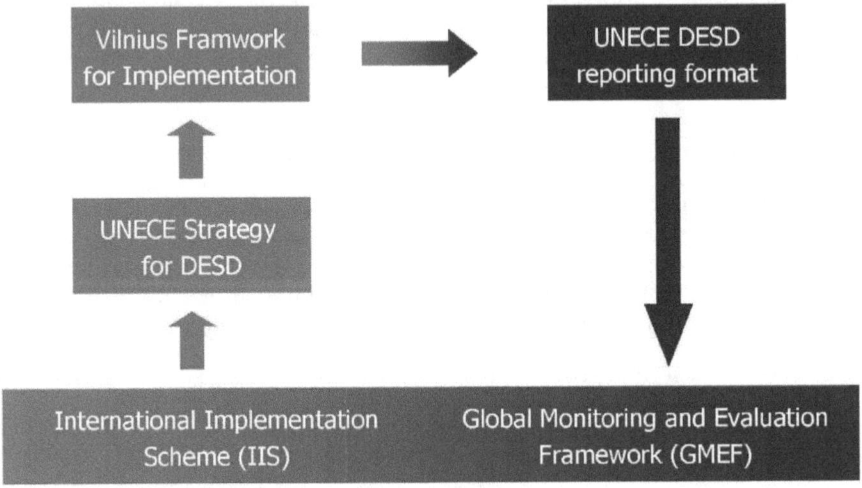

Figure 101: Summary of UNECE regional DESD implementation and monitoring[2003]

"The UNECE Strategy for ESD remained a unique example of the regional implementation of ESD among the different initiatives developed in the framework of the United Nations Decade of Education for Sustainable Development,

2002 Despite the fact that *DESD* is officially scheduled only until 2014, the UNECE strategy and implementation is the only framework explicitly adhering to the very notion of *ESD*: strictly speaking, this commitment cannot be properly scheduled. Moreover, it must be considered a future investment whose duration must be extended to *"2015 and beyond"*.
See United Nations Economic Commission for Europe (UNECE); United Nations Economic and Social Council (ECOSOC) (eds.) (2005f) (cf. *footnote 391* op. cit.), p. 14.
See *Figure 101* in chapter IX 6.4.5 *Summary* on page 434.

2003 This scheme serves to graphically arrange the regional UNECE *DESD* implementation and monitoring, and UNESCO's global implementation (*International Implementation Scheme*) and monitoring frameworks (*Global Monitoring and Evaluation Framework*). Both the *UNECE Strategy for DESD* and *Vilnius Framework for Implementation* are considered to meet global requirements of implementation. In a very similar vein, the UNECE *DESD* reporting format contributes to UNESCO's international agenda of monitoring and evaluation.

and hence served as an example for other regions."[2004] Moreover, given the UNECE case in which a comprehensive and representative base of information is available, the approach sets a shining example of how *ESD* data can be gathered, processed and interpreted effectively and quantitatively.

6.5 Latin America

"The Latin America and Caribbean Region (LAC) has developed its Regional Plan and the other United Nations Regions are under way."[2005]

In full alignment with international principles, *DESD* was launched separately in the Latin American and Caribbean region:[2006] it was first mentioned during the *Ibero-American Conference on Sustainable Development* held in Rio de Janeiro from 31 May to 2 June 2005, and mentioned for the last time during the conference on *Education for Sustainable Development: New Approaches for the Future* held in Kingston, Jamaica from 18 to 20 October 2005.[2007] Despite the fact of different launch platforms, both regions share a common *DESD* strategy. Its genesis was remarkably expedient: the draft version of the regional strategy *Building Education for Sustainable Development in Latin America and the Caribbean*[2008] had been posted online for comments by November 2006.[2009] An online forum had been established, highlighting discussions, observations

---

2004 See United Nations Economic Commission for Europe (UNECE); United Nations Economic and Social Council (ECOSOC) (eds.) (2007a) (cf. *footnote 1774* op. cit.), p. 7.

2005 See UNESCO (ed.) (2005f) (cf. *footnote 37* op. cit.), p. 11; UNESCO (ed.) (2005j) (cf. *footnote 44* op. cit.), p. 14.

2006 *International Implementation Scheme* (IIS); Spanish version: Plan de Aplicación Internacional.
Cf. Oficina Regional de Educación de la UNESCO para América Latina y el Caribe (OREALC); UNESCO (eds.) (2005a): Decenio de las Naciones Unidas de la Educación para el Desarrollo Sostenible 2005–2014. Plan de Applicación Internacional. Proyecto. Santiago de Chile: UNESCO Santiago, pp. 43 et seqq.
See *Table 46* in chapter IX 6.5 *Latin America* on page 436.
Cf. *Figure 57* in chapter IX 1.1 *Regional strategies* on page 258.

2007 Cf. UNESCO (ed.) (2007k) (cf. *footnote 4* op. cit.), p. 37.

2008 Original Spanish title: *Estrategia Regional: Construyendo una Educación para el Desarrollo Sostenible en América Latina y el Caribe.*
Cf. UNESCO (ed.) (2007k) (cf. *footnote 4* op. cit.), p. 37; UNESCO; The Earth Charter Initiative (ECI) (eds.) (Marzo 2007) (cf. *footnote 113* op. cit.), p. 13; UNESCO (ed.) (2007f) (cf. *footnote 427* op. cit.), pp. 8–9.

2009 Cf. UNESCO (Enero-Abril 2007): Encuentro Latinoamericano: Construyendo una Educación para el Desarrollo Sostenible en América Latina. San José, Costa Rica, 31 de octubre–2 de noviembre, 2006. Reseña. Volume 6, Issue 1. San José, Costa Rica. (HORIZONTE SANITARIO, 1).

and suggestions taking place regionally.[2010] Firmly determined to create momentum for and commitment to action through a participatory and open-access approach, consensus had finally been created at regional level. The online forum had been closed down by March 2007. Consequently, the strategy was published immediately the very same month.[2011]

Table 46: *ESD-related commitment of implementation in Latin America and the Caribbean*[2012]

Regional activity	*Information*
Multi-stakeholder initiative on regional Andean co-operation (Lima, Perú, 2002)	Sub-regional launch of the *Andes-Amazon Plan for Environmental Communication and Education*[2013]
International conference of regional ministers for the environment (Panamá, November 2003)	Creation of the *Latin-American and Caribbean Programme on Environmental Education for Sustainable Development*[2014]
International Seminar on *Education for Sustainable Development: A Contribution from Science Education* (Buenos Aires, Argentina; July 2004)	Preparing *DESD* and identifying key issues and strategies to generate favourable behaviour and attitudes towards sustainable development

2010 Cf. Oficina Regional de Educación de la UNESCO para América Latina y el Caribe (OREALC) (ed.) (2009b): Políticas, estrategias y planes regionales, subregionales y nacionales en educación para el desarrollo sostenible y la educación ambiental en América Latina y el Caribe. Decenio de las Naciones Unidas de la Educación para el Desarrollo Sostenible 2005–2014. OREALC/2009/PI/H/2. Edited by Carol Salgado; Eloísa Tréllez Solís. Santiago de Chile: UNESCO Santiago, p. 39.

2011 Cf. Organización de Estados Iberoamericanos para la Educación, la Ciencia y la Cultura (OEI) (ed.) (2007) (cf. *footnote 1223* op. cit.); UNESCO (ed.) (August 2007) (cf. *footnote 693* op. cit.), p. 7.

2012 Cf. UNESCO (ed.) (2007k) (cf. *footnote 4* op. cit.), pp. 37–42; UNESCO (ed.) (August 2007) (cf. *footnote 693* op. cit.), p. 7; UNESCO (ed.) (2007f) (cf. *footnote 427* op. cit.), pp. 8–9; Oficina Regional de Educación de la UNESCO para América Latina y el Caribe (OREALC) (ed.) (2009b) (cf. *footnote 2010* op. cit.), pp. 35 et seqq; UNESCO (ed.) (2010a) (cf. *footnote 1843* op. cit.).

2013 Original Spanish title: *Plan Andino-Amazónico de Comunicación y Educación Ambiental* (PANACEA).
Cf. Oficina Regional de Educación de la UNESCO para América Latina y el Caribe (OREALC) (ed.) (2009b) (cf. *footnote 2010* op. cit.), pp. 45–47.

2014 Original Spanish title: *Programa Latinoamericano y del Caribe de Educación Ambiental en el Marco del Desarrollo Sostenible* (PLACEA).
Cf. Oficina Regional de Educación de la UNESCO para América Latina y el Caribe (OREALC) (ed.) (2009b) (cf. *footnote 2010* op. cit.), pp. 41–44.

Caribbean Regional Conference on Education for Sustainable Development: *New Approaches for the Future* (Kingston, Jamaica; 18 to 20 October 2005)	Regional launch of *DESD*, discussing main challenges of *ESD* in the region and highlighting *DESD* as a process encompassing physical, biological, social, cultural and economic aspects
International Seminar on *Environmental Education for Sustainable Development* (Santiago, Chile; January 2005)	Launching *DESD* in the Andean-Amazon region and presenting a work plan on regional implementation
Latin America Regional Mobilisation Meeting (San José, Costa Rica; 31 to 2 November 2006)	Promoting action and implementation by articulating a common regional agenda for *ESD*, developing the first draft of the regional implementation strategy, establishing an online-forum for debate and comments
Caribbean Teachers Colleges meeting on *ESD* (Montego Bay, Jamaica; 28 to 29 June 2006 / Kingston, Jamaica; 22 to 23 August 2006)	Exploratory workshop discussions on teacher education to address sustainability
YouthPATH (Youth Poverty Alleviation through Tourism and Heritage)	Training for sustainable and innovative employment in the area of natural and cultural heritage tourism, management and interpretation of heritage attractions, site assessment, heritage tourism product identification and assessment, business start-up and life skills
Publication of the CD-ROM Series entitled *Awareness for Sustainability*	Series of CD-ROMs aiming at renovating science teaching in the region and creating educational materials on the sustainable use of natural resources
Publication of the book *Sustainable Development: Its Environmental and Educative Aspects*	Offering an interdisciplinary *DESD* approach articulating multiple viewpoints related to scientific, socio-economic, environmental and education-related inquiries
Electronic discussion list for teacher educators	Promoting *ESD* through an electronic discussion list in order to re-orient teacher education to addressing sustainability

The driving impulse for a strategy of regional *DESD* implementation in Latin America and the Caribbean was made apparent at the 2006 multi-stakeholder conference in San José aimed at highlighting regional *ESD*-related actions.[2015] One of the principal objectives was to develop and reach a consensus on a regional Latin-American strategy.[2016] Additionally, the conference partici-

2015 Cf. UNESCO (ed.) (August 2007) (cf. *footnote 693* op. cit.), p. 6.

2016 The strategy's scope is applied *qua* one-region approach to the Latin American continent as well as to the Caribbean islands.
Cf. UNESCO (Enero-Abril 2007) (cf. *footnote 2009* op. cit.), p. 1.

pants aim to strengthen interdisciplinary linkages between *ESD* and regional issues such as HIV / AIDS prevention and increasing the literacy rate. Further issues raised are:

- Integrating peace, security, environment and sustainable development;
- Promoting value-based education;
- Incorporating *ESD* into formal and non-formal education;
- Searching for interdisciplinary approaches; and
- Defining fields of priority for implementing the regional strategy.

The regional strategy has two parts:

1. *Final declaration*[2017] equivalent to an executive strategic summary; and
2. *Regional strategy for Latin America and the Caribbean,*[2018] similar to a plan of action or implementation, and accompanied by a regional *Strategies of Communication and Education for Sustainable Development.*[2019]

The final declaration considers *DESD* to be *"an opportunity to find ways of forging alliances between the different educational communities involved and between countries. This is a point in time which will prove crucial for the strengthening of our processes and organisations as well for defending what we have already achieved. The Decade is also an opportune moment for revisiting and critically evaluating not only our progress and results in education but equally the mistakes, failures, regresses and stagnation in our region".*[2020]

2017 Cf. UNESCO; The Earth Charter Initiative (ECI) (eds.) (Marzo 2007) (cf. *footnote 113* op. cit.), pp. 10–18.

2018 Cf. UNESCO; The Earth Charter Initiative (ECI) (eds.) (Marzo 2007) (cf. *footnote 113* op. cit.), pp. 17–18.

2019 Original Spanish title: *Estrategias de comunicación y educación para el desarrollo sostenible.*
Cf. Oficina Regional de Educación de la UNESCO para América Latina y el Caribe (OREALC) (ed.) (2008) (cf. *footnote 1223* op. cit.).

2020 Translation from Spanish into English: *"Por ello, la Década es una oportunidad para refrendar compromisos estableciendo alianzas con las distintas comunidades educativas implicadas y entre países. Se trata de un momento decisivo para fortalecer nuestros procesos y organizaciones, así como para defender los logros alcanzados. La Década es también oportuna para revisar y evaluar críticamente, tanto los avances y éxitos obtenidos en educación, como los errores, fracasos, retrocesos y estancamientos de la actividad en nuestra Región".*
See UNESCO; The Earth Charter Initiative (ECI) (eds.) (Marzo 2007) (cf. *footnote 113* op. cit.), p. 17.

In preparing regional implementation of *DESD*, twenty-one member states of the Latin American and Caribbean region plus Spain and the United States of America[2021] agreed upon nine guiding principles:[2022]

a) Making every social and institutional effort necessary to address *ESD*;
b) Integrating and harmonising educational policies;
c) Establishing normative indicators in support of *ESD*;
d) Supporting communication and information campaigns relating to *DESD*;
e) Strengthening co-operation and strategic associations;
f) Referring to *The Earth Charter* as an ethical and educational benchmark;
g) Fostering processes of monitoring and evaluation;
h) Setting *ESD* as a high priority on respective national agendas; and
i) Collecting and disseminating experiences, information and good practices.

6.5.1 Regional context

Implementing *DESD* in Latin America and the Caribbean is a substantial and difficult task. *"However, there are difficulties in implementing the ambitious theoretical objectives outlined. At this point in time there is no single member state nor any practice of development that might be called sustainable and indicators show that a sustainable state of affairs is still far from being realised."*[2023]

The critical question to be answered relates to what makes *ESD* particularly relevant in the Latin American and Caribbean region. In other words, why must this region be targeted by a separate, case-specific and properly strategic approach to *ESD*? Here follows a brief outline of the obstacles to be confronted, followed by the implications for the implementation of *DESD*.[2024]

2021 I.e. Argentina, Belize, Bolivia, Brazil, Chile, Colombia, Costa Rica, Cuba, Ecuador, El Salvador, Spain, Guatemala, French Guiana, Honduras, Mexico, Nicaragua, Panama, Paraguay, Peru, the Dominican Republic, Uruguay, the United States and Venezuela.
Cf. UNESCO; The Earth Charter Initiative (ECI) (eds.) (Marzo 2007) (cf. *footnote 113* op. cit.), pp. 19–20.
Cf. *Figure 57* in chapter IX 1.1 *Regional strategies* on page 258.

2022 Cf. UNESCO; The Earth Charter Initiative (ECI) (eds.) (Marzo 2007) (cf. *footnote 113* op. cit.), p. 18; Vilela, Miriam (2010) (cf. *footnote 827* op. cit.).

2023 Translation from Spanish into English: *"Sin embargo, persisten las dificultades para operacionalizar los ambiciosos enunciados teóricos; a la fecha, ningún país ni estilo de desarrollo se asume como sostenible y los indicadores muestran que esa posibilidad está lejana".*
See UNESCO; The Earth Charter Initiative (ECI) (eds.) (Marzo 2007) (cf. *footnote 113* op. cit.), p. 11.

2024 Cf. Organización de Estados Iberoamericanos para la Educación, la Ciencia y la Cultura (OEI); Instituto Internacional de Planeamiento de la Educación (IIPE); UNESCO (eds.) (2006): Informe sobre las Tendencias sociales y educativas en

Firstly, the *socio-economic* background of the continent presents a substantial challenge. Poverty and precarious living conditions are of major concern, and many are excluded from prosperity,[2025] income distribution and productivity is highly diverse and uneven[2026] and low-skilled labour and services are often poorly remunerated.[2027] Sectors of lower productivity and income are not integrated. High unemployment rates and significant informality are characteristics of most Latin American countries.[2028] The rates of national economic development are hugely diverse and are frequently affected by all kinds of externalities. Growth take place primarily in urban areas, and such rural development as there is is primarily dependent on natural resources.[2029]

Secondly, the *historical* and *socio-cultural* background must be considered. In most countries society is not equitably represented, but rather split or frag-

America Latina. 2006. Edited by Néstor Lopez. Paris / Buenos Aires / Madrid: UNESCO publishing; Servicio de Publicaciones; Talleres Trama S.A.; Organización de Estados Iberoamericanos para la Educación, la Ciencia y la Cultura (OEI); Instituto Internacional de Planeamiento de la Educación (IIPE); UNESCO (eds.) (2007): Informe sobre las Tendencias sociales y educativas en America Latina. 2007. Paris / Buenos Aires / Madrid: UNESCO publishing; Servicio de Publicaciones; Talleres Trama S.A.; Organización de Estados Iberoamericanos para la Educación, la Ciencia y la Cultura (OEI); Instituto Internacional de Planeamiento de la Educación (IIPE); UNESCO (eds.) (2008): La escuela y los adolescentes. Informe sobre las Tendencias sociales y educativas en America Latina. 2008. Edited by Néstor Lopez. Paris / Buenos Aires / Madrid: UNESCO publishing; Servicio de Publicaciones; Talleres Trama S.A. See *Figure 103* in chapter IX 6.5.1 *Regional context* on page 445.

2025 Cf. Organización de Estados Iberoamericanos para la Educación, la Ciencia y la Cultura (OEI); Instituto Internacional de Planeamiento de la Educación (IIPE); UNESCO (eds.) (2006) (cf. *footnote 2024* op. cit.), p. 18; Organización de Estados Iberoamericanos para la Educación, la Ciencia y la Cultura (OEI); Instituto Internacional de Planeamiento de la Educación (IIPE); UNESCO (eds.) (2007) (cf. *footnote 2024* op. cit.), pp. 39 et seqq.

2026 Cf. Soubbotina, Tatyana P. (2004) (cf. *footnote 86* op. cit.), pp. 14, 27–30, 31–34.

2027 Cf. Organización de Estados Iberoamericanos para la Educación, la Ciencia y la Cultura (OEI); Instituto Internacional de Planeamiento de la Educación (IIPE); UNESCO (eds.) (2008) (cf. *footnote 2024* op. cit.), pp. 47 et seqq.

2028 Cf. Organización de Estados Iberoamericanos para la Educación, la Ciencia y la Cultura (OEI); Instituto Internacional de Planeamiento de la Educación (IIPE); UNESCO (eds.) (2006) (cf. *footnote 2024* op. cit.), pp. 31, 33, 87–88, 91, 93, 96; Organización de Estados Iberoamericanos para la Educación, la Ciencia y la Cultura (OEI); Instituto Internacional de Planeamiento de la Educación (IIPE); UNESCO (eds.) (2007) (cf. *footnote 2024* op. cit.), pp. 46 et seqq.

2029 Cf. Organización de Estados Iberoamericanos para la Educación, la Ciencia y la Cultura (OEI); Instituto Internacional de Planeamiento de la Educación (IIPE); UNESCO (eds.) (2006) (cf. *footnote 2024* op. cit.), pp. 14, 19; Organización de Estados Iberoamericanos para la Educación, la Ciencia y la Cultura (OEI); Instituto Internacional de Planeamiento de la Educación (IIPE); UNESCO (eds.) (2007) (cf. *footnote 2024* op. cit.), p. 87.

mented into different identities.[2030] While societies encompass a rich diversity of different cultures and traditions, such as indigenous peoples or *mestizos*, many ethnic minority groups are neither socio-economically nor politically enfranchised.[2031] Racial discrimination and conflicts occur frequently, and nationalist tendencies are apparent.[2032]

Thirdly, the *political* framework is beset by weak institutions, considerable levels of bureaucracy, deficiencies in democratic processes and in the participation of civil society.[2033] Furthermore, corruption, populism and nepotism destroy reliability and allow uncertainty to flourish.[2034]

2030 Cf. Organización de Estados Iberoamericanos para la Educación, la Ciencia y la Cultura (OEI); Instituto Internacional de Planeamiento de la Educación (IIPE); UNESCO (eds.) (2006) (cf. *footnote 2024* op. cit.), p. 35; Organización de Estados Iberoamericanos para la Educación, la Ciencia y la Cultura (OEI); Instituto Internacional de Planeamiento de la Educación (IIPE); UNESCO (eds.) (2007) (cf. *footnote 2024* op. cit.), p. 16.

2031 Cf. Organización de Estados Iberoamericanos para la Educación, la Ciencia y la Cultura (OEI); Instituto Internacional de Planeamiento de la Educación (IIPE); UNESCO (eds.) (2007) (cf. *footnote 2024* op. cit.), pp. 38, 107, 138 et seqq.

2032 Cf. Organización de Estados Iberoamericanos para la Educación, la Ciencia y la Cultura (OEI); Instituto Internacional de Planeamiento de la Educación (IIPE); UNESCO (eds.) (2006) (cf. *footnote 2024* op. cit.), p. 14; Organización de Estados Iberoamericanos para la Educación, la Ciencia y la Cultura (OEI); Instituto Internacional de Planeamiento de la Educación (IIPE); UNESCO (eds.) (2007) (cf. *footnote 2024* op. cit.), pp. 112 et seqq.

2033 Cf. Organización de Estados Iberoamericanos para la Educación, la Ciencia y la Cultura (OEI); Instituto Internacional de Planeamiento de la Educación (IIPE); UNESCO (eds.) (2006) (cf. *footnote 2024* op. cit.), p. 154; Andelman, Marta (2009): Argentina and Education for Sustainable Development. In: Chalkley, Brian; Haigh, Martin J.; Higgitt, David (eds.): Education for sustainable development. Papers in honour of the United Nations Decade of Education for Sustainable Development (2005–2014). London / New York: Routledge, pp. 245–250.
See *Figure 102* in chapter IX 6.5.1 *Regional context* on page 442.

2034 Cf. Organización de Estados Iberoamericanos para la Educación, la Ciencia y la Cultura (OEI); Instituto Internacional de Planeamiento de la Educación (IIPE); UNESCO (eds.) (2006) (cf. *footnote 2024* op. cit.), p. 19; Organización de Estados Iberoamericanos para la Educación, la Ciencia y la Cultura (OEI); Instituto Internacional de Planeamiento de la Educación (IIPE); UNESCO (eds.) (2008) (cf. *footnote 2024* op. cit.), p. 113.

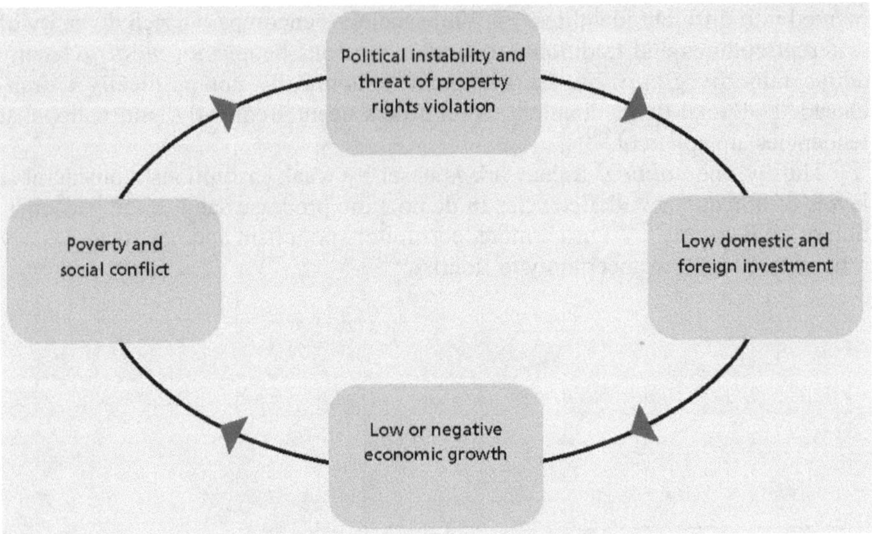

Figure 102: The vicious circle of political instability[2035]

Fourthly, the *educational* background of most of the countries concerned is alarming. Access to quality education is frequently contingent on gender and social background or position,[2036] and access to quality education is lacking.[2037]

2035 This figure causally relates socio-economic challenges with political instability that is still considered one of the most prevailing factors of inhibiting development in the Latin American and Caribbean region.
See Soubbotina, Tatyana P. (2004) (cf. *footnote 86* op. cit.), p. 34.

2036 Cf. Organización de Estados Iberoamericanos para la Educación, la Ciencia y la Cultura (OEI); Instituto Internacional de Planeamiento de la Educación (IIPE); UNESCO (eds.) (2006) (cf. *footnote 2024* op. cit.), pp. 65–68, 105, 135–137, 146 et seqq; Organización de Estados Iberoamericanos para la Educación, la Ciencia y la Cultura (OEI); Instituto Internacional de Planeamiento de la Educación (IIPE); UNESCO (eds.) (2007) (cf. *footnote 2024* op. cit.), p. 65.

2037 Cf. Organización de Estados Iberoamericanos para la Educación, la Ciencia y la Cultura (OEI); Instituto Internacional de Planeamiento de la Educación (IIPE); UNESCO (eds.) (2006) (cf. *footnote 2024* op. cit.), pp. 20, 37, 48, 55; Organización de Estados Iberoamericanos para la Educación, la Ciencia y la Cultura (OEI); Instituto Internacional de Planeamiento de la Educación (IIPE); UNESCO (eds.) (2007) (cf. *footnote 2024* op. cit.), pp. 78 et seqq; Macedo, Beatriz; Salgado, Carol (2007): Educación ambiental y educación para el desarrollo sostenible en América Latina. Forum de Sostenibilidad (FS). Cátedra UNESCO. In: análisis, Issue 1, pp. 29–37, p. 30.

Illiteracy is a major problem.[2038] From a regional perspective, levels of qualification differ considerably and knowledge is unequally distributed.[2039] Awareness of environmental, let alone sustainable issues as a whole is generally low. A redefinition of education as a medium of social and cultural cohesion and representation is necessary.[2040] School curricula and pedagogical concepts must therefore be re-oriented towards holistic educational concepts,[2041] open forms of schooling, dialogues and contextualised knowledge instead of the encyclopaedic reproduction of knowledge.[2042] Public expenditure for education is usually not sufficient to meet the need and demand for quality education.[2043]

Fifthly, *social* background matters. There are huge disparities in society,[2044] and this inequality is not only a major concern in the sphere of education. Even where it does exist, social welfare, security systems and public services are usually poor in quality, inefficient and not universally accessible.[2045] Large parts of society are still excluded.[2046] Decisions are either non-consensual or unrepresen-

---

2038 Cf. Organización de Estados Iberoamericanos para la Educación, la Ciencia y la Cultura (OEI); Instituto Internacional de Planeamiento de la Educación (IIPE); UNESCO (eds.) (2006) (cf. *footnote 2024* op. cit.), pp. 31, 45, et seqq.

2039 Cf. Soubbotina, Tatyana P. (2004) (cf. *footnote 86* op. cit.), pp. 35–42; Organización de Estados Iberoamericanos para la Educación, la Ciencia y la Cultura (OEI); Instituto Internacional de Planeamiento de la Educación (IIPE); UNESCO (eds.) (2006) (cf. *footnote 2024* op. cit.), pp. 14, 117.

2040 Cf. Organización de Estados Iberoamericanos para la Educación, la Ciencia y la Cultura (OEI); Instituto Internacional de Planeamiento de la Educación (IIPE); UNESCO (eds.) (2006) (cf. *footnote 2024* op. cit.), p. 37.

2041 Cf. UNESCO Education Sector (ed.) (2008) (cf. *footnote 27* op. cit.).

2042 *Adult education*, for instance, is still marginalised and not yet incorporated sufficiently into curricula as part of a holistic understanding of education.
Cf. Organización de Estados Iberoamericanos para la Educación, la Ciencia y la Cultura (OEI); Instituto Internacional de Planeamiento de la Educación (IIPE); UNESCO (eds.) (2006) (cf. *footnote 2024* op. cit.), pp. 39, 54, 72, 163; Organización de Estados Iberoamericanos para la Educación, la Ciencia y la Cultura (OEI); Instituto Internacional de Planeamiento de la Educación (IIPE); UNESCO (eds.) (2007) (cf. *footnote 2024* op. cit.), pp. 91 et seqq; Organización de Estados Iberoamericanos para la Educación, la Ciencia y la Cultura (OEI); Instituto Internacional de Planeamiento de la Educación (IIPE); UNESCO (eds.) (2008) (cf. *footnote 2024* op. cit.), p. 17.

2043 This means salaries, buildings and material resources in general.
Cf. Organización de Estados Iberoamericanos para la Educación, la Ciencia y la Cultura (OEI); Instituto Internacional de Planeamiento de la Educación (IIPE); UNESCO (eds.) (2007) (cf. *footnote 2024* op. cit.), p. 125.

2044 Cf. Macedo, Beatriz; Salgado, Carol (2007) (cf. *footnote 2037* op. cit.), p. 30.

2045 Cf. Organización de Estados Iberoamericanos para la Educación, la Ciencia y la Cultura (OEI); Instituto Internacional de Planeamiento de la Educación (IIPE); UNESCO (eds.) (2007) (cf. *footnote 2024* op. cit.), pp. 22–25.

2046 Cf. Organización de Estados Iberoamericanos para la Educación, la Ciencia y la Cultura (OEI); Instituto Internacional de Planeamiento de la Educación (IIPE);

tative. Societies are faced with the demographic transitions of a fast growing population and mega-cities are on the rise.[2047]

Sixthly, the *legal* framework of the *rule of law* continues to display its many insufficiencies.[2048] Human, civil and political rights are still violated. Trials are not conducted independently of political considerations, and corruption in general is a major problem. Conflicts with neighbouring countries are quite frequent and peace, stability and friendly relations amongst stakeholders within the region remain desirable yet unrealised *steady states*.[2049]

UNESCO (eds.) (2006) (cf. *footnote 2024* op. cit.), pp. 20, 33, 57; Organización de Estados Iberoamericanos para la Educación, la Ciencia y la Cultura (OEI); Instituto Internacional de Planeamiento de la Educación (IIPE); UNESCO (eds.) (2007) (cf. *footnote 2024* op. cit.), p. 28.

2047 Cf. Organización de Estados Iberoamericanos para la Educación, la Ciencia y la Cultura (OEI); Instituto Internacional de Planeamiento de la Educación (IIPE); UNESCO (eds.) (2006) (cf. *footnote 2024* op. cit.), pp. 34, 62;Organización de Estados Iberoamericanos para la Educación, la Ciencia y la Cultura (OEI); Instituto Internacional de Planeamiento de la Educación (IIPE); UNESCO (eds.) (2007) (cf. *footnote 2024* op. cit.), p. 56.

2048 Cf. Organización de Estados Iberoamericanos para la Educación, la Ciencia y la Cultura (OEI); Instituto Internacional de Planeamiento de la Educación (IIPE); UNESCO (eds.) (2007) (cf. *footnote 2024* op. cit.), p. 26.

2049 Cf. Organización de Estados Iberoamericanos para la Educación, la Ciencia y la Cultura (OEI); Instituto Internacional de Planeamiento de la Educación (IIPE); UNESCO (eds.) (2007) (cf. *footnote 2024* op. cit.), pp. 122 et seqq.

Figure 103: Challenges of DESD implementation in Latin America and the Caribbean[2050]

As a consequence, successful application of *DESD* to the Latin America region requires the strategy to address local situations and needs in two specific ways:

1. Adapting *DESD* to the regional structure (*structural adjustment*); and
2. Adapting contents of *DESD* to the regional situation (*content adjustment*).

As regards the structural question, the strategy proposes a *component approach*. *DESD* is primarily considered a holistic, synergetic platform on which to link existing educational programmes and initiatives while stressing their particular relevance to furthering sustainable development. *"Considering sustainability as a potential (source) of integrating and creating synergies between multiple is-*

2050 The Latin American and Caribbean region is facing multiple challenges regarding *DESD* implementation. Almost any state sector is involved to certain extent.

sues pertaining to education, it is evident that education addressing environment, interculturalism, peace, human rights, poverty, health and gender equality, amongst others, is a crucial component of (ESD)."[2051]

Where contents are concerned, the most driving issues have already been raised. The following aspects and issues expressly mentioned in the strategy do play a driving role in terms of systematic *DESD* implementation in Latin America:[2052]

2051 Translation from Spanish into English: "*Considerando que el concepto de sostenibilidad cuenta con el potencial de integrar y crear sinergias entre multiplicidad de temáticas educativas, se hace evidente que la educación ambiental, intercultural, para la paz, los derechos humanos, el combate contra la pobreza, la salud y la equidad de género, entre otras vertientes, son componentes esenciales de una educación para el desarrollo sostenible*".
See UNESCO; The Earth Charter Initiative (ECI) (eds.) (Marzo 2007) (cf. *footnote 113* op. cit.), p. 11.

2052 Cf. UNESCO; The Earth Charter Initiative (ECI) (eds.) (Marzo 2007) (cf. *footnote 113* op. cit.), pp. 10–11.
See *Table 47* in chapter IX 6.5.1 *Regional context* on page 447.

Table 47: Issues and challenges of DESD implementation in Latin America[2053]

Dimensions			
Environmental	*Social*	*Economic*	*Cultural*
Biodiversity	Discrimination	Growth	Discrimination
Energy	Poverty	Development	Interculturalism
Waste disposal	Gender equality	Consumption	Understanding
	Health	Production	Representation
	Civics	Welfare	Diversity
	Emancipation	Income distribution	Emancipation
	Education		
	Democracy		
Education			
Structure	*Demands*	*Issues*	*Criteria*
Access	Quality	Illiteracy	Interdisciplinary
Formal	Dialogue	Poverty	Holistic
Non-formal	Integration	Tolerance	Integrated
Informal	Monitoring	Environment	Context-based
Institutions	Evaluation	Health (HIV / AIDS)	Intercultural
Co-operation	Consensus	Civil society	Multi-perspective
Training	Synergy effects	Peace / Justice	Needs-based
Networks	Capacity-building	Democracy	Interactive
		Governance	Values-driven
			Locally relevant
			Participatory
			Multi-method
			Critical thinking
			Problem-solving
			Qualitative
			Proactive

2053 Cf. UNESCO; The Earth Charter Initiative (ECI) (eds.) (Marzo 2007) (cf. *footnote 113* op. cit.), pp. 10–11.

6.5.2 Contents

The *vision* of *ESD* in Latin America and the Caribbean is that of an overall public policy which is fully in line with other educational processes facilitating the inspirational, contextual and integral formation of human beings concerning the promotion of the following:[2054]

- Values of sustainability;
- Knowledge of cultural pluralism;
- Respect for the nature and life;
- Integrity of eco-systems;
- Economic justice and social and gender equality;
- Application of human rights;
- Tolerance of ambiguity;
- Dialogue;
- Co-existence;
- Peace.

The vision statement illustrates two major challenges that arise in reference to *DESD* in Latin America and the Caribbean. Given the multitude of inter-related *ESD* issues relevant to the region, the two following functions are performed:[2055]

a) It reveals some conceptual *opaqueness* regarding the nature and definition of *DESD*; and
b) It confirms that the regional interpretation of *DESD* is far too complex in scope in order to be dealt with properly.

In the primary vision all processes of environmental destruction and contamination will have been reversed by the end of *DESD*.[2056] In its educational and communicative programmes the strategy also envisions substantial progress in building just and sustainable societies.

2054 Cf. Oficina Regional de Educación de la UNESCO para América Latina y el Caribe (OREALC); UNESCO (eds.) (2004): Educación para el Desarrollo Sostenible. Edited by Daniel Gil-Pérez; Amparo Vilches. Santiago de Chile: UNESCO Santiago; UNESCO; The Earth Charter Initiative (ECI) (eds.) (Marzo 2007) (cf. *footnote 113* op. cit.), p. 12.
Cf. chapter VII 1 *Vision* on page 149.

2055 Cf. González-Gaudiano, Edgar (2009) (cf. *footnote 659* op. cit.).

2056 Cf. Oficina Regional de Educación de la UNESCO para América Latina y el Caribe (OREALC); UNESCO (eds.) (2005b): Plan educativo regional para el Desarrollo sostenible. Edited by Beatriz Macedo. Santiago de Chile: UNESCO Santiago, p. 2.

Four *objectives* are being formulated to address the particular regional context of Latin America (and the Caribbean). These are:[2057]

1. Making sure that *DESD* is known and promoted in all countries of the region;
2. Ensuring that governments support and finance the implementation of *DESD*;
3. Focusing on international co-operation and private sector commitment to carry out plans for region-specific implementation; and
4. Forming a strong education-based community capable of incorporating principles of sustainability into all levels of formal education as well as beyond, into informal and non-formal education.

With the intention of specifying the provisions which are stated as the vision and the objectives, the regional strategy defines six consecutive *principles* of implementation.[2058]

Table 48: Principles of DESD implementation in Latin America[2059]

Principle	*Contents*
Proclamation of joint action	• Provides a complex and integrated perspective • Combines social and institutional efforts in *ESD* • Seeks better standards of living (quality of life)
Integration and harmonisation of educational policies	• Involves each country • Addresses all levels and forms of teaching as well as informal and non-formal education • Involves governmental authorities as well as institutions of civil society • Improves educational practice related to *ESD*
Formulation of normative indicators	• Expresses *ESD* in a binding, cross-cutting and interdisciplinary way • Accompanies *ESD* with procedures, instruments and implementing tools • Provides resources to enable momentum building and co-ordinating initiatives

2057 Cf. UNESCO; The Earth Charter Initiative (ECI) (eds.) (Marzo 2007) (cf. *footnote 113* op. cit.), p. 13; Fien, John (2010) (cf. *footnote 817* op. cit.).

2058 See *Table 48* in chapter IX 6.5.2 *Contents* on page 449.

2059 Cf. UNESCO; The Earth Charter Initiative (ECI) (eds.) (Marzo 2007) (cf. *footnote 113* op. cit.), pp. 13–14; Makrakis, Vassilio (2010) (cf. *footnote 1544* op. cit.).

Principle	*Contents*
Communication and information[2060]	• Raises public awareness of types of development, social structures, methods of production and sustainable lifestyles • Supports social networking and other means of communication • Makes available new information and communication technologies
Co-operation and strategic associations	• Facilitates stakeholder interaction on the local, national, regional and global stage • Creates platforms for the co-ordination and exchange of experiences • Contributes to investment in human and financial resources and institutional *ESD* infrastructure
Monitoring and evaluation	• Generates objectives and benchmark indicators (qualitative and quantitative) • Defines methods and procedures of participatory, continuing and interactive evaluation • Encourages stakeholder commitment through incentives

Each member state is requested to identify those persons responsible for defining areas of *priorities*. These must be based upon the global and regional *DESD* principles of implementation and ought to address the particular characteristics, interests, needs and opportunities of every single member state. Relevant guidelines that have to be taken into consideration are:[2061]

a) Embedding *DESD* and the regional action plan for Latin America at national, sub-national and local level;
b) Introducing the formulation and application of integrated and inter-sectoral public policies for the furtherance of *ESD*;
c) Strengthening national normative benchmarks for the judicial, administrative, budgetary and operational implementation of *DESD*;
d) Supporting research and development of curricula at all educational levels including non- and informal education enabling *ESD*-related initiatives to be integrated into national educational systems;
e) Promoting value-based and principle-oriented professional teacher training at the levels of primary, secondary and higher education;

2060 Cf. Oficina Regional de Educación de la UNESCO para América Latina y el Caribe (OREALC) (ed.) (2008) (cf. *footnote 1223* op. cit.).

2061 Cf. UNESCO; The Earth Charter Initiative (ECI) (eds.) (Marzo 2007) (cf. *footnote 113* op. cit.), pp. 14–15; Oficina Regional de Educación de la UNESCO para América Latina y el Caribe (OREALC) (ed.) (2008) (cf. *footnote 1223* op. cit.).

f) Managing context-dependent contents and appropriate didactic and pedagogical approaches;
g) Communicating *ESD* effectively;
h) Forging interdisciplinary links between sciences, economics, politics, arts and humanities;
i) Providing public access to *ESD*-related educational materials and instruments necessary for the programmatic implementation of *ESD* in an efficient and effective way;
j) Institutionalising platforms, networks and co-operation between involved civic stakeholders;
k) Encouraging fundraising and disseminating *ESD* practices showing educational initiative;
l) Optimising civic education by providing information related to formal, non-formal and informal mechanisms of *ESD*;
m) Stimulating the creation of integrated civic councils on the implementation and evaluation of principal stakeholders during *DESD*;
n) Relating *ESD* to initiatives already in progress as a point of departure for its application;
o) Creating public momentum in environmental education at national and international level;
p) Promoting collaboration between existing programmes;[2062]
q) Disseminating good or best-practice examples for increased visibility;
r) Reporting progress, challenges and experiences;
s) Elaborating national action plans for *DESD* implementation;
t) Increasing youth participation throughout *DESD* conception and implementation of programmes and action;
u) Evaluating results and achievements in an object-driven, criteria-based and indicator-oriented approach in the short, medium and long term; and
v) Designing follow-up programmes and ongoing activities.

Multi-*stakeholder* participation and cross-*sectoral* co-operation is expressly mentioned and recognised to be a prerequisite for regional *DESD* implementation in Latin America. However, due to various restrictions[2063] the strategy focuses on principal actors that are likely to have a substantial impact on the success of its implementation. These target groups are shown in the following tabulation.[2064]

2062 Examples are the *United Nations Decade for the Promotion of a Culture of Peace and Non-Violence* or the *World Programme for Human Rights Education*.

2063 Examples include infrastructure, transfer and reach; financial, materialistic and human resources; and information.

2064 See *Table 49* in chapter IX 6.5.2 *Contents* on page 452.

Table 49: Principle stakeholders of DESD implementation in Latin America[2065]

Stakeholder category	*Description*
Decision-makers	• Execute political, technical and administrative responsibility • Enable associations between authorities and governmental functionaries, legislative bodies, entrepreneurs and civil society (non-governmental organisations, networks and initiatives)
Experts	• Contribute knowledge, skills and expertise • Address members of the educational, scientific and technological elite • Extend invitations to professionals in the education sector and experts in traditional knowledge societies
Facilitators or inhibitors	• Influence positively or negatively according to rank • Consider trade union leaders and civil society commitment (groups with expertise or *DESD* affinity) • Encourage religious organisations, journalists, political parties
Beneficiaries	• Make use of *DESD*, particularly advantaging children, youth, senior citizens, indigenous population and other disadvantaged groups

The strategy is directed towards the building of momentum and the creation of synergies by bringing together the actors involved in order to:[2066]

- Stimulate communication and proactive action between the sectors;
- Promote dialogue and the exchange of information and experiences as well as participation and implementation; and
- Provide evaluation, follow-ups and research.

Besides the non-mandatory stakeholders, there are international organisations acting in fulfilment of their mandate for the implementation of *DESD* globally and regionally. As far as *ESD* in Latin America is concerned, these mandatory organisations are from the United Nations system. They provide both leadership and support and guidance for the processes of monitoring and evaluation.[2067]

2065 Cf. UNESCO; The Earth Charter Initiative (ECI) (eds.) (Marzo 2007) (cf. *footnote 113* op. cit.), pp. 15–16.

2066 Cf. UNESCO; The Earth Charter Initiative (ECI) (eds.) (Marzo 2007) (cf. *footnote 113* op. cit.), p. 15; Oficina Regional de Educación de la UNESCO para América Latina y el Caribe (OREALC) (ed.) (2008) (cf. *footnote 1223* op. cit.).

2067 See *Table 50* in chapter IX 6.5.2 *Contents* on page 453.

Table 50: International organisation commitment of DESD implementation in Latin America[2068]

Scope	International organisation	
International	*United Nations Educational, Scientific and Cultural Organization* (UNESCO)	
	United Nations Environment Programme (UNEP)	*Programa de las Naciones Unidas para el Medio Ambiente* (PNUMA)
	World Health Organisation (WHO)	*Organización Mundial de la Salud* (OMS)
	Food and Agriculture Organisation (FAO)	*Organización de las Naciones Unidas para la Agricultura y la Alimentación* (FAO)
	United Nations International Children's Emergency Fund (UNICEF)	
	United Nations Development Programme (UNDP)	*Programa de las Naciones Unidas para el Desarrollo* (PNUD)
	United Nations Population Fund (UNFPA)	*Fondo de Población de las Naciones Unidas* (FNUAP)
Regional (Latin America)	Regional UNESCO office for education in Latin America and the Caribbean based in Santiago de Chile	*Oficina Regional de Educación para América Latina y el Caribe con sede en Santiago de Chile, Chile* (OREALC / UNESCO Santiago)
	Regional education project for Latin America and the Caribbean	*Proyecto Regional de Educación para América Latina y el Caribe* (PRELAC)
	Regional programme on environmental education for Latin America and the Caribbean	*Programa Latinoamericano y del Caribe de Educación Ambiental* (PLACEA)

The success of *DESD* implementation in Latin America also depends on solid *financing*. All stakeholders are requested to assure appropriate access to the required resources. The strategy aims in the first instance to raise public awareness of decision makers' traceable spending on educational processes. This may substantially contribute to more favourable budgetary conditions for *ESD* financing. Secondly, governments are required to devise specific budgets and allocate resources to *DESD* exclusively, and other programmes accordingly. Thirdly, governments must provide strong economic incentives in order to finance *ESD*-related projects, programmes and activities at all levels, and including scholarship programmes. Fourthly, it is important that *ESD* should be in-

2068 This table serves as summary of primary *DESD* stakeholder organisations – both international and regional – in Latin America and the Caribbean region.
Cf. UNESCO; The Earth Charter Initiative (ECI) (eds.) (Marzo 2007) (cf. *footnote 113* op. cit.), p. 18.

volved in already existing and ongoing bi- and multi-lateral programmes at either the national or international level. In this respect, benefiting from *synergy effects* is absolutely possible. This type of resource-saving co-operation may lead to non-profit or foundational organisations.

DESD implementation in Latin America and the Caribbean is self-generating and primarily based upon selected best practices. At the very core is the idea of disseminating examples of *ESD* activities and programmes through which more and more stakeholders are invited to participate. Put differently, the implementing process starts rather informally and acquires greater formality as structures of programme planning, dialoguing and co-operation are erected. Given means of guidance and facilitation, this procedural approach explicitly takes into account the region-specific circumstances of limited access to formalised or institutionalised provisions.[2069] The regional implementation of *DESD* is deliberately oriented towards culture-related *ESD* issues.[2070]

According to feedback obtained from monitoring, regional commitment remains ambivalent. As documented, the reporting stage has only been partially accomplished because in providing the feedback requested by the regional *questionnaires*[2071] not all countries and national commissions complied.[2072] Reporting in Latin America and the Caribbean is roughly based on the *UNECE report format*.[2073] Slight modifications and adaptations have been made mainly through

---

2069 Cf. Oficina Regional de Educación de la UNESCO para América Latina y el Caribe (OREALC); UNESCO (eds.) (2005b) (cf. *footnote 2056* op. cit.), pp. 2–4.

2070 This may be done by referring to the benefits of cultural plurality, diversity, development and education.
Cf. Oficina Regional de Educación de la UNESCO para América Latina y el Caribe (OREALC); UNESCO (eds.) (2005b) (cf. *footnote 2056* op. cit.), pp. 3–4; UNESCO; The Earth Charter Initiative (ECI) (eds.) (Marzo 2007) (cf. *footnote 113* op. cit.), pp. 8, 10, 11, 35.

2071 Cf. Oficina Regional de Educación de la UNESCO para América Latina y el Caribe (OREALC) (2008c) (cf. *footnote 1213* op. cit.); UNESCO (ed.) (2008h) (cf. *footnote 219* op. cit.), pp. 3–8; Tilbury, Daniella (July 2009) (cf. *footnote 1807* op. cit.), p. 191.

2072 For instance, unlike Mexico and Brazil, other influential member states of the region, such as Argentina or Venezuela, entirely refused to take part in *DESD* and to engage in *ESD*.
Cf. Gerner, Martin (30/07/2009) (cf. *footnote 407* op. cit.); UNESCO Section for DESD Coordination (ed.) (2009) (cf. *footnote 116* op. cit.), p. 79; Andelman, Marta (2009) (cf. *footnote 2033* op. cit.); González-Gaudiano, Edgar (2009) (cf. *footnote 659* op. cit.).

2073 Cf. United Nations Economic Commission for Europe (UNECE) (26/10/2006) (cf. *footnote 413* op. cit.); United Nations Economic Commission for Europe (UNECE) (ed.) (2009) (cf. *footnote 1789* op. cit.), pp. 51–69.
See *Figure 104* in chapter IX 6.5.2 *Contents* on page 455.

the addition of an additional *glossary*[2074] on learning terminology and a short *briefing catalogue*[2075] on *DESD*.

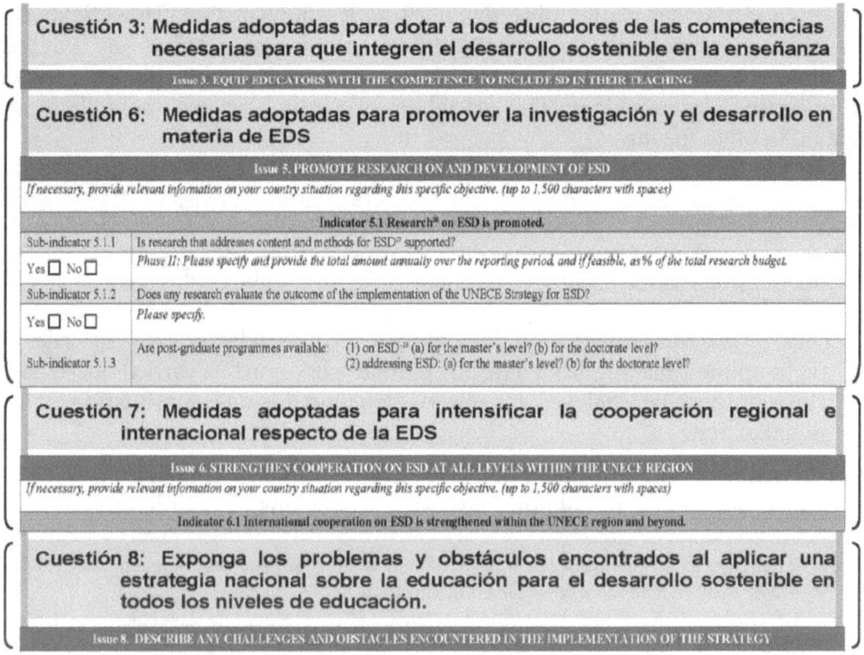

Cuestión 3: Medidas adoptadas para dotar a los educadores de las competencias necesarias para que integren el desarrollo sostenible en la enseñanza

Issue 3. EQUIP EDUCATORS WITH THE COMPETENCE TO INCLUDE SD IN THEIR TEACHING

Cuestión 6: Medidas adoptadas para promover la investigación y el desarrollo en materia de EDS

Issue 5. PROMOTE RESEARCH ON AND DEVELOPMENT OF ESD

If necessary, provide relevant information on your country situation regarding this specific objective. (up to 1,500 characters with spaces)

Indicator 5.1 Research[a] on ESD is promoted.	
Sub-indicator 5.1.1	Is research that addresses content and methods for ESD[a] supported?
Yes ☐ No ☐	*Phase II: Please specify and provide the total amount annually over the reporting period, and if feasible, as % of the total research budget.*
Sub-indicator 5.1.2	Does any research evaluate the outcome of the implementation of the UNECE Strategy for ESD?
Yes ☐ No ☐	*Please specify.*
Sub-indicator 5.1.3	Are post-graduate programmes available: (1) on ESD[a] (a) for the master's level? (b) for the doctorate level? (2) addressing ESD: (a) for the master's level? (b) for the doctorate level?

Cuestión 7: Medidas adoptadas para intensificar la cooperación regional e internacional respecto de la EDS

Issue 6. STRENGTHEN COOPERATION ON ESD AT ALL LEVELS WITHIN THE UNECE REGION

If necessary, provide relevant information on your country situation regarding this specific objective. (up to 1,500 characters with spaces)

Indicator 6.1 International cooperation on ESD is strengthened within the UNECE region and beyond.

Cuestión 8: Exponga los problemas y obstáculos encontrados al aplicar una estrategia nacional sobre la educación para el desarrollo sostenible en todos los niveles de educación.

Issue 8. DESCRIBE ANY CHALLENGES AND OBSTACLES ENCOUNTERED IN THE IMPLEMENTATION OF THE STRATEGY

Figure 104: DESD reporting in Latin America and the Caribbean compared to UNECE[2076]

2074 Cf. Oficina Regional de Educación de la UNESCO para América Latina y el Caribe (OREALC) (2008b) (cf. *footnote 1213* op. cit.).

2075 Cf. Oficina Regional de Educación de la UNESCO para América Latina y el Caribe (OREALC) (2008a): El Monitoreo y la Evaluación Mundial de la Ejecución de la Actividades del DEDS. Directrices para la respuesta al cuestionario. Published by: UNESCO. Oficina Regional de Educación de la UNESCO para América Latina y el Caribe (OREALC). Santiago de Chile.

2076 This figure is a compilation of two *DESD* report formats. Comparing them undoubtedly shows evidence that the Latin American way of reporting is largely based on the UNECE format. Positively speaking, this fact may support the argument of UNECE serving as good-practice example of regional *DESD* implementation. Critically speaking, any proper or genuine reporting strategy could be adopted for the Latin American and Caribbean region in order to meet region-specific needs and priorities.
Cf. United Nations Economic Commission for Europe (UNECE) (26/10/2006) (cf. *footnote 413* op. cit.), pp. 7, 9, 10, 11; Oficina Regional de Educación de la UNESCO para América Latina y el Caribe (OREALC) (2008c) (cf. *footnote 1213* op. cit.), pp. 7, 11, 12, 13.

6.5.3 Fieldwork experiences

To begin with, it must be taken into account that research based upon individual experience provides neither objective nor limitless information. Thus, fieldwork experiences cannot serve as representative samples of proving any kind of credible evidence. However, the type of research permits and facilitates methods of in-depth opinion-making. This would not or hardly have been possible by referring to other means.

In the case of monitoring *DESD* implementation in Latin America and the Caribbean, experience-based research is interesting and advisable for two reasons:

1. *Lack of publications*: there is comparatively little published, officially accessible data; and
2. *Lack of insights*: researchers must always face knowledge gaps. In order to avoid opinion-making from a distance, field work must be carried out on site. This can best be achieved by observation, inquiry and consultation of regional experts.

In contrast to several informal briefings, different formally conducted *interviews* constitute the corpus, in both oral and written accounts,[2077] and have been used

2077 The majority of interviewees were affiliated with an institutional mandate; only a few are of truly independent, *freelance* backgrounds.
Cf. Böhmer, Karl (19/06/2008): UNESCO y la Década de las Naciones Unidas "Educación para el desarrollo sostenible" en América Latina. Universidad ARCIS; UNESCO. Interview. Format: mp3. Santiago de Chile; Samaniego, Joseluis (07/07/2008): UNESCO y la Década de las Naciones Unidas "Educación para el desarrollo sostenible" en América Latina. Comisión Económica Para América Latina y el Caribe (CEPAL/ECLAC). Interview. Format: mp3. Santiago de Chile; Ossa, Vicente (17/07/2008): UNESCO y la Década de las Naciones Unidas "Educación para el desarrollo sostenible" en América Latina. United Nations Development Programme (UNDP/PNUD) Chile. Interview. Format: mp3. Santiago de Chile; Hollander, Astrid; Salgado, Carol (23/07/2008) (cf. *footnote 1810* op. cit.); Arrué Rodriguez, Rodrigo (24/07/2008): UNESCO y la Década de las Naciones Unidas "Educación para el desarrollo sostenible" en América Latina. Comisión Nacional del Medio Ambiente (CONAMA) Chile. Interview. Format: mp3. Santiago de Chile; Gallardo, Tito; Gajardo Gabelo, Octavio (24/07/2008): UNESCO y la Década de las Naciones Unidas "Educación para el desarrollo sostenible" en América Latina. Ministerio de Educación (MINEDUC); UNESCOP Chile. Interview. Format: mp3. Santiago de Chile; Gallopin, Gilberto (29/08/2008): UNESCO y la Década de las Naciones Unidas "Educación para el desarrollo sostenible" en América Latina. UNESCO / Comisión Económica Para América Latina y el Caribe (CEPAL/ECLAC). Interview. Format: mp3. Buenos Aires; Berrios, Fernando (23/09/2008): UNESCO y la Década de las Naciones Unidas "Educación para el desarrollo sostenible" en América Latina. UNESCO Perú. Interview. Format: mp3. Lima; Macedo, Beatriz (02/08/2010): UNESCO y la Década de las Naciones Unidas "Educación para el desarrollo sostenible" en América Latina.

for further content analysis. Respective sources have been anonymised according to general principles of empirical social research. Thus, purposely any conclusion can be drawn neither about individual statements nor institutional preferences of the interviewee.[2078] Questions are mainly standardised and based on a questionnaire.

The chapters of the *questionnaire* are logically defined and pre-structured. They are arranged in order to gradually deduce contents:

- *Sustainability* (1–3): addressing issues of topicality, aspects and problems of *ESD* in Latin America and the Caribbean;
- *Institutions* (4–5): relating to the particular role of institutions and their strategic approach to *ESD*;
- *Implementation* (6–9): obtaining knowledge of instruments, focal issues, priorities and projects in place regionally;
- *Networking* (10–11): raising the issues of cross-cutting co-operation and spillover or synergy effects; and
- *Cultural education*[2079] (12–14): dealing with culture, its pivotal function in the course of *DESD* and the criteria of cultural education in consideration of the fact that *culture* is considered a regional focal point.

6.5.4 Results

Topicality: How would you describe public awareness and topical relevance in view of ESD within society of your region?

Generally speaking, public awareness and the topical relevance of *ESD* in the Latin America and Caribbean region are considered marginal. This finding is evidenced by:

Former regional specialist in charge of ESD / Oficina Regional de Educación de la UNESCO para América Latina y el Caribe (OREALC/UNESCO Santiago). Interview. Format: doc (Questionnaire). Paris.

2078 The author takes full account of the information provided and at the same time guarantees both the validity of data and confidentiality vis-à-vis contributing interviewees (*informed consent*). All results subsequently presented in a consolidated version are traceable to single narrative accounts and respective statements.
Cf. Hopf, Christel (2005): Forschungsethik und qualitative Forschung. In: Flick, Uwe; Kardorff, Ernst von; Steinke, Ines (eds.): Qualitative Forschung. Ein Handbuch. Reinbek bei Hamburg: Rowohlt-Taschenbuch-Verlag (Rororo Rowohlts Enzyklopädie, 55628), pp. 589–600, pp. 591–592.

2079 Cf. chapter II 2.4 *Cultural sustainability* on page 24, chapter VI 2.2 *Expertise* on page 131, chapter VII 4 *Dimensions* on pages 153 et seqq, and chapter VII 15 *Summary* on pages 195 et seqq.

- Considerable *ignorance* of *ESD* both as a technical and programmatic term due to inconsistent, insufficient or lacking explanation and conceptualisation;[2080]
- Marginal knowledge, perception, awareness and *visibility* of *ESD* in public;[2081]
- Limited *commitment* and capabilities due to poor mobilisation of citizens and minimal bottom-up participation;[2082] and
- Notable divergence of *interests*, support and needs subject to differing priorities.[2083]

However, the need for substantial changes globally is increasingly recognised[2084] by some national agendas, predominantly emphasising the environmental dimension of *ESD*.[2085] Still, it has not been fully transformed into a concern at an overall regional level. Some countries take the initiative in setting up programmes, pieces of legislation and civic discourse on environmental education. Conversely, all other domains of *ESD* – economic, social and cultural – are even more under-represented. A holistic and regional approach to *ESD* through public awareness and topical relevance remains, for now, a distant vision.

Aspects: Which are relevant aspects of ESD to be necessarily covered within your respective region?

The aspects considered most relevant to be taken into account within the Latin America and Caribbean region pertain primarily to interdisciplinary awareness-raising and capacity-building. With regard to the subject matter of *ESD*, however, opinions are rather diverse, ranging from more abstract issues, such as:

- Strengthening civic education;[2086]
- Changing mindsets through capacity-building;[2087] or
- Sensibilising stakeholders to cross-cutting approaches;[2088]

to more concrete visions whose main aspects are:

- Definitions of *ESD* content-wise through examples of best practice;[2089]

2080 Cf. interviewee C, interviewee D, interviewee E, interviewee F, and interviewee I.
2081 Cf. interviewee A, interviewee C, interviewee E, interviewee G, and interviewee I.
2082 Cf. interviewee A, and interviewee H.
2083 Cf. interviewee C, interviewee G, and interviewee I.
2084 Cf. interviewee D, interviewee F, and interviewee G.
2085 Cf. interviewee C.
2086 Cf. interviewee B.
2087 Cf. interviewee B, and interviewee I.
2088 Cf. interviewee A, and interviewee F.
2089 Cf. interviewee C.

- Promotion of environmental education through more public and private investment in environmental issues;[2090]
- Encouragement of educational reform towards a greater emphasis on the acquisition of personal competences and responsibilities at every stage;[2091]
- Applying alternative pathways of regional development by taking stock of current concerns[2092] and different dimensions;[2093] and
- Development of regional strategies and context-based indicators for *ESD*.[2094]

Education in the broadest sense is the central, driving aspect of *ESD* in the region. This applies both to the need for structural changes and orientation towards the subject matter of *ESD*.

Problems: Which are major problems and concerns with respect to ESD?

The major problems and concerns related to *ESD* in Latin America and the Caribbean are raised according to different focal issues. Challenges are threefold and refer to:

- *Mobilisation and commitment*: the added value provided by *DESD* and the implicit or explicit incentives for institutional and civic participation by policy-makers and stakeholders receive insufficient explanation;[2095]
- *Co-ordination*: there is an urgent need for consistency in the use of technology in defining *ESD* consistently within the region.[2096] Generally, the increase in international bureaucracy is criticised and institutional effectiveness is openly questioned.[2097] In terms of the co-operative and managerial practices of *DESD*, uncertainty remained over the approach of *ESD*: namely, is it bottom-up or top-down? The translation of *ESD* into practice is often difficult;[2098] and
- *Resources*: financial and disciplinary restrictions[2099] can negatively influence *ESD* implementation in the matter of the efficient and effective allocation of resources.[2100] Because of substantial conflicts of interest,[2101] strategic targets must be prioritised.[2102]

2090 For example: scarcity of resources, contamination, biodiversity, climate change, forest degradation, energy, etc.
Cf. interviewee A, interviewee D, interviewee E, interviewee G, and interviewee I.

2091 Cf. interviewee H.

2092 For example: distributive inequality, ownership, poverty, rule of law, etc.

2093 Cf. interviewee G.

2094 Cf. interviewee G.

2095 Cf. interviewee C, interviewee D, interviewee E, interviewee G, interviewee H, and interviewee I.

2096 Cf. interviewee A, and interviewee E.

2097 Cf. interviewee C, interviewee D, and interviewee G.

2098 Cf. interviewee B.

2099 For example: budget deficits, inflation, growth orientation, financial crisis, etc.

2100 Cf. interviewee A, interviewee C, interviewee E, and interviewee I.

Several typically structural reasons can inhibit stakeholders from subscribing to *ESD*. The additional-cost criterion and the limited resources available for *DESD* are by far the most prevailing within the region.

Institutional role: With regard to institutions, how would you state your mission regarding DESD?

Consensus is reached upon the pivotal role assigned to institutions. However, institutional power is considered limited in the case of *DESD*. In Latin America and the Caribbean, there are three explanations for this:

- Institutions in charge of *ESD* simply do not exist or are still emerging;[2103]
- Institutions are not sufficiently charged with the exercise of legislative, executive or judicial authority for the promotion of *ESD*;[2104] or
- Institutions do not perform effectively, due to excessive bureaucracy,[2105] absent institutional linkages[2106] or the inability to co-operate and facilitate.[2107]

The role of regional institutions in charge of co-ordinating and implementing the goals of *DESD*[2108] has been poorly developed. This is not only because of weak institutional bodies in the matter of resources or facilities, but rather results from deficiencies in inter-agency co-operation.[2109] Besides, no particular institutional role has been ascribed to UNESCO in terms of contributions to *ESD* at the regional level.

Strategy: In accordance with the implementation principles of DESD, how would you de-fine your institutional role and strategic approach within this process?

Accepting *education* as the primary concern of *DESD*,[2110] a summary follows of how all institutions have in general perceived their role in *ESD* in Latin America and the Caribbean:

- *Information and publishing*: institutions are to provide and publish background information and regional analyses of *ESD*-related issues. These tasks often run on minimal budgets or off third-party (or extra-budgetary) financing;[2111]

2101 For example: too many mandates and decades parallel in process.
2102 Cf. interviewee F.
2103 Cf. interviewee E, and interviewee F.
2104 Cf. interviewee G.
2105 Cf. interviewee C.
2106 Cf. interviewee I.
2107 Cf. interviewee D, interviewee F, and interviewee G.
2108 Cf. interviewee H.
2109 Cf. interviewee D.
2110 Cf. interviewee F.
2111 Cf. interviewee A, and interviewee I.

- *Assistance and consultancy*: institutions are to provide the technical guidance requested principally for establishing structures of interactive *ESD* networking.[2112] Consultancy needs to be binding, continuous, coherent and above all based on analyses;[2113] and
- *Promotion and multiplication*: institutions are to share their expertise in *ESD* *qua* regional think tanks by providing multiplier effects.[2114]

To conclude, the strategic approach of institutions is oriented towards foundation and facilitation. No concrete means of either implementing or monitoring *ESD* forms part of any institutional approach.

Instruments: Which instruments are being used and how are they applied in order to monitor the implementation of DESD?

Region-specific instruments of implementing and monitoring *ESD*[2115] have hardly been developed, let alone deployed.[2116] In Latin America and the Caribbean, systematic approaches of applying instruments focusing on *ESD* in an interdisciplinary way are rarer.[2117] By contrast, many initiatives rely on informal networks and platforms originating in personal experience, assigned resources and institutional expertise.[2118] Action plans are driven by numerous motives and developed rather in a *step-by-step* and spontaneous manner.[2119]

Monitoring the regional implementation of *ESD* using globally valid, cross-cutting indicators must be treated with great analytical caution.

Focal issues: Which are your preferred fields of work in terms of implementing DESD?

In Latin America and the Caribbean, the focal issues of *DESD* implementation are twofold and distinguish between:

- *Structure*: significant concerns include the provision of technical assistance for awareness-raising and capacity-building,[2120] and the construction of regional *ESD* platforms in order to promote *ESD* in public;[2121] and

---

2112 For example: both in civil-society, private, public and academic projects. Cf. interviewee A, interviewee C, and interviewee G.

2113 Cf. interviewee D, and interviewee G.

2114 Cf. interviewee A, interviewee C, interviewee F, and interviewee I.

2115 Cf. interviewee H.

2116 Cf. interviewee F, and interviewee I.

2117 Cf. interviewee C, and interviewee G.

2118 For example: round table platforms consisting of *non-governmental organisations* (NGO), universities, companies and governmental bodies. Cf. interviewee E, and interviewee F.

2119 Cf. interviewee E.

2120 For example: developing educational materials for teachers and other stakeholders. Cf. interviewee C.

2121 Cf. interviewee C, interviewee D, interviewee E, and interviewee H.

- *Content*: beside *ESD*, the most pressing issues concern how the programmes *Millennium Development Goals* (MDG) and *Education for All* (EFA) might best be executed. In the case of *ESD*, environmental education certainly exerts the strongest influence.[2122] Cultural education is also mentioned as a relevant issue which concerns cultural heritage and cultural diversity.[2123]

It must be recognised that *DESD* cannot be dealt with as a single issue. It must instead be considered as one of many global initiatives. Priorities must be outlined in full awareness of the scarcity of resources and budgetary limitations, and this applies to this region in particular.[2124] What has happened in the case of *DESD* is that some focal issues that had previously been established now share certain aspects of *ESD*. *DESD* constitutes an international *code-share process*.

Priorities: According to the four domains of DESD, which priorities are considered to be most relevant to be taken into consideration within your region?

In view of the four prescribed domains of *DESD*,[2125] there is no clear-cut regional prioritisation or preference towards a particular one within Latin America and the Caribbean. All aspects are considered to be equally important and complementary:[2126]

- *Promoting and improving basic education*: it is quality education that really matters as a substantial basis for *ESD*;[2127]
- *Re-orienting existing education programmes*: it is acquired awareness that finally induces means of *ESD* implementation;[2128]
- *Developing public understanding and awareness*: it is sensibilised, mobilised and committed regional stakeholders who initiate vital interdisciplinary and context-based *ESD* capacity-building;[2129] and
- *Training*: it is *Public-Private-Partnerships* (PPP) which may be said to be platforms for disseminating and applying *ESD* materials.[2130]

The range of opinions reveals the most critical, but at the same time interchangeable message for Latin America and the Caribbean: a) any domain of

2122 For instance: integrating the business sector into environmental education, providing legal provisions for environmental protection, compensation mechanisms and voluntary contributions, or encouraging initiatives meeting with international obligations, for example: on biodiversity, climate change, renewable energy, etc.
Cf. interviewee A, interviewee D.

2123 Cf. interviewee F.

2124 Cf. interviewee F.

2125 Cf. chapter IX 2.2 *Domains* on page 278.

2126 Cf. interviewee B, interviewee G, and interviewee I.

2127 Cf. interviewee A, and interviewee C.

2128 Cf. interviewee A, and interviewee H.

2129 Cf. interviewee A, interviewee C, interviewee D, interviewee G, and interviewee H.

2130 Cf. interviewee F.

DESD is crucial as far as issues of education are concerned and addressed,[2131] and b) as long as processes eventually change *status-quo* situations towards *ESD*.

Projects: What kind of ESD-related projects do you or does your institution realise or directly support?

Carrying out *ESD*-related projects in Latin America and the Caribbean depends by and large on the institutional background. However, success is reliant on the individual or collective effort.[2132] Throughout the region different projects are in place.[2133] They are either run by *ESD*-affiliated institutions or initiated independently. UNESCO offers special *kick-off* projects for mobilising stakeholders and disseminating educational materials for teachers, students and the public.[2134] Most regional projects are dedicated exclusively to issues of environmental education,[2135] while some are devoted to communicating *ESD* and a number address cultural topics relating to *ESD*.[2136] Interdisciplinary workshops, seminars and courses on capacity-building are fairly under-represented.[2137]

There is a growing demand for environmental education, although it of course constitutes only one dimension of *ESD*.[2138] Consequently, the *holistic*, multi-dimensional notion of *ESD* is not sufficiently realised or is only addressed. This may be due to deficits in communication or irrelevance in practice.

Interrelation: To what extent is DESD interrelated with other existing and ongoing educational processes?

The interrelation between *DESD* and other existing and ongoing educational processes is unclear, particularly in Latin America and the Caribbean where institutional affiliations are rather fragile. On the one hand, programmes focusing on education are themselves separate, self-contained and independent. On the other hand, there is to some extent both inter-institutional collaboration and overlaps with regard to contents.[2139] *DESD* is an interdisciplinary and an intersectoral effort, and this is why *ESD* ranges between two principal positions:

2131 Namely learning, teaching and training.
2132 Cf. interviewee C.
2133 Cf. interviewee A, interviewee E, interviewee H, and interviewee I.
2134 Cf. interviewee C, interviewee F, and interviewee H.
2135 For example: climate change, energy, water and drought, resource efficiency, mega-cities, etc.
Cf. interviewee A.
2136 For example: indigenous minorities, cultural heritage, traditional ways of production and consumption, diversity of languages, etc.
2137 Cf. interviewee G.
2138 Cf. interviewee C.
2139 Cf. interviewee C.

- *Autonomy*: the standard case consists of more or less independent strategic regional planning. Institutional arrangements, cross-sectoral participation or joint actions are largely uncommon. This institutionally independent approach is particularly criticised in the case of the parallel instigation of *ESD*-related activities.[2140] However, good practices of regional co-ordination through inter-institutional collaboration do exist.[2141] Institutional linkages with UNESCO regarding *ESD* are less frequent,[2142] even though there is a pronounced demand for more institutional co-operation at the regional level in the provision of platforms for formal *ESD* co-operation; and
- *Inter-dependence*: institutional co-operation and collaboration on *ESD* is not always intentional and very often occasional.[2143] Scheduled and formalised interaction takes place as soon as platforms are established.[2144] This applies primarily to *ESD* in the fields of *scientific*[2145] and *political*[2146] dialogue.[2147] Due to separate budgetary planning and accounting, administrative co-operation is usually impossible and programmes and projects are thus carried out independently.[2148]

Organising and directing regional *ESD* co-operation and collaboration among institutions and stakeholders remains important but, equally, challenging. This applies to most regional organisations in charge of *ESD*-related issues, including UNESCO.

Synergy effects: If applicable, in which way do you benefit from other programmes or processes in place in terms of expertise and resources?

As a consequence of the limited institutional ties within Latin America and the Caribbean there is little documented evidence of synergy effects in terms of

2140 Cf. interviewee B.

2141 For example: developing a consolidated regional vision upon the *Millennium Development Goals* (MDG).
Cf. interviewee D.

2142 Cf. interviewee A, interviewee D, interviewee E, interviewee F, interviewee G, and interviewee I.

2143 Cf. interviewee A, and interviewee E.

2144 Cf. interviewee I.

2145 Namely, *ESD* co-operation with schools, universities and research institutes in terms of research, teaching and formation.
Cf. interviewee I.

2146 For example: *ESD* round-table co-operation among political (governmental) institutions of education, sciences and culture, and United Nations institutions, bodies and agencies in charge of aspects of *ESD*, namely the *Food and Agriculture Organisation* (FAO), the *United Nations Development Programme* (UNDP) and the *United Nations Environment Programme* (UNEP).

2147 Cf. interviewee F.

2148 Cf. interviewee G.

ESD.[2149] To some extent, institutional synergies do exist at regional level in terms of operational co-operation.[2150] However, if this is the case, synergy effects apply only at national level.[2151] What are certainly more important are the established channels of informal communication. Furthermore, beneficial *spill-over effects* can emerge from sharing and adopting examples of best practice.[2152] Irrespective of formal co-operation, informal communication[2153] and good practices are both potentially fruitful options for directing efforts towards pathways of regional development.[2154]

Making use of synergy effects is an important way of sharing workloads and responsibilities. It is obvious that this economic principle is not adequately adopted. According to its present regional structure, *ESD* can neither fulfil the *United-Nations-delivery-as-one* approach[2155] nor live up to any *UNESCO-delivery-as-one* approach.

Culture: Which role does culture play in the ESD implementation process?

Frequently, culture is perceived as only an *add-on category*. This is certainly not the case in Latin America and the Caribbean: the predominance of cultural issues is remarkable.[2156] Once one is aware of it, culture does matter. This applies to *ESD*. Hence, three aspects of culture are considered vital for successful *ESD* implementation:

- *Cultural knowledge*: learning from each other's cultural value bases,[2157] critically evaluating individual behaviour (self-interest) and institutional structures (political power).[2158] Establishing a socio-cultural consensus on *ESD* in view of ethnic traditions, modernity and development;[2159]
- *Interculturalism*: practising intercultural dialogue and exchanging multi-cultural expertise.[2160] Changing perspectives, stimulating critical thinking and

2149 Cf. interviewee D.

2150 For example: operative co-operation in terms of *Millenniums Development Goals* (MDG) with different United Nations institutions, bodies and agencies. Cf. interviewee A, and interviewee F.

2151 Cf. interviewee E.

2152 Cf. interviewee I.

2153 Cf. interviewee G.

2154 Cf. interviewee F, and interviewee I.

2155 Cf. interviewee D.

2156 Cf. interviewee I.

2157 For example: culture-bound *ESD* conceptions and identifications of land, water, air, etc, and rethinking concepts of prevention or protection when addressing ethnic minorities or indigenous groups, for instance.

2158 Cf. interviewee C, and interviewee G.

2159 Cf. interviewee A, and interviewee I.

2160 Cf. interviewee E, and interviewee H.

questioning established practices.[2161] Elaborating and applying intercultural codes of conduct; and

- *Cultural diversity*: promoting and developing projects on cultural diversity. Fostering regional affiliations with cultural heritage. Associating cultural industries either within the context of or in line with *ESD*.[2162]

Culture is an underlying aspect of both development and change. Existing regional awareness of culture is a key factor in any economic, social and environmental transformation. Culture perfectly illustrates and underpins the necessity of *ESD*.

Criteria: How feasible are cultural criteria with regard to cultural education as part of ESD?

The conception of *cultural education* is occasionally misleading, since it is not immediately self-explanatory. *Cultural education* describes the process of raising awareness and capacity-building in cultural practices, beliefs, customs and traditions through forms of education. Culture is the *chip* of society and the *nucleus* of any kind of development, be it social, economic, environmental or indeed any other kind of development. Societies are culturally constructed realities and *cultural education* can therefore enable positive momentum in *ESD* vision-building. Normatively speaking, cultural criteria can be formulated as follows:

- *ESD* acknowledges and recognises cultural diversity;[2163]
- *ESD* anticipates any kind of standard-setting on cultural issues;[2164]
- *ESD* applies alternative teaching methods which may be characterised as holistic, interdisciplinary, empathetic, communicative, interactive, and experimental;[2165]
- *ESD* guarantees liberty and understanding for indigenous knowledge and learning systems;[2166] and
- *ESD* both protects cultural identity and simultaneously encourages future-oriented sustainable development.[2167]

Devising cultural criteria for *cultural education* in relation to *ESD* is *pioneer* or *grass-roots* work, particularly in Latin America and the Caribbean. Not only is it worthwhile to integrate cultural education into the *ESD* framework appropri-

2161 Cf. interviewee G.
2162 Cf. interviewee A, and interviewee F.
2163 Cf. interviewee F.
2164 Cf. interviewee A, and interviewee G.
2165 Cf. interviewee A, and interviewee C.
2166 Cf. interviewee A.
2167 For example: through certified cultural industries, balancing innovation and efficiency by enhancing health and living conditions.
Cf. interviewee F, and interviewee I.

ately, but cultural education also offers enriching and innovative approaches of self-reflection. This cultural awareness is even more crucial when referring to practices of implementing *ESD*. These means must not only be compatible with cultural understanding, but must be based upon it.

Cultural education: Which means are appropriate to foster cultural education on ESD project stage?

Cultural education can be applied and fostered at multiple levels. This roughly drafted outline is one way to draw attention to particular interrelations between cultural education and *ESD*:

- Raising awareness of multiple forms of heterogeneous ethnicity;[2168]
- Changing cultural mindsets through capacity-building and training of auto-reflection and critical-thinking capabilities;[2169]
- Documenting and protecting unique cultural practices through patents or certificates;[2170]
- Appreciating the comparative advantage of cultural heritage based on enriching differences due to ethnic and cultural diversity;[2171]
- Making use of palpable fusion and synergy effects from living cultures; and
- Promoting public awareness and protecting modes of cultural diversity in schools underwritten by de-centralised school programmes.[2172]

To sum up, cultural education is to be appreciated as equally important and relevant compared to the established corresponding *foci* of environmental and economic education, or socialisation, respectively. Additionally, the regional perception, reflection and practice of cultural education in Latin America and the Caribbean is evidence of the growing need for further conceptualisation of cultural education as concerns *ESD*-related issues and impacts.

6.5.5 Issues

In documents and interview data[2173] the catalogue of regionally-relevant issues is considerable in size, and the scope of *ESD*-interrelated topics is complex.[2174]

2168 Cf. interviewee A, interviewee B, and interviewee E.

2169 Cf. interviewee C.

2170 Cf. interviewee A, and interviewee F.

2171 Cf. interviewee D, and interviewee F.

2172 Cf. interviewee A.

2173 Cf. Böhmer, Karl (19/06/2008) (cf. *footnote 2077* op. cit.); Samaniego, Joseluis (07/07/2008) (cf. *footnote 2077* op. cit.); Ossa, Vicente (17/07/2008) (cf. *footnote 2077* op. cit.); Hollander, Astrid; Salgado, Carol (23/07/2008) (cf. *footnote 1810* op. cit.); Arrué Rodriguez, Rodrigo (24/07/2008) (cf. *footnote 2077* op. cit.); Gallardo, Tito; Gajardo Gabelo, Octavio (24/07/2008) (cf. *footnote 2077* op. cit.); Gallopin, Gilberto

Educational initiatives such as quality *Education for All* (EFA) and the *United Nations Literacy Decade* (UNLD) are the most important beyond the accomplishment of the *Millennium Development Goals* (MDG).[2175]

Without question, education is vital to development. Hence, global efforts in education need to be extended beyond more regionally-relevant issues of employment and poverty reduction[2176] as well as topics of social, gender and legal equity.[2177]

(29/08/2008) (cf. *footnote 2077* op. cit.); Berrios, Fernando (23/09/2008) (cf. *footnote 2077* op. cit.); Macedo, Beatriz (02/08/2010) (cf. *footnote 2077* op. cit.).

2174 Cf. González-Gaudiano, Edgar (2009) (cf. *footnote 659* op. cit.).

2175 Cf. Macedo, Beatriz (2005): Educación para Todos, Educación Ambiental y Educación para el Desarrollo Sostenible. Debatiendo las Vertientes de la Década de la Educación para el Desarrollo Sostenible. Published by: Oficina Regional de Educación de la UNESCO para América Latina y el Caribe (OREALC). Oficina Regional de Educación de la UNESCO para América Latina y el Caribe (OREALC). Santiago de Chile; UNESCO; Oficina Regional de Educación de la UNESCO para América Latina y el Caribe (OREALC) (eds.) (2007b) (cf. *footnote 480* op. cit.); UNESCO; Oficina Regional de Educación de la UNESCO para América Latina y el Caribe (OREALC) (eds.) (2007c): Situación Educativa de América Latina y el Caribe: Garantizando la Educación de Calidad para Todos. Informe Regional de revisión y Evaluación del progreso de América Latina y el Caribe hacia la Educación para Todos en el marco del Proyecto Regional de Educación (EPT/PRELAC) – 2007. Santiago de Chile: UNESCO Santiago, pp. 7–10, 15 et seqq, 47 et seqq; Hirmas R., Carolina; Eroles, Daniela (eds.) (2008b): Convivencia democrática, inclusión y cultura de paz: Lecciones desde la práctica educativa innovadora en América Latina. Edited by Rosa Blanco. Santiago de Chile: UNESCO Santiago; Pehuén Editores; Salesianos Impresores S.A. (Colección Innovemos, III), pp. 13 et seqq; Oficina Regional de Educación de la UNESCO para América Latina y el Caribe (OREALC); innovemos – Red Regional de Innovaciones Educativas; Organización de Estados Iberoamericanos para la Educación, la Ciencia y la Cultura (OEI) (eds.) (2009a): Experiencias educativas de segunda oportunidad. Lecciones desde la práctica innovadora en América Latina. Edited by Rosa Blanco. Santiago de Chile: SDL impresores (Colección Innovemos, IV), pp. 37 et seqq.

2176 Cf. Konrad-Adenauer-Stiftung (ed.) (2005): Diálogo Político. Educación y pobreza. Publicación trimestral de la Konrad-Adenauer-Stiftung A. C. Buenos Aires (Diálogo Político, N° 4 – Diciembre, 2005); Messina, Graciela; Pieck, Enrique; Castañeda, Elsa (eds.) (2008): Educación y Trabajo. Lecciones desde la práctica innovadora en América Latina. Edited by Elvia María Acuña. Santiago de Chile: UNESCO Santiago (Colección Innovemos, I), pp. 25, 37–38.

2177 For example: children's rights, right to education.
Cf. Konrad-Adenauer-Stiftung (ed.) (2005) (cf. *footnote 2176* op. cit.), pp. 135 et seqq; Frigerio, Graciela; Diker, Gabriela (Junio 2008): Infancia y derechos: las raíces de la sostenibilidad. Aportes para un porvenir. Santiago de Chile: Andros Ltda., pp. 9–15; Oficina Regional de Educación de la UNESCO para América Latina y el Caribe (OREALC) (ed.) (2009a): Educación para la paz, la convivencia democrática y los

Issues of sustainability are related primarily to the environment.[2178] Certainly, *"(e)nvironmental education can suggest paths allowing us to move beyond 'sustainable development', to travel other paths and to seek breaches in this new closing circle".*[2179] Consequently, other domains must also be addressed in order to comply with *ESD*. In contrast to some discerning claims that other aspects of *ESD* have been insufficiently included, the cultural domain is regionally relevant and comparatively well-known. *"Since culture is one of the mainsprings of development, the cultural aspects of development are as important as its economic aspects, which individuals and peoples have the fundamental right to participate in and enjoy."*[2180] Major strands of *ESD*-related cultural issues are *cultural education* and *cultural diversity*. Within the regional context,

---

derechos humanos. San José de Costa Rica 24 al 28 de Noviembre 2008. Santiago de Chile: Salesianos Impresores S.A. (Jornadas de Cooperación, III), pp. 31 et seqq. See *Figure 105* in chapter IX 6.5.5 *Issues* on page 472.

2178 Cf. Oficina Regional de Educación de la UNESCO para América Latina y el Caribe (OREALC); UNESCO (eds.) (2004) (cf. *footnote 2054* op. cit.), pp. 3 et seqq; Organización de Estados Iberoamericanos para la Educación, la Ciencia y la Cultura (OEI) (ed.) (2006c): Educación para el desarrollo sostenible II. Edited by José Gutiérrez Pérez; Teresa Pozo Llorente; Eloísa Tréllez Solís. Madrid: Servicio de Publicaciones (Revista Iberoamericana de Educación, N° 41), pp. 21 et seqq; Organización de Estados Iberoamericanos para la Educación, la Ciencia y la Cultura (OEI) (ed.) (2006a) (cf. *footnote 678* op. cit.), pp. 17–24, 25 et seqq; Organización de Estados Iberoamericanos para la Educación, la Ciencia y la Cultura (OEI) (ed.) (2006b): Educación para el desarrollo sostenible I. Década de la Educación para un Futuro Sostenible (2005–2014): un punto de inflexión necesario en la atención a la situación del planeta. Edited by José Gutiérrez Pérez; Teresa Pozo Llorente; Eloísa Tréllez Solís. Madrid: Servicio de Publicaciones (Revista Iberoamericana de Educación, N° 40 II), pp. 125 et seqq; Quiroga Martínez, Rayén (ed.) (Octubre 2007): El séptimo objetivo del Milenio en América Latina y el Caribe: avances al 2007. LC/L.2782-P/E. Edited by División de Estadistica y Protecciones Económicas. Santiago de Chile: Naciones Unidas (estudios estadísticos y prospectivos, 57), pp. 11 et seqq; Macedo, Beatriz; Salgado, Carol (2007) (cf. *footnote 2037* op. cit.), pp. 30 et seqq; Barton C., Jonathan R.; Jordán F., Ricardo; León A., Silvia Mabel, et al. (eds.) (Diciembre 2007): Cuán sustentable es la Región Metropolitana de Santiago? Metodologías de evaluación de la sustentabilidad. Documento del Proyecto/LC/W.170. Santiago de Chile: Naciones Unidas (CEPAL – Colección Documentos de proyectos), pp. 23 et seqq; Sauvé, Lucie; Berryman, Tom (2009): Challenging a "Closing Circle": Alternative Research Agendas for the ESD Decade. In: Chalkley, Brian; Haigh, Martin J.; Higgitt, David (eds.): Education for sustainable development. Papers in honour of the United Nations Decade of Education for Sustainable Development (2005–2014). London / New York: Routledge, pp. 229–232, p. 230; Oficina Regional de Educación de la UNESCO para América Latina y el Caribe (OREALC) (ed.) (2009b) (cf. *footnote 2010* op. cit.), pp. 28, 31–32.

2179 See Sauvé, Lucie; Berryman, Tom (2009) (cf. *footnote 2178* op. cit.), p. 232.

2180 See *5. Principle of the complementarity of economic and cultural aspects of development* UNESCO (ed.) (2005a) (cf. *footnote 42* op. cit.), p. 5.

cultural education refers to building the capacity to profit from systems of cultural knowledge and historical references that support the agenda of *DESD*.[2181]

Cultural education in particular *"[...] aims to pass on cultural heritage to young people, to enable them to create their own (...) (ways of cultural expressions) and to contribute to their global development (emotional and cognitive)"*.[2182] This can be achieved through *"(r)ecognising the importance of traditional knowledge (...) and in particular the knowledge systems of indigenous peoples, and its positive contribution to sustainable development (...)"*.[2183] Moreover, *"(c)ultural diversity is a rich asset for individuals and societies. The protection, promotion and maintenance of cultural diversity are an essential requirement for sustainable development for the benefit of present and future generations"*.[2184] In fact, there is a remarkable awareness of *cultural diversity* regionally,[2185] by which is meant the plurality of cultural practices[2186] and the awareness of the need to protect them.[2187]

2181 For example: regional approaches and strategies in favour of *cultural education* and *ESD* in Latin America and the Caribbean and in Europe.
Cf. Restrepo Arcila, Roberto Arturo (ed.) (2000): El vuelo de la serpiente. Desarrollo sostenible en la América prehispánica. Volume Primera edición. Santafé de Bogotá: Siglo del Hombre Editores; Federal Ministry for Education, Culture and Science; KulturKontakt Austria (eds.) (2006): Promoting Cultural Education in Europe. A Contribution to Participation, Innovation and Quality. European Specialist Conference in the Framework of the 2006 Austrian EU Presidency. Conference Report. Graz, 8–10 June 2006. Graz; Kono, Toshiyuki (2007) (cf. *footnote 83* op. cit.), p. 270; Gambini, Barbara (2009) (cf. *footnote 83* op. cit.), p. 125; Hirmas R., Carolina; Eroles, Daniela (eds.) (2008b) (cf. *footnote 2175* op. cit.), pp. 38–42; Oficina Regional de Educación de la UNESCO para América Latina y el Caribe (OREALC); innovemos – Red Regional de Innovaciones Educativas; Organización de Estados Iberoamericanos para la Educación, la Ciencia y la Cultura (OEI) (eds.) (2009a) (cf. *footnote 2175* op. cit.), p. 47.

2182 See and cf. Köhler, Karl-Heinz (2006): Thesen zur kulturellen Bildung. Praxis der unesco-projekt-schulen und konzeptionelle Überlegungen. In: Deutsche UNESCO-Kommission e. V. (DUK) (ed.): forum der unesco-projekt-schulen. Kulturelle Bildung. Beiträge der unesco-projekt-schulen. Zeitschrift der UNESCO-Projektschulen, Sonderheft Nr. 3. Bonn: Bonner Universitäts-Buchdruckerei, pp. 6–12, p. 6; Federal Ministry for Education, Culture and Science; KulturKontakt Austria (eds.) (2006) (cf. *footnote 2181* op. cit.), p. 26.

2183 See digit 8 UNESCO (ed.) (2005a) (cf. *footnote 42* op. cit.), p. 2.

2184 See *6. Principle of sustainable development* UNESCO (ed.) (2005a) (cf. *footnote 42* op. cit.), p. 5; UNESCO (2007) (cf. *footnote 78* op. cit.).

2185 Cf. Hirmas R., Carolina; Blanco, Rosa (eds.) (2008a): Educación y diversidad cultural. Lecciones desde la práctica innovadora en América Latina. Santiago de Chile: UNESCO Santiago; Pehuén Editores (Colección Innovemos, 2), pp. 41 et seqq.

2186 Cf. Macedo, Beatriz (2005): Compromisos Educativos Establecidos por la Década. Published by: Oficina Regional de Educación de la UNESCO para América Latina y el Caribe (OREALC). Oficina Regional de Educación de la UNESCO para América

To this end, there are comprehensive pedagogic approaches available in awareness-raising, ranging from training materials to appropriate tool kits for application.[2188] In addition, examples of good practices document how awareness of *cultural diversity* can be promoted in schools.[2189]

Latina y el Caribe (OREALC). Santiago de Chile; Macedo, Beatriz (2005) (cf. *footnote 2175* op. cit.), p. 5; Hirmas R., Carolina; Blanco, Rosa (eds.) (2008a) (cf. *footnote 2185* op. cit.), pp. 113 et seqq; Oficina Regional de Educación de la UNESCO para América Latina y el Caribe (OREALC) (ed.) (2010) (cf. *footnote 480* op. cit.), p. 9.

2187 Cf. Oficina Regional de Educación de la UNESCO para América Latina y el Caribe (OREALC); UNESCO (eds.) (2004) (cf. *footnote 2054* op. cit.), pp. 7, 19, 23; UNESCO (ed.) (2005a) (cf. *footnote 42* op. cit.); Konrad-Adenauer-Stiftung (ed.) (2007): Diálogo Político. Regulación de los medios. Publicación trimestral de la Konrad-Adenauer-Stiftung A. C. Buenos Aires (Diálogo Político, Nº 3 – Septiembre, 2007), pp. 133–147.

2188 Cf. UNESCO; Oficina Regional de Educación de la UNESCO para América Latina y el Caribe (OREALC) (eds.) (2005a): Diversidad cultural. Materiales para la formación docente y el trabajo de aula. Santiago de Chile: UNESCO Santiago (3); UNESCO (2006) (cf. *footnote 1333* op. cit.); Lasonen, Johanna (2009) (cf. *footnote 73* op. cit.); Oficina Regional de Educación de la UNESCO para América Latina y el Caribe (OREALC); MInisterio de Educación Chile (MINEDUC) (eds.) (2009b): Re-creo mi Identidad. Las Guías de Actividades Patrimoniales. Edited by Francisca Gallegos; Genoveva Moncada; Patricia Gallardo. Santiago de Chile: UNESCO Santiago.

2189 Cf. Deutsche UNESCO-Kommission e. V. (DUK) (ed.) (2006): forum der unesco-projekt-schulen. Kulturelle Bildung. Beiträge der unesco-projekt-schulen. In: Zeitschrift der UNESCO-Projektschulen, Volume 2006, Issue 3. Bonn: Bonner Universitäts-Buchdruckerei; Köhler, Karl-Heinz (2006) (cf. *footnote 2182* op. cit.), p. 11.

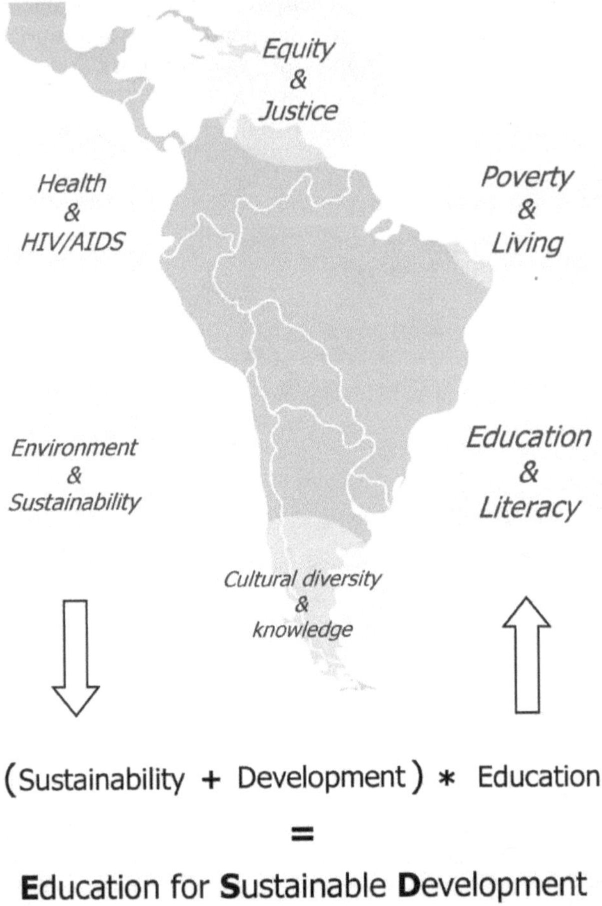

Figure 105: Driving concerns and ESD–related issues in Latin America and the Caribbean[2190]

Recalling the three components of *ESD* – education, sustainability and development – it must be stated that education is the one and only dominating issue in Latin America and the Caribbean. Development issues remain vital, particularly in the field of poverty reduction and living conditions. Sustainability, by contrast, plays a minor role in practice.

2190 *ESD* in Latin America and the Caribbean can be described as process of setting priorities. Issues of education and literacy, poverty and living, equity and justice, or health by far outweigh topics of environment and sustainability, to put it bluntly.

6.5.6 Achievements

Taking into account the consolidated results of research in relation to the *Regional strategy for Latin America and the Caribbean,*[2191] the following positive effects for *ESD* in the Latin America and Caribbean region can be observed:

a) On an institutional[2192] level:
- Existence of awareness towards sustainability;
- Familiarity with concepts of sustainable development;
- Prioritisation of education and particularly environmental education;[2193]
- Provision of framework conditions[2194] and platforms of best practice;[2195]
- Awareness of interdisciplinary approaches and appropriate efforts towards managing subject matter set in context; and

b) On a societal level:
- Nascent consciousness and increasing public momentum towards environmental sustainability;
- Evolving platforms (predominantly informal) and co-operative networks in civil society;
- Rising attentiveness to culture, cultural diversity and cultural education.

6.5.7 Challenges

General obstacles have been identified globally, and most of them are reflective of regional challenges within Latin America and the Caribbean. Once again, considering research data against the ambitious *Regional strategy for Latin America and the Caribbean*[2196] and the regional *Communication strategy on*

2191 Cf. UNESCO; The Earth Charter Initiative (ECI) (eds.) (Marzo 2007) (cf. *footnote 113* op. cit.), pp. 10–18.

2192 In this particular context, institutions are those entities directly or indirectly mandated to *DESD* unless not otherwise affiliated. This primarily refers to UNESCO institutions, but equally includes regional United Nations bodies.

2193 Cf. Oficina Regional de Educación de la UNESCO para América Latina y el Caribe (OREALC) (ed.) (2009b) (cf. *footnote 2010* op. cit.), p. 88.

2194 For example: strategy, communication, criteria and indicators, reporting structures, etc. Cf. Oficina Regional de Educación de la UNESCO para América Latina y el Caribe (OREALC) (ed.) (2010) (cf. *footnote 480* op. cit.), pp. 7–8.

2195 Cf. innovemos – Red Regional de Innovaciones Educativas (2010): Desarrollo sostenible. Published by: Oficina Regional de Educación de la UNESCO para América Latina y el Caribe (OREALC).

2196 Cf. UNESCO; The Earth Charter Initiative (ECI) (eds.) (Marzo 2007) (cf. *footnote 113* op. cit.), pp. 10–18.

ESD,[2197] predominantly negative effects and negative conclusions must be stated in relation to *ESD*:[2198]

a) On an institutional level:

- Lack of definition and clarity in general conceptualisation of *ESD*;[2199]
- Lack of government involvement and compliance,[2200] effective co-ordination[2201] and making use of intended synergies;[2202]
- Lack of methodological information and guidance for the development of *ESD*-related processes;[2203]
- Lack of momentum in promoting implementation of *ESD*;
- Gap between structural information and applicable knowledge;[2204]
- Limited commitment to *ESD* agenda-setting and monitoring;[2205]

2197 Cf. Oficina Regional de Educación de la UNESCO para América Latina y el Caribe (OREALC) (ed.) (2008) (cf. *footnote 1223* op. cit.).

2198 Cf. UNESCO Section for DESD Coordination (ed.) (2009) (cf. *footnote 116* op. cit.), p. 57.

2199 This is particularly the case in reference to the conceptual difference between *ESD* and environmental education.
Cf. Oficina Regional de Educación de la UNESCO para América Latina y el Caribe (OREALC) (ed.) (2009b) (cf. *footnote 2010* op. cit.), pp. 34, 55, 85.

2200 There are few qualitatively significant national initiatives, not only in the matter of environmental education but also in the matter of *ESD* in general. Only five out of forty-four countries in the region (Chile, México, Uruguay, Jamaica and Costa Rica) are even taking part!
Cf. Oficina Regional de Educación de la UNESCO para América Latina y el Caribe (OREALC) (ed.) (2009b) (cf. *footnote 2010* op. cit.), pp. 51, 53–54, 81.

2201 Cf. Oficina Regional de Educación de la UNESCO para América Latina y el Caribe (OREALC) (ed.) (2009b) (cf. *footnote 2010* op. cit.), p. 48.

2202 Namely the strengthening of structural synergy effects, instead of mostly unintentional *coincidences* in the definitions and phraseology of *ESD*.
Cf. Oficina Regional de Educación de la UNESCO para América Latina y el Caribe (OREALC) (ed.) (2009b) (cf. *footnote 2010* op. cit.), pp. 48, 87; Wals, Arjen E. J. (July 2009) (cf. *footnote 533* op. cit.), p. 201.

2203 This might be done by including research expertise of UNESCO institutes in *ESD*. For example: public access to *ESD* didactics, pedagogic approaches, such as educational materials and instruments, especially those related to social, economic and cultural domains of *ESD*.
Cf. Gerner, Martin (11/08/2009) (cf. *footnote 407* op. cit.).

2204 In particular in recognising which networks of educators for sustainability do exist and how to enter them in order to facilitate the exchange of knowledge, best practice and *ESD*-related experience.
Cf. Macedo, Beatriz; Salgado, Carol (2007) (cf. *footnote 2037* op. cit.), pp. 33, 36.

2205 There was a poor rate of feedback to the call for regional reporting (33 %).
Cf. Oficina Regional de Educación de la UNESCO para América Latina y el Caribe (OREALC) (ed.) (2009b) (cf. *footnote 2010* op. cit.), pp. 34, 49, 51.

- Uncertainty towards *ESD* assessment as a result of non-existent region-specific criteria for normative implementation and monitoring indicators;[2206]
- Lack of relevant resources and funding;[2207] and

b) On a societal level:
- Lack of public awareness of sustainable development;
- Lack of meaning, context and visibility of *ESD*;
- Little interest in, commitment to and support for implementation, monitoring and communication of *ESD* and additionally a lack information campaigns that might rectify this;[2208]
- Lack of *ESD* communication and multi-stakeholder participation;
- Perception of *ESD* as being too formal education-centric;
- Difficulties in translating public awareness into behavioural change;
- Lack of *ESD*-trained resource persons, teachers and prominent multipliers.

6.5.8 Summary

The Latin America and Caribbean region is faced with multiple obstacles that require considerable structural and programmatic efforts. For various reasons, *DESD* has not been considered as an integrated approach but rather as an imposed and resource-consuming *add-on*. Thus, *ESD* in its multi-dimensionality is not set high on the regional agendas.

Generally speaking, there is no successful and consistent strategic approach to addressing *ESD* regionally. Some critics even argue that *ESD* does not play an important role on any agenda at all.[2209] As a result, *DESD* has little or no impact in Latin America and the Caribbean. However, certain select efforts are being made and there is a possibility that impact might be made by regional initiatives.[2210]

Policies of empty shells may pose a major threat to *ESD* in the region: that is, structures without contents. It is highly questionable whether *DESD* can be called a *living strategy*[2211] in the matter of being actively used to stimulate regional action at the various policy-levels and of being frequently re-visited, up-

2206 There are few examples of embedding *DESD* and the respective regional action plan at national, sub-national and local level.

2207 Cf. Oficina Regional de Educación de la UNESCO para América Latina y el Caribe (OREALC) (ed.) (2009b) (cf. *footnote 2010* op. cit.), p. 83.

2208 Cf. Oficina Regional de Educación de la UNESCO para América Latina y el Caribe (OREALC) (ed.) (2009b) (cf. *footnote 2010* op. cit.), p. 48.

2209 Cf. Andelman, Marta (2009) (cf. *footnote 2033* op. cit.).

2210 Cf. Frigerio, Graciela; Diker, Gabriela (Junio 2008) (cf. *footnote 2177* op. cit.); Oficina Regional de Educación de la UNESCO para América Latina y el Caribe (OREALC) (ed.) (2009b) (cf. *footnote 2010* op. cit.).

2211 See UNESCO Section for DESD Coordination (ed.) (2009) (cf. *footnote 116* op. cit.), p. 24.

dated, re-confirmed, re-endorsed and shared by all relevant stakeholders. It is mainly an issue of simple pretence or achieving something in line with *ESD*.

Regional approaches to *DESD* implementation and monitoring vary considerably between UNECE and the Latin America and Caribbean region. The UNECE approach has been explained, comprehensively and systematically structured by beginning with the strategy and implementation scheme and then moving onto practices and publication. In contrast, the approach of Latin America and Caribbean is quite different because it is more experimental in character. Published and disseminated *ESD* practices are initially intended to produce spillover effects. This kind of *me-too strategy* requires active involvement, but it will continue to be limited unless appropriate structures of dissemination and communication are constructed.[2212]

Gathering *ESD*-related data in terms of regional information and feedback policy has been challenging. This is mainly dependent on the existence and availability of as well as the access to relevant sources that may be said to favour a qualitative approach. Based upon the data available, UNESCO does not appear to exercise leadership functions on regional level with any significance. This applies neither to structural guidance,[2213] nor to the contents of its programmes.[2214] In this respect, UNESCO does not constitute the *ESD* driving force, and in those ways in which it does, it does so with notable limitations.

7 Conclusion

The implementation of *DESD* is at the heart of UNESCO's ambitious mandate as *lead agency*, not only because of the multitude of issues involved, but also due to the number of structures that must necessarily be developed and activated. The intention of this chapter was to provide an in-depth understanding of the entire framework of *DESD* implementation and monitoring.

Firstly, the preparatory stage is characterised primarily by processes of description. *DESD* offers conditions not marked by the ease of operation within them, but is characterised instead by broad and undefined topics, uncertainty as to the identity of stakeholders and ambiguous declarations of intent. UNESCO employs a highly value-driven approach through defining and concretising certain principles that originate in concepts of good governance and in UNESCO's

2212 Cf. Oficina Regional de Educación de la UNESCO para América Latina y el Caribe (OREALC); UNESCO (eds.) (2005b) (cf. *footnote 2056* op. cit.), pp. 2–4.

2213 For instance, limited influence or support on the development and genesis of the regional *DESD* strategy, or little structural or programmatic interdependence and institutional co-operation.

2214 Above all, defining and conceptualising *ESD* within the regional context.

perception of itself,[2215] and these principles are applied to the implementation of *DESD*. The principle of regional implementation is certainly among the most prominent of these.[2216]

Secondly, UNESCO divides its functional contribution to *DESD* into two separate parts: on the one hand, the *dual role* consists of the United Nations *lead agency* mandate as the *international co-ordinator and facilitator* of *DESD*, as outlined in the *International Implementation Scheme* (IIS) and in respective regional strategies.[2217] On the other hand, UNESCO carries out real initiatives as a substantive, *ESD*-implementing stakeholder as proposed by the *UNESCO Action plan*. In the course of *DESD*, the greatest attention is drawn to UNESCO in its role as the *international co-ordinator and facilitator* of *DESD*, and UNESCO's role is ambivalent for two reasons. On the one hand, the question of successful *DESD* leadership cannot be answered *in extenso*, since UNESCO's steering and management of *DESD* is complemented and directed by other (regional) organisations. On the other hand, UNESCO is held fully responsible. Irrespective of outsourced units of implementation, any *DESD*-related malfunction is ultimately attributed to limited institutional commitment on the part of UNESCO. This problem is subject first and foremost to the conceptual planning of interpreting the *lead agency* mandate. It can be characterised in a twofold way by the pattern of co-occurring aspects: highlighting the principle of heterogeneous and regional implementation policies, and the institutional leadership mandate. In other words, there is a discrepancy between regional implementation and the efforts of global leadership. In order to avoid these inconsistencies and even contradictions, there is demand for either more normative institutional drive (*guidance*) or enhanced means of displaying charismatic leadership.[2218] Since normative actions are limited in the case of *DESD*, UNESCO's leadership qualities must primarily exhibit trickle-down effects at the regional level.

Thirdly, UNESCO organises *DESD* monitoring in reference to the *Global Monitoring and Evaluation Framework* (GMEF).[2219] Given the regional contexts and indicators, this process of *bureaucratic* leadership is one of the most difficult. However, monitoring is designed in a centralised and systematic way in order to achieve at least some comparability of results. For reasons of accountability, it may turn out to be problematic that reviewing *DESD* is conducted exclusively *in-house*.[2220] There is no independent, external assessment of perform-

2215 Cf. Gerner, Martin (2008) (cf. *footnote 259* op. cit.), p. 28.
Cf. *Figure 60* in chapter IX 1.10 *Summary* on page 276.

2216 Cf. chapter IX 1 *Principles of implementation* on pages 257 et seqq.

2217 Cf. *Figure 63* in chapter IX 2.3 *Summary* on page 289.
See *Figure 106* in chapter IX 7 *Conclusion* on page 479.

2218 Cf. chapter VI 2 *Leadership* on pages 123 et seqq.

2219 See *Figure 106* in chapter IX 7 *Conclusion* on page 479.

2220 Cf. chapter IX 5.4 *Evaluation* on page 378.

ance, since most experts have been or are still affiliated with UNESCO in direct or indirect ways, in some functional nexus or another. The risk of biased information or data is substantial.

Fourthly, and finally, two concrete examples of regional *DESD* implementation and monitoring illustrate quantitatively and qualitatively how UNESCO deals with differing contexts and challenging framework conditions. The major differences are varying levels of dedication to and familiarity with *ESD*-related issues. In consequence, the organisation's performance can provisionally be described twofold: *DESD* is successful in that it deploys considerable expertise and continuing commitment within the Europe and North America (UNECE) and Asia and the Pacific region. By contrast, *DESD* is insignificant or of very little importance in other regions, such as Latin America and the Caribbean in particular. *"Presently, it appears that the only strategies which are consistently monitored and fully endorsed by countries in the regions are the UNECE ESD Strategy and, to some extent, the regional ESD strategy for the Asia-Pacific."*[2221]

The success of *DESD* implementation and monitoring is barely measurable on a global scale. Unless regional strategies are what UNESCO makes plain to be most desirable as a guiding principle, all consequences ranging from accomplishment to failure must be taken into account. Between the theoretic-normative intent of *DESD* and its factual accomplishment in reality, there has been some kind of conceptual discrepancy or ambiguity right from the very beginning.

2221 See UNESCO Section for DESD Coordination (ed.) (2009) (cf. *footnote 116* op. cit.), p. 24.

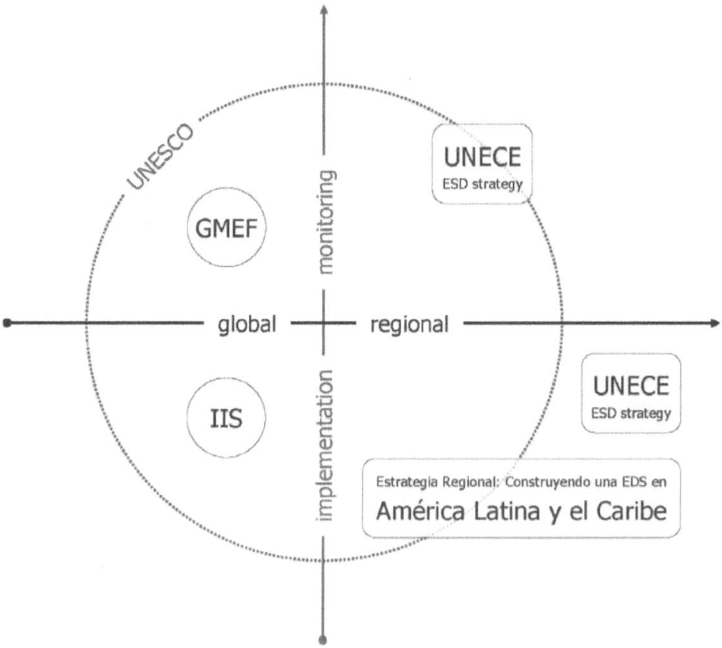

Figure 106: Complexity of UNESCO's DESD leadership mandate[2222]

2222 This figure is aimed at graphically summarising *DESD* implementation. For this purpose, two continuous dimensions can be distinguished: one that is describing rather the implementation than the monitoring of *DESD*; another one that is referring rather to the global than regional scope of *DESD*. Both views are incorporated into the organisational ambit of UNESCO. In terms of the global commitment towards implementing and monitoring *DESD*, UNESCO provides professional guidance by establishing respective frameworks, namely the *International Implementation Scheme* (IIS) and the *Global Monitoring and Evaluation Framework* (GMEF). As to regional commitment, functional responsibilities and technical competencies are primarily delegated to regional-level stakeholders. However, this very fact does not exempt UNESCO from its role as *lead agency*. Given two examples of regional implementation, the mandate is carried out differently. With respect to the UNECE region, there is a largely independent, self-contained *ESD* strategy that is only affiliated with UNESCO as regards its *ESD* contents. Monitoring *DESD* is partially shared with UNESCO's expertise. With respect to the Latin American and Caribbean region, there is an *ESD* strategy that is attached to multiple stakeholders, among them the regional office of UNESCO. Monitoring *DESD* is primarily carried out on the basis of the UNECE *ESD* strategy.

X Conclusion

After detailed and comprehensive consideration, this chapter will finally draw a conclusion. Compared to the initial intentions, what are the principal results of research to be reviewed and critically acclaimed? Starting with the analytic framework, the criteria-based summary represents the core component of a conclusion drawn on UNESCO's DESD leadership role. Prior to providing future perspectives, the executive summary includes rather general implications for global leadership mandates.

1 Framework of analysis

Analysis has purposefully been designed in a twofold and deductive way, addressing the global research question by splitting its various aspects into single-issue research questions. This approach of document and data analysis is facilitated by the application of relevant theory-based criteria.[2223]

1.1 Research questions

Recalling the point of departure, the question was how UNESCO fulfils its leadership and co-ordination mandate as *lead agency* in the course of the *United Nations Decade of Education for Sustainable Development* (2005–2014).[2224]

2223 Cf. chapter I 3 *Structure* on page 4, and chapter IV 5 *Research assignment* on page 94.
2224 Cf. chapter I 3 *Structure* on page 5.

In order to adequately theorise on the UNESCO *lead agency* mandate and its structural background, this global research question has been translated into chapter-based sub-items, namely:[2225]

- What is the primary concern to be discussed in depth?
- Which key terms require direct clarification prior to further considerations?
- Which theoretical setting best serves to support the research objective?
- Which methodological approach provides a suitable connection between theory and research objectives?
- To what extent does UNESCO provide regulatory frames of reference that may facilitate *DESD*?
- Which features and competences constitute and define the UNESCO mandate for *DESD* leadership?
- In what way is *DESD* grounded and affiliated to evolutions in practice?
- Which means of force and effect does UNESCO employ in order to facilitate effective implementation of *DESD*?
- How does UNESCO co-ordinate and monitor the implementation of *DESD*?
- What are the principal results of research to be reviewed and critically acclaimed?

1.2 Set of criteria

Given the preferred theoretical approach and methodological framework, seven criteria have been found adequate to address each of these research questions. Consequently, the quality of the UNESCO *lead-agency* mandate has been taken into consideration according to the following:[2226]

2225 Cf. chapter I 3 *Structure* on page 5.

2226 Cf. chapter IV 2.2 *Criteria* on pages 75 et seqq.
See *Table 51* in chapter X 1.2 *Set of criteria* on page 483.

Table 51: Set of research criteria

Functions	*Criterion*	*Aspects*
Standard-setting – Policy advice – Monitoring	Effectiveness	• Implementation and monitoring • Co-ordination
	Efficiency	• Proportionality • Flexibility • Validity
	Compliance	• Responsibility • Commitment • Accountability
	Leadership	• Promotion • Integration • Consultancy • Governance
	Topicality	• Continuity • Frequency • Image • Visibility • Communication
	Context	• Resources • Structure • Expertise
	Power	• Deciding • Institutional • Productive

1.3 Consolidation

Moreover, the research objectives can be correlated with the set of criteria. However, each research question relates to its respective criteria in a different way.[2227] That is the reason why multiple criteria may correspond to one single question.

2227 See *Table 52* in chapter X 1.4 *Consolidation* on page 484.

Table 52: Matrix of research-question related lead-agency criteria of ESD

Criterion / *Research question*	Effectiveness	Efficiency	Compliance	Leadership	Topicality	Context	Power
What is the primary concern to be discussed in depth?							
Which key terms require clarification prior to further considerations?							
Which theoretical setting best serves to support the research objective?							
Which methodological approach provides a suitable connection between theory and research objectives?							
To what extent does UNESCO provide regulatory frames of reference that may facilitate *DESD*?	✓	✓	✓	✓	✓	✓	✓
Which features and competences constitute and define the UNESCO mandate for *DESD* leadership?	✓	✓		✓	✓	✓	✓
In what way is *DESD* grounded and affiliated to evolutions in practice?	✓	✓	✓	✓	✓	✓	✓
Which means of force and effect does UNESCO employ in order to facilitate effective implementation of *DESD*?	✓	✓	✓			✓	✓
How does UNESCO co-ordinate and monitor the implementation of *DESD*?	✓	✓	✓	✓	✓	✓	✓
What are the principal results of research to be reviewed and critically acclaimed?							

2 Summary

Each particular criterion merits close attention. Thus, providing a summary comprises:

1. Recalling and explaining the criterion within the particular *DESD* context (*hypothesis*); followed by
2. Providing qualifying arguments by referring to processed resources driven by relevant research objectives (*supported arguments*); and
3. Concluding by means of well-balanced reasoning upon achievement of objectives *(synthesis)*.

2.1 Effectiveness

UNESCO's role as *lead agency* of *DESD* is effective, if specific *DESD* objectives of organisations are accomplished accordingly; and this means promoting education as a basis of learning for a more sustainable human society and integrating sustainable development into education systems at all levels.[2228]

One must be fully aware of the object to be evaluated. It is not the effectiveness of the *DESD* regime itself that matters, but UNESCO's effectiveness at problem-solving. What also matters is the concept of *functional effectiveness* which is directed towards UNESCO's efforts in the case of the *DESD* context, its codification, legitimacy, inclusion, representation and distribution of power. As a result, UNESCO's functional effectiveness has implications most prominently for the organisational performance in implementing *DESD* and also in monitoring and co-ordination.[2229]

One must be clear about the point of reference for evaluating effectiveness. Due to the *elusive* nature of *DESD*, predefined *means* hardly exist. So far no particular standards or units of repeatable measurement have been devised. What is important is *relative improvement* rather than hypothetically approaching some kind of *collective optimum*. As a consequence, the question of the problem-solving capacity of UNESCO and its mandatory link with *DESD* is addressed. This applies to two aspects of these objectives in particular:

- *Education for ESD*: does UNESCO manage to give an enhanced profile to the central role of education and learning in the common pursuit of sustainable development by fostering an increased quality of teaching and learning through *ESD*?

2228 Cf. chapter VII 6 *Objectives* on page 160, and chapter IV 2.2.1 *Effectiveness* on pages 76 et seqq.

2229 Cf. chapter VI 3 *Scope* on page 143.

Yes, UNESCO does strengthen the role of education in all its aspects through *ESD*. Firstly, because education forms part of the organisation's *ESD* vision and mission statement;[2230] secondly because educational issues are raised multi-dimensionally by linking them with economic, ecological, societal and cultural aspects;[2231] thirdly because education is *the* focal issue, fundamental thrust and priority, and driving competence of UNESCO;[2232] fourthly because the nature of education is clearly reflected in line with the *ESD* principles and characteristics;[2233] fifthly because it is primarily stakeholders with expertise in education who are addressed;[2234] sixthly because education does play a pivotal role in sustainable development from the very beginning[2235] and finally because multiple educational initiatives are closely and intentionally related with *ESD* by UNESCO.[2236]

- *Development for ESD*: Does UNESCO's approach help countries to make progress towards development, through the medium of and in combination with *ESD* efforts?

Yes, UNESCO does facilitate progress in the field of development through *ESD*, particularly in order to reach the *Millennium Development Goals* (MDGs), because by definition *ESD* is oriented towards development that is both driven by and directed towards aspects of sustainability;[2237] because UNESCO enriches the notion of development by extending and diversifying its scope in relation to multiple perspectives in the range of economic, but also social, environmental and cultural matters;[2238] because the organisation feels tightly bound to interna-

2230 Cf. chapter VII 1 *Vision* on page 149, chapter VII 2 *Mission* on page 151.
2231 Cf. chapter VII 4 *Dimensions* on page 156.
2232 Cf. chapter V 1 *Global assignment* on page 98, chapter VI 1 *Competences* on page 122, chapter VII 6 *Objectives* on page 160, and chapter VII 11 *Thrusts* on page.
2233 Cf. chapter VI 2 *Leadership* on page 123, and chapter VII 8 *Principles* on page 163.
2234 Cf. chapter VII 12 *Stakeholders* on pages 167 et seqq.
2235 Cf. chapter VII 15 *Summary* on page 195.
2236 Cf. *Figure 58* in chapter IX 1.2.1 *Programmes* on page 265.
2237 Cf. chapter II 3.1 *Sustainable development* on page 27, and chapter V 4 *Monitoring* on page 27.
2238 Cf. *Table 20* in chapter VII 5 *Perspectives* on page 158, chapter IX 2.2.3 *Developing public awareness of sustainability* on page 282, and chapter IX 3.4.2 *Section I: Education for Sustainable Development* on page 309.

tional initiatives, particularly in the area of development,[2239] and finally because *ESD* provides a long-term vision for commitment and investment.[2240]

Effectiveness is most likely to be achieved if and when UNESCO manages to address the following challenges to the *DESD* regime:[2241]

1. Definition

The question of how to explain and categorise *DESD* and its components remains vital. Irrespective of different attempts made by UNESCO to define the essence of *DESD*, in the view of many stakeholders the conceptualisation of *ESD* was vague.[2242] This is primarily due to the multi-faceted notion of *sustainability*.[2243] The lack of understanding and conceptual ambiguity is particularly evident in different cultural settings and regional contexts.[2244] Obviously, there have been major UNESCO-centred failures in providing definitions of *ESD* that are sufficient and applicable to various contexts.

2. Conceptualisation

The question of how to consolidate different *ESD* perspectives of understanding into one coherent framework is addressed by participatory proceedings.[2245] From the beginning UNESCO has opted for multi-stakeholder codification under the major leadership of the organisation's education sector, in order to create momentum and commitment for the implementation of *ESD*.[2246] This process of establishing the framework for *DESD* has been completed on time and successfully.[2247]

3. Communication

The question of how to communicate the key messages of *DESD* institutionally and publicly remains essential. Positively communicating *ESD* has been one of

2239 Cf. chapter IX 1.2.1 *Programmes* on page 259, *Table 28* in chapter IX 1.2.1 *Programmes* on page 260, chapter IX 2 *UNESCO's contributions* on page 276, chapter IX 2.2.1 *Promoting and improving basic education* on page 280, chapter IX 2.2.3 *Developing public awareness of sustainability* on page 282, chapter IX 4.3 *Characteristics* on page 344, chapter IX 6.5.4 *Results* on page 462, and chapter IX 6.5.5 *Issues* on page 468.

2240 Cf. chapter VII 10 *Timeline* on page 165, and chapter IX 6.4.2 *Contents* on page 409.

2241 Cf. chapter VII 3 *Challenges* on page 152.

2242 Cf. chapter II 4.1 *Concept* on page 31.

2243 Cf. chapter II 2 *Sustainability* on page 21.

2244 Cf. chapter VII 3 *Challenges* on page 152, chapter IX 6.5.4 *Results* on page 458, and chapter IX 6.5.7 *Challenges* on page 474.

2245 Cf. chapter IX 1.4 *Participatory*on page 268.

2246 Cf. chapter IX 2.2.3 *Developing public awareness of sustainability* on page 282, and chapter IX 3 *International Implementation Scheme* on page 290.

2247 Cf. chapter IX 2.2.3 *Developing public awareness of sustainability* on page 282, and chapter IX 3.2 *Drafting history* on page 298.

the major challenges from the beginning. It is most probable that the correct strategy was implemented far too late.[2248] Valuable time elapsed and initial momentum was lost. In particular, two developments at regional level have been taking place: on the one hand, autonomous regional strategies of communicating *ESD* have been evolving independently,[2249] but, on the other hand, there has simultaneously been some delay and even complete standstill in certain regional contexts due to the lack of institutional guidance in communicating *ESD* communication.[2250] Stakeholder representation has evidently not been achieved by means of implementation, but has rather been dependent on effective communication provided by the organisation's communication sector.[2251] UNESCO's *ESD* communication can hardly be considered sufficient.

4. *Operationalisation*

The question of how to ensure proper implementation and co-ordination of *DESD* inevitably leads one to question aspects of its legitimacy, inclusion and distribution of power. The acceptance expressed towards implementation of *ESD* has been ensured by the consensus of participation[2252] and built on UNESCO's mandate in educational issues.[2253] The process of operationalising *DESD* has been professionally led or guided by UNESCO, starting with the provision of defining roles,[2254] followed by means of implementation[2255] and concluded with appropriate monitoring instruments.[2256] To a certain extent, this process is conceptually inconsistent because regional strategies are desirable yet at the same time subject to UNESCO's requirements for implementation and monitoring. Moreover, an imbalance in the institutional distribution of power may be what leads to challenges posed to the legitimacy of its leadership.

One must be acquainted with different techniques of measurement. Assessing *DESD* effectiveness is not about comparing regional case studies,[2257] and regime performance should instead be assessed using sound criteria. Considering UNESCO's functional effectiveness and organisational performance in the

2248 Cf. chapter IX 2.2.3 *Developing public awareness of sustainability* on page 282, and chapter IX 4.3 *Characteristics* on page 344.

2249 Cf. chapter IX 1.1 *Regional strategies* on page 257, chapter IX 6.4 *Europe and North America* on pages 397 et seqq, and chapter IX 7 *Conclusion* on page 478.

2250 Cf. chapter IX 6.5 *Latin America* on page 438.

2251 Cf. chapter IX 2.2.3 *Developing public awareness of sustainability* on page 282.

2252 Cf. chapter VII 8 *Principles* on page 163, and chapter VII 9 *Characteristics* on page 164.

2253 Cf. chapter VI 1 *Competences* on page 122.

2254 Cf. chapter IX 2 *UNESCO's contributions* on page 276.

2255 Cf.chapter IX 3 *International Implementation Scheme* on page 289.

2256 Cf. chapter IX 5 *Monitoring* on page 358.

2257 Cf. chapter IV 4.1 *Qualitative approach* on page 88.

matter of implementing, monitoring and co-ordinating *DESD*, three scenarios of results which might serve as benchmarks of effectiveness are conceivable:[2258]

1. To what extent does *DESD* produce *output* in the sense of real activity?

In the course of *DESD*, UNESCO addresses *ESD* in two ways, both of which themselves constitute meaningful *output*. However, at the same time, they promise the creation of further *output*. In the first place, the *platform for ESD* has been established as a genuine *ESD* co-ordination activity. This platform provides options for refining and promoting the vision of *ESD*, and it facilitates the transition towards sustainable development through all forms of learning and public awareness, especially through networking, exchange of expertise and interaction among multiple stakeholders of *ESD*.[2259] In second place, *opportunities for ESD* have been set up by UNESCO through mechanisms of implementation and monitoring which are primarily directed towards revisable strategies at various levels in order to strengthen capacity for *ESD* and to create new opportunities to incorporate *ESD* into respective efforts towards education reform.[2260]

2. How does *DESD* generate *outcome* in the sense of affecting behaviour normatively?

Behavioural effectiveness is what *ESD* is ultimately directed to realise. It is, however, most difficult to judge. Firstly, the time horizon is fairly limited: an independent attempt at assessment will be only possible by the end of *DESD*. Secondly, comparing situations *ex ante* and *ex post* is a method which either lacks suitable benchmarks or relevant counterfactuals or depends on potentially biased information due to organisational self-interest.[2261] Nonetheless, UNESCO fosters an ambitious indicator-based approach of not only considering *marketable outputs*, but also including *behavioural outcomes* of *ESD* related to commitment, best practice (*spillover*) and multiplier effects.[2262] This bears not only conceptual difficulties, but also considerable differences between the regional and global scales.[2263]

3. In what way does *DESD* create *impact* in the sense of broader consequences or long-term results?

2258 Cf. chapter IV 4.2 *Quantitative approach* on page 93.

2259 Cf. chapter IX 1.2.2 *Platforms* on page 265, and chapter IX 3.5 *Summary* on page 340.

2260 Cf. chapter IX 2.1 *Functions* on page 277, chapter IX 3.4.6 *Launch* on page 334, chapter IX 6.1 *Introduction* on page 382, and *Table 39* in chapter IX 6.2 *Specifics* on page 386.

2261 Cf. chapter IX 3.4.4 *Section III: Implementation and Evaluation* on page 324.

2262 Cf. *Table 31* in chapter IX 3.4.4 *Section III: Implementation and Evaluation* on page 326, chapter IX 5.2 *Indicators* on pages 361 et seqq, chapter IX 6.4.4 *Reporting* on page 433, and chapter IX 6.5.6 *Achievements* on page 473.

2263 Cf. chapter IX 7 *Conclusion* on page 478.

In contrast to the assessment of *ESD output* and *outcome* effectiveness, *ESD* impacts are less concerned with fulfilling objectives within fixed time frames, but reach instead far beyond the given period of time.[2264] It is almost impossible to integrate impact assessment into the *DESD* framework. Whether UNESCO finally addresses the *ESD* vision in a manner that allows the effective creation of prospects is a question with little probability of being answered within the ten-year period of *DESD*. For all that, there are promising developments under way due in part to the commitment of UNESCO, and amongst others, the steadily growing public visibility of sustainable issues.[2265] However, the question of how to act on the request for an effective *DESD* follow-up remains challenging.[2266]

As a preliminary result, UNESCO's *effectiveness* in relation to *ESD* is ambiguous. It can be addressed in a twofold way. The first objective of promoting education as a learning basis for a more sustainable human society is being successfully met. This is mainly due to the huge normative expertise of UNESCO in the field of education.[2267] The second objective of integrating sustainable development into education systems at all levels is being met with greater difficulty. On the one hand, the organisation shows great effectiveness in its coordination by providing the platform for *ESD*. On the other hand, there are limits to the contribution that can be made in terms of the implementation and monitoring of *ESD*. This is mainly due to problems of providing explicit definitions, timely communication and consistent *operationalisation* of *ESD*.

2.2 Efficiency

UNESCO's fulfilment of its role as *lead agency* of *DESD* is efficient if the given objectives can be achieved at reasonable ratio of cost to value. More precisely, efficiency relates to an optimal resource allocation in terms of the proportionality between the sources applied and the outcomes expected, the flexibility in making use of resources, and the validity of officially accepted means.[2268]

In the case of UNESCO and *DESD*, available resources can be optimally allocated if these three requirements are met accordingly:

1. *Proportionality* of *ESD* can be characterised as a *triad trade-off* between the mandate, resources and outcomes. From the mandate's point of view,

2264 Cf. chapter VII 6 *Objectives* on page 160.
2265 Cf. *Figure 7* in chapter II 4.1 *Concept* on page 32.
2266 Cf. chapter VII 12.1 *United Nations affiliation* on page 170, and chapter IX 3.2 *Drafting history* on page 294.
Cf. Bory-Adams, Aline (2010) (cf. *footnote 37* op. cit.), p. 178.
2267 Cf. chapter V 3 *Standard-setting* on page 109.
2268 Cf. chapter IV 2.2.2 *Efficiency* on pages 80 et seqq.
Cf. Bory-Adams, Aline (2010) (cf. *footnote 37* op. cit.), p. 178.

UNESCO has taken on an ambitious and comprehensive leadership assignment in *ESD*.[2269] Considering the regular resource endowment of *ESD*, both financial and human resources are the subject of careful calculation compared to both the extensive mandate and the overall UNESCO budget.[2270] Taking into account budgetary spending on *ESD* on the part of UNESCO alone, the *added value* would certainly be rather limited. Considering, however, that *DESD* functions as a multi-stakeholder approach and presuming that UNESCO acts more as the *initiator* for *ESD*, the ratio might be more balanced. However, the functional assignment of UNESCO does not support this restricted concept. Conversely, the *ESD* mandate actually requests the full range of leadership qualities from UNESCO.[2271]

2. *Flexibility* of resource application is subject to the principles of *DESD*.[2272] UNESCO acknowledges not only region-oriented and stakeholder-driven means of *ESD*, but also promotes de-centralised solutions.[2273] On the one hand, such procedures are a matter of organisational conviction, and not only in the case of *DESD*. On the other hand, it is also a necessary consequence of the ubiquitous scarcity of resources.[2274]
3. *Validity* refers to the extent to which practices of resource use are publicly accepted. Methodological guidelines of how to make the most use of resources in support of *ESD* are officially proposed, but not imposed by UNESCO.[2275] On the contrary: the organisation encourages the creation of diverse and innovative means of promoting and implementing *ESD* in order to attain the greatest institutional and public support possible.[2276]

2269 Cf. chapter VI 1 *Competences* on page 122, and chapter VI 2.1 *Lead agency* on page 125.

2270 Cf. chapter VI 2.3.1 *Staffing* on page 134, and chapter VI 2.3.2 *Financing* on pages 134 et seqq. and 141.

2271 Cf. chapter IX 2.1 *Functions* on page 277.

2272 Cf. chapter IX 1.1 *Regional strategies* on page 257.

2273 Cf. chapter IX 1.6 *Multi-level* on page 270, chapter IX 1.9 *Innovative* on page 275, chapter IX 3.4.3 *Section II: Stakeholders and Strategies* on page 311, chapter IX 3.4.4 *Section III: Implementation and Evaluation* on page 313, chapter IX 1.3 *Bottom-up* on page 351, chapter IX 5.2 *Indicators* on page 364, chapter IX 6.1 *Introduction* on page 383, and chapter IX 6.4.2 *Contents* on page 409.

2274 Cf. chapter VI 2.3.1 *Staffing* on page 134, and chapter VI 2.3.2 *Financing* on page 135.

2275 Cf. chapter VI 2.1 *Lead agency* on page 125, chapter IX 2 *UNESCO's contributions* on page 277, chapter IX 2.2.1 *Promoting and improving basic education* on page 280, chapter IX 2.2.4 *Training* on page 287, chapter IX 6.4.2 *Contents* on page 423, and chapter IX 6.5.5 *Issues* on page 471.

2276 Cf. chapter VI 2.1 *Lead agency* on page 125, chapter IX 1.9 *Innovative* on page 275, chapter IX 6.5.4 *Results* on page 316, chapter IX 6.2 *Specifics* on page 393, chapter IX 6.4.2 *Contents* on page 409, chapter IX 6.4.4 *Reporting* on page 432, and chapter IX 6.5.2 *Contents* on page 451.

As a preliminary result, the efficiency of UNESCO's *ESD* performance is complex, because a comparison with its official *status*, placed among the United Nations educational priorities,[2277] reveals that *DESD* is severely under-resourced. This general tendency towards scarce institutional resources is apparent in the provision of financial support and in the employment of persons in charge of *ESD* professionally. Considering the regular UNESCO budget in particular, only a marginal percentage is allocated to *ESD* activities.[2278] Without extra-budgetary funding and voluntary donations, outsourced responsibilities or transferred competences, as well as commitment from non-profit bodies, *DESD* would simply fail, or at the very least be far from operationally effective.

2.3 Compliance

UNESCO's role as *lead agency* of *DESD* encourages compliance as long as substantial momentum and commitment are being generated for *ESD*, both of which relate to encouraging either explicit-active or tacit-passive fulfilment of the *DESD* mandate.[2279]

Considering compliance amongst the guiding regime criteria, UNESCO is requested to foster provisions related to compliance in the course of *DESD*.[2280] With regard to the type or domain of compliance, it must be noted that *DESD* is not legally binding.[2281] This means that accountability on the part of *ESD* cannot be enforced through the *hard-law* means of *de-jure* compliance.[2282] The major constraint is that *DESD* has not been based upon an adopted source of international law which would ultimately guarantee legally binding effects.[2283] However, under favourable conditions, *soft law* may possibly induce rather similar *de-facto* consequences.[2284] For that reason, in consideration of its genesis and framework, *DESD* has been classified as a *soft-law regime*.[2285] Compliance can

2277 Cf. chapter VI 2.3.1 *Staffing* on page 134, chapter VI 2.3.2 *Financing* on page 136, and chapter VII 12.2 *UNESCO affiliation* on page 174.
2278 Cf. chapter *Table 19* in chapter VI 2.3.2 *Financing* on page 141.
2279 Cf. chapter IV 2.2.3 *Compliance* on pages 80 et seqq.
Cf. Bory-Adams, Aline (2010) (cf. *footnote 37* op. cit.), p. 178.
2280 Cf. chapter III 2.2 *Approaches* on page 61, chapter III 3 *Closing remarks* on page 70 and chapter VIII 1.6 *Summary* on pages 237 et seqq.
2281 Cf. chapter V 3 *Standard-setting* on page 106, chapter VIII 1.1 *Sources* on page 199, and chapter IX 6.4.2 *Contents* on page 409.
2282 Cf. chapter VIII 1 *Theoretical setting* on page 199.
2283 Cf. chapter VIII 1.1 *Sources* on page 199, chapter VIII 1.2 *Challenges* on page 202, chapter VIII 1.3 *Gradual normativity* on page 206, and chapter VIII 3 *Conclusion* on page 251.
2284 Cf. chapter VIII 1.5 *Compliance* on page 229.
2285 Cf. chapter VIII 1.3 *Gradual normativity* on page 212, chapter VIII 1.4 *Soft law* on page 226, and chapter VIII 1.6 *Summary* on page 239.

be considered to be primarily a concept of degree or, in other words, an issue of relative normativity;[2286] there can in fact be limited, gradual or dynamic commitment towards *DESD*. Moreover, UNESCO emphasises the importance of *de-facto* compliance with *ESD* that is outcome-oriented and driven towards tangible impacts.[2287] Compliance and causality are not necessarily linked: there might be simultaneous instances of corresponding behaviour yet an absence of any underlying *ESD*-related nexus.[2288] Finally, compliance with *ESD* does not necessarily have any bearing on the matter of regime effectiveness: compliance cannot be the exclusive and compulsory indicator of effectiveness, because compliance involves explicit-active commitment rather than sometimes unintentional, tacit-passive fulfilment.[2289]

As a result of UNESCO's expertise with normative instruments,[2290] in the context of *DESD*, the organisation promotes a threefold set of principles in order to foster compliant stakeholder behaviour.[2291] All of them are fully in line with *soft-law* enforcement:[2292]

1. Not coercing compliance.[2293] *DESD* has been defined as the fostering of commitment developed out of leadership qualities and relevant skills of management;[2294]
2. Connecting nations by launching particular programmatic activities[2295] which are directed to create *me-too momentum* with UNESCO *eo ipso* setting a

2286 Cf. chapter VIII 1.6 *Summary* on page 237.
2287 Cf. chapter VIII 1.4 *Soft law* on page 224.
2288 This is comparable to existing processes being in place simultaneously and creating synergy effects accordingly. For instance, environmental education programmes automatically contribute to *DESD*.
2289 Cf. chapter IV 2.2.3 *Compliance* on page 81.
2290 Cf. chapter V 3 *Standard-setting* on page 108.
2291 Cf. chapter V 3 *Standard-setting* on page 108, chapter V 5 *Conclusion* on page 119, chapter VI 1 *Competences* on page 122, and chapter VIII 1.3 *Gradual normativity* on page 207.
2292 Cf. chapter VIII 1.4 *Soft law* on page 226.
2293 Cf. chapter III 1.2 *Regimes* on page 39, chapter IV 2.2.3 *Compliance* on page 82, chapter VIII 1.5 *Compliance* on pages 227 and 228, and chapter VIII 2.2 *Monitoring* on page 250.
2294 Cf. chapter VI 4 *Conclusion* on page 147chapter VIII 1.6 *Summary* on page 238, chapter IX 1.4 *Participatory* on page 268, and chapter IX 1.8 *Evidence-based* on page 274.
2295 Cf. chapter IX 1.7 *Cross-cutting* on page 271, chapter IX 2 *UNESCO's contributions* on page 277, chapter IX 2.2.3 *Developing public awareness of sustainability* on page 282, chapter IX 3 *International Implementation Scheme* on pages 289 et seqq, chapter IX 4.3 *Characteristics* on page 344, chapter IX 5.1 *Drafting history* on page 361, chapter IX 6.1 *Introduction* on page 382, and chapter IX 6.5.2 *Contents* on page 452.

good example[2296] in order to demonstrate that benefits outweigh the costs of commitment to *ESD*;[2297] and

3. Shaping expectations and promoting processes of common understanding.[2298] Beside the more explicit and active commitment of leadership and *me-too strategies*, important effects of generating a binding force can be achieved through more passive aspects.[2299] Of course, the whole discourse on *ESD* initiated by UNESCO and its stakeholders already constitutes a significant implicit by-product within the gradual process towards extra-legal compliance.[2300]

UNESCO's regime performance in fulfilling the *DESD* mandate on *de-facto* consequences of compliance is dependent on distinct variables.[2301] Given this, the question is how UNESCO manages to create compliance with *ESD* ranging in attitudinal manifestation from *beneficial*, supportive or facilitative, and still *pending* or undecided to *obstructive*.[2302]

2296 Cf. chapter IX 2.3 *Summary* on page 288, *Figure 63* in chapter IX 2.3 *Summary* on page 289, and chapter IX 4 *UNESCO Action plan* on pages 340 et seqq.

2297 Cf. chapter VIII 3 *Conclusion* on page 252, chapter IX 6.5.8 *Summary* on page 476.

2298 Cf. chapter VIII 1.4 *Soft law* on page 225, and chapter IX 1.4 *Participatory* on page 268.

2299 Cf. chapter IX 1.9 *Innovative* on page 275.

2300 Cf. chapter V 3 *Standard-setting* on page 107, chapter V 3.2 *Illustration* on page 115.

2301 Cf. chapter IV 2.2.3 *Compliance* on page 82, chapter VIII 1.5 *Compliance* on page 228, chapter VIII 1.6 *Summary* on page 238, and chapter VIII 1.6 *Summary* on page 239.

2302 See *Table 53* in chapter X 2.3 *Compliance* on page 495.

Table 53: Compliance-related variables of ESD

Category	*Criterion*	*Assessment*	*Reasons*
Institutional setting	Infrastructure	*Beneficial*	• Involves multiple functional capacities[2303] • Establishes certain strategic synergies with UNESCO's functional assignment of standard-setting,[2304] monitoring[2305] and policy advice[2306]
	Hierarchy	*Obstructive*	• Creates complexity of UNESCO decision-making bodies[2307] • Misses the opportunity of lean structures and autonomous decision-making[2308] • Installs an excess of international bureaucracy[2309]
	Transparency	*Pending*	• Provides access to relevant information and networks[2310] • Limits insights into monitoring and checking results for plausibility[2311]

2303 Cf. chapter VII 12 *Stakeholders* on pages 167 et seqq, chapter IX 1.2 *Synergy effects* on page 258, chapter IX 1.2.3 *Communities* on page 267, chapter IX 1.4 *Participatory* on page 269, chapter IX 1.7 *Cross-cutting* on page 271, chapter IX 2.2.3 *Developing public awareness of sustainability* on page 282, chapter IX 3 *International Implementation Scheme* on page 290, chapter IX 3.4.3 *Section II: Stakeholders and Strategies* on page 310, and chapter IX 3.4.6 *Launch* on page 338.

2304 Cf. chapter VIII 2.1 *Standard-setting* on page 246, chapter IX 5.2 *Indicators* on page 361, and chapter IX 6.5.4 *Results* on page 466.

2305 Cf. chapter V 3.1.2 *Recommendation* on page 113, chapter V 4 *Monitoring* on page 115, chapter IX 3.4.4 *Section III: Implementation and Evaluation* on pages 313 et seqq, and chapter IX 5.5 *Summary* on page 381.

2306 Cf. chapter VIII 2.3 *Policy advice* on page 250, and chapter IX 2.2.3 *Developing public awareness of sustainability* on page 282.

2307 Cf. *Table 34* in chapter VII 12.2 *UNESCO affiliation* on page 179.

2308 Cf. chapter III 1.3 *Institutions* on page 43, and *Table 33* in chapter VII 12.2 *UNESCO affiliation* on page 175.

2309 Cf. chapter IX 6.5.4 *Results* on pages 459 et seqq.

2310 Cf. chapter VI 2.1 *Lead agency* on page 125, chapter IX 1.2.1 *Programmes* on page 260, chapter IX 2.2.2 *Re-orienting existing education programmes* on page 281, chapter IX 2.2.3 *Developing public awareness of sustainability* on page 282, chapter IX 3.4.3 *Section II: Stakeholders and Strategies* on page 311, chapter IX 4.3 *Characteristics* on page 344, chapter IX 6.5.2 *Contents* on pages 450 and 452, and chapter IX 6.5.4 *Results* on pages 459 et seqq.

2311 Cf. chapter IX 6.5.4 *Results* on page 460, chapter IX 6.5.7 *Challenges* on page 475, chapter IX 6.5.8 *Summary* on page 476, and chapter IX 7 *Conclusion* on page 477.

Category	*Criterion*	*Assessment*	*Reasons*
	Responsiveness	*Pending*	• Provides means and channels of communication[2312] • Fails to introduce corporate designs of desired conceptual meaning[2313]
	Reputation	*Supportive*	• Draws on UNESCO's technical and normative expertise[2314]
	Responsibilities	*Beneficial*	• Organises de-centralised functional UNESCO units[2315] • Delegates competences[2316]

2312 Cf. chapter V 2.1.2 *Framework* on page 103, chapter V 3.1.2 *Recommendation* on page 113, chapter VII 3 *Challenges* on page 153, chapter VII 8 *Principles* on page 164, chapter VII 9 *Characteristics* on page 165, chapter VIII 1.6 *Summary* on page 239, chapter VIII 2.2 *Monitoring* on pages 248 and 250, chapter IX 2.2.3 *Developing public awareness of sustainability* on page 282, chapter IX 2.2.3 *Developing public awareness of sustainability* on page 282, chapter IX 3.4.4 *Section III: Implementation and Evaluation* on page 313, chapter IX 4.3 *Characteristics* on pages 346 et seqq, chapter IX 6.4.2 *Contents* on page 409, chapter IX 6.5.2 *Contents* on page 450, and chapter IX 6.5.4 *Results* on page 465.

2313 Cf. chapter II 4.1 *Concept* on page 31, chapter II 5 *Conclusion* on page 35, chapter VII 3 *Challenges* on page 152, chapter IX 3.4.6 *Launch* on page 333, chapter IX 6.5.2 *Contents* on page 448, and chapter IX 6.5.7 *Challenges* on page 474.

2314 Cf. chapter V 1 *Global assignment* on page 98, chapter V 1.1 *Functions* on pages 99 and 100, chapter V 1.2 *Role* on pages 101, chapter V 3 *Standard-setting* on pages 104 and 108, and chapter VI 2.2 *Expertise* on page 131.

2315 Cf. *Table 11* in chapter III 1.5 *Conclusion* on page 54, chapter VII 12 *Stakeholders* on pages 167 et seqq, chapter VII 12.1 *United Nations affiliation* on page 168, chapter VIII 1.5.1 *Positivist perspective* on page 231, chapter VIII 2.2 *Monitoring* on page 249, and chapter IX 5.4 *Evaluation* on page 379.

2316 Cf. chapter IX 3.4.4 *Section III: Implementation and Evaluation* on page 313, chapter IX 6.1 *Introduction* on page 382, and chapter IX 6.2 *Specifics* on pages 383 and 385.

Category	*Criterion*	*Assessment*	*Reasons*
	Accountability	*Pending*	• Offers UNESCO monitoring structures[2317] • Restricts external data validation[2318]
	Benefits	*Facilitative*	• Communicates *added value*[2319]
	Efficiency	*Pending*	• Achieves validity and limited flexibility of resources[2320] • Applies UNESCO resources disproportionally[2321]
	Flexibility	*Beneficial*	• Encourages UNESCO-embedded, in-house but de-centralised solutions[2322]

2317 Cf. chapter V 3.1.2 *Recommendation* on page 113, chapter V 3.2 *Illustration* on page 114, chapter V 4 *Monitoring* on page 115, chapter V 4.2 *Summary* on page 118, chapter VI 2.1 *Lead agency* on page 125, chapter VI 3.2 *Implementation* on page 147, chapter VII 12.2 *UNESCO affiliation* on page 178, chapter VIII 2.2 *Monitoring* on page 250, chapter VIII 3 *Conclusion* on page 252, chapter IX 1.2.2 *Platforms* on page 266, chapter IX 1.7 *Cross-cutting* on page 271, chapter IX 3.2 *Drafting history* on page 294, chapter IX 3.4.3 *Section II: Stakeholders and Strategies* on page 312, chapter IX 3.4.4 *Section III: Implementation and Evaluation* on pages 313 et seqq, chapter IX 3.4.5 *Section IV: Programming the Decade* on page 329, chapter IX 4.3 *Characteristics* on pages 344 et seqq, chapter IX 5 *Monitoring* on page 358, chapter IX 5.2 *Indicators* on page 361, chapter IX 5.5 *Summary* on pages 380 seqq, *Figure* in chapter IX 5.5 *Summary* on page 382, chapter IX 6.4.2 *Contents* on page 409, *Figure 100* in chapter IX 6.4.2 *Contents* on page 429, chapter IX 6.4.4 *Reporting* on page 432, *Figure 101* in chapter IX 6.4.5 *Summary* on page 434, chapter IX 6.5.1 *Regional context* on page 447, and chapter IX 6.5.2 *Contents* on page 450.

2318 Cf. chapter IX 5.4 *Evaluation* on page 378, chapter IX 5.5 *Summary* on page 381, and chapter IX 7 *Conclusion* on page 477.

2319 Cf. chapter II 4.2 *United Nations Decade of Education for Sustainable Development* on page 33, chapter III 2.2 *Approaches* on page 61, chapter VI 2.1 *Lead agency* on page 125, chapter VII 1 *Vision* on page 149, chapter VII 9 *Characteristics* on page 165, chapter VIII 1.6 *Summary* on page 239, and chapter IX 3.4.1 *Introduction* on page 308.

2320 Cf. chapter VI 2.3.1 *Staffing* on page 134.

2321 Cf. chapter VI 2.3.2 *Financing* on page 141, and chapter VI 4 *Conclusion* on page 147.

2322 Cf. chapter VI 2.3.1 *Staffing* on page 134, chapter VI 2.3.2 *Financing* on page 135, chapter VIII 1.4 *Soft law* on page 226, chapter VIII 2.3 *Policy advice* on page 250, chapter IX 1.1 *Regional strategies* on pages 257 et seqq, chapter IX 3.4.3 *Section II: Stakeholders and Strategies* on page 311, chapter IX 3.4.4 *Section III: Implementation and Evaluation* on page 313, chapter IX 3.4.4 *Section III: Implementation and Evaluation* on pages 313 et seqq, chapter IX 5.2 *Indicators* on pages 364 and 366, chapter IX 5.2 *Indicators* on pages 361 et seqq, chapter IX 5.3 *Reporting* on page 374, chapter IX 5.5 *Summary* on page 381, chapter IX 6 *Regional implementation* on pages 382 et seqq, chapter IX 6.1 *Introduction* on page 383, chapter IX 6.2 *Specifics* on pages 383, 384 and 385, chapter IX 6.4.5 *Summary* on page 433, chapter IX 6.5.1 *Regional context* on page 445, and chapter IX 7 *Conclusion* on page 477.

Category	*Criterion*	*Assessment*	*Reasons*
Context	Frameworks	*Pending*	• Dovetails existing UNESCO initiatives and programmes[2323] • Lacks resources and dispersed structures[2324]
	Consensus	*Supportive*	• Sharing of UNESCO values, means and objectives[2325] • Invalidates voting behaviours[2326]
	Legitimacy	*Beneficial*	• Forms part of the UNESCO constitutional framework[2327] • Adheres to principles of regional and cultural diversity[2328]

2323 Cf. chapter IX 1.2 *Synergy effects* on pages 258 et seqq, chapter IX 3.4.1 *Introduction* on page 308, chapter IX 3.4.3 *Section II: Stakeholders and Strategies* on page 311, chapter IX 3.4.4 *Section III: Implementation and Evaluation* on page 313, chapter IX 3.4.5 *Section IV: Programming the Decade* on page 329 on page 329, chapter IX 3.4.6 *Launch* on page 333, chapter IX 6.4.2 *Contents* on page 409, chapter IX 6.5.1 *Regional context* on page 445, chapter IX 6.5.2 *Contents* on page 453, and chapter IX 6.5.4 *Results* on pages 464 et seqq.

2324 Cf. chapter VI 2.1 *Lead agency* on page 125, chapter VI 2.3 *Resources* on pages 133 et seqq, chapter VI 4 *Conclusion* on pages 147 and 147, chapter VII 12.2 *UNESCO affiliation* on page 177, chapter VIII 2.1 *Standard-setting* on page 244, chapter IX 1.2.2 *Platforms* on page 267, chapter IX 5.4 *Evaluation* on page 379, and chapter IX 6.5.7 *Challenges* on page 475.

2325 Cf. chapter II 4.2 *United Nations Decade of Education for Sustainable Development* on page 33, chapter II 5 *Conclusion* on page 36, chapter III 1.3 *Institutions* on page 43, chapter III 1.4 *Synthesis* on page 52, chapter V 3 *Standard-setting* on page 104, chapter VI 2 *Leadership* on page 123, chapter VII 1 *Vision* on page 150, chapter VII 6 *Objectives* on page 160, chapter VII 8 *Principles* on page 163, chapter VII 9 *Characteristics* on page 164, chapter IX 1.2.1 *Programmes* on page 259, chapter IX 2.2.1 *Promoting and improving basic education* on page 279, chapter IX 2.2.2 *Reorienting existing education programmes* on page 282, chapter IX 2.2.3 *Developing public awareness of sustainability* on page 282, chapter IX 3.2 *Drafting history* on page 294, chapter IX 3.3 *Framework* on page 302, chapter IX 3.4.3 *Section II: Stakeholders and Strategies* on page 312, chapter IX 3.4.4 *Section III: Implementation and Evaluation* on pages 313 et seqq, chapter IX 4.3 *Characteristics* on page 346, chapter IX 6.4.2 *Contents* on page 409, chapter IX 6.5.2 *Contents* on page 450, chapter IX 6.5.4 *Results* on page 459, and chapter IX 7 *Conclusion* on page 476.

2326 Cf. chapter VIII 1.2 *Challenges* on page 201, and chapter VIII 1.3 *Gradual normativity* on page 206.

2327 Cf. chapter III 2.7 *Conceptions* of order on page 67, chapter V 3 *Standard-setting* on pages 104 and 107, chapter V 3.1 *Instruments* on pages 110 et seqq, *Figure 18* in chapter V 3.2 *Illustration* on page 115, and *Figure 37* in chapter VIII 1.2 *Challenges* on page 203.

2328 Cf. chapter II 2.2 *Social sustainability* on page 23, chapter II 2.4 *Cultural sustainability* on page 24, chapter II 4.2 *United Nations Decade of Education for Sustainable De-*

Category	*Criterion*	*Assessment*	*Reasons*
Content	Obligation	*Pending*	• Promotes UNESCO *soft-law* provisions[2329] • Envisages and prioritises *de-facto* commitment[2330] • Avoids *de-jure* enforcement[2331]
	Legalisation	*Pending*	• Produces positive, extra-legal and UNESCO-attributed outcomes[2332] • Confronts trends of reluctance towards further legalisation of normative instruments[2333]

velopment on page 34, chapter II 5 *Conclusion* on page 35, chapter V 1 *Global assignment* on page 98, chapter VI 2.2 *Expertise* on page 131, chapter VIII 1.5 *Compliance* on page 228, chapter IX 1.1 *Regional strategies* on page 257, chapter IX 4.2 *Drafting history* on page 343, chapter IX 6.3 *Close-up* on page 395, chapter IX 6.4.2 *Contents* on page 409, chapter IX 6.5.4 *Results* on page 466, chapter IX 6.5.4 *Results* on page 466, and chapter IX 6.5.5 *Issues* on page 470.

2329 Cf. chapter VIII 1.2 *Challenges* on pages 202 and 206, and *Figure 56* in chapter VIII 3 *Conclusion* on page 253.

2330 Cf. chapter V 3 *Standard-setting* on page 105, chapter V 3.2 *Illustration* on page 115, chapter VIII 1.3 *Gradual normativity* on page 215, chapter VIII 1.5 *Compliance* on page 229, chapter VIII 2.1 *Standard-setting* on pages 243, 244 and 246, and chapter VIII 3 *Conclusion* on page 254.

2331 Cf. chapter VIII 1.5 *Compliance* on page 229, and chapter VIII 2.1 *Standard-setting* on page 245.

2332 Cf. chapter V 3 *Standard-setting* on page 107, chapter VI 1 *Competences* on page 122, chapter VI 3.1 *Co-ordination* and facilitation on page 144, chapter VIII 1.3 *Gradual normativity* on page 210, chapter VIII 1.4 *Soft law* on page 217, *Table 31* in chapter IX 3.4.4 *Section III: Implementation and Evaluation* on page 326, chapter IX 3.4.4 *Section III: Implementation and Evaluation* on pages 313 et seqq, and chapter IX 4.3 *Characteristics* on page 344.

2333 Cf. chapter III 2.7 *Conceptions* of order on page 68, chapter V 3.1 *Instruments* on page 110, chapter VIII 1.2 *Challenges* on page 201, chapter VIII 3 *Conclusion* on page 217, and chapter IX 7 *Conclusion* on page 477.

Category	Criterion	Assessment	Reasons
Target	Stakeholder	*Facilitative*	• Achieves continuing and voluntary commitment[2334] • Addresses both general and specific participation[2335] • Enhances UNESCO's unique networking capacities[2336]
Miscellaneous	Time	*Facilitative*	• Makes use of *windows of opportunity*[2337] • Concentrates on limited UNESCO-scheduled time frames[2338]
	Place	*Pending*	• Accepts the centralised UNESCO steering through monitoring and co-ordination[2339] • Implements de-centralised strategies[2340]

2334 Cf. chapter V 3.1 *Instruments* on page 111, chapter VI 2.3.2 *Financing* on page 135, chapter VII 8 *Principles* on page 163, chapter VIII 1.2 *Challenges* on page 205, chapter VIII 1.4 *Soft law* on page 226, chapter IX 1.4 *Participatory* on page 268, and chapter IX 6.4.2 *Contents* on page 425.

2335 Cf. chapter II 2.2 *Social sustainability* on page 23, chapter IV 2.2.7 *Power* on page 84, chapter VIII 1.3 *Gradual normativity* on page 213, chapter VIII 1.4 *Soft law* on page 220, chapter VIII 2.1 *Standard-setting* on page 244, chapter IX 1.5 *Multi-sphere* on page 269, chapter IX 1.7 *Cross-cutting* on page 271, chapter IX 2.1 *Functions* on page 277, chapter IX 3.3 *Framework* on page 306, chapter IX 3.4 *International Implementation Scheme* on page 307, chapter IX 6.2 *Specifics* on page 385, chapter IX 6.4.2 *Contents* on page 409, and chapter IX 6.5.2 *Contents* on page 451.

2336 Cf. chapter III 1.1 *Networks* on pages 38 et seqq, *Figure 11* in chapter III 1.5 *Conclusion* on page 54, chapter III 3 *Closing remarks* on page 69, chapter V 1.1 *Functions* on page 99, chapter VI 2.1 *Lead agency* on page 125, chapter VII 12.2 *UNESCO affiliation* on page 174, chapter IX 1.2.1 *Programmes* on page 260, chapter IX 2.2.1 *Promoting and improving basic education* on page 280, chapter IX 2.2.4 *Training* on page 288, chapter IX 3.3 *Framework* on page 303, chapter IX 3.4.3 *Section II: Stakeholders and Strategies* on pages 311 and 311, chapter IX 3.4.4 *Section III: Implementation and Evaluation* on pages 313 et seqq, chapter IX 4.3 *Characteristics* on page 347, chapter IX 5.3 *Reporting* on page 376, and chapter IX 6.5.6 *Achievements* on page 473.

2337 Cf. chapter III 2.7 *Conceptions* of order on page 68, chapter IV 2.2.6 *Context* on page 83, and chapter IX 4.3 *Characteristics* on page 346.

2338 Cf. chapter VI 2.1 *Lead agency* on page 126, chapter VII 10 *Timeline* on page 165, and chapter IX 3.4.5 *Section IV: Programming the Decade* on page 329.

2339 Cf. chapter VII 12.1 *United Nations affiliation* on page 171, chapter VII 12.2 *UNESCO affiliation* on page 174, and chapter IX 7 *Conclusion* on page 477.

2340 Cf. chapter VI 2.3.1 *Staffing* on page 134, chapter VIII 2.3 *Policy advice* on page 250, chapter IX 3.4.3 *Section II: Stakeholders and Strategies* on page 311, chapter IX 3.4.4 *Section III: Implementation and Evaluation* on pages 313 et seqq, and chapter IX 5.2 *Indicators* on page 364.

Category	*Criterion*	*Assessment*	*Reasons*
	Agenda	*Supportive*	• Construction of issues, tasks and fully-fledged discourses[2341] • Creating links and continuity with global and UNESCO efforts[2342]

A considerable part of the UNESCO framework does support and contribute to *DESD* compliance. This applies to the organisational infrastructure, global reputation, shared responsibilities, joint benefits, creative flexibility, value-based consensus and acknowledged legitimacy in particular. By contrast, the hierarchical structure of UNESCO's construction of *DESD* may inhibit compliance. Some factors remain undecided and both contribute to and inhibit *DESD* compliance. This relates primarily to the transparency of information, responsiveness of communication, stakeholder accountability in monitoring, resource efficiency, the synergy effects of sharing frameworks, and the consequences of obligation and further legalisation.

Keeping these arguments in mind, it remains highly notional whether *ESD* can achieve a standardised quality in the future. The issue of compliance is ultimately addressed by means of the three functional aspects of UNESCO:

- Standard-setting is possible if the normative character and *de-facto* binding nature of *DESD* is commonly accepted. Further progress must be made in the domains of hierarchy, obligation and legalisation;
- Monitoring is possible if mechanisms of monitoring and assessment of *DESD* are fully established and applied. Further progress must be made in the domains of efficiency, accountability and frameworks; and
- Policy advice is desirable if particular codes of conduct towards *DESD* are recommended and implemented. Further progress must be made in the domains of transparency and responsiveness.

As a preliminary result, UNESCO's actions in the field of *compliance* with *DESD* are directed for the most part towards the creation of momentum and commitment. Most of UNESCO's institutional and contextual framework condi-

2341 Cf. chapter IV 2.2.6 *Context* on page 83, chapter IV 2.2.7 *Power* on page 84, chapter V 1.2 *Role* on page 101, chapter IX 2.2.3 *Developing public awareness of sustainability* on page 282, chapter IX 3.2 *Drafting history* on page 293, chapter IX 3.4.3 *Section II: Stakeholders and Strategies* on page 312, chapter IX 3.4.4 *Section III: Implementation and Evaluation* on pages 313 et seqq, and chapter IX 6.4.2 *Contents* on page 409.

2342 Cf. chapter VI 2.2 *Expertise* on page 131, chapter VI 3.1 *Co-ordination* and facilitation on page 144, chapter VII 12.2 *UNESCO affiliation* on page 177, chapter IX 1.2.1 *Programmes* on pages 262 and 263, *Figure 58* in chapter IX 1.2.1 *Programmes* on page 265, chapter IX 2.1 *Functions* on page 278, and chapter IX 3.4.1 *Introduction* on page 308.

tions support commitment to *ESD*. Improvements can be made within the ambit of organisational hierarchy, responsibility and accountability.

2.4 Leadership

UNESCO's role as *lead agency* of *DESD* is leadership-oriented, where the organisation manages to exercise meaningful influence on the change of behavioural patterns in relation to *ESD*.[2343]

The degree of leadership is subject to the results of substantial negotiation and is dependent on both *charismatic* and *bureaucratic* leadership.[2344] In the first instance, UNESCO rises to the challenge of charismatic leadership because the *ESD* vision of change has been explicitly formulated.[2345] Secondly, the organisation is mandated for bureaucratic *DESD* leadership. Given its *lead-agency* mandate, UNESCO is held responsible for designing the strategic approach and managing the process of global implementation.[2346] This aligns with the very nature of UNESCO as *lead agency*, both in general[2347] as well as for *DESD* in all requisite aspects.[2348] These professional leadership qualities are of particular relevance in the matters of:

a) The promotion of *ESD* values: UNESCO focuses on value-driven strategies.[2349] Nonetheless, the value-based and normative character of *ESD* has either not been made sufficiently clear or not been unanimously understood;[2350]

2343 Cf. chapter IV 2.2.4 *Leadership* on pages 82 et seqq.
2344 Cf. *Figure 20* in chapter VI 2 *Leadership* on page 124.
2345 Cf. chapter VII 1 *Vision* on pages 149 et seqq, and chapter VII 2 *Mission* on pages 151 et seqq.
2346 Cf. chapter VII 3 *Challenges* on page 128.
2347 Cf. chapter VI 2.1 *Lead agency* on page 125.
2348 Legitimacy, launching, partners, relevance, design, structures, instruments, and public relations are among the salient aspects of this.
Cf. *Figure 21* in chapter VI 2.1 *Lead agency* on page 128, and chapter VI 2.1 *Lead agency* on pages 125 et seqq.
2349 Cf. chapter II 3.1 *Sustainable development* on page 27, III 1.3 *Institutions* on page 43, chapter III 1.4 *Synthesis* on page 52, chapter V 3 *Standard-setting* on page 104, chapter VII 1 *Vision* on pages 149 and 150, chapter VII 8 *Principles* on page 163, chapter VII 9 *Characteristics* on page 164, chapter VII 13 *Milestones* on page 192, chapter VIII 1.4 *Soft law* on page 226, chapter IX 2.2.1 *Promoting and improving basic education* on page 279, chapter IX 2.2.3 *Developing public awareness of sustainability* on page 282, chapter IX 3.2 *Drafting history* on page 294, chapter IX 3.3 *Framework* on page 302, chapter IX 3.4.3 *Section II: Stakeholders and Strategies* on page 312, chapter IX 3.4.4 *Section III: Implementation and Evaluation* on pages 313 et seqq, chapter II 5 *Conclusion* on page 34, chapter IX 4.3 *Characteristics* on page 344, chapter IX 6.4.2 *Contents* on pages 409 et seqq, chapter IX 6.5 *Latin America* on page 438, chapter IX 6.5.2 *Contents* on page 450, and chapter IX 7 *Conclusion* on page 476.

b) Integration of *ESD* stakeholders: UNESCO aims to foster and guide stakeholder commitment through the establishment of platforms for processes of *ESD* decision-making.[2351] This functional co-ordination has seen rather ambivalent success, with particular differences in regional perspective;[2352] and
c) Consultancy and governance: UNESCO successfully facilitates the implementation of *ESD*-related subjects[2353] in line with principles of governance[2354] and by providing appropriate means of technical advice.[2355]

It may provisionally be stated that UNESCO's *leadership* functionalities are wholly applicable to the framework of *DESD*. Given the institutional restrictions and varying contextual conditions, disparities that occur in leading *DESD* are more likely to be a result of bureaucratic shortcomings on the part of the *lead agency* than they are to be directly attributable to UNESCO's charismatic approach.[2356] Promisingly, UNESCO has initiated a meaningful institutional drive in order to exert an active influence on the course of *DESD*. However, behavioural changes towards *ESD* depend on leadership qualities *and* the appropriate

---

2350 Cf. chapter II 2 *Sustainability* on pages 18 and 21, chapter VII 3 *Challenges* on page 152, and chapter IX 6.5.7 *Challenges* on page 474.

2351 Cf. chapter IV 2.2.4 *Leadership* on page 82, chapter V 3 *Standard-setting* on page 105, chapter VI 2.1 *Lead agency* on page 125, chapter VII 3 *Challenges* on page 153, chapter VII 6 *Objectives* on page 161, chapter VII 12.2 *UNESCO affiliation* on page 177, chapter VII 12.3 *Miscellaneous affiliation* on page 182, chapter VIII 2.3 *Policy advice* on page 250, chapter VIII 2.2 *Monitoring* on page 286, chapter IX 3.4.4 *Section III: Implementation and Evaluation* on page 313, chapter IX 5.2 *Indicators* on page 362, chapter VI 3.1 *Co-ordination* and facilitation on page 368, and chapter IX 7 *Conclusion* on page 476.

2352 Cf. chapter VII 8 *Principles* on page 163, chapter VII 9 *Characteristics* on page 164, chapter IX 6.5.7 *Challenges* on page 474, chapter IX 6.5.8 *Summary* on page 476, and chapter IX 7 *Conclusion* on pages 477 and 478.

2353 Cf. chapter III 2.5 *Regime theory* on page 64, chapter III 2.8 *Conclusion* on page 69, chapter VII 11 *Thrusts* on page 166, chapter IX 3.3 *Framework* on page 301, chapter IX 3.4 *International Implementation Scheme* on page 307, chapter IX 3.4.4 *Section III: Implementation and Evaluation* on page 313, chapter VII 5 *Perspectives* on page 338, chapter IX 6.4.2 *Contents* on pages 409 et seqq, chapter IX 6.4.4 *Reporting* on page 432, chapter IX 6.4.5 *Summary* on page 434, chapter IX 6.5.2 *Contents* on page 452 and 454, chapter IX 6.5.8 *Summary* on page 476, and chapter IX 7 *Conclusion* on page 477.

2354 Cf. chapter III 1.4 *Synthesis* on page 52, chapter IV 2.2.4 *Leadership* on page 82, chapter V 3 *Standard-setting* on page 105, chapter VIII 1.4 *Soft law* on page 225, chapter VIII 1.4 *Soft law* on page 226, chapter IX 1 *Principles of implementation* on page 256, chapter IX 1.10 *Summary* on page 276, and chapter IX 3.4.4 *Section III: Implementation and Evaluation* on page 313.

2355 Cf. chapter V 2.1 *Instruments* on page 102, chapter VII 12.2 *UNESCO affiliation* on page 174, chapter IX 1.7 *Cross-cutting* on page 271, and chapter IX 3.4.6 *Launch* on page 335.

2356 Cf. chapter IX 7 *Conclusion* on pages 477.

allegiance. UNESCO will therefore have to pay only part of the bill for success or failure.

2.5 Topicality

UNESCO's role as *lead agency* of *DESD* is considered current as long as the organisational performance can be characterised as proactive and anticipatory by taking advantage of a *window of opportunity*[2357] in addressing *ESD*.[2358]

UNESCO has thoroughly succeeded in actively setting *ESD* in continuity with past, existing and ongoing processes in the discourses of education, sustainability and development.[2359] Drawing attention to its numerous aspects, the organisation manages to establish a nexus with the current topics and formative debates of *ESD*.[2360] Moreover, UNESCO aims to address future-thinking and the fostering of perspectives that reach far beyond the official *DESD* schedule.[2361] This means that follow-up actions – whether already scheduled or not – are most likely to incorporate the idea of *DESD* into their respective programmes.[2362]

UNESCO has sustained a considerable frequency of action, particularly when launching *DESD*.[2363] It is important that pace is not lost, but instead that the rate of acceptance is maintained or even improved.[2364] This applies primarily

---

2357 Cf. chapter IV 2.2.6 *Context* on page 83, and chapter VIII 1.5 *Compliance* on page 228.

2358 Cf. chapter IV 2.2.5 *Topicality* on pages 83 et seqq.

2359 Cf. chapter II 2 *Sustainability* on pages 19 and 20, chapter II 5 *Conclusion* on page 36, chapter VI 1 *Competences* on page 121, chapter VI 2.2 *Expertise* on page 131, chapter VII *Background* on page 149, chapter VII 12.1 *United Nations affiliation* on page 170, chapter VII 13 *Milestones* on pages 186 et seqq, chapter VII 15 *Summary* on page 195, *Figure 36* in chapter VII 15 *Summary* on page 196, chapter IX 1.2.1 *Programmes* on page 259, *Figure 58* in chapter IX 1.2.1 *Programmes* on page 265, and chapter IX 6.2 *Specifics* on page 383.

2360 Cf. chapter II 1.3 *Teaching* on page 18, chapter VI 2.1 *Lead agency* on page 125, chapter VII 1 *Vision* on page 150, chapter VII 3 *Challenges* on page 153, and chapter VII 10 *Timeline* on page 165.

2361 Cf. chapter VII 12.1 *United Nations affiliation* on page 170, and *Table 23* in chapter VII 14 *United Nations decades* on page 193.

2362 Cf. chapter VI 2.1 *Lead agency* on page 127, chapter VII *Background* on page 149, chapter IX 3.2 *Drafting history* on page 294, and chapter IX 6.5.2 *Contents* on pages 451 and 452.
Cf. Bory-Adams, Aline (2010) (cf. *footnote 37* op. cit.), p. 178.

2363 Cf. chapter IX 6.2 *Specifics* on page 384, *Table 39* in chapter IX 6.2 *Specifics* on page 386, and *Figure 98* in chapter IX 6.2 *Specifics* on page 394.

2364 Cf. *Figure 62* in chapter IX 2.2.3 *Developing public awareness of sustainability* on page 287.

to enhancing the visibility of *ESD*-related actions and results, and achieving pro-active *ESD* agenda-setting.

UNESCO has been making efforts to propagate the key message of *ESD*.[2365] According to feedback information gathered through public discourse, the *ESD* image transfer only takes place to a limited extent,[2366] because there is, in comparison to the positive intentions of *DESD* as a fully-fledged regime,[2367] relatively little coverage in the media and equally little receipt of public attention.[2368] Obviously, the beneficial effects of *ESD* do insufficiently redound to UNESCO.[2369] Acknowledging existent differences in regional and global perceptions, beyond the *ESD*-related community, mutual awareness is rather marginal; ignorance or reservations towards *ESD* are considerable.[2370] This may be due either to the fact that *DESD* has not been pushed in a sufficiently timely manner or because methods of communication have been inadequately used. The formats and media of communication are current, innovative and they appeal to the different target-groups and stakeholders.[2371] As a direct consequence of this, the official *DESD* communication strategy has entered into effect a good deal after the launch of *DESD*.[2372] Valuable time, and with it opportunities for immediate lobbying and anticipatory publicity, has elapsed.

UNESCO's options in terms of *topicality* are numerous and charged with potential. On the one hand, the public presence of *ESD* is insufficient, and in this

---

2365 Cf. chapter VIII 1.6 *Summary* on page 239, chapter IX 2.2.3 *Developing public awareness of sustainability* on pages 282 et seqq, chapter IX 3.4.4 *Section III: Implementation and Evaluation* on page 313, chapter IX 6.5 *Latin America* on pages 438 et seqq, chapter IX 6.5.2 *Contents* on pages 450 and 452, chapter IX 6.5.4 *Results* on page 460, and chapter IX 6.5.8 *Summary* on page 476.

2366 Cf. chapter IX 6.5.4 *Results* on pages 458 and 459, and chapter IX 6.5.7 *Challenges* on page 474.

2367 Cf. chapter III 1.4 *Synthesis* on pages 52 et seqq, chapter IX 3.4.4 *Section III: Implementation and Evaluation* on page 313, chapter IX 3.5 *Summary* on page 340, and chapter IX 6.5.2 *Contents* on page 451.

2368 Cf. chapter VII 12.3 *Miscellaneous affiliation* on page 182.

2369 Cf. chapter IX 7 *Conclusion* on page 477.

2370 Cf. chapter VIII 2.2 *Monitoring* on pages 249 and 249, chapter IX 3.4.3 *Section II: Stakeholders and Strategies* on page 319, chapter IX 5.4 *Evaluation* on page 379, chapter IX 6.5.4 *Results* on page 458, and chapter IX 6.5.7 *Challenges* on page 475.

2371 Cf. chapter VI 2.1 *Lead agency* on page 125, chapter VIII 2.2 *Monitoring* on page 249, chapter IX 1.9 *Innovative* on page 275, chapter IX 2.2.3 *Developing public awareness of sustainability* on page 282, chapter IX 3.3 *Framework* on page 304, chapter IX 3.4.3 *Section II: Stakeholders and Strategies* on page 312, chapter IX 3.4.4 *Section III: Implementation and Evaluation* on pages 313 et seqq.

2372 Cf. chapter VII 8 *Characteristics* on page 165, chapter IX 2.2.3 *Developing public awareness of sustainability* on page 282, chapter IX 4.3 *Characteristics* on page 346, chapter IX 6.5 *Latin America* on page 438, chapter IX 6.5.4 *Results* on page 463, chapter IX 6.5.7 *Challenges* on page 475, and chapter X 2.1 *Effectiveness* on page 488.

respect, opportunities for lobbying and the proactive communication of *ESD* have not been seized with enough consistent vigour from the very beginning. On the other hand, the future is promising: in relation to the concept of *economies of scale*, once *DESD* has gained critical importance and sufficient *drive*,[2373] UNESCO's long-run costs and efforts in securing campaigns for the publicity, visibility, image and communication of *ESD* may drastically drop. At the same time, attaching value to the *real* substance of *ESD* increases noticeably. Nonetheless, the challenge of making the voice of both the organisation and *DESD* heard by a sufficiently large audience is one that remains, and in this case the *window of opportunity* for *DESD* is still open.

2.6 Context

UNESCO's role as *lead agency* of *DESD* is context-driven when the organisation takes into proper consideration the variability of circumstances, surroundings, background, settings or requirements while fulfilling its mandate.[2374]

The context of *DESD* is determined by its stakeholders. This refers to the degree to which individual preferences are integrated into the situational order, particularly in terms of:

a) *Resources*: Does UNESCO provide sufficient financial and human resources;
b) *Structure*: Does UNESCO promote an appropriate structural environment; and
c) *Expertise*: Does UNESCO speak to sufficient levels of competences in order to make knowledge and skills available?

As to resources: UNESCO's course of action is certain but rather limited. The majority of the *DESD* leadership mandate is covered and its core requirements funded by UNESCO.[2375] However, both according to the budget and in comparison with organisational leadership requirements, *DESD* cannot be considered UNESCO's highest priority.[2376] Since stakeholders depend either on proper *ESD* financing or additional funding, regular resources are neither sufficiently nor persistently distributed, by either UNESCO or the participating member

2373 For instance, through to trickle-down or multiplying (*snowball*) effects.
Cf. chapter II 1.2 *Training* on page 17, chapter IX 3.4.3 *Section II: Stakeholders and Strategies* on page 311, chapter IX 3.4.4 *Section III: Implementation and Evaluation* on page 313, chapter IX 6.5.4 *Results* on page 461, and chapter IX 7 *Conclusion* on page 477.
Cf. Alvarez, José Enrique (2006) (cf. *footnote 141* op. cit.), p. 347.

2374 Cf. chapter IV 2.2.6 *Context* on pages 83 et seqq.

2375 Cf. chapter VI 2.3.2 *Financing* on page 135, and chapter X 2.2 *Efficiency* on page 492.

2376 Cf. *Figure 24* in chapter VI 2.3.2 *Financing* on page 137.

states.[2377] Extra-budgetary financing and project-bound resources also apply to UNESCO's functioning.[2378]

In the case of structure, UNESCO aims to focus on different structural settings. The most essential contribution in order to meet different political, economic, social and cultural needs has been made in considering regional solutions and approaches towards *ESD*.[2379] Nonetheless, no (significant) extra resources for *DESD* have been allocated to the five UNESCO regions, a fact which may give the impression that regions take on the management of *ESD en passant*.[2380] Moreover, regionally addressing specifics only serves as one approach in coping with variegation: the regional divisions of UNESCO represent a manageable compromise.[2381] In order to obtain realistic, needs-based structures in relation to *DESD*, the organisation has been explicitly encouraging appropriate subregional and local structures.[2382]

In the case of expertise, prior to the development of skills and knowledge, the relevant competences of *ESD* must first be formulated and communicated.[2383] Still, the dissemination of the *elusive* concept of *ESD* as a strategic approach to competence-building has been complex: particularly at a regional scale, *DESD* communication has not contributed to understanding in a sufficiently timely or comprehensive manner.[2384] This has meant that a considerable lack of acceptance and a great understatement of the relevance of *ESD* are in evidence.[2385] At the same time, UNESCO's own expertise and its role in leading educational efforts, such as *DESD*, are not suitably called on.[2386] Once effective awareness of *ESD* has been raised, UNESCO promotes adequate methods of competence-building through multiple means and at multiple levels.[2387] For in-

2377 Cf. chapter VI 2.3.2 *Financing* on page 135.

2378 Cf. *Figure 23* in chapter VI 2.3.2 *Financing* on page 135.

2379 Cf. chapter IX 1.1 *Regional strategies* on page 257, chapter IX 6.4.2 *Contents* on page 409, and chapter IX 7 *Conclusion* on page 477.

2380 Cf. *Figure 57* in chapter IX 1.1 *Regional strategies* on page 258, chapter IX 1.2 *Synergy effects* on page 258, and chapter IX 1.2.1 *Programmes* on page 259.

2381 Cf. chapter IX 7 *Conclusion* on page 477.

2382 Cf. chapter IX 1.6 *Multi-level* on page 270.

2383 Cf. *Figure 41* in chapter IX 5.2 *Indicators* on page 363.

2384 Cf. chapter II 3.2 *Characteristics* on page 28, and chapter X 2.1 *Effectiveness* on page 487.

2385 Cf. chapter IX 6.5.7 *Challenges* on page 474, and chapter IX 6.5.8 *Summary* on page 476.

2386 Cf. chapter V 2 *Formulation of global policies and policy advice* on page 102, chapter V 5 *Conclusion* on page 119, chapter VI 1 *Competences* on page 121, chapter VI 2.2 *Expertise* on page 131, *Table 17* in chapter VI 2.2 *Expertise* on page 132, and chapter VI 2.2 *Expertise* on page 133.

2387 Cf. chapter V 5 *Conclusion* on page 119, chapter VI 2.1 *Lead agency* on page 125, chapter IX 3 *International Implementation Scheme* on pages 289 et seqq, chapter IX 3.4.4 *Section III: Implementation and Evaluation* on page 313, chapter IX 5

stance, given the heterogeneity of *ESD* stakeholders,[2388] UNESCO fosters the creation of multi-level platforms of dialogue for sharing *ESD*-related information and experience, and for developing appropriately collaborative activities.[2389]

It may be preliminarily stated that UNESCO's role of determining the context of *DESD* ranges from proactive commitment to passive acceptance. This applies to a) the proactive implementation of structures, b) the active sharing of expertise and practices, and c) the actively depreciating or passive underestimation of resource provision. Context matters greatly, and of course, it does have tremendous consequences and feedback effects on structural arrangements and expertise. That is to say, performance might certainly be much more effective if circumstances such as the availability of resources were taken into more conscious account.

2.7 Power

UNESCO's role as *lead agency* of *DESD* endows it with power as long as the organisation succeeds in harnessing productive creativity by emphasising its *DESD* leadership function. This applies to UNESCO's power of decision, its institutional power and its productive power.[2390]

Power of decision may be related to the assertion and implementation of decisions subject to the provisions of material and normative resources.[2391] UNESCO adheres firmly to the transparency of decision-making in accordance with the *normative set-up* of the *DESD* leadership mandate.[2392] This implies that strategic decisions are to be taken proactively and in the anticipation of different scenarios including, above all, the risk of failure.[2393] Apart from UNESCO's professionalism in performance in spite of changing contexts, diverging expectations and constrained resources, the pressure of uncertainty is inevitable.[2394] In the course of *DESD*, UNESCO has addressed this particular challenge mainly through delegating the power of implementing decisions and the processes lead-

---

Monitoring on pages 358 et seqq, chapter IX 6.4.2 *Contents* on page 409, chapter IX 6.5.2 *Contents* on page 449, and chapter IX 6.5.4 *Results* on page 461.

2388 Cf. chapter VII 12.3 *Miscellaneous affiliation* on page 182, and chapter IX 2 *UNESCO's contributions* on page 277.

2389 Cf. chapter IX 1.2.1 *Programmes* on page 265, and chapter IX 1.2.3 *Communities* on page 267.

2390 Cf. chapter IV 2.2.7 *Power* on pages 83et seqq.

2391 Cf. chapter III 1.3 *Institutions* on page 43, and chapter IV 2.2.7 *Power* on page 84.

2392 Cf. chapter VI 2 *Leadership* on page 123, chapter IX 1.2.2 *Platforms* on page 265, chapter IX 6.4.2 *Contents* on page 409, and chapter IX 6.5.2 *Contents* on page 453.

2393 Cf. chapter VI 2.1 *Lead agency* on page 74, chapter V 1.1 *Functions* on page 99, chapter VI 2 *Leadership* on page 123, and chapter IX 3.2 *Drafting history* on page 294.

2394 Cf. chapter VIII 1.4 *Soft law* on page 219.

ing to such decisions to decentralised stakeholder bodies.[2395] Ultimately, this principle of *creative subsidiarity*[2396] may conflict with UNESCO's overall accountability for the *DESD* mandate.[2397]

Because of the non-binding nature of *DESD*, UNESCO's institutional power is preset to exercising the primarily facilitative and influencing aspects of leadership,[2398] and, therefore, with regard to normative matters, the organisation's strategy in relation to *DESD* is driven by *soft-law*.[2399] *Grosso modo*, UNESCO's unique selling power as an institution consists of setting *DESD* high on global agendas and creating *living structures* of *ESD*.[2400] Those combine stakeholder orientation[2401] with appropriate institutionalised frameworks.[2402] As a result, it is not *de-jure* compliance with provisions, but *de-facto* commitment that serves as a meaningful indicator of sufficient leadership power as an institution.[2403] In the case of regionally empowered solutions, UNESCO's performance remains rather ambiguous, ranging between the promising and the questionable.[2404]

Promoting productivity within institutional settings is challenging. Bureaucratic leadership *eo ipso* is frequently, and misleadingly, perceived as in opposition to creative solutions to problems,[2405] whereas in fact both success and failure depend on the managerial culture of the institution.[2406] In the matter of *DESD*, creative productivity is to a certain extent but not entirely determined by

---

2395 Cf. chapter IX 3.5 *Summary* on page 340, and chapter IX 6.2 *Specifics* on page 384.

2396 Cf. chapter VII 8 *Principles* on page 163, chapter IX 3.4.3 *Section II: Stakeholders and Strategies* on page 312, and chapter IX 6.4.2 *Contents* on page 422.

2397 Cf. chapter III 1.3 *Institutions* on page 43, and chapter III 2.2 *Approaches* on page 61.

2398 Cf. chapter VI 2 *Leadership* on page 124, chapter IX 1.2.2 *Platforms* on page 266, chapter IX 6.4.2 *Contents* on page 409, and chapter X 2.4 *Leadership* on page 502.

2399 Cf. chapter III 1.4 *Synthesis* on page 53, and chapter VIII 3 *Conclusion* on pages 251, 252 and 254.

2400 Cf. chapter IV 2.2.6 *Context* on page 83, chapter IV 2.2.7 *Power* on page 84, chapter VI 2.1 *Lead agency* on page 125, chapter VI 2.3.1 *Staffing* on page 134, chapter IX 3.4.4 *Section III: Implementation and Evaluation* on pages 313 et seqq, and chapter IX 6.5 *Latin America* on page 439.

2401 E.g., through participation, guidance and assistance, etc.
Cf. chapter VII 8 *Characteristics* on page 164, and chapter IX 1 *Principles of implementation* on page 256.

2402 Through, for example, agenda-setting activities, co-ordination schemes, etc.
Cf. chapter III 1.3 *Institutions* on page 43, chapter VI 2.1 *Lead agency* on page 125, chapter VIII 2.3 *Policy advice* on page 250, and chapter IX 3.3 *Framework* on page 306.

2403 Cf. chapter V 3 *Standard-setting* on pages 105 and 108, chapter V 3.2 *Illustration* on page 115, and chapter VIII 2.1 *Standard-setting* on page 246.

2404 Cf. chapter IX 6.5.8 *Summary* on page 475.

2405 Cf. chapter VI 2 *Leadership* on page 123, chapter VI 4 *Conclusion* on page 147, and chapter VIII 1.6 *Summary* on page 240.

2406 Cf. chapter VI 2 *Leadership* on page 124.

UNESCO's structural provisions.[2407] However, substantial results in *ESD*[2408] are developed by both UNESCO *and* its contributing regime stakeholders.[2409] Conversely, UNESCO's independent and directly attributable share in productivity coincides with the mandated *dual role* of the organisation: firstly, co-ordinating and facilitating *DESD* – identifying problems and deficits, defining objectives, and proposing viable solutions and, secondly, implementing and monitoring *DESD* – developing strategies and taking effective action.[2410] Irrespective of *frictional losses* that are mainly attributable to bureaucracy,[2411] UNESCO is working ambitiously in support of turning *DESD* into a process oriented towards productivity and outcomes.[2412]

It may also be stated preliminarily that the power UNESCO exerts in relation to *DESD* amounts to a *tightrope walk* between mainstreaming *ESD* in a participatory manner and autonomously leaving its *genuine* institutional mark. It should not be doubted that the unfolding of creative potential is linked inextricably with bureaucratic leadership. As far as *DESD* decision-making is concerned, UNESCO operates consistently and influentially unless the power of decision has been delegated. Once further co-ordination has been required in order to come to a joint decision within some particular field of action, UNESCO aims to provide contributing *ESD* stakeholders with a sufficiently stimulating framework. Institutional power differs considerably in regional scope but, this notwithstanding, UNESCO's approach to *ESD* favours *living structures* of *de-facto* commitment over *de-jure* compliance in particular. Concerning institutional productivity, UNESCO ensures genuine *added value* through its *dual* mandate

---

2407 Cf. chapter VI 2.2 *Expertise* on page 132, and *Figure 24* in chapter VI 2.3.2 *Financing* on page 133.

2408 Such as output, outcome and impact.
Cf. chapter IX 3.4.4 *Section III: Implementation and Evaluation* on page 313.

2409 Cf. chapter III 1.4 *Synthesis* on page 51, chapter III 3 *Closing remarks* on page 70, chapter IV 2.2.4 *Leadership* on page 82, and chapter IX 6.5.2 *Contents* on page 452.

2410 Cf. chapter VI 2.1 *Lead agency* on page 125, chapter VII 12.1 *United Nations affiliation* on page 173, chapter IX 2.1 *Functions* on page 277, *Figure 63* in chapter IX 2.3 *Summary* on page 289, chapter IX 4.1 *Objectives* on page 340, and chapter IX 7 *Conclusion* on page 477.

2411 These might include time-consuming processes of co-ordination and approval, distortions through hierarchical communication and constraints of budgetary spending.
Cf. chapter II 1.1 *Learning* on page 13, *Figure 24* in chapter VI 2.3.2 *Financing* on page 133, *Figure 26* in chapter VI 2.3.2 *Financing* on page 142, and chapter VIII 2.2 *Monitoring* on page 248.

2412 Cf. chapter III 1.2 *Regimes* on page 39, chapter III 2.4 *Nexus* on page 63, chapter IV 4.1 *Qualitative approach* on page 89, chapter IV 4.2 *Quantitative approach* on page 93, chapter VIII 1.4 *Soft law* on page 224, chapter VIII 2.1 *Standard-setting* on page 241, chapter IX 3.4.4 *Section III: Implementation and Evaluation* on pages 313 et seqq, chapter IX 4.3 *Characteristics* on page 344, chapter IX 5.1 *Drafting history* on page 360, and chapter IX 5.2 *Indicators* on pages 361 et seqq.

of co-ordination and facilitation, respectively, and implementation. Essentially, the organisation's power can be characterised as facilitative and supportive.

2.8 Synthesis

Moving now towards a synthesised analysis of UNESCO's mandate as *lead agency* of *DESD* and taking into consideration the adapted regime criteria, the organisation performs with varying degrees of success.[2413] In general, the trend appears to be promising: UNESCO-led *DESD* bears good prospects. Challenges are predominantly due to the fact of regional *upheavals*.[2414]

In terms of functional *effectiveness* , UNESCO has succeeded in linking educational issues to those of sustainable development, and although this has not always been sufficiently clear in definitions and communication, the conception of *DESD* has been well highlighted and made visibly operable. This applies to the implementation, monitoring and co-ordination of *DESD*.

In the matter of *efficiency*, UNESCO has been allocated resources disproportionately, a fact which does not reflect the importance and priority accorded to *DESD*. UNESCO's recognisably flexible application of resources cannot compensate for this.

In the matter of *compliance*, UNESCO has succeeded in building momentum and commitment for *DESD*. The attainment of stakeholder responsibility and accountability for *DESD* is ultimately dependent upon structural decisions taken by the organisation.

In the matter of *leadership*, UNESCO has been tasked with promoting *DESD*. This has been achieved to a certain extent only with charismatic leadership, and thus remains challenging. With regard to bureaucratic leadership, the organisation has managed to set *DESD* onto the agenda and to integrate it into the global context. Because of its substantial expertise, UNESCO has been successful in *DESD* consultancy in line with principles of governance.

In the matter of *topicality*, UNESCO has managed to establish and provide continuity in aspects pertaining to *DESD*. Improvements in the public image of *DESD* depend largely on pace, communication and visibility.

In the matter of *context*, UNESCO has been constrained in making adjustments to the structure, to relatively limited resources for *DESD* which ultimately challenges the organisation to make adequate use of its incontestable expertise in matters of content and technicality.

Lastly, in the matter of *power*, UNESCO has been enormously productive in dealing with the main requests of the *DESD* mandate. In accordance with the

2413 Cf. chapter IV 2.2 *Criteria* on page 75.
2414 See *Table 54* in chapter X 2.8 *Synthesis* on page 512.

ruling principle of *DESD*, UNESCO's institutional power of decision is related above all to the organisation's regional performance.

Table 54: Synthesis of UNESCO's performance as DESD lead agency

Functions	*Criterion*	*Aspects*	*Executive summary*
Standard-setting – Policy advice – Monitoring	Effectiveness	Implementation and monitoring	• Definition, conceptualisation, communication and operationalisation of *ESD* • Developing the *International Implementation Scheme* (IIS) and *Global Monitoring and Evaluation Framework* (GMEF)
		Co-ordination	• Platforms for *ESD*
	Efficiency	Proportionality	• *Trade-off* relation between *ESD* mandate, resources and outcomes
		Flexibility	• Ability to adjust scarcity of *ESD* resources to the stakeholders and changing regional conditions
		Validity	• Support and acceptance of guidelines of *ESD* resource application
	Compliance	Responsibility	• *Soft-law* enforcement of *ESD*
		Commitment	• *De-facto* *ESD*-oriented standard-setting capability
		Accountability	• Transparency of *ESD* structures for *ESD* participation, momentum and co-operation
	Leadership	Promotion	• Understanding the values of *ESD*
		Integration	• Bureaucratic drive in support of *ESD* and links with existing and ongoing initiatives
		Consultancy	• Enabling *ESD* to be realised
		Governance	• Guidance and steering of *ESD* processes and stakeholders
	Topicality	Continuity	• Strategic nexus of *ESD* add-on and follow up
		Frequency	• Agenda setting in favour of *ESD*
		Image	• Availability of *ESD*-related information and transfer (window of opportunity)
		Visibility	• Outward public manifestation and recognition of *ESD*

		Communication	• Publicity and strategies of *ESD* dissemination • Developing the *Framework for a DESD Communication Strategy in support of DESD* (*DESD* Communication Strategy)
	Context	Resources	• Provision and distribution of marginal *ESD* resources
		Structure	• Political and societal goodwill towards regional *ESD* scenarios
		Expertise	• *ESD* dialoguing and co-operative structures of exchanging views
	Power	Deciding	• Subsidiarity of *ESD* decision-making
		Institutional	• Set-up of structures in support of the *DESD* agenda
		Productive	• Accomplishment of the *DESD* mandate in terms of co-ordination, facilitation and implementation
Rating scale of issues		Accomplished	Attainable / Challenging

In summary, UNESCO's performance as the *DESD lead agency* ranges between accomplished, attainable and challenging. According to the chosen regime criteria, UNESCO performs best in the effective implementation, monitoring and co-ordination of *DESD*. Promising action has been undertaken in ensuring compliance and providing evidence for UNESCO's institutional power. UNESCO's leadership role has been more contrastive in the matters of efficiency, leadership and context. The topicality of *DESD* remains the sphere of activity most in need of attention, with the image, frequency, visibility and communication of *ESD* in particular need of attention. Ultimately, UNESCO's leadership role is not self-contained but instead highly interrelated with other processes in place. Indeed, because of its (non-)legal set-up and institutional structure, there has been significant stakeholder interdependence from the very launch of *DESD*. This may of course have complicated UNESCO's efforts.

3 Implications

Taking into conscious account the difficulties of taking a broad view, the question of what UNESCO's *lead-agency* mandate might possibly mean for global leadership mandates in general inevitably arises. What has been observed is the tendency towards institutionally-driven leadership mandates.[2415] These assignments may potentially serve to popularise the concept of *lead agency*. Consequently, on an international scale, leadership criteria shall be deemed high in demand.[2416]

An international *lead agency* may theoretically be defined in terms of seven, but still non-exhaustive, regime-related elements: effectiveness, efficiency, compliance, leadership, topicality, context, and power.[2417] Each item ought from a practical perspective to be *customised* to regime-specific requirements in order to guarantee explicit significance in explanation. Besides it is important to mention that these criteria originate from different but thoroughly interdisciplinary backgrounds. They incorporate quite different approaches both in theory and methodology, most notably addressing aspects and reconciling positions of public international law and political science, among others.[2418] The proposed catalogue may possibly serve as shining example of including them successfully into the respective framework of research.

2415 Cf. chapter VI 2.2 *Expertise* on page 132, chapter V 5 *Conclusion* on page 119, chapter VI 2.1 *Lead agency* on page 125, *Table 23* in chapter VII 14 *United Nations decades* on page 193.

2416 Cf. chapter III 2.8 *Conclusion* on page 69, chapter III 3 *Closing remarks* on page 70, chapter IV 2.2 *Criteria* on page 75, *Table 12* in chapter IV 2.3 *Overview* on page 84, and chapter VIII 2.2 *Monitoring* on page 247.

2417 See *Figure 107* on page 515.

2418 Examples of multiple sources applied in support of respective *lead agency* criteria: regime theory (effectiveness), theory of allocation (efficiency, context), game theory (compliance), rational choice (effectiveness, efficiency), management (leadership, power, topicality), (new) institutionalism (context, power), soft law (compliance, effectiveness), social (contract) theory (compliance, context, topicality, power), international political economy (compliance, effectiveness, power) etc.
Cf. chapter I 4 *Notion* on page 5.

Figure 107: General guidelines proposed for global leadership mandates[2419]

In a nutshell, these presented findings and implications support the following concluding theses:

1. The performance of globally acting *lead agencies* may be assessed by means of particular sets of criteria;
2. In doing so the adequately determined international organization's functional mandate serves as decisive basis for assessment and valuation;
3. A catalogue of criteria can be considered appropriate and conducive if it is theoretically grounded, science-based and coherently deduced in terms of methodology;
4. Results of organizational topic-related advocacy must be considered in a differentiated way and tend to deviate from established normative standards of evaluation; and

2419 The figure displays compiled characteristics and guidelines that are suggested for analysing and assessing global leadership mandates. Depending on the context each criterion may be subdivided, adapted and prioritised according to individual requirements.

5. There is noticeable tendency towards subject-bound and institution-driven mandates of leadership that increasingly require qualifying respective performances and rating related prospects of success.

4 Prospects

DESD is an ongoing process, and until 2014 UNESCO is expected to carry on work as its *lead agency*. Specific mechanisms of follow-up have not yet been scheduled. However, after 2015, *ESD* is likely to have several follow-up developments. Once recognised and established as a fundamental principle, *ESD* will certainly be respected and promoted by and integrated into multiple follow-up initiatives, programmes or further normative mechanisms. No one can seriously question the desirability of winning acceptance for the idea that *"(...) Education for Sustainable Development based on the interdependence of environment, economy, society and cultural diversity, is the key to a better and more just world of the 21st century".*[2420] In this respect, UNESCO's contribution to the leading of *DESD* at least constitutes the foundations on which future achievements will be based.

5 En guise de conclusion

Guided initially by the intentions of providing a comprehensive and general overview of the *United Nations Decade of Education for Sustainable Development* (2005–2014), and illustrating the focal points of regional implementation of the *United Nations Decade of Education for Sustainable Development* (2005–2014), the aims and objectives of the Decade could have been fulfilled. On the one hand, *DESD* has been introduced in its multi-faceted aspects alongside the UNESCO leadership mandate. On the other hand, this particular *lead-agency* mandate has been applied to the regional implementation practice of *DESD*.

To return to the overall research question of how UNESCO fulfills its leadership and co-ordination mandate as the *lead agency* in the course of *DESD*: yes, definitively UNESCO can be considered thoroughly qualified and has succeeded in making meaningful steps towards accomplishing the primary organisational assignment. Sure enough, the regional impacts vary noticeably in reality. Above all, these distortions between ambition and reality have been evidenced throughout the process of implementation. Relating *DESD* to UNESCO standard-setting and policy advice has been of ultimately minor significance. By contrast, much

2420 See Bokova, Irina (2009) (cf. *footnote 89* op. cit.).
See *Figure 108* on page 518.

more attention could have been paid to how monitoring processes may lead to particular mindsets and individual commitment towards *DESD*.

It was noted right at the beginning that Albert Einstein claimed to *"never think of the future. It comes soon enough"*.[2421] UNESCO's efforts have been right in drawing attitudes towards the opposite conviction. It is because of *ESD* that one might feasibly profess to be *"more interested in the future than the past, because that's where I am thinking of living"*. Einstein's insights obviously require some refinement in order to resolve these obvious contradictions. UNESCO's reply would be unambiguously clear: in the final reckoning, it is behaviour now and in the future that matters.

2421 Cf. chapter I 1 *Preface* on page 1.

Figure 108: Successfully paving the way for future steps on DESD[2422]

2422 This is part of an image campaign expressing the progress on *ESD* as well as the firm and *fail-safe* guidance that is directed towards sustainable development. See UNESCO (ed.) (2007k) (cf. *footnote 4* op. cit.), p. 7.

Bibliography

Monographs and authored books

Alvarez, José Enrique (2006): International organizations as law-makers. Oxford: Oxford University Press.

Aust, Anthony (2006): Handbook of international law. Volume Reprint. Cambridge: Cambridge University Press.

Bartholomäi, Reinhard (1997): Sustainable Development und Völkerrecht. Nachhaltige Entwicklung und intergenerative Gerechtigkeit in der Staatenpraxis. Baden-Baden: Nomos Verlagsgesellschaft (Gießener Abhandlungen zum Umweltrecht, 2).

Blaze Corcoran, Peter; Maathai, Wangari (2005): The Earth Charter in action. Amsterdam: KIT Publishers BV.

Bleckmann, Albert (1982): Grundprobleme und Methoden des Völkerrechts. Freiburg im Breisgau / München: Alber Verlag (Kolleg Rechtstheorie, Sonderband 1).

Bohnsack, Ralf (2007): Rekonstruktive Sozialforschung. Einführung in qualitative Methoden. Volume 6. durchgesehene und aktualisierte Auflage. Opladen: Verlag Barbara Budrich (UTB Erziehungswissenschaft Sozialwissenschaft, 8242).

Boyle, Bill; Christie, Tom (1996): Issues in setting standards. Establishing comparabilities. London: Routledge Falmer.

Breitmeier, Helmut; Young, Oran R.; Zürn, Michael (2006): Analyzing international environmental regimes. From case study to database. Cambridge, Massachusetts: MIT Press (Global Environmental Accord: Strategies for Sustainability and Institutional Innovation).

Brownlie, Ian (2002): Principles of public international law. Volume 5. edition, reprinted. Oxford: Clarendon Press.

Burgstaller, Markus (2005): Theories of compliance with international law. Leiden: Martinus Nijhoff Publishers; Brill Academic Publishers (Developments in International Law, 52).

Carson, Rachel (1962 / 2002): Silent spring. Volume 40th anniversary edition / 1st Mariner Books edition. Boston: Houghton Mifflin.

Choucri, Nazli (1995): Global accord. Environmental challenges and international responses. Volume 1. paperback edition. Cambridge, Massachusetts: MIT Press (Global Environmental Accord: Strategies for Sustainability and Institutional Innovation).

Cizek, Gregory J. (2001): Setting performance standards. Concepts, methods, and perspectives. Mahwah, New Jersey: Lawrence Erlbaum Associates.

Cizek, Gregory J.; Bunch, Michael B. (2006): Standard setting. A guide to establishing and evaluating performance standards on tests. Thousand Oaks, California: SAGE Publications.

Conforti, Benedetto (1995): Diritto internazionale. Volume 4. edizione, ristampa (con aggiornamenti). Napoli / Padova: Edizione Scientifica (Diritto internazionale, 16).

Cropley, Arthur J. (2005): Qualitative Forschungsmethoden. Eine praxisnahe Einführung. Volume 2. überarbeitete Auflage. Eschborn bei Frankfurt am Main: Klotz.

Deppermann, Arnulf (2001): Gespräche analysieren. Eine Einführung. Volume 2. durchgesehene Auflage. Opladen: Leske & Budrich (Qualitative Sozialforschung, 3).

Dicke, Klaus (1994): Effizienz und Effektivität internationaler Organisationen. Darstellung und kritische Analyse eines Topos im Reformprozeß der Vereinten Nationen. Berlin / Kiel: Duncker & Humblot (VIIR 116).

Dicke, Klaus; Hüfner, Klaus (1987): Die Leistungsfähigkeit des VN-Systems. Politische Kritik und wissenschaftliche Analyse. Bonn: Deutsche Gesellschaft für die Vereinten Nationen; UNO-Verlag (UN-Texte, 37).

Dietz, Hella (1998): Der soziologische Neo-Institutionalismus von James G. March und Johan P. Olsen. Auf dem Weg zur eigenständigen Methodologie oder Katalysator und Korrektiv für gegenwärtige politikwissenschaftliche Theorien? Semesterarbeit WS 1997 / 1998. Supervised by: Wiesenthal, Helmut. Berlin. Humboldt-Universität Berlin, Fachbereich Sozialwissenschaften. Available online: http://www.hwiesenthal.de/public/div/dietz/Institutionalismus.txt [Accessed on 19/05/2009].

Doehring, Karl (1999): Völkerrecht. Ein Lehrbuch. Heidelberg: C. F. Müller Verlag.

Doehring, Karl (2004): Völkerrecht. Ein Lehrbuch. Volume 2. neubearbeitete Auflage. Heidelberg: C. F. Müller Verlag (Großes Lehrbuch).

Fischer-Lescano, Andreas; Teubner, Gunther (2006): Regime-Kollisionen. Zur Fragmentierung des globalen Rechts. Volume Originalausgabe. Frankfurt am Main: Suhrkamp (Suhrkamp Taschenbuch Wissenschaft, 1803).

Flick, Uwe (2006): Qualitative Sozialforschung. Eine Einführung. Volume 4. Auflage, vollständig überarbeitet und erweiterte Neuausgabe. Reinbek bei Hamburg: Rowohlt-Taschenbuch-Verlag (Rororo Rowohlts Enzyklopädie, 55654).

Fridtjof Nansens Institutt / The Fridtjof Nansens Institute (ed.) (2005): The Commission on Sustainable Development. A Study of Institutional Design, Distribution of Capabilities and Entrepreneurial Leadership. Edited by Stine Madland Kaasa. Lysaker: Fridtjof Nansen Institute (FNI report, 5).

Frigerio, Graciela; Diker, Gabriela (Junio 2008): Infancia y derechos: las raíces de la sostenibilidad. Aportes para un porvenir. Santiago de Chile: Andros Ltda.

Gehring, Thomas (2002): Die Europäische Union als komplexe internationale Organisation. Wie durch Kommunikation und Entscheidung soziale Ordnung entsteht. Volume 1. Auflage. Baden-Baden: Nomos Verlagsgesellschaft.

Gerner, Martin (2008): Global Governance und Internationales Ressourcenmanagment – aktuelle Aspekte, Entwicklung und Herausforderungen. Seminar paper. Supervised by: Schorlemer, Sabine von. Dresden. Technische Universität Dresden, Juristische Fakultät / Lehrstuhl für Völkerrecht, Recht der EU und Internationale Beziehungen. Available online: http://www.sef-bonn.org/download/veranstaltungen/2007/2007_abschluss_ressourcen_paper_Martin_Gerner_de.pdf [Accessed on 10/12/2010].

Guzman, Andrew T. (2008): How international law works. A rational choice theory. New York: Oxford University Press.

Hasse, Raimund; Krücken, Georg (2005): Neo-Institutionalismus. Volume 2. vollständig überarbeitete Auflage. Bielefeld: Transcript-Verlag.

Heusel, Wolfgang (1991): "Weiches" Völkerrecht. Eine vergleichende Untersuchung typischer Erscheinungsformen. Volume 1. Auflage. Baden-Baden: Nomos Verlagsgesellschaft.

Hobe, Stephan; Kimminich, Otto (2004): Einführung in das Völkerrecht. Volume 8. vollständig neu bearbeitete und erweiterte Auflage. Tübingen / Basel: A. Francke Verlag.

Hoof, G. J. H. (Fried) van (1983): Rethinking the sources of international law. Deventer / Boston / Frankfurt am Main: Kluwer Law and Taxation Publishers.

Hörtreiter, Isabel (2007): Die Vereinten Nationen und Wirtschaftsunternehmen – zwischen Kooperation und Kontrolle. Steuerungsformen zur Stärkung menschenrechtlicher Unternehmensverantwortung unter dem Dach der Vereinten Nationen. Frankfurt am Main: Peter Lang GmbH.

Inglis, Christine (2008): Planning for cultural diversity. Paris: UNESCO publishing (Fundamentals of Educational Planning, 87).

Institut international de planification de l'éducation (IIPE) (ed.) (2009): Former des acteurs du développement durable. Les défis relevés par le Pôle Développement Durable des Chaires UNESCO en France. Edited by Patrick Blandin. Paris: UNESCO workshops.

Ipsen, Knut; Menzel, Eberhard; Epping, Volker (2004): Völkerrecht. Volume 5. völlig neu bearbeitete Auflage. München: Verlag C. H. Beck.

Jones, Phillip Worner; Coleman, David (2005): The United Nations and education. Multilateralism, development and globalisation. London / New York: Routledge Falmer.

Kailitz, Steffen (2007): Schlüsselwerke der Politikwissenschaft. James G. March / Johan P. Olsen, Rediscovering Institutions. The Organizational Basis of Politics, New York / London 1989. pp. 278–281. Wiesbaden: VS Verlag für Sozialwissenschaften; GWV Fachverlage GmbH Wiesbaden (SpringerLink).

Klabbers, Jan (1996 / 1998): The concept of treaty in international law. The Hague: Kluwer Law International.

Krajewski, Markus (2006): Wirtschaftsvölkerrecht. Heidelberg: C. F. Müller Verlag.

Kremser, Holger (1996): "Soft Law" der UNESCO und Grundgesetz. Dargestellt am Beispiel der Mediendeklaration. Frankfurt am Main / New York: Peter Lang GmbH (Schriften zum internationalen und zum öffentlichen Recht, 10).

Kuhn, Katina (März 2006): Zur kulturellen Dimension nachhaltiger Entwicklung – Eine metatheoretische und diskursanalytische Bestandsaufnahme. INFU-Diskussionsbeiträge 28/06. Supervised by: Michelsen, Gerd; Adomßent, Maik; Barth, Matthias and Godemann, Jasmin. Lüneburg. Universität Lüneburg / University of Lüneburg, Institut für Umweltkommunikation (INFU). Available online: http://www.leuphana.de/fileadmin/user_upload/Forschungseinrichtungen/infu/files/pdf/infu-reihe/28_06_000.pdf [Accessed on 22/06/2010].

Lamnek, Siegfried (2005): Qualitative Sozialforschung. Lehrbuch. Volume 4. vollständig überarbeitete Auflage. Weinheim: Beltz-Verlag (Beltz-PVU).

Leicht, Alexander; Plum, Jacqueline; Fuchs, Max (2007): Kulturelle Bildung für nachhaltige Entwicklung. Sankt Augustin / Berlin: Konrad-Adenauer-Stiftung (IM PLENUM).

Lind, Agneta (2009): Literacy for all. Making a difference. Paris: UNESCO publishing (Fundamentals of Educational Planning, 89).

López Ospina, Gustavo (2003): Planetary Sustainability in the Age of the Information and Knowledge Society. For a Sustainable World and Future. Working toward 2015. ED-2004/WS/15. Paris / Quito: UNESCO publishing.

López Ospina, Gustavo (2005): Construcción de un futuro sostenible. Década de una educación por un desarrollo sostenible 2005–2014. Volume Primera edición. Quito: UNESCO publishing.

Mahler, Claudia; Mihr, Anja; Toivanen, Reetta (2009): The United Nations Decade for Human Rights Education and the inclusion of national minorities. Volume 1. Auflage. Frankfurt am Main: Peter Lang Publishing Incorporation.

March, James G.; Olsen, Johan P. (1989): Rediscovering Institutions. The organizational basic of politics. Volume 1.edition, 3. print. New York: Free Press.

Mayring, Philipp (2002): Einführung in die qualitative Sozialforschung. Eine Anleitung zu qualitativem Denken. Volume 5. überarbeitete und neu ausgestattete Auflage. Weinheim: Beltz-Verlag (Beltz Studium).

Nelson, Jane (2002): Building partnerships. Cooperation between the United Nations system and the private sector. New York: UN Department of Public Information; United Nations Publications.

North, Douglass Cecil (1990 / 2007): Institutions, institutional change and economic performance. Volume 24. print. Cambridge: Cambridge University Press (Political Economy of Institutions and Decisions).

North, Richard D. (2005): Sustainable Development: A concept with a Future? Volume First Edition. Berlin: Comdok GmbH (OccasionalPaper, 11).

Novak Talavera, Fabián; García Corrochano Moyano, Luis (2000): Derecho Internacional Público. Introducción y fuentes. Volume 1. edición. Lima: Pontificia Universidad Católica del Perú Fondo Editorial (Derecho internacional público / Fabián Novak Talavera Luis García-Corrochano Moyano, Tomo I).

Novak Talavera, Fabián; García Corrochano Moyano, Luis (2001): Derecho Internacional Público. Sujetos de derecho internacional. Volume 1. edición. Lima: Pontificia Universidad Católica del Perú Fondo Editorial (Derecho internacional público / Fabián Novak Talavera Luis García-Corrochano Moyano, Tomo II, Volumen I).

Novak Talavera, Fabián; García Corrochano Moyano, Luis (2002): Derecho Internacional Público. Sujetos de derecho internacional. Volume 1. edición. Lima: Pontificia Universidad Católica del Perú Fondo Editorial (Derecho internacional público / Fabián Novak Talavera Luis García-Corrochano Moyano, Tomo II, Volumen II).

Peters, Brainard Guy (2005): Institutional theory in political science. The 'new institutionalism'. Volume 2. edition. London: Continuum.

Rutherford, Malcolm (1994 / 2008): Institutions in Economics. The Old and the New Institutionalism. Volume Reprint. Cambridge: Cambridge University Press (Historical Perspectives in Modern Economics).

Rychen, Dominique Simone; Salganik, Laura Hersh (2001): Defining and selecting key competencies. Seattle: Hogrefe & Huber; Key DeSeCo publications.

Rychen, Dominique Simone; Salganik, Laura Hersh (2003): Key competencies for a successful life and a well-functioning society. Cambridge, Massachusetts: Hogrefe & Huber; Key DeSeCo publications.

Schneider, Volker; Janning, Frank (2006): Politikfeldanalyse. Akteure, Diskurse und Netzwerke in der öffentlichen Politik. Wiesbaden: VS Verlag für Sozialwissenschaften; GWV Fachverlage GmbH Wiesbaden (Springer-11776 [Dig. Serial]).

Schröder, Peter (2011): Politische Strategien. Potsdam: Friedrich-Naumann-Stiftung für die Freiheit.

Schweisfurth, Theodor (2006): Völkerrecht. Tübingen: Mohr Siebeck.

Scott, William A. H.; Gough, Stephen R. (2003): Sustainable development and learning. Framing the issues. Volume 1. edition. London / New York: Routledge Falmer.

Scott, William Richard (Dick) (2001): Institutions and organizations. Volume 2nd edition. Thousand Oaks, California: SAGE Publications.

Scott, William Richard (Dick) (2008): Institutions and organizations. Ideas and interests. Volume 3rd edition. Los Angeles: SAGE Publications.

Senden, Linda (2004): Soft law in European Community law. Oxford: Hart Publishing (Modern studies in European law, 1).

Shaw, Malcolm N. (2008): International Law. Volume 6th edition. Cambridge UK / New York: Cambridge University Press.

Sloan, Blaine (1991): United Nations General Assembly resolutions in our changing world. Ardsley-on-Hudson, New York: Transnational Publishers; Brill Academic Publishers.

Soubbotina, Tatyana P. (2004): Beyond economic growth. An introduction to sustainable development. HD75.S684 2000. Volume 2. edition. Supported by: Sheram, Katherine A. Washington, D. C.: World Bank (WBI learning resources series).

Strati, Antonio (2000): Theory and method in organization studies. Paradigms and choices. London: SAGE Publications.

Strauss, Anselm Leonard (1987): Grundlagen qualitativer Sozialforschung. Datenanalyse und Theoriebildung in der empirischen soziologischen Forschung. Volume 2. Auflage. München: Fink, 1998 (UTB für Wissenschaft, 1776, Soziologie).

Symonides, Janusz; Volodin, Vladimir (1996): UNESCO and Human Rights. Standard-Setting Instruments Major Meetings Publications. Selection of documents and introduction SHS-96/WS/8. Supported by: Rivet, Sophie. Paris: UNESCO workshops.

The World Conservation Union (IUCN); United Nations Environment Programme (UNEP); World Wide Fund For Nature (WWF) (1991): Caring for the earth. A strategy for sustainable living. Gland, Switzerland: The World Conservation Union (IUCN) (IUCN Strategies For Sustainable Development Handbook Series).

UNESCO (2007n): Conventions, Recommendations, Declarations and Charters adopted by UNESCO (1948–2006). Paris / Leiden: UNESCO publishing; Martinus Nijhoff Publishers (UNESCO reference works series, 2).

United Nations (ed.) (1993): Agenda 21. United Nations Conference on Environment and Development (UNCED), 3–14 June 1992, Rio de Janeiro, Brazil. A/CONF.151/26/Rev.1(Vol.I). Volume 1993. New York: UN Department of Public Information (1).

United Nations; Brundtland, Gro Harlem (1991): Our common future. (In 1987 published and transmitted to UN General Assembly as annex to document A/42/42). Volume 13. imprint. Oxford: Oxford University Press (Oxford paperbacks).

Verdross, Alfred; Simma, Bruno (1984 / 2010): Universelles Völkerrecht. Theorie und Praxis. Volume 3. Auflage, unveränderter Nachdruck. Berlin: Duncker & Humblot.

Victor, David G.; Raustiala, Kal; Skolnikoff, Eugene (1998): The implementation and effectiveness of international environmental commitments. Theory and practice. Cambridge, Massachusetts: MIT Press.

Walgenbach, Peter; Meyer, Renate E. (2008): Neoinstitutionalistische Organisationstheorie. Stuttgart: Kohlhammer.

Weiss, Edith Brown (2000): Engaging countries. Strengthening compliance with international environmental accords. Volume 1. paperback edition. Cambridge, Massachusetts: MIT Press.

Young, Oran R. (1999b): Governance in world affairs. Ithaca, New York: Cornell University Press.

Edited volumes and collections

Adomßent, Maik; Henze, Christa (eds.) (2007): UN Decade of Education for Sustainable Development – The Contribution from Europe. Conference Report. Documentation of the International Conference in the context of the German Presidency of the Council of the European Union. Berlin, 24–25 May 2007. Bonn: Bonner Universitäts-Buchdruckerei.

Altner, Günter; Michelsen, Gerd (eds.) (2005): Baustelle Hochschule. Nachhaltigkeit als neues Fundament für Lehre und Forschung. München: oekom Verlag (Politische Ökologie, 93).

Armstrong, David; Brunée, Jutta (eds.) (2009): Routledge Handbook of International Law. London: Routledge (Routledge International Handbooks).

Atteslander, Peter; Cromm, Jürgen (eds.) (2003): Methoden der empirischen Sozialforschung. Volume 10. neu bearbeitete und erweiterte Auflage. Berlin: de Gruyter (De-Gruyter-Studienbuch).

Australian Research Institute in Education for Sustainability (ARIES); Macquarie University Sydney; Australian Government Department of the Environment and Water Resources (eds.) (2006): Development of a National Approach to Monitoring, Assessment and Reporting on the Decade of Education for Sustainable Development. Summarising Documented Experiences on the Development of ESD Indicators and Networking with Expert Groups on ESD Indicators. Sydney: Photospin.

Austrian Federal Ministry for Education, the Arts and Culture (BMUKK) (ed.) (2006): Resolution adopted by the participants of the EU Presidency Conference on "ESD towards responsible Global Citizenship". Vienna, 13–15 March 2006. Vienna.

Barton C., Jonathan R.; Jordán F., Ricardo; León A., Silvia Mabel, et al. (eds.) (Diciembre 2007): Cuán sustentable es la Región Metropolitana de Santiago? Metodologías de evaluación de la sustentabilidad. Documento del Proyecto/LC/W.170. Santiago de Chile: Naciones Unidas (CEPAL – Colección Documentos de proyectos).

Bauer, Steffen; Biermann, Frank (eds.) (2004): Partners or Competitors? Policy Integration for Sustainable Development between United Nations Agencies. The Case of the United Nations Environment Programme and the United Nations Development Programme. 2004 Berlin Conference on the Human Dimensions of Global Environmental Change: Greening of Policies-Interlinkages and Policy Integration. Berlin.

Becker, Egon; Jahn, Thomas; Stieß, Immanuel, et al. (eds.) (1997): Sustainability: A Cross-Disciplinary Concept for Social Transformations. Paris / Frankfurt am Main: UNESCO publishing (Management of Social Transformation (MOST) Policy Papers, 6).

Bell, Imogen (ed.) (2002): Eastern Europe, Russia and Central Asia. Volume Third edition. London: Publications Office of the European Union / Europa Publications Ltd. (Regional Surveys of the World).

Bernecker, Roland; Leicht, Alexander (eds.) (1998): Kultur und Entwicklung. Zur Umsetzung des Stockholmer Aktionsplans. Bonn: Deutsche UNESCO-Kommission.

Bhola, Harbans S.; Valdivielso Gómez, Sofía (eds.) (2008): Signposts to literacy for sustainable development. Complementary studies. Supported by: Ouane, Adama. Hamburg: UNESCO Institute for Lifelong Learning.

Bodansky, Daniel; Brunée, Jutta; Hey, Ellen (eds.) (2007): The Oxford handbook of international environmental law. Oxford: Oxford University Press (Oxford handbooks).

Bohnsack, Ralf; Marotzki, Winfried; Meuser, Michael (eds.) (2006): Hauptbegriffe qualitativer Sozialforschung. Volume 2. Auflage. Opladen: Budrich (UTB Erziehungswissenschaft Sozialwissenschaft, 8226).

Centre for Environment and Sustainability (GMV); Chalmers University of Technology; University of Gothenburg (eds.) (2009): The Gothenburg Recommendations on Education for Sustainable Development. Adopted November 12, 2008. Edited by Pernilla Ottosson; Bo E. Samuelsson. Göteborg: Eskils Tryckeri.

Centre for Environment Education (CEE); South Asia Youth Environment Network (SAYEN) (eds.) (2007): Sustainable Development: An Introduction. Ahmedabad (Internship Series, Volume 1).

Chalkley, Brian; Haigh, Martin J.; Higgitt, David (eds.) (2009): Education for sustainable development. Papers in honour of the United Nations Decade of Education for Sustainable Development (2005–2014). London / New York: Routledge.

COMHAR Sustainable Development Council; ECO-UNESCO (eds.) (2007): Education for Sustainable Development in Ireland. Research Project compiled by ECO-UNESCO. Research Project on ESD commissioned by COMHAR SDC and undertaken by ECO-UNESCO. Edited by Elaine Nevin; Derek Ginnetty. Dublin: ECO-UNESCO.

Council of Ministers of Education, Canada; Environment Canada; Canadian Commission for UNESCO (eds.) (2007): Report to UNECE and UNESCO on Indicators of Education for Sustainable Development. Report for Canada. Prepared by the Council of Ministers of Education, Canada in collaboration with Environment Canada and The Canadian Commission for UNESCO. Ottawa: UNESCO Canada.

Council of the European Union (ed.) (2006): Renewed Sustainable Development Strategy. Review of the EU Sustainable Development Strategy (EU SDS) – Renewed Strategy. 10917/06. Brussels: Publications Office of the European Union / Europa Publications Ltd.

Deutsche UNESCO-Kommission e. V. (DUK) (ed.) (2003a): Nachhaltigkeit lernen: Hamburger Erklärung der Deutschen UNESCO-Kommission zur Dekade der Vereinten Nationen "Bildung für nachhaltige Entwicklung" (2005–2014). Bonn: Deutsche UNESCO-Kommission.

Deutsche UNESCO-Kommission e. V. (DUK) (ed.) (2007): Education for Sustainable Development Worldwide. Conference Report. International Workshop on the UN Decade of Education for Sustainable Development. 28–29 November 2006, Bonn. Edited by Alexander Leicht; Charlotte Schmitz; Lina Franken. Bonn: Deutsche UNESCO-Kommission / German Commission for UNESCO.

Deutscher Bundestag (ed.) (1998): Konzept Nachhaltigkeit. Vom Leitbild zur Umsetzung = The concept of sustainability. Abschlußbericht der Enquete-Kommission "Schutz des Menschen und der Umwelt – Ziele und Rahmenbedingungen einer nachhaltig zukunftsverträglichen Entwicklung" des 13. Deutschen Bundestages. Bonn / Berlin: Deutscher Bundestag Referat Öffentlichkeitsarbeit (Drucksache 13/11200, 98,4).

Dyroff, Hans-Dieter (ed.) (1994): Weltdekade für kulturelle Entwicklung (1988–1997). Deutsche Beiträge. Bonn: Deutsche UNESCO-Kommission.

Elias, Derek; Sachathep, Karampreet (eds.) (2009): ESD Currents: Changing Perspectives from the Asia-Pacific. ESD/09/OS/002-1000. Bangkok: UNESCO publishing.

European Commission (ed.) (1999): Bologna Declaration. On the European space for higher education. Bologna / Brussels: Publications Office of the European Union / Europa Publications Ltd.

European Commission; Secretariat-General (eds.) (2008a): A sustainable future in our hands. A Guide to the EU's Sustainable Development Strategy. Brussels: Publications Office of the European Union / Europa Publications Ltd.

European Commission; Secretariat-General (eds.) (2008b): Progress on EU Sustainable Development Strategy. Final Report. Brussels / Rotterdam: ECORYS Nederland BV.

Evans, Malcolm David (ed.) (2006): International Law. Volume 2. edition. Oxford: Oxford University Press.

Federal Ministry for Education, Culture and Science; KulturKontakt Austria (eds.) (2006): Promoting Cultural Education in Europe. A Contribution to Participation, Innovation and Quality. European Specialist Conference in the Framework of the 2006 Austrian EU Presidency. Conference Report. Graz, 8–10 June 2006. Graz.

Federal Ministry of Education and Research (BMBF) (ed.) (2002): Report of the Federal Government on education for a sustainable development. Translation of Bundestag document No. 14/7971 from January 3, 2002. Bonn: BMBF Publik.

Federal Ministry of Education and Research (BMBF) (ed.) (2006): Research for Sustainability. Framework programme of the German Federal Ministry of Education and Research (BMBF) for a sustainable, innovative society. Berlin: BMBF Publik.

Flick, Uwe; Kardorff, Ernst von; Steinke, Ines (eds.) (2005): Qualitative Forschung. Ein Handbuch. Reinbek bei Hamburg: Rowohlt-Taschenbuch-Verlag (Rororo Rowohlts Enzyklopädie, 55628).

Foreign Office of the Federal Republic of Germany / German Commission for UNESCO (ed.) (2007): The Role of UNESCO. Contribution to the Debate by Germany. Berlin / Bonn: Gebrüder Kopp.

Forum for the Future; Higher Education Partnership for Sustainability (HEPS) (eds.) (2004): Learning and skills for sustainable development. Developing a sustainability literate society. Guidance for Higher Education Institutions. Edited by Fiona Brookes; Elizabeth White. London: Severnprint.

Gallopin, Gilberto (ed.) (March 2003): A systems approach to sustainability and sustainable development. LC/L.1864-P/I. Santiago de Chile: Naciones Unidas (medio ambiente y desarrollo, 64).

Goncalves G., María Paola (ed.) (1998): A Cultural Decade. Reflections on the World Decade for Cultural Development 1988–1997. CLT-98AVSI8. Paris: UNESCO publishing (Studies and Reports of the Unit of Cultural Research and Management, 5).

Haddad, Caroline (ed.) (2005): A Situational Analysis of Education for Sustainable Development in the Asia-Pacific Region. ESD/05/OP/396-1000. Volume Revised Edition. Supported by: Elias, Derek; Nakayama, Shuichi and Hargreaves, Lucy. Bangkok: UNESCO publishing.

Hafner, Gerhard; Seidl-Hohenveldern, Ignaz (eds.) (1998): Liber amicorum Professor Ignaz Seidl-Hohenveldern. In honour of his 80th birthday. Supported by: Rest, Alfred; Hafner, Gerhard and Loibl, Gerhard et al. The Hague: Kluwer Law International.

Hasenclever, Andreas; Rittberger, Volker (eds.) (2007): Macht und Ohnmacht internationaler Institutionen. Festschrift für Volker Rittberger. Frankfurt am Main: Campus Verlag.

Hirmas R., Carolina; Blanco, Rosa (eds.) (2008a): Educación y diversidad cultural. Lecciones desde la práctica innovadora en América Latina. Santiago de Chile: UNESCO Santiago; Pehuén Editores (Colección Innovemos, 2).

Hirmas R., Carolina; Eroles, Daniela (eds.) (2008b): Convivencia democrática, inclusión y cultura de paz: Lecciones desde la práctica educativa innovadora en América Latina. Edited by Rosa Blanco. Santiago de Chile: UNESCO Santiago; Pehuén Editores; Salesianos Impresores S.A. (Colección Innovemos, III).

Hüfner, Klaus; Reuther, Wolfgang (eds.) (2005): UNESCO-Handbuch. Volume Neuausgabe, 2. Auflage. Bonn: UNO-Verlag.

Jachtenfuchs, Markus; Knodt, Michèle (eds.) (2002): Regieren in internationalen Institutionen. Festschrift für Beate Kohler-Koch. Opladen: Leske & Budrich.

Kälin, Walter; Baldegger, Mirjam (eds.) (2006): Völkerrecht. Eine Einführung. Volume 2. Auflage. Bern: Stämpfli.

Keohane, Robert O. (ed.) (1989): International institutions and state power. Essays in international relations theory. Boulder: Westview Press.

Kirton, John J.; Trebilcock, Michael J. (eds.) (2004): Hard choices, soft law. Voluntary standards in global trade, environment, and social governance. Aldershot / Burlington, Vermont: Ashgate Dartmouth (Global environmental governance).

Koch, Sascha; Schemmann, Michael; Göhlich, Michael (eds.) (2009): Neo-Institutionalismus in der Erziehungswissenschaft. Grundlegende Texte und empirische Studien. Organisation und Pädagogik 6. Volume 1. Auflage. Wiesbaden: VS Verlag für Sozialwissenschaften.

Konrad-Adenauer-Stiftung (ed.) (2005): Diálogo Político. Educación y pobreza. Publicación trimestral de la Konrad-Adenauer-Stiftung A. C. Buenos Aires (Diálogo Político, N° 4 – Diciembre, 2005).

Konrad-Adenauer-Stiftung (ed.) (2007): Diálogo Político. Regulación de los medios. Publicación trimestral de la Konrad-Adenauer-Stiftung A. C. Buenos Aires (Diálogo Político, N° 3 – Septiembre, 2007).

Koskenniemi, Martti (ed.) (2007): Sources of international law. Volume Reprinted. Aldershot: Ashgate Dartmouth (The Library of Essays in International Law, 5).

Krasner, Stephen D. (ed.) (2004): International regimes. Volume 11. print. Ithaca, New York: Cornell University Press.

Lecours, André (ed.) (2005): New Institutionalism. Theory and Analysis. Toronto / Buffalo / Toronto: University of Toronto Press (Studies in Comparative Political Economy and Public Policy, 23).

Lowe, Vaughan; Fitzmaurice, Malgosia (eds.) (1996 / 2008): Fifty years of the International Court of Justice. Essays in honour of Sir Robert Jennings. Cambridge: Cambridge University Press; Grotius Publications.

Maclean, Rupert; Fien, John; Park, Man-Gon (eds.) (2009): Work, Learning and Sustainable Development. Opportunities and Challenges. Dordrecht: Springer Netherlands (Springer-11648 [Dig. Serial], 8).

Messina, Graciela; Pieck, Enrique; Castañeda, Elsa (eds.) (2008): Educación y Trabajo. Lecciones desde la práctica innovadora en América Latina. Edited by Elvia María Acuña. Santiago de Chile: UNESCO Santiago (Colección Innovemos, I).

Meyer, Heinz-Dieter (ed.) (2006): The new institutionalism in education. Albany, New York: State University of New York Press.

Miles, Edward L. (ed.) (2002): Environmental regime effectiveness. Confronting theory with evidence. Cambridge, Massachusetts: MIT Press (Global Environmental Accord: Strategies for Sustainability and Institutional Innovation).

Möllers, Christoph; Vosskuhle, Andreas; Walter, Christian (eds.) (2007): Internationales Verwaltungsrecht. Tübingen: Mohr Siebeck (Jus internationale et Europaeum, 16).

Morris, Julian (ed.) (2002): Sustainable Development. Promoting progress or perpetuating poverty? London: Profile Books Ltd.

Mörth, Ulrika (ed.) (2004): Soft law in governance and regulation. An interdisciplinary analysis. Cheltenham / Northampton: Edward Elgar Publishing.

Mutua, Makau (ed.) (2007): Standard Setting in Human Rights: Critique and Prognosis. Volume Paper No. 2007-013. New York: BUFFALO Legal Studies Research Paper Series (Human Rights Quarterly, Vol. 29).

NSW Ageing and Disability Department (ed.) (1998): Standards In Action Manual. Edited by Margarete Verick; Deborah Fullwood. Sydney: Ageing and Disability Department.

Oficina Regional de Educación de la UNESCO para América Latina y el Caribe (OREALC) (2008a): El Monitoreo y la Evaluación Mundial de la Ejecución de la Actividades del DEDS. Directrices para la respuesta al cuestionario. Published by: UNESCO. Oficina Regional de Educación de la UNESCO para América Latina y el Caribe (OREALC). Santiago de Chile.

Oficina Regional de Educación de la UNESCO para América Latina y el Caribe (OREALC) (ed.) (2008): Estrategias de comunicación y educación para el desarrollo sostenible. Edited by David Solano. Santiago de Chile.

Oficina Regional de Educación de la UNESCO para América Latina y el Caribe (OREALC) (2008b): Marco Mundial de Monitoreo y la Evaluación de la Ejecución de las Actividades del DEDS. Glosario para la untilización del cuestionario. Published by: UNESCO. Oficina Regional de Educación de la UNESCO para América Latina y el Caribe (OREALC). Santiago de Chile.

Oficina Regional de Educación de la UNESCO para América Latina y el Caribe (OREALC) (2008c): Marco Mundial de Monitoreo y la Evaluación de la Ejecución de las Actividades del DEDS. Contexto y Estructura del la Educación para el Desrrollo Sostenible (EDS) en los estados miembros. Cuestionario 1. Published by:

UNESCO. Oficina Regional de Educación de la UNESCO para América Latina y el Caribe (OREALC). Santiago de Chile.

Oficina Regional de Educación de la UNESCO para América Latina y el Caribe (OREALC) (ed.) (2009a): Educación para la paz, la convivencia democrática y los derechos humanos. San José de Costa Rica 24 al 28 de Noviembre 2008. Santiago de Chile: Salesianos Impresores S.A. (Jornadas de Cooperación, III).

Oficina Regional de Educación de la UNESCO para América Latina y el Caribe (OREALC) (ed.) (2009b): Políticas, estrategias y planes regionales, subregionales y nacionales en educación para el desarrollo sostenible y la educación ambiental en América Latina y el Caribe. Decenio de las Naciones Unidas de la Educación para el Desarrollo Sostenible 2005–2014. OREALC/2009/PI/H/2. Edited by Carol Salgado; Eloísa Tréllez Solís. Santiago de Chile: UNESCO Santiago.

Oficina Regional de Educación de la UNESCO para América Latina y el Caribe (OREALC) (ed.) (2010): Activity Review 2009. OREALC/2010/PI/H/1. Santiago de Chile: UNESCO Santiago.

Oficina Regional de Educación de la UNESCO para América Latina y el Caribe (OREALC); innovemos – Red Regional de Innovaciones Educativas; Organización de Estados Iberoamericanos para la Educación, la Ciencia y la Cultura (OEI) (eds.) (2009a): Experiencias educativas de segunda oportunidad. Lecciones desde la práctica innovadora en América Latina. Edited by Rosa Blanco. Santiago de Chile: SDL impresores (Colección Innovemos, IV).

Oficina Regional de Educación de la UNESCO para América Latina y el Caribe (OREALC); MInisterio de Educación Chile (MINEDUC) (eds.) (2009b): Re-creo mi Identidad. Las Guías de Actividades Patrimoniales. Edited by Francisca Gallegos; Genoveva Moncada; Patricia Gallardo. Santiago de Chile: UNESCO Santiago.

Oficina Regional de Educación de la UNESCO para América Latina y el Caribe (OREALC); UNESCO (eds.) (2004): Educación para el Desarrollo Sostenible. Edited by Daniel Gil-Pérez; Amparo Vilches. Santiago de Chile: UNESCO Santiago.

Oficina Regional de Educación de la UNESCO para América Latina y el Caribe (OREALC); UNESCO (eds.) (2005a): Decenio de las Naciones Unidas de la Educación para el Desarrollo Sostenible 2005–2014. Plan de Applicación Internacional. Proyecto. Santiago de Chile: UNESCO Santiago.

Oficina Regional de Educación de la UNESCO para América Latina y el Caribe (OREALC); UNESCO (eds.) (2005b): Plan educativo regional para el Desarrollo sostenible. Edited by Beatriz Macedo. Santiago de Chile: UNESCO Santiago.

Organización de Estados Iberoamericanos para la Educación, la Ciencia y la Cultura (OEI) (ed.) (2006a): Educación para el desarrollo sostenible I. Década de la Educación para un Futuro Sostenible (2005–2014): un punto de inflexión necesario en la atención a la situación del planeta. Edited by José Gutiérrez Pérez; Teresa Pozo Llorente; Eloísa Tréllez Solís. Madrid: Servicio de Publicaciones (Revista Iberoamericana de Educación, N° 40 I).

Organización de Estados Iberoamericanos para la Educación, la Ciencia y la Cultura (OEI) (ed.) (2006b): Educación para el desarrollo sostenible I. Década de la Educación para un Futuro Sostenible (2005–2014): un punto de inflexión necesario en la atención a la situación del planeta. Edited by José Gutiérrez Pérez; Teresa Pozo Llorente; Eloísa Tréllez Solís. Madrid: Servicio de Publicaciones (Revista Iberoamericana de Educación, N° 40 II).

Organización de Estados Iberoamericanos para la Educación, la Ciencia y la Cultura (OEI) (ed.) (2006c): Educación para el desarrollo sostenible II. Edited by José Gutiérrez Pérez; Teresa Pozo Llorente; Eloísa Tréllez Solís. Madrid: Servicio de Publicaciones (Revista Iberoamericana de Educación, N° 41).

Organización de Estados Iberoamericanos para la Educación, la Ciencia y la Cultura (OEI) (ed.) (2007): Construyendo una Educación para el Desarrollo Sostenible en América Latina y el Caribe. Estrategia Regional. Madrid / San José / Paris: UNESCO Santiago; Servicio de Publicaciones.

Organización de Estados Iberoamericanos para la Educación, la Ciencia y la Cultura (OEI); Instituto Internacional de Planeamiento de la Educación (IIPE); UNESCO (eds.) (2006): Informe sobre las Tendencias sociales y educativas en America Latina. 2006. Edited by Néstor Lopez. Paris / Buenos Aires / Madrid: UNESCO publishing; Servicio de Publicaciones; Talleres Trama S.A.

Organización de Estados Iberoamericanos para la Educación, la Ciencia y la Cultura (OEI); Instituto Internacional de Planeamiento de la Educación (IIPE); UNESCO (eds.) (2007): Informe sobre las Tendencias sociales y educativas en America Latina. 2007. Paris / Buenos Aires / Madrid: UNESCO publishing; Servicio de Publicaciones; Talleres Trama S.A.

Organización de Estados Iberoamericanos para la Educación, la Ciencia y la Cultura (OEI); Instituto Internacional de Planeamiento de la Educación (IIPE); UNESCO (eds.) (2008): La escuela y los adolescentes. Informe sobre las Tendencias sociales y educativas en America Latina. 2008. Edited by Néstor Lopez. Paris / Buenos Aires / Madrid: UNESCO publishing; Servicio de Publicaciones; Talleres Trama S.A.

Organization for Economic Cooperation & Development (OECD) (ed.) (2005): The Definition and Selection of Key Competences. Executive Summary. Paris: Key DeSeCo publications.

Pérez Cuéllar, Javier de (ed.) (1995 / 1996): Our creative diversity. Report of the World Commission on Culture and Development. CLT-96/WS-6. Volume 2. edition, revised. Paris: UNESCO publishing.

Persson, Torsten (ed.) (1997): Nobel Lectures. Economic sciences. 1991–1995. Supported by: The Nobel Foundation. Singapore: World Scientific Publishing Company (Nobel lectures).

Pies, Ingo; Winning, Alexandra von (eds.) (2006): Die UN-Dekade "Bildung für eine nachhaltige Entwicklung" und der Beitrag des Global Compact. Eine wirtschaftsethische Perspektive. Halle an der Saale: Lehrstuhl für Wirtschaftsethik an der Martin-Luther-Universität Halle-Wittenberg; Universitäts- und Landesbibliothek Sachsen-Anhalt (Diskussionspapier / Lehrstuhl für Wirtschaftsethik, Martin-Luther-Universität Halle-Wittenberg, 06,5).

Pigozzi, Mary Joy (ed.) (1999): Education in Emergencies and for Reconstruction: A developmental approach. UNICEF/PD/ED/99-1. New York: UNICEF Programme Division Education (Working Paper Series).

Powell, Walter Woody; DiMaggio, Paul Joseph (eds.) (1991 / 2004 / 2008): The new institutionalism in organizational analysis. Volume Reprint. Chicago / London: University of Chicago Press.

Quiroga Martínez, Rayén (ed.) (Octubre 2007): El séptimo objetivo del Milenio en América Latina y el Caribe: avances al 2007. LC/L.2782-P/E. Edited by División de Estadistica y Protecciones Económicas. Santiago de Chile: Naciones Unidas (estudios estadísticos y prospectivos, 57).

Restrepo Arcila, Roberto Arturo (ed.) (2000): El vuelo de la serpiente. Desarrollo sostenible en la América prehispánica. Volume Primera edición. Santafé de Bogotá: Siglo del Hombre Editores.

Schuchardt, Erika; Mbeki, Thabo (eds.) (2005): Brückenbau: 15 Jahre Begegnungsschulen im Südlichen Afrika. Erfolgsmodell deutscher Auswärtiger Kulturpolitik. Berlin: IBA.

Senge, Konstanze; Hellmann, Kai-Uwe; Scott, William Richard (Dick) (eds.) (2006): Einführung in den Neo-Institutionalismus. Volume 1. Auflage. Wiesbaden: VS Verlag für Sozialwissenschaften.

Shelton, Dinah (ed.) (2000): Commitment and Compliance. The Role of Non-Binding Norms in the International Legal System. Oxford: Oxford University Press.

Shelton, Dinah (ed.) (2003): Commitment and Compliance. The Role of Non-Binding Norms in the International Legal System. Volume Published new in paperback. Oxford / New York: Oxford University Press.

Sinclair, Timothy J. (ed.) (2004): Global Governance. London / New York: Routledge Chapman & Hall (Critical Concepts in Political Science, Volume I).

Sinclair, Timothy J. (ed.) (2004 / 2006): Global Governance: Critical Concepts in Political Science. London / New York / London: Taylor & Francis, Inc.; Routledge (Critical Concepts in Political Science, Volume II).

Skubiszewski, Krzysztof; Bernhardt, Rudolf (eds.) (1981): Die Bedeutung der Resolutionen der Generalversammlung der Vereinten Nationen. Volume 1. Auflage. Baden-Baden: Nomos Verlagsgesellschaft (Fünftes Deutsch-Polnisches Juristen-Kolloquium).

The Earth Charter Initiative (ECI) (ed.) (2000): The Earth Charter. San José, Costa Rica: Earth Charter Center.

The World Conservation Union (IUCN); University of Cambridge (eds.) (2006): The Future of Sustainability. Re-thinking Environment and Development in the Twenty-first Century. Report of the IUCN Renowned Thinkers Meeting, 29–31 January 2006. Edited by William M. (Bill) Adams. Cambridge: The World Conservation Union (IUCN).

Tooley, James; Dixon, Pauline (eds.) (2005): Private Education is Good for the Poor: A Study of Private Schools Serving the Poor in Low-Income Countries. White Paper. Washington, D. C.: Cato Institute (Policy Studies).

UN Department of Economic and Social Affairs (ed.) (1992): United Nations Conference on Environment & Development. Agenda 21. Rio de Janeiro, Brazil, 3–14 June 1992. Edited by Division for Sustainable Development. New York: United Nations.

UN Department of Economic and Social Affairs (ed.) (2002): Plan of Implementation of the World Summit on Sustainable Development. Johannesburg, South Africa, 26 August –4 September 2002. DPI/2305. Edited by Division for Sustainable Development. New York: UN Department of Public Information; United Nations Publications.

Underdal, Arild; Young, Oran R. (eds.) (2004): Regime consequences. Methodological challenges and research strategies. Dordrecht: Kluwer Academic Publishers.

UNESCO (ed.) (1945): Constitution of the United Nations Educational, Scientific and Cultural Organization. Adopted in London on 16 November 1945. Volume 2004 edition. Paris: UNESCO workshops (Basic texts).

UNESCO (ed.) (1987a): Report by the Director-General on the proposed setting-up of an Intergovernmental Committee to be responsible for following and evaluating the implementation of the World Decade for Cultural Development. Executive Board. 126 EX/24. Paris: UNESCO publishing.

UNESCO (ed.) (1987b): World Decade for Cultural Development Report by the Director-General. General Conference Twenty-fourth Session, Paris 1987. 24 C/23. Paris: UNESCO publishing.

UNESCO (ed.) (1990a): World Decade for Cultural Development 1988–1997. Statutes and Rule of Procedures. CC-89/WS-21. Paris: UNESCO workshops.

UNESCO (ed.) (1990b): World Decade for Cultural Development 1988–1997. Plan of Action. CC-89/WS-20. Paris: UNESCO workshops.

UNESCO (ed.) (1990c): World Decade for Cultural Development 1988–1997. Strategy for the Implementation of the Plan of Action. CC-89/WS-19. Paris: UNESCO workshops.

UNESCO (ed.) (1990 / 2000): World Declaration on Education for All. Adopted by the World Conference on Education for All. Meeting Basic Learning Needs, Jomtien, Thailand, 5–9 March 1990. ED-2000/WS/27. Edited by Ulrika Peppler Barry. Paris: UNESCO publishing.

UNESCO (ed.) (1991): Report by the Director-General on the Process in the implementation of the aims and programmes of the World Decade for Cultural Development. General Conference Twenty-sixth Session, Paris 1991. 26 C/94. Paris: UNESCO publishing.

UNESCO (ed.) (1992): Resolutions. Records of the General Conference. Twenty-sixth Session Paris, 15 October–7 November 1991. Paris: UNESCO workshops (1).

UNESCO (ed.) (1996): Learning: The treasure within. Report to UNESCO of the International Commission on Education for the Twenty-first Century. Edited by Jacques Delors. Paris: UNESCO publishing; Editions Odile Jacob.

UNESCO (ed.) (1997a): Resolutions and Recommendations adopted by various bodies and organizations of the United Nations System concerning the World Decade for Cultural Development. Intergovernmental Committee of the World Decade for Cultural Development; Fifth regular session (Paris, 21–25 April 1997). CLT/DEC/1997/05. Paris: UNESCO publishing.

UNESCO (ed.) (1998): Action Plan on Cultural Policies for Development. adopted in by the Intergovernmental Conference on Cultural Policies for Development. 2 April 1998, Stockholm, Sweden. Paris / Stockholm: UNESCO Networking & Information Section.

UNESCO (ed.) (2000): The Dakar Framework for Action: Education for All: Meeting our Collective Commitments. Adopted by the World Education Forum Dakar, Senegal, 26–28 April 2000. ED-2000/WS/27. Edited by Ulrika Peppler Barry. Paris: UNESCO publishing.

UNESCO (ed.) (2001): UNESCO Universal Declaration on Cultural Diversity. General Conference 31st session. Volume No. 1, 2002. Paris: Copyright Bulletin (Vol. XXXVI).

UNESCO (ed.) (2002a): Approved Programme and Budget 2002–2003. 31 C/5 Approved. Paris: UNESCO workshops.

UNESCO (ed.) (2002b): Cultural Diversity: A Conceptual Platform. Sustainable Diversity: The indivisibility of culture and development. Edited by Katérina Stenou. Paris: UNESCO publishing (Cultural Diversity Series, No. 1).

UNESCO (ed.) (2002c): Education for Sustainability. From Rio to Johannesburg: Lessons learnt from a decade of commitment. Paris: UNESCO publishing.

UNESCO (ed.) (2002d): Enhancing Global Sustainability. Preparatory Committee for the World Summit on Sustainable Development (WSSD) 3rd Session New York, 25 March 2002. Position Paper and Proposals by UNESCO. Paris / New York: UNESCO publishing.

UNESCO (ed.) (2002e): Knowledge for sustainable development. An insight into the Encyclopedia of life support systems. 3 Bände. Oxford / Paris / London: UNESCO publishing; Encyclopedia of Life Support Systems (EOLSS) Publishers (Environment and Development series).

UNESCO (ed.) (2002f): Medium-Term Strategy for 2002–2007. 31 C/4 Approved. Paris: UNESCO workshops.

UNESCO (ed.) (2003a): Decisions adopted by the Executive Board at its 166th session. Executive Board. 166 EX/Decisions. Paris: UNESCO publishing.

UNESCO (ed.) (2003b): United Nations Decade of Education for Sustainable Development (2005–2014). Framework for the International Implementation Scheme. 32 C/INF.9. Paris: UNESCO publishing.

UNESCO (ed.) (July 2003): United Nations Decade of Education for Sustainable Development (January 2005 – December 2014). Framework for a Draft International Implementation Scheme. Paris: UNESCO publishing.

UNESCO (ed.) (2004a): Approved Programme and Budget 2004–2005. 32 C/5 Approved. Paris: UNESCO workshops.

UNESCO (ed.) (2004b): Educating for a sustainable future: Commitments and partnerships. Proceedings of the High-Level International Conference on Education for Sustainable Development at the World Summit on Sustainable Development. 2–3 September 2002, Johannesburg. Paris: UNESCO publishing.

UNESCO (ed.) (2004c): United Nations Decade of Education for Sustainable Development (2005–2014). Draft International Implementation Scheme. Paris: UNESCO publishing.

UNESCO (20/07/2004): High-Level Panel on the United Nations Decade of Education for Sustainable Development. Paris. Available online: http://portal.unesco.org/education/en/ev.php-URL_ID=32593&URL_DO=DO_TOPIC&URL_SECTION=201.html [Accessed on 13/10/2008].

UNESCO (ed.) (2005a): Convention on the Protection and Promotion of the Diversity of Cultural Expressions. General Conference 33rd session. CLT-2005/CONVENTION DIVERSITE-CULT REV. Paris: UNESCO publishing.

UNESCO (ed.) (2005b): Decisions adopted by the Executive Board at its 171st session. Draft international implementation scheme for the United Nations Decade of Education for Sustainable Development. 171 EX/Decisions. Paris: UNESCO publishing.

UNESCO (ed.) (2005c): Draft International Implementation Scheme for the United Nations Decade of Education for Sustainable Development. 171 EX/7. Paris: UNESCO publishing.

UNESCO (ed.) (2005d): Education for Sustainable Development. Public information. memobpi. Paris: Bureau of Public Information (BPI).

UNESCO (ed.) (2005e): Guidelines and Recommendations for Reorienting Teacher Education to Address Sustainability. Education for Sustainable Development in Action. ED-2005/WS/66 Technical Paper N° 2 – 2005. Paris: UNESCO workshops.

UNESCO (ed.) (2005f): Report by the Director-General on the United Nations Decade of Education for Sustainable Development. International Implementation Scheme and UNESCO's Contribution to the Implementation of the Decade. 172 EX/11. Paris: UNESCO publishing.

UNESCO (ed.) (2005g): UN Decade of Education for Sustainable Development: Links between the Global Initiatives in Education. Education for Sustainable Development in Action. Technical Paper N°1. Paris: UNESCO workshops.

UNESCO (ed.) (2005h): UNESCO and Sustainable Development. Edited by Monique Perrot-Lanaud; Sabrina Sidhu; Stéphanie Tang; Marine Samson. Paris: UNESCO publishing.

UNESCO (ed.) (2005i): UNESCO's Contribution to the Implementation of the United Nations Decade of Education for Sustainable Development (2005–2014). Report by the Director-General on the United Nations Decade of

Education for Sustainable Development: International Implementation Scheme and UNESCO's Contribution to the implementation of the decade. 172 EX/INF.4. Paris: UNESCO publishing.

UNESCO (ed.) (2005j): United Nations Decade of Education for Sustainable Development (2005–2014). International Implementation Scheme. ED/DESD/2005/PI/01. Paris: UNESCO workshops.

UNESCO (ed.) (2006a): Approved Programme and Budget 2006–2007. 33 C/5 Approved. Paris: UNESCO workshops.

UNESCO (ed.) (2006b): Definitions of legal terms concerning normative and standard setting instruments. Paris: UNESCO publishing.

UNESCO (ed.) (2006c): Drivers and Barriers for Implementing Sustainable Development in Higher Education. Education for Sustainable Development in Action. Göteborg Workshop December 7–9, 2005. ED-2006/WS/63 Technical Paper N° 3. Edited by John Holmberg; Bo E. Samuelsson. Paris: UNESCO publishing.

UNESCO (ed.) (2006d): Education for Sustainable Development Toolkit. Education for Sustainable Development in Action. Learning & Training Tools N°1. Edited by Rosalyn McKeown; Charles Hopkins; Regina Rizzi; Marianne Chrystalbride. Paris: UNESCO workshops.

UNESCO (ed.) (2006e): Follow-up to 166 EX/DECISION 3.6.1 concerning the proposal for the elaboration of an education programme for the sustainable management of freshwater resources. Report by the Director-General on the development of an intersectoral strategy on education for the management of freshwater resources. 174 EX/INF.13. Paris: UNESCO publishing.

UNESCO (ed.) (2006f): Framework for the UN DESD International Implementation Scheme. ED/DESD/2006/PI/1. Paris: UNESCO workshops.

UNESCO (ed.) (2006g): Highlights on Progress to Date. January 2006. Paris: UNESCO publishing.

UNESCO (ed.) (2006h): Highlights on Progress to Date. September 2006. Paris: UNESCO publishing.

UNESCO (ed.) (2006i): Promotion for a Global Partnership for the UN Decade of Education for Sustainable Development (2005–2014). The International Implementation Scheme for the Decade in brief. ED-2006/WS/60. Paris: UNESCO workshops.

UNESCO (ed.) (2006j): UNESCO-Private Sector Partnerships: Making a Difference. ERC/CFS/MLT/2006/PI/1. Paris: UNESCO publishing.

UNESCO (ed.) (2007a): Asia-Pacific Guidelines for the Development of National ESD Indicators. APE/ESD/07/OP/022-1000. Edited by Daniella Tilbury; Sonja Janousek; Leanne Denby; Derek Elias; Joel E. Bacha. Bangkok: UNESCO Asia and Pacific Regional Bureau for Education.

UNESCO (ed.) (2007b): Drivers and Barriers for Implementing Learning for Sustainable Development in Pre-School through Upper Secondary and Teacher Education. Education for Sustainable Development in Action. Göteborg Workshop 27–29 March 2006. Technical Paper N° 4. Edited by Inger Björneloo; Eva Nyberg. Paris: UNESCO publishing.

UNESCO (ed.) (2007c): Education for Sustainable Development: Linking Learning and Happiness. APE/ESD/07/OP/065-500. Edited by Joel E. Bacha; Sombath Somphone; Lawrence Surendra. Bangkok: UNESCO Asia and Pacific Regional Bureau for Education.

UNESCO (Enero-Abril 2007): Encuentro Latinoamericano: Construyendo una Educación para el Desarrollo Sostenible en América Latina. San José, Costa Rica, 31 de octubre–2 de noviembre, 2006. Reseña. Volume 6, Issue 1. San José, Costa Rica. (HORIZONTE SANITARIO, 1). Available online: http://www.ujat.mx/publicaciones/horizonte_sanitario/ediciones/2007_ene_abril/5_resenas.pdf [Accessed on 23/11/2007].

UNESCO (ed.) (2007d): Framework for a DESD Communication Strategy in support of the UN Decade of Education for Sustainable Development. ED-2007/WS/20. Paris: UNESCO workshops.

UNESCO (ed.) (2007e): Good Practices in Education for Sustainable Development: Teacher Education Institutions. Education for Sustainable Development in Action. Good Practices N°1. Edited by Rosalyn McKeown. Paris: UNESCO workshops.

UNESCO (ed.) (2007f): Highlights on DESD Progress to Date. January 2007. Paris: UNESCO publishing.

UNESCO (ed.) (2007g): Highlights on DESD Progress to Date. April 2007. Paris: UNESCO publishing.

UNESCO (ed.) (2007h): Monitoring and assessing progress during the UNDESD in the Asia-Pacific Region: A quick guide to developing national ESD indicators. APE/ESD/07/OP/022-1500. Edited by Daniella Tilbury; Sonja Janousek; Leanne Denby; Derek Elias; Joel E. Bacha. Bangkok: UNESCO Asia and Pacific Regional Bureau for Education.

UNESCO (ed.) (2007i): Natural Disaster Preparedness and Education for Sustainable Development. APE/ESD/07/OP/006-2000. Bangkok: UNESCO Asia and Pacific Regional Bureau for Education.

UNESCO (ed.) (2007j): Report by the Director-General on the follow-up to decisions and resolutions adopted by the Executive Board and the General Conference at their previous sessions. Progress in the development of cross-sectoral capacity-building programmes. 176 EX/5 Add.2. Paris: UNESCO publishing.

UNESCO (ed.) (2007k): The UN Decade of Education for Sustainable Development (DESD 2005–2014). The First Two Years. Paris: UNESCO publishing.

UNESCO (ed.) (2007l): UN Decade of Education for Sustainable Development 2005–2014. The DESD at a glance. ED/2005/PEQ/ESD/3. Paris: UNESCO publishing.

UNESCO (ed.) (2007m): United Nations Decade of Education for Sustainable Development (2005–2014). Summary of the UNESCO Action Plan For DESD. Final Draft. Paris: UNESCO publishing.

UNESCO (ed.) (August 2007): Progress Report by the Director-General on the United Nations Decade of Education for Sustainable Development (2005–2014). 177 EX/9 Annex III. Paris: UNESCO publishing.

UNESCO (ed.) (2008a): Approved Programme and Budget 2008–2009. 34 C/5 Approved. Paris: UNESCO workshops.

UNESCO (ed.) (2008b): Convention on the Protection and Promotion of the Diversity of Cultural Expressions. Culture in Sustainable Development: Insights for the future implementation of art. 13. CE/08/Throsby/Art.13. Edited by David Throsby. Sydney: UNESCO publishing.

UNESCO (ed.) (2008c): DESD Quarterly Highlights. December 2008. Paris: UNESCO publishing.

UNESCO (ed.) (2008d): DESD Quarterly Highlights. July 2008. Paris: UNESCO publishing.

UNESCO (ed.) (2008e): Medium-Term Strategy for 2008–2013. 34 C/4 (CLD-8.8). Paris: UNESCO workshops.

UNESCO (ed.) (2008f): Report by the Director-General on the development and management of intersectoral platforms. Executive Board. 179 EX/16. Paris: UNESCO publishing.

UNESCO (ed.) (2008g): The contribution of early childhood education to a sustainable society. The Role of Early Childhood Education for a Sustainable Society Göteborg, Sweden, 2–4 May 2007. ED-2008/WS/14 – CLD 3427.7. Edited by Ingrid Pramling Samuelsson; Yoshie Kaga. Paris: UNESCO publishing.

UNESCO (ed.) (2008h): UN DESD Global Monitoring and Evaluation Framework (GMEF). Operational Plan. Edited by Daniella Tilbury. Paris: UNESCO publishing.

UNESCO (ed.) (2009a): Draft Programme and Budget 2010–2011. Revised version. 35 C/5 Draft. Paris: UNESCO workshops (Volumes 1and 2).

UNESCO (ed.) (2009b): Guidelines and procedures for the UNITWIN/UNESCO Chairs Programme. ED/HED/UNITWIN/2006/PI/1 rev. 4. Paris: UNESCO publishing.

UNESCO (ed.) (2010a): Youth Poverty Alleviation Through Tourism and Heritage An Educational Tool for Sustainable Development Youth PATH. Introduction to Youth Poverty Alleviation Tourism and Heritage. An Educational Tool for Sustainable Development. Kingston: Pear Tree Press.

UNESCO; Asia-Pacific Centre of Education for International Understanding (APCEIU) (eds.) (2007a): Two Concepts, One Goal: Education for International Understanding (EIU) and Education for Sustainable Development (ESD). TH/2007/PI/H/3. Bangkok / Seoul: UNESCO Asia and Pacific Regional Bureau for Education.

UNESCO; Federal Ministry of Education and Research (BMBF); Deutsche UNESCO-Kommission e. V. (DUK) (eds.) (2009a): Bonn Declaration. UNESCO World Conference on Education for Sustainable Development. 31 March–2 April 2009, Bonn, Germany. Bonn: Deutsche UNESCO-Kommission.

UNESCO; Oficina Regional de Educación de la UNESCO para América Latina y el Caribe (OREALC) (eds.) (2005a): Diversidad cultural. Materiales para la formación docente y el trabajo de aula. Santiago de Chile: UNESCO Santiago (3).

UNESCO; Oficina Regional de Educación de la UNESCO para América Latina y el Caribe (OREALC) (eds.) (2007b): Quality Education for All: A Human Rights Issue. Educational policies within the framework of the II Intergovernmental Meeting of the Regional Project in Education for Latin America and the Caribbean (EFA/PRELAC). Background document. March 29–30, 2007; Buenos Aires, Argentina. Santiago de Chile: UNESCO Santiago.

UNESCO; Oficina Regional de Educación de la UNESCO para América Latina y el Caribe (OREALC) (eds.) (2007c): Situación Educativa de América Latina y el Caribe: Garantizando la Educación de Calidad para Todos. Informe Regional de revisión y Evaluación del progreso de América Latina y el Caribe hacia la Educación para Todos en el marco del Proyecto Regional de Educación (EPT/PRELAC) – 2007. Santiago de Chile: UNESCO Santiago.

UNESCO; The Earth Charter Initiative (ECI) (eds.) (2007d): Good Practices in Education for Sustainable Development Using the Earth Charter. Education for Sustainable Development in Action. Good Practices No. 3. Paris / San José: Earth Charter Center; UNESCO publishing.

UNESCO; The Earth Charter Initiative (ECI) (eds.) (Marzo 2007): Encuentro Latinoamericano: Construyendo una Educación para el Desarrollo Sostenible. Estrategia Regional: Construyendo una Educación para el Desarrollo Sostenible en América Latina y el Caribe. Paris / San José: Producciones ALPI.

UNESCO; Thomson Foundation (eds.) (2008a): Media as partners in education for sustainable development: A Training and Resource Kit. CI/COM/2008/PI/2. Edited by Eleanor Bird; Richard Lutz; Christine Warwick. Paris: UNESCO publishing (UNESCO Series on Journalism Education).

UNESCO; UNESCO Associated Schools (eds.) (2008b): First Collection of Good Practices for Quality Education. ED-2008/WS/41. Edited by Amina Hamshari. Paris: UNESCO Press.

UNESCO; UNESCO Associated Schools (eds.) (2009b): Second Collection of Good Practices. Education for Sustainable Development. ED-2009/WS/11. Edited by Amina Hamshari. Paris: UNESCO Press.

UNESCO; United Nations Environment Programme (UNEP); Méta (Media, Ecology and Technology Association), et al. (eds.) (2002 / 2008): www.youthXchange.net – towards sustainable lifestyles. training kit on responsible consumption. THE GUIDE. Paris / New York: United Nations Publications.

UNESCO; United Nations University (UNU) (eds.) (2005b): International Conference on Globalization and Education for Sustainable Development. Sustaining the Future. Nagoya, Japan, 28–29 June 2005. Paris: UNESCO publishing.

UNESCO Culture Sector (ed.) (1997): From weaving to websites ... UNESCO celebrates culture. Culture and Development. Rethinking development: the World Decade for Cultural Development, 1988–1997. Edited by Malachy Quinn. Paris: Paragraphic L'UNION.

UNESCO Education Sector (ed.) (2005): Contributing to a More Sustainable Future: Quality Education, Life Skills and Education for Sustainable Development. ED/PEQ/IQL/2005/PI/H/2. Paris: UNESCO publishing.

UNESCO Education Sector (ed.) (2007): Good Practices in the UNECE region. Education for Sustainable Development in Action. ED-2007/WS/31 Good Practices N° 2. Paris: UNESCO workshops.

UNESCO Education Sector (ed.) (2008): Quality Education, Equity and Sustainable Development. A holistic vision through UNESCO's four World Education Conferences 2008–2009. Paris: UNESCO publishing.

UNESCO Education Sector (ed.) (March 2009): UNESCO Strategy for the Second Half of the United Nations Decade of Education for Sustainable Development. Supporting Member States and other stakeholders in addressing global sustainable development challenges through ESD. Education for Sustainable Development in Action / 2010/ED/UNP/DESD/PI/1. Paris: UNESCO workshops.

UNESCO Section for DESD Coordination (ed.) (2009): Learning for a sustainable world. Review of Contexts and Structures for Education for Sustainable Development. 2009 DESD Global Report. Edited by Daniella Tilbury; Saïd Belkachla; Abelardo Brenes; Elaine Unterhalter; Pierre Varcher; Roel van Raiij; Alex Michalos; Govinda Rangachar; Shivali Lawale; Overson Shumba. Paris: UNESCO workshops.

UNESCO Bangkok (ed.) (2007): Asia-Pacific UN DESD Interagency Steering Committee. Draft Meeting Report. Eighth Meeting. Bangkok: UNESCO Asia and Pacific Regional Bureau for Education.

United Nations (ed.) (1945): Charter of the United Nations. San Francisco / New York: UN Treaty Collection (Certified True Copies).

United Nations (ed.) (1948): Universal Declaration of Human Rights. A/RES/217(III)[A]. Geneva / New York: United Nations Publications (Resolutions adopted by the General Assembly during its 3rd session, 1).

United Nations (ed.) (1969): Vienna Convention on the Law of Treaties. Vienna: United Nations Publications (Treaty Series, 2).

United Nations (ed.) (1987a): Declaration on the Right to Development. Resolution adopted by the General Assembly. A/RES/41/128. New York: United Nations (Resolutions and decisions adopted by the General Assembly during its 41st session, 53).

United Nations (ed.) (1987b): Report of the World Commission on Environment and Development. General Assembly Resolution. A/RES/42/187. New York: United Nations.

United Nations (ed.) (1987c): Report of the World Commission on Environment and Development. Brundtland Report (Annex "Our Common Future"). A/43/427. New York: United Nations.

United Nations (ed.) (1989 / 1990): Convention on the Rights of the Child. A/RES/44/25. New York: United Nations.

United Nations (ed.) (1992 / 1993): Resolution on the report of the second Committee. Institutional arrangements to follow up the United Nations Conference on Environment and Development. A/RES/47/191. New York: United Nations.

United Nations (ed.) (2000): United Nations Millennium Declaration. Resolution adopted by the General Assembly [without reference to a Main Committee (A/55/L.2)]. A/RES/55/2. New York: United Nations.

United Nations (ed.) (2001): Towards global partnerships. A/RES/55/215. New York: United Nations.

United Nations (ed.) (2002a): Report of the World Summit on Sustainable Development. Johannesburg, South Africa, 26 August–4 September 2002. A/CONF.199/20. New York: United Nations Publications.

United Nations (ed.) (2002b): Resolution adopted by the General Assembly [on the report of the Third Committee (A/56/572)]. United Nations Literacy Decade: Education for All. A/RES/56/116. New York: United Nations.

United Nations (ed.) (2002c): Towards global partnerships. A/RES/56/76. New York: United Nations.

United Nations (ed.) (2002 / 2003): United Nations Decade of Education for Sustainable Development. Resolution adopted by the General Assembly. A/RES/57/254. New York: United Nations.

United Nations (ed.) (2003a): International Decade for Action, "Water for Life", 2005–2015. Resolution adopted by the General Assembly. A/RES/58/217. New York: United Nations.

United Nations (ed.) (2003b): Sustainable development: United Nations Decade of Education for Sustainable Development. Report of the Second Committee. A/58/486. New York: United Nations.

United Nations (ed.) (2003c): The Road from Johannesburg. World Summit on Sustainable Development. What Was Achieved and the Way Forward. New York: United Nations.

United Nations (ed.) (2004a): Sustainable development: United Nations Decade of Education for Sustainable Development. Report of the Second Committee. A/59/483/Add.7. New York: United Nations.

United Nations (ed.) (2004b): United Nations Decade of Education for Sustainable Development. Resolution adopted by the General Assembly on the report of the Second Committee (A/58/486). A/RES/58/219. New York: United Nations.

United Nations (ed.) (2004c): United Nations Decade of Education for Sustainable Development. Fifty-ninth session Second Committee. Japan: draft resolution. A/C.2/59/L.9. Paris: United Nations.

United Nations (ed.) (2004d): United Nations Decade of Education for Sustainable Development. Fifty-ninth session Second Committee. Draft resolution on the basis of informal consultations held on draft resolution A/C.2/59/L.9. A/C.2/59/L.24. Paris: United Nations.

United Nations (ed.) (2005a): Towards global partnerships. Enhanced cooperation between the United Nations and all relevant partners, in particular the private sector. Report of the Secretary-General. A/60/214. New York: United Nations.

United Nations (ed.) (2005b): United Nations Decade of Education for Sustainable Development. Resolution adopted by the General Assembly on the report of the Second Committee (A/59/483/Add.7). A/RES/59/237. New York: United Nations.

United Nations (ed.) (2012): The future we want. United Nations Conference on Sustainable Development (Rio+12), 20–22 June 2012, Rio de Janeiro, Brazil. A/CONF.216/L.1. Rio de Janeiro; New York: United Nations.

United Nations; UNESCO (eds.) (1994): Rethinking development. World Decade for Cultural Development 1988–1997. Edited by Birgitta Leander. Paris: UNESCO publishing (Culture Plus).

United Nations Commission for Sustainable Development (CSD); United Nations Economic and Social Council (ECOSOC) (eds.) (2003): Report on the eleventh session (27 January 2003 and 28 April–9 May 2003). Official Records, Supplement No. 9. E/2003/29 / E/CN.17/2003/6. New York: United Nations.

United Nations Conference on Trade and Development (UNCTAD); UNESCO; United Nations Children's Fund (UNICEF) (eds.) (2001): Education for All and Sustainable Development in LDCs. Issue Paper. Third United Nations Conference on the Least Developed Countries (LDC III) Brussels, 14–20 May 2001. Interactive Thematic Session on Education for All 16 May 2001. Brussels: UNESCO publishing.

United Nations Economic and Social Council (ECOSOC) (ed.) (2003): Future programme, organization and methods of work of the Commission on Sustainable Development. Resolutions 2003/61. E/2003/INF/2/Add.4. New York: United Nations.

United Nations Economic and Social Council (ECOSOC); United Nations Commission for Sustainable Development (CSD) (eds.) (1996): Report on the Fourth Session (18 April–3 May 1996). Official Records, Supplement No. 8. E/CN.17/1996/38. New York: United Nations.

United Nations Economic and Social Council (ECOSOC); United Nations Commission for Sustainable Development (CSD) (eds.) (1998): Report on the Sixth Session (22 December 1997 and 20 April–1 May 1998). Official Records, Supplement No. 9. E/CN.17/1998/20. New York: United Nations.

United Nations Economic Commission for Europe (UNECE) (ed.) (2006): UNECE Strategy for Education for Sustainable Development. Guidance for reporting. Expert Group on Indicators for ESD. Geneva: United Nations.

United Nations Economic Commission for Europe (UNECE) (26/10/2006): Format for Reporting on Implementation of the UNECE Strategy for Education for Sustainable Development. Within the framework of the United Nations Decade of Education for Sustainable Development (2005–2014). ECE/CEP/AC.13/2006/5/Add.1. UNECE Steering Committee on Education for Sustainable Development. Geneva. Available online: http://www.unece.org/env/esd/Implementation/Documents/ReportingFormat.E.doc [Accessed on 06/11/2007].

United Nations Economic Commission for Europe (UNECE) (ed.) (2009): Learning from each other. The UNECE Strategy for Education for Sustainable Development. ECE/CEP/159. Geneva / New York: United Nations Publications.

United Nations Economic Commission for Europe (UNECE); United Nations Economic and Social Council (ECOSOC) (eds.) (2003a): Draft Terms of Reference of the Task Force on Education for Sustainable Development. First regional meeting on education for sustainable development. Geneva, 19–20 February 2004. CEP/AC.13/2004/4. New York: United Nations.

United Nations Economic Commission for Europe (UNECE); United Nations Economic and Social Council (ECOSOC) (eds.) (2003b): Draft UNECE Strategy for Education for Sustainable Development. First regional meeting on education for sustainable development. Geneva, 19–20 February 2004. CEP/AC.13/2004/3. New York: United Nations.

United Nations Economic Commission for Europe (UNECE); United Nations Economic and Social Council (ECOSOC) (eds.) (2003c): Fifth Ministerial Conference "Environment for Europe" Kiev, Ukraine, 21–23 May 2003. Declaration by the Environment Ministers of the region of the United Nations Economic Commission for Europe (UNECE). ECE/CEP/94/Rev.1. New York: United Nations.

United Nations Economic Commission for Europe (UNECE); United Nations Economic and Social Council (ECOSOC) (eds.) (2003d): Fifth Ministerial Conference "Environment for Europe", Kiev, Ukraine, 21–23 May 2003. Statement on Education for Sustainable Development by the UNECE Ministers of the Environment. ECE/CEP/102/Rev.1. New York: United Nations.

United Nations Economic Commission for Europe (UNECE); United Nations Economic and Social Council (ECOSOC) (eds.) (2003e): Framework for the Post-Kiev Work on Education for Sustainable Development. CEP/2003/22. New York: United Nations.

United Nations Economic Commission for Europe (UNECE); United Nations Economic and Social Council (ECOSOC) (eds.) (2003f): Work Programme of the Task Force on Education for Sustainable Development. First regional meeting on education for sustainable development. Geneva, 19–20 February 2004. CEP/AC.13/2004/5. New York: United Nations.

United Nations Economic Commission for Europe (UNECE); United Nations Economic and Social Council (ECOSOC) (eds.) (2004a): Draft Vilnius Framework for the Implementation of the UNECE Strategy for Education for Sustainable Development. High-level meeting of Environment and Education Ministries (Vilnius, 17–18 March 2005). CEP/AC.13/2005/4. New York: United Nations.

United Nations Economic Commission for Europe (UNECE); United Nations Economic and Social Council (ECOSOC) (eds.) (2004b): Draft UNECE Strategy for Education for Sustainable Development. High-level meeting of Environment and Education Ministries (Vilnius, 17–18 March 2005). CEP/AC.13/2005/3. New York: United Nations.

United Nations Economic Commission for Europe (UNECE); United Nations Economic and Social Council (ECOSOC) (eds.) (2004c): Draft UNECE Strategy for Education for Sustainable Development. Eleventh session (Geneva, 13–15 October 2004). CEP/2004/15 / CEP/AC.13/2004/8/Rev.1. New York: United Nations.

United Nations Economic Commission for Europe (UNECE); United Nations Economic and Social Council (ECOSOC) (eds.) (2004d): Draft UNECE Strategy for Education for Sustainable Development. Addendum. Explanatory Notes. Second regional meeting on education for sustainable development (Rome, 15–16 July 2004). CEP/AC.13/2004/8/Add.2. New York: United Nations.

United Nations Economic Commission for Europe (UNECE); United Nations Economic and Social Council (ECOSOC) (eds.) (2004e): Draft UNECE Strategy for Education for Sustainable Development. Background. Second regional meeting on education for sustainable development (Rome, 15–16 July 2004). CEP/AC.13/2004/8/Add.1. New York: United Nations.

United Nations Economic Commission for Europe (UNECE); United Nations Economic and Social Council (ECOSOC) (eds.) (2004f): Draft UNECE Strategy for Education for Sustainable Development. Explanatory Notes. Second regional meeting on education for sustainable development Rome, 15–16 July 2004. CEP/AC.13/2004/8/Add.2. Geneva: United Nations.

United Nations Economic Commission for Europe (UNECE); United Nations Economic and Social Council (ECOSOC) (eds.) (2004g): Framework for the Implementation of the UNECE Strategy for Education for Sustainable Development. Eleventh session (Geneva, 13–15 October 2004). CEP/2004/17 / CEP/AC.13/2004/10. New York: United Nations.

United Nations Economic Commission for Europe (UNECE); United Nations Economic and Social Council (ECOSOC) (eds.) (2004h): Provisional Agenda. High-level meeting of Environment and Education Ministries, Vilnius, 17–18 March 2005. CEP/AC.13/2005/1. New York: United Nations.

United Nations Economic Commission for Europe (UNECE); United Nations Economic and Social Council (ECOSOC) (eds.) (2004i): Report on the Tenth Session 20–22 October 2003. ECE/CEP/116. New York: United Nations.

United Nations Economic Commission for Europe (UNECE); United Nations Economic and Social Council (ECOSOC) (eds.) (2005a): Chair's Summary. High-level meeting of Environment and Education Ministries, Vilnius, 17–18 March 2005. CEP/AC.13/2005/5. New York: United Nations.

United Nations Economic Commission for Europe (UNECE); United Nations Economic and Social Council (ECOSOC) (eds.) (2005b): Draft work plan for the implementation of the UNECE Strategy for Education for Sustainable Development, 2005-2007 (Geneva, 13–14 December 2005). For adoption by the Steering Committee UNECE Steering Committee on Education for Sustainable Development. CEP/AC.13/2005/8. New York: United Nations.

United Nations Economic Commission for Europe (UNECE); United Nations Economic and Social Council (ECOSOC) (eds.) (2005c): Indicators for Education for Sustainable Development. Progress Report on the work of the Expert Group. First meeting, Geneva, 13–14 December 2005. CEP/AC.13/2005/9. New York: United Nations.

United Nations Economic Commission for Europe (UNECE); United Nations Economic and Social Council (ECOSOC) (eds.) (2005d): Report of the Meeting. High-level meeting of Environment and Education Ministries, Vilnius, 17–18 March 2005. CEP/AC.13/2005/2. New York: United Nations.

United Nations Economic Commission for Europe (UNECE); United Nations Economic and Social Council (ECOSOC) (eds.) (2005e): UNECE Strategy for Education for Sustainable Development. Report of the High-level meeting of Environment and Education Ministries (Vilnius, 17–18 March 2005). CEP/AC.13/2005/3/Rev.1. New York: United Nations.

United Nations Economic Commission for Europe (UNECE); United Nations Economic and Social Council (ECOSOC) (eds.) (2005f): UNECE Strategy for Education for Sustainable Development. High-level meeting of Environment and Education Ministries (Vilnius, 17–18 March 2005). CEP/AC.13/2005/3/Rev.1. New York: United Nations.

United Nations Economic Commission for Europe (UNECE); United Nations Economic and Social Council (ECOSOC) (eds.) (2005g): Vilnius Framework for the Implementation of the UNECE Strategy for Education for Sustainable Development. High-level meeting of Environment and Education Ministries (Vilnius, 17–18 March 2005). CEP/AC.13/2005/4/Rev.1. New York: United Nations.

United Nations Economic Commission for Europe (UNECE); United Nations Economic and Social Council (ECOSOC) (eds.) (2006): Report of the Meeting. First meeting, Geneva, 13–14 December 2005. CEP/AC.13/2005/7. New York: United Nations.

United Nations Economic Commission for Europe (UNECE); United Nations Economic and Social Council (ECOSOC) (eds.) (2007a): Environment for Europe – Chair's Summary. Sixth Ministerial Conference "Environment for Europe" Belgrade, 10–12 October 2007. ECE/BELGRADE.CONF/2007/9. Edited by Saša Dragin. New York: United Nations.

United Nations Economic Commission for Europe (UNECE); United Nations Economic and Social Council (ECOSOC) (eds.) (2007b): Indicators for Education for Sustainable Development. Progress report on the work of the Expert Group. Second meeting, Geneva, 4–5 December 2006. ECE/CEP/AC.13/2006/5. New York: United Nations.

United Nations Economic Commission for Europe (UNECE); United Nations Economic and Social Council (ECOSOC) (eds.) (2007c): Report of the Meeting. Second meeting, Geneva, 4–5 December 2006. ECE/CEP/AC.13/2006/3. New York: United Nations.

United Nations Economic Commission for Europe (UNECE); United Nations Economic and Social Council (ECOSOC) (eds.) (2007d): Sixth Ministerial Conference "Environment for Europe" Belgrade, 10–12 October 2007. Declaration "Building Bridges to the Future" by Ministers of the region of the United Nations Economic Commission for Europe (UNECE). ECE/BELGRADE.CONF/2007/8. New York: United Nations.

United Nations Environment Programme (UNEP) (ed.) (1972): Stockholm Declaration. Declaration of the United Nations Conference on the Human Environment. The United Nations Conference on the Human Environment, 5–16 June 1972. Stockholm / Nairobi: United Nations.

United Nations Environment Programme (UNEP); UNESCO (eds.) (1975): The Belgrade Charter. A Global Framework for Environmental Education. 13 to 22 October 1975. Belgrade: United Nations.

United Nations Environment Programme (UNEP); UNESCO (eds.) (1977 / 1978): Tbilisi Declaration. Intergovernmental Conference on Environmental Education, 14–26 October 1977. Final Report ED/MD/49. Edited by George Francis. Paris: United Nations.

United Nations Global Compact (ed.) (2007a): Enhancing Partnership Value. A Tool for Assessing Sustainability and Impact. New York: United Nations Global Compact Office.

United Nations Global Compact (ed.) (2007b): Joining Forces for Change. Demonstrating innovation and impact through UN-Business Partnerships. New York: United Nations Global Compact Office.

United Nations University (UNU); UNESCO; International Association of Universities (IAU) (eds.) (2002): Ubuntu Declaration. On Education and Science and Technology for Sustainable Development. WSSD Johannesburg Summit. New York: United Nations.

Vitzthum, Wolfgang Graf; Bothe, Michael (eds.) (2007): Völkerrecht. Volume 4. neu bearbeitete Auflage. Supported by: Dolzer, Rudolf; Hailbronner, Kay and Klein, Eckard et al. Berlin: de Gruyter (Recht).

Wade, Ros; Parker, Jenneth (eds.) (2008): EFA-ESD Dialogue: Educating for a sustainable world. ED.2008/WS/49. Paris: UNESCO publishing (Education for sustainable development policy dialogue, 1).

Witthaus, Michele; McCandless, Karen; Lambert, Rebecca (eds.) (2010): Tomorrow today. Supported by: Nicklin, Sean and Cornwell, Ben. Leicester, United Kingdom: Tudor Rose; UNESCO publishing.

World Bank (ed.) (2003): Sustainable development in a dynamic world. Transforming institutions, growth, and quality of life. 24705. New York: Oxford University Press (World development report, 25).

Woyke, Wichard (ed.) (2008): Handwörterbuch internationale Politik. Volume 11. überarbeitete und aktualisierte Auflage. Opladen: Budrich (UTB für Wissenschaft, 702).

Young, Oran R. (ed.) (1999a): The effectiveness of international environmental regimes. Causal connections and behavioral mechanisms. Cambridge, Massachusetts: MIT Press.

Young, Oran R.; King, Leslie A; Schroeder, Heike (eds.) (2008): Institutions and environmental change. Principal findings, applications, and research frontiers. Cambridge, Massachusetts: MIT Press.

Yusuf, Abdulqawi A. (ed.) (2007): Normative action in education, science and culture. Essays in commemoration of the sixtieth anniversary of UNESCO. Volume French edition. Paris / Leiden / Boston: UNESCO publishing; Martinus Nijhoff Publishers (UNESCO reference works series, 1).

Journals and magazines

Abbott, Kenneth W.; Snidal, Duncan (2000): Hard Law and Soft Law in International Governance. In: International Organization, Volume 54, Issue 3, pp. 421–456. Available online: http://papers.ssrn.com/sol3/papers.cfm?abstract_id=1402966 [Accessed on 15/06/2009].

Alkoby, Asher (2008): Theories of Compliance with International Law and the Challenge of Cultural Difference. In: Journal of International Law and International Relations, Volume 4, Issue 1, pp. 151–198. Available online: http://papers.ssrn.com/sol3/papers.cfm?abstract_id=1113846 [Accessed on 10/06/2009].

Andresen, Steinar (2007): The Effectiveness of UN Environmental Institutions. In: International Environmental Agreements: Politics, Law and Economics, Volume 7, Issue 4, pp. 317–336. Available online: http://www.fni.no/doc&pdf/SA-IEA-2007-1.PDF [Accessed on 20/05/2009].

Bernstein, Stephen; Hannah, Erin (2008): Non-state global standard setting and the WTO: Legitimacy and the need for regulatory space. In: Journal of International Economic Law, Volume 11, Issue 3, pp. 575–608. Available online: http://jiel.oxfordjournals.org/cgi/reprint/11/3/575, first published: 19 July 2008 [Accessed on 06/02/2009].

Biermann, Frank; Bauer, Steffen (2004): Assessing the effectiveness of intergovernmental organisations in international environmental politics. In: Global Environmental Change, Volume 14, Issue 2, pp. 189–193. Available online: http://www.sciencedirect.com/science?_ob=MImg&_imagekey=B6VFV-4CVRMHD-B-1&_cdi=6020&_user=1592544&_orig=mlkt&_coverDate=07%2F31%2F2004&_sk=999859997&view=c&wchp=dGLbVlW-zSkzk&md5=05bdfa69b13b02b77e7862c12f854ab5&ie=/sdarticle.pdf [Accessed on 10/06/2009].

Bothe, Michael (1980): Legal and Non-Legal Norms – a meaningful distinction in international relations? In: Netherlands Yearbook of International Law Review, Volume 11 / XI, pp. 65–95.

Boyle, Alan E. (1999): Some Reflections on the Relationship of Treaties and Soft Law. In: International and Comparative Law Quarterly, Volume 48, October 1999, pp. 901–913. Available online: http://journals.cambridge.org/action/displayAbstract?fromPage=online&aid=1529232 [Accessed on 19/01/2010].

Cunliffe, S. Alex (1996): The UNHCR as Lead Agency in the Former Yugoslavia. In: The Journal of Humanitarian Assistance. Available online: http://jha.ac/1996/04/01/the-unhcr-as-lead-agency-in-the-former-yugoslavia/ [Accessed on 25/10/2010].

D'Amato, Anthony (2008): International Soft Law, Hard Law, and Coherence. In: Northwestern Public Law Research Paper, 08-01. Available online: http://papers.ssrn.com/sol3/papers.cfm?abstract_id=1103915 [Accessed on 15/06/2009].

D'Aspremont, Jean (2008): Softness in International Law: A Self-Serving Quest for New Legal Materials. In: European Journal of International Law (EJIL), Volume 19, Issue 9, pp. 1075–1093. Available online: http://papers.ssrn.com/sol3/papers.cfm?abstract_id=1265511 [Accessed on 15/06/2009].

Deutsche UNESCO-Kommission e. V. (DUK) (ed.) (2003b): Tätigkeitsbericht 2002. Vertrauen schaffen, Nachhaltigkeit gestalten. Bonn: Deutsche UNESCO-Kommission (Online-Magazin der Deutschen UNESCO-Kommission, 7).

Fastenrath, Ulrich (1993): Relative Normativity in International Law. In: European Journal of International Law (EJIL), Volume 4, Issue 3, pp. 305–340. Available online: http://207.57.19.226/journal/Vol4/No3/art1.pdf [Accessed on 15/06/2009].

Frowein, Jochen Abraham (1989): The Internal and External Effects of Resolutions by International Organizations. In: Zeitschrift für ausländisches öffentliches Recht und Völkerrecht (ZaöRV) / Heidelberg Journal of International Law (HJIL), Volume 49, pp. 778–790. Available online: http://www.zaoerv.de/49_1989/49_1989_4_a_778_790.pdf [Accessed on 11/06/2009].

Fuchs, Max (2002): Dialog zwischen den Kulturen. Kulturtheoretische und -politische Anmerkungen. Online-Magazin der Deutschen UNESCO-Kommission. In: unesco heute online, Volume März 2002, Issue 3. Available online: http://deposit.ddb.de/ep/netpub/28/34/66/972663428/_data_dync/_stand_Dezember_2006/302/kulturdialog.htm [Accessed on 22/06/2010].

Gersen, Jacob E.; Posner, Eric A. (2008): Soft Law. In: Stanford Law Review / University of Chicago, Public Law and Legal Theory Working Paper, Volume March 2008, Issue 213, pp. 2–50. Available online: http://papers.ssrn.com/sol3/papers.cfm?abstract_id=1113537 [Accessed on 15/06/2009].

Goldmann, Matthias (2009): Inside Relative Normativity: From Sources to Standard Instruments for the Exercise of International Public Authority. In: German Law Journal, Volume 9, Issue 11, pp. 1865–1908. Available online: http://papers.ssrn.com/sol3/papers.cfm?abstract_id=1348811 [Accessed on 15/06/2009].

Grendstad, Gunnar; Selle, Per (1995): Cultural Theory and the New Institutionalism. In: Journal of Theoretical Politics, Volume 7, Issue 1, pp. 5–27. Available online: http://jtp.sagepub.com/cgi/reprint/7/1/5 [Accessed on 10/06/2009].

Heyvaert, Veerle (2009): Hybrid Norms in International Law. In: London School of Economics & Political Science (LSE) Legal Studies Working Papers, Volume 6, pp. 1–26. Available online: http://papers.ssrn.com/sol3/papers.cfm?abstract_id=1342366 [Accessed on 15/06/2009].

Hillgenberg, Hartmut (1998): Soft Law im Völkerrecht. In: Zeitschrift für Europarechtliche Studien (ZEUS), Volume Vol. 1, Issue 1, pp. 81–102.

Hillgenberg, Hartmut (1999): A Fresh Look at Soft Law. In: European Journal of International Law (EJIL), Volume 10, Issue 3, pp. 499–515. Available online: http://docstore.ingenta.com/cgi-bin/ds_deliver/1/u/d/ISIS/50787041.1/oup/ejilaw/1999/00000010/00000003/art00499/A88AD78329A1972F12450709874AE5A0D734586E74.pdf?link=http://www.ingentaconnect.com/error/delivery&format=pdf [Accessed on 15/06/2009].

Hofer, Thomas; McGuire, Douglas (2003): Beyond the International Year of Mountains: A Preliminary Assessment by the FAO, the United Nations Lead Agency for IYM2002. In: Mountain Research and Development, Volume 23, Issue 1, pp. 80–83. Available online: http://www.bioone.org/doi/pdf/10.1659/0276-4741%282003%29023%5B0080%3ABTIYOM%5D2.0.CO%3B2 [Accessed on 25/10/2010].

Imber, Mark F. (1993): The United Nations' role in sustainable development. In: Environmental Politics, Volume 2, Issue 4, pp. 121–136.

Jabloner, Clemens; Okresek, Wolf (1983): Theoretische und praktische Anmerkungen zu Phänomenen des "soft law". In: Österreichische Zeitschrift für öffentliches Recht und Völkerrecht, Volume 34, Issue 2, pp. 217–241.

Jönsson, Christer (1996): From 'Lead Agency' to 'Integrated Programming': The Global Response to AIDS in the Third World. Green Globe Yearbook 1996. Fridtjof Nansen Institute. In: Green Globe Yearbook (GGY), pp. 65–72. Available online: http://www.fni.no/YBICED/96_06_jonsson.pdf [Accessed on 25/10/2010].

Kaasa, Stine Madland (2007): The UN Commission on Sustainable Development: Which Mechanisms Explains Its Accomplishments? In: Global Environmental Politics, Volume 7, Issue 3, pp. 107–130. Available online: http://www.fni.no/doc&pdf/smk_gep_2007.pdf [Accessed on 20/05/2009].

King, Kenneth (1993): Multilateral agencies in the construction of the global agenda on education. In: Comparative Education, Volume 43, Issue 3, pp. 377–391.

King, Kenneth (2007): Multilateral agencies in the construction of the global agenda on education. In: Comparative Education, Volume 43, Issue 3, pp. 377–391. Available online: http://dx.doi.org/10.1080/03050060701556331 [Accessed on 11/05/2009].

Klabbers, Jan (1996a): The Redundancy of Soft Law. In: Nordic Journal of International Law, Volume 65, Issue 2, pp. 167-182(16). Available online: http://web.ebscohost.com/ehost/pdf?vid=3&hid=8&sid=c7b61a38-63da-4155-b088-b26550e54076%40sessionmgr8 [Accessed on 15/06/2009].

Klabbers, Jan (1998b): The Undesirability of Soft Law. In: Nordic Journal of International Law, Volume 67, Issue 4, pp. 381-391(11). Available online: http://web.ebscohost.com/ehost/pdf?vid=3&hid=8&sid=c7b61a38-63da-4155-b088-b26550e54076%40sessionmgr8 [Accessed on 15/06/2009].

Lee, Kelley (1998): Shaping the future of global health cooperation: where can we go from here? World Health. In: The Lancet, Volume 351, March 21, pp. 899–902. Available online: http://www.science direct.com/science?_ob=MImg&_imagekey=B6T1B-3SY8P7F-D-3&_cdi=4886&_user=2891414&_pii=S01406 73697114556&_origin=search&_coverDate=03%2F21%2F1998&_sk=996480893&view=c&wchp=dGLzVzz-z SkzV&md5=599a26fc7556db18db49abaeaed2dbaa&ie=/sdarticle.pdf [Accessed on 25/10/2010].

Macedo, Beatriz; Salgado, Carol (2007): Educación ambiental y educación para el desarrollo sostenible en América Latina. Forum de Sostenibilidad (FS). Cátedra UNESCO. In: análisis, Issue 1, pp. 29–37. Available online: http://www.ehu.es/temporalcatedra/revista/numero_1/01_03macedo.pdf [Accessed on 02/08/2010].

Mazuelos Bellido, Ángeles (2004): Soft Law: ¿Mucho ruido y pocas nueces? In: Revista Electrónica de Estudios Internacionales, Issue 8, pp. 1–40. Available online: http://www.reei.org/reei8/MazuelosBellido_reei8_.pdf [Accessed on 10/05/2010].

Monroe, Martha C.; Fien, John (2005): The Role Environmental Education Might Play in the Decade for Education for Sustainable Development. In: Applied Environmental Education & Communication, Volume 4, Issue 3, pp. 203–206.

Oestreich, Joel E. (1998): UNICEF and the Implementation of the Convention on the Rights of the Child. In: Global Governance, Volume 4, Issue 183, pp. 183–198.

Pugh, Michael; Cunliffe, S. Alex (1997): The Lead Agency Concept in Humanitarian Assistance: The Case of the UNHCR. In: Security Dialogue, Volume 28, Issue 1, pp. 17–30. Available online: http://sdi.sagepub.com/content/28/1/17.full.pdf+html [Accessed on 25/10/2010].

Shaffer, Gregory; Pollack, Mark A. (2008): How Hard and Soft Law Interact in International Regulatory Governance: Alternatives, Complements and Antagonists. Inaugural Conference 2008 Paper. In: Society of International Economic Law (SIEL), Issue 45, pp. 1–68. Available online: http://papers.ssrn.com/sol3/papers.cfm?abstract_id=1156867 [Accessed on 15/06/2009].

Sjöblom, Gunnar (1993): Some Critical Remarks on March and Olsen's Rediscovering Institutions. In: Journal of Theoretical Politics, Volume 5, Issue 3, pp. 397–407. Available online: http://jtp.sagepub.com/cgi/reprint/5/3/397 [Accessed on 15/06/2009].

Skjærseth, Jon Birger; Stokke, Olav Schram; Wettestad, Jørgen (2006): Soft Law, Hard Law, and Effective Implementation of International Environmental Norms. In: Global Environmental Politics, Volume 6, Issue 3, pp. 104–120. Available online: http://www.fni.no/doc&pdf/JBS-OSS-JW-GEP-2006-3.pdf [Accessed on 20/05/2009].

Skodvin, Tora; Andresen, Steinar (2006): Leadership Revisited. Negotiating International Environmental Regimes. In: Global Environmental Politics, Volume 6, Issue 3, pp. 13–28. Available online: http://www.fni.no/doc&pdf/SA-GEP-2006-3.pdf [Accessed on 20/05/2009].

Sloan, Blaine (1987): General Assembly resolutions revisited. Forty years later. In: British year book of international law, Volume 58, Issue 8, pp. 39–150.

Stiftung Wissenschaft und Politik (SWP) / Deutsches Institut für Internationale Politik und Sicherheit (ed.) (2011): SWP-Aktuell. Berlin: Stiftung Wissenschaft und Politik (SWP).

Stokke, Olav Schram (2007): Qualitative Comparative Analysis, Shaming, and International Regime Effectiveness. In: Journal of Business Research, Volume 60, Issue 5, pp. 501–511. Available online: http://www.fni.no/doc&pdf/OSS-JBR-2007.PDF [Accessed on 20/05/2009].

Suchman, Mark C. (1995): Managing legitimacy: strategic and institutional approaches. In: Academy of Management Review, Volume 20, Issue 3, pp. 571–610. Available online: http://web.ebscohost.com/ehost/pdf?vid=1&hid=9&sid=2796b956-029e-469d-828b-a015b93dba05%40sessionmgr4 [Accessed on 25/06/2009].

Taylor, Jerry (August 2002): Sustainable Development. A Dubious Solution in Search of a Problem. The Cato Institute. In: Policy Analysis, Issue 449. Available online: http://www.cato.org/pubs/pas/pa449.pdf [Accessed on 09/04/2008].

Tilbury, Daniella (2007): Evaluating the UN Decade of Education for Sustainable Development (DESD). Monitoring and Evaluation during the UN Decade of Education for Sustainable Development. In: Journal of Education for Sustainable Development, Volume Vol. 1, Issue 2, pp. 239–254. Available online: http://jsd.sagepub.com/cgi/reprint/1/2/239.pdf [Accessed on 10/06/2009].

Tilbury, Daniella (July 2009): Tracking Our Progress: A Global Monitoring and Evaluation Framework for the UN DESD. In: Journal of Education for Sustainable Development, Volume 3, Issue 2, pp. 189–193. Available online: http://jsd.sagepub.com/content/3/2/189.full.pdf+html [Accessed on 19/07/2010].

Underdal, Arild (1992): The Concept of Regime 'Effectiveness'. In: Cooperation and Conflict, Volume 27, Issue 3, pp. 227–240. Available online: http://cac.sagepub.com/cgi/reprint/27/3/227 [Accessed on 10/09/2009].

Underdal, Arild (1998): Explaining Compliance and Defection. Three Models. In: European Journal of International Relations, Volume 4, Issue 1, pp. 5–30. Available online: http://ejt.sagepub.com/cgi/reprint/4/1/5 [Accessed on 10/06/2009].

UNESCO (2003): UNESCO and The International Decade of Education for Sustainable Development (2005–2015). In: Connect, Volume 28, Issue 1, pp. 1–28. Available online: http://unesdoc.unesco.org/images/0013/001306/130632e.pdf [Accessed on 10/10/2007].

UNESCO (2005): International Implementation Scheme for the UN Decade of Education for Sustainable Development (2005–2014). In: Connect, Volume 30, Issue 1, pp. 1–28. Available online: http://unesdoc.unesco.org/images/0014/001401/140147e.pdf [Accessed on 10/10/2007].

UNESCO (2006): UNESCO's role, vision and challenges for the UN Decade of Education for Sustainable Development (2005–2014). In: Connect, Volume 31, 1-2, pp. 1–28. Available online: http://unesdoc.unesco.org/images/0014/001469/146976e.pdf [Accessed on 10/10/2007].

Wals, Arjen E. J. (July 2009): A Mid-DESD Review. Key Findings and Ways Forward. In: Journal of Education for Sustainable Development, Volume 3, Issue 2, pp. 195–204. Available online: http://jsd.sagepub.com/content/3/2/195.full.pdf+html [Accessed on 21/07/2010].

Weil, Prosper (1982 / 1983): Vers une normativité relative en droit international? / Towards Relative Normativity in International Law. In: Revue General de Droit International Public (RGDIP) / American Journal of International Law, Volume 86 / 77, 1 / 3, pp. 5-47 / 413-442. Available online: http://www.jstor.org/stable/pdfplus/2201073.pdf [Accessed on 15/06/2009].

Wiliams, Colin C.; Millingtin, Andrew C. (2004): The diverse and contested meanings of sustainable development. In: Geographical Journal, Volume 170, Issue 2, pp. 99–104. Available online: http://www3.interscience.wiley.com/journal/118752331/abstract?CRETRY=1&SRETRY=0 [Accessed on 19/01/2010].

Young, Oran R. (2002): Evaluating the success of international environmental regimes: Where are we now? In: Global Environmental Change, Volume 12, Issue 1, pp. 73–77. Available online: http://www.sciencedirect.com/science?_ob=MImg&_imagekey=B6VFV-45J5TBG-4-2&_cdi=6020&_user=1592544&_orig=mlkt&_coverDate=04%2F30%2F2002&_sk=999879998&view=c&wchp=dGLzVlz-zSkzV&md5=54ce231928638af3f90e5c01ca1932d3&ie=/sdarticle.pdf [Accessed on 10/06/2009].

Young, Oran R.; Zürn, Michael (2006): The International Regimes Database: Designing and Using a Sophisticated Tool for Institutional Analysis. In: Global Environmental Politics, Volume 6, Issue 3, pp. 121–143. Available online: http://web.ebscohost.com/ehost/pdf?vid=1&hid=9&sid=37efb417-a4f2-4a4d-96b8-723f0b346bc1%40SRCSM2 [Accessed on 10/06/2009].

Articles

Abi-Saab, Georges (2007): Conclusions. General Conclusions. In: Yusuf, Abdulqawi A. (ed.): Normative action in education, science and culture. Essays in commemoration of the sixtieth anniversary of UNESCO. French edition. Paris / Leiden / Boston: UNESCO publishing; Martinus Nijhoff Publishers (UNESCO reference works series, 1), pp. 417–423.

Andelman, Marta (2009): Argentina and Education for Sustainable Development. In: Chalkley, Brian; Haigh, Martin J.; Higgitt, David (eds.): Education for sustainable development. Papers in honour of the United Nations Decade of Education for Sustainable Development (2005–2014). London / New York: Routledge, pp. 245–250.

Beisheim, Marianne; Lode, Birgit; Simon, Nils (2011): Ein Rat für Nachhaltige Entwicklung. Vor der Rio-Konferenz 2012: Optionen zur Reform der VN-Nachhaltigkeitsinstitutionen. In: Stiftung Wissenschaft und Politik (SWP) / Deutsches Institut für Internationale Politik und Sicherheit (ed.): SWP-Aktuell. Berlin: Stiftung Wissenschaft und Politik (SWP), Volume 46, pp. 1–8.

Béland, Daniel (2005): Ideas, Interests, and Institutions: Historical Institutionalism Revisited. In: Lecours, André (ed.): New Institutionalism. Theory and Analysis. Toronto / Buffalo / Toronto: University of Toronto Press (Studies in Comparative Political Economy and Public Policy, 23), pp. 29–50.

Benedek, Wolfgang (2007): Fostering Access to Education and Knowledge. The Normative Implications of Education for All (EFA): The Right to Education. In: Yusuf, Abdulqawi A. (ed.): Normative action in education, science and culture. Essays in commemoration of the sixtieth anniversary of UNESCO. French edition. Paris / Leiden / Boston: UNESCO publishing; Martinus Nijhoff Publishers (UNESCO reference works series, 1), pp. 311–329.

Betz, Joachim (2007): Macht und Ohnmacht der internationalen Finanzinstitutionen – IWF und Weltbank. In: Hasenclever, Andreas; Rittberger, Volker (eds.): Macht und Ohnmacht internationaler Institutionen. Festschrift für Volker Rittberger. Frankfurt am Main: Campus Verlag, pp. 314–342.

Bhola, Harbans S. (2008): Adult Literacy for Sustainable Development: Creating a Knowledge-based Discourse for Action. In: Bhola, Harbans S.; Valdivielso Gómez, Sofía (eds.): Signposts to literacy for sustainable development. Complementary studies. Hamburg: UNESCO Institute for Lifelong Learning, pp. 1–76.

Bilder, Richard B. (2003): Beyond Compliance: Helping Nations Cooperate. In: Shelton, Dinah (ed.): Commitment and Compliance. The Role of Non-Binding Norms in the International Legal System. Published new in paperback. Oxford / New York: Oxford University Press, pp. 65–73.

Boisson de Chazournes, Laurence (2007): Elaborating and Implementing UNESCO's Standard-setting Instruments. Monitoring, Supervision and Coordination of the Standard-setting Instruments of UNESCO. In: Yusuf, Abdulqawi A. (ed.): Normative action in education, science and culture. Essays in commemoration of the sixtieth anniversary of UNESCO. French edition. Paris / Leiden / Boston: UNESCO publishing; Martinus Nijhoff Publishers (UNESCO reference works series, 1), pp. 51–73.

Bory-Adams, Aline (2010): Looking beyond the Decade: UNESCO's contribution. In: Witthaus, Michele; McCandless, Karen; Lambert, Rebecca (eds.): Tomorrow today. Leicester, United Kingdom: Tudor Rose; UNESCO publishing, pp. 175–178.

Börzel, Tanja; Risse, Thomas (2002): Die Wirkung internationaler Institutionen. Von der Normanerkennung zur Normeinhaltung. In: Jachtenfuchs, Markus; Knodt, Michèle (eds.): Regieren in internationalen Institutionen. Festschrift für Beate Kohler-Koch. Opladen: Leske & Budrich, pp. 141–182.

Boyle, Alan E. (2006): Soft Law in International Law-Making. In: Evans, Malcolm David (ed.): International Law. 2. edition. Oxford: Oxford University Press, pp. 141–158.

Charney, Jonathan L. (2003): Compliance With International Soft Law. In: Shelton, Dinah (ed.): Commitment and Compliance. The Role of Non-Binding Norms in the International Legal System. Published new in paperback. Oxford / New York: Oxford University Press, pp. 115–118.

Chinkin, Christine (2003): Normative Development in the International Legal System. In: Shelton, Dinah (ed.): Commitment and Compliance. The Role of Non-Binding Norms in the International Legal System. Published new in paperback. Oxford / New York: Oxford University Press, pp. 21–42.

Combes, Bernard P. Y. (2009): The United Nations Decade of Education for Sustainable Development (2005–2014): Learning to Live Together Sustainably. In: Chalkley, Brian; Haigh, Martin J.; Higgitt, David (eds.): Education for sustainable development. Papers in honour of the United Nations Decade of Education for Sustainable Development (2005–2014). London / New York: Routledge, pp. 215–219.

Cowhey, Peter F. (2004 / 2006): The international telecommunications regime. The political roots of regimes for high technology. In: Sinclair, Timothy J. (ed.): Global Governance: Critical Concepts in Political Science. London / New York / London: Taylor & Francis, Inc.; Routledge (Critical Concepts in Political Science, Volume II), Volume International Organization 44 (2) (1990): 169-199, pp. 426–456.

Cox, Robert W. (2004 / 2006): The Executive Head. An Essay on Leadership in International Organization. In: Sinclair, Timothy J. (ed.): Global Governance: Critical Concepts in Political Science. London / New York / London: Taylor & Francis, Inc.; Routledge (Critical Concepts in Political Science, Volume II), Volume International Organization 23 (2) (1969): 205-230, pp. 199–224.

DiMaggio, Paul Joseph; Powell, Walter Woody (1991 / 2004 / 2008): Introduction. In: Powell, Walter Woody; DiMaggio, Paul Joseph (eds.): The new institutionalism in organizational analysis. Reprint. Chicago / London: University of Chicago Press, pp. 1–38.

Dupuy, Pierre-Marie (2007): Beyond Treaty Law: The Influence of the Legal Instruments Adopted by UNESCO on General International Law. The Impact of Legal Instruments Adopted by UNESCO on General International Law. In: Yusuf, Abdulqawi A. (ed.): Normative action in education, science and culture. Essays in commemoration of the sixtieth anniversary of UNESCO. French edition. Paris / Leiden / Boston: UNESCO publishing; Martinus Nijhoff Publishers (UNESCO reference works series, 1), pp. 371–384.

Ebbesson, Jonas (2007): Public Participation. In: Bodansky, Daniel; Brunée, Jutta; Hey, Ellen (eds.): The Oxford handbook of international environmental law. Oxford: Oxford University Press (Oxford handbooks), pp. 681–703.

Eisemann, Pierre Michel (2007): Elaborating and Implementing UNESCO's Standard-setting Instruments. Introduction. In: Yusuf, Abdulqawi A. (ed.): Normative action in education, science and culture. Essays in commemoration of the sixtieth anniversary of UNESCO. French edition. Paris / Leiden / Boston: UNESCO publishing; Martinus Nijhoff Publishers (UNESCO reference works series, 1), pp. 25–30.

Faundez, Julio (2007): Promoting Dignity, Equality and Mutual Respect among Human Beings. Introduction. In: Yusuf, Abdulqawi A. (ed.): Normative action in education, science and culture. Essays in commemoration of the sixtieth anniversary of UNESCO. French edition. Paris / Leiden / Boston: UNESCO publishing; Martinus Nijhoff Publishers (UNESCO reference works series, 1), pp. 177–195.

Fernandez, Alfred (2007): Fostering Access to Education and Knowledge. Ensuring Equal Opportunities in Education. In: Yusuf, Abdulqawi A. (ed.): Normative action in education, science and culture. Essays in commemoration of the sixtieth anniversary of UNESCO. French edition. Paris / Leiden / Boston: UNESCO publishing; Martinus Nijhoff Publishers (UNESCO reference works series, 1), pp. 331–339.

Fien, John (2010): The private sector and education for sustainable development. In: Witthaus, Michele; McCandless, Karen; Lambert, Rebecca (eds.): Tomorrow today. Leicester, United Kingdom: Tudor Rose; UNESCO publishing, pp. 52–53.

Fien, John; Goldney, David; Murphy, Tom (2009): Rethinking Development: As if the Planet and its People Really Mattered. In: Maclean, Rupert; Fien, John; Park, Man-Gon (eds.): Work, Learning and Sustainable Development. Opportunities and Challenges. Dordrecht: Springer Netherlands (Springer-11648 [Dig. Serial], 8), pp. 19–33.

Finnemore, Martha (2004 / 2006): International organizations as teachers of norms. The United Nations educational, scientific, and cultural organization and science policy. In: Sinclair, Timothy J. (ed.): Global Governance: Critical Concepts in Political Science. London / New York / London: Taylor & Francis, Inc.; Routledge (Critical Concepts in Political Science, Volume II), Volume International Organization 47 (4) (1993): 565-597, pp. 302–335.

Francioni, Francesco (1996 / 2008): International 'soft law': a contemporary assessment. In: Lowe, Vaughan; Fitzmaurice, Malgosia (eds.): Fifty years of the International Court of Justice. Essays in honour of Sir Robert Jennings. Cambridge: Cambridge University Press; Grotius Publications, pp. 167–180.

Gambini, Barbara (2009): Cultural Assumptions against Sustainability: An International Survey. In: Chalkley, Brian; Haigh, Martin J.; Higgitt, David (eds.): Education for sustainable development. Papers in honour of the United Nations Decade of Education for Sustainable Development (2005–2014). London / New York: Routledge, pp. 111–127.

Ginkel, Hans van (2010): For our common future: education for sustainable development. In: Witthaus, Michele; McCandless, Karen; Lambert, Rebecca (eds.): Tomorrow today. Leicester, United Kingdom: Tudor Rose; UNESCO publishing, pp. 29–31.

González-Gaudiano, Edgar (2009): The Decade of Education for Sustainable Development: Challenges and Opportunities in México. In: Chalkley, Brian; Haigh, Martin J.; Higgitt, David (eds.): Education for sustainable development. Papers in honour of the United Nations Decade of Education for Sustainable Development (2005–2014). London / New York: Routledge, pp. 273–275.

Gough, Annette (2009): Towards a Synthesis. In: Maclean, Rupert; Fien, John; Park, Man-Gon (eds.): Work, Learning and Sustainable Development. Opportunities and Challenges. Dordrecht: Springer Netherlands (Springer-11648 [Dig. Serial], 8), pp. 71–74.

Haigh, Martin J. (2009): Promoting Environmental Education for Sustainable Development: The Value of Links between Higher Education and Non-Governmental Organizations (NGOs). In: Chalkley, Brian; Haigh, Martin J.; Higgitt, David (eds.): Education for sustainable development. Papers in honour of the United Nations Decade of Education for Sustainable Development (2005–2014). London / New York: Routledge, pp. 175–197.

Hartmann, Eva-Maria (2002): 10 Jahre nach Rio. Auf dem Weg zum Weltgipfel für nachhaltige Entwicklung. In: Deutsche UNESCO-Kommission e. V. (DUK) (ed.): forum der unesco-projekt-schulen. Nachhaltigkeit. Zeitschrift der UNESCO-Projektschulen, Sonderheft Nr. 1. Bonn, pp. 4–9.

Harty, Siobhán (2005): Theorizing Institutional Change. In: Lecours, André (ed.): New Institutionalism. Theory and Analysis. Toronto / Buffalo / Toronto: University of Toronto Press (Studies in Comparative Political Economy and Public Policy, 23), pp. 51–79.

Hasenclever, Andreas; Mayer, Peter (2007): Einleitung. Macht und Ohnmacht internationaler Institutionen. In: Hasenclever, Andreas; Rittberger, Volker (eds.): Macht und Ohnmacht internationaler Institutionen. Festschrift für Volker Rittberger. Frankfurt am Main: Campus Verlag, pp. 9–37.

Hass, Peter M. (2003): Compliance Theories. Choosing to Comply: Theorizing from International Relations and Comparative Politics. In: Shelton, Dinah (ed.): Commitment and Compliance. The Role of Non-Binding Norms in the International Legal System. Published new in paperback. Oxford / New York: Oxford University Press, pp. 43–64.

Higgitt, David (2009a): Approaching the UN Decade of Education for Sustainable Development: Prospects and Challenges. In: Chalkley, Brian; Haigh, Martin J.; Higgitt, David (eds.): Education for sustainable development. Papers in honour of the United Nations Decade of Education for Sustainable Development (2005–2014). London / New York: Routledge, pp. 1–12.

Higgitt, David (2009b): Finding Space for Education for Sustainable Development in the Enterprise Economcy. In: Chalkley, Brian; Haigh, Martin J.; Higgitt, David (eds.): Education for sustainable development. Papers in honour of the United Nations Decade of Education for Sustainable Development (2005–2014). London / New York: Routledge, pp. 99–110.

Hopf, Christel (2005): Forschungsethik und qualitative Forschung. In: Flick, Uwe; Kardorff, Ernst von; Steinke, Ines (eds.): Qualitative Forschung. Ein Handbuch. Reinbek bei Hamburg: Rowohlt-Taschenbuch-Verlag (Rororo Rowohlts Enzyklopädie, 55628), pp. 589–600.

Hopkins, Charles (2010): From Tbilisi to Bonn: an important journey in the historical context of ESD. In: Witthaus, Michele; McCandless, Karen; Lambert, Rebecca (eds.): Tomorrow today. Leicester, United Kingdom: Tudor Rose; UNESCO publishing, pp. 23–25.

Jepperson, Ronald L. (1991 / 2004 / 2008): Institutions, Institutional Effects, and Institutionalism. In: Powell, Walter Woody; DiMaggio, Paul Joseph (eds.): The new institutionalism in organizational analysis. Reprint. Chicago / London: University of Chicago Press, pp. 143–163.

Keohane, Robert O. (1989a): Neoliberal Institutionalism: A Perspective on World Politics. In: Keohane, Robert O. (ed.): International institutions and state power. Essays in international relations theory. Boulder: Westview Press, pp. 1–20.

Keohane, Robert O. (2004 / 2006b): Institutionalization in the United Nations General Assembly. In: Sinclair, Timothy J. (ed.): Global Governance: Critical Concepts in Political Science. London / New York / London: Taylor & Francis, Inc.; Routledge (Critical Concepts in Political Science, Volume II), Volume International Organization 23 (4) (1969): 859-896, pp. 225–262.

Kirton, John J.; Trebilcock, Michael J. (2004): Introduction: Hard Choices and Soft Law in Sustainable Governance. In: Kirton, John J.; Trebilcock, Michael J. (eds.): Hard choices, soft law. Voluntary standards in global trade, environment, and social governance. Aldershot / Burlington, Vermont: Ashgate Dartmouth (Global environmental governance), pp. 3–30.

Kiss, Alexandre (2003): Commentary and Conclusions. In: Shelton, Dinah (ed.): Commitment and Compliance. The Role of Non-Binding Norms in the International Legal System. Published new in paperback. Oxford / New York: Oxford University Press, pp. 223–242.

Klabbers, Jan (2007): The redundancy of soft law. In: Koskenniemi, Martti (ed.): Sources of international law. Reprinted. Aldershot: Ashgate Dartmouth (The Library of Essays in International Law, 5), Volume Nordic Journal of International Law 65: 167–182, 1996, pp. 189–204.

Koch, Sascha; Schemmann, Michael (2009a): Entstehungskontexte und Grundlegungen neo-institutionalistischer Organisationsanalyse. In: Koch, Sascha; Schemmann, Michael; Göhlich, Michael (eds.): Neo-Institutionalismus in der Erziehungswissenschaft. Grundlegende Texte und empirische Studien. Organisation und Pädagogik 6. 1. Auflage. Wiesbaden: VS Verlag für Sozialwissenschaften, pp. 20–27.

Koch, Sascha; Schemmann, Michael (2009b): Neo-Institutionalismus und Erziehungswissenschaft – Eine einleitende Verhältnisbestimmung. In: Koch, Sascha; Schemmann, Michael; Göhlich, Michael (eds.): Neo-Institutionalismus in der Erziehungswissenschaft. Grundlegende Texte und empirische Studien. Organisation und Pädagogik 6. 1. Auflage. Wiesbaden: VS Verlag für Sozialwissenschaften, pp. 7–18.

Köhler, Karl-Heinz (2005): Nachhaltigkeit lernen. Zur UN-Dekade und möglichen Beiträgen der unesco-projekt-schulen. In: Deutsche UNESCO-Kommission e. V. (DUK) (ed.): forum der unesco-projekt-schulen. Nachhaltigkeit. Zeitschrift der UNESCO-Projektschulen, Sonderheft Nr. 1. Bonn: Bonner Universitäts-Buchdruckerei, pp. 5–7.

Köhler, Karl-Heinz (2006): Thesen zur kulturellen Bildung. Praxis der unesco-projekt-schulen und konzeptionelle Überlegungen. In: Deutsche UNESCO-Kommission e. V. (DUK) (ed.): forum der unesco-projekt-schulen. Kulturelle Bildung. Beiträge der unesco-projekt-schulen. Zeitschrift der UNESCO-Projektschulen, Sonderheft Nr. 3. Bonn: Bonner Universitäts-Buchdruckerei, pp. 6–12.

Kono, Toshiyuki (2007): Safeguarding the World's Cultural and Natural Heritage. UNESCO and Intangible Cultural Heritage from the Viewpoint of Sustainable Development. In: Yusuf, Abdulqawi A. (ed.): Normative action in education, science and culture. Essays in commemoration of the sixtieth anniversary of UNESCO. French edition. Paris / Leiden / Boston: UNESCO publishing; Martinus Nijhoff Publishers (UNESCO reference works series, 1), pp. 249–280.

Krott, Maximilian (2002): Evaluation of Transdisciplinary Research. In: UNESCO (ed.): Knowledge for sustainable development. An insight into the Encyclopedia of life support systems. 3 Volumes. Oxford / Paris / London: UNESCO publishing; Encyclopedia of Life Support Systems (EOLSS) Publishers (Environment and Development series), Volume 3, pp. 965–973.

Lasonen, Johanna (2009): Intercultural Education: Promoting Sustainability in Education and Training. In: Maclean, Rupert; Fien, John; Park, Man-Gon (eds.): Work, Learning and Sustainable Development. Opportunities and Challenges. Dordrecht: Springer Netherlands (Springer-11648 [Dig. Serial], 8), pp. 187–202.

Lecours, André (2005): New Institutionalism: Issues and Questions. In: Lecours, André (ed.): New Institutionalism. Theory and Analysis. Toronto / Buffalo / Toronto: University of Toronto Press (Studies in Comparative Political Economy and Public Policy, 23), pp. 3–25.

Leicht, Alexander (2005): Nachhaltigkeit lernen. Die UN-Dekade „Bildung für nachhaltige Entwicklung (2005–2014)" in Deutschland. In: Deutsche UNESCO-Kommission e. V. (DUK) (ed.): forum der unesco-projekt-schulen. Ziel: Zukunftsfähigkeit. Beiträge zur UN-Dekade "Bildung für nachhaltige Entwicklung". Ergebnisse der 40. Jahrestagung der UNESCO-Projektschulen. Zeitschrift der Deutschen UNESCO-Kommission, Sonderheft Nr. 3. Bonn: Bonner Universitäts-Buchdruckerei, pp. 15–17.

Lepsius, Oliver (2007): Standardsetzung und Legitimation. In: Möllers, Christoph; Vosskuhle, Andreas; Walter, Christian (eds.): Internationales Verwaltungsrecht. Tübingen: Mohr Siebeck (Jus internationale et Europaeum, 16), pp. 345–373.

Lim, Gary; Zach Abdullah, Khaeril (2009): Sustainable Development by Instinct, Challenges, and Opportunities in the Decade. In: Chalkley, Brian; Haigh, Martin J.; Higgitt, David (eds.): Education for sustainable development. Papers in honour of the United Nations Decade of Education for Sustainable Development (2005–2014). London / New York: Routledge, pp. 269–272.

Linn, Monika; Sochirca, Angela (2010): Learning from each other. In: Witthaus, Michele; McCandless, Karen; Lambert, Rebecca (eds.): Tomorrow today. Leicester, United Kingdom: Tudor Rose; UNESCO publishing, pp. 26–28.

Lode, Birgit (2011): What do you think should be the two or three highest priority political outcomes of the United Nations Conference on Sustainable Development (Rio+20), scheduled for Rio de Janeiro in June 2012? In: Natural Resources Forum, Volume 35, Issue 4, pp. 334–342. Available online: http://online library.wiley.com/doi/10.1111/j.1477-8947.2011.01409.x/abstract [Accessed on 16/12/2011].

Macedo, Beatriz (2005): Compromisos Educativos Establecidos por la Década. Published by: Oficina Regional de Educación de la UNESCO para América Latina y el Caribe (OREALC). Oficina Regional de Educación de la

UNESCO para América Latina y el Caribe (OREALC). Santiago de Chile. Available online: http://www.unesco.cl/medios/biblioteca/documentos/compromisos_decada_desarrollo_sostenible_congreso_investigacion_educativa.pdf [Accessed on 17/06/2008].

Macedo, Beatriz (2005): Educación para Todos, Educación Ambiental y Educación para el Desarrollo Sostenible. Debatiendo las Vertientes de la Década de la Educación para el Desarrollo Sostenible. Published by: Oficina Regional de Educación de la UNESCO para América Latina y el Caribe (OREALC). Oficina Regional de Educación de la UNESCO para América Latina y el Caribe (OREALC). Santiago de Chile. Available online: http://www.unesco.cl/medios/biblioteca/documentos/educacion_para_todos_ambiental_para_desarrollo_sostenible_debatiendo_vertientes_decada_educacion_desarrollo_sostenible.pdf [Accessed on 17/06/2008].

Magraw Barstow, Daniel; Hawke, Lisa D. (2007): Sustainable Development. In: Bodansky, Daniel; Brunée, Jutta; Hey, Ellen (eds.): The Oxford handbook of international environmental law. Oxford: Oxford University Press (Oxford handbooks), pp. 613–638.

Makrakis, Vassilio (2010): Strategies to reinforce the role of ICT in teaching and learning for sustainability. In: Witthaus, Michele; McCandless, Karen; Lambert, Rebecca (eds.): Tomorrow today. Leicester, United Kingdom: Tudor Rose; UNESCO publishing, pp. 169–171.

March, James G.; Olsen, Johan P. (2004): The new institutionalism. Organizational factors in political life. In: Sinclair, Timothy J. (ed.): Global Governance. London / New York: Routledge Chapman & Hall (Critical Concepts in Political Science, Volume I), Volume The American Political Science Review, Vol. 78, No. 3. (1984), pp. 734-749, pp. 271–299.

Matsuura, Koïchiro (2007): Foreword. In: Yusuf, Abdulqawi A. (ed.): Normative action in education, science and culture. Essays in commemoration of the sixtieth anniversary of UNESCO. French edition. Paris / Leiden / Boston: UNESCO publishing; Martinus Nijhoff Publishers (UNESCO reference works series, 1), pp. 11–14.

Merkel, Christine; Gördel, Bettina (2002): Die vergessene Priorität von Rio. Bildung für nachhaltige Entwicklung. In: Deutsche UNESCO-Kommission e. V. (DUK) (ed.): forum der unesco-projekt-schulen. Nachhaltigkeit. Zeitschrift der UNESCO-Projektschulen, Sonderheft Nr. 1. Bonn, pp. 13–19.

Meyer, John W.; Rowan, Brian (1991 / 2004 / 2008a): Institutionalized Organizations: Formal Structure as Myth and Ceremony. In: Powell, Walter Woody; DiMaggio, Paul Joseph (eds.): The new institutionalism in organizational analysis. Reprint. Chicago / London: University of Chicago Press, pp. 41–62.

Meyer, John W.; Rowan, Brian (2009b): Institutionalisierte Organisationen. Formale Struktur als Mythos und Zeremonie. In: Koch, Sascha; Schemmann, Michael; Göhlich, Michael (eds.): Neo-Institutionalismus in der Erziehungswissenschaft. Grundlegende Texte und empirische Studien. Organisation und Pädagogik 6. 1. Auflage. Wiesbaden: VS Verlag für Sozialwissenschaften, pp. 28–56.

Minsch, Jürg (2005): Nachhaltigkeit: Aufforderung zur Weiterentwicklung der offenen Gesellschaft. Essay mit ökologisch-ökonomischem Repertoire. In: Deutsche UNESCO-Kommission e. V. (DUK) (ed.): forum der unesco-projekt-schulen. Ziel: Zukunftsfähigkeit. Beiträge zur UN-Dekade "Bildung für nachhaltige Entwicklung". Ergebnisse der 40. Jahrestagung der UNESCO-Projektschulen. Zeitschrift der Deutschen UNESCO-Kommission, Sonderheft Nr. 3. Bonn: Bonner Universitäts-Buchdruckerei, pp. 6–14.

Mitchell, Ronald B. (2007): Compliance Theory. Compliance, Effectiveness, and Behaviour Change in International Environmental Law. In: Bodansky, Daniel; Brunée, Jutta; Hey, Ellen (eds.): The Oxford handbook of international environmental law. Oxford: Oxford University Press (Oxford handbooks), pp. 893–921.

North, Douglass Cecil (1997): Economic Performance Through Time. Nobel Prize Lecture. December 9, 1993. In: Persson, Torsten (ed.): Nobel Lectures. Economic sciences. 1991–1995. Singapore: World Scientific Publishing Company (Nobel lectures), pp. 112–126.

O'Connell, Mary Ellen (2003): The Role of Soft Law in a Global Order. In: Shelton, Dinah (ed.): Commitment and Compliance. The Role of Non-Binding Norms in the International Legal System. Published new in paperback. Oxford / New York: Oxford University Press, pp. 100–114.

Pötter, Bernhard (2002): Was wurde aus der Agenda 21. Bilanz der Halbherzigkeiten. In: Deutsche UNESCO-Kommission e. V. (DUK) (ed.): forum der unesco-projekt-schulen. Nachhaltigkeit. Zeitschrift der UNESCO-Projektschulen, Sonderheft Nr. 1. Bonn, pp. 10–12.

Richmond, Mark (2010): Envisioning, coordinating and implementing the UN Decade of Education for Sustainable Development. In: Witthaus, Michele; McCandless, Karen; Lambert, Rebecca (eds.): Tomorrow today. Leicester, United Kingdom: Tudor Rose; UNESCO publishing, pp. 19–22.

Röhl, Hans Christian (2007): Internationale Standardsetzung. In: Möllers, Christoph; Vosskuhle, Andreas; Walter, Christian (eds.): Internationales Verwaltungsrecht. Tübingen: Mohr Siebeck (Jus internationale et Europaeum, 16), pp. 319–343.

Ruggie, John Gerard (2004 / 2006): International regimes, transactions, and change. Embedded liberalism in the postwar economic order. In: Sinclair, Timothy J. (ed.): Global Governance: Critical Concepts in Political Science. London / New York / London: Taylor & Francis, Inc.; Routledge (Critical Concepts in Political Science, Volume II), Volume International Organization 36 (2) (1982): 379-415, pp. 387–425.

Sauvé, Lucie; Berryman, Tom (2009): Challenging a "Closing Circle": Alternative Research Agendas for the ESD Decade. In: Chalkley, Brian; Haigh, Martin J.; Higgitt, David (eds.): Education for sustainable development. Papers in honour of the United Nations Decade of Education for Sustainable Development (2005–2014). London / New York: Routledge, pp. 229–232.

Schemmann, Michael (2009): Das unausgeschöpfte Potential des Neo-Institutionalismus – Die Verknüpfung der analytischen Ebenen als zukünftiger Forschungsfokus. In: Koch, Sascha; Schemmann, Michael; Göhlich, Michael (eds.): Neo-Institutionalismus in der Erziehungswissenschaft. Grundlegende Texte und empirische Studien. Organisation und Pädagogik 6. 1. Auflage. Wiesbaden: VS Verlag für Sozialwissenschaften, pp. 347–358.

Schmidt, Christiane (2005): Analyse von Leitfadeninterviews. Kapitel 5.10. In: Flick, Uwe; Kardorff, Ernst von; Steinke, Ines (eds.): Qualitative Forschung. Ein Handbuch. Reinbek bei Hamburg: Rowohlt-Taschenbuch-Verlag (Rororo Rowohlts Enzyklopädie, 55628), pp. 447–456.

Schorlemer, Sabine von (2007): Elaborating and Implementing UNESCO's Standard-setting Instruments. UNESCO Dispute Settlement. In: Yusuf, Abdulqawi A. (ed.): Normative action in education, science and culture. Essays in commemoration of the sixtieth anniversary of UNESCO. French edition. Paris / Leiden / Boston: UNESCO publishing; Martinus Nijhoff Publishers (UNESCO reference works series, 1), pp. 75–105.

Schrijver, Nico (2007): Beyond Treaty Law: The Influence of the Legal Instruments Adopted by UNESCO on General International Law. UNESCO's Role in the Development and Application of International Law: An Assessment. In: Yusuf, Abdulqawi A. (ed.): Normative action in education, science and culture. Essays in commemoration of the sixtieth anniversary of UNESCO. French edition. Paris / Leiden / Boston: UNESCO publishing; Martinus Nijhoff Publishers (UNESCO reference works series, 1), pp. 385–405.

Selby, David (2009): The Firm and Shaky Ground of Education for Sustainable Development. In: Chalkley, Brian; Haigh, Martin J.; Higgitt, David (eds.): Education for sustainable development. Papers in honour of the United Nations Decade of Education for Sustainable Development (2005–2014). London / New York: Routledge, pp. 199–213.

Senge, Konstanze (2006): Zum Begriff der Institution im Neo-Institutionalismus. In: Senge, Konstanze; Hellmann, Kai-Uwe; Scott, William Richard (Dick) (eds.): Einführung in den Neo-Institutionalismus. 1. Auflage. Wiesbaden: VS Verlag für Sozialwissenschaften, pp. 35–47.

Shelton, Dinah (2003a): Commentary and Conclusions. In: Shelton, Dinah (ed.): Commitment and Compliance. The Role of Non-Binding Norms in the International Legal System. Published new in paperback. Oxford / New York: Oxford University Press, pp. 449–463.

Shelton, Dinah (2003b): Editor's Concluding Note. The Role of Non-binding Norms in the International Legal System. In: Shelton, Dinah (ed.): Commitment and Compliance. The Role of Non-Binding Norms in the International Legal System. Published new in paperback. Oxford / New York: Oxford University Press, pp. 554–556.

Shelton, Dinah (2003c): Law, Non-Law and the Problem of 'Soft Law'. In: Shelton, Dinah (ed.): Commitment and Compliance. The Role of Non-Binding Norms in the International Legal System. Published new in paperback. Oxford / New York: Oxford University Press, pp. 1–18.

Shelton, Dinah (2006d): International Law and 'Relative Normativity'. In: Evans, Malcolm David (ed.): International Law. 2. edition. Oxford: Oxford University Press, pp. 159–185.

Shelton, Dinah (2007e): Equity. In: Bodansky, Daniel; Brunée, Jutta; Hey, Ellen (eds.): The Oxford handbook of international environmental law. Oxford: Oxford University Press (Oxford handbooks), pp. 639–662.

Simma, Bruno (1981): Zur völkerrechtlichen Bedeutung von Resolutionen der UN-Generalversammlung. In: Skubiszewski, Krzysztof; Bernhardt, Rudolf (eds.): Die Bedeutung der Resolutionen der Generalversammlung der Vereinten Nationen. 1. Auflage. Baden-Baden: Nomos Verlagsgesellschaft. Fünftes Deutsch-Polnisches Juristen-Kolloquium, Volume 2, pp. 45–76.

Thomas, Elwyn (2009): Sustainable Development: The Challenges and Prospects for a Sustainability Curriculum. In: Maclean, Rupert; Fien, John; Park, Man-Gon (eds.): Work, Learning and Sustainable Development. Opportunities and Challenges. Dordrecht: Springer Netherlands (Springer-11648 [Dig. Serial], 8), pp. 77–92.

Tilbury, Daniella (2010): Change for a better world: assessing the contribution of the DESD. In: Witthaus, Michele; McCandless, Karen; Lambert, Rebecca (eds.): Tomorrow today. Leicester, United Kingdom: Tudor Rose; UNESCO publishing, pp. 146–148.

Underdal, Arild (2002a): Conclusions. Patterns of Regime Effectiveness. In: Miles, Edward L. (ed.): Environmental regime effectiveness. Confronting theory with evidence. Cambridge, Massachusetts: MIT Press (Global Environmental Accord: Strategies for Sustainability and Institutional Innovation), pp. 433–466.

Underdal, Arild (2002b): Methods of analysis. In: Miles, Edward L. (ed.): Environmental regime effectiveness. Confronting theory with evidence. Cambridge, Massachusetts: MIT Press (Global Environmental Accord: Strategies for Sustainability and Institutional Innovation), pp. 47–62.

Underdal, Arild (2002c): One question, two answers. In: Miles, Edward L. (ed.): Environmental regime effectiveness. Confronting theory with evidence. Cambridge, Massachusetts: MIT Press (Global Environmental Accord: Strategies for Sustainability and Institutional Innovation), pp. 3–46.

Underdal, Arild (2004d): Methodological challenges in the Study of Regime Effectiveness. In: Underdal, Arild; Young, Oran R. (eds.): Regime consequences. Methodological challenges and research strategies. Dordrecht: Kluwer Academic Publishers, pp. 27–48.

UN-HABITAT (2010): Education for sustainable cities. In: Witthaus, Michele; McCandless, Karen; Lambert, Rebecca (eds.): Tomorrow today. Leicester, United Kingdom: Tudor Rose; UNESCO publishing, pp. 42–44.

Valdivielso Gómez, Sofía (2008): Luggage for a Journey: From Functional Literacy and Development to Integral Literacy and Sustainable Development. In: Bhola, Harbans S.; Valdivielso Gómez, Sofía (eds.): Signposts to literacy for sustainable development. Complementary studies. Hamburg: UNESCO Institute for Lifelong Learning, pp. 79–171.

Varwick, Johannes (2008): Völkerrecht / Internationales Recht. In: Woyke, Wichard (ed.): Handwörterbuch internationale Politik. 11. überarbeitete und aktualisierte Auflage. Opladen: Budrich (UTB für Wissenschaft, 702), pp. 541–548.

Vilela, Miriam (2010): Integrating sustainability in teaching and learning: the role of the Earth Charter. In: Witthaus, Michele; McCandless, Karen; Lambert, Rebecca (eds.): Tomorrow today. Leicester, United Kingdom: Tudor Rose; UNESCO publishing, p. 48.

Weiss, Edith Brown (2003): Conclusions: Understanding Compliance with Soft Law. In: Shelton, Dinah (ed.): Commitment and Compliance. The Role of Non-Binding Norms in the International Legal System. Published new in paperback. Oxford / New York: Oxford University Press, pp. 535–553.

Woods, Ngaire (2004 / 2006): Good Governance in International Organizations. In: Sinclair, Timothy J. (ed.): Global Governance: Critical Concepts in Political Science. London / New York / London: Taylor & Francis, Inc.; Routledge (Critical Concepts in Political Science, Volume II), Volume Global Governance 5 (1) (1999): 39-61, pp. 361–383.

Young, Oran R. (1999a): Regime Effectiveness: Taking Stock. In: Young, Oran R. (ed.): The effectiveness of international environmental regimes. Causal connections and behavioral mechanisms. Cambridge, Massachusetts: MIT Press, pp. 249–279.

Young, Oran R. (2004b): The Consequences of International Regimes. In: Underdal, Arild; Young, Oran R. (eds.): Regime consequences. Methodological challenges and research strategies. Dordrecht: Kluwer Academic Publishers, pp. 3–24.

Young, Oran R.; Levy, Marc A. (1999): The Effectiveness of International Environmental Regimes. In: Young, Oran R. (ed.): The effectiveness of international environmental regimes. Causal connections and behavioral mechanisms. Cambridge, Massachusetts: MIT Press, pp. 1–32.

Yusuf, Abdulqawi A. (2007a): Beyond Treaty Law: The Influence of the Legal Instruments Adopted by UNESCO on General International Law. Introduction. In: Yusuf, Abdulqawi A. (ed.): Normative action in education, science and culture. Essays in commemoration of the sixtieth anniversary of UNESCO. French edition. Paris / Leiden / Boston: UNESCO publishing; Martinus Nijhoff Publishers (UNESCO reference works series, 1), pp. 369–370.

Yusuf, Abdulqawi A. (2007b): Elaborating and Implementing UNESCO's Standard-setting Instruments. UNESCO Practices and Procedures for the Elaboration of Standard-setting Instruments. In: Yusuf, Abdulqawi A. (ed.): Normative action in education, science and culture. Essays in commemoration of the sixtieth anniversary of UNESCO. French edition. Paris / Leiden / Boston: UNESCO publishing; Martinus Nijhoff Publishers (UNESCO reference works series, 1), pp. 31–49.

Zemanek, Karl (1998): Is the Term 'Soft Law' Convenient? In: Hafner, Gerhard; Seidl-Hohenveldern, Ignaz (eds.): Liber amicorum Professor Ignaz Seidl-Hohenveldern. In honour of his 80th birthday. The Hague: Kluwer Law International, pp. 843–862.

Newspapers and periodicals

Michelsen, Gerd (08/05/2007): Interview Talk with Aline Bory-Adams (UNESCO, Paris). Education for Sustainable Development International. Online-Magazine "Education for Sustainable Development". In: BNE-Journal, Volume May 2007, Issue 1, pp. 1–8. Available online: http://www.bne-portal.de/coremedia/generator/pm/en/Issue__001/Downloads/02__Interview/Interview_20Bory-Adams.pdf [Accessed on 10/01/2010].

Singer, S. Fred (22/04/2011): The Sustainable Development Hoax. In: American Thinker, April 2011. Available online: http://www.americanthinker.com/2011/04/the_sustainable_development_ho.html [Accessed on 29/04/2011].

Online publications and electronic sources

Bokova, Irina (2009): UNESCO in a Globalised World: New Humanism for the 21st Century. Mission statement by the Director-General of UNESCO. 15 November 2009. UNESCO. Available online: http://www.unesco.org/new/en/unesco/o-junesko/o-junesko/generalnyi-direktor-junesko-irina-bokova/programnoe-zajavlenie [Accessed on 02/11/2010].

Conference of European Rectors (CRE); Centre for Natural Resources (1993 / 1994): Copernicus University Charter for Sustainable Development. Published by: Association of European Universities. Available online: http://www.eso.ed.ac.uk/pdfs/CopernicusUpdate2000.pdf [Accessed on 12/01/2010].

Deutsche UNESCO-Kommission e. V. (DUK) (2007): Bildung für Nachhaltige Entwicklung (BNE)-Portal. Supported by: Sobieraj, Anke and Diepenbrock, Freya. Published by: Deutsche UNESCO-Kommission e. V. (DUK) and Bundesministerium für Bildung und Forschung (BMBF). Deutsche UNESCO-Kommission e. V. (DUK); Freie Universität Berlin. Available online: http://www.bne-portal.de/coremedia/generator/unesco/de/01__Startseite/Startseite.html [Accessed on 08/10/2007].

Deutsche UNESCO-Kommission e. V. (DUK) (2007): Kultur – Deutsche UNESCO-Kommission. Supported by: Offenhäußer, Dieter; Schlünkes, Kurt and Möller, Lutz. Available online: http://www.unesco.de/kultur.html?&L=0 [Accessed on 08/10/2007].

Deutsche UNESCO-Kommission e. V. (DUK) (2007): Nachhaltigkeit lernen – Deutsche UNESCO-Kommission. www.bne-portal.de. Supported by: Offenhäußer, Dieter; Schlünkes, Kurt and Möller, Lutz. Available online: http://www.unesco.de/esd.html [Accessed on 08/10/2007].

Dhillon, Sam (2008): UNESCO Intersectoral Platform: Education for sustainable development. Published by: UNESCO. Available online: http://portal.unesco.org/fr/ev.php-URL_ID=43019&URL_DO=DO_PRINTPAGE&URL_SECTION=201.html [Accessed on 22/01/2009].

Dow Jones Sustainability Indexes (DJSI) (2009): Corporate sustainability. Published by: SAM Indexes GmbH. Available online: http://www.sustainability-index.com/07_htmle/sustainability/corpsustainability.html [Accessed on 13/01/2010].

Dow Jones Sustainability Indexes (DJSI) (2009): Global Sustainability Index. Published by: SAM Indexes GmbH. Available online: http://www.sustainability-index.com/ [Accessed on 13/01/2010].

Elias, Victoria (2007): Overview of the UNECE Strategy on ESD process. Annex 3. European ECO-Forum. Available online: http://209.85.135.104/search?q=cache:ja-xxD20Gy4J:www.eco-forum.org/E_ig/Vilnus_report/

ANNEX_3_eco-forum%2520and%2520the%2520process.doc+Overview+of+the+UNECE+Strategy+on+ESD+process&hl=de&ct=clnk&cd=1&gl=de&client=firefox-a [Accessed on 06/11/2007].

innovemos – Red Regional de Innovaciones Educativas (2010): Desarrollo sostenible. Published by: Oficina Regional de Educación de la UNESCO para América Latina y el Caribe (OREALC). Available online: http://www.redinnovemos.org/content/view/1151/183/lang,sp [Accessed on 12/08/2010].

International Court of Justice (2009): Statute of the International Court of Justice. Available online: http://www.icj-cij.org/documents/index.php?p1=4&p2=2&p3=0#CHAPTER_II [Accessed on 22/09/2009].

Shelton, Dinah; Jonge Oudraat, Chantal de; Simmons, P. J. (1999 / 2009): Commitment and Compliance: What Role for International Soft Law? Presentation review. Supported by: Blavin, Jonathan. Carnegie Endowment for International Peace. Available online: http://www.carnegieendowment.org/events/index.cfm?fa=eventDetail&id=47 [Accessed on 15/05/2009].

SocialFunds.com (2000): The First Global Sustainability Index Turns One. Published by: Social Responsibility Investment Center (SRI World Group Inc.). Available online: http://www.socialfunds.com/news/print.cgi?sfArticleId=376 [Accessed on 13/01/2010].

The Magna Charta Observatory (September 1988): Magna Charta Universitatum Europaeum. Available online: http://www.magna-charta.org/pdf/mc_pdf/mc_english.pdf [Accessed on 12/10/2010].

UNESCO (ed.) (1997b): The Declaration of Thessaloniki. International Conference on Environment and Society: Education and Public Awareness for Sustainability. 8–12 December 1997. Available online: http://portal.unesco.org/education/es/file_download.php/d400258bf583e49cd49ab70d6e7992f6Thessaloniki+declaration.doc [Accessed on 22/10/2007].

UNESCO (2004): Education. Concepts. Published by: UNESCO Education Sector. Available online: http://portal.unesco.org/education/en/ev.php-URL_ID=23292&URL_DO=DO_PRINTPAGE&URL_SECTION=201.html [Accessed on 04/08/2009].

UNESCO (2006): Teaching and Learning for a Sustainable Future. A multimedia teacher education programme. CD-ROM. Published by: UNESCO. (Educating for a Sustainable Future). Available online: http://www.unesco.org/education/tlsf/ [Accessed on 15/10/2007].

UNESCO (2007): General introduction to the standard-setting instruments of UNESCO. Published by: UNESCO. Available online: http://portal.unesco.org/en/ev.php-URL_ID=23772&URL_DO=DO_PRINTPAGE&URL_SECTION=201.html [Accessed on 10/02/2009].

UNESCO (2007): Key Action Themes. Cultural Diversity. Published by: UNESCO Education Sector. Available online: http://www.unesco.org/en/esd/themes/cultural-diversity/ [Accessed on 26/10/2007].

UNESCO (2007): Welcome to Education for Sustainable Development. UNESCO. Available online: http://portal.unesco.org/education/en/ev.php-URL_ID=27234&URL_DO=DO_TOPIC&URL_SECTION=201.html [Accessed on 26/10/2007].

UNESCO (2008): Education Sector Headquarters Organizational Chart. Slightly adapted and modified version. UNESCO Education Sector. Available online: http://www.unesco.org/education/sector/organigramme.ppt [Accessed on 25/03/2010].

UNESCO (2008): Education Today Newsletter. Education for All by 2015. Available online: http://portal.unesco.org/education/en/ev.php-URL_ID=46227&URL_DO=DO_TOPIC&URL_SECTION=201.html [Accessed on 24/10/2008].

UNESCO (2009): International Decades proclaimed by the United Nations General Assembly. Published by: UNESCO Education Sector. Available online: http://portal.unesco.org/en/ev.php-URL_ID=7590&URL_DO=DO_TOPIC&URL_SECTION=201.html [Accessed on 04/08/2009].

UNESCO (2009): UN Decade of Education for Sustainable Development. DESD in Close-up. Published by: UNESCO Education Sector. Available online: http://cms01.unesco.org/en/esd/decade-of-esd/ [Accessed on 04/08/2009].

UNESCO (ed.) (2010b): UNESCO regions. Worldwide. Map. Available online: http://www.unesco.org/new/fileadmin/MULTIMEDIA/HQ/BPI/EPA/images/media_services/regions_worldwide.jpg [Accessed on 23/06/2010].

UNESCO; International Association of Universities (IAU); COPERNICUS-CAMPUS; Association of University Leaders for a Sustainable Future (ULSF) (2001): Global Higher Education for Sustainability Partnership

(GHESP). Lüneburg Declaration. Universität Lüneburg / University of Lüneburg. Available online: http://www.iau-aiu.net/sd/rtf/sd_dluneburg.rtf [Accessed on 13/01/2010].

UNESCO; International Association of Universities (IAU); COPERNICUS-CAMPUS; Association of University Leaders for a Sustainable Future (ULSF) (2002): Global Higher Education for Sustainability Partnership (GHESP). Memorandum of Understanding. Available online: http://www.iau-aiu.net/sd/pdf/mou.pdf [Accessed on 13/01/2010].

UNESCO; International Association of Universities (IAU); COPERNICUS-CAMPUS; Association of University Leaders for a Sustainable Future (ULSF) (2004): Global Higher Education for Sustainability Partnership (GHESP). WSSD Type II Partnership. Action Plan. Available online: http://portal.unesco.org/eduction/en/files/37578/11037253463GHESP_Action_Plan_December_04.pdf/GHESP_Action_Plan_December_04.pdf [Accessed on 13/01/2010].

UNESCO Natural Sciences (2009): UNESCO's Man and the Biosphere Programme (MAB). UNESCO. Available online: http://portal.unesco.org/science/en/ev.php-URL_ID=6393&URL_DO=DO_TOPIC&URL_SECTION=201.html [Accessed on 12/01/2010].

United Nations (1992): Rio Declaration on Environment and Development. Annex I of the Report of the United Nations Conference on Environment and Development, 12/08/1992, Rio de Janeiro. A/CONF. 151/26 (Vol. I). (1). Available online: http://www.un.org/documents/ga/conf151/aconf15126-1annex1.htm [Accessed on 10/10/2007].

United Nations (ed.) (2009): International Decades Designated by the General Assembly. Periods, topics and respective resolutions. R02086. United Nations Dag Hammarskjöld Library. Available online: http://lib-unique.un.org/lib/unique.nsf/Link/R02086 [Accessed on 04/08/2009].

United Nations Global Compact (2007): Issues. Business and Sustainable Development. Available online: http://www.unglobalcompact.org/Issues/partnerships/business_development.html [Accessed on 10/12/2008].

Universität Bayreuth (2009): Ziele der Forschungsstelle for das Recht der Nachhaltigen Entwicklung der Universität Bayreuth (FoRNE). Published by: Rechts- und wirtschaftswissenschaftliche Fakultät / Lehrstuhl Öffentliches Recht I. Available online: http://www.forne.uni-bayreuth.de/de/Ziele/index.html [Accessed on 03/08/2009].

Recordings, films and digital media

Centre for Environment Education (CEE); UNESCO (2007): Comprendre l'Éducation pour le développement durable. ED/EO/KMS/031. Directed by: Nambiar, Prithi. Supported by: Mewada, Ashok (Compilation). Format: CD (Image). Paris: UNESCO Multimedia Archives.

Deutsche UNESCO-Kommission e. V. (DUK) (ed.) (2002): forum der unesco-projekt-schulen. Nachhaltigkeit. In: Zeitschrift der UNESCO-Projektschulen, Volume 2002, Issue 1. Bonn.

Deutsche UNESCO-Kommission e. V. (DUK) (ed.) (2005a): forum der unesco-projekt-schulen. Ziel: Zukunftsfähigkeit. Beiträge zur UN-Dekade "Bildung für nachhaltige Entwicklung". Ergebnisse der 40. Jahrestagung der UNESCO-Projektschulen. In: Zeitschrift der Deutschen UNESCO-Kommission, Volume 2005, Issue 3. Bonn: Bonner Universitäts-Buchdruckerei.

Deutsche UNESCO-Kommission e. V. (DUK) (ed.) (2005b): forum der unesco-projekt-schulen. Nachhaltigkeit. In: Zeitschrift der UNESCO-Projektschulen, Volume 2005, Issue 1. Bonn: Bonner Universitäts-Buchdruckerei.

Deutsche UNESCO-Kommission e. V. (DUK) (ed.) (2006): forum der unesco-projekt-schulen. Kulturelle Bildung. Beiträge der unesco-projekt-schulen. In: Zeitschrift der UNESCO-Projektschulen, Volume 2006, Issue 3. Bonn: Bonner Universitäts-Buchdruckerei.

Deutsche UNESCO-Kommission e. V. (DUK) (ed.) (2006): UNESCO heute. UN-Dekade "Bildung für nachhaltige Entwicklung". In: Zeitschrift der Deutschen UNESCO-Kommission, Volume 2006, Issue 1. Bonn: Bonner Universitäts-Buchdruckerei.

Lectures

Bory-Adams, Aline; Wals, Arjen E. J. (14/05/2009): DESD Global Monitoring and Evaluation process. Fourth International RCE Conference 2009: UNESCO DESD Coordination Section. Taken place on 14/05/2009. Montreal. Presented by: United Nations University. Available online: http://www.ias.unu.edu/resource_centre/8.50%20WALS%20Presentation.ppt [Accessed on 21/07/2010].

Combes, Bernard P. Y. (12/05/2010): Ressources DESD. Paris. E-Mail to: Gerner, Martin.

Gellhorn, Ernest (15/04/2002): Standard-Setting. George Mason University. Manuscript. Officially released and issued on 15/04/2002, Fairfax, Virginia.

Jansen, Dorothea (27/06/2000): Der neue Institutionalismus. Antrittsvorlesung: Deutsche Hochschule für Verwaltungswissenschaften Speyer. Taken place on 27/06/2000. Speyer. Presented by: Lehrstuhl für Soziologie der Organisation. Available online: http://www.hfv-speyer.de/JANSEN/download/SpeyererVortr%C3%A4geInstitutionalismus.pdf [Accessed on 18/05/2009].

Matsuura, Koïchiro (01/03/2005): Address by Mr Koïchiro Matsuura Director-General of the United Nations Educational, Scientific and Cultural Organization (UNESCO) on the occasion of the International launch of the United Nations Decade on Education for Sustainable Development (2005–2014). DG/2005/036. Manuscript. Officially released and issued on 01/03/2005, United Nations Headquarters, New York.

Mayor, Federico (21/01/1988): Address by Mr Federico Mayor Director-General of the United Nations Educational, Scientific and Cultural Organization (UNESCO) on the occasion of the launching of the World Decade for Cultural Development. Manuscript. Officially released and issued on 21/01/1988, Paris.

Mayor, Federico (17/10/1992): Address by Mr Federico Mayor at the opening of the World Congress for Education and Communication on Environment and Development (ECO-ED). Education for Sustainable Development: Taking up the Challenge of Rio. DG/92/43. Manuscript. Officially released and issued on 17/10/1992, Toronto, Ontario.

UNESCO (05/07/2003): Position Paper. Education for Sustainable Development. Eighth Draft. Manuscript. Officially released and issued on 05/07/2003, Paris.

General Assembly: Press Release on the endorsement of the Johannesburg Declaration and the Johannesburg Plan of Action and the scheduled adoption of resolution 57/254. Fifty-seventh General Assembly Plenary 78th Meeting (AM). GA/10125. Press release. Issued on 12/12/2002. New York. Available online: http://www.un.org/News/Press/docs/2002/ga10125.doc.htm [Accessed on 15/09/2009].

United Nations (20/12/2002): Fifty-seventh session United Nations General Assembly 78th plenary meeting Friday, 20 December 2002, 10 a.m. New York. Official Records. A/57/PV.78. Published by: United Nations. General Assembly. New York. Available online: http://daccessdds.un.org/doc/UNDOC/GEN/N02/757/69/PDF/N0275769.pdf?OpenElement [Accessed on 27/05/2009].

United Nations (2003): Fifty-eighth session Second Committee. Allocation of agenda items to the Second Committee. A/C.2/58/1. General Assembly. New York. Available online: http://daccessdds.un.org/doc/UNDOC/GEN/N03/529/60/PDF/N0352960.pdf?OpenElement [Accessed on 17/10/2008].

United Nations (19/09/2003): 2nd plenary meeting. Official Records. A/58/PV.2. Published by: United Nations. General Assembly. New York. Available online: http://daccessdds.un.org/doc/UNDOC/GEN/N03/526/76/PDF/N0352676.pdf?OpenElement [Accessed on 17/10/2008].

United Nations (20/10/2003): Second Committee Summary record of the 15th meeting. Official Records. A/C.2/58/SR.15. General Assembly. New York. Available online: http://daccessdds.un.org/doc/UNDOC/GEN/N03/566/97/PDF/N0356697.pdf?OpenElement [Accessed on 17/10/2008].

United Nations (23/12/2003): 78th plenary meeting. Official Records. A/58/PV.78. General Assembly. New York. Available online: http://daccessdds.un.org/doc/UNDOC/GEN/N04/208/47/PDF/N0420847.pdf?OpenElement [Accessed on 17/10/2008].

United Nations (10/12/2004): Second Committee Summary record of the 14th meeting Held at Headquarters, New York, on Monday, 18 October 2004, at 10 a.m. Official Records. A/C.2/59/SR.14. Published by: United Nations. General Assembly. New York. Available online: http://daccess-dds-ny.un.org/doc/UNDOC/GEN/N04/558/24/PDF/N0455824.pdf?OpenElement [Accessed on 13/01/2010].

Wals, Arjen E. J. (13/05/2009): Towards non-prescriptive and emergent indicator frameworks for self-determined sustainability with a planetary conscience. Fourth International RCE Conference 2009: Wageningen University. Taken place on 13/05/2009. Montreal. Presented by: United Nations University. Available online: http://www.ias.unu.edu/resource_centre/Assessment%20Arjen%20Wals.pdf [Accessed on 21/07/2010].

Interviews

Arrué Rodriguez, Rodrigo (24/07/2008): UNESCO y la Década de las Naciones Unidas "Educación para el desarrollo sostenible" en América Latina. Comisión Nacional del Medio Ambiente (CONAMA) Chile. Interview. Format: mp3. Santiago de Chile.

Berrios, Fernando (23/09/2008): UNESCO y la Década de las Naciones Unidas "Educación para el desarrollo sostenible" en América Latina. UNESCO Perú. Interview. Format: mp3. Lima.

Böhmer, Karl (19/06/2008): UNESCO y la Década de las Naciones Unidas "Educación para el desarrollo sostenible" en América Latina. Universidad ARCIS; UNESCO. Interview. Format: mp3. Santiago de Chile.

Gallardo, Tito; Gajardo Gabelo, Octavio (24/07/2008): UNESCO y la Década de las Naciones Unidas "Educación para el desarrollo sostenible" en América Latina. Ministerio de Educación (MINEDUC); UNESCOP Chile. Interview. Format: mp3. Santiago de Chile.

Gallopin, Gilberto (29/08/2008): UNESCO y la Década de las Naciones Unidas "Educación para el desarrollo sostenible" en América Latina. UNESCO / Comisión Económica Para América Latina y el Caribe (CEPAL/ECLAC). Interview. Format: mp3. Buenos Aires.

Gerner, Martin (30/07/2009): DESD: Monitoring and evaluating. Informal briefing. Interviewee: Lawale, Shivali. Format: Personal notes. Paris.

Gerner, Martin (10/08/2009): DESD in progress. Informal briefing. Interviewee: Laboulle, Olivier. Format: Personal notes. Paris.

Gerner, Martin (11/08/2009): International Institute for Educational Planning (IIEP) and DESD. Informal briefing. Interviewee: Göttelmann-Duret, Gabriele. Format: Personal notes. Paris.

Gerner, Martin (14/09/2009): DESD and UNECE. Informal briefing. Interviewee: Bolshakova, Marianna. Format: Personal notes. Geneva.

Hollander, Astrid; Salgado, Carol (23/07/2008): UNESCO y la Década de las Naciones Unidas "Educación para el desarrollo sostenible" en América Latina. Oficina Regional de Educación para América Latina y el Caribe (OREALC). Interview. Format: doc (Questionnaire). Santiago de Chile.

Macedo, Beatriz (02/08/2010): UNESCO y la Década de las Naciones Unidas "Educación para el desarrollo sostenible" en América Latina. Former regional specialist in charge of ESD / Oficina Regional de Educación de la UNESCO para América Latina y el Caribe (OREALC/UNESCO Santiago). Interview. Format: doc (Questionnaire). Paris.

Ossa, Vicente (17/07/2008): UNESCO y la Década de las Naciones Unidas "Educación para el desarrollo sostenible" en América Latina. United Nations Development Programme (UNDP/PNUD) Chile. Interview. Format: mp3. Santiago de Chile.

Samaniego, Joseluis (07/07/2008): UNESCO y la Década de las Naciones Unidas "Educación para el desarrollo sostenible" en América Latina. Comisión Económica Para América Latina y el Caribe (CEPAL/ECLAC). Interview. Format: mp3. Santiago de Chile.

Glossary

A posteriori	Latin expression meaning *posterior to* and depending on experience or empirical evidence.
A priori	Latin expression meaning *prior to* and non-depending of experience.
Accountability	*Responsibility* explicitly on demand for taken decisions and expected actions.
Ad hoc	Latin expression applied to spontaneously designed for specific problems or tasks that are not universally applicable and therefore usually not adaptable to other purposes.
Added value	Attributed to finance, describing extra competitive edges through features of specific items of interest while deviating from *standard* expectations through providing an excess of something without adding additional costs.
African Union (AU)	International *organisation* established in 2000 / 2002 and founded as the *Organization of African Unity* (OAU) in 1963 to promote co-operation among the independent nations of Africa.
Agenda 21	Action plan to the 1992 *United Nations Conference on Environment and Development* held in Rio de Janeiro, Brazil.
Assessment	Process of well-balanced opinion-making and judgement about something or somebody (*evaluation*).
Assignment	Task, *mission* or particular piece of work attributed to somebody.
Association of South East Asian Nations (ASEAN)	International geo-political and economic *organisation* located in Southeast Asia. Formed in 1967, its aims encompass reconciling accelerated economic growth with social progress and cultural *development* among its members, protecting peace and stability within the region, and providing participatory platform opportunities for member countries.
Belgrade Declaration	Ministerial *declaration* adopted in 2007 urging *UNECE* countries to further strengthen efforts for the *implementation* of the *UNECE Strategy for ESD* at all levels by the end of *DESD*.
Best (or good) practice	Viable solution serving as shining example.

Best Practices and Local Leadership Programme (BLP)	Global *network* of government agencies, local authorities and their associations, professional and academic *institution*s and grassroots *organisation*s established in 1997 and dedicated to the identification and exchange of successful solutions for *sustainable development*.
Biennium	Latin expression describing the time period of two years.
Binding	State of being obliged to comply, as result of existing legal provisions, for example.
Bologna Declaration	Main guiding document of the so called *Bologna process* adopted in 1999 converging European higher *education* systems through creating the *European Higher Education Area* (EHEA).
Bona fide	Latin expression meaning *in good faith* expressing the legal principle of tacit compliance based on the state of moral honesty and line of conduct.
Bonn Declaration	Final document adopted in 2009 at the *UNESCO World Conference on Education for Sustainable Development* addressing achievements and challenges for the second half of *DESD*.
Bottom up	Directional process of grounded planning from the lowest towards the higher positions.
Briefing	Mostly informal narrative account of exchanging specific information.
Brundtland Report	See *Report of the World Commission on Sustainable Development Our Common Future*.
Budget	Given amount of tangible and intangible *resources* available to persons or *institution*s including the plan of spending it over a certain period of time.
Calculus approach	Strategic cost-benefit thinking based on rational utility calculations depending on individual preferences.
Capacity-building	Process of developing the ability to understand, apply or act appropriately within certain *context*s.
Charter of the United Nations	Signed and taken effect in 1945, the charter is the constituting treaty of the international *organisation* of *United Nations* that legally binds members of the international community to universally valid provisions.
Civil society (CS)	Umbrella *concept* of citizenry composed of the totality of voluntary civic and social *organisation*s, non-state *institution*s dedicated to the functioning of society, and privately-owned commercial *institution*s of the economy.

Civil Society Organisation (CSO)	Non-state interest group, such as *non-governmental organisations*, trade unions, faith-based *institution*s, indigenous peoples' movements, foundations, companies and others, raising particular concerns and dedicated to *commitment*.
Clearinghouse	*Organisation*al *conception* of collecting and exchanging information and *expertise*-related data on behalf of people, members or miscellaneous entities.
Coastal Regions and Small Islands (CSI)	Global platform for environmentally sound, socially equitable, culturally respectful and economically viable (sustainable) *development* in *coastal regions and small islands* through mitigation and conflict management.
Code of conduct	*Institution*alised, codified or otherwise co-ordinated behaviour.
Coercion	Practice of forcing another party to behave against its will by applying sources of intimidation, force or some threatening course of action.
Collective Consultation of Non-governmental Organisations (CCNGO)	Key mechanism created by *UNESCO* within the *Education* Sector facilitating reflection, continuous dialogue and joint action between *NGO* and *UNESCO* in different thematic areas.
Commitment	Willingness or promise of dedicating *resources*, such as energy, time, *power* or *expertise*, to specific processes in order to achieve certain goals and objectives.
Comparative advantage	Making the most possible use of an opportunity with respect to others.
Competence	Ability of performing well or accomplishing successfully.
Compliance	Deed of obeying *de facto* or *de jure* expectations, rules or legal provisions.
Concept	Interrelated idea or principle.
Conception	Process of forming an idea or plan.
Connect	*UNESCO*'s international newsletter for science, technology and environmental *education* launched in 1976.
Constitution	Legally *binding* treaty-like instrument prescribing fundamental *organisation*al principles and establishing respective structure, procedures, *power*s and duties.
Content analysis	Systematically exploring, extracting, condensing and re-arranging information to *concept*s according to respective *research question*s.

Context	Surroundings, particular circumstances, environment, background or settings that implicitly or explicitly determine, specify, clarify or shape the character or meaning of given situations.
Convention	*Framework* structures of international co-operation reflecting shared or common *stakeholder* understanding with varying extents of legally-*binding* provisions.
Convention on the Protection and Promotion of the Diversity of Cultural Expressions	Legally *binding UNESCO* instrument adopted in 2005 directed to take into consideration *cultural diversity* and incorporating culture as strategic element in national and international *development* policies.
Convention on the Rights of the Child (CRC)	Legally *binding* instrument adopted in 1989 incorporating the full range of human (civil, cultural, economic, political, and social) rights into the international *commitment* towards promoting and protecting the well-being of all children.
Co-ordination	Ability of facilitating or making *stakeholder*s work together effectively in an organised way through appropriate *ex ante* and *ex post* provisions.
Copernicus University Charter for Sustainable Development	Signed in 1993 as direct response to the 1992 *United Nations Conference on Environment and Development* (*Agenda 21 / Earth Summit*) in Rio de Janeiro in raising consciousness among European universities about essential co-operation towards *sustainability*.
Counterfactual	Hypothetical way of thinking, reasoning and developing scenarios vis-à-vis alternative opportunities and solutions.
CSD	See *United Nations Commission for Sustainable Development*.
Cultural approach	Individual behaviour influenced by collective socio-cultural patterns and particular conditions of view of life.
Cultural diversity	*Concept* of comprising the manifold ways in which the cultures of groups and societies find their expression passed on and expressed within and among groups and societies through varied ways of cultural heritage, and augmented and transmitted through the variety of cultural expressions and through diverse modes of artistic creation, production, dissemination, distribution and enjoyment by multiple means and technologies.
Database	Collection of sorted, stored, organised and retrievable information.

De facto	Latin expression meaning *by the fact* and *for all intents and purposes*, in legal terminology referring to *factual* actions in practice, but not necessarily ordained by law or actuality without being officially established. Opposite of *de jure*.
De jure	Latin expression concerning law as (only) *normative* and justiciable principle of legal *commitment* referring to *according to the law* or *by right*. Opposite of *de facto*.
Declaration	Legally non-*binding* instrument of promulgating general principles intended to inspire action in specific fields as well as subscribing to moral *commitment*s and fostering consensus.
Declaration of intent	Legally non-*binding* statement or document hypothetically outlining prospective intentions and programmatic actions.
Declaration on the Right to Development (UNDRD)	Legally non-*binding* instrument adopted in 1986 considering *development* as participatory, equitable, non-discriminatory, transparent and accountable process while respecting all *standard*s of human rights at the same time.
Delors Report	See *Report of the Independent Commission on Education for the 21st Century Learning: The Treasure Within*.
DESD	Official abbreviation for *United Nations Decade of Education for Sustainable Development*.
DESD Secretariat or Section for DESD Co-ordination (ED/UNP/DESD)	Principal *UNESCO* unit of *DESD* located in Paris providing oversight, advice and backstopping, and supporting *co-ordination* and *network*ing with different programme and thematic areas.
Development	Process of improving and building human capacity in order to facilitate socio-economic progress.
Dimension	Technical term referring to certain aspects, thrusts, self-contained domains, realms or focal issues.
Do ut des	Latin expression meaning *I give so that you may give, too* as Roman principle and corresponding reciprocal *strategy* of equivalent retaliation and unanimously shared expectations. See *tit-for-tat*.
Earth Summit	See *United Nations Conference on Environment and Development*.

Economic Commission for Latin America and the Caribbean / Comisión Económica para América Latina y el Caribe (ECLAC / CEPAL)	Headquartered in Santiago de Chile, one of the five regional commissions of the *United Nations* founded in 1948 with the purpose of contributing to the economic and social *development* of Latin America and the Caribbean through co-ordinating actions and reinforcing economic ties among countries and with other nations of the world.
Economy of scale	Long-run *concept* of comparative cost advantages in business due to increased size and scale of *output* per unit.
ECOSOC	See *United Nations Economic and Social Council.*
Education	Continuing process of learning, training and teaching in order to develop applicable skills and knowledge.
Education for All (EFA)	Global movement led by *UNESCO* and initiated by *UNESCO*, *UNDP*, *UNFPA*, *UNICEF* and the *World Bank* at the *World Conference on Education for All* in 1990 aiming at universalising primary *education* and massively reducing illiteracy through meeting learning needs of all children, youth and adults vis-à-vis quality basic *education* by 2015.
Education for Sustainable Development (ESD)	Integrating the principles, values and practices of *sustainable development* into all aspects of *education* and learning by providing every individual with the opportunity to acquire values, competencies, knowledge and skills in order to enable everybody to contribute towards socially just, culturally promising, economically viable and ecologically sustainable societies.
Effectiveness	Degree of achieving desired or intended results in functional perspective.
Efficiency	Economic principle of achieving particular goals based on the least-cost criterion.
Eo ipso	Latin expression meaning *by or from the thing itself* similar to the English idioms of *by the same token*, *of itself* or *on its own account.*
Erga omnes	Latin expression describing rights and obligations directed towards all or in relation to everyone.
ESD	Official abbreviation for *Education for Sustainable Development.*
ESD Caucus	Flexible regional platform facilitating counterpart communication and *stakeholder* co-operation, and building regional *momentum* through concerted actions on *Education for Sustainable Development* (ESD).

ESD Hub	Multi-*stakeholder* platform dedicated to exchanging relevant information, *expertise* and *best practice*s on *Education for Sustainable Development* (ESD).
ESD Inter-sectoral Platform	*UNESCO* in-house body directed to provide opportunity for strengthening pre-existing internal *co-ordination* mechanisms on *Education for Sustainable Development* (ESD).
Estoppel	Originally ancient French expression indicating the legal principle of impeding the party from denying, contradicting or alleging certain facts owing to that very party's previous conduct, allegation, or denial expressed or implied through deed, acts or representation. See *venire contra factum proprium*.
European Union (EU)	Hybrid, supra-national and inter-governmental economic and political union and partnership between European countries in order to guarantee peace, prosperity and freedom based on voluntary regional integration.
Evaluation	*Assessment* of results according to predefined criteria and scopes.
Ex ante	Latin expression meaning *beforehand* being related to future performance.
Ex post	Latin expression meaning *afterward* being related to past performance.
Ex professo	Latin expression referring to profound expert *competence*s arising from professional capacity and background.
Expertise	Specific expert knowledge, skills or applied capacities in particular subjects, activities or professional realms.
Facilitation	Enabling or making action and processes possible or easier.
Fait accompli	French expression for an *accomplished fact* that is usually considered irreversible.
Favor seriositatis	Term coined in non-*standard* Latin applied in legal terminology for moral *commitment* corresponding approximately to seriously taken *accountability*, reliability or certainty of expectations.
Food and Agriculture Organisation (FAO)	*United Nations specialised agency* founded in 1945 in order to lead international efforts to defeat hunger by means of negotiating agreements, debating policies and being a neutral source of knowledge and information.

Framework	Formalised systems' structures consisting of a set of assumptions, ideas or rules of systems, sometimes provisional by nature.
Game theory	Mathematical attempt at capturing rational decision-making behaviour in strategic situations, games or interactions based on interdependent choices and preferences among economic agents.
General principles of law	Principles essentially providing mechanism of addressing international issues not already subject either to treaty provisions or to *binding* customary rules.
Global governance	*Concept* of the complex of formal and informal *institutions*, international *order*, co-operative mechanisms, multi-*stakeholders* relationships, *networks* and processes between and among states, markets, citizens and *organisations*, both inter- and non-governmental, through which – in the absence of global government – collective interests and policies on the global scale are articulated and managed, rights and obligations are established, and differences in processes are mediated.
Global Higher Education for Sustainability Partnership (GHESP)	Initiative formed in 2002 of international *organisations* with a strong *commitment* to making *sustainability* the major focus of higher *education* by combining forces to mobilise universities and higher *education institutions* to support *sustainable development*.
Global Initiative on HIV / AIDS and Education (EDUCAIDS)	Launched in 2004 to support countries by promoting, developing and supporting comprehensive *education* sector-based responses to *HIV / AIDS*, in particular focusing on children and young people.
Global Monitoring and Evaluation Framework (GMEF)	Operational plan establishing formalised mechanisms for assessing progress during *DESD* in terms of reviewing changes in *context* structures, processes and learning, and *outcomes* and *impacts* by combining self-*reporting*, participatory *monitoring* and expert *evaluation*.
Global Sustainability Index	Launched in 1999 as the first global indexes tracking the financial performance of leading *sustainability*-driven companies worldwide.
Good governance	*Normative* principle of *institution*al quality management and capacity enhancement with respect to autonomy, *efficiency*, rationality, training, *participation*, *accountability*, transparency and fairness.
Green Economy	Business concept discussed and adopted at the *United Nations Conference on Sustainable Development* (Rio+12) in order to encourage and foster economically viable solutions of sustainable development.

Grosso modo	Latin expression meaning *by and large*.
Guidance	Strategic help or advice provided by more experienced persons or *institution*s.
Guidelines	Officially introduced rules or instructions serving as jointly honoured principles for individual or collective decision-making.
Hard law	Legally *binding* instruments, laws and treaties. Opposite of *soft law*.
High-Level Panel on the DESD (HLP)	Series of *leadership* meetings initiated in 2004 and composed of leading experts in order to give *DESD guidance* to *UNESCO*.
Human Immunodeficiency Virus / Acquired Immuno-Deficiency Syndrome (HIV / AIDS)	Disease of the human immune system caused by the human immunodeficiency virus progressively reducing the *effectiveness* of the immune system and leaving individuals susceptible to opportunistic infections and tumours.
Impact	Long-term results.
Implementation	Process of carrying out or turning tasks, plans, *mandate*s or *vision*s into practice.
Indicator	Means, tool or sign of depicting suitable, measurable, achievable, realistic and timely changes in performance.
Information and Communication Technologies (ICT)	Modern information technology based on all available technical means used to handle vocal, pictorial, textual and numerical information and to support communication, including computers, *network*ing hard- and software (internet), telephony, broadcast media, audio and video processing and trans*mission*.
Institution	Comprehensive pattern or rule-based system embedding multiple *stakeholder*s, representing durable social entities directed to produce stability of expectation in interdependent relations and consisting of certain principles, *norm*s and rules.
Institutionalism	Method of inquiry focused on *institutions*.
Inter-Agency Committee for the DESD (IAC)	Constituted in 2006 to ensure harmonious international *co-ordination*, exchange, support and funding of *DESD* at all levels, particularly considering an effective forum to timely and coherently integrate the *ESD* agenda into the work of the *United Nations* family.
International customary law	Recognised source of international law, along with *general principles of law* and treaties, derived from custom.

International Implementation Scheme (IIS)	Broad non-prescriptive *framework* for all partners to contribute to *DESD* providing *context*ual *guidance*, *network*ing opportunities and strategic management of challenges in order to facilitate *ESD*.
Inter-Sectoral Working Group on ESD (IWG)	Set up in 2005 as participatory and integrated *UNESCO* platform in order to link all programme sectors and offices, institutes and regional offices with *DESD*.
Interview	Specifically designed narrative account of standardised communication in rather formal situations or settings.
Intra vires	Latin expression literally meaning *within powers* and legally complying with acting under certain legal *power*, *mandate*, *competence* or authority. Opposite of *ultra vires*.
Ius cogens	Latin expression for *compelling law* as fundamental principle of peremptory and unalienable *norm*s of international law unanimously shared by the international community.
Kiev Declaration	Document adopted by the *UNECE* environment ministers in 2003 articulating *commitment* to enhanced cooperation on environmental protection and *sustainable development* in terms of *implementation* and *monitoring* within and beyond *UNECE*.
Lacunae	Latin expression meaning *gaps* addressing the lack of legal provisions or sources determining *normative context*s.
Lead agency	Representing some formally appointed, *mandate*d, designated or otherwise legitimated *institution*al body which is officially launched and scheduled for carrying out a particular *mission*.
Leadership	Ability, process and position of influencing, organising and directing people to accomplish common goals both by means of charismatic behaviour, intelligence, *vision* or values, and bureaucratic function, situational interaction or entrepreneurial *power*.
Legitimacy	Generalised perception or assumption of actions to be desirable, proper, recognised or appropriate within some socially constructed *context* of *norm*s, values, beliefs and definitions.
Lex feranda	Latin expression meaning *future law*.
Lex lata	Latin expression meaning *current law*.

Literacy Initiative for Empowerment (LIFE)	Global strategic *framework* for the *implementation* of the *United Nations Literacy Decade* (UNLD) (2003–2012) in order to meet the *Education for All* (EFA) goals particularly focusing on adult literacy and out-of-school children.
Local and Indigenous Knowledge Systems (LINKS)	*UNESCO* cross-cutting project of interdisciplinary and inter-sectoral action launched in 2002 involving all five *UNESCO* programme sectors and aiming at empowering local and indigenous peoples in biodiversity governance and *sustainable development* by advocating full recognition of their unique knowledge, know-how and practices.
Magna Charta Universitatum Europaeum	Proposal adopted among rectors of European universities in 1988 to celebrate the deepest values and shared inheritance of European university traditions, to encourage strong bonds considering common aims and common methodologies of exploring and disseminating knowledge, and to universally inspire any extra-European university of joining.
Mandate	Legal capacity of authority, *power* and *order* assigned to governments, *institution*s or *organisation*s in order to carry out certain *assignment*s, such as functional *leadership* in international law.
Memorandum of understanding	Bilateral or multilateral agreement between parties expressing convergence of will, indicating an intended common, consolidated line of action.
Me-too-strategy	Competitive approach based on imitating or copying behaviour and action of others.
Millennium Declaration	See *United Nations Millennium Declaration*.
Millennium Development Goals (MDG)	Eight goals acknowledged by all *United Nations* member states in 2000 through the *United Nations Millennium Declaration* to be achieved by 2015 and committing world leaders to specific targets and *indicator*s to combat poverty, hunger, disease, illiteracy, environmental degradation and discrimination against women.
Millennium Summit	See *United Nations Millennium Summit*.
Mission	Formal statement of the programmatic purposes and practices of *institution*s, companies or *organisation*s, usually being deduced from visions and serving as a kind of *framework* or *context* for carrying out strategic actions by officially spelling out the overall goal, providing *guidance* in decision-making through programmatic practice and *operationalisation*.

Momentum	Literally applied to classical mechanics describing the ability to keep increasing or developing impetus or stimuli.
Monitoring	Process of *reporting developments* and systematically evaluating tasks, *implementation* activities and mandatory *assignments*.
Monitoring and Evaluation Expert Group (MEEG)	Expert group established by *UNESCO* in 2007 for providing *guidance* on the preparation and *implementation* of the *Global Monitoring and Evaluation Framework for the DESD* (GMEF), drawing on specific regional approaches of *monitoring* and *evaluation*, and offering technical advice and support to the *DESD Secretariat* to assess the global progress in the *implementation* of *DESD* as well as *UNESCO*'s contribution to *DESD implementation*.
Nash-equilibrium	Set of mixed reciprocal strategies for finite, non-cooperative games between two or more players whereby no player can improve his or her payoff by changing their *strategy*. Each player's *strategy* is an optimal solution based on the anticipated rational *strategy* of the other players in the game.
Network	Relative permanent, not formally arranged, non-hierarchic modes of communication relations fostered by interdependence and commonly shared presuppositions of behaviour or behavioural orientations.
New institutionalism	Positivist *concept* in *organisation*al theory and sociology comprising of *institution*al analysis based on rejection of rational-actor models, interest in interacting *institution*s as independent variables, turn towards cognitive, *context*ual and cultural explanations, and interest in properties of supra-individual units of analysis that cannot be reduced to aggregations or direct consequences of individuals' attributes or motives.
Non-governmental organisation (NGO)	*Institution* operating often globally and independent from any government with established, effective and autonomous *competence*s in governing and decision-making with respect to particular trans-disciplinary fields of action.
Norm	Implicitly or explicitly expressed rule, *standard* or pattern of conduct complied by group members in terms of appropriate value and belief, attitude or expected behaviour.
Norm cascade	Process of gradual *binding*, internalising and diffusing *norm*s from *normative* ideas to the point of *norm*-oriented patterns and *norm*-consistent behaviours.

Normative action	Any type of (legally) *binding* decision and instrument suitable to generate substantial results.
Normativity	Degree of gradually setting *standard*s and rules of behaviour, ranging between relative (*soft law*) and absolute (*hard law*).
Operationalisation	Extract of relevant objectives, instruments and means-end relations for the purpose of practical employment.
Opinio iuris (sive necessitatis)	Latin expression meaning *opinion of law (or necessity)* in terms of any accepted domain or manifest practice requiring legal provisions either in conformity with or desirable of turning into *international customary law*.
Opportunity costs	Costs of the neglected opportunity and related to the next-best option among several mutually exclusive choices.
Order	System of rules and customs in order to create certainty of expectations either through *binding* contracts reflected in *constitution*s, laws and other sources, or by organising community through *codes of conduct* and moral obligation.
Organización de Estados Iberoamericanos para la Educación, la Ciencia y la Cultura (OEI)	International *organisation* dating back to 1949 for inter-governmental co-operation between the Latin American countries in the field of *education*, science, technology and culture in the *context* of the integral *development*, democracy and regional integration.
Organisation	*Institution* with established, effective and autonomous *competence*s in governing and decision-making with respect to particular realms of action.
Organisation for Economic Co-operation and Development (OECD)	International economic *organisation* founded in 1961 aimed to stimulate economic progress and world trade being committed to democracy and market economy in order to support sustainable economic growth, boost employment, raise living *standard*s, maintain financial stability, assist other countries' economic *development* and contribute to growth in world trade.
Organization of American States (OAS)	International *organisation* established in 1948 comprising of member states of the American continent dedicated to provide the regional forum for achieving an *order* of peace and justice, promoting solidarity, strengthening collaboration, and defending sovereignty, territorial integrity, and independence.
Our common future	See *Report of the World Commission on Sustainable Development Our Common Future*.

Outcome	Result or effect of actions or events referring to the level of performance or achievement of changing behaviour implying or demanding for quantification.
Output	Quality and quantity of generating principles, *norm*s, rules, procedures and decisions out of factual activities or processes.
Pacta sunt servanda	Latin expression meaning *agreements must be kept* as basic principle based on good faith of *binding*ly contracting parties in civil and international law. See *hard law*.
Pareto-optimum	*Conception* of economic *efficiency* and income distribution named after the Italian economist Vilfredo Pareto claiming the optimal allocation of *resources* whenever changing to different allocation no individual player can be better off without compromising any other individual player worse off.
Participation	Act of taking part in and contributing to activities, projects, processes or events, and exerting influence and informed ownership vis-à-vis political, economic, management or other social decisions.
Policy advice	Formulating policies and recommending codes of conduct as de-centralised, case-dependent, issue-related and *stakeholder*-oriented *strategy* or *framework*.
Policy cycle	Tool applied for analyzing and illustrating (global) policy making and advice.
Poverty Reduction Strategy Paper (PRSP)	Plan prepared by countries through the participatory process of ownership and broad-based support involving domestic *stakeholder*s as well as external *development* partners describing macro-economic, structural, social policies and programmes to be pursued in order to promote growth, to reduce poverty as well as to comply with external financing needs and associated sources of financing (debt relief).
Power	Ability, opportunity, strength, authority, right or *responsibility* to shape, influence, guide, decide or control.
Prisoner's dilemma	Fundamental problem in *game theory* demonstrating why two people might not co-operate, even if it is in both their best interests to do so, and leading to both a *Nash-equilibrium* and *pareto-suboptimal* solution, still.
Public-Private-Partnership (PPP)	Issue-related platform of mixed project-based co-operation funded and operated both by government and private sector.

Qualitative	Inductive research paradigm connected with how good something is rather than with how much of it there is. Opposite of *quantitative*.
Quantitative	Deductive research paradigm connected with the amount or number of something rather than with how good it is. Opposite of *qualitative*.
Questionnaire	Both *qualitative* and *quantitative* research instrument consisting of a written series of questions and other prompts for the purpose of gathering target-group-related information from respective respondents.
Rapporteur	French expression meaning *reporter* used in international legal and political *contexts* referring to an officially appointed person being responsible for investigating and *reporting* on certain issues, processes, situations or negotiations.
Rational choice	Theoretical paradigm and *framework* of modelling decision-making assuming the social and economic behaviour in line with the *calculus approach* regarding utility maximisation and individual preferences.
Recommendation	Non legally-*binding*, declaratory and flexible instrument proposing *code of conduct* or action, such as *convention*, *recommendation*, charter, *framework* or plan of action.
Reference Group for the DESD	Advisory group composed of experts in different spheres of *ESD* in 2006 set up to functionally assist the *DESD Secretariat* and *UNESCO*, particularly in strategic planning, such as for the *co-ordination* and mobilisation of *DESD stakeholder*s.
Regime	Patterned behaviours of high-level social *institution*s consisting of agreed upon principles, *norm*s, rules, procedures and programmes that govern interactions of actors in specific domains or particular political arenas without carrying *stakeholder* status.
Regime theory	*Framework* of thought in the realm of international *regime*s examining conditions of international co-operation and governance directed towards understanding agenda-setting processes and creating appropriate *institution*al arrangements for legislative and *institution*al bargaining.
Report of the Independent Commission on Education for the 21st Century Learning: The Treasure Within (*Delors Report*)	Proposal made in 1996 by the chairman and former European Commission president Jacques Delors of rethinking modes of learning in societies and identifying four founding pillars of *education*: learning to be, learning to know, learning to do, and learning to live together.

Report of the World Commission on Sustainable Development Our Common Future (*Brundtland Report*)	Final report of the so called *Brundtland Commission*, named after the chairperson Gro Harlem Brundtland, formally appointed by the *United Nations General Assembly* in 1983 by *resolution* 38/161 as the *World Commission on Environment and Development* (WCED), entitled *Our Common Future*, and welcomed by the *United Nations General Assembly* in 1987 by *resolution* 42/187.
Reporting	Compiling and presenting different kinds of information or data either voluntarily or on request.
Research question	Formulated scope of investigation.
Resources	Physical or virtual entities or qualities with limited availability (scarcity).
Responsibility	Duty to deal with or to take care of something or somebody complementary to prescribed rights.
Rio Declaration	Final document of the *United Nations Conference on Environment and Development* addressing the integrity of the global environmental and *development*al system by linking economic progress with environmental protection and establishing new, equitable, global and multi-*stakeholder* partnerships.
Soft law	Legally non-*binding* instruments without contracting *power*. Opposite of *hard law*.
Southern Africa Development Community (SADC)	Inter-governmental *organisation* of southern African states complementing the role of the *African Union* (AU) and aiming at furthering socio-economic co-operation and integration as well as political and security co-operation.
Southern Africa Development Co-ordination Conference (SADCC)	Formed in 1980 and predecessor regional *organisation* of the *Southern Africa Development Community* (SADC).
Stakeholder	Person or entity (group, *organisation*, company, system, etc.) with legal or corporate affiliation directly involved with or affected by certain action.
Standard	Measure of instrumental alignment in terms of *compliance* or technical objectives limited to specific purpose and scope. Performance versus content / *de facto* versus *de jure* (legal *commitment*s)
Standard-setting	Proper following of some prescribed rational system of rules or procedures resulting in the *assignment* of benchmarks enabling to differentiate between two or more states or degrees of performance.
Strategy	Plan of action intended and designed to achieve a particular objective or purpose.

Subsidiarity	*Organisation*al principle of de-centralisation considering matters to be handled or controlled by the smallest, lowest or least centralised competent local authority. See *top down*.
Sui generis	Latin expression literally referring to *of its own kind*, *genus* or *unique* in its characteristics.
Sustainability	Meeting the needs of the present without compromising the ability of prospect generations to meet their own needs.
Sustainability literacy	Ability to develop awareness, recognition and knowledge towards *sustainability*.
Sustainable Development (SD)	Social, economic and environmental and cultural capacity to maintain an intentional path of continuing *development* by taking equally into account the need for dynamic learning of individuals and *organisation*s that economic and social progress depend critically on the preservation of the natural resource base with effective measures to prevent environmental degradation.
Synergy effect	Additional positive energy, *power*, success or results released through strategic interaction and collaboration.
Teacher Training Initiative for sub-Saharan Africa (TTISSA)	Ten-year programme designed to dramatically improve teacher training capacities in sub-Saharan countries by assisting countries to synchronise their policies, teacher *education* and labour practices with national *development* priorities for *Education for All* (EFA) and the *Millennium Development Goals* (MDG) .
The Earth Charter	*Declaration*, initiative and *vision* launched in 2000 of fundamental ethical principles for building a just, sustainable and peaceful global society in the 21st century by seeking to inspire people through the sense of global inter-dependence and shared *responsibility* for the well-being of present and future generations.
The Gothenburg Recommendations on Education for Sustainable Development	Call on governments, *civil society* and educators to prioritise processes that develop and strengthen *ESD* being fully in line with the *International Implementation Scheme* (IIS) and *The Earth Charter*.
Theoretical sampling	Tool of *qualitative* research referring to the process of choosing adequate points of comparison as analytic frames.

Tit-for-tat	Reciprocal *strategy* of equivalent retaliation that is highly effective and applicable in *game theory*. See *do ut des*.
Top down	Directional process of subsidiary planning from the highest towards the lower positions. See *subsidiarity*.
Topicality	State of being timely of thematic interest.
Trade-off	Economic principle of two or more contrasting objectives.
Trans-National Corporation (TNC)	Corporation or enterprise operating across borders through managing production or delivery of goods and services in multiple countries.
Travaux préparatoires	French expression meaning *preparatory works* related to official records which document negotiation processes.
Triangulation	Methodological principle of using independent pieces of information through combining various techniques in order to improve the validity of research.
Ultra vires	Latin expression literally meaning *beyond powers* and legally referring to excesses of *mandate* or *competences*. Opposite of *intra vires*.
UNECE	See *United Nations Economic Commission for Europe*.
UNECE Committee on Environmental Policy (CEP)	Annual multi-*stakeholder* meetings dating back to 1971 providing collective policy direction in the area of environment and *sustainable development*, preparing ministerial meetings, developing international environmental law and supporting international initiatives in the *UNECE* region.
UNECE Expert Group on ESD indicators	*UNECE* body assigned to measure the *effectiveness* of *DESD implementation* within the *UNECE* region by endorsing respective *ESD indicators* and *monitoring*.
UNECE Secretariat	Organisational *UNECE* structure divided into different strategic units and functional divisions.
UNECE Steering Committee on ESD	*UNECE* body supported by the *UNECE secretariat* and including representatives from member states' *educational* and environmental sector and other *stakeholders* with observer status assigned to decide on implementing the *UNECE strategy*, and to guide and review the process.
UNECE Strategy for Education for Sustainable Development	Regional *DESD strategy* adopted in 2005 by the *United Nations Economic Commission for Europe* (UNECE).
UNESCO	See *United Nations Educational, Scientific and Cultural Organization*.

UNESCO (programme) sectors	Five concrete thematic and policy-style approaches for *education*, natural sciences, social and human sciences, culture, communication and information.
UNESCO Action plan	*UNESCO*'s genuine *DESD implementation* initiative approved in 2007 by the *Inter-Sectoral Working Group on ESD* (IWG) considered as comprehensive inter-sectoral plan outlining the proper programme with approved *budget* for the *implementation* of *DESD*.
UNESCO Associated Schools Project Network (ASPnet)	Global *network* of *education*al *institution*s around the world ranging from pre-schools, primary, secondary and vocational schools to teacher training *institution*s, founded in 1953, and working in support of international understanding, peace, intercultural dialogue, *sustainable development* and quality *education* in practice.
UNESCO Chair	Project which is part of the *University Twinning and network scheme* (UNITWIN) established in 1992 as a global *network* of co-operation, teaching and research among chairholders in the strategic realm of *UNESCO*.
UNESCO Director-General	Representative and executive head authority of *UNESCO* elected every four years by the *UNESCO General Conference*.
UNESCO Executive Board	*Constitution*al organ of *UNESCO* elected by the *UNESCO General Conference mandate*d to approve the programme work and corresponding *budget* estimates, and to ensure the effective and rational execution of the programme by the *UNESCO Director-General*.
UNESCO General Conference	*UNESCO* member states' representation meeting every two years for discussing and adopting the main lines of work by setting programmes and *budget*, usually as proposed beforehand by the *UNESCO Executive Board*.
UNESCO Institute for Lifelong Learning (UIL)	Non-profit, policy-driven, international research, training, information, assistance, documentation and publishing centre of *UNESCO* based in Hamburg promoting lifelong learning policy and practice focusing on adult learning and *education*.
UNESCO International Institute for Educational Planning (IIEP)	Centre for training and research created in 1963 specialised in *education*al planning and management providing training, research and technical assistance run by *UNESCO* and headquartered in Paris.

UNESCO scientific institutes	Specialised *UNESCO* departments situated around the world supporting and technically assisting the *UNESCO (programme) sectors*, cluster and national offices, and regional bureaux.
UNESCO Secretariat	Executive branch of *UNESCO* translating the programmes into day-to-day reality consisting of the *UNESCO Director-General* and staff divided into professional and general service of programme sectors, support sectors, central services, field offices, and institutes and centres.
UNESCO Universal Declaration on Cultural Diversity	Legally non-*binding* instrument adopted in 2001 recognising *cultural diversity* as common heritage of humanity and considering its safeguarding an ethical imperative that ought to be inseparable from respect for human dignity.
UNESCO World Conference on Education for Sustainable Development	Mid-term *DESD* conference held in Bonn in March 2009 dedicated to exchanging *best practice*s, developing mechanisms for enhanced co-operation, highlighting relevance, promoting international exchange, reviewing the regional *implementation* progress, and developing culturally appropriate strategies for the ongoing process.
UNESCO's Man and the Biosphere Programme (MAB)	Launched in 1977 aiming to set and promote the scientific interdisciplinary basis for improving the relationships between people and their environment globally through research, *capacity-building*, training, communications in ecosystem conservation and rational use of natural *resources*, particularly targeted at the ecological, social and economic *dimension*s of biodiversity.
UNICEF-United Nations Girls' Education Initiative (UNGEI)	Partnership of *organisation*s launched in 2000 driven by the objectives of the *Millennium Development Goals* (MDG) and *Education for All* (EFA) committed to narrowing the gender gap in primary and secondary *education* by accelerating action on girls' *education*.
United Nations (UN)	International *organisation* founded in 1945 after the Second World War committed to maintaining international peace and security, developing friendly relations among nations and promoting social progress, and better living *standard*s and respect for human rights.
United Nations International Children's Emergency Fund (UNICEF)	*United Nations organisation* established in 1946 to provide long-term humanitarian and *development*al assistance to children and mothers focusing on child survival and *development*, basic *education* and gender equality, *HIV / AIDS* and children, child protection, and policy advocacy and partnerships.

United Nations Commission for Sustainable Development (CSD)	Created in 1992 to ensure effective follow-up of the *United Nations Conference on Environmental and Development* to monitor and report on *implementation* at the local, national, regional and international levels by ensuring the high visibility of *sustainable development* issues within the *United Nations* system and helping to improve the *United Nations co-ordination* of environment and *development* activities in the fields of fresh water, health and solid wastes.
United Nations Conference on Environment and Development	Summit held in Rio de Janeiro, Brazil, in 1992 to discuss solutions for global problems of poverty, war and the growing gap between industrialised and developing countries, and to introduce the paradigm of *sustainable development* into the global environmental system, above all.
United Nations Conference on Sustainable Development (Rio+12)	Follow-up summit of the 1992 *United Nations Conference on Environment and Development* held in Rio de Janeiro, Brazil, in 2012 to challenge the issue of climate change and to strategically focus on innovative green markets with sustainable products instead.
United Nations decade	Single-issued and mostly inter-dependent initiative at regional or global scale based on *mandate* or *assignment* and scheduled for a particular period of time.
United Nations Decade for Human Rights Education	Ten-year period of time proclaimed by the *United Nations* and led by *UNESCO* from 1995 until 2004 dedicated to human rights *education* globally through training, dissemination and information.
United Nations Decade of Education for Sustainable Development (DESD)	Ten-year period of time proclaimed by the *United Nations* and led by *UNESCO* from 2005 until 2014 dedicated to promoting *education* for *sustainable development* at local, sub-national, national, regional and international level.
United Nations Development Group (UNDG)	*United Nations* platform formed in 1997 uniting most of the *United Nations* funds, programmes, agencies, departments and offices providing system-wide *guidance* to co-ordinate, harmonise and align *United Nations development* activities meant to deliver more coherent, effective, efficient support and to countries seeking to attain internationally agreed *development* goals, including the *Millennium Development Goals* (MDG).

United Nations Development Programme (UNDP)	*United Nations* global *development network* merged in 1965 and 1972 to an *organisation* advocating for change and connecting countries to knowledge, experience and *resources* to help people build better lives by means of expert advice, training and technical support.
United Nations Economic and Social Council (ECOSOC)	*United Nations* organ established under the *Charter of the United Nations* as the principal organ to co-ordinate economic, social and related work of the *United Nations* specialised agencies, functional commissions and five regional commissions facilitating international co-operation on *standard*s-making and problem-solving in economic and social issues.
United Nations Economic Commission for Europe (UNECE)	One of five regional commissions of the *United Nations* set up in 1947 consisting of countries in Europe and North America directed to promote pan-European economic integration through dialogue, co-operation, analysis, *policy advice* and assistance to governments in the fields of economic co-operation and integration, energy, environment, housing and land management, gender, population, statistics, timber, trade, and transport.
United Nations Educational, Scientific and Cultural Organization (UNESCO)	*United Nations specialised agency* in 1945 *mandate*d to contribute to peace, universal respect and security by promoting international collaboration through *education*, science, and culture divided into five strategic programme sectors.
United Nations Environment Programme (UNEP)	Thematic programme of the *United Nations* launched in 1972 in the realm of environment performing as multi-*stakeholder* catalyst, advocate, educator and facilitator to promote the efficient use of *resources* and *sustainable development* of the global environment.
United Nations General Assembly	Main deliberative, policymaking and representative organ of the *United Nations* established in 1945 under the *Charter of the United Nations* for taking decisions on questions on peace and security, admission of new members and *budget*ary matters, granting members states the right to vote, and establishing subsidiary organs for the performance of its functions.
United Nations Global Compact	Strategic policy initiative and global platform launched in 2000 convening *United Nations* agencies, labour and *civil society* together with companies and businesses (corporate citizenship) committed to aligning operations and strategies with universally accepted principles in the areas of human rights, labour, environment and anti-corruption.

United Nations High Commissioner for Refugees (UNHCR)	*Mandate*d agency established in 1950 to lead and co-ordinate international action to protect refugees and resolve refugee problems worldwide by safeguarding the rights and well-being of refugees, ensuring everyone's right to seek asylum, and helping stateless people.
United Nations Human Settlements Programme (UN-HABITAT)	Self-contained programme since 2001 *mandate*d to promote socially and environmentally sustainable towns and cities with the goal of providing adequate shelter for all by means of *monitoring* and research, policy *development*, *capacity-building*, and financing for housing and urban *development*.
United Nations Literacy Decade (UNLD)	Scheduled from 2003 to 2012, this *United Nations decade* aims to extend the use of literacy to those who do not currently have access to it in order to enable people everywhere to communicate effectively within their own communities and with the outside world.
United Nations Millennium Declaration	Final document adopted by the *United Nations General Assembly* at the *United Nations Millennium Summit* of world leaders at the headquarters of the *United Nations* in September 2000 consisting of eight chapters and key objectives that are commonly known as *Millennium Development Goals* (MDG) .
United Nations Millennium Summit	Strategic meeting among world leaders at the *United Nations* headquarters in September 2000 intended to discuss the role of *United Nations* at the turn of the twenty-first century. See *United Nations Millennium Declaration*.
United Nations Population Fund (UNFPA)	International *development* agency, founded in 1969, *mandate*d to promote the right of every woman, man and child to lives of health and equal opportunity through policies of reducing poverty and ensuring safe conditions of pregnancy, birth and growing-up free of *HIV / AIDS*, and by promoting programmes for treating every girl and woman with dignity and respect.
United Nations resolution	Non legally-*binding*, declaratory, formal document adopted by any *United Nations* body, for the most part the *United Nations General Assembly*.
United Nations specialised agency	*Organisation*s incorporated into the system of the *United Nations* by the *United Nations Economic and Social Council* (ECOSOC) acting under articles 57 and 63 of the *Charter of the United Nations*.

United Nations University (UNU)	Launching academic activities in 1975, the *institution* is dedicated to the generation and transfer of knowledge, and the strengthening of individual and *institutional* capacities in furtherance of the purposes and principles of the *Charter of the United Nations*. The *mission* is to contribute to efforts to resolve pressing global problems of human survival, *development* and welfare in the realm of the *United Nations* through collaborative research, capacity *development* and advisory services.
Universal Declaration of Human Rights (UDHR)	Adopted in 1948, this document sets forth for the first time the inalienable fundamental human rights and freedoms for all peoples and all nations as common *standard* of achievements to be universally protected.
University Twinning and network scheme (UNITWIN)	*UNESCO* programme established in 1992 directed to advance research, training and programme *development* in all of *UNESCO*'s fields of *competence* by building university *networks* and encouraging inter-university co-operation through the transfer of knowledge across borders.
Usus	Latin expression referring to the specific custom or habit applied in legal practice.
Venire contra factum proprium	Latin expression and legal principle that nobody can base oneself in contradiction to its genuine previous conduct. See *estoppel*.
Via regia	Latin expression related to the best possible and viable approach or solution.
Vilnius Framework	*Framework* drafted in 2005 for implementing the *UN-ECE Strategy for Education for Sustainable Development*.
Vision	Future-oriented and stylised ability of positive utopian thinking directed towards a desirable steady state.
Window of opportunity	Idiom describing the short and decisive period of time during which an advantageous chance must be acted on or otherwise will be missed.
World Bank	International financial *institution* founded in 1944 and headquartered in Washington, D.C. providing financial assistance (loans and credits) and assigned to reducing world poverty.
World Commission on Environment and Development (WCED)	See *Report of the World Commission on Sustainable Development Our Common Future*.
World Conference on Education for All	Conference of launching *EFA* held 1990 in Jomtien, Thailand.

World Decade for Cultural Development	Scheduled from 1988 to 1997, this *United Nations decade* aimed to acknowledge the cultural *dimension* of *development*, to affirm and enrich cultural identities, to broaden *participation* in culture, and to promote international cultural co-operation.
World Health Organisation (WHO)	*United Nations specialised agency* established in 1948 as a co-ordinating authority on international public health responsible for providing *leadership* on global health matters, shaping the health research agenda, setting *norm*s and *standard*s, articulating evidence-based policy options, providing technical support to countries, and *monitoring* and assessing health trends.
World Summit on Sustainable Development (WSSD)	International conference held in 2002 in Johannesburg, South Africa, constituting the *implementation* groundwork and way for action as follow-up to the *Agenda 21* of the 1992 *United Nations Conference on Environment and Development.*
Youth Poverty Alleviation through Tourism and Heritage (YouthPATH)	Training and empowerment programme designed and implemented to engage young people in true partnership with *UNESCO* considered as active participants and partners in multi-level project work.

Subject index

A

B

C

D

E

F

G

H

I

J

K

L

M

N

O

P

U

V

W

Y

Dresdner Schriften zu Recht und Politik der Vereinten Nationen
Papers on Law and Policy of the United Nations

Herausgegeben von Sabine von Schorlemer

Band 1 Sabine von Schorlemer (Hrsg.): „Wir, die Völker (...)" – Strukturwandel in der Weltorganisation – Konferenzband. Konferenz aus Anlass des 60-jährigen Bestehens der Vereinten Nationen vom 27.–29. Oktober 2005 in Dresden in Kooperation mit dem Zentrum für Internationale Studien (ZIS) und der Deutschen Gesellschaft für die Vereinten Nationen (DGVN). 2006.

Band 2 Philipp von Hülsen: Die Vereinten Nationen als Gesetzgeber im Kosovo. Rechtmäßigkeitsanforderungen an Rechtssetzungsakte der UNMIK am Beispiel der Unternehmensprivatisierung durch die Kosovo Trust Agency. 2007.

Band 3 Sabine von Schorlemer (Hrsg.): Die Vereinten Nationen und neuere Entwicklungen der Frauenrechte. 2007.

Band 4 Tina Miller: Die Frage der Rückkehr palästinensischer Flüchtlinge, unter Berücksichtigung der Lösungsansätze der Vereinten Nationen. 2007.

Band 5 Isabel Hörtreiter: Die Vereinten Nationen und Wirtschaftsunternehmen – zwischen Kooperation und Kontrolle. Steuerungsformen zur Stärkung menschenrechtlicher Unternehmensverantwortung unter dem Dach der Vereinten Nationen. 2007.

Band 6 Ariane Wewers: Die Pflicht der EU-Partner zur Koordinierung in internationalen Organisationen und auf internationalen Konferenzen (Art. 19 EUV). Die Praxis der GASP dargestellt am Beispiel der Vereinten Nationen. 2009.

Band 7 Niklas Keller: Die „Principles on Housing and Property Restitution for Refugees and Displaced Persons" der Vereinten Nationen. Die Lösung der Wohnraum- und Eigentumsproblematik bei der Rückkehr von Flüchtlingen und Displaced Persons. 2009.

Band 8 Martin Ramsperger: Die Terrorismusbekämpfung im Rahmen der Europäischen Sicherheits- und Verteidigungspolitik (ESVP). 2009.

Band 9 Sabine von Schorlemer: Kindersoldaten und bewaffneter Konflikt. Nukleus eines umfassenden Schutzregimes der Vereinten Nationen. 2009.

Band 10 Lauri Philipp Rothfritz: Die Konvention der Vereinten Nationen zum Schutz der Rechte von Menschen mit Behinderungen. Eine Analyse unter Bezugnahme auf die deutsche und europäische Rechtsebene. 2010.

Band 11 Arlett Rassel: Strafgerichtsbarkeit über Angehörige der Friedenstruppen in UN-geführten Missionen. Unter besonderer Berücksichtigung von Sexualstraftaten. 2010.

Band 12 Dirk Monsau: Vereinte Nationen und Korruptionsbekämpfung. 2010.

Band 13 Jana Hertwig: Die Europäische Union und die Bekämpfung der Verbreitung von Massenvernichtungswaffen. Theorie und Praxis der europäischen Nichtverbreitungsstrategie. 2010.

Band 14 Jana Hertwig / Sylvia Maus / Almut Meyer zu Schwabedissen / Matthias Schuler (eds.): Global Risks. Constructing World Order through Law, Politics and Economics. 2010.

Band 15 Sabine von Schorlemer / Elena Schulte-Herbrüggen (Hrsg.): 1989–2009: 20 Jahre UN-Kinderrechtskonvention. Erfahrungen und Perspektiven. 2010.

Band 16 Philip Michael Winkler: Technologietransfer im Recht der UNESCO. 2012.

Band 17 Martin Gerner: Lead Agency. UNESCO´s Global Leadership and Co-ordination Role for the United Nations Decade of Education for Sustainable Development (2005–2014). 2013.

www.peterlang.de

FSC
www.fsc.org
MIX
Papier | Fördert gute Waldnutzung
FSC® C083411

Kolibri 360 GmbH
Ferdinand-Jühlke-Straße 7
99095 Erfurt, Deutschland
produktsicherheit@kolibri360.de